The Journals of
Charlotte Forten Grimké

THE SCHOMBURG LIBRARY OF
NINETEENTH-CENTURY BLACK WOMEN WRITERS

General Editor, Henry Louis Gates, Jr.

Titles are listed chronologically; collections that include works published over a span of years are listed according to the publication date of their initial work.

The Journals

of

Charlotte Forten Grimké

Edited by
BRENDA STEVENSON

New York   Oxford
OXFORD UNIVERSITY PRESS
1988

Oxford University Press

Oxford   New York   Toronto
Delhi   Bombay   Calcutta   Madras   Karachi
Petaling Jaya   Singapore   Hong Kong   Tokyo
Nairobi   Dar es Salaam   Cape Town
Melbourne   Auckland

and associated companies in
Beirut   Berlin   Ibadan   Nicosia

Library of Congress Cataloging-in-Publication Data

Forten, Charlotte L.
The journals of Charlotte Forten Grimké.
(The Schomburg library of nineteenth-century black
women writers)
Bibliography: p.
1. Forten, Charlotte L.—Diaries.   2. Afro-American
teachers—Diaries.   I. Stevenson, Brenda.   II. Title.
III. Series.
LA2317.F67A3   1988   371.1′0092′4 [B]   87-31266
ISBN 0-19-505238-2
ISBN 0-19-505267-6 (set)

The journals of Charlotte Forten Grimké are reproduced courtesy of the Moorland-
Spingarn Research Center, Howard University, Washington, D.C.

2 4 6 8 10 9 7 5 3 1

Printed in the United States of America
on acid-free paper

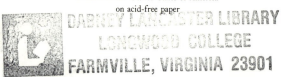

The
Schomburg Library
of
Nineteenth-Century
Black Women Writers
is
Dedicated
in Memory
of
PAULINE AUGUSTA COLEMAN GATES

1916–1987

PUBLISHER'S NOTE

FOREWORD
In Her Own Write

Henry Louis Gates, Jr.

One muffled strain in the Silent South, a jarring chord and a vague and uncomprehended cadenza has been and still is the Negro. And of that muffled chord, the one mute and voiceless note has been the sadly expectant Black Woman, ...

The "other side" has not been represented by one who "lives there." And not many can more sensibly realize and more accurately tell the weight and the fret of the "long dull pain" than the open-eyed but hitherto voiceless Black Woman of America.

. . . as our Caucasian barristers are not to blame if they cannot *quite* put themselves in the dark man's place, neither should the dark man be wholly expected fully and adequately to reproduce the exact Voice of the Black Woman.

—ANNA JULIA COOPER, *A Voice From the South* (1892)

The birth of the Afro-American literary tradition occurred in 1773, when Phillis Wheatley published a book of poetry. Despite the fact that her book garnered for her a remarkable amount of attention, Wheatley's journey to the printer had been a most arduous one. Sometime in 1772, a young African girl walked demurely into a room in Boston to undergo an oral examination, the results of which would determine the direction of her life and work. Perhaps she was shocked upon entering the appointed room. For there, perhaps gathered in a semicircle, sat eighteen of Boston's most notable citizens. Among them were John Erving, a prominent Boston merchant; the Reverend Charles Chauncy, pastor of the Tenth Congregational Church; and John Hancock, who would later gain fame for his signature on the Declaration of Independence. At the center of this group was His Excellency, Thomas Hutchinson, governor of Massachusetts, with Andrew Oliver, his lieutenant governor, close by his side.

Why had this august group been assembled? Why had it seen fit to summon this young African girl, scarcely eighteen years old, before it? This group of "the most respectable Characters in *Boston*," as it would later define itself, had assembled to question closely the African adolescent on the slender sheaf of poems that she claimed to have "written by herself." We can only speculate on the nature of the questions posed to the fledgling poet. Perhaps they asked her to identify and explain—for all to hear—exactly who were the Greek and Latin gods and poets alluded to so frequently in her work. Perhaps they asked her to conjugate a verb in Latin or even to translate randomly selected passages from the Latin, which she and her master, John Wheatley, claimed that she "had made some Progress in." Or perhaps they asked her to recite from memory key passages from the texts of John Milton and Alexander Pope, the two poets by whom the African claimed to be most directly influenced. We do not know.

We do know, however, that the African poet's responses were more than sufficient to prompt the eighteen august gentlemen to compose, sign, and publish a two-paragraph "Attestation," an open letter "To the Publick" that prefaces Phillis Wheatley's book and that reads in part:

We whose Names are under-written, do assure the World, that the Poems specified in the following Page, were (as we

verily believe) written by Phillis, a young Negro Girl, who
was but a few Years since, brought an uncultivated Barbarian
from *Africa,* and has ever since been, and now is, under the
Disadvantage of serving as a Slave in a Family in this Town.
She has been examined by some of the best Judges, and is
thought qualified to write them.

So important was this document in securing a publisher for
Wheatley's poems that it forms the signal element in the
prefatory matter preceding her *Poems on Various Subjects, Religious and Moral,* published in London in 1773.

Without the published "Attestation," Wheatley's publisher
claimed, few would believe that an African could possibly
have written poetry all by herself. As the eighteen put the
matter clearly in their letter, "Numbers would be ready to
suspect they were not really the Writings of Phillis." Wheatley and her master, John Wheatley, had attempted to publish
a similar volume in 1772 in Boston, but Boston publishers
had been incredulous. One year later, "Attestation" in hand,
Phillis Wheatley and her master's son, Nathaniel Wheatley,
sailed for England, where they completed arrangements for
the publication of a volume of her poems with the aid of the
Countess of Huntington and the Earl of Dartmouth.

This curious anecdote, surely one of the oddest oral examinations on record, is only a tiny part of a larger, and
even more curious, episode in the Enlightenment. Since the
beginning of the sixteenth century, Europeans had wondered aloud whether or not the African "species of men," as
they were most commonly called, *could* ever create formal
literature, could ever master "the arts and sciences." If they
could, the argument ran, then the African variety of humanity was fundamentally related to the European variety. If not,
then it seemed clear that the African was destined by nature

to be a slave. This was the burden shouldered by Phillis Wheatley when she successfully defended herself and the authorship of her book against counterclaims and doubts.

Indeed, with her successful defense, Wheatley launched two traditions at once—the black American literary tradition *and* the black woman's literary tradition. If it is extraordinary that not just one but both of these traditions were founded simultaneously by a black woman—certainly an event unique in the history of literature—it is also ironic that this important fact of common, coterminous literary origins seems to have escaped most scholars.

That the progenitor of the black literary tradition was a woman means, in the most strictly literal sense, that all subsequent black writers have evolved in a matrilinear line of descent, and that each, consciously or unconsciously, has extended and revised a canon whose foundation was the poetry of a black woman. Early black writers seem to have been keenly aware of Wheatley's founding role, even if most of her white reviewers were more concerned with the implications of her race than her gender. Jupiter Hammon, for example, whose 1760 broadside "An Evening Thought. Salvation by Christ, With Penitential Cries" was the first individual poem published by a black American, acknowledged Wheatley's influence by selecting her as the subject of his second broadside, "An Address to Miss Phillis Wheatly [*sic*], Ethiopian Poetess, in Boston," which was published at Hartford in 1778. And George Moses Horton, the second Afro-American to publish a book of poetry in English (1829), brought out in 1838 an edition of his *Poems By A Slave* bound together with Wheatley's work. Indeed, for fifty-six years, between 1773 and 1829, when Horton published *The Hope of Liberty*, Wheatley was the *only* black person to have published a book of imaginative literature in English. So central was this black woman's role in the shaping of the Afro-American literary tradition that, as one historian has maintained, the history of the reception of Phillis Wheatley's poetry *is* the history of Afro-American literary criticism. Well into the nineteenth century, Wheatley and the black literary tradition were the same entity.

But Wheatley is not the only black woman writer who stands as a pioneering figure in Afro-American literature. Just as Wheatley gave birth to the genre of black poetry, Ann Plato was the first Afro-American to publish a book of essays (1841) and Harriet E. Wilson was the first black person to publish a novel in the United States (1859).

Despite this pioneering role of black women in the tradition, however, many of their contributions before this century have been all but lost or unrecognized. As Hortense Spillers observed as recently as 1983,

> With the exception of a handful of autobiographical narratives from the nineteenth century, the black woman's realities are virtually suppressed until the period of the Harlem Renaissance and later. Essentially the black woman as artist, as intellectual spokesperson for her own cultural apprenticeship, has not existed before, for anyone. At the source of [their] own symbol-making task, [the community of black women writers] confronts, therefore, a tradition of work that is quite recent, its continuities, broken and sporadic.

Until now, it has been extraordinarily difficult to establish the formal connections between early black women's writing and that of the present, precisely because our knowledge of their work has been broken and sporadic. Phillis Wheatley, for example, while certainly the most reprinted and discussed poet in the tradition, is also one of the least understood. Ann Plato's seminal work, *Essays* (which includes biographies and poems), has not been reprinted since it was published a cen-

tury and a half ago. And Harriet Wilson's *Our Nig,* her
compelling novel of a black woman's expanding consciousness in a racist Northern antebellum environment, never received even *one* review or comment at a time when virtually
all works written by black people were heralded by abolitionists as salient arguments against the existence of human slavery. Many of the books reprinted in this set experienced a
similar fate, the most dreadful fate for an author: that of
being ignored then relegated to the obscurity of the rare book
section of a university library. We can only wonder how
many other texts in the black woman's tradition have been
lost to this generation of readers or remain unclassified or
uncatalogued and, hence, unread.

This was not always so, however. Black women writers
dominated the final decade of the nineteenth century, perhaps
spurred to publish by an 1886 essay entitled "The Coming
American Novelist," which was published in *Lippincott's
Monthly Magazine* and written by "A Lady From Philadelphia." This pseudonymous essay argued that the "Great
American Novel" would be written by a black person. Her
argument is so curious that it deserves to be repeated:

> When we come to formulate our demands of the Coming
> American Novelist, we will agree that he must be native-
> born. His ancestors may come from where they will, but we
> must give him a birthplace and have the raising of him. Still,
> the longer his family has been here the better he will represent
> us. Suppose he should have no country but ours, no traditions
> but those he has learned here, no longings apart from us, no
> future except in our future—the orphan of the world, he
> finds with us his home. And with all this, suppose he refuses
> to be fused into that grand conglomerate we call the "Amer-
> ican type." With us, he is not of us. He is original, he has
> humor, he is tender, he is passive and fiery, he has been

taught what we call justice, and he has his own opinion about
it. He has suffered everything a poet, a dramatist, a novelist
need suffer before he comes to have his lips anointed. And
with it all he is in one sense a spectator, a little out of the
race. How would these conditions go towards forming an
original development? In a word, suppose the coming novelist
is of African origin? When one comes to consider the subject,
there is no improbability in it. One thing is certain,—our
great novel will not be written by the typical American.

An atypical American, indeed. Not only would the great
American novel be written by an African-American, it would
be written by an African-American *woman:*

Yet farther: I have used the generic masculine pronoun
because it is convenient; but Fate keeps revenge in store. It
was a woman who, taking the wrongs of the African as her
theme, wrote the novel that awakened the world to their
reality, and why should not the coming novelist be a woman
as well as an African? She—the woman of that race—has
some claims on Fate which are not yet paid up.

It is these claims on fate that we seek to pay by publishing
The Schomburg Library of Nineteenth-Century Black Women
Writers.
    This theme would be repeated by several black women
authors, most notably by Anna Julia Cooper, a prototypical
black feminist whose 1892 *A Voice From the South* can be
considered to be one of the original texts of the black feminist movement. It was Cooper who first analyzed the fal-
lacy of referring to "the Black man" when speaking of black
people and who argued that just as white men cannot speak
through the consciousness of black men, neither can black
men "fully and adequately . . . reproduce the exact Voice of
the Black Woman." Gender and race, she argues, cannot be

conflated, except in the instance of a black woman's voice, and it is this voice which must be uttered and to which we must listen. As Cooper puts the matter so compellingly:

> It is not the intelligent woman vs. the ignorant woman; nor the white woman vs. the black, the brown, and the red,—it is not even the cause of woman vs. man. Nay, 'tis woman's strongest vindication for speaking that *the world needs to hear her voice*. It would be subversive of every human interest that the cry of one-half the human family be stifled. Woman in stepping from the pedestal of statue-like inactivity in the domestic shrine, and daring to think and move and speak,—to undertake to help shape, mold, and direct the thought of her age, is merely completing the circle of the world's vision. Hers is every interest that has lacked an interpreter and a defender. Her cause is linked with that of every agony that has been dumb—every wrong that needs a voice.
>
> It is no fault of man's that he has not been able to see truth from her standpoint. It does credit both to his head and heart that no greater mistakes have been committed or even wrongs perpetrated while she sat making tatting and snipping paper flowers. Man's own innate chivalry and the mutual interdependence of their interests have insured his treating her cause, in the main at least, as his own. And he is pardonably surprised and even a little chagrined, perhaps, to find his legislation not considered "perfectly lovely" in every respect. But in any case his work is only impoverished by her remaining dumb. The world has had to limp along with the wobbling gait and one-sided hesitancy of a man with one eye. Suddenly the bandage is removed from the other eye and the whole body is filled with light. It sees a circle where before it saw a segment. The darkened eye restored, every member rejoices with it.

The myopic sight of the darkened eye can only be restored when the full range of the black woman's voice, with its own special timbres and shadings, remains mute no longer.

Similarly, Victoria Earle Matthews, an author of short stories and essays, and a cofounder in 1896 of the National Association of Colored Women, wrote in her stunning essay, "The Value of Race Literature" (1895), that "when the literature of our race is developed, it will of necessity be different in all essential points of greatness, true heroism and real Christianity from what we may at the present time, for convenience, call American literature." Matthews argued that this great tradition of Afro-American literature would be the textual outlet "for the unnaturally suppressed inner lives which our people have been compelled to lead." Once these "unnaturally suppressed inner lives" of black people are unveiled, no "grander diffusion of mental light" will shine more brightly, she concludes, than that of the articulate Afro-American woman:

And now comes the question, What part shall we women play in the Race Literature of the future? . . . within the compass of one small journal ["Woman's Era"] we have struck out a new line of departure—a journal, a record of Race interests gathered from all parts of the United States, carefully selected, moistened, winnowed and garnered by the ablest intellects of educated colored women, shrinking at no lofty theme, shirking no serious duty, aiming at every possible excellence, and determined to do their part in the future uplifting of the race.

If twenty women, by their concentrated efforts in one literary movement, can meet with such success as has engendered, planned out, and so successfully consummated this convention, what much more glorious results, what wider spread success, what grander diffusion of mental light will not come forth at the bidding of the enlarged hosts of women writers, already called into being by the stimulus of your efforts?

And here let me speak one word for my journalistic sisters

who have already entered the broad arena of journalism. Before the "Woman's Era" had come into existence, no one except themselves can appreciate the bitter experience and sore disappointments under which they have at all times been compelled to pursue their chosen vocations.

If their brothers of the press have had their difficulties to contend with, I am here as a sister journalist to state, from the fullness of knowledge, that their task has been an easy one compared with that of the colored woman in journalism.

Woman's part in Race Literature, as in Race building, is the most important part and has been so in all ages. . . . All through the most remote epochs she has done her share in literature. . . .

One of the most important aspects of this set is the republication of the salient texts from 1890 to 1910, which literary historians could well call "The Black Woman's Era." In addition to Mary Helen Washington's definitive edition of Cooper's *A Voice From the South,* we have reprinted two novels by Amelia Johnson, Frances Harper's *Iola Leroy,* two novels by Emma Dunham Kelley, Alice Dunbar-Nelson's two impressive collections of short stories, and Pauline Hopkins's three serialized novels as well as her monumental novel, *Contending Forces*—all published between 1890 and 1910. Indeed, black women published more works of fiction in these two decades than black men had published in the previous half century. Nevertheless, this great achievement has been ignored.

Moreover, the writings of nineteenth-century Afro-American women in general have remained buried in obscurity, accessible only in research libraries or in overpriced and poorly edited reprints. Many of these books have never been reprinted at all; in some instances only one or two copies are extant. In these works of fiction, poetry, autobiography, biography, essays, and journalism resides the mind of the nineteenth-century Afro-American woman. Until these works are made readily available to teachers and their students, a significant segment of the black tradition will remain silent.

Oxford University Press, in collaboration with the Schomburg Center for Research in Black Culture, is publishing thirty volumes of these compelling works, each of which contains an introduction by an expert in the field. The set includes such rare texts as Johnson's *The Hazeley Family* and *Clarence and Corinne*, Plato's *Essays*, the most complete edition of Phillis Wheatley's poems and letters, Emma Dunham Kelley's pioneering novel *Megda*, several previously unpublished stories and a novel by Alice Dunbar-Nelson, and the first collected volumes of Pauline Hopkins's three serialized novels and Frances Harper's poetry. We also present four volumes of poetry by such women as Mary Eliza Tucker Lambert, Adah Menken, Josephine Heard, and Maggie Johnson. Numerous slave and spiritual narratives, a newly discovered novel—*Four Girls at Cottage City*—by Emma Dunham Kelley (-Hawkins), and the first American edition of *Wonderful Adventures of Mrs. Seacole in Many Lands* are also among the texts included.

In addition to resurrecting the works of black women authors, it is our hope that this set will facilitate the resurrection of the Afro-American woman's literary tradition itself by unearthing its nineteenth-century roots. In the works of Nella Larsen and Jessie Fauset, Zora Neale Hurston and Ann Petry, Lorraine Hansberry and Gwendolyn Brooks, Paule Marshall and Toni Cade Bambara, Audre Lorde and Rita Dove, Toni Morrison and Alice Walker, Gloria Naylor and Jamaica Kincaid, these roots have branched luxuriantly. The eighteenth- and nineteenth-century authors whose works are presented in this set founded and nurtured the black women's literary tradition, which must be revived, explicated, analyzed, and debated before we can understand more completely the formal shaping of this tradition within a tradition, a coded literary universe through which, regrettably, we are only just beginning to navigate our way. As Anna Cooper said nearly one hundred years ago, we have been blinded by the loss of sight in one eye and have therefore been unable to detect the full *shape* of the Afro-American literary tradition.

Literary works configure into a tradition not because of some mystical collective unconscious determined by the biology of race or gender, but because writers read other writers and *ground* their representations of experience in models of language provided largely by other writers to whom they feel akin. It is through this mode of literary revision, amply evident in the *texts* themselves—in formal echoes, recast metaphors, even in parody—that a "tradition" emerges and defines itself.

This is formal bonding, and it is only through formal bonding that we can know a literary tradition. The collective publication of these works by black women now, for the first time, makes it possible for scholars and critics, male and female, black and white, to *demonstrate* that black women writers read, and revised, other black women writers. To demonstrate this set of formal literary relations is to demonstrate that sexuality, race, and gender are both the condition and the basis of *tradition*—but tradition as found in discrete acts of language use.

A word is in order about the history of this set. For the past decade, I have taught a course, first at Yale and then at Cornell, entitled "Black Women and Their Fictions," a course that I inherited from Toni Morrison, who developed it in the mid-1970s for Yale's Program in Afro-American Studies. Although the course was inspired by the remarkable accomplishments of black women novelists since 1970, I gradually extended its beginning date to the late nineteenth century, studying Frances Harper's *Iola Leroy* and Anna Julia Cooper's *A Voice From the South*, both published in 1892. With the discovery of Harriet E. Wilson's seminal novel, *Our Nig* (1859), and Jean Yellin's authentication of Harriet Jacobs's brilliant slave narrative, *Incidents in the Life of a Slave Girl* (1861), a survey course spanning over a century and a quarter emerged.

But the discovery of *Our Nig*, as well as the interest in nineteenth-century black women's writing that this discovery generated, convinced me that even the most curious and diligent scholars knew very little of the extensive history of the creative writings of Afro-American women before 1900. Indeed, most scholars of Afro-American literature had never even read most of the books published by black women, simply because these books—of poetry, novels, short stories, essays, and autobiography—were mostly accessible only in rare book sections of university libraries. For reasons unclear to me even today, few of these marvelous renderings of the Afro-American woman's consciousness were reprinted in the late 1960s and early 1970s, when so many other texts of the Afro-American literary tradition were resurrected from the dark and silent graveyard of the out-of-print and were reissued in facsimile editions aimed at the hungry readership for canonical texts in the nascent field of black studies.

So, with the help of several superb research assistants—including David Curtis, Nicola Shilliam, Wendy Jones, Sam Otter, Janadas Devan, Suvir Kaul, Cynthia Bond, Elizabeth Alexander, and Adele Alexander—and with the expert advice of scholars such as William Robinson, William Andrews, Mary Helen Washington, Maryemma Graham, Jean Yellin, Houston A. Baker, Jr., Richard Yarborough, Hazel Carby, Joan R. Sherman, Frances Foster, and William French, dozens of bibliographies were used to compile a list of books written or narrated by black women mostly before 1910. Without the assistance provided through this shared experience of scholarship, the scholar's true legacy, this project could not have been conceived. As the list grew, I was struck by how very many of these titles that I, for example, had never even heard of, let alone read, such as Ann Plato's *Essays*, Louisa Picquet's slave narrative, or Amelia Johnson's two novels, *Clarence and Corinne* and *The Hazeley Family*. Through our research with the Black Periodical Fiction and Poetry Project (funded by NEH and the Ford Foundation), I also realized that several novels by black women, including three works of fiction by Pauline Hopkins, had been serialized in black periodicals, but had never been collected and published as books. Nor had the several books of poetry published by black women, such as the prolific Frances E. W. Harper, been collected and edited. When I discovered still another "lost" novel by an Afro-American woman (*Four Girls at Cottage City*, published in 1898 by Emma Dunham Kelley-Hawkins), I decided to attempt to edit a collection of reprints of these works and to publish them as a "library" of black women's writings, in part so that I could read them myself.

Convincing university and trade publishers to undertake this project proved to be a difficult task. Despite the commercial success of *Our Nig* and of the several reprint series of women's works (such as Virago, the Beacon Black Women Writers Series, and Rutgers' American Women Writers Series), several presses rejected the project as "too large," "too limited," or as "commercially unviable." Only two publishers recognized the viability and the import of the project and, of these, Oxford's commitment to publish the titles simultaneously as a set made the press's offer irresistible.

While attempting to locate original copies of these exceedingly rare books, I discovered that most of the texts were housed at the Schomburg Center for Research in Black Culture, a branch of The New York Public Library, under the direction of Howard Dodson. Dodson's infectious enthusiasm for the project and his generous collaboration, as well as that of his stellar staff (especially Diana Lachatanere, Sharon Howard, Ellis Haizip, Richard Newman, and Betty Gubert), led to a joint publishing initiative that produced this set as part of the Schomburg's major fund-raising campaign. Without Dodson's foresight and generosity of spirit, the set would not have materialized. Without William P. Sisler's masterful editorship at Oxford and his staff's careful attention to detail, the set would have remained just another grand idea that tends to languish in a scholar's file cabinet.

I would also like to thank Dr. Michael Winston and Dr. Thomas C. Battle, Vice-President of Academic Affairs and the Director of the Moorland-Spingarn Research Center (respectively) at Howard University, for their unending encouragement, support, and collaboration in this project, and Esme E. Bhan at Howard for her meticulous research and bibliographical skills. In addition, I would like to acknowledge the aid of the staff at the libraries of Duke University, Cornell University (especially Tom Weissinger and Donald Eddy), the Boston Public Library, the Western Reserve Historical Society, the Library of Congress, and Yale University. Linda Robbins, Marion Osmun, Sarah Flanagan, and Gerard Case, all members of the staff at Oxford, were extraordinarily effective at coordinating, editing, and producing the various segments of each text in the set. Candy Ruck, Nina de Tar, and Phillis Molock expertly typed reams of correspondence and manuscripts connected to the project.

I would also like to express my gratitude to my colleagues who edited and introduced the individual titles in the set. Without their attention to detail, their willingness to meet strict deadlines, and their sheer enthusiasm for this project, the set could not have been published. But finally and ultimately, I would hope that the publication of the set would help to generate even more scholarly interest in the black women authors whose work is presented here. Struggling against the seemingly insurmountable barriers of racism *and* sexism, while often raising families and fulfilling full-time professional obligations, these women managed nevertheless to record their thoughts and feelings and to *testify* to all who dare read them that the will to harness the power of collective endurance and survival is the will to write.

The Schomburg Library of Nineteenth-Century Black Women Writers is dedicated in memory of Pauline Augusta Coleman Gates, who died in the spring of 1987. It was she who inspired in me the love of learning and the love of literature. I have encountered in the books of this set no will more determined, no courage more noble, no mind more sublime, no self more celebratory of the achievements of all Afro-American women, and indeed of life itself, than her own.

A NOTE FROM
THE SCHOMBURG CENTER

Howard Dodson

The Schomburg Center for Research in Black Culture, The New York Public Library, is pleased to join with Dr. Henry Louis Gates and Oxford University Press in presenting The Schomburg Library of Nineteenth-Century Black Women Writers. This thirty-volume set includes the work of a generation of black women whose writing has only been available previously in rare book collections. The materials reprinted in twenty-four of the thirty volumes are drawn from the unique holdings of the Schomburg Center.

A research unit of The New York Public Library, the Schomburg Center has been in the forefront of those institutions dedicated to collecting, preserving, and providing access to the records of the black past. In the course of its two generations of acquisition and conservation activity, the Center has amassed collections totaling more than 5 million items. They include over 100,000 bound volumes, 85,000 reels and sets of microforms, 300 manuscript collections containing some 3.5 million items, 300,000 photographs and extensive holdings of prints, sound recordings, film and videotape, newspapers, artworks, artifacts, and other book and nonbook materials. Together they vividly document the history and cultural heritages of people of African descent worldwide.

Though established some sixty-two years ago, the Center's book collections date from the sixteenth century. Its oldest item, an Ethiopian Coptic Tunic, dates from the eighth or ninth century. Rare materials, however, are most available for the nineteenth-century African-American experience. It is from these holdings that the majority of the titles selected for inclusion in this set are drawn.

The nineteenth century was a formative period in African-American literary and cultural history. Prior to the Civil War, the majority of black Americans living in the United States were held in bondage. Law and practice forbade teaching them to read or write. Even after the war, many of the impediments to learning and literary productivity remained. Nevertheless, black men and women of the nineteenth century persevered in both areas. Moreover, more African-Americans than we yet realize turned their observations, feelings, social viewpoints, and creative impulses into published works. In time, this nineteenth-century printed record included poetry, short stories, histories, novels, autobiographies, social criticism, and theology, as well as economic and philosophical treatises. Unfortunately, much of this body of literature remained, until very recently, relatively inaccessible to twentieth-century scholars, teachers, creative artists, and others interested in black life. Prior to the late 1960s, most Americans (black as well as white) had never heard of these nineteenth-century authors, much less read their works.

The civil rights and black power movements created unprecedented interest in the thought, behavior, and achievements of black people. Publishers responded by revising traditional texts, introducing the American public to a new generation of African-American writers, publishing a variety of thematic anthologies, and reprinting a plethora of "classic texts" in African-American history, literature, and art. The reprints usually appeared as individual titles or in a series of bound volumes or microform formats.

The Schomburg Center, which has a long history of supporting publishing that deals with the history and culture of Africans in diaspora, became an active participant in many of the reprint revivals of the 1960s. Since hard copies of original printed works are the preferred formats for producing facsimile reproductions, publishers frequently turned to the Schomburg Center for copies of these original titles. In addition to providing such material, Schomburg Center staff members offered advice and consultation, wrote introductions, and occasionally entered into formal copublishing arrangements in some projects.

Most of the nineteenth-century titles reprinted during the 1960s, however, were by and about black men. A few black women were included in the longer series, but works by lesser known black women were generally overlooked. The Schomburg Library of Nineteenth-Century Black Women Writers is both a corrective to these previous omissions and an important contribution to Afro-American literary history in its own right. Through this collection of volumes, the thoughts, perspectives, and creative abilities of nineteenth-century African-American women, as captured in books and pamphlets published in large part before 1910, are again being made available to the general public. The Schomburg Center is pleased to be a part of this historic endeavor.

I would like to thank Professor Gates for initiating this project. Thanks are due both to him and Mr. William P. Sisler of Oxford University Press for giving the Schomburg Center an opportunity to play such a prominent role in the set. Thanks are also due to my colleagues at The New York Public Library and the Schomburg Center, especially Dr. Vartan Gregorian, Richard De Gennaro, Paul Fasana, Betsy

Pinover, Richard Newman, Diana Lachatanere, Glenderlyn Johnson, and Harold Anderson for their assistance and support. I can think of no better way of demonstrating than in this set the role the Schomburg Center plays in assuring that the black heritage will be available for future generations.

PREFACE

Brenda Stevenson

The five journals of Charlotte Forten Grimké compose a wonderful historical text filled with invaluable thoughts and observations for both the scholar and general reader interested in the most significant events and persons of the nineteenth century. The journals are particularly enlightening with regard to antebellum issues of civil rights, familial structure and relations, education, feminism, religion, and cultural diversity and expression. Moreover, one cannot read Grimké's diaries without gaining extensive insight into the lifestyles, attitudes, and activities of an important minority within the antebellum black community—the free black elite. Grimké also gives a unique and personal view of the Civil War and Reconstruction eras. Of equal value is the record that these journals provide of the innermost ideals, feelings, and ideas— political, social, intellectual, and romantic—of a black female struggling to reach maturity and make her mark in a period of unparalleled political and social change in the history of the American republic.

A previous edition of Charlotte Grimké's journals was published in 1953. The editor, Ray Allen Billington, presented large portions of the first four journals but excluded over one-third of their text. In so doing and in omitting the fifth journal altogether, Billington denied his readers knowledge of some of Grimké's most important relationships, as well as vital aspects of her self-education and philosophical thoughts. Furthermore, since the Billington edition, scholars have uncovered crucial information that sheds new light on

Grimké's lifestyle and personal relationships. In preparing this new edition of the Grimké journals, therefore, I wanted not only to include the entire text but also to provide annotation that reflected the most recent scholarship on Grimké's life.

The Grimké journals are a superb document, easily comparable in detail, breadth, and historical importance to Mary Chesnut's Civil War diary. The value of this text is enhanced by the fluidity of Charlotte Grimké's writing style, her excellent grammatical skills, and the clarity of her expression. As the journals are a testament to Grimké's scholarly achievements and literary accomplishments, there was little need to alter the original text except to impose certain minor changes to aid the reader. Of those changes, the most significant was the addition of bracketed information spelling out the names of people whose identity Grimké continually obscured through her constant use of initials, abbreviations, and nicknames. I have attempted to identify as many of these people as possible and to explain their relationships to Grimké in the notes that follow the journals. Identification was not always possible, however, given that several people had names with the same initials and given that Grimké often provided little contextual information to indicate clearly who these people were. When I was completely unable to determine a person's identity, no bracketed information was provided. When there was some doubt about identification, a bracketed name was provided but was followed by a question mark to let the reader know about my uncertainty.

Charlotte Grimké rarely misspelled words or those names that she gave in full. Generally, the spelling errors that she did make have been retained in the text. Occasionally, the notation [*sic*] was inserted following a misspelling or gap in phrasing that would be particularly confusing to the reader. In addition, there were remarkably few errors in dates of journal entries. The most significant was that of the first entry in Journal One. Grimké began keeping her diary on Wednesday, May 24, 1854, although she recorded the date as Wednesday, May 22, 1854. This correction has been made in the text. Elsewhere, two journal entry dates fell out of sequence and were placed back into chronological order.

This edition of the journals of Charlotte Forten Grimké includes annotation of those events and persons that were most significant in her life. A decision was made, given time and space constraints, not to provide comprehensive annotation of the creative and literary artists that Grimké mentions in her entries. Thus the notes at the end of this volume are primarily historical and biographical in nature.

I would like to express my appreciation to the following persons who aided me in preparing this book. John Blassingame was a continuous source of support and knowledge. He allowed me to use the resources of the Frederick Douglass Papers and the Afro-American Studies Program at Yale University to complete much of the work on the journals. Esme Bhan at the Moorland-Spingarn Research Center at Howard University provided me with much information about various aspects of the text and supporting materials. The editorial skills of Marion Osmun and Joan Bossert at Oxford University Press helped to bring clarity to this work. Gwendolyn Williams, Janet Giarratano, and Dorothy Motton patiently typed the journals and other related texts. Henry

Louis Gates, Jr., was as patient and resourceful an editor and friend as anyone could want. These people have given generously of their time and energy to the successful completion of this project. For any errors and shortcomings that the book might have, however, I accept sole responsibility.

CONTENTS

CHRONOLOGY

August 17, 1837	Charlotte Forten was born in Philadelphia, Pennsylvania, to Robert Bridges and Mary Virginia Woods Forten.
August 1840	Mary Virginia Woods Forten died of consumption.
November 1853	Charlotte Forten (hereafter CF) moved from Pennsylvania to Salem, Massachusetts, where she resided in the home of Charles Lenox Remond, his wife, Amy Matilda (Williams Cassey) Remond, and their children, Sarah Cassey Smith and Henry Cassey. Charlotte enrolled in the Higginson Grammar School where Mary Shepard was principal.
March 1855	CF graduated from the Higginson Grammar School with "decided éclat"; her poem "A Parting Hymn" was selected as the best from her class and honored at graduation. She immediately enrolled in the Salem Normal School. Her poem "To W.L.G. on Reading His 'Chosen Queen'" was published in the *Liberator* magazine.
September 1855	CF joined the Salem Female Anti-Slavery Society.
Fall 1855	Robert Bridges Forten, his second wife, Mary, and their two sons, Wendell and Edmund Quincy, moved from Pennsylvania to Canada.

June 18, 1856	CF accepted a position as teacher in the Epes Grammar School, Salem.
July 22, 1856	CF graduated from the Salem Normal School and read "Poem for Normal School Graduation" at the ceremony.
August 15, 1856	Amy Matilda (Williams Cassey) Remond died.
August 24, 1856	CF's poem for her graduation from the Salem Normal School was published in the *Liberator*.
January 17, 1857	CF's uncle Joseph Purvis, of Byberry, Pennsylvania, died.
June 12, 1857	CF left Salem for Philadelphia to recuperate from a respiratory tract illness.
July 28, 1857	CF left Philadelphia to return to her teaching post at the Epes Grammar School in Salem. She again stayed in the home of Charles Remond with her friend Sarah Cassey Smith.
August 28, 1857	CF's cousin William Purvis, son of Harriet and Robert Purvis, died.
December 12, 1857	CF and Sarah Cassey Smith moved from the home of Charles Remond to that of his sister, Caroline Remond, and her husband, Joseph Putnam.
December 16, 1857	CF completed a short story entitled "The Lost Bride" and submitted it for publication, unsuccessfully, to the *Ladies Home Journal*.
1858	Robert Forten, his second wife, Mary, and their two sons moved from Canada to England.

March 3, 1858	CF resigned her teaching post at the Epes Grammar School due to poor health. Subsequently, she returned to Pennsylvania where she taught the younger children of Robert and Harriet Purvis at Byberry.
May 20, 1858	CF's poem "Flowers" was accepted by Bishop Daniel Payne for publication in the *Christian Recorder*. He paid her $1 for its use.
June 18, 1858	CF's "Glimpses of New England," an essay, was published in the *National Anti-Slavery Standard*.
July 26, 1858	CF wrote the poem "The Angel's Visit" and submitted it for publication in the *Anglo-African Magazine*.
January 15, 1859	CF's poem "The Two Voices" was published in the *National Anti-Slavery Standard*.
April 30, 1859	CF accepted a teaching post at the Higginson Grammar School in Salem for the fall of 1859.
May 27, 1859	CF's poem "The Wind Among the Poplars" was published in the *Liberator*.
September 1859	CF moved to Salem to teach at the Higginson School.
January 14, 1860	CF's poem "The Slave Girl's Prayer" was published in the *National Anti-Slavery Standard*.
Spring 1860	CF resigned her teaching post due to poor health, traveled to Bridgewater to recuperate, and then tried a water cure facility in Worcester under the care of Dr. Seth Rogers.

September 1860	CF resumed teaching in Salem.
October 1860	CF resigned her teaching post due to poor health and returned to Philadelphia.
May 1861	CF went to Byberry to care for her ill cousin, Robert Purvis, Jr.
Fall 1861	CF moved to Philadelphia where she taught in the Lombard Street School run by her Aunt Margaretta Forten.
March 19, 1862	Cousin Robert Purvis, Jr., died of consumption.
Summer 1862	CF moved to Salem to teach summer classes at the Higginson Grammar School.
August 9, 1862	CF and Mary Shepard visited the home of John Greenleaf Whittier in Amesbury. Whittier advised CF that she should travel to Port Royal, South Carolina, to teach the contraband slaves.
September 14, 1862	CF returned to Philadelphia so she could apply to the Port Royal Relief Association for sponsorship to South Carolina.
October 22, 1862	CF left for Port Royal, South Carolina, to teach under the auspices of the Port Royal Relief Association.
December 12, 1862	Letter from CF descriptive of her first experiences in the South Carolina Sea Islands was published in the *Liberator*.
December 19, 1862	CF's "Interesting Letter from Miss Charlotte L. Forten [,] St. Helena Island, Beaufort, S.C. [,] Nov. 27, 1862" was published in the *Liberator*. It described the

	Thanksgiving celebration held at the Sea Islands.
January 23, 1863	CF's "New Year's Day on the Islands of South Carolina, 1863" was published in the *Liberator*.
February 19, 1863	Colonel Thomas Higginson of the First South Carolina Volunteers requested that CF accompany his regiment on an expedition to Florida. She was to serve as teacher to the regiment.
March 26, 1863	CF was unable to join Higginson's regiment in Florida because General David Hunter ordered the evacuation of the troops stationed in Jacksonville, Florida.
July 22, 1863	CF volunteered as a nurse to treat wounded soldiers of the 54th Massachusetts after their bloody defeat at Fort Wagner, South Carolina.
July 31, 1863	CF sailed from Port Royal for a two-month vacation up North.
October 16, 1863	CF returned to St. Helena Island.
March 2, 1864	CF's father, Robert Bridges Forten, joined the Union army.
April 25, 1864	Sergeant-Major Robert Bridges Forten died of typhoid fever at the Forten family home in Philadelphia.
May 1864	CF resigned her position as teacher on St. Helena Island and returned to Philadelphia.
May/June 1864	CF's essays, "Life on the Sea Islands," Parts I and II, were published in the *Atlantic Monthly*.

October 1865	CF accepted a position as Secretary of the Teachers Committee of the New England Branch of the Freedmen's Union Commission and moved to Boston.
February 1868	CF completed her essay "Waiting for the Verdict."
1869	CF's translation of the French novel *Madame Thérèse; or, The Volunteers of '92*, by Emile Erckmann and Alexandre Chatrain, was published by Scribner's.
1871–1872	CF was employed as a teacher at the Shaw Memorial School in Charleston, South Carolina.
1872–1873	CF taught in the black preparatory high school later known as Dunbar High in Washington, D.C.
1873–1878	CF held the position of first-class clerk in the Fourth Auditor's Office of the U.S. Treasury Department.
1874	CF wrote the poem "Charles Sumner."
1876	CF wrote the essays, "The Centennial Exposition" and "From Washington."
December 19, 1878	CF married the Reverend Francis Grimké, minister of the Fifteenth Street Presbyterian Church in Washington, D.C.
January 1, 1880	CFG's daughter, Theodora Cornelia Grimké, was born.
June 10, 1880	Theodora Cornelia Grimké died.
1885	CFG wrote the poems, "A June Song" and "Charlotte Corday," and the essays, "On

Mr. Savage's Sermon: 'The Problem of the Hour' " and "One Phase of the Race Question."

1885–1889   CFG and her husband lived in Jacksonville, Florida, where Francis Grimké was the minister of the Laura Street Presbyterian Church.

1888   CFG wrote the poem "At Newport."

1889   CFG wrote the essay "Colored People in New England." She and her husband returned to Washington, D.C., where Francis Grimké was pastor of the Fifteenth Street Presbyterian Church.

1890   CFG wrote the poem "The Gathering of the Grand Army."

1893   CFG wrote the poem "In Florida." In June, her essay "Personal Recollections of Whittier" was published in the *New England Magazine*.

1894–1898   CFG and her husband acted as the legal guardians of Francis Grimké's niece, Angelina Weld Grimké.

1896   CFG became a founding member of the National Association of Colored Women.

1890s   CFG wrote the following essays: "The Umbrian and Roman School of Art"; "The Flower Fairies' Reception"; "At the Home of Frederick Douglass"; and "Midsummer Days in the Capitol: 'The Corcoran Art Gallery.' " She also wrote the poem "Wordsworth."

| 1905 | Archibald Grimké and his daughter, Angelina, moved into the home of Charlotte and Francis Grimké. |
| July 22, 1914 | CFG died in Washington, D.C. |

PEOPLE IN THE JOURNALS

Below is a list of family members, friends, and historically significant figures mentioned in Charlotte Forten Grimké's journals.

Celia Babcock. Daughter of Cecelia Remond (Babcock) and James Babcock of Salem.

Nathaniel Banks. Prominent politician from Waltham, Massachusetts, who served as the governor of his native state and as speaker of the House of Representatives.

Maria Barnes. Classmate and friend of Charlotte Forten Grimké at the Higginson Grammar School and the Salem Normal School.

Henry Ward Beecher. Prominent clergyman, lecturer, editor, and abolitionist from Litchfield, Connecticut.

Sarah Brown ("Brownie"). Classmate and friend of Charlotte Forten Grimké at the Higginson Grammar School and the Salem Normal School.

William Wells Brown. Noteworthy black abolitionist, lecturer, and writer.

Anthony Burns. Fugitive slave from Alexandria, Virginia, captured in Boston in May 1854, and later tried, found to be the property of Charles Suttle, and returned to slavery.

Elizabeth Buffum (Chace). Prominent abolitionist, suffragist, and prison-reform advocate from Providence, Rhode Island.

Francis ("Frank") Cassey. Youngest son of Amy Matilda (Williams Cassey) Remond and Joseph Cassey of Philadelphia.

Henry Cassey. Son of Amy Matilda (Williams Cassey) Remond and Joseph Cassey of Philadelphia.

Sarah ("Sallie," "Sis") Cassey Smith (Watson). Daughter of Amy Matilda (Williams Cassey) Remond and Joseph Cassey of Philadelphia.

Maria Weston Chapman. Prominent abolitionist and editor from Weymouth, Massachusetts.

Miss Chase. Friend of Charlotte Forten Grimké in Salem and a member of the Salem Female Anti-Slavery Society.

Mrs. Chew. Friend of the Forten family in Philadelphia.

Lydia Maria Child. Prominent writer, editor, abolitionist, and reformer.

P. Elizabeth ("Lizzie") Church. Classmate of Charlotte Forten Grimké at the Higginson Grammar School and the Salem Normal School.

Frederick Douglass. Renowned black civil rights advocate, writer, editor, lecturer, and diplomat.

Sarah Mapps Douglass (Douglass). Prominent black teacher and abolitionist in Philadelphia.

George Downing. Noteworthy black businessman, abolitionist, Underground Railroad agent in New York City, and owner of the Sea Girt Hotel in Newport, Rhode Island.

J. C. Dutch (Captain). Commander of the U.S. blockading vessel *Kingfisher* during the Civil War.

Richard Edwards. Principal of the Salem Normal School.

Mrs. Farbeaux. Friend of the Forten family in Philadelphia.

Charlotte Forten. Charlotte Forten Grimké's paternal grandmother who was active in Philadelphia's abolitionist circles.

Edmund Quincy Forten. Half-brother of Charlotte Forten Grimké.

Harriet Forten (Purvis). Charlotte Forten Grimké's paternal aunt who was a prominent abolitionist and the wife of Robert Purvis.

James Forten, Jr. Charlotte Forten Grimké's paternal uncle.

James Forten, Sr. Charlotte Forten Grimké's paternal grandfather, as well as a prominent businessman and abolitionist in Philadelphia.

James Forten, III. Son of Charlotte Forten Grimké's paternal uncle, James Forten, Jr.

Margaretta Forten. Charlotte Forten Grimké's paternal aunt, as well as an abolitionist and teacher in Philadelphia.

Mary Forten. Charlotte Forten Grimké's stepmother.

Robert Bridges Forten. Charlotte Forten Grimké's father and an active abolitionist.

Sarah Louise Forten (Purvis). Charlotte Forten Grimké's paternal aunt, the wife of Joseph Purvis, an abolitionist, writer, and women's rights advocate.

Thomas Deas Forten. Charlotte Forten Grimké's paternal uncle.

Wendell Forten. Charlotte Forten Grimké's half-brother.

William Deas Forten. Charlotte Forten Grimké's paternal uncle.

Stephen Seymonds Foster. Prominent abolitionist, author, reformer, and clergyman from Canterbury, New Hampshire.

John C. Frémont. Abolitionist, military officer, and politician who ran for president on the Republican ticket in 1856.

Octavius Brooks Frothingham. Important clergyman and antislavery spokesman in Salem and later New York City.

William Furness. Prominent Unitarian clergyman and abolitionist in Philadelphia.

Frances (Dana) Gage. Prominent abolitionist and women's rights advocate who was a nurse and missionary among the Sea Island blacks.

William Lloyd Garrison. Renowned radical abolitionist, reformer, and editor of the *Liberator*.

Jacob Gilliard. A ship's barber from Baltimore who was the husband of Helen Putnam of Salem.

Quincy Gillmore (Brigadier General). U.S. army officer who temporarily relieved General David Hunter as commander of the Department of the South in June 1863.

Mary Grew. Notable abolitionist, women's rights advocate, and

Quaker minister who was secretary of the Philadelphia Female Anti-Slavery Society.

Mattie Griffiths.   Important abolitionist, lecturer, and author.

Francis Grimké.   Charlotte Forten Grimké's husband, prominent black minister, and civil rights advocate.

Edward ("Ned") Hallowell (Major).   An officer in the 54th Massachusetts who became the regiment's commander after the death of Col. Robert Gould Shaw in July 1863.

Thomas Wentworth Higginson.   Prominent abolitionist, minister, and writer from Cambridge, as well as commanding officer of the First South Carolina Volunteers during the Civil War.

Ada Hinton.   Lifelong friend of Charlotte Forten Grimké.

Lucretia (Lucy) Hopper.   Friend and classmate of Charlotte Forten Grimké's cousin, Harriet ("Hattie") Purvis.

Charles Hovey.   Notable abolitionist, temperance supporter, and merchant.

Samuel Gridley Howe.   Politician, abolitionist, and organizer of the Vigilance Committee of Boston.

Elizabeth Hunn.   Daughter of John Hunn, the storekeeper on St. Helena Island.

John Hunn.   Quaker who traveled to St. Helena Island to open a store for the newly freed slaves in residence there.

David Hunter (General).   U.S. army commander of the Department of the South during most of the Civil War.

Hutchinsons (Asa and John).   Prominent abolitionists and singers who often toured New England to support the antislavery cause.

Amy Ives.   Salem abolitionist who served as president of the Salem Female Anti-Slavery Society.

Abigail Kelley (Foster).   Prominent women's rights advocate and abolitionist.

Jean Lander.   Supervisory nurse for the Union troops stationed at Beaufort, South Carolina, during the Civil War.

Nancy Lenox (Remond).   Salem caterer and hairdresser and wife of John Remond.

Luca Family. Prominent black singers and instrumentalists who often performed at antislavery events.

Elizabeth ("Lizzie") Magee (Remond). Friend of Charlotte Forten Grimké and the second wife of Charles Lenox Remond.

Harriet Martineau. Prominent English writer, political economist, reformer, and supporter of abolition.

J. Miller McKim. Prominent Philadelphia abolitionist who was largely responsible for the establishment of the Port Royal Relief Association.

James Montgomery (Colonel). U.S. army commander of the Second South Carolina Volunteers.

Lucretia (Coffin) Mott. Prominent women's rights' advocate, Quaker minister, and abolitionist who helped organize the Seneca Falls Convention in 1848.

Ellen Murray. Teacher of the freed slaves on St. Helena Island.

William Cooper Nell. Prominent black abolitionist, journalist, politician, and historian from Boston.

Toussaint L'Ouverture. Renowned black military and political figure of the Haitian Revolution.

Theodore Parker. Prominent abolitionist, Unitarian clergyman, and scholar from Lexington, Massachusetts.

Daniel Alexander Payne. Prominent black activist, educator, historian, and bishop of the African Methodist Episcopal Church.

Elizabeth (Palmer) Peabody. Well-known scholar, Transcendentalist, and supporter of abolition, women's rights, and education reform from Billerica, Massachusetts.

Wendell Phillips. Prominent Boston reformer, most active as an abolitionist and supporter of women's rights, labor reform, and academic conservatism.

Edward L. Pierce. Boston lawyer, abolitionist, and soldier who supervised the activities of the Sea Island contraband slaves until General Rufus Saxton assumed this responsibility in April 1862.

Sarah Pitman. Friend and classmate of Charlotte Forten Grimké from the Salem Normal School.

Charles ("Charlie") Burleigh Purvis. Son of Charlotte Forten Grimké's paternal aunt Harriet Forten (Purvis) and Robert Purvis, Sr.

Emily Purvis. Daughter of Charlotte Forten Grimké's paternal aunt Sarah Louise Forten (Purvis) and Joseph Purvis.

Harriet ("Hattie") Purvis. Daughter of Charlotte Forten Grimké's paternal aunt Harriet Forten (Purvis) and Robert Purvis, Sr.

Joseph Purvis, Sr. Black abolitionist and businessman who was married to Sarah Louise Forten (Purvis).

Robert Purvis, Jr. Son of Charlotte Forten Grimké's paternal aunt Harriet Forten (Purvis) and Robert Purvis, Sr.

Robert Purvis, Sr. Prominent black abolitionist and businessman who was instrumental in the development of the Underground Railroad in Pennsylvania and who was married to Harriet Forten (Purvis).

William Purvis. Son of Charlotte Forten Grimké's paternal aunt Harriet Forten (Purvis) and Robert Purvis, Sr.

Adelaide ("Addie," "Ada") Putnam. Daughter of Jane and George Putnam of Salem.

Edward ("Eddie") Putnam. Son of Caroline Remond (Putnam) and Joseph Putnam of Salem.

Georgianna ("Georgie") Putnam. Daugher of Jane and George Putnam of Salem.

Helen ("Ellen") Putnam (Gilliard). Daughter of Jane and George Putnam of Salem and the wife of Jacob Gilliard.

Jane Putnam. Daughter of Jane and George Putnam of Salem.

(Mrs.) Jane Putnam. Hair salon owner in Salem and the wife of George Putnam.

Joseph Putnam. Son of Jane and George Putnam, husband of Caroline Remond, teacher, and businessman.

Louisa Victoria Putnam. Daughter of Caroline Remond (Putnam) and Joseph Putnam of Salem.

Caroline Remond (Putnam). Owner of a hair salon in Salem, wife of Joseph Putnam, and the daughter of Nancy Lenox and John Remond.

Cecelia Remond. Owner of a wig shop in Salem, wife of James Babcock, and the daughter of Nancy Lenox and John Remond.

Charles Lenox Remond. Prominent abolitionist and the first black lecturing agent of the Massachusetts Anti-Slavery Society, Charlotte Forten Grimké's Salem host from 1853 to 1857, and the son of Nancy Lenox and John Remond.

John Remond. Salem caterer and hairdresser and a prominent abolitionist married to Nancy Lenox.

John Lenox Remond. Son of Nancy Lenox and John Remond of Salem and the husband of Ruth Rice of Newport, Rhode Island.

Maritchie Juan Remond. Daughter of Nancy Lenox and John Remond and owner of a wig shop with her sister Cecelia Remond (Babcock).

Nancy Remond (Shearman). Oldest child of Nancy Lenox and John Remond of Salem and the wife of James Shearman, an oyster dealer.

Sarah Parker Remond. Prominent abolitionist, lecturing agent for the American Anti-Slavery Society, and the daughter of Nancy Lenox and John Remond.

Ruth Rice (Remond). Friend from Newport, Rhode Island, whom Charlotte Forten Grimké met in Salem, and the wife of John Lenox Remond.

Susan Rice. Sister of Ruth Rice (Remond).

Seth Rogers (Dr., Captain). Physician who owned a hydropathic clinic in Worcester, Massachusetts, was prominent in abolitionist circles, and served as a surgeon to the First South Carolina Volunteers.

Amanda Ruggles. Teacher to the freedmen on St. Helena Island and sister of T. Edwin Ruggles.

T. Edwin Ruggles. Plantation superintendent on St. Helena Island.

Rufus Saxton (Brigadier General). Administrator of the abandoned plantations and remaining residents on the Sea Islands during Union military occupation for much of the Civil War.

Robert Gould Shaw (Colonel). U.S. army commander of the 54th Massachusetts.

Helen ("Ellen") Shearman. The eldest daughter of Nancy Remond and James Shearman of Salem.

James Shearman. Salem oyster dealer married to Nancy Remond.

Mary Shepard. Principal of the Higginson Grammar School in Salem.

Robert Smalls. Slave from Beaufort, South Carolina, who as a skilled seaman escaped to Union naval lines with a Confederate boat, served as pilot for the U.S. military, and later became a noted politician.

Gerrit Smith. Prominent businessman, abolitionist, lecturer, and philanthropist born in Utica, New York.

Mrs. James McCune Smith. Wife of the prominent black New York physician, abolitionist, writer, and scholar.

William Still. Prominent black civil rights advocate, Underground Railroad agent, and writer in Philadelphia.

Charles Sumner. Senator, orator, and abolitionist from Boston who was instrumental in the formation of the Republican Party and radical Reconstruction policy following the Civil War.

David Thorpe. Plantation superintendent on St. Helena Island.

Laura Towne. Teacher and physician among the freedmen on St. Helena Island.

Tacie Townsend. Quaker friend of Charlotte Forten Grimké and the second wife of her uncle Robert Purvis, Sr.

Harriet Tubman. Slave from Dorchester County, Maryland, who escaped to freedom in 1849, but returned to the South numerous times to help as many as 300 other slaves escape; also served as a nurse, scout, and cook for the Union army during the Civil War.

Denmark Vesey. Prominent Charleston ex-slave who planned an extensive slave revolt to occur on July 14, 1822, but who was betrayed by informants, eventually captured, tried, and hung.

Mary Webb. Free black dramatist who performed throughout the Northeast.

Daniel Webster ("Dangerfield"). Fugitive slave from Athensville, Virginia, who was arrested, tried in Philadelphia in April 1859, and acquitted.

Elizabeth Whittier. Sister of John Greenleaf Whittier, the poet.

John Greenleaf Whittier. Celebrated poet, abolitionist, and editor, as well as a longtime friend of the Forten family.

Amy Matilda (Williams Cassey) Remond. Wife of Charles Lenox Remond and Charlotte Forten Grimké's Salem hostess from 1853 until her death in 1856.

Mrs. Peter Williams. Mother of Amy Matilda (Williams Cassey) Remond and widow of the prominent black New York clergyman and abolitionist.

Nelly Winsor. Plantation superintendent on St. Helena Island.

Annie Woods (Webb). Charlotte Forten Grimké's maternal aunt.

Mary Virginia Woods (Forten). Charlotte Forten Grimké's mother who was popular in Philadelphia's free black elite society and in abolitionist circles; she died in 1840 at the age of twenty-six.

The Journals of
Charlotte Forten Grimké

INTRODUCTION

Brenda Stevenson

The diaries in this volume provide not only an account of the life of Charlotte Forten Grimké but also visual "slices" of the lives and characters of an enormous range of nineteenth-century persons with whom she came in contact, briefly and intimately. Scholar, reformer, teacher, and writer, she presented within her journals varied and intriguing glimpses of antebellum American life in her quest to express her feelings, to record her daily activities, and to document noteworthy public events and the activities of her friends and family. It is fortunate that Charlotte Grimké was such a keen observer and meticulous recorder of such events, for her journal survives as an important chronicle of one woman's struggles and accomplishments during this most important era in U.S. history.[1]

Charlotte Forten was born on August 17, 1837 in Philadelphia, Pennsylvania. She was the only child of Robert Bridges Forten (1813–1864) and his first wife, Mary Virginia Woods Forten (1816–1840), who died when Charlotte was only three. The Forten family was among the most prestigious and wealthy of the Philadelphia free black community. Moreover, they used their financial and social standing to support local and regional reform movements, most particularly the efforts to abolish slavery and to establish legal equality for free blacks. Charlotte's earliest paternal ancestor in this country had been an African slave, but that was five generations before her birth. She represented the fourth generation of Fortens who were born free, a generation that

3

would live long enough to realize some of the political goals that her family of activists advocated. James Forten, Sr., Charlotte's paternal grandfather, initially articulated these ideals that so profoundly influenced the lives of his children and his granddaughter in particular.[2]

James Forten was born on September 2, 1766. His father, Thomas Forten, died when James was only seven, which meant that he would have to accept, as a youth, the responsibility for the support of his mother and sister. Consequently, he left the Quaker School of Anthony Benezet in 1775 to begin work at a local grocery store. At the outset of the Revolutionary War, he requested that his mother allow him to join the patriot forces and so, in 1780, became powder boy aboard the *Royal Luis*. Sometime thereafter, the crew suffered a decided defeat by the British *Amphyon*, and all of the survivors, including young Forten, were taken prisoner. The commander of the *Amphyon*, Captain Beasely, employed the youth as a companion to his son, who was about the same age. James Forten proved to be clever and entertaining in this role and soon won the affection of his young master and the captain, who proposed that Forten return to England with him and therefore escape the harsh life he was destined to have on a prison ship. Forten declined the offer so that his actions would not be construed as traitorous to his country. Accordingly, Beasely had him transferred to the British ship *Old Jersey*, but commended him to the ship's captain and requested that the young free black be placed on the list of exchange prisoners. In so doing, Beasely assured the eventual release of Forten, for it was not unusual for the British to sell "patriot" black prisoners to the West Indies as slaves. Forten was released from the prison ship after about seven months. He then returned to his home in Philadelphia, but left soon after to accompany his brother-in-law to England. There he resided for a year and learned of the abolitionists' struggle in that society.[3]

When James Forten returned to Philadelphia from England, he did not immediately become involved in abolitionist efforts, but sought to receive some skilled training with which he could provide financial support for his mother and widowed sister. He soon became an apprentice to the sailmaker Robert Bridges. Forten learned quickly, was hardworking and ambitious. His efforts impressed Bridges and in 1786, at the age of twenty, Forten became foreman of Bridges' racially mixed work crew. This was quite an accomplishment for a young black man in late eighteenth-century Philadelphia where the large majority of free black males were unskilled day laborers and the women primarily laundresses and domestics. Yet James Forten intended to accomplish much more; and so he did. He held the position of foreman from 1786 until Mr. Bridges retired in 1798. At that time, Forten was able to buy the company, which flourished under his ownership. He studied his craft well and patented a unique and lucrative device for the handling of sails.[4]

The success of Forten's company gave him and his family the financial security he believed was so important for their survival and comfort in the racially antagonistic world of antebellum Philadelphia. He provided the Fortens with the material comforts of the day—a stately home, opportunities for travel, fine private educations, and access to social and cultural activities. It was his desire that his family should have all the opportunities for advancement and happiness that his financial and emotional support could provide. Moreover, once he became established financially, he worked diligently to change the status of free blacks in American society so that their opportunities would be equal to those of white Americans.

In 1800, James Forten was among other prominent Philadelphia free blacks who, led by the Reverend Absalom Jones, petitioned the U.S. Congress to end the African slave trade, establish guidelines for the gradual abolition of slavery, and provide legislation to weaken the Fugitive Slave Act of 1793.[5] The Congress voted 85 to 1 not to consider the petition.[6]

Forten and his peers, however, were not discouraged in their determination to gain legal and economic equality for blacks. In 1813, Charlotte's grandfather published a pamphlet of five letters rebutting statements supportive of legislation that would ban the entrance of free blacks into the state of Pennsylvania. Moreover, he was an adamant critic of the American Colonization Society. The members of the society, which has formed in December 1816, proposed the voluntary removal of free blacks from the United States to some location in Africa or elsewhere. Most members did not support abolition, but offered a ready remedy for the social and economic problems that they believed free blacks imposed on American society. Colonizationists, as they were called, couched their appeal to blacks in "benevolent" terms, asserting that prejudiced whites in the United States would never accept blacks as full citizens. Outside the country, however, blacks could live more peaceably and "freely." Forten and other free black activists, on the other hand, believed that blacks and whites had equal intellectual and physical capabilities, that blacks had contributed much to the creation and development of the United States as a nation, and thus should have equal access to the country's resources and equal protection under its laws. Free blacks should not be forced to move elsewhere, Forten maintained, but should receive the appropriate training to enable them to live productive lives in American society. He supported protest meetings against the colonizationist movement in both 1817 and 1819. In 1830, Forten was one of the driving forces behind a National Negro Convention held in Philadelphia. Participants of this convention not only condemned colonizationist efforts, but also discussed strategies to expand the rights of free blacks and abolish slavery. Black reformers held several similar meetings during the 1830s, and Forten figured prominently in all of them.[7]

This was an important decade for all blacks within the nation, for it was during these years that disparate antislavery efforts became united in powerful organizations, locally and regionally. James Forten and most of the adult members of his household were at the forefront of these efforts. He served as both an advisor to and financial supporter of William Lloyd Garrison and his efforts to establish the *Liberator* magazine in 1831. Giving freely of his time and energy, Forten helped create a well-organized and widespread antislavery movement. Indeed, his home was often the site of meetings of pioneering abolitionists from England, New England, and New York as well as Pennsylvania. Some of the organizational meetings of the American Anti-Slavery Society, for example, were held there in 1833. Forten served on the Board of Managers of this society for several years. He also promoted other reform movements of the era—in particular, the temperance movement and women's rights. As a founding member and presiding officer of the American Moral Reform Society from 1835 until his death in 1842, he helped formulate the guiding principles of this organization, which were temperance, economy, nonresistance, and fraternal love. The Forten home of the 1830s was a hub of radical thought and activity, and certainly none of its members could have escaped the influence of such dedication and activity.[8] Into this household Charlotte Forten was born in 1837.

James Forten and his wife, Charlotte, Sr. (1784–1884), taught their children to take responsibility both for their lives and for the fate of their race. Scholarship, morality, achievement, selfless dedication to the improvement of the political and economic conditions of blacks—these were the important elements of the socialization process that took place at 92 Lombard Street during Charlotte's childhood as well as during her father's. James and his wife had eight children, four sons and four daughters. Among them, Margaretta, Sarah, Harriet, and Robert Forten were the most politically active.[9]

The three sisters were particularly prominent in abolitionist circles. Their dedication to important political and social issues, as well as their poise and kindness, inspired the young John Greenleaf Whittier, a close family friend, to write the following poem, entitled "To the Daughters of James Forten":

> Sisters!—the proud and vain may pass ye by
> With the rude taunt and cold malicious eye;
> Point the pale hand deridingly and slow,
> In scorn's vile gesture at the darker brow;
> Curl the pressed lip with sneers which might befit
> Some mocking spirit from the nether pit;
> Yet, from a heart whence Truth and Love have borne
> The last remains of Prejudice and Scorn,
> From a warm heart, which, thanks to God, hath felt
> Pride's charm to loosen and its iron melt,
> Fervent and pure let this frail tribute bear
> A Brother's blessing and a Brother's prayer.

And what, my sisters, though upon your brows
The deeper coloring of your kindred glows
Shall I less love the workmanship of Him
Before whose wisdom all our own is dim?
But for the White, and for the Black be still?
Let the thought perish, while the heart can feel
The blessed memory of your grateful zeal,
While it can prize the excellence of mind
The chaste demeanor and the state refined,
Still are ye all my sisters, meet to share
A Brother's blessing and a Brother's prayer.[10]

Forten's daughters, his wife, and his future daughter-in-law (Mary Virginia Woods)[11] were all founding members of the Philadelphia Female Anti-Slavery Society in 1833, an organization that figured prominently in their activities. Margaretta (1808–1875), teacher and administrator of a school for black children in Philadelphia, had a special interest in education and would serve on the society's educational committee for several years. Moreover, she was one of the few remaining founding members who still supported the organization when it dispersed in 1870. Sarah, her younger sister, also served on the Female Anti-Slavery Society's Board of Managers, representing the organization at the Anti-Slavery Convention of American Women in 1837. Harriet Forten herself was a delegate to this conference in 1837 and 1838.[12]

A writer, Sarah Forten (Purvis) used her craft in support of the political causes of her day. Several of her poems and essays related to the subject of black civil rights appeared in the *Liberator* from 1831 to 1837 under the pen names "Ada" and "Magwasca." Sarah worked primarily with other women

in her efforts to secure universal emancipation, and like many
black women involved in the movement, was painfully aware
of the racism of women who participated in such events with
her. Not surprisingly, therefore, one of her most well-known
poems is one in which she addressed the issue of racism
among female reformers. The occasion that prompted the
writing of this poem was the opening of the Anti-Slavery
Convention of American Women held in New York City in
1837.[13] The poem read in part:

> We are thy sisters. God has truly said,
> That of one blood the nations he has made.
> O, Christian woman! in a Christian land,
> Canst thou unblushing read this great command?
> Suffer the wrongs which wring our inmost heart,
> To draw one throb of pity on thy part!
> Our skins may differ, but from thee we claim
> A sister's privilege and a sister's name.[14]

Sarah Forten and her sister Harriet were also active supporters of women's rights and representative of a growing
number of antebellum women who believed in the equality
of the sexes. They especially understood the great social and
political changes women could help to effect and believed
women had a contribution to make to society. Their husbands,
the brothers Robert and Joseph Purvis, held similar views.
Harriet's spouse, Robert, was a particularly influential abolitionist as well as an advocate of temperance and women's
rights. Young Charlotte Forten was very impressed with her
Uncle Robert's activism and enlightened perspective, and she
drew personal comfort and intellectual delight when in the
company of her Aunt Harriet, Mr. Purvis (as she called her
uncle), and her cousins Robert, Jr., and Hattie, who were

about the same age as she. In their home and in her grand-parents' Charlotte met and heard some of the most important members of the abolitionist movement, locally and nationally.

Charlotte's uncle, Robert Purvis, Sr., was born in Charleston, South Carolina, in 1810, the son of a wealthy English cotton broker, William Purvis, and a free woman of Moorish-Jewish descent, Harriet Judah Purvis. His family moved to Philadelphia in 1819, where he and his two brothers completed their private education. William Purvis planned to move his family permanently to England, but died before he could do so in 1826. The family thus remained in Philadelphia. Young, wealthy, and intelligent, Robert Purvis was a welcome addition to Philadelphia's free black community. He strengthened his ties to this community when, in September 1831, he married Harriet Forten. It was about this time that he became actively involved in the abolitionist movement.[15]

A year before his marriage to Harriet, Purvis had several lengthy discussions with William Lloyd Garrison about abolition. No doubt he had similar discussions with members and friends of the Forten family. Moreover, Purvis was present at meetings from which the American Anti-Slavery Society emerged. This society was founded in 1833, and he served as its vice-president for several years. An active man, he was president of the Pennsylvania Anti-Slavery Society from 1845 to 1850 and a long-term member of the Pennsylvania Society for Promoting the Abolition of Slavery. He made his greatest impact with his work on the Underground Railroad in Pennsylvania and was responsible for helping many fugitive slaves gain their freedom in Canada. Purvis was also instrumental in the organization and day-to-day activities of the first Underground Railroad group called the

Vigilance Committee of Philadelphia. He served as its president during the entire period of its tenure (1839–1844) as well as chairman of the successor organization, the General Vigilance Committee, from 1852 to 1857. In 1844, he and his family moved from Philadelphia to nearby Byberry in Bucks County, Pennsylvania. At his home, Purvis constructed a trap door in the floor where he could hide fugitive slaves from authorities.[16]

Robert Purvis was as concerned with the poor social and political conditions of free blacks as he was with the plight of slaves. The education of black youth was especially important to him. In 1833, he helped to organize the Philadelphia Library of Colored Persons and was among a group of prominent free blacks who tried to establish a manual labor college for blacks in New Haven, Connecticut, in the early 1830s. Within his own township of Byberry, Purvis pressured public officials to allow black children to attend local public schools by refusing to pay his local taxes, which were substantial due to his extensive property holdings. His own children were educated mostly in private Quaker schools and by tutors.[17]

Although the 1830s was a decade characterized by a marked increase of activity by free blacks with regard to abolition and civil rights, their position in Pennsylvania continued to decline. In 1838, for example, white mobs in Philadelphia destroyed an orphanage for black children by setting fire to it, tried to burn down one black church, and vandalized another. This was also the year voters adopted a new Pennsylvania state constitution that disfranchised free blacks. Activists, including Robert Purvis and other members of the Forten family, worked tirelessly to prevent the adoption of this constitution. Purvis chaired a committee that jointly wrote

"An Appeal of Forty Thousand Citizens Threatened with Disfranchisement, to the People of Pennsylvania." Charlotte's father, Robert Bridges Forten, was a member of this committee as well as another group of free blacks who addressed the state legislature regarding the rights of free blacks in a protest document entitled the "Memorial of 30,000 Disfranchised Citizens of Philadelphia to the Honorable Senate and House of Representatives."[18]

Like his brother-in-law, Robert Forten was deeply committed to his race and dedicated to efforts to improve the status of blacks in America. It was a commitment that his father demanded of him and that he expected of his daughter. Born in 1813 and educated privately, Charlotte's father was considered by family, friends, and acquaintances as the most talented of his clan. As a young man, he was known locally as a mathematician, poet, and orator. It was during his youth that he constructed a nine-foot telescope that was exhibited at Philadelphia's Franklin Institute. And it was at an early age that he began to participate in various antislavery organizations and activities. Forten was a member of the Young Men's Anti-Slavery Society of Philadelphia and served on its Board of Managers from 1835 to 1836. He also was a member of the Philadelphia Vigilance Committee and the New England Anti-Slavery Society.[19]

Robert Forten's activities document his dedication to antislavery and civil rights, and yet the years of frustration and anger he sustained while growing up as a talented black man in a racist society took its toll. He found it impossible to live a productive and happy life in the United States and moved abroad, first to Canada in 1855 and then to England in 1858. Initially, when considering a move from Pennsylvania, Forten had thought of taking his second wife, Mary, and their two sons, Edmund and Wendell, to Massachusetts to live.[20] Charlotte, then an adolescent studying in Salem, Massachusetts, noted in her diary that she looked forward to having her family together in "a pleasant New England home."[21] However, the outcome of the trial of Anthony Burns, an escaped slave from Alexandria, Virginia, who had since his escape resided in Boston, persuaded Charlotte's father that life in Massachusetts for a black family would be little better than in Pennsylvania.[22] Charlotte concluded of the decision: "To my great disappointment, father has decided not to remove to New England. He is, as I feared he would be, much prejudiced against it on account of the recent slave case, or, he says, he is so against Boston, and I think he intends that feeling to the whole state at least."[23]

Little information descriptive of Robert Forten's life in Canada is available. What is known, however, is that he did have some financial problems that hindered him from giving Charlotte much aid, if any, after 1855. While in England from 1858 to 1862, he worked as a commercial agent. In 1862 Robert Forten returned to the United States to enlist in the Union forces then at war with the Confederacy. Although his family counseled him not to expose himself to the harshness of military life, he was determined to join the U.S. army and did so at Camp William Penn on March 2, 1864. His initial rank was that of a private in Company A of the 43rd U.S. Colored Infantry. A month later, he was promoted to sergeant-major and transferred to Maryland, where he was to help recruit black soldiers. Forten became ill almost immediately after reaching Maryland and, on April 18, 1864, requested sick leave to return to his family home in Philadelphia. Robert Forten died of typhoid fever on April 25,

1864. He was the first black to receive a military funeral in Philadelphia.[24]

Charlotte's father and other politically active family members must have had a tremendous impact on her. She grew up in a home where abolition and equal rights for blacks were key issues to discuss and act upon. Daily she was in the presence of important designers and participants in the abolitionist and civil rights movements. William Lloyd Garrison, John Greenleaf Whittier, Harriet Martineau, William Nell, and Charles Remond were but a few of the prominent abolitionists who visited the Forten and Purvis homes. Moreover, there were present in her family and their groups of friends several impressive female activists who served as important role models for Charlotte. Her mother, grandmother, and aunts were all well-educated, hardworking, morally upright, socially astute women who quite willingly gave much of their energy, financial resources, and time to abolition, civil rights, and the general improvement of conditions within the free black community. Charlotte's mother, Mary Virginia Woods Forten, who was described by her contemporaries as a "beautiful mulatto," was herself a member of a prominent abolitionist family of Philadelphia. Undoubtedly, the young mother believed that her little girl too would grow up to participate in such worthy activities. Unfortunately, Mary Virginia Forten died when Charlotte was quite young and thus was unable to influence her child directly.[25] Yet Charlotte's relatives provided recollections of her mother that served as an inspiration to her as she grew older. As a young woman, Charlotte was able to articulate her curiosity about her mother and openly discussed her with others. One day, for example, Charlotte noted in her diary: "This eve. Mr.

P. [urvis] talked with me about my dear lost mother; I love to hear of her."[26] She also gained some valuable information about her mother by reading some of her correspondence, which Charlotte's maternal aunt, Annie Woods Webb, had saved. After reading some of her mother's letters one night, Charlotte wrote: "Last night I lay awake, thinking of my mother's letters. What a pure and noble character they reveal. She must indeed have been just such a being as I have always fondly imagined."[27]

After Mary Virginia Forten died, Charlotte's paternal grandmother, Charlotte Forten, Sr., and her aunts—particularly Margaretta, who was unmarried—took over the maternal role in her life. Her grandmother and Margaretta lived in the Forten family home on Lombard Street as Charlotte was growing up, and so it was natural for her to feel close to them. She retained strong feelings for them even after 1845, when her father remarried and they moved out of the house. Her diaries are filled with loving concern over her aging grandmother's health. A typical entry, one dated February 28, 1857, reads: "Hattie [Purvis] thinks grandmother doesn't look so well, and it is plain to see that she is growing old. This makes me feel very anxious. I *wish* I could see her, and oh! I wish most earnestly that I could have averted the sorrow and fatigue she has lately endured. But it could not be. I can only give her my love and grateful sympathy."[28] She also often wrote affectionately of her Aunt Margaretta. On returning from her school in Salem one day in 1854, Charlotte found a letter from Margaretta Forten. She noted her surprise in her journal: "it was unexpected, and made me very happy. It was so kind, so cheering that it seemed almost like hearing the gentle affectionate voice of my dear aunt."[29]

Because her aunts and their families lived so near each other, Charlotte benefited from an extended family network that was particularly close-knit. She spent many of her childhood days at the Forten family home at 92 Lombard Street, but would also often visit her aunts Sarah and Harriet Purvis in nearby Bucks County. She adored her cousins and the beauty of the land surrounding their homes, spending many summer days riding, reading, playing games, acting out plays, discussing important issues, picking flowers and berries, and generally enjoying herself. And it seems she never was as relaxed or happy as when surrounded by family. After she moved to Salem in late 1853, Charlotte often thought of the happy times she had spent with her large family and wished once again to be in their presence. Yet she was not one for leisurely vacations at home. She had left Philadelphia to complete her education, which to her was a lofty pursuit. Her personal needs, even family affection, she maintained, were unimportant in comparison.[30]

On May 24, 1854, Charlotte Forten began to keep a journal. At the time, she was sixteen years old and had moved to Salem, Massachusetts, from her native Pennsylvania just six months before to complete her studies. At home, Charlotte had received years of private instruction from tutors since Robert Forten had refused to send her to the poorly equipped and racially segregated schools designated for black children in Philadelphia. When an opportunity came for her to receive an excellent public school education outside of Philadelphia, Charlotte was sent. Mr. Forten discovered from friends that Salem had integrated schools of sound reputation. It was also the location of a fine normal school which her father wanted her eventually to attend so that she could prepare for a teaching career. This profession, he believed, would give Charlotte some practical skill with which to aid her race, for there were few well-trained teachers available to the black community. Moreover, he surmised, such a profession would allow Charlotte some secure means of financial support.

It is not clear from reading the diaries whether Charlotte ever really wanted to become a teacher. It seems as though she preferred the life of a scholar or writer. The young Miss Forten was, however, eager to please her father and to contribute to the uplift of her race and, therefore, she was determined to complete her studies successfully. "I will spare no effort to become what he desires that I should be; . . . to prepare myself well for the responsible duties of a teacher, and to live for the good that I can do my oppressed and suffering fellow-creatures." [31]

Robert Forten arranged that his precocious but shy daughter reside in the Salem home of old friends, the prominent abolitionist Charles Lenox Remond and his wife, Amy Matilda (Williams Cassey) Remond. Charlotte's hostess was the daughter of the Reverend Peter Williams of New York, a well-known abolitionist who had been an associate and friend of James Forten, Sr. Amy Williams's first marriage was to Joseph Cassey, a wealthy black activist from Philadelphia and friend of the Fortens. The Casseys and their children— Alfred, Peter, Sarah, Henry, and Frank—had been neighbors of the Fortens when Charlotte was growing up living just a few houses away at 113 Lombard Street. Robert Forten knew the Casseys well and the children had been Charlotte's playmates. Mr. Cassey died in 1848, and some time later, his widow married Charles Lenox Remond. It was to their home that Charlotte came to live in 1853. Again, she was surrounded by some of the most renowned political activists of the day. [32]

Her Salem host, Charles Lenox Remond, was perhaps the most important black participant in the integrated abolitionist movement before the rise of Frederick Douglass. Remond was born in 1810 in Salem, the son of free black parents, John and Nancy Remond. He and his siblings attended Salem's public schools. Given Remond's refined appearance, eloquence of speech, intelligence, and commitment to abolition, it was not surprising to his contemporaries that, in 1838, he was chosen as the first black lecturing agent of the Massachusetts Anti-Slavery Society. Two years later, Remond served as delegate for the American Anti-Slavery Society when attending the World's Anti-Slavery Convention in London. There he refused to support gender-segregated seating, but instead gave up his seat on the floor of the meeting hall to sit in the gallery with female participants. Remond became a popular speaker abroad and lectured on abolition before audiences in England and Ireland. He returned to Boston in December 1841 with a petition signed by over 60,000 Irishmen who supported abolition in the United States.[33]

Charles Remond remained active as an orator and supporter of the abolitionist cause and was still in the forefront of the movement during Charlotte's stay in his home. In fact, it was while she resided with the Remonds that she met William Lloyd Garrison, Wendell Phillips, John Whittier, Abigail and Stephen Foster, Lydia Maria Child, Maria Chapman, William C. Nell, William Wells Brown, and other noted abolitionists. Many of these persons were close friends of Charlotte's family and the Remonds, and so they wholeheartedly welcomed her into their fold.

Her host's sister, Sarah Parker Remond, did not live with her brother, but was a frequent visitor. A lecturer for the American Anti-Slavery Society, Miss Remond inspired Charlotte with stories of her lecturing tours at home and abroad. On March 6, 1857, for example, Charlotte wrote: "Last night Miss R. entertained me with an account of her tour, and of the delightful day she spent with Mr. [Wendell] Phillips. . . . I listened with most unwearied attention until the 'small hours of the morn' stole upon us."[34]

Other members of the Remond family were involved in the abolitionist movement too. Charlotte was particularly close to Caroline Remond Putnam and her husband, Joseph. Caroline Remond's in-laws (Jane and George Putnam) and their children (Helen [Gilliard], Georgiana, Adelaide, and Jane) were among Charlotte's favorite companions. Other Salem friends included Cecelia Remond Babcock, Nancy Remond Shearman, her husband, James, and their daughter, Ellen. These persons—along with the Casseys, Sarah and Henry—comprised the small circle of black abolitionists and intellectuals that Charlotte interacted with daily and considered her Salem family. Together they surveyed the latest political events, attended lecture series of political and literary subjects, traveled to Boston and other nearby cities to attend abolitionist conventions and fairs, and gave each other the emotional support to continue their efforts.[35]

Although lonely at times, Charlotte came to enjoy Salem and her new friends. It was not long before she began to think of Mrs. Amy Remond as a surrogate mother, and Sarah and Henry as her sister and brother. She was particularly close to Mrs. Remond, whom she described as "[t]he loveliest of women, the best and kindest of friends to me."[36] Thus Mrs. Remond's death, on August 15, 1856, was one of the saddest events of Charlotte's adolescence. It precipitated one of a series of deep depressions that she suffered while residing in Salem. Times of personal loss apparently robbed her of support, comfort, and hope, making her commitment to the larger struggle of her race seem that much more futile. It was during these periods of despair that she dwelt on the near impossibility of trying to survive and achieve something worthwhile in a fundamentally oppressive society. "Often I think there is nothing worth living for. Nothing!" she sighed. "Those whom we love best die and leave us. We are a poor, oppressed people, with very many trials, and very few friends. The Past, the Present, the Future are alike dark and dreary for us. . . . Oh! for strength," she concluded. "[S]trength she concluded. "[S]trength to bear the suffering, to do the work bravely, unfalteringly!"[37]

Charlotte remained in the Remond home for several months after the death of her hostess, but the warmth and friendly charm of the household was lost to her forever. She retained her close ties to Mrs. Remond's daughter, Sarah Smith. Her relationship with Charles Remond, however, gradually deteriorated due to his disagreeable disposition. Charlotte tried to relieve some of the tension within the Remond household by arranging to board in that portion of the house occupied by Sarah, but the change did not have the desired effect. Thus Charlotte and Sarah both moved from the home of Charles Lenox Remond to that of his sister, Mrs. Caroline Remond Putnam, on December 12, 1857. Home life was pleasant once more for Charlotte. She again was able to share intellectual conversations and political pursuits with other members of a politically active household. She particularly enjoyed the "brotherly" affection of Caroline's husband, Joseph Putnam.[38]

Her "society," as Charlotte referred to her friends—the Remonds, Putnams, and Casseys—was extremely important to her psychological well-being. She felt akin to them in spirit and perspective and was therefore able to entrust them with strong emotional ties reminiscent of those she had with her own family and intimates in Pennsylvania. Hesitant to confront her friends who may have momentarily offended her because she feared the disruption it would bring to the circle of intimates, Charlotte had little patience with those who were not willing to sacrifice hurt feelings for the sake of external peace. She noted, for example, several "unfortunate" disputes between Caroline Remond Putnam and her sister, Miss Sarah Parker Remond. Charlotte liked and admired both of these women but was critical of them because they were "always getting offended at trifles."[39] "Such things are *very* unpleasant," she wrote. "Our society is so exceedingly small, it does seem as if they might dwell in peace together. These constant dissensions between people with whom I necessarily come in close contact, are so *very* disagreeable, that I sometimes wish myself far away from Salem."[40]

As time passed, Charlotte came to know and love Salem. Its climate, political activism, and particularly its intellectual offerings suited her tastes. She was well aware of the racism of some of its residents and various instances of institutionalized discrimination, but in comparison with Philadelphia, she found Salem much less oppressive. On those occasions when she had to leave New England for Pennsylvania, Charlotte was routinely apprehensive of the treatment she would receive in her racially hostile home state. She recorded a typical encounter while visiting Philadelphia on June 17, 1857: "On reaching the city," Charlotte recalled, "Mrs. P.[utnam] and I were *refused* at two ice cream saloons, successively. Oh, how terribly I felt! Could say but few words. Mrs. P. told one of the people some wholesome truths, which cannot be soon forgotten. It is dreadful! dreadful! I cannot stay in such a place. I long for N.[ew] E.[ngland]."[41] Charlotte's essay entitled "Glimpses of New England," published in the *National Anti-Slavery Standard* in June 1858, was her tribute to Salem and New England.[42]

During the first year and a half of her stay in Salem, Charlotte was a student at the Higginson Grammar School. Under the direction of Miss Mary Shepard and her three assistants—Elizabeth Jelly, Mary Horton, and Mary Stowers—the 201 female pupils attending Higginson along with Charlotte received instruction in spelling, reading, writing, English grammar, arithmetic, modern geography, and American history. Intellectually, Charlotte thrived at the school from which she graduated with "decided éclat" in March 1855 (the actual graduation ceremony did not, however, take place until almost a year later). Charlotte's poem "A Parting Hymn" was chosen at the time of her official graduation on February 12, 1856 as the best submitted by her class, and she gained a modest local reputation as a young poet of some merit. In fact, she had begun to submit her poetry for publication a year before. In March 1855, a poem that she wrote in praise of William Lloyd Garrison was published in the *Liberator* magazine.[43] Always modest to a fault, Charlotte submitted the poem with only her initials as a clue to its authorship. Thus she was slightly annoyed when her Aunt Margaretta recognized its author.[44] Charlotte entered the Salem Normal School after her final examinations at Higginson and graduated in July 1856, at which time she wrote another poem called simply "Poem for Normal School Graduation." It was published in the *Liberator* in August 1856.[45]

Charlotte lamented the end of her school days, but she

pursued knowledge even more avidly in the years following the end to her formal education than she had as a student. She most often spent her free time studying French, German, Latin, European and classical history, and reading the works of both her contemporaries and of the great authors of the past. Charlotte was particularly fond of good literature and searched for companions with similar tastes. Fortunately, she found such persons in her "society" of housemates and their local relations. Still, she deemed her studies her "closest friends" and approached them with a vitality and passion rarely expressed in other facets of her life. A typical week of self-imposed study was rigorous. On January 5, 1857 she noted: "Still alone, and should be lonesome were not my time so constantly occupied,—teaching all day and reading and studying all the evening. Translated several passages from the 'Commentaries,' and finished the 'Conquest of Mexico.' "[46] The following evening she read and criticized Tennyson.[47] The afternoon of the seventh she spent studying Latin.[48] The next evening she dedicated herself to translating Caesar, a task of which she wrote: "Find it rather difficult, but am determined to persevere. Excelsior! shall be my motto, now and forever."[49] On the ninth, she relaxed and attended a concert by the pianist Thalberg, but followed this with a thorough reading of the *Liberator* when she returned home.[50]

Such was the scholar's life that young Charlotte Forten chose for herself. To pursue her studies in this uninhibited manner she considered a wonderful blessing. Deeply religious, Charlotte believed that God had indeed chosen her for a particular mission—to use her natural talents to inspire and improve her race. Denial of this calling, Charlotte believed, could jeopardize her own Christian salvation. She explained her feelings about this "mission" in a poem entitled "The

Improvement of Colored People," which she wrote in 1856. It read in part:

> In the earnest path of duty,
>> With the high hopes and hearts sincere,
> We, to useful lives aspiring,
>> Daily meet to labor here.
>>> . . . . . .
>
> Not the great and gifted only
>> He appoints to do his will,
> But each one, however lowly,
>> Has a mission to fulfill.
>
> Knowing this, toil we unwearied,
>> With true hearts and purpose high;—
> We would win a wreath immortal
>> Whose bright flowers ne'er fade and die.[51]

Ambition, vanity, and pleasure associated with the acquisition of knowledge, Charlotte concluded, were merely indicative of her selfish and unworthy nature, sins for which she found it necessary to repent.[52] She attributed her need for love and attention to her failure as a Christian, "born as we are to the stern *performance* of *duty* rather than the *pursuit* of *happiness*."[53] Charlotte profoundly believed that "true *un*selfishness must ever be a source of the purest and highest happiness."[54] If she was unhappy, therefore, it was the result of her own moral failure.

Charlotte's insistence on selfless dedication to her race—which in her mind denied her the right of such basic human needs as love, pride, and concern for "self-culture"—was at best a burdensome ideal that caused her immeasurable frustration during her youth. It was a goal that, in time, Charlotte came to know as unattainable. As a young adult, however, she could not accept this rationally and failed to appreciate the valuable contributions she could and did make. Thus a pervasive sense of unworthiness and insecurity characterized Charlotte's adolescence and young adulthood. Several lengthy entries in her diary reveal her stern self-criticism, shame, and guilt. One such entry, dated June 15, 1858, reads:

> Have been under-going a thorough self-examination. The result is a mingled feeling of sorrow, shame and self-contempt. Have realized more deeply and bitterly than ever in my life my own ignorance and folly. Not only am I without the gifts of Nature, wit, beauty and talent; without the accomplishments which nearly every one of my age, whom I know, possesses; but I am not even *intelligent*. And for *this* there is not the *shadow* of an excuse. Have had many advantages of late years; and it is entirely owing to my own want of energy, perseverance and application, that I have not improved them. It grieves me deeply to think of this. I have read an immense quantity, and it has all amounted to nothing, because I have been too indolent and foolish to take the trouble of *reflecting*. Have *wasted* more time than I dare think of, in idle daydreams, one of which was, how much I should know and do before I was twenty-one. And here I am nearly twenty-one, and only a *wasted life* to look back upon.—Add to intellectual defects a disposition whose despondency and fretfulness have constantly led me to look on the dark side of things, and effectually prevented me from contributing to the happiness of others; whose contrariness has often induced me to do those things which I ought not to have done, and to leave undone those things which I ought to have done, and wanted to do,— and we have as dismal a picture as one could look upon; and yet hardly dismal enough to be faithful. Of course, I want to try to reform. But how to begin![55]

Miss Forten's unhappiness and frustration during the period chronicled in her first three journals not only derived from a growing sense of failure with regard to her mission but also from the deteriorating relationship with her father, Robert Forten.

Knowing how highly she valued her education, it is not surprising that Charlotte felt alienated from her father when on two occasions—in September 1854 and March 1855—he asked that she leave Salem and return home immediately. Both times Charlotte wrote to him and pleaded to stay until graduation. Both times her father relented, but her relationship with him suffered. It declined steadily as the distance between them grew.[56]

Charlotte came to Salem in 1853 hoping her father and stepfamily would soon relocate to Massachusetts, where together they could establish a home.[57] She was therefore very disappointed when Robert Forten decided in 1855 to move his family to Canada. Once he left the country, Charlotte received little communication from him, which prompted her to believe that his interest in and affection for his only daughter had somehow diminished. His silence was slow torture to her. Charlotte's journal documents the profound sense of abandonment she experienced as a result of her father's apparent coldness. "I too have known but little of a father's love," she wrote in 1857. "It is hard for me to bear. To thee, alone, my journal, can I say with tears how *very* hard it is. I *have* a loving heart, though some may doubt it, and I long for a parent's love—for the love of my only parent; but it seems denied me; I know not why."[58]

Charlotte's estrangement from her father posed practical problems, too, for she was left with no financial support except that which she earned herself. When her father's aid ceased, she was a full-time student at the Salem Normal School and suddenly was unable to pay some of her school expenses as well as her room and board to the Remonds. Her growing indebtedness was another source of frustration and depression. "All my day dreams of independence and usefulness," she noted, "seems to have been dissipated one by one. And harder and sterner become the realities of life."[59] Charlotte thought that her financial problems were solved when, in June 1856, she accepted an offer to teach in the Epes Grammar School in Salem for an annual salary of $200. She was the first black to be offered such a position in the city and so was, momentarily, a bit proud of herself. Yet, by late 1856, her health had begun to fail and eventually forced her to take a leave of absence from her teaching position. Temporarily unable to earn a living, she returned to Philadelphia. When Charlotte finally did receive a letter from her father in May 1857, she realized he had sent her several other letters which she had never received.[60] She was relieved to discover that her father had not "forsaken" her, but the relationship was never completely mended. Several months later he wrote again to her in response to a request for financial assistance, stating that he was, as Charlotte described it, *"utterly unable"* to help her.[61] Charlotte did make some mention of possibly joining her father after he moved to England in 1858, but the plans never solidified.[62]

As Charlotte's relationship with her father disintegrated, she seemed to think more of her deceased mother and of the loving relationship they would have had if she had lived. Charlotte's fantasies of her mother depicted a beautiful, warm, loving woman to whom an unhappy and often ill daughter could always turn for comfort.[63] Charlotte conveyed these feelings in a poem she wrote in 1858, "The Angel's Visit." In this poem, she describes the needs of a woman, weary of life, who pleads with her angel mother to

> . . . guide and soothe thy sorrowing child;
>   And if 'tis not His will
> That thou shouldst take me home with thee,
>   Protect and bless me still;
> For dark and dreary had been my life
>   Without thy tender smile,
> Without a mother's loving care,
>   Each sorrow to beguile.

In a later verse, the mother offers her daughter comforting guidance:

> She gently drew me to her side,
>   She pressed her lips to mine,
> And softly said, "Grieve not, my child,
>   A mother's love is thine.
> I know the cruel wrongs that crush
>   The young and ardent heart;
> But falter not; keep bravely on,
>   And nobly bear thy part."

The poem ends with the angel mother promising her daughter that she will live to see a "brighter day" when her goals will be accomplished if she continues to lead a "noble and unselfish life."[64]

This poem is particularly interesting because it reveals the solace Charlotte finds in thoughts of death and everlasting life. But while she did think longingly of death as an end to loneliness and frustration, she never contemplated suicide. To do so would have been a sin, for she accepted the Christian principle that one's death was solely God's choice. Charlotte could only hope that God would help her achieve her mission so that she would enjoy a peaceful life after death.

Although for days and weeks at a time Charlotte thought much about her mother, her fantasies did not bring her long-lasting comfort. In fact, she did not actually mourn her real mother, whom she had hardly known, but a mother figure to whom she could turn for comfort. Charlotte continued to grieve the loss of her surrogate mother, Amy Matilda Remond. Meanwhile, female family members—particularly her paternal grandmother and aunts Harriet Purvis, Margaretta Forten, and Annie Woods Webb—brought her a great deal of solace, though they could never be the parents she so missed.

Charlotte's unhappiness and negative self-perception undoubtedly also stemmed from the racism and rejection of whites with whom she came in contact daily. During her adolescence and early adulthood, she felt the racism of classmates and, later, of teachers in Salem. Early on, there were some schoolmates, Elizabeth ("Lizzie") Church and Sarah Brown ("Brownie"), for example, who won Charlotte's confidence as true friends, but for the most part, she found her Salem classmates racist and generally unsympathetic to the abolitionists' cause to which she had dedicated herself.[65]

A shy, sensitive, sometimes angry and defensive adolescent, Charlotte absolutely refused to compromise her standards with regard to friends. In June 1854, for instance, she wrote in her journal about her classmates at Higginson: "Would that those with whom I shall recite to-morrow could sympathize with me in this; would that they could look upon all God's creatures without respect to color, feeling that it is character alone which makes the true man or woman! I earnestly hope that the time will come when they will feel thus."[66] A year later, while enrolled in the Normal School, her tone was decidedly more angry: "I wonder that every colored person is not a misanthrope," she wrote. "Surely we have everything to make us hate mankind. I have met girls in the school-room—they have been thoroughly kind and cordial to me—perhaps the next day met them in the street—they feared to recognize me; these I can but regard now with scorn and contempt, once I liked them, believing them incapable of such measures. Others give the most distant recognition possible. I, of course, acknowledge no such recognition, and they soon cease entirely. These are but trifles," she concluded, "[b]ut to those who experience them, these apparent trifles are most wearing and discouraging; even to the child's mind they reveal volumes of deceit and heartlessness, and early teach a lesson of suspicion and distrust."[67] Charlotte did grow suspicious of the racial attitudes of whites and usually withheld her judgment of a person until she found out if they held the "correct" views on racial issues. She was, however, able to establish a few meaningful relationships with some of her schoolroom associates, most particularly a deep friendship with Miss Mary Shepard, Charlotte's principal at the Higginson Grammar School.

Indeed, Charlotte's acceptance of Mary Shepard's good intentions in aiding and befriending her sole black student was almost immediate. Charlotte found her teacher not only intelligent and friendly but, most important, an advocate of antislavery. On May 26, 1854, she recorded in her journal: "Had a conversation with Miss Mary Shepard about slavery; she is, as I thought, thoroughly opposed to it."[68] The next day, Charlotte "spent a delightful hour" with Miss Shepard, examining engravings of various locations in Europe, discussing religious persecution, and reading "exquisite pieces of poetry."[69] As their friendship grew, Charlotte continually documented her affection and respect for Mary in her journal. Miss Shepard proved an invaluable friend and an important intellectual mentor. A constant companion, Mary often pro-

vided Charlotte with money, job nominations, introductions
to literary friends, and emotional support. She was particularly kind to Charlotte during her bouts with lung fever. On
June 4, 1857, for example, Charlotte recorded: "This evening
my too kind friend Miss S. came in, bringing some exquisite
flowers and spent some time with me. It was so delightful to
have her here. . . . She, with her usual self-sacrificing
kindness and generosity wishes me to spend a few weeks in
the country at her expense." Charlotte's response to Mary's
offer was typical: "I feel as if I *ought* not to do it . . . it
would not be just to her. I *know* that it would not be. . . .
I—so unworthy—am blest indeed, in having so very kind a
friend."[70]

Certainly Charlotte judged her own character and actions
more harshly than she did those of her friends and family.
She was particularly generous in her assessment of those
whites whom she believed had overcome their racism and
were involved actively in the abolitionist movement. She also
praised those who offered her genuine acceptance and friendship. And while Charlotte was familiar with the overt racial
hostility of most whites in mid-nineteenth-century America,
she continued to be angered and hurt when faced with
discrimination or outright rejection.

Yet as a young adult, Miss Forten never realized the
enormous impact that she had on whites with whom she came
in contact. Her insecurity and extreme modesty blinded her
to their appreciation of her demeanor, intelligence, and accomplishments. These persons—primarily abolitionists, intellectuals, and literary artists—viewed her as exceptional in
character and talent. Her close friend, John Greenleaf Whittier, for example, described Charlotte to Theodore Dwight
Weld as "a young lady of exquisite refinement, quiet culture

and ladylike and engaging manners, and personal appearance." "I look upon her as one of the most gifted representatives of her class," he concluded.[71] A writer for the *Salem
Register* wrote of Charlotte in 1856: "She presented in her
own mental endowments and propriety of demeanor an honorable vindication of the claims of her race to the rights of
mental culture and privileges of humanity."[72]

Perhaps Charlotte's negative self-esteem resulted from her
subconscious inculcation of popular views of black inferiority.
Publicly she never wavered in her belief in the natural
equality of the races and, indeed, dedicated her life to asserting
through personal example the legitimacy of that doctrine. Yet
privately she struggled not so much with the basic premise
of natural equality, but with the question of whether members
of her race were willing to work diligently to achieve the
reality of equality, given their limited access to it. Her
criticism of blacks, as of herself, was often severe, and it was
difficult for her to accept their moral nobility, much more so
than it was for her to recognize the nobility of whites. She
described her good friend, Henry Cassey, for example, as a
young black man with a "noble nature, and high aspirations,
both moral and mental." She went on, however, to sharply
contrast his nobility with those of other black males, noting
that these characteristics of Henry made "him a different
being from the generality of colored young men that one
sees;—though I know that the unhappy circumstances in
which these are placed, are often more to blame than they
themselves."[73]

Charlotte certainly adopted white standards for beauty that
caused her to think of herself as unattractive when by all
accounts she was a pretty woman. While she was visiting
John Whittier's home in 1862, for example, the poet's sister,

Elizabeth, presented her with a portrait of an Italian woman that everyone there thought resembled Charlotte. Miss Forten noted of the incident, however: "I utterly failed to see it: *I* thought the Italian girl very pretty, and I know myself to be the very opposite."[74] On another occasion Charlotte described a friend of her cousin Hattie Purvis as quite attractive, with "just such long, light hair, and beautiful blue eyes. . . . She is a little poetess,—a sweet, gentle creature. I have fallen quite in love with her."[75] When describing the face of a wounded black soldier in the 54th Massachusetts, she again indicated her standards for beauty. "He has such a good, honest face. It is pleasant to look at it—although it is black."[76] Thus Charlotte herself internalized racist attitudes that undoubtedly would have a negative effect on her self-image.

While issues of race continued to figure largely in Charlotte's life, her health problems became a major source of frustration as early as 1856. Like so many of her friends and family, she suffered from respiratory ailments that not infrequently imposed an immense physical and emotional burden on her. The consequences of such ailments were familiar to Charlotte. Her mother, her friends, including Amy Matilda Remond, Sarah Smith's husband, Joseph Putnam, and her cousins, Robert and William Purvis, had all died of respiratory disease by the time Charlotte reached her twenty-fifth birthday.[77] So it wasn't surprising that she would spend time and energy protecting her own health and nursing her sick loved ones.

Charlotte first began to suffer from severe headaches and respiratory illnesses in November 1856, not long after she accepted a teaching position at the Epes Grammar School, at which time she was disabled for two weeks. Charlotte was intermittently ill for the next six months and, in May 1857, contracted a cold so severe that she was forced to return to Philadelphia to rest and regain her health. Her inability to work, and therefore to support herself financially, was particularly stressful. On June 7, 1857, for example, she noted in her journal: "Dr. G. came, and examined my lungs. Advises me not to enter school again this summer. Shall be glad to rest if it can only be arranged so that I may have school again in the Fall. If it cannot be so, I know not what I *shall* do. . . . Feel that I would rather risk anything than give up my school entirely."[78] Charlotte was relieved when, two days later, Mr. Richard Edwards, the principal of the Salem Normal School who had initially nominated her for the teaching post, assured her that her job would be secure.[79] Thus she spent part of the summer recuperating in the Forten family home in Philadelphia and in nearby Bucks County with her aunts Harriet and Sarah Purvis.[80] Her health, however, was never fully restored.

Charlotte returned to Salem in July 1857 to resume her teaching position at Epes, but was forced to resign in early March 1858 due to illness. Her resignation became town news when an announcement appeared in the *Salem Register*.[81] The decision to leave her post at Epes was a particularly difficult one. While Charlotte very much wanted her job, she felt that if she did not make an effort to restore her health completely it would assure her a life of uselessness and dependency. To avoid such a life, the independent young woman concluded: "I would ten thousand times rather die than that."[82]

Following her resignation, Charlotte returned to Pennsylvania where she rested, taught the younger children of Harriet Purvis, and wrote poems and essays for publication. Although her health had interrupted her teaching career, the less hectic pace of the Purvis household in Byberry allowed her to focus on professional writing. She received her first payment for writing, a modest sum of one dollar, from Bishop Daniel Payne of the *Christian Recorder* magazine, on May 20, 1858, for a poem entitled "Flowers."[83] The next month, her essay "Glimpses of New England" appeared in the *National Anti-Slavery Standard.*[84] In 1859, two poems—"The Two Voices" and "The Wind Among the Poplars"—appeared in print."[85] And in January 1860, Charlotte's poem "The Slave Girl's Prayer" was published in the *National Anti-Slavery Standard.*[86]

Miss Forten was serious about her efforts to become a good writer. And if her health continued to be impaired, she hoped that perhaps she could support herself through writing. As usual, however, her confidence was low. As critical of her works as of herself, she noted upon publication of "Glimpses of New England": "To my great astonishment see that my poor 'Glimpses' are published in the 'Standard.' They are not worth it."[87] On another occasion, she wrote similarly: "Commenced writing a story . . . 'Twas commenced on the impulse of the moment. 'Tis not possible that it will ever be finished—or if finished, worth publishing. I'm *quite sure* it will not."[88] Nonetheless, she vowed to persevere in her efforts.

Charlotte remained with her family until September 1859, when she again returned to Salem to teach with Miss Shepard in the Higginson Grammar School. By the spring, however, she became ill with "lung fever" and resigned her post. Charlotte then traveled to Bridgewater and later to Worcester to seek physical therapy at the water cure establishment of Dr. Seth Rogers.[89] By the fall of 1860, she had recuperated enough to resume work, but again became seriously ill in late

October 1860 and had to return to Philadelphia. There she rested but remained active in the abolitionist cause while she taught in a school for black children run by her Aunt Margaretta. Charlotte returned to Salem during the summer of 1862 to teach summer classes, and on August 9, 1862, she and Mary Shepard visited John Whittier at his home in Amesbury. It was during this visit that Whittier suggested to Charlotte that she could render a great service to her people if she went to teach among the contraband slaves who had run away to Union camps in the Confederate South.[90]

On October 22, 1862, Charlotte Forten sailed from New York for Port Royal, South Carolina, where she remained for about eighteen months. Under the auspices of the Port Royal Relief Association, Charlotte secured the position of teacher among the contraband slaves of the South Carolina Sea Islands. She was among hundreds of teachers from the Northeast who had come South for various reasons, but primarily to prepare the recently released slaves for their new role as free citizens of the United States.

The first teachers came to South Carolina in March 1862. Five months before, in November 1861, Commander S. F. Dupont and his naval fleet were successful in their attack on Confederate batteries located in the Port Royal Sound. As a result, the wealthy planters who occupied the Sea Islands off the coast of South Carolina evacuated their plantations, reluctantly leaving behind approximately ten thousand "uncooperative" slaves. The U.S. government confiscated the remaining slaves as "contraband of war" for the use of Union forces. These slaves officially became free on July 17, 1862, when the U.S. Congress determined that all slaves who belonged to rebels and were presently behind Union lines were free. The newly freed slaves, however, were responsible to the local U.S. military officers and agents and under their protection. The adults were put to work, primarily in the fields growing and harvesting that most important of crops— King Cotton. And many of the children reported to schools established throughout the region by Northern agencies organized to lend assistance and guidance.[91]

Charlotte Forten was among the first black teachers aiding the Southern contraband and, at the time she arrived, the first and only one stationed on St. Helena Island. Proportionately, there continued to be a very small number of blacks who were trained as teachers. Moreover, some agencies were less than cooperative in their efforts to place qualified black teachers in these positions. Charlotte Forten, for example, initially tried to reach South Carolina under the auspices of the Boston Educational Commission, later renamed the New England Freedman's Aid Society. After several unsuccessful attempts to gain their sponsorship in August 1862, she returned to Philadelphia where she retained the support of the Port Royal Relief Association of that city.[92]

Miss Forten believed that working among the contraband slaves of South Carolina would afford her an excellent opportunity to help her race. Frustrated by the restrictions of poor health, she welcomed the opportunity to travel South where she hoped the mild climate would allow her to remain tolerably healthy while she performed the "noble" task of preparing illiterate blacks for their roles as free Americans. She expressed her feelings about past disappointments and future opportunities on the occasion of her twenty-fifth birthday: "Tisn't a very pleasant thought," she remarked,

> that I have lived a quarter of a century, and am so very, very ignorant. Ten years ago, I hoped for a different fate at

twenty-five. But why complain? The accomplishments, the society, the delights of travel which I have dreamed of and longed for all my life, I am now convinced can never be mine. If I can go to Port Royal, I will try to forget all these desires. I will pray that God in his goodness will make me noble enough to find my highest happiness in doing my duty.[93]

From the very beginning of her stay on St. Helena Island, Charlotte thought fondly of the contraband slaves with whom she came in contact. Sensitive to their plight of trying to adjust to the status of free persons, she was quick to explain that their cultural expression and lifestyles, which seemed peculiar and sometimes crude to Northerners, were largely a result of their past as slaves.[94] Yet like the other teachers and missionaries who came to instruct the contraband, Charlotte sometimes was both amused and repulsed by the social and religious practices of the Sea Island blacks. Overall, however, she appreciated their friendly and deferential manner, their determination to gain freedom and educate their children, and particularly their affectionate treatment of loved ones and friends. Her general fondness for the adults as well as her students caused her to be solicitous of their individual and group needs, especially their health and material welfare.[95]

Miss Forten's primary task on St. Helena Island was to teach the contraband children the rudiments of a formal education. Placed in a one-room schoolhouse with children of all ages, Charlotte taught reading, writing, spelling, history, and math. She also instructed the other blacks on proper moral and social behavior. Freedman aid societies, such as the one that sponsored Charlotte's work, strongly advocated this kind of informal but instructive contact between contraband slaves and their Northern workers. It was indeed a

necessity, these organizations argued, if contraband blacks
were to become useful and acceptable free members of American society. Thus, early on, many Northerners hoped to
begin to "reconstruct" the South by instilling in these blacks
Northern cultural values and practices.[96] Charlotte, who was
an avid assimilationist, was no different in this respect from
her white peers and adamantly believed that blacks would
never be accepted as equals to whites in society if they
remained culturally distinct. Certainly she enjoyed the culture
of the Sea Island blacks, especially their unique singing style,
but she was greatly relieved that the contraband were con-
forming to Northern mores, such as solemnizing their relationships through legal marriage.[97]

Most of her time on St. Helena was happy. It was undoubtedly the most challenging period of her life, a time of
immense personal growth. As the first black teacher among
the contraband who resided there, Charlotte faced the mixed
feelings of both teachers and military personnel. Although
she reported that most of the Union whites she interacted
with were pleasant, she did note that initially she felt no
"congeniality" among those with whom she lived.[98] This
feeling, however, would change when old abolitionist friends
and acquaintances arrived later. Yet, during the first few
months, she was decidedly lonely. The contraband slaves did
not greet her with open arms, and having served whites all
their lives, they found it difficult to accept Charlotte's position
as equal to that of the Anglo-American teachers. The black
domestic staff at Oaklands, where she resided, were unpre-
pared to wait on her and questioned a white resident as to the
young black woman's background and position. It was only
a year later, after hearing her play the piano, that as Colonel

Thomas Wentworth Higginson reported to his wife, they began to view her with the same respect as they did whites.[99]

Colonel Higginson was one of several close friends that Charlotte acquired while residing on St. Helena Island. A native of Massachusetts, Thomas Higginson had been a dedicated abolitionist who gained widespread notoriety in 1854 when he tried unsuccessfully to aid in the escape of the fugitive slave Anthony Burns, who was then on trial in Boston. Higginson was by profession a Unitarian minister and lived in Worcester, Massachusetts. When Charlotte saw him in South Carolina during the fall of 1862, she recalled that she had seen him the summer before drilling soldiers of the all-white 51st Massachusetts before they left for duty in the South, and she remembered his enthusiasm in commanding the troops. Such a man, "so full of life and energy" and so obviously dedicated to the black race, was "the one best fitted to command a regiment of colored soldiers," she thought.[100] So did General Rufus Saxton, commander of the Union forces in the Port Royal region, who decided to place Higginson in command of the First South Carolina Volunteers, a regiment of Sea Island blacks.[101]

Charlotte followed closely the recruitment and training of this historical regiment, and both blacks and white abolitionists hoped that they would soon impress America with their bravery and determination. Colonel Higginson thought highly of Charlotte, too, particularly of her intellect, kindness, and genuine desire to help her race. Thus it was not surprising that he tried to recruit her as a teacher for his men on their campaign to Florida in 1863. Charlotte was thrilled at the opportunity. "So much depends on these men," she noted. "If I can help them in any way I shall be glad to do so."[102]

Yet she was never able to join the regiment since the Union army in Florida was losing ground. Higginson and his men were eventually evacuated and returned to Port Royal.[103]

Meanwhile, Charlotte remained on St. Helena Island where she befriended other military personnel and teachers. Although she initially felt no "congeniality" with the other residents, as time passed, she came to know them better, share experiences, work with them, and socialize more frequently and as a result was able to build some sound friendships. She shared the responsibility of teaching with two others—Ellen Murray of Milton, Massachusetts, and Laura Towne from Shoemakertown, Pennsylvania. Miss Towne, whom Charlotte described as "housekeeper, physician, everything, here," and the "most indispensable person on the place," was among the first of the Freedmen Aid Society representatives to arrive on the island, coming during the summer of 1862. She and Miss Murray had already established a school for the contraband children in the local Baptist church when Charlotte arrived.[104] Charlotte's group of friends also included Elizabeth Hunn, who came with her from Philadelphia, and Elizabeth's father, John Hunn, who opened a store for the ex-slaves on the island.[105]

Miss Forten became fond of several plantation superintendents as well, including David Thorpe, a student from Brown University, and Edwin Ruggles and his sister, Amanda, who were Charlotte's closest neighbors. Reuben Tomlinson, a member of the staff of General Rufus Saxton who was particularly interested in the educational activities of the ex-slaves on the island, and Edward L. Pierce, special agent of the Treasury Department and general coordinator of all the activities related to the contraband, were also among Charlotte's acquaintances.[106]

In addition, Charlotte met and was very impressed with Colonel Robert Gould Shaw, son of the noted abolitionist Francis Shaw of New York and commander of the all-black 54th Massachusetts regiment. She was moved by Colonel Shaw's gentlemanly qualities, intellect, and his great appreciation for his position as commander of the first regiment of free blacks from the North to be engaged in the Civil War.[107] "I am perfectly charmed with Col. S.," Charlotte wrote during the summer of 1863. "He seems to me in every way one of the most delightful persons I have ever met. . . . To me he seems a thoroughly lovable person. And there is something so exquisite about him. The perfect breeding," she concluded, "how evident it is. . . . I have seen him but once, yet I cannot help feeling a really affectionate admiration for him."[108] Thus Charlotte was stunned by the death of Colonel Shaw at the bloody battle of Fort Wagner on Morris Island, South Carolina, on July 18, 1863. "That our noble, beautiful young Colonel is killed, and the regt. cut to pieces!" she wrote upon receiving the news of the outcome of the battle.[109] The bravery that Shaw exhibited left a lasting impression on her. Several years later, in 1871, she returned to South Carolina to teach at the Shaw Memorial School in Charleston. Moreover, in the small collection of photographs retained in her papers, there is an autographed picture of Shaw.[110]

While her third and fourth journals are filled with descriptions and anecdotes of the lives and culture of the people of the island, Charlotte never established close social relationships with the black ex-slaves she came to know. She noted her meeting with Harriet Tubman, the famous escaped slave who returned South several times to aid the escape of other slaves, but she never became friends with her. Tubman was then employed by the Union army as spy, scout, and nurse. It seems Charlotte had difficulty considering these blacks her peers because of their cultural differences, personal histories, and lack of intellectual sophistication. She felt much more comfortable with well-educated Northerners, such as the other teachers, plantation superintendents, and army officers in the area.[111] By far the most important relationship that Charlotte established on St. Helena Island was her deep romantic attachment to the white surgeon in Higginson's First South Carolina Volunteers, Dr. Seth Rogers, whom she had met a few years before.

As Charlotte entered young adulthood, her journal indicates that her longing for love and attention became less focused on a parental relationship and more centered on a romantic one. At age twenty-one, for example, she wrote:

> I long for one earnest sympathizing soul to be in close communion with my own. I long for the pressure of a loving hand in mine, the touch of loving lips upon my aching brow. I long to lay my weary head upon an earnest heart, which beats for me,—to which *I* am dearer far than all the world beside. There is none, for me, and never will be. I could only love one whom I could look up to, and reverence and that *one* would never think of such a poor little ignoramus as I. But what a selfish creature I am. This is a forlorn old maid's reverie.[112]

There is no suggestion in her journal, however, that Charlotte established a romantic relationship before she left for South Carolina in 1862. She does note that local gossip in Philadelphia viewed her and Henry Cassey as romantically involved. Charlotte implicitly denied this rumor, though her concern over not having received any letters from Henry once she went to St. Helena perhaps would suggest a deeper emotional involvement than she was willing to admit.[113]

When Charlotte arrived in South Carolina, she was understandably lonely—not only was she trying to adjust to a strange, new environment, but she was participating in a "revolutionary" social experiment with persons she did not know who were quite different in background from her. So she was more than pleased to learn that an old friend, Dr. Seth Rogers of Worcester, Massachusetts, would soon arrive.[114]

Charlotte first met Dr. Rogers during the spring of 1860, when she frequented his water cure establishment in Worcester. This experience firmly established in Charlotte's mind a growing affection and regard for him. Writing of that time in Worcester, she noted: "The excellent Dr. R. did me a world of good—spiritually as well as physically. To me he seems one of the best and noblest types of manhood I ever saw. In my heart I shall thank him always."[115] Two years later, she met the doctor and his wife, Bell, at an abolitionist meeting held on the Fourth of July at Framingham, Massachusetts. "How glad I was to see the Dr. again," she recalled. "But it grieved me to see him looking so far from well. . . . He is certainly one of the most thoroughly good men in the world."[116] Later that summer, Charlotte spent time with Dr. Rogers in Worcester, riding with him, accompanying him to his home, and seeing him professionally at his clinic.[117]

Seth Rogers arrived at Camp Saxton, South Carolina, during the latter part of December 1862. When Charlotte traveled to the camp on New Year's Day 1863 to celebrate the Emancipation Proclamation, she was elated to see her friend and physician again. "Just as my foot touched the plank, on landing," she noted, "a hand grasped mine and well known voice spoke my name. It was my dear and noble friend, Dr. Rogers. I cannot tell you . . . how delighted I was to see him; how *good* it was to see the face of a friend from the North, and *such* a friend."[118] Their friendship flourished. Entry after entry in Charlotte's diary describe the times they spent together—taking walks and riding horseback, having dinner, traveling together to nearby plantations, playing chess, reading to one another, and just talking about themselves, their work, and literature.[119]

It is not certain how profoundly Dr. Rogers felt about Charlotte, for the journal only depicts her feelings. It does tell us, however, that Rogers certainly devoted a great deal of time and energy to her while they were in South Carolina. Moreover, it was his suggestion that they write to one another when they could not visit often. And apparently Dr. Rogers was happy with Colonel Higginson's request that Charlotte join their regiment during the Florida campaign. He also sent her gifts, read to her when she was ill, and was generally very attentive.[120] Although his gestures appear to have been romantic in intent, Charlotte explained on February 2, 1863 that Dr. Rogers wanted her to think of him "as a brother." "And I will gladly do so," she responded.[121]

Whether Charlotte and Seth continued to view their relationship in this light is uncertain, but her journal entries from this period seem to indicate that she was very much in love with the young doctor whom she found "impossible to resist."[122] Charlotte admitted that she not only thought of him "constantly," but found him to be noble, handsome, and exciting, both intellectually and physically.[123] His presence brought her *"unspeakable* happiness."[124] Consider, for example, a journal entry that Charlotte made in early 1863:

He [Dr. Rogers] came home to dine with us, and then we—just he and I—had the loveliest horseback ride to Mr. Thorpe's place. It was lovely through those pines and we found the most exquisite jessamine. . . . Nothing c'ld be more perfect that the color, more delicious than the fragrance. Dr. R. broke off long sprays and twined them around me. I felt grand as a queen. . . . Mr. T.[horpe] . . . was not at home, so we made no stay. Dear A.* I can give you no idea of the ride homeward. I know only that it was the most delightful ride I ever had in my life. The young moon—just a silver bow—had a singular, almost violet tinge, and all around it in the heavens was a rosy glow, deepening every moment, which was wonderfully beautiful. . . . How wild and unreal it all seemed and what happiness it was.[125]

The love and passion that Charlotte felt for Rogers inspired her to express her fear that he would be killed in battle: "The thought makes my heart ache," she noted. "I am willing to give up my life—which is nothing—but I do not want one so good and noble as he to die yet."[126]

Charlotte did not forget that Dr. Rogers was married and white. He in turn, seeming to anticipate the possibility of a more intimate relationship with her, tried to quell it by insisting that Charlotte regard him as a brother and by reminding her of his wife. Charlotte viewed these as "noble" gestures and was apt to respond to them by feeling closer to him. She documented, for example, an incident when Seth sent her a note that his wife had sent to him: "He has sent . . . also a little note of Bell's full of touching and beautiful affection," Charlotte wrote. "Indeed it is very kind of him to let me see this little note. It somehow brings me nearer to him."[127]

* A. [mi inconnu] was the name that Charlotte gave her journal.

Charlotte's journal indicates that she and Dr. Rogers continued to have a close relationship throughout most of 1863. In fact, when Charlotte traveled back to Philadelphia for a much needed rest in July of that year, Dr. Rogers, along with some of her other friends, were aboard the same ship with her. Moreover, Charlotte visited Worcester during her vacation. When she returned to St. Helena in October, a large party of associates, including Rogers, accompanied her. One of the last times she mentions him—and then only slightly—was on October 16, 1863, in an entry describing her trip back to South Carolina: "In spite of the pleasant company with me (Dr. R., . . .) had a rather dreary voyage." Charlotte remained in South Carolina until late May 1864. Rogers, on the other hand, resigned from his post in the Union army in December 1863, and went back to Worcester. Obviously, the relationship suffered after his departure, but the lack of reference to him in her journal following her return from the North may indicate a slow deterioration that had begun sometime earlier.[128]

Overall, Charlotte's experiences on St. Helena Island were fruitful. She wrote of her time among the contraband in two letters addressed to William Lloyd Garrison, which were subsequently published in the *Liberator* in 1862. A two-part article, which Charlotte called "Life on the Sea Islands," appeared in the *Atlantic Monthly* in 1864.[129] It was a rewarding and exciting period of her life not only because opportunities existed for it to be so, but also because she had acquired the emotional maturity necessary to realistically perceive and act on these opportunities. After a troubled and prolonged adolescence, she was long overdue for the happiness and sense of fulfillment that she obtained while working among the ex-slaves. Unfortunately, her health began to fail

again. That circumstance, and undoubtedly her father's un-
timely death on April 25, 1864, precipitated her decision to
return to the North for good where she hoped to recover her
health and draw comfort from her family.[130]

Various aspects of Charlotte Forten's life after her departure
from St. Helena Island in 1864 are unclear. If indeed she
did continue to chronicle her activities in journal form, most
of that record has since been lost to the public. What does
remain is a brief diary that she kept from 1885 until 1892.
Other information descriptive of her life also exists, but it is
fragmentary.

In spite of the absence of substantive documentation, however, we do know that Charlotte did not remain very long in
Philadelphia once she left the South. Her health was poor,
and she wrote to her friend John Whittier from Detroit
during the summer of 1865 to solicit his aid in securing her
a place in the sanatorium of Dioclesian Lewis at Lexington,
Massachusetts. For reasons that are unclear, Charlotte never
went to Lexington. Instead, in October 1865, she accepted a
position as Secretary of the Teachers Committee of the New
England Branch of the Freedmen's Union Commission for a
salary of ten dollars a week.[131] Located in Boston, Charlotte
socialized with her many New England friends and continued
with her personal studies. Her pursuit to master the French
language culminated in her translation of Emile Erckmann
and Alexandre Chatrain's novel *Madame Thérèse; or, The
Volunteers of '92*, which Scribner's published in 1869.[132] As
Secretary of the Teachers Committee, Charlotte acted as
liaison between the teachers in the South who tutored the ex-
slaves and those in the North who supplied them with financial
and material support through the auspices of the Commission.
She held this position until October 1871.[133]

Miss Forten worked diligently for the committee and, given her own experience, was of great assistance to the teachers in the field, but it appears that she was not completely satisfied with her job. Writing to her old abolitionist friend Lucy Chase in 1867, Charlotte disclosed that she wanted to go South again to work as soon as her health allowed her to do so. "I think I shall try to go to Florida, next year," she wrote. "I long to enter into the work again. I feel that I ought to go South, if I am able to teach." [134] Again, Charlotte was terribly depressed about her health and its obstruction to the fulfillment of her mission. "Oh, if one could only be well!" she continued in her letter to Chase. "I am disgusted with myself. I feel as if my life were a failure. Not one of its long-cherished aspirations has yet been fulfilled." [135] Three years later John Whittier wrote on her behalf to Charles Sumner with regard to Charlotte's qualifications for a job that she wanted in the Boston Public Library. [136] She did not obtain that position, but she did resign her post at the Freedmen's Union Commission in the fall of 1871 to teach for a year at the (Robert Gould) Shaw Memorial School in Charleston, South Carolina. [137] She then moved to Washington, D.C., where from 1872 until 1873 she was a teacher in a black preparatory high school (later named Dunbar High) under the direction of Alexander Crummell. Charlotte left this position to accept a job as first-class clerk in the Fourth Auditor's Office of the U.S. Treasury Department. [138]

Charlotte stayed in Washington for almost the remainder of her life. Her first few years in the capital were no doubt spent working, meeting new friends, renewing old acquaintances, writing, and studying. She also enjoyed the stimulating company of her cousin, Charles Burleigh Purvis, who was at that time a surgeon in the Freedmen's Hospital at Howard

University.[139] Charlotte continued to suffer from poor health, and kind but chauvinistic friends, such as John Whittier, wished that "the poor girl could be better situated—the wife of some good, true man who could appreciate her as she deserves."[140] Several years later, Whittier's wish for "the poor girl" came true. During her late thirties, Charlotte met and fell in love with a young, black graduate student who was twelve years her junior—Francis Grimké. The two were married in December 19, 1878.[141]

Grimké's background was so very different from Charlotte's that it is diffficult to believe the two ever met, fell in love, and married. Charlotte was not only much older than Francis but physically ill. In addition, she had been reared in the privileged surrounding of an elite free black society. Francis, on the other hand, was born a slave. He and his brothers, Archibald and John, were the illegitimate sons of the wealthy Charleston planter Henry Grimké and his slave mistress Nancy Weston. When Henry died, Francis and his brothers were inheritied by their half-brother, E. Montague Grimké, in spite of their father's will stipulating that they were to be freed upon Henry's death. When Montague Grimké threatened to sell Francis, the youth escaped for a time and worked as the valet of a Confederate officer from 1861 to 1863. It was during this time that Charlotte was in South Carolina, teaching slaves who had run away to join the Union lines. When Montague Grimké discovered Francis's whereabouts, he had him imprisoned, and during this incarceration the youth fell ill. After recovering, he was sold to a Confederate officer. His tenure as a slave ended with the defeat of the Confederate forces in 1865.[142]

For the next several years Francis Grimké dedicated himself to acquiring an exceptional education. With the aid of a local woman of liberal thought, he attended for a short while the Morris Street School in Charleston. He and his brother, Archibald, then traveled North. In 1866, both enrolled at Lincoln University in Pennsylvania, and Francis graduated as class valedictorian in 1870. Two years later, he received his master's degree. After briefly working at Lincoln as a financial agent, Francis went to study law at Howard University in 1874. It was probably during this year in Washington that he met Charlotte. Sometime thereafter he decided not to pursue a law career and instead went to Princeton Theological Seminary from which he graduated in 1878. His education at Lincoln and Princeton was partially sponsored by the well-known abolitionist and feminist, Angelina Grimké Weld. Mrs. Weld, who had left the South with her sister Sarah because they disapproved of the institution of slavery, discovered in 1868 that Francis and his brothers were her mulatto nephews. She accepted them as legitimate members of her family and remained supportive of their activities from that time on.[143] Francis Grimké was ordained by the Presbytery of Washington, D.C., in 1878. That same year he married Charlotte and accepted a position as pastor at the Fifteenth Street Presbyterian Church in Washington.[144]

Intelligent, sensitive, morally upright, and fiercely dedicated to his profession and race, Francis Grimké was certainly the husband Charlotte and her friends hoped that she would have some day. The two set up house in Washington, and Charlotte retired from public work. They had one child, Theodora Cornelia, who died as an infant in 1880. Given Charlotte's age and persistent bad health, it was inconceivable that she could bear another child, though she dearly loved children.

Charlotte now viewed her mission as intimately intertwined

with that of her husband's, and thus she dressed and acted as a missionary. Francis Grimké used his pulpit as a religious forum to attack discrimination. He and Charlotte wrote and published many essays that were critical of racial oppression. They obviously worked well together, combining fierce intellectual acumen with a passionate commitment to alleviating the racial hostility prevalent in late nineteenth- and early twentieth-century America.[145]

In 1885, Charlotte and her husband left Washington to reside in Jacksonville, Florida, where Grimké had accepted the pastorate at the Laura Street Presbyterian Church. They remained there for four years but then returned to Washington and the Fifteenth Street Presbyterian Church. Although they were both busy with missionary work and the many commitments that Grimké's growing political influence mandated, Charlotte and her husband continued to pursue an intellectual life. They both regularly attended two weekly reading groups, one on Friday and the other on Sunday, where they discussed art, literature, history, politics, religion, and any other topic of interest to the members of the societies.[146]

After her marriage, Charlotte continued her interest in writing poetry and essays. Her poems from that period include "A June Song" (1885), "Charlotte Corday" (1885), "At Newport" (1888), "The Gathering of the Grand Army" (1890), and "In Florida" (1893). Only a handful of essays that she wrote during the 1880s and 1890s survive: "On Mr. Savage's Sermon: 'The Problem of the Hour'" (1885), a lengthy letter addressed to the editor of the *Boston Commonwealth*; "One Phase of the Race Question" (1885), another letter written to the *Commonwealth* editor; "Colored People in New England" (1889), which was sent to the editor of

The Evangelist; and "Personal Recollections of Whittier" (1893), which appeared in the *New England Magazine*. Four other essays, probably written during the 1890s, were not assigned a specific date of completion: "The Umbrian and Roman School of Art"; "The Flower Fairies' Reception"; "At the Home of Frederick Douglass"; and "Midsummer Days in the Capitol: 'The Corcoran Art Gallery.' "[147]

The last decade of the nineteenth century was a busy one for Charlotte, not only because of her intellectual pursuits, writing, and missionary work, but also because of her special relationship with her niece, Angelina Weld Grimké. Angelina Grimké was the only child of Francis Grimké's brother, Archibald. From 1894 to 1898, Archibald, who held a law degree from Harvard, served as consul to Santo Domingo, and Charlotte and her husband acted as Angelina's legal guardians while her father was out of the country. Charlotte always had a deep affection for her niece, who was born just two years after Charlotte's infant daughter died. When Archibald and his wife, Sarah Stanley, separated, Charlotte became an important maternal figure in Angelina's life. Moreover, after 1905, Archibald and Angelina Grimké moved into Charlotte's home, where they remained until well after her death in 1914. Their permanent inclusion in Charlotte's house enlivened it socially and intellectually—further cementing the bond between aunt and niece. As always, Charlotte was surrounded by well-educated, political activists. And she must have drawn immense pleasure from the fact that this time it was her own home that was the hub of activity. Although continually ill, she was undoubtedly happy to be among her loved ones, to be cared for by a "noble" and loving husband whose mission was so compatible with her own, and to be able to pursue her intellectual growth and development.[148]

Charlotte Forten Grimké died in her home in Washington, D.C., on July 22, 1914, at the age of seventy-six. She had been confined to her bed for thirteen months before her death. During that time, she was nursed by her husband, who remained devoted to her. His obituary of Charlotte written the day after her death read in part:

> Mrs. Grimké had a lovely disposition, was sweet and gentle, and yet she was a woman of great strength of character. She was a lady in the best sense of that term—a woman of great refinement. There was not the slightest trace of coarseness about her in any shape or form. She never grew old in spirit—she was always young, as young as the youngest. She had a fine mind, carefully trained and cultivated by hard study and by contact [with] the best literature and with cultured people. She had the keenest appreciation for all that was best in literature and art. She loved books and pictures and flowers and everything that was beautiful and soul-uplifting. She had also charming manners—she was always thoughtful, always considerate for others, never allowing the thought of self to intrude or to interfere with the comfort and happiness of others. The plane upon which her life, inner and outer, moved was always high.[149]

JOURNAL ONE
Salem, May 24, 1854–
December 31, 1856

A wish to record the passing events of my life, which, even if quite unimportant to others, naturally possess great interest to myself, and of which it will be pleasant to have some remembrance, has induced me to commence this journal. I feel that keeping a diary will be a pleasant and profitable employment of my leisure hours, and will afford me much pleasure in other years, by recalling to my mind the memories of other days, thoughts of much-loved friends from whom I may then be separated, with whom I now pass many happy hours, in taking delightful walks, and holding "sweet converse"; the interesting books that I read; and the different people, places and things that I am permitted to see.

Besides this, it will doubtless enable me to judge correctly of the growth and improvement of my mind from year to year.

—C. L. F., *Salem, May 1854.*

Wednesday, May 24, 1854—Rose at five. The sun was shining brightly through my window, and I felt vexed with myself that he should have risen before me; I shall not let him have that advantage again very soon. How bright and beautiful are these May mornings! The air is so pure and balmy, the trees are in full blossom, and the little birds sing sweetly. I stand by the window listening to their music, but suddenly remember that I have an Arithmetic lesson which employes me until breakfast; then to school, recited my lessons, and commenced my journal. After dinner practised a music lesson, did some sewing, and then took a pleasant walk by the water. I stood for some time admiring the waves as they rose and fell, sparkling in the sun, and could not help envying a party of boys who were enjoying themselves in a sailing boat. On my way home, I stopped at Mrs. [Caroline] Putnam's[1] and commenced reading "Hard Times," a new story by Dickens. The scene opens in a very matter-of-fact school, where teacher and committee deal in stern facts, and allow no flights of fancy in the youthful minds committed to their charge. One interesting little girl is severely reprimanded for wishing a carpet of flowers (not natural ones); while a repulsive looking boy receives much praise for a very long definition of the word "horse," which seems quite unintelligible to every one else. I anticipate to much pleasure in reading this story.— Saw some agreeable friends, [Jonathan] McBuffum[2] and his family from Lynn, prepared tea, and spent the evening in writing.

Thursday, May 25—Did not intend to write this evening, but have just heard of something that is worth recording;— something which must ever rouse in the mind of every true friend of liberty and humanity, feelings of the deepest indignation and sorrow. Another fugitive [Anthony Burns] from bondage has been arrested;[3] a poor man, who for two short months has trod the soil and breathed the air of the "Old Bay State," was arrested like a criminal in the streets of her capital, and is now kept strictly guarded,—a double police force is required, the military are in readiness; and all this is done to prevent a man, whom God has created in his own image, from regaining that freedom with which, he, in common with every other human being, is endowed. I can only hope and pray most earnestly that Boston will not again disgrace herself by sending him back to a bondage worse than death; or rather that she will redeem herself from the disgrace which his arrest alone has brought upon her. The weather is gloomy and my feelings correspond with it, how applicable now are the words of the immortal Cowper,—

> "My ear is pained,
> My soul is sick with every day's report
> Of wrong and outrage, with which earth is filled;
> There is no flesh in man's obdurate heart,
> It does not feel for man; the nat'ral bond
> Of brotherhood, is severed as the flax.
> He finds his fellow guilty of a skin
> Not coloured like his own; and having power
> T'enforce the wrong, for such a worthy cause
> Dooms and devotes him as his lawful prey."

Friday, May 26, 1854—Had a conversation with Miss Mary Shepard[4] about slavery; she is, as I thought, thoroughly opposed to it, but does not agree with me in thinking that the churches and ministers are generally supporters of the infamous system; I believe it firmly. Mr. [Albert] Barnes, one of the most prominent of the Philadelphia clergy, who does not profess to be an abolitionist, has declared his belief that 'the American church is the bulwark of slavery.' Words cannot express all that I feel; all that is felt by the friends of Freedom, when thinking of this great obstacle to the removal of slavery from our land. Alas! that it should be so. I was much disappointed in not seeing the eclipse, which, it [*sic*] was expected to be the most entire that has taken place for years, but the weather was rainy and the sky obscured by clouds, so after spending half the afternoon on the roof of the house in eager expectation, I saw nothing; heard since that the sun made his appearance for a minute or two, but I was not fortunate enough to catch even the momentary glimpse of him. Father[5] left yesterday for Providence and N.[orth] Bedford; thinks he will return tomorrow evening. I write to the sound of music sweet; Sarah [Cassey Smith][6] is playing the "Bords Du Rhin," and I imagine myself standing on the banks of that beautiful river which flows so placidly past the happy homes of Germany. All around is lovely and calm; the sun is shedding his last rays upon the distant hills, and the gentle warbling of the shepherd's flute is heard as he returns home with his flock. I wish that this delightful day-dream could last, but it cannot, and I must rouse myself from it and return to sober reality. It is already time that I should be indulging in nightly dreams.—

> "Ah—visions less beguiling far,
> Than waking dreams by daylight are."

Saturday, May 27.—Have been very busy all morning, sweeping, dusting, sewing, and doing sundry other little things which are always to be done on Saturday.—Spent a delightful hour in the afternoon at Miss [Mary] Shepard's, looking with her and Miss [Elizabeth] Church,[7] over some beautiful engravings, representing those parts of France, Italy and Switzerland in which the persecuted Waldenses lived. Some of the scenery was very lovely, with smooth lakes and quiet valleys; sparkling streams on the banks of which cattle and sheep were very demurely grazing, and near them small groups of peasants in their pretty and fanciful costume; the spirit of repose seems breathed around.—And then we turn to another scene where the lofty mountains rise in grandeur to the very clouds; how sublime, how very grand they appear! The views were all beautiful, and looking at them has increased my desire to visit these countries. Miss Shepard showed us some of her beautiful books, and read one or two exquisite pieces of poetry. I enjoyed myself very much.— Returned home, read the Anti-Slavery papers, and then went down to the depot to meet father; he had arrived in Boston early in the morning, regretted very much that he had not reached there in the evening before to attend the great meeting at Faneuil Hall. He says that the excitement in Boston is very great; the trial of the poor man[8] takes place on Monday. We scarcely dare to think of what may be the result; there seems to be nothing too bad for those Northern tools of slavery to do.

Sunday, May 28. A lovely day; in the morning I read in the Bible and wrote letters; in the afternoon took a quiet walk in Harmony Grove, and as I passed by many 'an unknown grave,' the question 'who sleeps below?' rose often to my mind, and led to a long train of thoughts, of who those departed ones might have been, how much beloved, how deeply regretted and how worthy of such love and such regret.

I love to walk on the Sabbath, for all is so peaceful; the noise and labor of every-day life has ceased; and in perfect silence we can commune with Nature and with Nature's God. Spent the evening very pleasantly at Mrs. [Cecelia] Babcock's.[9]

Tuesday, May 30.   Rose very early and was busy until nine o'clock; then, at Mrs. Putnam's urgent request, went to keep store for her while she went to Boston to attend the Anti-Slavery Convention.[10] I was very anxious to go, and will certainly do so to-morrow; the arrest of the alleged fugitive will give additional interest to the meetings, I should think. His trial is still going on and I can scarcely think of anything else; read again to-day as most suitable to my feelings and to the times, "The Runaway Slave at Pilgrim's Point," by Elizabeth B. Browning; how powerfully it is written! how earnestly and touchingly does the writer portray the bitter anguish of the poor fugitive as she thinks over all the wrongs and sufferings that she has endured, and of the sin to which tyrants have driven her but which they alone must answer for! It seems as if no one could read this poem without having his sympathies roused to the utmost on behalf of the oppressed. After a long conversation with my friends on their return, on this all-absorbing subject, we separated for the night, and I went to bed, weary and sad.

Wednesday, May 31.   The last day of spring. She has not been very pleasant this year, until within a few weeks, during which her smiles have been so bountiful and bright, her character so very lovable, that we part from her with regret. Sarah [Cassey Smith] and I went to Boston in the morning. Everything was much quieter—outwardly than we expected, but still much real indignation and excitement prevail. We walked past the Court-House, which is now lawlessly converted into a prison, and filled with soldiers, some of whom

were looking from the windows, with an air of insolent
authority, which made my blood boil, while I felt the strongest contempt for their cowardice and servility. We went to
the meeting, but the best speakers were absent, engaged in
the most arduous and untiring efforts in behalf of the poor
fugitive; but though we missed the glowing eloquence of
[Wendell] Phillips,[11] [William Lloyd] Garrison,[12] and
[Theodore] Parker,[13] still there were excellent speeches made,
and our hearts responded to the exalted sentiments of Truth
and Liberty which were uttered. The exciting intelligence
which occasionally came in relation to the trial, added fresh
zeal to the speakers, of whom Stephen Foster[14] and his wife
[Abigail Kelley][15] were the principal. The latter addressed,
in the most eloquent language, the women present, entreating
them to urge their husbands and brothers to action, and also
to give their aid on all occasions in our just and holy cause.—
I did not see father the whole day; he, of course, was deeply
interested in the trial.—Dined at Mr. Garrison's; his wife is
one of the loveliest persons I have ever seen, worthy of such
a husband. At the table, I watched earnestly the expression
of that noble face, as he spoke beautifully in support of the
non-resistant principles to which he has kept firm; his is
indeed the very highest Christian spirit, to which I cannot
hope to reach, however, for I believe in resistance to tyrants,
and would fight for liberty until death. We came home in
the evening, and felt sick at heart as we passed through the
streets of Boston on our way to the depot, seeing the military
as they rode along, ready at any time to prove themselves the
minions of the South.

Thursday, June 1. I am keeping store for Mrs. Putnam
again. Miss [Sarah Parker] Remond[16] is still in Boston, and
Mrs. [Nancy] R.[emond][17] has gone also; father and Aunt

Harriet [Purvis] [18] are there. The trial is over at last; the commissioner's decision will be given to-morrow. We are all in the greatest suspense; what will that decision be? Alas! that any one should have the power to decide the right of a fellow being to himself! It is thought by many that he will be acquitted of the *great crime* of leaving a life of bondage, as the legal evidence is not thought sufficient to convict him. But it is only too probable that they will sacrifice him to propitiate the South, since so many at the North dared oppose the passage of the infamous Nebraska Bill. Miss [Helen] Putnam [19] was married this evening. Mr. [Octavius B.] Frothingham performed the ceremony, and in his prayer alluded touchingly to the events of this week; he afterwards in conversation with the bridegroom, (Mr. [Jacob] Gilliard), [20] spoke in the most feeling manner about this case,— his sympathies are on the right side. The wedding was a pleasant one; the bride looked very lovely; and we enjoyed ourselves as much as is possible in these exciting times. It is impossible to be happy now.

Friday, June 2.   Our worst fears are realized; the decision was against poor [Anthony] Burns, and he has been sent back to a bondage worse, a thousand times worse than death. [21] Even an attempt at rescue was utterly impossible; the prisoner was completely surrounded by soldiers with bayonets fixed, a canon loaded, ready to be fired at the slightest sign. To-day Massachusetts has again been disgraced; again has she showed her submissions to the Slave Power; and Oh! with what deep sorrow do we think of what will doubtless be the fate of that poor man, when he is again consigned to the horrors of slavery. With what scorn must that government be regarded which cowardly assembles thousands of soldiers to satisfy the demands of slaveholders; to deprive of his freedom a man, created in God's own image, whose sole offense is the color of his skin! And if resistance is offered to this outrage, these soldiers are to shoot down American citizens without mercy; and this by express orders of a government which proudly boasts of being the freest in the world; this on the very soil where the Revolution of 1776 began; in sight of the battlefield, where thousands of brave men fought and died in opposing British tyranny, which was nothing compared with the American oppression of today. In looking over my diary, I perceive that I did not mention that there was on the Friday night after the man's arrest, an attempt made to rescue him,[22] but although it failed, on account of there not being men enough engaged in it, all honor should be given to those who bravely made the attempt. I can write no more. A cloud seems hanging over me, over all our persecuted race, which nothing can dispel.

Sunday, June 4. A beautiful day. The sky is cloudless, the sun shines warm and bright, and a delicious breeze fans my cheeks as I sit by the window writing. How strange it is that in a world so beautiful, there can be so much wickedness, on this delightful day, while many are enjoying themselves in their happy homes, not poor Burns only, but millions beside are suffering in chains; and how many Christian ministers to-day will mention him, or those who suffer with him? How many will speak from the pulpit against the cruel outrage on humanity which has just been committed, or against the many, even worse ones, which are committed in this country every day? Too well do we know that there are but very few, and these few alone deserve to be called the ministers of Christ, whose doctrine was 'Break every yoke, and let the oppressed go free.'—During the past week, we have had a vacation, which I had expected to enjoy very much, but it was, of course, impossible for me to do so. To-morrow school[23] commences, and although the pleasure I shall feel in again seeing my beloved teacher,[24] and in resuming my studies will be much saddened by recent events, yet they shall be a fresh incentive to more earnest study, to aid me in fitting myself for laboring in a holy cause, for enabling me to do much towards changing the condition of my oppressed and suffering people. Would that those with whom I shall recite to-morrow could sympathize with me in this; would that they could look upon all God's creatures without respect to color, feeling that it is character alone which makes the true man or woman! I earnestly hope that the time will come when they will feel thus.—I have several letters to write to-day to send by Aunt Harriet [Purvis] who leaves for Philadelphia tomorrow. Father left yesterday, he has not yet decided to come here to live; he will write and tell me what he has determined to do, as soon as he has consulted mother.[25] I fear he has not now a very favorable opinion of Massachusetts; still I hope they will come; I long to see the children[26] again.

Monday, June 5. Rose very early, after passing a sleepless night.—Studied my lesson, and then went to school. Miss [Elizabeth] Church and I counted the merits of the first and second classes for Miss Shepard; after school, had an hour's conversation with her about slavery and prejudice. I fully appreciate her kindness, and sympathy with me; she wishes me to cultivate a Christian spirit in thinking of my enemies; I know it is right, and will endeavor to do so, but it does seem very difficult. Aunt Harriet [Purvis] left at two o'clock to-day; we shall be quite lonesome now that she and father have both gone; their departure has made me feel a little homesick, but I will not indulge the feeling. The weather is very warm and makes one feel very much disposed to be idle. This is a beautiful evening, and I have just been enjoying a pleasant walk by moon-light.—And now to bed.

Tuesday, June 6. Studied my lesson, then went to school. How pleasant it is after a few days separation, to see our kind teacher and the happy faces around her again, and to resume our studies with renewed energy and perseverance! The day has been so beautiful and bright that it seems as if not a single moment should be wasted. After school Henry [Cassey] [27] and I went to Mr. [Charles] Hoffman's garden and walked through the hot houses. We saw some very splendid cactuses, some of a bright scarlet color, others of the deepest crimson. Their gorgeous hues seemed fitter for "the clime of the East, the land of the sun," than for our colder climate. Then we stopped to admire the graceful and beautiful fuchsias, and saw some superb emblem of "devotion." I love flowers; they beautify our homes, and seem to diffuse cheerfulness as well as fragrance around us; and there are no purer or more beautiful ornaments than these natural ones.—Began to read "A Peep at Number Five." I like it very much; Miss Shepard gave me a slight sketch of the author who was a very lovely person. To know something of the author always adds greatly to the interest of a book.—In the evening, wrote until bed-time.

Wednesday, June 7. After school returned home and did some ironing, then practised a music lesson. In the afternoon read Mr. [Theodore] Parker's sermon on "The New Crime Against Humanity," written with his usual truthful eloquence. I wish that I could have heard him deliver it. This subject naturally possesses the greatest interest for me. Adelaide [Putnam] [28] and her sister and Helen [Gilliard] spent the evening with us, so we had plenty of music. Addie played some beautiful pieces, my favorite airs, and Jenny sang several pretty songs; she has a very sweet voice. Felt disappointed that Miss Remond could not come. I like to be in her society; she is always attractive, without making any particular effort to be so.

Thursday, June 8. Rain! rain! rain has been pouring in torrents nearly all day; but we should not complain, for it is much needed. I hope after a refreshing bath, our roses will soon be in bloom. As I sat writing in the afternoon, I said to Mrs. [Amy Matilda] Remond,[29] "I wish I had the power, said to be possessed by clairvoyants of knowing what others are doing in distant places. I should like to know what they are doing at home at this moment," she did not think it would always be a pleasure to possess this knowledge.—Practised for two hours. Then did some sewing during the rest of the evening.

Saturday, June 10. Received two letters, one from father. The other from Annie [Woods Webb].[30] Letters from home! how eagerly expected, how gladly welcomed they are! To my great disappointment, father has decided not to remove to New England. He is, as I feared he would be, much prejudiced against it on account of the recent slave case, or, he says, he is so against Boston, and I think he intends that feeling to the whole state at least. I shall write to-morrow, and use every argument I can think of, to induce him to change his opinion. I do not wish to have my long-cherished plan of our having together a pleasant New England home, defeated. In the afternoon went to impart the unwelcome tidings to Miss [Sarah Parker] Remond, who assured me that she had been quite certain of it before. She had a volume of Mrs. Browning's poems, from which I read "Promethus Bound" and "Casa Guidi Windows." Her poetry is so very different from most that I have read, so thoroughly original and beautiful, that I love to read it. The evening was delightful, and I enjoyed my walk home in the pale moonlight.

Monday, June 12.   Did not feel very well this morning, but was much better after taking a walk. After school went with Sarah [Cassey Smith] and Henry [Cassey] to the pastures. I enjoyed the novelty of wandering over the hills, and ascending some of the highest of them, had a fine view of the town and harbor. It seemed like a beautiful landscape; and I wished for the artist's power or the poet's still richer gift to immortalize it. I stood and watched the last rays of the glorious sun as it slowly disappeared behind the hills, lending a beautiful tinge to the water of a winding, romantic little stream that flowed at our feet; and felt so much delighted that it was with reluctance that I left the spot, and turned my steps homeward. I expect to have much enjoyment there during the summer. Found Mrs. [Amy Matilda] Remond waiting for us very impatiently, as she wished to go out. I felt quite tired after our long walk over the hills, and after performing some examples in Arithmetic, gladly sought repose.

Tuesday, June 13.   One of the loveliest days of this lovely month; regretted that I had not time to take a long walk, which gives me the truest enjoyment of this delightful weather. After school, stayed with Miss [Mary] Shepard, who was writing some sentiments for a fair, I wondered how she could write them so easily and rapidly; they were all excellent, and one so very amusing that I wish I dared insert it here. How often have I invoked in vain the spirit of song; the muse is always most unyielding, despite my assurances, that should she deign to bless me, my first offering should be upon the shrine of Liberty. On my return home, after eating supper, helped to clear away the things,—our 'help' having very ungraciously deserted us.—Then read a very interesting description of "Holyrood House," and of Edinburgh and its environs. I love to read of Scotland, of its beautiful and romantic 'lochs[,]' its ancient castles, lofty mountains, and the honest independent spirit of its people. And who that has read the glowing descriptions of Scott and Burns, would not wish to visit their beloved home, the land which they have immortalized?—Sewed for an hour. Then went to bed.

Wednesday, June 14.—Studied my lessons; helped Mrs. [Amy Matilda] Remond to get breakfast, after which, went to school.—Made a pudding for dinner.—Practised for two hours. Commenced reading "The Last Leaf from Sunny Side," which Miss Shepard had lent me; it is very interesting, the memoir of a beautiful life. Toward evening went down town with Addie [Putnam] to the shop. Miss [Sarah] Remond was reading Moore's "Life of Byron"; I looked over it for a few minutes and became deeply interested in it. One almost forgets the faults of the great poet in admiration of his wonderful genius, and his many noble traits of character.—In the evening, went to Mrs. [Jane] Putnam's,[31] and heard some delightful music.

Friday, June 16. Another delightful morning, the sky is cloudless, the sun is shining brightly; and, as I sit by the window, studying, a robin redbreast perched on the large apple tree in the garden, warbles his morning salutation in my ear;—music far sweeter to me than the clearer tones of the Canary birds in their cages, for they are captives, while he is free! I would not keep even a bird in bondage. In the afternoon, Miss [Elizabeth] Church and I looked over the engravings in "The Homes of American Authors" which

Miss Shepard had kindly lent us. We gazed admiringly on the beautiful homes of Irving, Longfellow, Bryant, Hawthorne, Lowell, and many other distinguished writers and orators. "Sunny Side," the residence of Irving, is particularly beautiful. And Bryant's home is very lovely, situated in a retired spot on the banks of a clear, winding stream, and surrounded by graceful trees. I thought at first that it was my ideal of a poet's home, but when I turned to Dana's residence, I found it hard to decide between them. The latter stands on a rock over-hanging the sea, and I thought how often the poet probably sat at his window, and gazed upon the boundless expanse of waters, until its sublime influence entered his soul, and inspired him to write of the beautiful and the grand. The 'Homes' are all very beautiful, fit residence for their gifted inmates.

After school I went to the pastures, and saw some Indians who were encamped there. They were not in any way remarkable, except, indeed, it might be for untidiness. I soon turned away and roamed over the hills, thinking of the great changes that had befallen the sons of the forest since they wandered here, the bold and free possessors of the soil. It is very sad to think of. I tried to banish it from my mind; and stood watching the beautiful sunset, and felt, as I always do, its soothing, and delightful power. We had a pleasant walk home through North Salem. Adelaide [Putnam] and her sister[32] spent the evening with us—Mrs. Putnam[33] came home yesterday; I have only seen her for a few moments, long enough to hear that all are well at home, and that she is much pleased with Philadelphia. To-morrow I must hear all the particulars about home and friends, that she has not had time to give me.

Saturday, June 17. A bad headache has prevented my

enjoying the fine weather to-day, or taking as much exercise as I generally do. Did some sewing on my return from school.—Read the "Liberator,"[34] then practised a music lesson. Late in the afternoon I went to Mrs. Putnam's, and listened to an account of her journey, and her visit to my home—home I must still call it, though I may never live there again; yet while those I love are there, it shall be "home, sweet home." Mrs. P.[utnam] left my letters with her baggage in New York. But of love, which cannot be left behind, I received as much as the most exacting affection could desire. In the evening Miss Sarah Remond read aloud Mr. Frothingham's sermon, whose stern truths shocked so many of his congregation. We, of course, were deeply interested in it, and felt grateful to this truly Christian minister for his eloquent defense of oppressed humanity. While Miss [Sarah Parker] R.[emond] was reading, Miss [Mary?] Osborne came in, and said she believed that we never talked or read anything but Anti-Slavery; she was quite tired of it. We assured her that she could never hear anything better; and said it was natural that we should speak and read much, on a subject so interesting to us. When I returned home, I found that Frank [Cassey][35] had brought me a large branch of the fragrant locust, which, he assured me, he had risked his life in obtaining. I could not help smiling, and think he had suddenly become extremely generous and self-sacrificing, while I told him that I could not prize too highly that which had been so dearly bought.

Sunday, June 18. Took a walk early in the morning which I enjoyed very much. The air felt so pure and refreshing, and was filled with the perfume of flowers and the music of birds. I had not time to go very far. Read for some time.— Then prepared dinner. In the afternoon went to Lynn to hear a lecture from Wendell Phillips.—The ride was very delightful. We passed the bay—how calm and beautiful the water looked, a light haze was over it, which made it look like a cloud in the distance. I longed to enjoy a sail on its bosom. I love the water, and sometimes think I could live 'on the ocean wave.' A delicious breeze was stirring, laden with the fragrance of locust and sweetbriar. It was indeed one of the loveliest days of summer. Mr. Phillips spoke eloquently and beautifully, as he always does, spoke earnestly of the recent slave case, and showed the position of Slavery and Freedom in this country, and the great strength and wickedness of the former. I wish I could transfer a few of those glowing words and noble sentiments to paper; but that is quite impossible. The Hutchinsons[36] were at the lecture, and sang very beautifully.—Mr. Phillips has promised to stay with us, the next time he comes to Salem.—We rode home in the quiet starlight; and saw a great number of fire-flies; they enlivened the dark road with their bright flashes and I amused myself by watching them.—Frank [Cassey] was much concerned lest a wagon whose rumbling we could hear, should get ahead of us; but to his great joy, this did not happen.—We were welcomed home by every demonstration of delight by Dash, who evidently did not like keeping house alone, which he told us as emphatically as a dog could tell it.

Monday, June 19. It is almost impossible to write of anything but heat to-day; indeed, it is almost impossible to write at all. Not a breath of air seems to be stirring. One can scarcely study. I can realize at last that summer has come, and made more beautiful this noble scenery; these rocks and hills, valleys and streams of N. [ew] England. In the afternoon there was every indication of a severe storm; we heard the distant rumbling of the thunder, which, I imagine must resemble the roaring of the sea; and saw several bright flashes of lightning; but little rain fell, and soon the clouds began to clear away, and we saw a beautiful rainbow. I stood watching it as it faded slowly away.—Then practised a music lesson. Read a little while.—Did some sewing in the evening.

Tuesday, June 20. Rose very early and took a pleasant walk in Danvers. I noticed that nearly every house we passed, however humble in other respects, was adorned with beautiful flowers. The sun had just risen and was shedding his bright rays over hills and trees, lending an additional charm to the beauty of the scene. As we returned home, while walking through Harmony Grove, a tiny striped squirrel bounded across the path and instantly hid itself among the trees on the hillside; I tried to coax him to come to me but without success. We visited little Albert's [?] grave; it was pleasant to think of the sweet, innocent child, not as having aught to do with the cold, damp earth at our feet, but as one of that bright band whose home is in a better and happier world.— Went to school. The weather was oppressively hot; one could scarcely study.—In the afternoon wrote a composition; subject, "A Day In June," which was very appropriate.—On my return home, commenced reading Macaulay's "History of England." I know that I shall like it, as I do everything that relates to England; there is a charm for me even in its very name. Did some needle work. Adelaide [Putnam] came over in the evening, and went with me to Miss [Mary] Shepard's; she was out but had left for me "Martin Merryvale," of which I read a number; it increases in interest.—I think it is written very much in Dickens' style.

Wednesday, June 21. Had anticipated much pleasure in taking a morning walk with Miss Shepard, but the weather was too chilly and disagreeable. What a change from yesterday! Bright smiling June seems to have given place to cloudy, gloomy November; but it will not be for a long time; she is too lovely to give us many frowns.—After school went home with Miss Shepard and stayed there for some time; she was talking to me of a lovely friend who in the midst of health had been suddenly taken away; it seemed very sad. I felt as if I had known her,—so good and so gifted, so very lovable as she must have been. I felt deeply interested, as I always do when conversing with Miss Shepard, and was surprised when I got home to find how late it was. Sewed very busily all the afternoon. In the evening went to Mr. [Joseph] Putnam's.[37]

Thursday, June 22. Copied my composition; then studied until breakfast. Went to school.—At recess read another number of "Martin Merrivale." After morning school, read [John Greenleaf Whittier's] "Moll Pitcher,"[38] to Mrs. [Amy Matilda] Remond. How very beautifully it is written! One can almost see the old witch and hear those frightful incantations, which so powerfully affected the young and beautiful girl, who sought her dismal abode. The poet's description of Nahant is exquisite, and has made me more desirous than ever of visiting that beautiful spot. I should love to wander on that beach.

> "Along whose verge and sceptre gull
> Her thin and snowy plumage laves—"
>
> . . . . . .
> "Around the blue and level main—
> Above, a sunshine rich, as fell,
> Brightening of old, with golden rain,
> The Isle Apollo loved so well!"

In the evening read for some time.—Then did some sewing; while I was sewing, tried to commit the above lines and some others to memory, but found it not very easy to do; my eyes and thoughts would wander to the beautiful poem, and the work was forgotten. At last I gave up both in despair, and went to take a walk with Sarah [Cassey Smith] and Adelaide [Putnam].

Friday, June 23. Saw some engravings of castles and mountains in Wales. The scenery was wild and beautiful. How very grand those mountains appear, towering to the very clouds! I should love to see them, and those old, ruined castles, now outgrown with ivy, whose stately rooms, once filled with the gay and the beautiful, are now desolate, and mouldering to decay.—After school, read in the "History of England."—Then did some sewing, while Sarah read aloud Mr. [Charles Lenox] Remond's[39] speech in the Convention, which I like very much.

Saturday, June 24. Rose very early and studied until school time.—In the afternoon, read Mrs. [Lydia Maria] Child's[40] "Memoir of Madame de Stael," which interested me very much. She was truly a wonderful and a highly gifted woman, I admire her character; and my admiration of Bonpart is considerably lessened since I know of his cowardly and unjust persecution of her.

Sunday, June 25. Have been writing nearly all day.—This afternoon went to Anti-Slavery meeting in Danvers, from which I have just returned. Mr. [Andrew] Foss spoke eloquently, and with that warmth and sincerity which evidently come from the heart. He said he was rejoiced that the people at the North were beginning to feel that slavery is no longer confined to the black man alone, but that they too must wear the yoke; and they are becoming roused on the subject at last. He spoke of the objections made by many of the Abolitionists, on the plea of their using too violent language; they say that the slave-holders are driven by it to worse measures; what they need is mild entreaty, etc., etc. But the petition against the Nebraska Bill,[41] couched in the very mildest terms by the clergymen of the North, was received even less favorably by the South, than the hardest sayings of the Abolitionists; and they were abused and denounced more severely than the latter have ever been.—As we walked home, Miss [Sarah Parker] Remond and I were wishing that we could have an anti-slavery meeting in the neighborhood every Sunday, and as well attended as this was. But it is now quite late, every one has retired to rest except myself. It is time that I should do so, as I wish to rise before the sun.

Monday, June 26. Went to the Essex Institute and saw many curiosities. Mr. [Henry] King showed us some specimens from his botanical garden, they were highly magnified: the first we saw was a very small portion of the green slime found in impure water; when seen through the microscope, it appeared like a large piece of seaweed and looked very beautiful.—Then we saw the first growth of a poor tree; every fibre and the many little cells of which it is composed were plainly visible; it resembled another, and still smaller portion of green slime when magnified. Mr. King told us that in the beginning every vegetable substance is composed of the same kind of cells and fibres; so that the largest elm tree in its first growth resembles this slimy substance. He showed us a very small water-seal[?] so highly magnified that we could see the heart and every palpitation very plainly.

Among the curiosities were Gov. Bradford's Christening blanket, mittens and shirt, which had a very odd and antique appearance. Dr. [Henry] Wheatland showed us a miniature canoe, and a Chinese hammock, composed of net silk with a border of beautiful feather work; a very elegant and pleasant conveyance for those Chinese ladies who cannot walk on account of the smallness of their feet. Their ideas of beauty and comfort are certainly very strange. I was much interested in the collection of shells and stones, and in the beautiful coral which always brings to my mind thoughts of the sea. The gentlemen kindly gave us much useful information, and we spent two hours there very pleasantly.

In the afternoon went to see Mrs. [Cecelia] B.[abcock]'s little girl,[42] who is very ill. On my return home, read for a short time, and then did some sewing.

Tuesday, June 27.   On my return from school found that Mrs. Alexander had arrived, and brought me a letter from Aunt Margaretta [Forten],[43] whose health is improving.— Made some pies for dinner. I had only time to attend to the baking of one of them; and that was declared to be "pretty good considering who made it," which expression I felt inclined to resent as implying some contempt of my skill in culinary matters. The other pies were unfortunate, Mary having forgotten that it was very probable they would burn by being left in the oven an unreasonably long time.

In the afternoon instead of attending to our usual exercises, we took our work to school and sewed while the compositions were read; I think "composition afternoons" are very pleasant.—Returned home and did some sewing; then read "Martin Merryvale," which increases in interest.

Wednesday, June 28.   Early in the morning went to the garden and watered the roses. They are in full bloom now, and looked very beautiful with the glittering dew-drops on their delicate leaves. The lillies will soon be open; I think they need a refreshing shower. Afterwards I took a walk alone. The weather was not very pleasant, but I walked by the water which is always beautiful to me, and stood for some time listening to the pleasant sound of the waves as they dashed against the rocks, and watching to see the cars cross the bridge; but the old steamhorse was in a contrary mood, for after moving forward and then back again several times he disappeared, and I saw him no more.—In the afternoon sewed very busily. In the evening went to Miss Shepard's and looked over some beautiful engravings, after spending a delightful hour with her, returned home.

Thursday, June 29. Studied, went to school, and on my return home did some washing. I felt in an uncommonly merry mood, and sang, laughed, and talked so gaily that Mrs. [Amy Matilda] Remond said she would like to employ such a pleasant washerwoman. In the evening sewed for some time, and afterwards read in Macaulay's "History of England."

Friday, June 30. Went with Lizzie [Church] to take a magnolia to one of Miss Shepard's friends. It was extremely fragrant; I can imagine how delightful it must be to ride for miles past these beautiful trees.—(Addie [Putnam] gave me some lovely moss-roses. I placed them on the table in my room, and as I sat sewing there toward evening, and inhaling their sweet perfume, they were delightful companions, and when occasionally, sad thoughts came to my mind, I looked on them and they seemed to me like beautiful messengers of happiness and peace).—In the evening did some more sewing, of which I must confess I am beginning to be heartily tired; I think it would be different if I had some one to read to me while I sew.—Wrote a long letter to Aunt Margaretta.

Saturday, July 1. When I awoke on this delightful morning, the first objects my eyes rested on were my sweet moss-roses. What a fragrant salutation they gave me!—Have been very busy all day, and felt quite tired in the evening, but went over to Adelaide [Putnam]'s, and after having some beautiful music, and walking among the flowers, feel quite refreshed.

Sunday, July 2. A delightful day—In the morning read several chapters in the New Testament. The third verse of the last chapter of Hebrews—"Remember them that are in bonds as bound with them" suggested many thoughts to my mind: *Remember the poor slave as bound with him.* How few even of those who are opposed to slavery realize this! If they felt thus so ardent, so untiring, would be their efforts that they would soon accomplish the overthrow of this iniquitous system. All honor for the noble few who do feel for the suffering bondman as *bound with him*, and act accordingly! In the evening wrote several letters; then took a walk with Adelaide and her sister. We thought we had never seen the clouds look so gorgeous. The setting sun had tinged them with the most brilliant hues. They seemed like temples of gold, or mountains of fire, rising from a sea of the deepest blue, and after enchanting the beholder by their glorious beauty, gradually fading away, as if by magic, from his sight.

Tuesday, July 4. The weather is intensely hot.—I arose with a distressing headache. The noise of cannons, guns, pistols, and every imaginable kind of firearms which the patriotic fired during the night was terrible, and effectually banished sleep from my pillow.—I passed the day at home, reading Miss Edgeworth's "Helen," which Miss Shepard had very kindly lent me.—Addie and her sister came over. The heat was almost insufferable, and we moved from room to room, and from window to window in the hope of finding a breath of air.—In the evening went over to Mrs. [Caroline] Putnam's, and felt truly grateful for a most refreshing breeze,

the first that I felt during the day. Staid there all night.—
Addie and I sat by the window until long after the last rocket
had ascended from the Common. We watched the beautiful
moon as she peeped out from a silvery cloud, and her soft
rays were reflected from the smooth clear water below.—It
was a lovely night and there was something very delightful
in its perfect repose after the heat and the tumult of the day.

Thursday, July 6. This has been a lovely day. We have
had a cool breeze from the "Northern clime" which is truly
refreshing after the intense heat of the last two days. At eleven
o'clock, Miss Shepard, instead of returning home, remained
in the school-room, and proposed that Lizzie and I should
remain with her, which we did very joyfully. We read
"Thorpe," an interesting story of English country life. It
contains many beautiful expressions of deep, earnest feeling,
and glorious thoughts through which is breathed the true
spirit of poetry, clothed in prosaic garb. In the evening took
a pleasant walk with several friends. Met Miss Shepard and
her friend Miss [Helen?] Creamer, to whom she introduced
me. I had read a book which she wrote and had felt a desire
to see her. Afterwards studied until ten o'clock.

Friday, July 7. This afternoon heard a very interesting
lecture on Equador, and received much useful information
concerning that beautiful country, the variety of its climate,
soil and productions; the grandeur of its mountain scenery;
the splendor of its capital, and the character, dress, and
manners of its inhabitants. On my return home, found that
Mrs. [Amy Matilda] Remond, with her usual kindness, had
arranged that I should take her place in the carriage. I had a
delightful ride on the sea shore. The waves looked very
beautiful as they rose and fell sparkling in the sunlight. And
in the distance, a steamboat which to us appeared to be

standing perfectly still, thought perhaps in reality it was gliding rapidly over the calm, and deep blue water of the bay, seemed like a single white cloud in the azure sky. We passed "High Rock," at the foot of which stood the residence of the far-famed "Moll Pitcher," the weird heroine of Whittier's beautiful poem. On the summit of this bold eminence stands the tasteful cottage of the Hutchinson family. It seems a fit abode for those gifted and warmhearted children of song. I enjoyed the ride the more because Mr. [Charles Lenox] Remond allowed me to drive nearly all the way.

Saturday, July 8. This morning took a very pleasant walk with Miss Shepard. We walked through Harmony Grove; the air was pure and balmy, and the trees and flowers looked very beautiful as they waved over the last resting place of many a loved and lost one. Miss Shepard read several exquisite poems written by the sister of Mrs. Hemans; they are full of deep, tender feeling, and one, a lament for the loss of her beloved and highly gifted sister, was particularly touching and beautiful. We talked of many things, and I felt pleased and happy as I always do in the society of my beloved teacher.—In the afternoon did some sewing.—Then read in Macaulay's "History of England." His account of the Norman Conquest is very interesting.—In the evening went to the Anti-Slavery meeting at Lyceum Hall. There were but very few present. Mr. [Andrew] Foss spoke eloquently for an hour, and then the meeting adjourned until to-morrow.

Sunday, July. Attended the meetings during the day and evening. I felt sorry and disappointed to see such a small number of persons present. The intense heat of the weather perhaps accounted for this. Though for such a cause I thought much more than that might have been endured. Very eloquent and interesting speeches were made by Mr. [William Lloyd]

Garrison and Mr. Foss in the afternoon and evening. After
tea I went to Miss [Sarah] Remond's where Mr. Garrison
had taken tea, and felt happier and better after listening to
the conversation of that truly good and great man.

Monday, July 10. I have seen to-day a portrait of Hawthorne, one of the finest that has ever been taken of him. He
has a splendid head. That noble, expansive brow bears the
unmistakeable impress of genius and superior intellect. And
in the depths of those dark, expressive eyes there is a strange,
mysterious influence which one feels in reading his works,
and which I felt most forcible when reading that thrilling
story "The Scarlet Letter." Yet there is in his countenance no
trace of that gloom which pervades some of his writings;
particularly that strange tale "The Unpardonable Sin" and
many of the "Twice Told Tales." After reading them, I had
pictured the author to myself as very dark and gloomy-
looking. But I was agreeably disappointed. Grave, earnest,
thoughtful, he appears but not gloomy. His sister, who, with
much kindness showed me his portrait, is very singular-
looking. She has an eerie, spectral look which instantly
brought to my mind the poem of "The Ancient Mariner,"
and for a moment gave me the strange, undefined feeling of
dread and yet of fascination which I so powerfully experienced
while reading that ghostly tale. But her cordial, pleasant
manner quickly dispelled this feeling. And I soon realized
that however peculiar she might appear, or be in reality, she
was no "shadowy visitant from another world," as at first I
could almost have fancied. She showed me another portrait
of Hawthorne taken when he was very young. His countenance, though glowing with genius, has more of the careless,
sanguine expression of youth than profound, elevated thought
which distinguishes his maturer years, and gives to his fine

face and to his deeply interesting writings that mysterious charm which is felt and acknowledged by all. Miss [Elizabeth] Hawthorne showed me a piece of the English yew, the "sepulchral yew," whose dark branches are seen in every country churchyard of England and seems there the emblem of mourning as the "weeping willow" here.

Tuesday, July 11. On my return from school copied the verses written by Miss Townsend on the death of Joseph. It was to me a sad task, and revived old memories of that dear cousin so good and so gifted who had dedicated himself to a "high and holy purpose"; who, but a boy in years, devoted himself to study beyond his strength, and "weary, worn at length," was compelled to relinquish all his bright hopes of future usefulness, and found in the silent grave that freedom and repose which was not granted to his brave, earnest spirit while on earth. And this comforted the many hearts who warmly loved him,—the certainty that he had gone to that "better land," where slavery and prejudice, sin and sorrow in every form, are unfelt and unknown.

Wednesday, July 12. Have been reading Irving's account of his visit to Abbotsford. How beautifully he describes the great poet and his family! One can almost see the kind noble face, and hear the full, clear tones of "the Great Magician of the north." Scott's magnificent mansion was not then completed and they were living in plainer style, but in such perfect love and happiness, as must have been most delightful to witness. And who does not envy Irving the hours spent in the society of the gifted poet? So genial, so warm-hearted, so truly noble as he was, ever causing his friends to forget his glory and his fame, and to think of him only as the kind and hospitable friend. And he the idol of his family and country, the admiration of the world, was noted for his child-like simplicity, and through enjoyment of all the social pleasures of life; his spirit free as his own loved mountain air, brave as the "Scottish clans" whose glorious deeds he has immortalized. Such a character was well worthy of all the glory which has been bestowed upon it, all the love and admiration with which he ever has been, and every will be regarded.

Thursday, July 13. This morning went with Lizzie [Church] to get a book for our dear teacher. We had a delightful walk. At recess read in the "Genius of Scotland," which is very interesting. I was much pleased with the description of the elegant city of Edinburgh, its splendid mansions, monuments, parks and numerous literary institutions. But what interested me most were the sketches of the gifted men who are the glory of Scotland—Professor Wilson, Burns, Drummond, the "Gentle Shepherd," Dr. Chalmers and many others. On my return home read an account of Irving's visit to Newstead Abbey. Byron was in a foreign land, but the home which his genius has consecrated, had been still more adorned by his intimate and admiring friends who then owned it. How delightful it must have been to visit those haunts which the poet loved, which his presence has made "sacred to genius"! I was much interested in the touching story of the "Little White Lady," that singular and unfortunate, yet somewhat gifted being, who so wildly worshipped the poet whom she had never seen.

Saturday, July 15. Have been very busy·to-day.—On my return from school did some sewing, and made some gingerbread.—Afterwards adopted "Bloomer" costume and ascended the highest cherry tree, which being the first feat of the kind ever performed by me, I deem worthy of note.— Obtained some fine fruit, and felt for the first time "monarch of all I surveyed," and then descended from my elevated position. In the evening spent some time very delightfully with Miss Shepard looking over her beautiful books and many elegant little curiosities.

Monday, July 17. This afternoon Miss Shepard allowed Lizzie [Church] and me to read a few pages of her journal which interested us very much; but we dared not appropriate any more of its precious contents. I have seen to-day a picture of a dear old English church. How beautiful and picturesque it was with its ivy wreathed spire and moss-covered walls! There could not be a lovelier spot than this consecrated to the worship of God. How delightful it would be to sit on the banks of the sparkling stream which winds so prettily among the ancient trees, and listen to the sweet music of the village bells as they chime the hour of prayer. Oh! England my heart yearns towards thee as to a loved and loving friend! I long to behold thee, to dwell in one of thy quiet homes, far from the scenes of my early childhood; far from the land, my native land—where I am hated and oppressed because God has given me a *dark skin*. How did this cruel this absurd prejudice ever exist? how can it exist? When I think of it a feeling of indignation rises in my soul too deep for utterance. This evening I have been thinking of it very much. When, Oh! when will these dark clouds clear away? When will the glorious light of Liberty and Justice appear? The prospect seems very gloomy. But I will try not to despond.

> "Truth crushed to the Earth, shall rise again,
> The eternal years of God are hers,
> But Error, wounded writhes in pain,
> And dies amid his worshippers!"

Wednesday, July 19. This afternoon went with our dear teacher and some of the scholars to Marblehead Beach. Miss

Hawthorne, the sister of the author, and Miss Anderson, our teacher's very dear friend, were of the party. I admired Miss A.[nderson]'s earnest, thoughtful face.—As we rode along the banks of Forest River, a sparkling stream which winds gracefully among the hills, we saw at a distance a beautiful grove. Figures were moving about among the trees; evidently a party was there, bent, like ourselves, on the enjoyment of this delightful summer day. We had a fine view of a part of the bay, and I noticed a miniature, rocky island. It was just such an island as I imagined "Monte Christo" must have been, and I thought how strange it would be if there was in those huge rocks, a secret cave where lie buried, untold treasures surpassing those of fairy-land. But my thoughts were soon recalled from their romantic, perhaps absurd wanderings to the beautiful reality before me. We were just entering a winding lane, where graceful elm-trees twined their branches, forming an arch of rich green foliage. Sweet-briar, and elder blossoms perfumed the air. And at a little distance we could see the white farmhouses peeping between the trees. It seemed to me as if I could feel the quiet beauty of the scene. And now we could distinctly hear the roaring of the waves. I shall never forget my emotions on first beholding the glorious ocean. I stood on the shore, listening to the wild sounds of the waves. They were of the richest emerald as they rose in grandeur, then suddenly falling broke into foam white as the drifting snow. Many mingled feelings rose to my mind. But above all others was that of perfect happiness. For liberty, glorious, boundless liberty reigned there supreme! How very grand were those immense rocks overhanging the sea! They seemed like guardian spirits of the waves.

We ensconsed ourselves among them in a delightful recess

shaded by a huge rock, and watched the waves as they dashed against the rocks, and rising high in the air at times almost enveloped us in a cloud of spray. We wandered on the beach for some time gathering a variety of beautiful stones and seaweed, and Miss Hawthorne gave me a singular stone, "to remember the place by," she said. After watching the glorious sunset, we rode home very pleasantly in the deepening twilight.

Friday, July 21. The weather is intensely hot. On my return from school, finding it impossible to sew, I tried the experiment of doing nothing, but only for a few moments; I found that more difficult than anything else. Read "Lalla Rookh," which, I think, has a peculiarly cooling influence even in its very name. How much I longed to be in that charming "Vale of Cashmere"! In the evening took a pleasant walk with Helen [Gilliard].

Sunday, July 23. Hot! hotter! Hottest! this bright, beautiful day is certainly the hottest of all. Why cannot one of those old Norwegian gods give us a puff of his icy breath ere we evaporate entirely?—Wrote several letters. I am sure they ought to be appreciated, for their warmth, if for nothing else, if they partook in the least degree of the writer's mood, which was certainly a "melting one."—Read "Sunny Side," a charming little story of a country clergyman's life.—In the evening we had a delightful, refreshing shower.

Monday, July 24. To-day Lizzie and I finished reading "The Genius of Scotland," and I return reluctantly from delightful imaginary wanderings "Among the braes o' Yarrow," and over many a "heathery dell" and "bonnie burn" of dear "auld Scotia," through the splendid halls of Abbotsford, and the humbler, but not less consecrated home of Burns, and from many a quiet home upon the hill-side where

the poor shepherd boy, neglected and unknown has caught
from his solitary communings with Nature the true spirit of
poetry, and breathed it forth in strains the most touching and
beautiful. How many of Scotland's sons have been thus gifted!
Again I have imagined myself standing on the banks of "Loch
Leven" and gazing on the stately old castle once the prison
of the beautiful and unfortunate Mary Stuart, or wandering
by the "classic Esk" or the "silver Tweed" near which so
many gifted bards have dwelt. I was much interested in the
life of the lovely young poetess, Mary Lundie Duncan[,]
"Sweet bird of Scotia's tuneful clime[,]" as one of our own
most gifted poetesses designates her. It seems very sad that
one so richly endowed with genius and goodness should pass
away so soon. Beautiful, happy Scotland! Well may her sons
be proud of her, and her greatest poet exclaim—

> "Oh Caledonia! stern and wild,
> Meet muse for a poetic child.
> Land of brown heath and shaggy wood—
> Land of the mountain and the flood.—
> Land of my sires! what mortal hand
> Could e'er unite the filial band
> That knits me to thy rugged strand?

This evening while we were sewing, S.[arah Cassey Smith]
read aloud Mrs. [Harriet Beecher] Stowe's "Sunny Memories of Foreign Lands." It is extremely interesting. Her
account of the trials of a sea voyage is very amusing. Mrs.
[Amy Matilda] Remond thought it ought to banish entirely
all my romantic ideas, as she calls them, of the delights of
going to sea, but she was mistaken; I do not think anything
could accomplish that.

Wednesday, July 26.   On my return from school, found a

letter awaiting me from Aunt Margaretta [Forten]; it was unexpected, and made me very happy. It was so kind, so cheering that it seemed almost like hearing the gentle affectionate voice of my dear aunt. Nothing can exceed the intense heat of the weather in Philadelphia, she says, I fear it will make her ill again, unless—but I must not think of what is so improbable.—This afternoon made several desperate attempts to iron a muslin dress, but overcome by the heat, I gave up in despair.—Went in search of Mary, whom I found scrubbing the steps, and persuaded her to change employments with me. So I scrubbed away very gayly, and afterwards prepared tea for her, while she ironed the unfortunate dress. It was quite pleasant to have anything to do with cold water on such a hot day. In the evening took a pleasant walk.— Then read in "Sunny Memories of Foreign Lands."

Friday, July 28.   This morning Miss Creamer, a friend of our teacher, came into the school. She is a very learned lady; a Latin teacher in Troy Seminary, and an authoress. I certainly did feel some alarm, when I saw her entering the room. But she was so very kind and pleasant that I soon felt more at ease. She asked us a few questions and told an amusing anecdote of one of her pupils. She seems to be a very nervous and excitable person, and I found myself frequently contrasting her appearance with that of our dear teacher, who looked so perfectly calm and composed, that I began to flatter myself that she was not experiencing any uneasiness about our acquitting ourselves creditably. I rather think that I was mistaken in this. But we felt very happy to hear her say afterwards that she was much pleased, and thought we did very well. I do think reading one's composition, before strangers is a trying task. If I were to tell Mrs. R.[emond] this, I know she would ask how I could expect to become what I often say I should like to be—an Anti-Slavery lecturer. But I think that I should then trust to the inspiration of the subject.—This evening read "Poems of Phillis Wheatley," an African slave, who lived in Boston at the time of the Revolution. She was a wonderful gifted woman, and many of her poems are very beautiful. Her character and genius afford a striking proof of the falseness of the assertion made by some that hers is an inferior race.

Saturday, July 29. This afternoon went to the pastures with Sarah R. [emond], Helen P. [utnam Gilliard], and the children to gather blackberries. There was a delightful breeze, and I must confess that I felt more inclined to sit on the rocks, and admire the beautiful prospect, than plunge among thorns and briars in search of berries,—to the great annoyance of Frank, who declared that I "should never get any berries, stopping every minute to look at the clouds and rocks as if I had never seen any before." After picking for some time, we came to a pleasant grove, and seating ourselves on the moss-covered rocks greatly enjoyed our lunch, and the delightful, rural spot in which it was taken. We returned home just as the sun was setting, and although we had not a great many berries, and felt rather tired, we all agreed that our "berrying" had been a very pleasant one.

Tuesday, August 1. To-day is the twentieth anniversary of British emancipation. The joy that we feel at an event so just and so glorious is greatly saddened by thoughts of the bitter and cruel oppression which still exists in our own land so proudly claiming to be "the land of the free." And how very distant seems the day when she will follow the example of "the mother country," and liberate her millions of suffering slaves! This morning I went with Mr. and Mrs. R. [emond] to the celebration at Abingdon. The weather was delightful, and a very large number of persons was assembled in the beautiful grove. Mr. Garrison, Wendell Phillips and many other distinguished friends of freedom were present and spoke eloquently. Mr. Garrison gave an interesting account of the rise and progress of the anti-slavery movement in Great Britain. I had not seen Mr. [Thomas Wentworth] Higginson[44] before. He is very fine looking, and has one of the deepest, richest voices that I have ever heard. I was much pleased with Mr. [John] M'Cluer, a genial, warm-hearted Scotchman who was arrested in Boston during the trial of Burns. He has a broad, Scotch accent which I was particularly delighted to hear as I have been reading very much about Scotland lately. The sadness that I had felt was almost entirely dissipated by the hopeful feelings expressed by the principal speakers. And still more pleasant to think that it was for a cause so holy that they had assembled then and there. Sarah and I had a sail in one of those charming little row-boats which are my particular favorites. It was very delightful to me to feel that I was so near the water; and I could not resist the temptation to cool my hands in the sparkling waves. I greatly enjoyed sitting under the shade of the noble pine trees and listening to the eloquent speeches in behalf of the slave; every sentiment of which met a warm response to my heart. On returning home we stopped in Boston and passed some time very pleasantly in the Common listening to the music which enlivened the stillness of the sultry night. It was quite late when we reached home. And I returned to rest feeling that this had been one of the happiest days of my life, and thinking hopefully of the happy glorious day when every fetter shall be broken, and throughout this land there shall no longer be a single slave!

Saturday, August 5. To-day vacation commenced.—How

busy we have been this morning in school! Lizzie [Church]
and I cleared the desks and drawers, arranged books and
papers, and put everything in order, rejoicing that we could
be of the slightest assistance to our dear teacher. I felt very
sad to part with that kind friend even for a few weeks. She
gently reproved me when we were parting, for not returning
her embrace. I fear she thought me cold, but it was not so.
I know not why it is that when I think and feel the most, I
say the least. I suppose it is my nature, not to express by
word or action who much I really feel. But it was real sorrow
that I parted from the beloved teacher to whom I owe so
much, so much more than I can ever repay, for the kindness
which has made this last few months so happy and useful to
me. She has supplied me with several excellent books to read
during vacation. This afternoon made some pies. In the
evening read the "Memoirs of Hannah More" (commenced
reading them).

Tuesday, August 8.   Miss Shepard has not gone away yet,
and this morning I took a delightful walk with her in
Harmony Grove. Never did it look so beautiful as on this
very loveliest of summer mornings, so happy, so peaceful
one almost felt like resting in that quiet spot, beneath the
soft, green grass. My teacher talked to me of a beloved sister
who is sleeping here. As she spoke, it almost seemed to me
as if I had known her; one of those noble, gentle, warm-
hearted spiritual beings, too pure and heavenly for this world.
Oh! how lovely it was this morning; all was so bright and
beautiful, and yet so calm. Again I parted with my dear
teacher, feeling how much I should miss her society, in which
I always find so much enjoyment. To-day I have been very
industrious, learning to weave hair,—having succeeded "tol-

erably," there is "room for improvement." I cannot say that it is a very pleasing occupation to me; it is rather too tedious for my restless nature which constantly craves excitement, action.—Commenced reading Longfellow's "Golden Legend."—Afterwards read for a while in "Hannah More," which interests me very much.

Thursday, August 10. Commenced reading "The House of the Seven Gables." That strange, mysterious, awful reality, that is constantly around ·and among us, that power which takes away from us so many of those whom we love and honor, or those who have persecuted and oppressed us, our bitter enemies whom we vainly endeavor not to hate. Oh! I long to be good, to be able to meet death calmly and fearlessly, strong in faith and holiness. But this I know can only be through one who died for us, through the pure and perfect love of Him, who was all holiness and love. But how can I hope to be worthy of His love while I still cherish the feeling towards my enemies, this unforgiving spirit? This is a question which I ask myself very often. Other things in comparison with this seem easy to overcome. But hatred of oppression seems to me so blended with hatred of the oppressor I cannot separate them. I feel that no other injury could be so hard to bear, so very hard to forgive, as that inflicted by cruel oppression and prejudice. How *can* I be a Christian when so many in common with myself, for no crime suffer so cruelly, so unjustly? It seems in vain to try, even to hope. And yet I still long to resemble Him that is really good and useful in life.

Wednesday, August 16. Finished reading "The House of Seven Gables." Have been spending some hours very pleasantly with Adelaide. This evening I had a conversation with

Mr. [William C.] N.[ell][45] about the "spiritual rappings."—He is a firm believer in their "spiritual" origin. He spoke of the different manner in which the different "spirits" manifested their presence,—some merely touching the mediums, others thoroughly *shaking* them, etc. I told him that I thought I required a very "thorough shaking" to make me a believer. Yet I must not presume to say that I entirely disbelieve that which the wisest cannot understand.

Thursday, August 17. My birthday—How much I feel to-day my own utter insignificance! It is true the years of my life are but few. But have I improved them as I should have done? No! I feel grieved and ashamed to think how very little I know of what I should know of what is really good and useful. May this knowledge of my *want* of knowledge be to me a fresh incentive to more earnest, thoughtful action, more persevering study! I trust, I believe it will.—Helen S.[hearman][46] and Ada [Putnam] and her sisters, spent the evening with us; and I had the pleasure of doing a wonderful thing—persuading Mrs. [Amy Matilda] R.[emond] to play and sing for us, which she did very sweetly.

Sunday, August 20. Read "Cowper's Poems" and "Hannah More." In the evening took a pleasant walk with Mrs. [Jane] P.[utnam] and her daughters in Harmony Grove.

Tuesday, August 22. Finished reading Mrs. Stowe's "Sunny Memories of Foreign Lands," which, I think, is one of the most entertaining books of travel that I have ever read.—Commenced reading Stevens' "Travels in the East."

Friday, August 25. Our usually quiet city has been quite noisy for the last two days with the drums and other accompaniments of the military.—I shall be thankful when their "muster" is over. I never liked soldiers, and since the disgraceful capture of poor Burns, they are more hateful to me than ever. Stevens' travels interest me very much, particularly his description of the temples of Egypt, and his voyage up the Nile.

Monday, August 28. This evening had a delightful ride on horseback in company with Mr. [Charles Lenox] Remond, his cousin Miss L.[enox] and Sarah [Cassey].—It was my first experience in equestrianism, and I enjoyed it exceedingly—all my pleasant anticipations were more than realized. We rode nearly ten miles. The weather was delightful, and I thought I had never seen the country look so beautiful. S.[arah] and I had a fine race, and returned home too much delighted to feel at all tired.

Tuesday, August 29. To-day we have an agreeable visitor; quite a distinguished daguerreotypist and artist. Mr. [Thomas] B.[all] from Cincinnati, whose genius and perseverance have triumphed even over prejudice so far as to make his elegant establishment one of the most profitable and fashionable in the country. This evening we had a pleasant family party, made still more pleasant by the unexpected arrival of Mr. N.[ell] who talked with me about music to my heart's content.

Thursday, August 31. Farewell to summer! Bright, beautiful summer; she is giving us at parting her very loveliest smiles. The delightful weather to-day tempted me to take an unusually long walk—to Marblehead Beach. I tried in vain to raise a party; everybody had something to prevent them from going except Henry [Cassey] who accompanied me. I felt deeply the grandeur, the sublimity of Old Ocean, as he thundered forth his mandates to the solitary rocks, which his rushing waves have washed for ages. I felt that:

> "There is society where none intrudes,
> By the deep sea—and music in its roar."

We had a very pleasant walk home in the evening. Of course everybody was surprised to hear that we had walked so far since dinner.

Sunday, September 3. Have just returned from walking in Harmony Grove with Mrs. [Amy Matilda] R. [emond] and Sarah [Cassey Smith].—Afterwards paid a visit to Miss [Sarah Parker] R. [emond]—What a beautiful night! The moonlight, the perfect stillness, broken only by the chirping of crickets, remind me of my country home; and my thoughts turn to the loved ones there with whom I have enjoyed so many quiet lovely evenings like this.—I imagine myself again sitting with father and mother in our pleasant porch, listening to the merry voices of my dear little brothers; and a delightful sensation of *home* enjoyment steals over me.—But it is only a dream. Good Night! dear friends. Pleasant dreams to you! I know mine will still be of you. May we soon meet again better, happier, more loving than ever!

Tuesday, September 5. Commenced reading the second volume of Stevens' "Travels."—I have suffered much to-day,—my friends Mrs. [Jane] P. [utnam] and her daughters were refused admission to the Museum, after having tickets given them, solely on account of their complexion. Insulting language was used to them.—Of course they felt and exhibited deep, bitter indignation; but of what avail was it? none, but to excite the ridicule of those contemptible creatures, miserable doughfaces who do not deserve the name of men. I will not attempt to write more.—No words can express my feelings, but these cruel wrongs cannot be much longer endured. A day of retribution must come. God grant that it may come very soon!

Sunday, September 10. How the rain is pouring to-day! Surely the clouds must be nearly exhausted from the quantity of tears they have shed for these last two days. But although so rainy, it is not a gloomy day to me. Mr. and Mrs. R.[emond] have gone to Manchester, and Sarah and I are keeping house.—This afternoon I finished reading the "Memoirs of Hannah More," then read for a while "The Course of Time." And now to guard effectually against "the blues" I will write to my dear grandmother, who is blessed with a most cheerful disposition; and send a "message of rebuke" to that eccentric bachelor—Uncle W.[illiam Forten] [47] for his indifference to our injunctions concerning the important Circular.

Monday, September 11. This evening I went with Adelaide [Putnam] and Henry [Cassey] to see representations of Niag[a]ra Falls, the Mammoth Cave, and those beautiful combinations of nature and art—Fairmont Water Works and Boston Common. The picture of the Mammoth Cave is beautiful. We could almost imagine that we were gazing on some region of fairy-land. The numberless crystals with which the rocky walls and ceiling are studded, glitter like diamonds in the torchlight. In our progress through the cave we see dark, fearful abysses, which are in striking contrast with the charming grottos. I should not think it possible any representation could give one a just conception of the sublimity of Niag[a]ra. The picture of Fairmont is excellent. The noble basin, the miniature waterfalls, suspension bridge, and the beautiful gardens on the banks of the Schuylkill looked exactly as I saw them last, and recalled to my mind many pleasing memories of delightful rambles there, with beloved friends, some of whom I shall see no more. But the Mammoth Cave was the most attractive feature of the exhibition, and it was truly magnificent. I said to Ada, "When the slaves are set free we shall certainly visit this beautiful, enchanted cavern."

Most despondingly she replied, "Then I fear we shall never behold it."

Wednesday, September 13.   This evening we made a cheerful little party round the fire in Mrs. [Amy Matilda] Remond's room—It seemed quite like a winter evening.—I read aloud from Stevens' "Travels in the East," his interesting account of a journey through the wilderness, and visit to Petra—the "city of rock."

Thursday, September 14.   Spent the evening at Mrs. Putnam's—We had quite a spirited discussion on Mr. [Charles] Sumner[48] and his party.—One or two recited poetry. Mrs. P.[utnam] wishes each of us to learn something to recite when we meet again.

Sunday, September 17.   Spent the afternoon at Mrs. [Jane] Putnam's. We read and recited poetry.—Some of Willis' "Sacred Poems" I think are very beautiful. We vainly tried to persuade Addie to read or recite. She played some very beautiful sacred tunes for us.—Her devotion to music conquers even her extreme unwillingness to make any display.— I was much interested in a conversation between Mrs. P.[utnam] and her grandson—little Eddie [Putnam], about slavery and prejudice.—I saw how hard she struggled to repress those deep, bitter emotions, which, I think she feels more strongly than many do, and to speak calmly to the child who listened with eager interest.—He is uncommonly intelligent and observing for one so young.

Monday, September 18.   Read awhile in Stevens' "Travels" which increases in interest.—In the evening, Ada [Putnam] and I kept store for Mrs. [Jane] P.[utnam].

Wednesday, September 20.   On my return from school was surprised to find that Mr. H. [?] had arrived from Philadelphia.—Of course I felt very glad to see any one from home. I inquired about Eliza, who, I fear has quite forgotten me.—In the afternoon took a pleasant walk with Adelaide.—Afterwards finished reading "Hard Times" which ends rather sorrowfully.

Friday, September 22.   Read Lowell's "Fable for Critics." It is an extremely amusing criticism on critics, and the leading American poets, including the author himself.—Studied a history lesson.—In the evening went to the Horticultural Exhibition, and saw some very fine fruit and some beautiful flowers.

Sunday, September 24.   Finished Stevens' "Travels in the East." I shall not soon forget his interesting description of the ancient temples, tombs and pyramids—those wonderful relics of the decayed splendor of that part of the old world.

Tuesday, September 26.   To-day Mr. and Mrs. R.[emond] left for Syracuse.—I know that we shall miss Mrs. Remond very much.— S.[arah Cassey Remond] is appointed principal housekeeper, and I assisted during her absence. Read a beautiful eulogium on Pascal. His character interested me greatly.—such a noble nature,—so brilliant, so profound, yet so perfectly simple and childlike. He was one to be loved and venerated.—When I read of the great and gifted ones of earth, I feel more deeply my own ignorance and insufficiency.—How very little after the most diligent and persevering study can I hope to resemble them!

Wednesday, September 27.   Have just received a letter from father, which contains a very unexpected summons.—I must return home next month.—It would give me much pleasure to see the loved ones there. But I cannot bear to think of leaving Salem, now that I have just begun to learn. Most earnestly do I wish to possess what is most invaluable,—a thorough education. I will write immediately and use every argument to induce father to permit me to remain a little longer.—I feel as if I *cannot* go now. Oh! I do hope that father will consent to my staying.

Saturday, September 30. My dear, kind teacher has written to father; I cannot but hope that *her* letter will have some effect.—My friends are very unwilling to have me go; they all sympathize with me in my desire to acquire all the knowledge that I possibly can.

Sunday, October 1. No one can call *this* a "melancholy day"—it is so very bright and beautiful. Miss [Sarah Parker] R. [emond] and I took breakfast with Mrs. [Caroline] P. [utnam]. Ada and I stood in the porch watching the little waves as they rose and sparkled like brilliants in the sunlight. It was a beautiful sight on this, most quiet and delightful of Sabbath mornings.—This afternoon commenced reading the "Wide Wide World." My anxiety to know what father's decision will be, almost prevents my thinking of anything else.

Tuesday, Oct. 3. This afternoon I had a lesson in teaching.—I heard the recitations of the third and fourth classes— we got along very pleasantly, and one pretty, rosy-cheeked little girl told me afterwards that she liked me *very* much for a teacher.—In the evening did some sewing, and read in Macaulay's "History of England."

Thursday, Oct. 5. Lizzie [Church] and I spent the evening with Miss Shepard, in her pleasant old-fashioned room. It was very delightful to be there with our teacher, who has the faculty of adapting herself to the society of all—young and old, and making the time pass more pleasantly than any one else can.—We read "Thorpe," which increases in interest, and gives one an excellent idea of life in a quiet English town.—I walked slowly home in the moonlight. It is exceedingly bright and beautiful now, and how lovely everything appears upon which it falls, the tops of the trees, the steeples of the churches, and the distant hills. (While the water ripples and sparkles beneath the silvery light of the moon.) It is so much more beautiful than the glaring light of day. This is the time for peaceful, happy thoughts, sweet remembrances of "days that are gone by."

Saturday, October 7.   This evening Mr. and Mrs. Remond arrived from Syracuse. W[illia]m. Wells Brown[49] accompanied them. He was improved greatly both in appearance and conversation during his residence in England.

Sunday, October 8.   This morning I had a delightful ride to Lawrence with Mr. and Miss [Sarah] R.[emond] and Mrs. B.[rown]. The country now looks very beautiful. The trees are tinted with the brilliant and gorgeous hues of autumn. We went to the anti-slavery meetings, which were extremely interesting and well-attended. I had the great pleasure of conversing with Mr. [William Lloyd] Garrison and Mr. [Wendell] Phillips. We were looking at some fine pictures of the queens of England, and afterwards at some grand old Italian and German cathedrals, and Mr. Phillips told me about some of them which he had visited. To me it was a great enjoyment and privilege to listen to the conversation of one so highly gifted.

There are some very picturesque little waterfalls formed by the great dam in Lawrence; the town itself is new—a busy manufacturing place, quite unlike quiet, old-fashioned Salem. I prefer the latter.

Wednesday, October 11.   Helen S[hearman] and I walked to Beverly. It was my first visit to this place, which is far more ancient-looking than Salem. The houses, the vehicles, and the people, had a most venerable appearance—even the children, I fancied, looked old. This evening studied arithmetic and read Macaulay.

Saturday, October 14. Last night I attended a concert by the "Luca family." The youngest of the brothers, a boy of sixteen, as a pianist is really wonderful. I regretted that they had not a larger audience, which they well deserved. They are staying with us.

Thursday, October 19. The "Luca Family"[50] are with us again; so that we have delightful music continually. The young pianist has composed a very beautiful schottish. We were trying to find a name for it, when Mrs. [Amy Matilda] Remond proposed that it should be called the "Liberty Schottish," and dedicated to Mr. Garrison, and this was agreed upon. Of course, Ada [Putnam] thoroughly appreciates our musical life, and is with us frequently.

This evening Sarah, Ada, and myself passed very pleasantly at Mrs. [Amy] Ives;[51] (There saw a very fine picture representing a scene in Napoleon's Russian campaign, during which the soldiers suffered so horribly. A soldier is dying; almost buried beneath the snow; one arm is draw [*sic*] closely around the dead body of a companion, perhaps a beloved son or brother, while the hand which convulsively grasps his musket has every muscle strained to the utmost. The expression of his face I shall never forget. Anguish and despair are blended with inflexible courage and determination in his compressed lips and flashing eyes.—I almost felt as if he could speak; but words could not have told more than did that painfully expressive face).

A Mr. D. [?] was present, with whose fiery enthusiastic nature I was pleased. We talked much about Napoleon, and Washington. Some one said that many persons refused to believe that the latter used profane language. I could not help saying that I believed that a person who would hold slaves would swear. Of course, the "Father of his Country" was eloquently defended from the charge of *willingly* holding slaves. For the rest of the evening our conversation was upon slavery.

Sunday, October 22.   Read some very beautiful poems of Mrs. Browning. The whole soul of the poetess is breathed forth in her writings. They seem like delicious music to reach the depths of our nature, to give us earnest, holy thoughts, and increase our love for the good and the beautiful.

Monday, October 23.   At last I have received the long expected letter, which to my great joy, contains the eagerly desired permission to remain. I thank father very much for his kindness, and am determined that so far as I am concerned, he shall never have cause to regret it. I will spare no effort to become what he desires that I should be; to prepare myself well for the responsible duties of a teacher, and to live for the good that I can do my oppressed and suffering fellow-creatures. Studied a lesson in Geology. This afternoon Miss Shepard lent Lizzie [Church] and me a beautiful volume, "Home Book of the Picturesque," which contains some very fine pictures of American scenery. One of them I admired particularly. It was a picturesque little cottage on the banks of the Hudson. The scenery around it was very beautiful and quiet—so *very* quiet. I thought it would be delightful to live there, with a few dear friends, far from the busy world; and yet to do much good in the world, to make others better and happier, and to be known by that good alone. Among the engravings were some of the noble Cattskill [*sic*] Mountains, and of the rivers and mountains of western Pennsylvania—

the beautiful valley of Wyoming I regarded with much interest as the scene of Campbell's far-famed poem which I have lately read.

Wednesday, October 25. A bright and beautiful October day. This afternoon took a long walk with my dear teacher and some of the girls.—We had a delightful ramble over the hills, and ascended one of the highest, which commands a fine view of the surrounding country. We saw Marblehead Beach, and glorious Old Ocean, which seemed to me like a dear friend whom I longed to be near. Salem with its venerable trees and houses, and winding streams, looked really beautiful. Far away in the distance were long ranges of ever-green hills. The whole was a magnificent panorama, painted by Nature with a skill that could never be rivalled by art. We gathered many beautiful wild flowers, and Miss Shepard and I made a bouquet for our gentle Lizzie, whose absence was the only drawback to the afternoon's enjoyment. We visited the "Dungeons," which are very singular mounds enclosing deep hollows, some of which contain water. It is supposed that they were made by some action of water, but, I believe, it has never been determined. We had a glorious sunset, and as we walked home in the quiet evening, I thought of the many times at home that I had longed for a ramble over the hills of New England, little imagining then that I should ever have the pleasure of many delightful ones. This evening studied arithmetic, and read Macaulay to Mrs. Remond.

Sunday, October 29. Went to the first of the course of anti-slavery lectures, which was given by Mr. Prince of Essex. It was excellent and very well-attended. The lecturer had not *quite* so much enthusiasm as I like, but he is interesting and warm-hearted. Miss Shepard was there, and she said that she was pleased with the lecture. I hope that she will be persuaded to attend the whole course. If she were better acquainted with the sentiments of the abolitionists, I do not think she could regard any of them as unchristian; but she would see them as they are—truly christian, noble hearted, devoted to the Right.

Wednesday, Nov.[ember] 1.   Commenced studying Natural Philosophy. Studied arithmetic and read Macaulay.

Thursday, November 2.   This morning our kind teacher, who is always doing something for our enjoyment and instruction, planned for some of us a visit to the Essex Institute. We saw some very old portraits. Among them were those of Dr. Holyoke, an eminent physician of Salem, who lived to be a hundred years old—John Higginson, the son of the first minister of Salem, from whom our school received its name— Gov. Bradstreet, Gov. Endicott, and the wife of Mr. Holyoke, the first president of Harvard College, a stately lady of the olden time. We saw the likeness of Oliver Cromwell, and the dark, severe countenance, I thought an index to the character of the stern Lord Protector.

Dr. [Henry] Wheatland showed us the first newspaper printed in Salem, and another also very old edited by a lady. Lizzie and I remarked that while the other paper contained no miscellaneous stories, the first article in the ladies' paper was a tragic story, with a most romantic title. Whether this would be ascribed to the *finer taste*, or to the weaker mind of our sex, I know not. I do know, however, that *my* appreciation of the generality of newspaper stories has greatly dimished [*sic*] of late.

We saw through a microscope, some infusoria—very minute insects which were found in fossil slate in Europe, and other specimens taken from ditches in this country—some of them are so exceedingly small that it is said to require one hundred and eighty-seven millions of them to weigh a single grain. Those we saw were highly magnified. We saw also through the microscope several other very small insects, and minute portions of leaves and of the rest of a plant which appeared very singular. We examined the eye of a common fly, which, when magnified[,] resembled a piece of lace.

Dr. Wheatland showed us some pictures of African huts near Cape Palmas—and told us that one of them was the residence of a priest or doctor, from whom the natives, when about to take a journey, procure charms, which they believe will effectually guard them from danger. When passing this place, they scatter a portion of food to the chickens, believing that the spirits of their deceased friends exist in them!

We saw a beautiful birch basket, made by some of the Tuscorora Indians, which showed great taste in the arrangement of colors; and some vessels made by them for containing water, exactly similar to those used by the East Indians. Dr. Wheatland said that this was a proof that man, as well and animals posses [*sic*] instinct—causing them to manufacture articles similar to those made by other nations, of whose very existence they were ignorant. I thought that it might also be probable, if, as is supposed the American Indians are descended from some of the inhabitants of Asia, that their ancestors in emigrating to this continent brought some of these vessels with them, and taught their children how to make them. We were much indebted to the kindness of Capt. [Henry] King and Dr. Wheatland for many interesting microscopic views, and much useful information about the old publications of the early settlers of Salem.

Sunday, November 5. This evening attended Mr. Remond's lecture at Lyceum Hall. It was excellent—on the never-failing topic which to us is all-important. Would it were so to every one! Not long should we have to mourn the existence of the terrible sin of slavery in our land. Read some of Mrs. Browning's beautiful poems, and Dr. Cheever's lecture on Bunyan. They are earnestly, beautifully written. Sometimes I feel that their deep religious thought is beyond my comprehension. Yet I cannot but acknowledge its truth, and admire its beauty and fervor.

Wednesday, November 8. This evening attended a lecture on Jerusalem and Damascus. It was very interesting, but as I have read so much about the Holy Land I should have preferred hearing a lecture on some subject with which I was less familiar. The lecturer—Rev. Mr. [Joseph] Thompson of New York, is evidently a very enthusiastic person, and he is certainly a fine lecturer. I was much interested in his account of the ruins of Baalbec—of that ancient city, situated in a fertile plain, near the large and beautiful city of Damascus, nothing is known—not even by whom it was founded, or when, and by what means destroyed. What a contrast must these desolate ruins present to the busy, flourishing city so near them! And how strange it seems that its history should be involved in such entire obscurity.

Friday, November 10. Finished reading, "Merkland" a beautiful Scottish story, which gives one a charming picture of life in Scotland; with its "lights and shadows" so simply yet vividly presented to our view that we feel almost unconsciously a warm sympathy and interest in them. Wrote a composition—subject—antiquities. It was most amusing to see the dismal, despairing faces when our teacher gave us the subject. We were truly a disconsolate band of youthful, inexperienced antiquarians; and the whole afternoon passed away before some of the mental relic-hunting expeditions were over. This evening studied arithmetic, read and copied some of Longfellow's exquisite poems, and read Macaulay.

Sunday, November 12. A rainy day. Read and wrote nearly all day. This evening attended an anti-slavery lecture by the Rev. Mr. [Thomas] Stone. He spoke with deep feeling. He is an earnest, truehearted man, who has suffered for the good cause.

Tuesday, November 14. This afternoon instead of the usual exercises, we had our work at school and read compositions. Many of them were both written and read beautifully. At Miss Shepard's invitation—Addie [Putnam] accompanied me to school. The children sang sweetly. I always love to hear the blending of those young voices. We enjoyed ourselves very much.—In the evening read some of the poems of those highly sigted [*sic*] sisters, Lucretia and Margaret Davidson. Studied Geography and wrote a letter. Afterwards Ada gave us some delightful music.

Wednesday, November 15. Have just returned from a lecture by Mr. [Josiah] Quincy. The lecturer contrasted the prosperity and customs of the North with that of the South, showing the great superiority of the former in all that contributes to the true enjoyment of life. Many of his remarks were extremely interesting—others very amusing. He spoke much of two of the most distinguished men of Virginia—Capt. John Smith, the brave heroic settler; and Randolph of Roanoke, the celebrated orator and statesman whose dying act of justice at least entitles his memory to respect. I can see but little merit in knowing and openly acknowledging the sin of slavery and even rebuking it as he did, and yet persisting in doing the wrong. Mr. Quincy, though evidently a man of somewhat liberal views is widely different from his truly liberty-loving brother. To divert my thoughts from American wickedness read Macaulay's character of Charles the Second— turned from the republican despotism of to-day to the monarchical tyranny of two centuries ago. The contrast is by no means very striking, as far as actually tyranny is concerned.

Saturday, November 18.   Rose before four—it was very dark and cold. Studied Philosophy.—Sewed all the afternoon very busily—This evening made some cakes, studied arithmetic and read Macaulay.—Afterwards Mr. [William Wells] B.[rown] arrived, and we talked about England. He talks continually about his daughters. They must be prodigies. I feel extremely curious to see them, and hope they are as finely educated and accomplished as he evidently thinks they are. Would that there were far more intelligent colored people! And yet we could hardly expect more of those, who have so many unsurmountable difficulties to contend with. But despite them all let our motto still be "Excelsior" and we cannot fail to make some improvement. At times I feel it almost impossible not to despond entirely of there ever being a better, brighter day for us. None but those who experience it can know what it is—this constant, galling sense of cruel injustice and wrong. I cannot help feeling it very often, it intrudes upon my happiest moments, and spreads a dark, deep gloom over everything.

Sunday, November 19.   Wrote a letter to my dear aunt. I can always write more freely to her than to any one else. Read Mrs. Browning's Poems.—This evening went to Mr. [William Wells] Brown's lecture. I thought that he spoke much better than he usually does. His manner was more animated. But although in private conversation he has greatly improved, I do not think he is a very good lecturer. As a writer, he is very highly spoken of by some of the leading English journals.

Tuesday, November 21. Attended a lecture by Rev. Mr. [Thomas Wentworth] Higginson of Worcester—subject "The Puritan Clergyman." It was very interesting and amusing; giving one an excellent idea of the manners and customs of the old Puritans. For some time he spoke sarcastically and severely about them; but afterwards paid a tribute of admiration and respect to their stern virtues and thorough consistency of action. I wished that my dear teacher had been there to hear the lecture, for she had a most enthusiastic love for the old Puritan fathers, and I knew she would appreciate it.

Wednesday, November 22. Studied arithmetic and philosophy and read Macaulay. Read "Wensley, a Story without a Moral," it was written by Edmund Quincy, but although he probably did not wish it to be known his incognito could not be long preserved. It is a pleasant story, and I enjoyed it the more for having some acquaintance with, and great admiration for, the noble-hearted author.

Thursday, November 23. This evening accompanied Miss Shepard on a visit to one of her friends—Miss Upton. They are very agreeable people, and I passed the evening pleasantly.—I told my dear teacher that if I could in the very least degree help to lessen the cruel, unjust prejudice which exists against us, I would go willingly. I think it hardly probable that I was so fortunate, but enjoyed the evening far more than I had anticipated. My beloved teacher and I walked home in the quiet starlight—star*shine* she said it might be called—and why not? we have sunshine and moonshine, and surely it is delightful—the light of those fair stars "which are the poetry of heaven." And more delightful it seemed to me with that dear friend, the remembrance of whose kind words and loving sympathy will remain, even after I have parted from her, one of the happiest of my life.

Friday, November 24.   Lizzie [Church] and I finished reading "Memorable Women," by Mrs. Crosland. It contained the memoirs of Lady Russell, the wife of the brave and upright, but unfortunate statesman—of Mrs. Piozzi— the intimate friend and hostess of Dr. Johnson—Madam D'Arblay—Margaret Fuller—and other gifted and noble- hearted women, whose memories will ever be regarded with the love and admiration to which their many virtues so justly entitle them. The character of Margaret Fuller interested me greatly; there is a charm even in reading of a nature so earnest and impassioned, combined with the richest mental endow- ments and possessing with all its defects so many qualities that were truly lovable, and worthy of the highest praise.

Sunday, November 26.   Finished reading "Ida May." It is extremely interesting but I do not think it compared with "Uncle Tom's Cabin." Still it shows plainly the evils of slavery, and may do much good. I read it with pleasure, as I do everything which is written in opposition to this ini- quitous system. This evening listened to one of the most eloquent and radical anti-slavery lectures that I have ever heard. It was given by Rev. Mr. [Charles] Hodges of Watertown, one of the few ministers who dare speak and act as freemen, obeying the Higher Law, and scorning all lower laws which are opposed to Justice and Humanity. His subject was the final issue of slavery, and he showed in the most conclusive manner how utterly impossible it is for liberty and slavery to exist in union; one of them must eventually triumph. He thinks that the latter will do so, and the country sink into inevitable ruin. And then on the ruins of the old republic, will be founded a new and glorious one, whose people will take warning from the fate of this, and form a union which shall be free from the curse of slavery.

Thursday, November 30. Thanksgiving Day.—Our usually quiet city is in quite a commotion this week. The preparations which we make at home for Christmas are made here for Thanksgiving. It is the time for "glad meetings round the social hearth," reunions of families and friends who may have been separated during the year. It is a pleasant custom, though often doubtless bringing sad as well as happy remembrances.—Spent the day in reading Byron and Mrs. Browning, and afterwards listened to Mr. [William Wells] Brown's entertaining account of some of his old-world experiences.

Sunday, December 3. Winter has come at last; cold, very cold, yet bright and beautiful. Last night I awoke, and the brilliant moonlight tempted me to go to the window. I looked out on the clear frosty night, and thought I had never seen the moon and stars look so beautiful. Their quiet light had such a soothing effect—calmed every disturbing thought and passion, and gave me a feeling of perfect peace. This morning read, and wrote to father, who has been quite ill. He informs me that Wendell [Forten] is in town going to Aunt Margaretta's school. I am very glad, and have no doubt that he will improve rapidly.

Evening. Have just returned from an interesting lecture by Mr. [William Lloyd] Garrison. I had the pleasure of shaking hands with the great and good man. He could scarcely have had a more disagreeable night. It is extremely windy and stormy. While I write the rain pours, and the wind blows a perfect hurricane. What a contrast to the quiet beauty of last night! And yet it is pleasant to sit by a cheerful fire and listen to the wild sound of the storm raging without.

Wednesday, December 6. Studied arithmetic and philosophy, and in the afternoon went to a sewing party, or "bee" as the New Englanders call it.—Such parties possess not the slightest attraction for me, unless they are for the anti-slavery fair. Then I always feel it both a duty and a pleasure to go. My teacher, with her usual kindness, gave me her Lyceum ticket. Dr. [Reighold] Solger was expected to lecture, but having another engagement Prof. [Louis] Agassiz supplied his place. The subject was the formation of animals, and though interesting and instructive, I felt somewhat disappointed, as I had heard him deliver a lecture nearly similar, and it did not quite compensate for what I had expected to hear about Europe.

Monday, December 4.   Wrote letters, read poetry, and studied history. This evening went to the anti-slavery sewing circle at Mrs. [Amy] Ives.—Nellie [Ives?] and I established ourselves at a pretty little table, and sewed and talked very very pleasantly. She is one of those intelligent, affectionate children whom it is impossible [not] to love. She was quite enthusiastic in her admiration of Mr. Garrison who had been staying with them, and we fully agreed with regard to his uncommon excellence.

Sunday, December 10.   Read Dr. Cheever's life of Bunyan, and "Adelaide Murray," a little Scottish story which my teacher recommended to me for Sunday reading. Took a long walk with Miss [Sarah Parker] Remond. We spoke of perfect sincerity and candor, how seldom they are found even in many whom the world calls good. She thought that she was a very little inclined to misanthropy. I think so; and feel the importance of guarding against this feeling to which every discovery we make of the faithlessness or unworthiness of others so strangely tempts us. In Miss R.[emond] I particularly admire the uncompromising sincerity which is a prominent trait of her character. This evening attended Rev. Mr.

[James] Appleton's lecture. I had expected to hear the most radical anti-slavery, nor was I disappointed. The lecturer forcibly and eloquently advocated the principles of moral action against slavery, denouncing all political action as being necessarily based on the Constitution, the very root of the evil; declared that the "timid good" were no accession to the anti-slavery ranks, but rather a hindrance to the work of freedom, which would be benefited by their leaving it; and that nothing but an open and manly denunciation of slavery, and those who support and apologize for it, or fear to speak against it, would ever be of the slightest avail. All of which, of course, had my entire sympathy and approbation.

Tuesday, December 12. Evening—Read aloud fifty-nine pages of Macaulay, and an interesting sketch of the distinguished philosopher, Sir Humphrey Davy.

Thursday, December 14. Spent this evening with our beloved teacher and Lizzie. We finished "Thorpe," which is *very* beautiful and interesting to the last. I passed an evening full of that quiet enjoyment which I always feel in the society of our dear friend and teacher, who possesses the invaluable power of making others happy. There was a charm, too, in the comfortable, old-fashioned room in which we were established for the evening. I have seldom enjoyed myself more.

Sunday, December 17. This evening Sarah [Cassey Smith]'s husband [Mr. Smith] arrived from California; Mr. [William C.] Nell and a Mr. Andrews accompanied him from Boston. We were very much surprised to see him. Of course Sarah is very happy. There was so much to be said, so many questions to be asked and answered, that we had nearly forgotten Lucy Stone's[52] lecture. We found the hall so much crowded that it was almost impossible to procure a seat. The lecture was earnest and impressive, and some parts of it very beautiful. It was an appeal to the noblest and warmest sympathies of our nature, in behalf of the oppressed. I saw many among her large and attentive audience, who had probably never attended an anti-slavery lecture before. I hope her touching appeal may not have been made in vain—that they may think rightly on this subject. And from noble *thoughts* spring noble *words* and *deeds*.

Monday, December 25. (Christmas Day. The return of this season brings to my mind many recollections both sad and pleasing[,] thoughts of home and the happy family meetings we have had on this delightful day. I imagine that I can see grandmother's loved countenance as she listens to the happy voices of the little ones around her wishing her a "Merry Christmas." The busy preparations for the grand dinner, the display of Christmas gifts, the pleasant salutations—I think of them all, and cannot help wishing that I could make one of the happy group assembled there. It is pleasant, too, to think of this as a day of festivity and rejoicing in other lands wherever is held in veneration the name of Him whose birth it commemorates. The sons and daughters of "Merrie England," from the stately palace to the humble cottage, the gay inhabitants of "sunny France" and the dwellers in beautiful Italy, gladly welcome and celebrate the Christmas holiday. And in the pleasant homes of Germany, little children are greeting eagerly the coming of the Christ-child, whose angelic beauty and liberal bounty are themes of universal wonder and delight. Busy hands are wreathing the Christmas tree, and merry voices are blending around the cheerful fire. In many homes there is happiness; but alas; in many others there is sorrow. The suffering poor, the oppressed and down-trodden of the earth, their hearts are sad to-day. For them the bright Christmas sun shines in vain, by

them the merry Christmas greetings are unheard. Their lives
are fraught with woe. Even on this bright day they are
unhappy. A great work lies before us to alleviate their
condition, to make their lives brighter and happier that they,
too, may enjoy this and every other gladsome season).

This morning, Sarah [Cassey Smith] and I went to Boston
to the Anti-Slavery Fair, in which I was somewhat disappointed, as many of the most beautiful articles had been sold,
and they had but very few books, mostly French and German.
The rooms were tastefully decorated with evergreens and
looked quite Christmas-like. In the afternoon, the boys accompanied me to the Museum. We saw a play entitled "The
Dream," which I did not think particularly interesting. I
want very much to see "Othello" or "Macbeth" or some other
of Shakespeare's grand tragedies. These lighter dramas possess
very little interest for me. In the evening returned to the
fair, and saw Mr. [Wendell] Phillips for a few moments.
His adopted daughter, Miss [Sarah Parker] Remond says,
is a lovely girl, and looks very much like Annie [Woods
Webb]. We expected Mr. Smith, but as he did not come
were obliged to return home much earlier than we had
intended.

Wednesday, December 27. A rainy disagreeable day. A
few days since a sheet of snow, dazzling white and beautiful,
covered the roofs of the house, the hills and the branches of
the evergreens. The merry jingle of sleigh-bells was heard,
and I was indulging the hope of soon having some delightful
rides. But the rain quite disregarding our comfort and pleasure has soiled and melted the beautiful snow, and ruined the
sleighing.—I did not feel well enough to attend school, and
have spent the day in various employments—studying arithmetic and philosophy, writing an abstract of the history of

New Jersey, reading Macaulay, and working on a New Year's gift for Mrs. [Amy Matilda] Remond.

Friday, December 29. At noon remained at the school-room with Miss [Mary] Shepard, and read to her sketches of the University of Frederick William at Berlin, and the home of Martin Luther, from "Notes of a Theological Student" by Rev. Mr. Hoppin. The author is an esteemed friend of our teacher. His writings are very beautiful, and his description of life in Germany I think extremely interesting. They manifest great admiration and love for the dear old "Fatherland."

Sunday, December 31. The last day of the old year. I can scarcely realize that I have spent the whole of it away from home. Yet, although separated from many of my dearest friends, this year has been to me a very happy one. Happy, because the field of knowledge, for the first time has seemed widely open to me; because I have studied here, and, I trust, learned more than during any other year of my life. I have been taught how very little I really know, and, with the knowledge of my ignorance, I feel an earnest desire to become very much wiser. There have been changes during the past year, which were far from pleasant to me, involving, as they did, the happiness of a beloved relative. But she appears satisfied, and I feel that *I* should be so. I have gained some new friends, a few of whom are very dear to me. One of them, my beloved teacher, has contributed very much to my happiness and improvement. Very great sources of happiness have been the frequent opportunities I have had of seeing and listening to the great pioneer of the anti-slavery cause, and those who have been with him its earliest, truest friends and most eloquent advocates. To-day finished "Dawning of Genesis" which contains very interesting sketches of the youth of

Sir Humphrey Davy, Dr. Adam Clarke, and other distinguished men; and the first volume of Macaulay. It contains the execution of Monmouth, and the immediate results of his rebellion. I was, at first deeply interested in the fortunes of the ill-fated duke, but afterwards felt indignant at his cowardice and meanness in deserting his faithful followers, and imploring his life at the hands of the revengeful and contemptible king.

New Year's Day, 1855. The new year has commenced on a bright, beautiful day.—This evening received a Philapena[?] present from Mr. Smith—Whittier's "Literary Recreations," which I have wanted very much. While I was working Sarah [Cassey Smith] read aloud from it an amusing story, and an excellent criticism on Thomas Carlyle's views of slavery.

Wednesday, January 3. This afternoon kept store for Mrs. Putnam. Commenced writing to Aunt M.[argaretta Forten]. But Eddie [Putnam] [53] and some little visitors were so uproarious in their amusements, that I had almost given up in despair, when Miss Shepard came in, exerted her magical influence over the little hand, taught them an amusing but less noisy play of which, as she laughingly declared, I was in a state of most benighted ignorance, and effectually quieted them.—This evening attended a lecture by Mr. Brace, on the ragged schools of England. The lecturer spoke in a very interesting manner; but to me it was very sad to hear of so much misery in the beautiful land which I have always loved, and earnestly longed to visit. But there is no doubt that these schools and the many other charitable institutions of Great Britain, aided and supported as they are by many of the noblest and most gifted of the land, have done very much and will continue to do much more towards relieving the suffering there.

Friday, January 5. After school read "The Hour and the Man" to Miss Shepard, while she was working on a birthday gift for a friend, which *must* be finished very soon. On my return home found some Christmas and New Year's presents, very useful ones, from Philadelphia. It is pleasant to receive the slightest token of remembrance from distant friends. Accompanying them was a kind note from my dear Aunt M. [argaretta]. Commenced reading Abbott's "History of Julius Caesar."

Sunday, January 7. Prepared dinner for Mary while she went to church. Read Dr. [George] Cheever and the Anti-Slavery papers.—Paid Adelaide [Putnam] a visit, and did some writing.

Monday, January 8. Looked over our English copy of Longfellow's poems. I think it is the most beautiful book I have ever seen. The engravings, the printing and the binding are executed with the greatest elegance, and enhance, if it can be enhanced, the fascination of the poetry. The book was a gift to Miss Shepard's brother. A more perfectly beautiful gift for the Near Year one could hardly desire.

Tuesday, January 9. Finished reading Abbott's "History of Julius Caesar."

Wednesday, January 10. Studied arithmetic and philosophy, and commenced Abbott's "History of Alfred the Great"—In the evening read aloud from "Literary Recreations."

Friday, January 12. This evening attended a lecture by Rev. Henry Ward Beecher[54] of Brooklyn. The subject was "patriotism." I thought the lecture extremely interesting, and many parts of it very touching and beautiful. His manner is not at all polished or elegant, but he says so many excellent things with such forcible earnestness or irresistible humor, that we quite forget it. As I had hoped, he bore his testimony against the wicked and unjust laws of our land, which it is not *patriotism* to make or to obey. He also eloquently advocated the right of women to vote; and paid a beautiful tribute to the lovely and noble-minded Lucretia Mott.[55] In listening to Mr. Beecher one feels convinced of his sincerity; and we would always rather know that a person *means* what he says, even if we differ from him.

Saturday, January 13. Copied a composition, which I wrote yesterday, on "winter."—Sewed very industriously all the afternoon and evening.—We had music and singing.— Afterwards Sarah read aloud and Henry amused us with enigmas and conundrums, which employed the Yankee faculty of "Guessing."

Sunday, January 14. A beautiful clear, but bitter cold day. Did not feel well enough to go out, though the bright sunshine tempted me strongly. Wrote letters and finished reading "Alfred the Great."

Monday, January 15. In school Lizzie [Church] and I commenced studying "The Second Book of History." This evening studied arithmetic and etymology, and commenced reading Wordsworth.

Wednesday, January 17. Commenced the second volume of Macaulay.

Saturday, January 20.

" 'Tis winter's jubilee: this day

His stores their countless treasures yield"

A bright or more beautiful winter's day I have never seen. We have had cloudy, stormy weather, snow and rain alternately nearly all the week, but the glorious sunshine of to-day fully compensates us. A robe of pure, white snow covers the trees and hills, contrasting beautifully with the dark branches of the evergreens. The air is mild and the sunlight warm and bright as on a day of spring. The sleigh bells are sounding merrily. I cannot but envy any one who is so fortunate as to have a sleigh ride to-day.—This afternoon went over to Adelaide's and had a delightful snow-balling with her music scholars, Emma and Ellie.—Afterwards Ada and I took a pleasant walk.

Sunday, January 21. Finished Mrs. Browning's Poems. One cannot read them without feeling an increased love for the good and beautiful. They have taught me to love and admire the gentle poetess, whom her friend, Miss Mitford, has called, "the priestess of poetry."—Read Wordsworth and the Anti-Slavery papers.

Monday, January 22. In the morning the rain poured in torrents, and all day the wind blew a perfect hurricane, but towards evening the clouds broke away and we had a glorious sunset. I had a fine view of it from Mrs. R.[emond]'s house which has a very pleasant and elevated situation. What strangely variable weather this is for a New England winter—tempests and calms, clouds and sunshine alternately as if it were April.

Tuesday, January 23. Read a report of one of [James Russell] Lowell's lectures on English poetry. They are very interesting and contain many beautiful thoughts which only a true poet could have. In the evening took a pleasant walk with my dear teacher, as far as the entrance of Harmony Grove. The moon was shedding a soft light over the beautiful spot, and the perfect quiet was only broken by the music of a tiny waterfall which the dark evergreens concealed from our sight. It was a lovely night. We stopped at Mrs. Putnam's and spent some time there in very animated conversation about slavery and prejudice. On my return home found a "surprise party" assembled there. Finished the evening very pleasantly with music, singing and conversation.

Wednesday, January 24. This evening attended a lecture by Mr. [John] Pierpont. His subject was, "The Effects of Physical Science upon the Moral World." He lacked animation, and his lecture was extremely uninteresting to me. I was much disappointed in it.

Thursday, January 25. Miss Shepard read to me some exquisite lines, "Canst Thou not Watch One Hour?" They are so very beautiful that I would not forget them, although I cannot ever hope to possess the spirit of Christian forbearance, and patience which they breathe. We think that Whittier must have written them. I hope that he did, for I can enjoy good and beautiful things so much more when I know that those who write them are themselves *good,* and devoted to the Right.

Saturday, January 27. In school studied a geographical description of France. I cannot even *think* of those beautiful, distant lands without a longing so earnest to behold them as makes the thought almost a painful one. I wish that I could cast away some of these day-dreams—forget these vain hopes of the Future, which I fear too often prevent me from engaging earnestly enough in the actual labor of the Present. There is so much to be done, and I can do so little—this feeling often oppresses and saddens me, and almost unconsciously I seek relief in the indulgence of those delightful dreams of days to come when great good shall be accomplished, and the glorious principles of Justice, Liberty and Truth everywhere triumphant. I *must* remember that the only hope of these depends upon the persevering efforts which we make to-day.

Sunday, January 28.   Wrote several letters. Took tea with Miss [Sarah] Remond. This evening read Wordsworth and did some writing.—Again the rain is pouring in torrents.

Monday, January 29.   This evening took a delightful ride by moonlight with Mr. [Charles Lenox] and Miss Remond and Mr. [William Wells] Brown—Attended a meeting which was addressed by Mr. B.[rown].

Tuesday, January 30.   Attended a lecture by Rev. Theodore Parker. I have long wished very much to see and hear this remarkable man, and my pleasant anticipation were fully realized. His subject was "The Anglo-Saxon Race." He gave an extremely interesting and instructive sketch of their origin and peculiar traits of character. And while he acknowledged their superiority in the sciences and in what is *practical* in life, he also showed how inferior they are generally to other races in imagination, love and appreciation of the beautiful, and true moral worth. He spoke of their aggressive spirit, which continually prompted them to make war upon and exterminate other races, and to take possession of their country, and of their strong love of individual liberty; but described them as too selfish to be fond of *equality*. One of their greatest failings is a lack of conscientiousness—they are *downright* before *men* but *not upright* before God. This somewhat exemplified by pauperism in England and slavery in America. Every eighth man in England is a pauper; every eighth man in America is *worse* than a pauper—he does not own the hands with which he works—the feet upon which he stands. Every eighth woman in America does not own herself nor the child upon her bosom.

Wednesday, January 31.   Again I have had the pleasure of hearing Mr. Parker. The lecture of this evening was even more interesting than the other; it was on the "character, condition and prospects of America." I will not attempt an account of it as I could not do it justice. I can only say that it was impressive and true—full of earnest thought and the warmest zeal for truth. Both this evening and last when he spoke of slavery it seemed to me as if I could *feel* the half suppressed sensation which it occasioned. It is *some* encouragement that nearly all the finest orators now are anti-slavery.

Thursday, February 1.   I can scarcely believe that the last winter month has commenced. How rapidly the months glide away! We pause to think of the Past or dream of the Future and our Present is already in the Past, our Future in the Present.—This afternoon we had some general exercises at school. Several visitors were present. Addie [Putnam] spent part of the afternoon with us. The girls read some excellent compositions, and sang beautifully.

Friday, February 2.   Read a lecture of Lowell's on Chaucer. It is very beautiful—so bright and fresh that, like Chaucer's own poetry it seems as if "flowers were springing up in it."

Sunday, February 4.   Read "Spectators among the Stars[,]" a review of two late English works which have for their subject, the stars and the probability or improbability of their being inhabited.—It gives me a dreamy, mysterious feeling to be brought as it were in such close communion with those distant starry worlds which

> . . . "Create
> In us such love and reverence from afar."

After reading of them I only feel that they are more mysterious, more incomprehensible to me than ever.

Tuesday, February 6.   The weather is intensely cold. Jack

Frost has festooned the windows with his most fanciful drapery.—This evening read Macaulay.

Wednesday, February 7. Attended a lecture by Mr. [George W.] Curtis on "Success." He is a very fine orator, his voice rich and musical, and his manner polished and elegant. The aim of the lecture was to show how often more worldly prosperity is confounded with true success and how widely dissimilar they are. He expressed many true and noble sentiments; and in conclusion spoke of America as more *prosperous* than *successful*. Success he declared to be a noble and higher aim than earthly prosperity.

Thursday, February 8. Compelled by a grand snow-storm and a severe cold to spend the day at home. Studied history, sewed, wrote, and read Macaulay.

Sunday, February 11. A great quantity of snow has fallen, and very beautiful it looks in the bright sunlight.—Wrote a composition, and read "Spectators among the Stars."

Wednesday, February 14. This afternoon had a sleigh ride—the first I have had this season. The hills look very beautiful in their snowy mantle. We met the Hutchinsons who seemed heartily glad to see Mr. [Charles Lenox] Remond. They have promised to visit Salem again, and I hope it will be seen. I admire those warm-hearted minstrels of the "Old Granite State."

Thursday, February 15. The day before examination, and a very busy day it is. The old school-room has been undergoing a thorough process of renovation, and looks really very bright and respectable. We had quite a dinner-party at the school-house, with Miss Shepard for the presiding genius, and a merry, delightful party it was.

Friday, February 16. Evening.—The dreaded examination day is over at last, and we feel very much relieved. The school-room was densely crowded. The girls did very well, and our teacher expressed herself much pleased. Everything passed off pleasantly, and everybody seemed very much delighted. I am extremely tired, but our dear teacher must be more so. I can scarcely bear to think how very soon I shall have to leave her. To me no one can ever supply her place.

Saturday, February 17. The excitement of yesterday has left me almost without strength to-day. We took our work to school and had some general exercises. Read Shakespeare's "King John" and Macaulay.

Sunday, February 18. Sat by the window with Wordsworth open before me, but looking oftenest at the beautiful blue sky, itself a glorious poem, and one which we have had the pleasure of reading but rarely of late. Wrote to father and Aunt Margaretta.

Monday, February 19. Amie [*sic*] Ives and Ada [Putnam] spent part of the evening with us. We had some very delightful music.

Tuesday, February 20. This afternoon attended the examination of the Bently School. Lizzie [Church] and I spent the evening with our dear teacher, and commenced reading "The Heir of Redclyffe" which is extremely interesting.

Saturday, February 24. Went with Miss Shepard and the first class to have our daguerreotypes taken, but they were not satisfactory and we were going to have them taken again.

Sunday, February 25. Finished reading Whittier's "Literary Recreations" which I liked very much.

Monday, February 26. Mrs. C. [aroline] Putnam's birthday. Spent the evening with her.

Tuesdsay, February 27. To-day we had our private examination. Writing constantly all day was extremely tiresome. Left the kind care of my beloved teacher. I feel that I owe her very much more than I can ever repay.—Finished reading "North and South" a very beautiful English story which relates particularly to the condition of the working classes.

Wednesday, February 28. This evening attended a very interesting and eloquent lecture on Switzerland, by Rev. Mr. [R. C.] Waterson.

Tuesday, March 6. Our class spent the evening at Miss Shepard's. We took the daguerreotypes which were handsomely finished in separate cases, arranged in one frame,—and a small work-box. Our teacher was much pleased with the presents.—We spent the evening very pleasantly. Lizzie [Church] and I remained long after the others had gone, sitting before the cheerful grate-fire and conversing with our friend, our teacher no longer.

Wednesday, March 7. This evening attended one of [James Russell] Lowell's Lectures on English Poetry. The subject of this was particularly "the imaginative faculty." I thought it very beautiful, and although I had previously read it, enjoyed it greatly. The poet's personal appearance is extremely unpretending. His figure is slight and rather short and his face, were it not for the whiskers and *moustache* which completely covers the lower part, would, I think look almost feminine. His voice is rich and musical, but scarcely loud enough for a lecturer. But the great beauty of his thoughts and language causes the listener to forget any minor deficiency. I have always admired him as one of the great Poets of Humanity.

Friday, March 9. Passed the evening quite pleasantly with most of our former class at Miss Dalton's. The girls were in high spirits, nearly all of them having triumphantly entered the High School. I hope very earnestly that father will consent to my entering the Normal School, or rather to my applying for admission. This week I have finished "Redclyffe" and commenced M'Leod's "Life of Sir Walter Scott."

Sunday, March 11. Read Wordsworth's beautiful poems on Yarrow, and "The White Doe of Rylstone."

Tuesday, March 13. Went through the examination and entered the Normal School. I have not yet heard from father; but as I had to give no pledge to remain a certain length of time, and this is the only opportunity I should have until another term, I thought it best to enter the school. It was with a very delightful sensation of relief that I received the welcome intelligence of my being admitted; for greatly had I feared it might be otherwise.

Wednesday, March 14. Heard Ralph Waldo Emerson lecture on France. The lecture was very interesting and entertaining though not particularly flattering does *his* estimate seem to be of the gay and fickle inhabitants of "la belle France." I had felt quite eager to hear the gifted men, who Wendell Phillips says, is thought in England to stand at the head of American literature. He is a fine lecturer, and a very peculiar-looking man.

Friday, March 16. To my great surprise, received a letter from father summoning me to return home as soon as possible. I feel deeply grieved; it seems harder than ever to leave now that I have just entered upon a course of study which I so earnestly hoped would thoroughly qualify me for the duties of a teacher. The few days I have spent at the Normal School have been very pleasant although I have felt a little strange and lonely. But the teachers are kind, and the teaching so thorough and earnest that it increases the love of knowledge and the desire to acquire it. Mr. [Richard]

Edwards[56] kindly assured me that he very much regretted my being obliged to leave. Although it would give me much pleasure to see my kind friends at home, I cannot but regret that I must go now, feeling as I do that a year longer at school would be of great benefit to me. This evening went to Miss Shepard who earnestly declared that I *must not* go, and who made me a very kind offer, which I do not think *can* be accepted with the little hope I now possess of being able to repay it.

Saturday, March 17. This morning Mr. Edwards came to see me, and told me that he had no doubt of my being able to obtain a situation as teacher here if I went through the Normal School. He wishes me to write to father and assure him of this. Miss Shepard urged me to consent to her writing to him about what she proposes. I do indeed feel obliged to her for her very great kindness to me, whether it be as she wishes it or not. I shall continue at school until I hear from home again, as Mr. Edwards said he would like to have me do so.

Sunday, March 18. Wrote a long letter to father, which I shall send with Miss S.[hepard]'s tomorrow. Spent the evening with Ada [Putnam] and Henry [Cassey], at Ellen Shearman's.

Wednesday, March 21. Have found it almost impossible to concentrate my mind upon my studies which, though difficult would be interesting to me, were it [not] for the anxious troubled thoughts which *will* intrude, and will continue to do so, I suppose, until I receive the decisive reply, which I long for and yet dread. Took tea with Mrs. Ruth Remond,[57] whom I see less frequently than any of the rest of the family, although she is a gentle, agreeable person, and I like her very much.

Saturday, March 24. To-day Mr. [Charles] and Mrs. [Amy Matilda] Remond went to Worcester, and Mrs. R.[emond] deputed me to be housekeeper until her return. Felt rather disappointed in not receiving a letter to-day. Puzzled my head over a syllogism, which I suspect, any one less stupid could understand instantly.

Sunday, March 25. Did a great deal of writing, went to see Ada who is quite sick, read Wordsworth and finished the second volume of Macaulay.

Wednesday, March 28. Received a few lines from father. To my very great joy he consents to my remaining in the Normal School. Aunt Margaretta also writes and asks if I wrote the lines to "W.L.G."[58] in the Liberator. If ever I write doggerel again I shall be careful not to sign my own initials. This evening attended a lecture on Hayti by Mr. Clark of Boston. The lecturer spoke eloquently of the Hay-. tians, from whom he had received much kindness; and paid a well-deserved tribute to the brave and unfortunate Toussaint. I was beginning to think him an earnest friend of freedom, when he proved to be a colonizationist[59] and then a very decided and unpleasant "change came o'er the spirit of my dream."

Friday, March 30. Commenced reading Ferguson's "History of Rome."

Sunday, April 1. A dismal rainy day. Read, and wrote five letters.

Tuesday, April 3. Had a difficult yet interesting lesson in Logic, which I am beginning to like very much. Colburn, the mathematician, visited the school to-day. His only re- markable feature is a very large nose which somebody says is a necessary appendage to all great men.

Wednesday, April 4. Remained a long while after school

to find the derivation of some words. I find far more beauty in the study of words than I had ever imagined it to possess. Stopped a few moments to see my dear friend Miss S. [hepard] who very kindly lent me her "Homes of American Authors."

Thursday, April 5.   Fast Day, and we have no school. Mr. [William C.] Nell spent the afternoon and evening with us. Read very interesting sketches of Bryant, Longfellow, Lowell, and Dana, from "Homes of American Authors." This evening finished M'Leod's "Life of Scott." More than ever do I love and admire Old Scotia's noblehearted and gifted son.

Saturday, April 7.   Spent the evening very delightfully with Miss [Mary] Shepard. We looked over some very beautiful pictures of Irish scenery. I will attempt no description of the grand old ruins of feudal castles, and ancient abbeys, with their Gothic windows and majestic towers so gracefully mantled by the rich, dark ivy, and overlooking some fairy lake, or the deep and dark blue Ocean. Over and around them seem to linger, like the shadows of departed ones, the solemn memories of the Past; and one cannot help feeling that only the richly gifted ones of the Present are privileged to lift the veil, and reveal to others the beauty and the grandeur of these 'mighty ministers of old Time.'

April.   Today Mr. [Richard] Edwards read one of Macaulay's "Lays of Ancient Rome"—one of the most spirited and beautiful poems I have ever heard. Its subject was the brave Horatius who alone sustained the attack of the whole Etruscan army while his friends cut down the bridge across the Tiber which led to Rome.

Tuesday, May 1.   ˙May-day; but tears instead of smiles are ushering in "the delicate-footed May." More and more pleasant becomes my Normal School life. Yet I have made but very few acquaintances, and cannot but feel that among all my school companions there is not a single one who gives me her full and entire sympathy. My studies are my truest friends.

Sunday, May 6. A lovely day. We had some visitors whom I cared not to see, their arrival interrupted a pleasant train of thoughts in which I was engaged; but perhaps it was best, for as usual I was building castles in the air! The gifted ones are privileged to indulge these dreams of future usefulness or glory; but for me on whom Nature has bestowed so little, it were better to try to improve that little; and I know that to do so I must toil unceasingly.

Saturday, May 12. Took a long and very pleasant walk with a number of our scholars and two of the teachers. We saw the process of rolling irons which was extremely interesting, and on our way home stopped at the pottery and saw the whole process of making earthen dishes which was more simple than I had supposed. I think that even the manufacture of things so common-place possesses both beauty and interest, to which Mr. Edwards' explanations added greatly.

Wednesday, May 23. We are reading my favorite "Lady of the Lake" at school. Mr. Edwards reads it so splendidly that it seems more beautiful to me than ever. I never read it without thinking of home and Uncle W. [illiam Forten].

Friday, May 25. This evening poor Mr. Smith died.[60] Although he has been ill many months his death seemed very sudden. He passed away as peacefully as an infant. Poor Sarah [Cassey Smith] is far more to be pitied than he who has gone where suffering is unknown. There is indeed something strange and awful in death. The mystery which envelops it can become known only to those who can never return to tell us. When we only *hear* of death we do not seem fully to realize it; but *when* we *see* it, when we watch the last struggle between the mortal frame and the immortal soul, how strongly are we impressed with its mysterious, all-conquering power!

Saturday, May 26. Stopped to say good-bye to my dear friend Miss S.[hepard] who is going to spend anniversary week with a friend. Poor Sarah suffers deeply. She has had very much trouble for one so young.

Sunday, May 27. A very lovely but sad day. I have seen the remains of poor Mr. Smith consigned to their last resting-place. His bereaved wife suffers deeply. I know of no real consolation that can be offered to hearts so deeply wounded as hers.

Wednesday, May 30. Ellen P.[utnam Gilliard] and I went to Boston. Went in to the anti-slavery convention for a short time; was not able to stay long. Mr. [Wendell] Phillips introduced Anthony Burns in the most beautiful manner. In the afternoon went to see the Panorama, which I liked very much. In the evening went to the meetings again. Mr. [Thomas Wentworth] Higginson gave a very interesting lecture; he is a particular favorite of mine. Mrs. Ernestine Rose spoke well but too long. Then Mr. Phillips spoke beautifully, eulogizing the former speaker—her consistency—her devotion to truth and right everywhere.

Thursday, May 31. Attended the meetings all day. Several very interesting speeches were made, in the afternoon an animated discussion on the Constitution was carried on between Mr. [William Lloyd] Garrison, Mr. [John] Pierpont, Mr. [Charles] Burleigh and others. In the evening Mr. Phillips made one of the most eloquent speeches I have ever heard even from his eloquent lips. Theodore Parker spoke; I was somewhat disappointed in him. The Hall was crowded; and while Wendell Phillips was speaking, I gazed on the hundreds of earnest faces, and thought that those glowing words so full of eloquence and truth could not be lost upon all of those to whom they were addressed.

Friday, June 1. Summer, the wayward loiterer has come at last. The song of the birds, melodious and sweet ushers her in. This morning returned to Salem; grateful indeed is its quietness and coolness after the noise and heat of Boston; the Common is the one bright beautiful spot of that crowded city which to my mind redeems it somewhat. As to its inhabitants, they are redeemed only by the few noble spirits— the best and noblest that the world has ever seen.

Wednesday, July 14. A month has elapsed since last I wrote in thee—my Journal; and conscience has busily whispered "What! has thy *daily* diary become a *monthly?*" Too busily occupied to heed the inward voice, days and hours have flown swiftly by—unheeded; for what scholar can fix his mind on other matters when that terrible event Examination draweth nigh? And so, my Journal thou hast been neglected. All our household save Sarah and myself have gone to the Framingham celebration, and we have locked up the house and are spending the day with our pleasant friends in Carltonville. Here all is cool, quiet and pleasant; and gratefully refreshing is coolness and quiet after the heat and noise of last night. The *patriots*, poor fools, were celebrating the anniversary of their vaunted *independence*. Strange that they cannot feel their own degradation—the weight of the chains which they have imposed upon themselves. We read "Rennoth," an interesting story of Napoleon's Russian campaign.

Monday, July 16, 1855. Examination Day. No further comment is needed.

Tuesday, July 17. I breathe freely—our trial is over; and happy are we to escape from the hot, crowded school-room—

for it has been densely crowded all day. This evening the scholars had a pleasant meeting in the school house and the last farewells were said. Ada [Putnam] and I walked home in the pleasant moonlight, and I spent the night at her house. Her mother [Jane Putnam] and I sat by the window—from which the water was plainly seen, sparkling beautifully in the moonlight, and conversed until after midnight.

Wednesday, July 18. Went to the school house early this morning; only Miss Weston was there; "deserted were our own good halls." I assisted Miss W.[eston] in putting away the books. Afterwards two of the other teachers came and the last "Good Bye" was said.

July. Received a letter from Aunt M.[argaretta] who will come on if possible with E.[liza?]. How glad I shall be to see them, for lonesome enough have I felt since school closed. I had no idea that I should miss the companions of my school hours so much. Had I but their entire sympathy I might truly be happy! but why should I repine; are we not to sacrifice rather than indulge self? Born as we are to the stern *performance* of *duty* rather than the *pursuit* of *happiness*.

Friday, July 27. Aunt M.[argaretta] and E.[liza?] have arrived and been warmly and gladly welcomed. It is indeed delightful to meet dear friends from whom we have long been parted,—to hear from *home voices*, "*news from home*."

Wednesday, August 1. Went with Aunt M.[argaretta] and a party of friends to the celebration at Abington. Our much-loved Garrison was not there, his absence could not fail to be felt. But Mr. Phillips and other able speakers were there and many eloquent speeches were made. We had a pleasant sail on the beautiful pond attached to the Grove; and passed altogether a delightful day.

Sunday, August 12. Had a delightful ride to Reading, to

an anti-slavery meeting. The road is beautiful and our Penn. [sylvania] friends warmly admired scenery which the eastern part of the Keystone State cannot boast of. Mr. Garrison and Mr. Phillips spoke very beautifully. To our great regret we were obliged to leave while Mr. Phillips was speaking. Our ride home was extremely pleasant.

Wednesday, August 15. Our household, the Putnams, and Miss S. [arah] P. [arker] R. [emond] spent part of the day at Marblehead Beach, took dinner on a huge rock; climbed the rocks, sat on one projecting far out into the sea, listening to the wild music of the waves, wandered along the sea-shore, bathed, and had a beautiful ride home in the early morning.

Friday, August 17. My eighteenth birthday. Spent the afternoon and evening very pleasantly at Mrs. Putnam's. Miss Brown[61] was there. I think I shall like her. Her father's fondness for her is rather too demonstrative. I guess she is a sensible girl. I enjoy talking with her about her European life. She is pleasant and communicative, and though coming lastly from England, has, I think, lived in France too much to acquire a great deal of that reserve which characterized the manners of the English.

Sunday, August 19. Aunt M. [argaretta] went to the anti-slavery meeting at Haverhill. To my regret I was not able to go. Read "The Days of Bruce" by Grace Aguilar and Scott's "Tales of a Grandfather," 1st Vol.

Sunday, August 26. Spent the evening at Mrs. Putnam's. Mr. Nell was there. We amused ourselves with making conundrums, reading and reciting poetry.

Thursday, August 30. To-day Aunt M. [argaretta] and E. [liza?] left. How lonesome we shall feel without them!

Saturday, September 1. "Bright summer, fare thee well!" Ada [Putnam] left early this morning for N. [ew] York, without my seeing her. I am very sorry, particularly as I wished to give her something. I shall be glad when school commences.

Saturday, September 8. Rec'd a long letter from Aunt M.[argaretta] who had a pleasant journey and arrived safely at home. Father intends removing to Canada.[62] I am glad, particularly on the children's account. Ada does not go on to Bath but will probably return home in a few weeks.

Sunday, September 9. Have been writing all day. This evening took a pleasant walk with Mrs. [Helen] Gilliard and Henry [Cassey]. Afterwards the moonlight was so beautiful I thought I would walk to Miss [Sarah Parker] R.[emond]'s. H.[enry] went with me. We staid a short time. I have been wondering what it is that attracts me in Miss R.[emond]. Sometimes she talks to me earnestly and as if she thought I understood what she was saying; but this is not often. Generally, it seems to me as if she treats me as if I were a silly child, with careless indifference. She is much older, far more experienced and intelligent than I and I know that I am not worthy of her companionship and can scarcely prevent myself from wishing that I did not love her as I do, as I love but very few in the world. How often do I wish that I had a sister my superior, yet who, despite her superiority and my unworthiness, would truly and fondly love me.

Wednesday, September 12. To-day school commenced. Most happy am I to return to the companionship of my studies, ever my most valued friends. It is pleasant to meet the scholars again; most of them greeted me cordially, and were it not for the thought that *will* intrude, of the want or *entire sympathy* even of those I know and like best, I should greatly enjoy their society. There is one young girl and only one—Miss Sarah Brown, who I believe thoroughly and heartily appreciates anti-slavery, *radical* anti-slavery and has no prejudice against color. I wonder that every colored person is not a misanthrope. Surely we have everything to make us hate mankind. I have met girls in the schoolroom—they have been thoroughly kind and cordial to me—perhaps the next day met them in the street—they feared to recognize me; these I can but regard now with scorn and contempt, once I liked them, believing them incapable of such measures. Others give the most distant recognition possible. I, of course, acknowledge no such recognition, and they soon cease entirely. These are but trifles, certainly to the great, public wrongs which we as a people are obliged to endure. But to those who experience them, these apparent trifles are most wearing and discouraging; even to the child's mind they reveal volumes of deceit and heartlessness, and early teach a lesson of suspicion and distrust. Oh! it is hard to go through life meeting contempt with contempt, hatred with hatred, fearing, with too good reason to love and trust hardly any one whose skin is white, however lovable, attractive and congenial in seeming. In the bitter, passionate feeling of my soul again and again there rises the question "When, oh! when shall this cease?" "Is there no help?" "How long oh! how long must we continue to suffer—to endure?" Conscience answers it is wrong, it is ignoble to despair; let us labor earnestly and faithfully to acquire knowledge, to break down the barriers of prejudice and oppression. Let us take courage, never ceasing to work,—hoping and believing that if not for us, for another generation there is a better, brighter day in store, when slavery and prejudice shall vanish before the glorious light of Liberty and Truth; when the rights of every colored man shall everywhere be acknowledged and respected, and he shall be treated as a *man* and a *brother*.

September. This evening Miss S. [arah] B. [rown] and I joined the Female Anti-Slavery Society.[63] I am glad to have persuaded her to do so. She seems an earnest hearted girl, in whom I cannot help having some confidence. I can only hope and pray that she will be true, and courageous enough to meet the opposition which every friend of freedom must encounter.

Wednesday, September. This afternoon Lizzie Dike, Lizzie Church and I commenced reading with Miss S. [hepard] Reed's "Lecture on English Literature," in connection with "Chamber's Encyclopedia." We shall read every Wednesday afternoon, and I cannot but hope and believe that they will be profitable as well as pleasant to us. It is exceedingly kind in Miss Shepard whose time is much occupied.

Friday, October 19. Walked to Marblehead with some of the girls to attend the teachers' meeting. Listened to one speech which I liked very much; and afterwards went with a pleasant party to Gun Rock; we returned in the evening to Marblehead and listened to a very beautiful lecture from Rev. Mr. Huntingdon, his subject was "Unconscious Tuition." But I felt a want, for among the many true and beautiful sentiments which he uttered not the faintest indication that he was even aware of the existence of that cruel and disgraceful system which refuses all teachings—all that can elevate and improve to millions of the inhabitants of this glorious republic. Had a pleasant walk to Salem in the moonlight with Miss Toft, Mr. Russell, and his niece, Miss B.

Sunday, October 21. The twentieth anniversary of the day on which beloved Garrison was mobbed and insulted in the streets of Boston.[64] To-day on the very spot where that little band of noble-hearted women so heroically maintained the right, the dauntless Pioneer of our glorious cause stands with many true-hearted co-workers, surrounded by hundreds of eager, sympathizing listeners. The men who dragged him with a rope around his neck through the streets of Boston, to their own shame, not his, would blush to confess it to-day. And even his bitter enemies are forced, despite themselves, to respect his self-sacrificing unfaltering devotion to Liberty and Truth. Dear, honored friends, I cannot be with you in your gathering to-day, but the light of your loved countenances,—the tones of your eloquent voices fall upon my grateful heart. This evening my necessary absence from the meeting in Boston, upon which my thoughts have dwelt all day, was somewhat compensated for by listening to an excellent and very interesting lecture from Rev. S. Johnson of Lynn. *The first of our course.*

Sunday, October 28. This has indeed been one of the happiest days of my life. Wendell Phillips, Mr. [Charles] Hovey, and Miss [Sallie] Holley and Miss Phillips have spent it with us, could it fail to be a happy one? Mr. Phillips is the most fascinating person I ever saw. That graceful affability which characterizes the truly great, he embodies, with all that is truly good and noble. Mr. Hovey is exceedingly entertaining. He has travelled much; and presented Mrs. [Amy Matilda] R.[emond] with a precious relic—a piece of mosaic pavement from the Baths of Caracalla, Rome, built sixteen hundred years ago. How strange it seems that sixteen centuries ago this stone was laid—almost incredible! While gazing on such relics a strange influence from the mighty mysterious Past comes over us conjuring up visions of that olden time, long past, but never to be forgotten; for the soul of man rests not in the Present nor soars in the great *Future*, which imagination paints for it, but also does it love to dwell in the deep, soul-stirring memories of the Past. Mr. Phillips' lecture was worthy of himself. I can bestow no higher praises upon it. Oh! it is a source of some consolation to feel—to know that some of the noblest minds—the greatest intellects of the age are enlisted in our behalf.

Friday, November 1. This evening heard Charles Sumner for the first time. He said many excellent things, but I cannot agree with very many of his views—particularly with his reverence for the Constitution and the Union. I believe, though greatly mistaken he yet has a warm, true heart, and certainly he is an elegant and eloquent orator. Though very different from, and inferior to Mr. Phillips, in my opinion.

Sunday, November 4. Mr. [J. B.] Swasey of Newburyport lectured. He is a new convert and a very zealous one. His lecture though rather long was on the whole a very good one.

Wednesday, November 7. This evening Lizzie D. [ike] and I read Reed's lectures with Miss Shepard. Our subject to-day was Chaucer whose beauty of character and rare genius must ever cause him to be an object of our warmest admiration and interest.

Sunday, November 11. Commenced "Plutarch's Lives." Rich in interest and information they are indeed worthy an attentive perusal. I long to know more of Grecian and Roman History, and doubtless much knowledge can be acquired by reading these lives of the most distinguished warriors, statesmen, and philosophers of both nations. Mr. [Charles Lenox] Remond's lecture this evening was excellent, though not quite so fiery as his speeches usually are. Took a delightful walk with Miss [Sarah Parker] R. [emond] and Sarah Kernewood to a beautiful place in the English style.

Monday, November 19. Prof. [Arnold] Guiot commenced his lectures on Physical Geography before our school to-day. They promise to be extremely interesting. This evening attended Mrs. [Mary] Webb's[65] readings; they were principally from Shakespeare. I was not very much pleased. I wish colored persons would not attempt to do anything of the kind unless they can compare favorably with others. But I know that I should not presume to criticize; and most sincerely hope if she has talent, it may be cultivated, and that she may succeed in her vocation, reflecting credit upon herself and her race.

Wednesday, November 21. To-day Prof. Guiot finished his lectures. Those of to-day were on the Creation. His theory is the geological one. Many parts of the lectures were too abstract and profound to be easily understood. But the grandeur of the subject, and the earnest eloquence of the orator failed not to make them deeply interesting.

Friday, November 23. We are to have vacation next week—Thanksgiving week. The happy voices of the girls as they spoke of "going home" made me feel rather home-sick. But as I cannot go to either of my homes—to Canada (where father has recently moved) or to Phila. [delphia], I must try not to think of them. This evening took a pleasant walk with Maria B. [arnes?] the most intimate of my school companions. She is an agreeable, intelligent girl, whom I wish very earnestly to interest in Anti-Slavery.

Sunday, November 25. Commenced "Paradise Lost." Feel quite ashamed of not having read it before. It is truly *beautiful* nay, more, *sublime*. And the circumstances under which it was written by a "poet, old and blind" adds greatly to the interest which the grandeur of the subject alone would excite. This evening Rev. J. [ames] F. [reeman] Clarke gave us an excellent lecture—one of the best we have had. His subject was the "Demoralization of the North by Slavery." Wrote long letters to father and Aunt M.[argaretta].

Monday, November 26.   This morning Sarah [Cassey Smith] and I took a long walk. The weather was delightful—as mild and pleasant as in May. It seemed strange when we looked at the naked branches so delicately traced on the deep blue sky.—Saw for the first time the Custom House of which I read Hawthorne's descriptions in the introduction to that thrilling story—the "Scarlet Letter." I should have known it at once by the description. I wonder that I have not visited it before.

Tuesday, November 27.   Quite tired of working. This afternoon stopped a while and paid a visit to Mrs. [Jane] P.[utnam] Sr. Afterwards went to Harmony Grove and saw Mr. Smith's tombstone. Hard it is to realize that beneath lie the remains of one who was with us a few short months ago! The belief of the Spiritualists is a beautiful, and must be a happy one. It is that the future world is on the same plan as this, but far more beautiful and without sin. Who could wish a more delightful home than this world—without sin or suffering of any kind?

Thursday, November 29.   Thanksgiving Day.—I fear I do not feel in a very thankful mood. Read "Wuthering Heights" a strange story of passion and sorrow, by the author [*sic*] of "Jane Eyre." Miss [Sarah Parker] R.[emond] spent the evening with us.

Saturday, December 1.   The first day of winter, a bright and beautiful day.

Sunday, December 2.   Wrote, studied and read "Paradise Lost" and a very interesting life of the renowned and good Plutarch.

Sunday, December 16.   Feel not a little self reproach for not paying more attention to thee, my Journal. But engaged in a constant, unwavering round of school duties, I have but very little worth committing to thy pages. This evening listened to a tolerably good lecture on slavery by Rev. Antoinette Brown. Her manner is too passive, and although she said some excellent things it was plain to be seen that she did not know as much on this subject as on that of Woman's Rights.

Tuesday, December 18. A dear, good man has spent the day at our school—Mr. [Samuel] May of Syracuse—one of the most delightful persons I have ever met. Mr. Russell introduced me to him, and he inquired with the greatest kindness after our family.

Wednesday, December 19. This afternoon Mr. May gave us an interesting lecture on the Idiot Schools. He eloquently portrayed the good and noble qualities necessary for the faithful teacher of an idiot school,—the untiring devotion, the self-sacrificing spirit, possessed in an eminent degree by every truly successful teacher in these schools especially. Other teachers have only to train the minds of their pupils;—the teacher of an idiot may be said to *make* the mind before training it—he may almost be said to *create* the materials which he is to work upon. He has trials to encounter far beyond what the most severely tried of other teachers has to endure, and far greater, if he is successful, should be the credit awarded to him. Mr. May also delivered before the Lyceum a lecture—extremely interesting and useful, on Magna Charta and the New Constitution of New York.

Sunday, December 23. This evening had the very great pleasure of hearing dear Mr. May speak on anti-slavery. It was one of the best lectures I have ever heard. And I thanked him with my whole heart for the beautiful and well deserved tribute which he paid Mr. Garrison, who is so very greatly unappreciated and misrepresented. He compared him to the fountain of the Black Forest of Germany where the mighty Danube—the great "anti-slavery stream" has its source; and failed not to mention the numerous valuable tributaries who have contributed to its mass of waters—ever receiving a new impulse from the great Fountain Head. He had a large, and extremely attentive audience.

Christmas Day, 1855. Alone; I do not know when I have been alone before on Christmas—never, I think.—Wrote a long letter to Aunt M. [argaretta]. While I was writing Mrs. [Helen] Gilliard came in and insisted on my accompanying her home. I spent part of the day and took dinner there. Came home in the afternoon and found Maria B. [arnes?]. She and Miss Putnam, who also came in, took tea with me, and in the evening M. [aria] and I went to hear Ralph Waldo Emerson, who lectured on Beauty. I liked his originality, though his manner is not particularly interesting. Altogether we were much pleased with the lecture.

Sunday, December 30. Yesterday, Mrs. [Amy Matilda] Remond, who has been attending the Boston Bazaar, came home, and brought with her Miss [Lucretia] Mott of Albany, who is a very agreeable person. Heard read, and read partly myself—"Caste" which is an interesting anti-slavery story.

This evening listened to an excellent lecture before our society, from Mr. Frothingham.

Tuesday, January 1, 1856. The first day of the New Year, and Nature wears a robe of spotless white in honor of his birth. Those nations whose *mourning* robes are white would say that she laments the death of the *Old,*—instead of rejoicing at the birth of the *New*. Doubtless there is good cause for both.—Read "Plutarch's Lives" which I think exceedingly instructive and interesting.—Went to school as usual.

Wednesday, January 2. Heard a lecture on Carlo Borromeo[,] the saintly Italian cardinal[,] by Mr. [Octavius B.] Frothingham. One cannot help admiring, though sincerely pitying the untiring self-sacrificing, but too often sadly mistaken devotion of his life.

Sunday, January 27. (Wrote a hymn for examination).[66] The last few weeks have been but successions of constant study, with but little variation. I have heard but one lecture—that of Mr. [Theodore] Parker, which was, of course, excellent. His subject was the "Productive Industry of the Age" and he contrasted it with the military achievements of the "olden time"; and strikingly showed the beneficial effects of the industry of our age. Every time I listen to this wonderful man, I become more deeply impressed with the magnificence of his intellect and the sincere goodness and nobleness of his heart. This evening Mr. [Charles] Hodges gave us a very good anti-slavery lecture. For the first time Mrs. Remond was obliged to introduce the lecturer; it was a great trial to her, but she did it well ne'ertheless. During this time remember Prof. Gajani on Pius 9th.

Saturday, February 2. This evening our beloved Mr. [William Lloyd] Garrison and his wife arrived.—Most gladly did we welcome them. The Remonds and Putnams spent the evening with us, and we had a delightful time. Mr. Garrison was very genial as he always is, and sang delightfully.

Sunday, February 3. This has been one of the happiest days of my life. More and more do I love and admire that great and good man. His wife is a lovely woman; it is indeed delightful to see so happy and noble a couple. This evening Mr. Garrison gave us one of the best lectures I ever heard him deliver. Always interesting to me, to-night he was unusually entertaining. Just before the lecture Mr. Innis announced the fact of Mr. [Nathaniel] Banks' election,[67] which was received with tumultous [*sic*] applause. Mr. G. [arrison] spoke beautifully of the *"Banks"* of Massachusetts impeding the onward progress of the waves of the southern despotism."

Monday, February 4. This morning Mr. and Mrs. G. [arrison] left. This was the first time they have staid with us since I have been here. And the pleasure, the great pleasure which I experienced from this visit, will prevent me from soon forgetting it.

Friday, February 8. Next week we shall have our examination. I dread it, and do most heartily wish it was over!

Tuesday, Friday 12. The last day of our examination. Thank Heaven it is over at last! I am completely tired out, and need rest, both in body and mind. We have got along very well. I could say pleasantly on the last afternoon, were it not for a new unpleasant remarks of Mr. Russell. The best way is to forget them as soon as possible. The exercises of the graduating class, on this afternoon were very interesting.

Wednesday, February 13. I should be sorry that we have vacation were it not that I need rest. This morning Mr. R[emond] left for Philadelphia. I felt very anxious to go, but it was impossible. We met at the school house, and formed a Normal Association. S. [allie] P. Chamberlain, Secretary, Mr. [Richard] Edwards, President, and Carrie Hawkins, Vice President.—My dear friend Miss [Mary]

Shepard is still seriously ill, though better than she has been; I saw her this evening. Mrs. Munger has left us forever. I like her, and shall always remember her kindly.

Thursday, February 14. This morning went to the school house and helped the teachers label the books, we labelled more than 700.—Valentine's Day; but no one has remembered me.—

Saturday, February 16. Went to Miss Shepard and read to her. She is better to-day.—

Sunday, February 17. Spent the day at home. This evening Mrs. [Amy Matilda] R.[emond], H.[elen Gilliard], S.[arah Cassey Smith] and I had quite a fiery mock debate on slavery, by way of practising. Read "Paradise Lost," and French "On the Study of Words," which is a charming as well as instructive little book.

Monday, February 18. This evening heard Dr. [William] Elder of Philadelphia lecture on Mental Science. It was somewhat strange and rambling but thoroughly original and entertaining.

Wednesday, February 20. This evening we were *surprised* by a Surprise Party—the Remonds and Mr. and Mrs. Gilliard. We passed the evening very pleasantly with music, dancing and conversation. I am exceedingly tired, and long for summer, hoping that with it will come to me the priceless blessing of health. Miss Upton has kindly promised me the remaining volumes of the "Queens of England," which I shall read as soon as I finish French.

Thursday, February 21. Still no news from Canada. I have heard from father but once since he removed thither. Only one letter during this long winter! It worries and grieves me. And not this alone, but my indebtedness to Mrs. [Amy Matilda] Remond, and many other things. All my day dreams of independence and usefulness, seems to have been dissipated one by one. And harder and sterner become the realities of life.

Saturday, March 1.   The first day of spring, and a lovely day it is. I would gladly go out and enjoy to the full the clear bracing air and the bright sunlight; but I was *wise* enough to take a severe cold and must pay the penalty by keeping a close prisoner on this delightful day. I have just heard that my beloved friend Miss Shepard is much better, and I feel better and happier for knowing it. A few evenings since attended a pleasant surprise party at Mr. P. [utnam]'s. Several of the company were dressed as ladies of the olden time, and very comical they looked in short skirts, high-heeled shoes, huge collars, and combs which are miniature steeples. I was persuaded to dress in full Bloomer costume, which I have since had good cause to regret, however.

Wednesday, March 5.   Quite tired of staying within doors, and playing the invalid. This evening we are to have a little play—"The Honeymoon," at Mrs. [Jane] P. [utnam]'s and as I am to take a part, I shall have wished for the pleasure of going out again.

Evening—The play passed off very pleasantly. Our *very* small audience deigned to speak most graciously of our respective performances. The hero and heroine of the play were a duke and duchess. I had the honor of being a sister of the latter. Of course I did not fail to appreciate my newly-acquired dignity.

Mr. [Jacob] Gilliard leaves for California to-morrow. He is an intelligent, agreeable person whom we shall greatly miss from our small circle. Finished French, and commenced the third volume of Macaulay.

Thursday, March 6.   Received a long and pleasant letter

from Sarah Brown. I was very glad to hear from her, and shall send her some anti-slavery tracts when I write. She is a most agreeable and good-hearted girl, interested in anti-slavery; but I do most earnestly hope to see her more so.—

Monday, March 10. This evening went to see "Hamlet." It is the first play of Shakespeare that I have seen and I enjoyed it very much. I suppose if I had ever seen any better acting than Mr. Marshall's I should not have been so pleased. The tragedy I have always liked very much; and many parts of it are as familiar as household words.

Tuesday, March 11. Went to hear the Misses Hall—the 'Singing Sisters!' They sang very sweetly. One of them has a particularly fine voice.—On returning home found a very old friend of our family—Mr. Coffin,—the former teacher of my father and uncles. I have seldom met any one who possessed such extensive and varied knowledge, and yet from his perfectly unassuming, and perhaps unrefined manner, a stranger would never suspect it. He is exceedingly entertaining, and as I know him to be a radical abolitionist I like him very much. His daughter has just entered our Normal School.

Wednesday, March 12. School commenced to-day. It is very pleasant to see the teachers and scholars again; one or two of them particularly. Miss Coffin seems good-natured but not particularly cordial. I'm afraid I shall not like her very much.—Our hard work, of course has not quite commenced so that I had time to spend the evening at Mrs. [Ellen] Shearman's and play whist, which I have just learned.

Thursday, March 13. We have commenced astronomy, which I know I shall like very much. Mrs. [Helen] Gilliard spent the evening with us, and after I had studied my lessons, we played several games of whist, as Mrs. Remond who has the greatest aversion to cards—finally gave her consent.

Friday, March 14. Had a very interesting lesson in the "School and Schoolmaster." I should be glad that we have it were it not for my dread of the essays which we shall be obliged to write. If I could only write on different subjects it would be pleasant; but to write them all on school teaching, will, I fear be very tedious, despite my real interest in that subject. But I will try to do the best I can. Lizzie D.[ike] tells me that our dear Miss Shepard is feeling almost well. I must see her to-morrow.

Saturday, March 15. After sewing very busily nearly all day, felt rather tired and unwell, and so, instead of going out, read Plutarch's "Life of Alexander." It is, as all his writings are, deeply interesting.

Sunday, March 16. Read and wrote, and studied astronomy. Miss S.[arah] Remond spent the evening with us.

March. To-day we had our election for those who are to write our poem, valedictory, and dissertation. Miss [Sarah C.] Pitman was chosen to write the dissertation; Lizzie Church the valedictory and my unworthy self to write the poem;[68] I most respectfully declined, but every one insists upon my doing it; so I suppose I must make the attempt. But it is a most formidable undertaking for me, and one which, I greatly fear, is quite beyond my powers.

Tuesday, April 1. My conscience reproaches me for neglecting thee so long, my Journal! but indeed I have had but little worth committing to thy pages.—This morning I heard the first robin. Most welcome are the cheering notes of the dear little "harbinger of spring." I have but little time for anything but study; my only amusements are an occasional game of whist on Friday or Saturday evening; and the reading for which I have time only on Sundays.

Wednesday, April 2. This afternoon I had a long conversation with Mr. [Richard] Edwards. He spoke very kindly to me, far more so than I deserve, and urged me to come back next term. When I very earnestly assured him that it was quite impossible, he asked me why in such a manner that I could not avoid telling him frankly. He said he would see if something could not be done. I said nothing, but I know too well that nothing *can* be done. Indeed though I very much wish to spend another term here, I desire nothing so much as some employment which shall enable me to pay my debts.—I hope I shall be fortunate enough to obtain some situation as a teacher.

Sunday, April 6. I have been reading Margaret Fuller's "Woman in the 19th Century," and liked it much. I am a warm admirer of the noble-hearted writer. She says so much about Goethe's writings that I felt more than ever anxious to read them, and have must [*sic*] commenced his "Wilhelm Meister," translated by Carlyle; but I am rather disappointed in it. Wilhelm seems to me to be so deficient in strength of character. The little Mignon I think is a beautiful though very singular character. I have a presentiment that I shall like the second volume better. I know, however, that these works lose very much of their beauty by translation. Oh, when shall I be able to read them in the original. I do most earnestly desire to; and I *will* if I live a few years longer. I am determined!

Thursday, April 10. Went to the depot this morning to bid Maria [Barnes] goodbye. Her health is so poor that she has been obliged to leave school. I am very sorry, for she has long sat with me, and I like her better than any one in our class. Last night she, Lucy Kingman, *Brownie* and I had a delightful walk.—I think I shall like Lucy K.[ingman].

She seems to be a girl of very sweet disposition, and excellent information.

Sunday, April 14. Went to Mrs. Putnam's yesterday afternoon, spent the evening in playing whist; and, as it rained very hard, stayed all night. How delightful it is this morning! The sky is cloudless, and the air delightful after last night's shower. From Mrs. P.[utnam]'s window I can see the river winding along, and hear it murmuring in sweet low tones. How kind it is to give me the benefit of its soliloquy; and I will not betray thy confidence, pleasant stream, not even to my Journal.

Afternoon. Home again. I have just finished an essay of eleven pages, on the "Organization of a School" which has employed me for some time. I hope Mr. Edwards will be indulgent enough to listen to its request.

> "*Don't* view me with a critic's eye.
> But pass my imperfections by.—"

Now to my Latin which I like better than anything else; and which will, I know be still more *interesting* to me when I commence to translate. I long to master "Virgil's lay" and Livy's "pictured page."

Wednesday, May 1. What a beautiful May day! Earth, air and sky unite in making it the loveliest of the year. My Journal! my Journal! From a daily thou hast well-nigh become a monthly. But my time is spent in hard study, and little is left for thoughts worth committing to thy pages. Sarah and Mr. R[emond] have gone to ride on horseback this lovely morning. How much I envy them! School and studies to-day as usual for me. It is hard to study when the air is so pure and refreshing, and the clouds so gloriously beautiful. I almost long to be the little bird I am watching cleaving the air with its light wing, and soaring far, far up into the deep blue of the sky.

Saturday, May 11. All day I have been worrying about that poem. That troublesome poem which has yet to be commenced. Oh! that I could become suddenly inspired and write as only great poets can write. or that I might write a beautiful poem of two hundred lines in my sleep as Coleridge did. Alas! in vain are all such longings. I must depend upon *myself* alone. And what can that self produce? Nothing, nothing but *doggerel!* This evening read Plutarch's "Lycurcus."

Friday, May 24. To-day Mr. [Robert] Purvis [69] arrived. I think he looks poorly. Felt glad to see him. We have vacation this week instead of next, for which I am sorry, because next week the Boston meetings take place.

Wednesday, May 29. Went up to Boston this afternoon with Mr. Purvis, Mrs. P. [utnam] and Miss L. R. We went to the Pillsbury Festival, which was a very brilliant and successful one. S. [arah Cassey] S. [mith] and her mother have been up since Monday;—Excellent speeches were made by our best speakers. Mr. [Wendell] P. [hillips] was as usual eloquent and fascinating. Mr. [Parker] Pillsbury spoke for a little while with deep feeling; his health is not entirely restored. I like him much. Had the happiness of seeing Mrs. [Maria W.] Chapman [70] for the first time. I think her the most beautiful woman I ever saw. Also the very great pleasure of seeing Mrs. Chase of R. [hode] I. [sland] to whom I wrote applying for the situation of governess. Her reply was a very kind letter. I love her for it. She is a lovely looking woman; I shall be glad to have such a friend. Went over to Chelsea and spent the night with Mrs. Morris. Met there a Miss

Frothingham, a cousin of [John Greenleaf] Whittier. Notwithstanding her relationship to my beloved poet, I cannot help thinking her a very uninteresting person. Had quite a discussion with her on Anti-Slavery. She is not radical. Mrs. Morris has an exquisite painting of the "Prisoner of Chillon" in his gloomy cell; at the moment when a ray of light streams through his casement, and there falls on his delighted ear the music of a bird.

"The sweetest song ear ever heard."

Sunday, June 1. The first day of summer—bright beautiful, but, in our N.[ew] E.[ngland] clime, fleeting summer. Oh how rapidly the weeks and months glide away! How necessary then that we work constantly unceasingly, if we would accomplish anything in the short space of time which is allotted us on earth. *Diem perdidi!* How much meaning in those two little words. May I never be obliged to say them of myself.

Wednesday, June 18. Amazing, wonderful news I have heard to-day! It has completely astounded me. I cannot realize it.—Mr. [Richard] Edwards called me into his room with a face full of such grave mystery, that I at once commenced reviewing my past conduct and wondering what terrible misdeed I, a very "model of deportment" had committed within the precincts of our Normal world. The mystery was most pleasantly solved. I have received the offer of a situation as teacher in one of the public schools [Epes Grammar School] of this city,—of this conservative, aristocratic old city of Salem!!! Wonderful indeed it is! I know that it is principally through the exertions of my kind teacher, although he will not acknowledge it.—I thank him with all my heart. I had a long talk with the Principal of the school [L. F.

Warren], whom I like very much. Again and again I ask myself—'Can it be true?' It seems impossible. I shall commence to-morrow.

Thursday, June 19. To-day a rainy and gloomy one, I have devoted to my new duties. Of course I cannot decide how I like them yet.—I thought it best to commence immediately, although the term has not quite closed. I could not write about it yesterday, the last day of my school life. Yet I cannot think it quite over until after the examination, in which Mr. Edwards has kindly arranged that I shall take part.

Saturday, June 21. I find the children rather boisterous and unmanageable, but Mr. Warren thinks there is a slight improvement in them. That is some comfort.

Monday, June 23. Went to my dear old school house to recite Latin. It was very pleasant to have them all greet me so gladly and kindly; but it made it seem harder than ever to leave.

Saturday, June 28. The weather is hot; the children restless, and I find a teacher's life not nearly as pleasant as a scholar's. But I do not despair. Oh! no! I have faith. Ever shall my motto be, "Labor omnia vincit." I found my scholars very pleasant and obliging. They bring me beautiful flowers every day. Many of them are interesting children. Other very far from being so.—May I be granted strength to do my duty in the great field of labor upon which I have entered.

Thursday, July 3. My dear friend Mrs. [Amy Matilda] Remond has been slightly unwell for some time. I am truly sorry that she will not be well enough to attend the celebration to-morrow. To-day there have been two arrivals. Mr. [Joseph] Putnam and my cousin Robert [Purvis, Jr.].[71] The latter a very unexpected one indeed. He looks much the same as usual. Only a very little older and more manly—that is all. Mr. Putnam, I have no doubt I shall like very much.

Friday, July 4.   To-day a large party of us, among whom were Miss Sarah P. Remond, Mr. [Joseph] and Mrs. [Caroline] P. [utnam], Mrs. [Jane] P. [utnam] Sr., and Mrs. G. [illiard] also cousin R. [obert] went to the Anti-Slavery celebration at Framingham. It was clear when we started, but before we reached Boston, the rain poured in torrents. However we went on to F. [ramingham], the meeting was held in the Hall in the morning, and was very interesting. In the afternoon adjourned to the grove, but it was too rainy to remain there long. When it was nearly time for us to return home the clouds cleared away and S. [arah], R. [obert] and I had a delightful walk through the grove. Some of the party regretted coming but we three did not, and agreed that we had a pleasant time despite the storm.

Wednesday, July 9.   This afternoon Robert, Sarah and I walked over to Lee's Garden in North Salem. Cousin R. [obert] has changed but little; is still a mischievous boy. Though he is very indifferent to me; though our natures are entirely dissimilar, yet I have ever loved and shall love him as a brother. Spent the evening at Miss Remond's and played whist. I like Mr. [Joseph] Putnam very much. He is very gentlemanly and intelligent.

Friday, July 18.   R. [obert] has gone and we miss his careless gayety much. This evening was spent at Mr. [Richard] Edwards' with our class. We had a very pleasant evening. Talked anti-slavery most of the time. Had a long talk with Mr. Clark who accompanied me home. He is a 'Liberty Party' man, and I vainly tried to persuade him that all political action was wrong. I like to hear him talk. He is so earnest and such a close reasoner.—Stood talking outside the gate until after eleven. My dear Mrs. [Amy Matilda] R.[emond] does not seem to improve. I fear she gets worse. This terribly oppressive heat is very unfavorable to her.

Saturday, July 19. This evening Mrs. [Peter] Williams[72] came. I am so glad to have her here. How patient our dear invalid is! Oh I would gladly suffer pain myself to relieve one so beloved, from suffering. I do wish I was able to do more for her.

Sunday, July 20. This evening Lucy R.—whom I love *very* much, for her own sake and her sister's—walked out Lafayette Street with me. We met Mr. Edwards who took me to his house, and there my poor poem was reviewed, for the last time. Mr. C.[lark] walked home with me, and we entered into a slight discussion, but not so lasting as our former one.

Monday, July 21. Attended the Examination this afternoon; we were examined in 'English Literature'; but the class did not distinguish itself, I grieve to say.

Tuesday, July 22. This afternoon we were examined in 'School and Schoolmaster.' Essays were read. Miss [Sarah C.] Pitman's D.[issertation], my poor poem, and Lizzie's V.[aledictory] which is a beautiful production; charming as dear Lizzie's self. Crowds of people were there. Our diplomas were awarded. I was lucky enough to get one. This evening we had a delightful meeting at the school house, our last. It was one of the pleasantest meetings we have had. And now I realize that my school days are indeed over. And many sad regrets I feel that it is indeed so. The days of my N.[ew] England school life, though spent far from home and early friends, have still been among the happiest of my life. I have been fortunate enough to receive the instruction of the best and kindest teachers; and the few friends I have made are warm and true.—New England! I love to tread thy soil,—tred by the few noble spirits,—Garrison, Phillips and others,—the truest and noblest in the land; to breathe the pure air of thy hills, which is breathed by them; to gaze upon the grand old rocks, "lashed by the fury of the ocean wave," upon thy granite hills, thy noble trees, and winding, sparkling streams to all of which a greater charm is added by the thought that *they* the good and gifted ones, have gazed upon them also.

Friday, July 25.   At Dr. [Henry] Wheatland's request took him that poor, miserable poem. I wish he would not have it published. It is *not worth* it. I think this will be the last of my attempts at poetizing. I am heartily ashamed of it.

Sunday, July 27.   Our beloved patient grows worse. She cannot endure this terrible oppressive heat. Oh! how much these weeks of illness have changed her. As I gaze upon her, lying on her bed of suffering, I can scarcely realize that it is indeed she, who a few, short months ago, seemed in such perfect health and spirits. Dear, dear friend, I earnestly, fondly hope that she will recover.

Friday, August 1.   Intended to go to the Celebration, and from thence to Bridgewater with Miss [Lucy] Kingman, but our dear Mrs R.[emond] is so much worse that none of us can leave. I very much fear that she will not be spared to us. But I cannot bear to think of it. God grant that it may not be so!

Wednesday, August 6.   Our dear invalid does not get better. Oh! this is a sad vacation to me. Every moment that I can spare I devote to her. All that love and care can do is done for her. I fear in vain. Still there is *some* hope; as the physician says she is not really worse to-day. At one time he gave her up entirely. I do not think he does now.

Friday, August 8. Mrs. R.[emond] does seem a little better to-day; and, feeling weary and worn, I consented to go with Miss Shepard and a few friends to Marblehead Beach.— The sun shone brightly when we started; and there was nothing ominous in the beautiful, fleecy, floating clouds, "islands of pearl on a sea of blue," above us. But ere we reached our place of destination the weather changed; dark clouds gathered, and the rain poured in torrents. We drove up to a pleasant old farm house; where Hugh Peters, one of the earliest and most eloquent ministers of Salem lived, in 1635 or 36. The people of the house were very kind, and showed us into a beautiful parlor, where we found some excellent books. We took our dinner in a delightful old barn; and passed a pleasant afternoon, lying on the straw, and listening to the music of "the swallows song in the eaves"; or to the deeper, wilder music of the waves, which we could see dashing furiously against the rocks. Lizzie C.[hurch] and Miss Hawthorne were with us.

Sunday, August 10. Our beloved friend is again very much worse. Oh! this suspense is dreadful! But I fear it will soon be over. Dr. G. now gives us no encouragement.

Friday, August 15. All is over! this morning between four and five, the dearly loved one passed away from us, to join the dwellers in the "Silent Land." The nurse and I sat up with her during the night,—

> "We watched her breathing through the night,
> Her breathing soft and low
> As in the breast the wave of life
> Kept heaving to and fro."

She is gone! Peacefully, without a murmur she passed away. The loveliest of women, the best and kindest of friends to me,—*her* place can never, never be filled.

Saturday, August 16.   The funeral takes place to-day.

Sunday, August 17.   My nineteenth birthday—the saddest I have ever known. Yesterday the remains of our dear friend were laid in the grave. Mr. and Mrs. Garrison, Mr. Phillips and many other friends who knew and loved her well were present. Truly might it be said of her,

> "None knew her but to love her,
> None named her but to praise."

I do not think there is in the world a more amiable or lovable person.—Poor dear Sarah, I pity her; she has had many trials for one so young.

Monday, August 18.   Our house is *very* lonely now, without the dearly loved mother and friend. *She* is indeed happy. We grieve for *ourselves* alone.—No one can ever supply her place to us,—Never!

Wednesday, August 20.   At the earnest solicitations of my good friend Helen G. [illiard] I went with the Putnams and Charles Lenox[73] to Lowell Island. It was a beautiful day and we caught plenty of fish.

Monday, September 1.   Bright, beautiful Summer has passed away. "Glad Summer—fare thee well!" To-day my school duties recommence. This has been a sad, sad vacation for me. Often I think there is nothing worth living for. Nothing! Those whom we love best die and leave us. We are a poor, oppressed people, with very many trials, and very few friends. The Past, the Present, the Future are alike dark and dreary for us. I know it is not right to feel thus. But I *cannot* help it always; though my own heart tells me that there is much to live for. That the more deeply we suffer, the nobler and holier is the work of life that lies before us! Oh! for strength; strength to bear the suffering, to do the work bravely, unfalteringly!

Sunday, September 7. This evening walked to Danvers, and heard an anti-slavery lecture from Mr. [William Wells] Brown. Liked it pretty well. Commenced "English Traits" which I shall like very much, I think.

Monday, September 8. Listened to Mr. [William Wells] Brown's drama. "The Kidnapper Kidnapped." It is quite interesting and very amusing.—Coming home Mr. [Charles Lenox] and Miss R.[emond] acted strangely I thought. The former's behavior is rather incomprehensible, at present,— very *sullen* and makes Sarah [Cassey Smith] and me feel rather unpleasantly.

Sunday, September 21. Took breakfast with the Putnam's and looked over some old papers and journeys of Mr. P.[utnam].

Tuesday, September 30. The last day of beautiful, "mellow, serene September"! Days,—weeks,—months! As we grow older how rapidly they glide away! Ever, ever we bid farewell to the Past, and welcome in the Future. Just finished Emerson's "English Traits,"—which I like *very* much. The author's views of English character are far more liberal than those of American travellers generally. He evidently appreciates dear old England; and, loving her as I do, I like his book and thank him for it with all my heart.

Sunday, October 5. Took a delightful walk to Cob's Spring in N.[ew] S.[alem] with S.[arah], Mr. and Mrs. P.[utnam] and Miss S.[arah] P. R.[emond]. Commenced "Hyperion."

Sunday, October 12. Another pleasant walk with the same

party, except Miss R. [emond]. These Sabbath walks are very pleasant. To-day we went to Castle Hill which commands a fine view of our pretty City of Peace, and her pleasant little country cousins—Beverly and Danvers.—"Hyperion" is beautiful,—truly *'poetic prose.'* The writer's constant and familiar mention of German authors, of which I know so very little, is rather provoking. But I am determined that I *will*, some time, be glad to read those noble works in their own rich and beautiful language.

Wednesday, October 15. To-day, Sarah Putnam[74] and I went into our dear Normal School. We have been there pretty often of late. It is very pleasant to see our loved teachers and the *few* pleasant companions who are left of our broken band.—This evening our sewing circle met at Mrs. Putnam's. Had a pleasant chat with Mr. P. [utnam] and Mr. Nell before it commenced and afterwards. Mr. N. [ell] lent me an old book of very interesting sketches of some old Greek poets.

Friday, October 17. Took a pleasant walk to the Fort with Mr. and Mrs. P. [utnam], Mr. N. [ell] and Sarah [Cassey Smith].—Had a game of whist.

Sunday, October 19. Heard an excellent lecture from Mr. [Frank] Appleton. One of the best I ever listened to. He spoke particularly of disunion.

Saturday, October 25. So utterly dispirited and weary have I been for these few days past that I have not felt like writing in thee my Journal. I have been troubled at school very much; and have felt most hopeless. So much so that I have not ventured to see my beloved friend Miss S. [hepard] who has met with a terrible loss; that of her beloved mother. I tremble for her; she is so weak herself. I have seen her but once since this sad event; for I feared that in my own despondency I might do her harm. But I must see her to-morrow. Dear, dear friend—most earnestly do I wish to do something, something for the happiness of one who has done so much for me.—This afternoon S. [arah] P. [itman?] and I called upon Mr. E. [dwards], Miss W. [eston], Lucy R., and Lizzie D. [ike]. Mr. and Mrs. P. [utnam] stopped in. What an attractive person he is! So much more attractive than Mr. R. [emond] whose gloomy countenance gives me a fit of the *blues* regularly every morning. And the *blues* are not the pleasantest companions in the world; particularly after one has been working hard all day, and wants to be cheered up at night. Prescott's "Conquest" is deeply interesting.

Sunday, October 26. Mr. [Charles Lenox] R. [emond] lectured for us this evening. His lecture was very good. I particularly liked what he said about Kansas. Everybody has so much sympathy for the sufferers there, and so little for the poor slave, who for centuries has suffered tenfold worse miseries.—Still I am glad that *something* has roused the people of the North at last.

October. Went with Mr. [Joseph] Putnam to hear Mr. [Richard] Dana, who taught me more about Kansas than I ever knew before. A very great political excitement prevails.

Monday, November 3. [Hon. Charles] Sumner came to-day. I read eagerly the account of his reception. Coming as it did from the *heart* of the people it must have been exceedingly gratifying to the noble man. I long to see him.

Saturday, November 8. Alas! for the hope of the people! Again has Might triumphed over Right; Falsehood over Truth; Slavery over Freedom. But these things cannot last much longer. Surely a just God will not permit them.

Sunday, November 9. Sarah [Cassey Smith] and I spent the afternoon at Mrs. [Cecelia] Babcock's making pies.

Wednesday, November 12.   This evening Mr. [William Wells] Brown read his excellent Drama. People were so much pleased with it that he has been invited to read it again.

Friday, November 14.   Spent the evening very pleasantly at Mr. Edwards'. A large party of us came back in the pouring rain, in high spirits; found Peter [Cassey] [75] just arrived from California. He looks remarkably well. Mr. [Charles Lenox] and Miss [Sarah Parker] R.[emond] are certainly going on their lecturing tour next week.

Sunday, November 16.   Mr. and Miss R.[emond] went to the Essex Co. meeting at Georgetown. I could not go but wanted to sadly. Mr. [Sumner] Ellis lectured. Very good lecture. Some parts of it surprisingly radical for him.

Tuesday, November 18.   Spent the evening with Miss S.[arah] Remond, who goes to-morrow. We shall miss her greatly. She is a very entertaining person.

Wednesday, November 19.   Peter [Cassey] brought Frank [Cassey] from Hopedale. Was too unwell to attend school. *Brownie* very kindly taught for me. Miss [Lucy] Kingman called this evening. How good and kind she is! She tried hard to induce me to return home with her and spend Thanksgiving week. But I cannot afford to go. I long to do so. Mr. and Mrs. P.[utnam] took tea with us. Afterwards, to our astonishment, who should walk in but Mr. [William C.] Nell. I felt too miserable to enjoy the evening much.

Thursday, November 20.   Still too unwell to attend school. All our household have gone except Henry and me. Oh! how *very*, very lonesome I shall feel without Sarah! Helen S.[hearman] is coming to spend the night with me.

Sunday, November 23.   Still unwell.—Oh! how wearily and drearily the hours pass away.—I have had many kind visitors,—Normal teachers and scholars but now they have all gone home to spend Thanksgiving week. Yesterday afternoon S. [arah] Putnam read to me; and Mr. Edwards came in.—I cannot go to hear my beloved [William Lloyd] Garrison tonight. It is *too bad!*

Monday, November 24. Felt enough better to read Prescott a little while. Afterwards committed to memory some parts of the "Prisoner of Chillon," and some of those exquisite 'Hebrew Melodies.' Head-ache, the consequence of course.

Wednesday, November 26. Sarah P. [itman?] commenced reading to me "The Hills of Shatemue" by the author of "Querchy." Like it exceedingly—walked a little way.

Thursday, November 27. Thanksgiving Day.—Dined at Mrs. [Ellen] Sherman's and rode home. Ellen is exceedingly kind to me. I must return it somehow.—This evening Sarah P. [itman?] finished reading "Hills of the Shatemue." It contains fine descriptions of the beautiful scenery in the Empire State. How much I should like to see it. Had a kind visit from Miss Weston.

Friday, November 28. Walked down town with Mrs. [Jane] P. [utnam] and Mrs. [Helen] G. [illiard]. A beautiful day.—Sat a while with Mrs. Caroline P. [utnam] in her very pretty improved store. Came home and wrote to Miss S. [arah] P. Remond, who has been successful. If I could only have accepted Miss Kingman's kind invitation to Bridgewater. But then—one can't always do what one wants to;—and there's an end on't.—Sarah wrote to me once. I wish she'd write again. Oh, how *very* much I have missed her!

Saturday, November 29. My dear Miss S. [hepard] came to see me and very kindly sent me "Undine" and "Sintram." This evening Lizzie C. [hurch] and Sarah P. [itman?] came in. Lizzie and I studied French. Afterwards read "Undine," a wild singular story from the German.

Sunday, November 30. The last day of autumn, and a very bright day it is. A light snow has fallen, and lies—a beautiful and spotless mantle on the hard ground, and the gaunt branches of the trees. Farewell to thee Autumn!— "Sweet Sabbath of the year!" Many and sad have the changes been since we last saw thee.—Many and sad may they be ere we see thee again.—The dreary Winter, the pleasant Spring, the glowing Summer will pass away.—Then shall we again behold thy sober face. *Some* of us;—*not* all, for many will be slumbering in the bosom of our dear old mother Earth.— Miss W. [eston] came to see me. Mr. E. [dwards] says I must not go to school to-morrow,—he will send one of the girls to teach for me. How very kind it is! Mr. [Joseph] P. [utnam] and E. [llen Shearman] have gone to the lecture. I could not go. Tried to study Latin with Henry; but did not succeed. My head seems to have scarcely any strength.— Altogether rather a restless and unsatisfactory day. A little letter writing accomplished.

Monday, December 1. A cold, cold winter's day.—Dr. G. forbids my going out until I see him again on Thursday. My poor school! What *will* become of it. But it can't be helped. Passed most of the day alone.—Sewed a little, studied a little Latin and French and finished "Sintram," which I like very much for its spirited wildness and singularity. Hear that Mr. Wesson's lecture of last night was very excellent. Wish I could have heard it. I crave anti-slavery food continually.

Tuesday, December 2. Sewed a little and read. Mrs. P. [utnam] and Mrs. G. [illiard] spent part of the afternoon with me. Had a number of visitors, among whom were Brownie, Miss S. [hepard] and Lucy R. Miss S. [hepard], with her usual kindness, brought me some books,—three volumes of "Queens of England." Commenced reading "Katherine Parr." Mrs. P.[utnam] thought Lucy R. a very interesting looking girl. She *is* one of the most interesting people I know. There is a depth of thought and beauty in her nature of which few who knew her slightly would dream. It seems quite wonderful to me, for one so young,—(I believe she is not eighteen).—Brownie is another charming and lovable girl, but less poetical and imaginative than Lucy.

Wednesday, December 3. A most gloomy day without.— Not particularly so within. During intervals of freedom from the headache translated "Esop's Fables." How much I love the beautiful Latin language! It always *rests* me, however weary and dispirited I may feel.—No letter from *Sarah* [Cassey Smith].—It is very strange. This afternoon received a very long and interesting letter from Sarah. Answered it and read "Queens of England."—My beloved Mr. [Samuel] May lectured this evening. It was a great grief to me not to hear him. I hear that his lecture was excellent.—Studied Latin again.

Thursday, December 4. Should have gone to school but Miss [Sarah Parker] R.[emond] came in and forbade it. How *very* kind she is! Finished fifth volume of "Queens of England"; Katherine Parr's life and part of Queen Mary's.

Friday, December 5. Did some sewing—Read "Conquest of Mexico," which increases in interest.—Mrs. P.[utnam] and E.[lizabeth] came in and entertained me with an account of a spiritual meeting, which they had been attending. Some of the manifestations were really quite wonderful.—Studied Latin.

Saturday, December 6. Attended school. My scholars were very glad to see me again. Came home rather tired.—Made some pies. Went down town to Mrs. P.[utnam]'s and Mrs.

B. [abcock]'s. Sewed. This evening Mr. [L. F.] Warren called and gave me some advice about school affairs which I will gladly follow. Read "Conquest of Mexico." Played solitary and whist with Ellen S. [hearman].

Sunday, December 7. Dined with Mr. and Mrs. P. [utnam]. Took a long walk. 'Twas *bitter* cold. Our little Common looks quite prettily in its mantle of pure white snow. Spent the evening as usual in reading and writing. A visit from Lucy and Miss W. [eston].

Monday, December 8. Went to the A. [nti]-S. [lavery] sewing circle at Miss [Lydia] Chase's. Only three or four were present. We had a very pleasant evening. Miss Chase showed us an inkstand which she had purchased at a children's Fair, held for the benefit of the Kansas sufferers. It's prettily carved out of a knot of oak,—and was sent to the Fair by Mrs. [Lydia Maria] Child, who had received it from a boy, who had read with great pleasure her "Letters from New York." How pleasant it must have been to the gifted lady to receive such a token! It is not strange that it was sent to her. No one could read *her* writings without the most enthusiastic admiration of the high-souled writer. I am sure that I cannot. "Philothea" is a book never to be forgotten. I always think of it with a feeling of grateful pleasure that it was written, and that I have had the delightful privilege of reading it.

Tuesday, December 9. After school spent the evening entirely alone,—thinking, reading the "Conquest," and writing. Tried to think cheerfully but, as usual, many sad thoughts *would* intrude,—thoughts of the unsatisfactory world, and of life, with its wearisome cares,—its constant *unrest*. But these thoughts must *not* gain ascendancy while the earnest and noble *labor* of life lies before me.—They shall not!

Wednesday, December 10. Went to my dear Normal School

and had some pleasant conversation with my friends. Took tea with Mrs. [Jane] P. [utnam] and Mrs. [Helen] G. [illiard]. Attended the Lyceum lecture. It was given by Professor [J.] Hoyt of Exeter. Subject—some of our popular fallacies.— One of the best lectures I ever listened to; thoroughly liberal in spirit, and abounding in passages of great truth and beauty. The popular fallacies he mentioned particularly were—the eager pursuit of material riches rather than worth. The confounding of *wealth* with *material* riches; of *law* with *legislative enactments;* of reverence with servility; of true *religion* with a more *religious creed.* Such lectures are truly *mental* and moral feasts, and cannot fail to accomplish a great good.

Thursday, December 11. Went to school.—Scholars decidedly improving.—Very encouraging. Read and studied Latin in the evening which I spent alone. Heard from Sarah through Henry.

Friday, December 12. Lizzie C. [hurch] and Sarah P. [itman?] called. We exchanged school experiences. None of them chance to be particularly pleasant. Spent most of the evening in sewing for E. [llen], building airy castles the while. Afterwards read the "Conquest" and played whist.

Saturday, December 13. Took my sewing and spent a very pleasant afternoon at Carltonville. Read "Tanglewood Tales," and enjoyed them exceedingly.

Sunday, December 14. One of the "dark days." Rains increasingly. Went to hear Mr. Woodbridge of Lowell lecture before our society. Excellent lecture. Principally an examination of the character of slavery.—Very few were present; not more than two dozen.—Read the "Conquest" and "Memoirs of Dr. Burney," by his daughter, Madame

D'Arklay. It tells me much that I wanted to know about such men as Burke, Dr. Johnson, etc.

Monday, December 15.   Our society met at Mrs. [Amy] Ives'. Came home and read Hawthorne's "Tanglewood Tales."

Tuesday, December 16.   Henry [Cassey] left for New York. He goes to California with Peter [Cassey]. More lonesome than ever now, and longing for Sarah's return. Ellen S. [hearman] is one of the kindest persons I know. I like her very much. Read my "Conquest."

Wednesday, December 17.   Went to the Normal and saw Mary O. [sborn] and my dear friend Miss R. and Lucy. Mr. Edwards kindly gave me a pass for Mr. Conway's lecture. It was a splendid lecture, subject "The Study of Words" which has always interested me greatly. Another rich and rare mental feast.

Thursday, December 18.   Piercing! piercing cold! I only write to record this as one of the coldest days.—Nearly froze, coming from school. Have been in a half torpid state ever since.—Only able to sew and read a little.

Friday, December 19.   Came home from school, weary and cold, but found something which refreshed and inspirited me,—filled me with joy and astonishment,—a letter from Whittier,—the 'Great Poet of Humanity'! It was an answer to one which I wrote to him—because—*I could not help it*; the Spirit moved me. *His* letter, most unexpected by me, is *very* kind and beautiful, most worthy of his noble self. I thank him for it with all my heart. A letter in *his own* handwriting. He can never know the happiness—the delight it gives me. But oh, it grieves me deeply to know that he is ill,—that his health has failed fearfully of late. How *could* we bear to lose him? I *will not* think that it is possible.

Saturday, December 20.   Spent the afternoon very delight-fully with my dear friend Miss S. [hepard]. Showed her my precious letter, which I would show to no one else in Salem. She appreciates it thoroughly; and kindly pardons my pre-sumption in writing to him,—the noblest poet, the noblest *man* of the age, with *very* few exceptions.

Sunday, December 21.   Have just returned from Parker Pillsbury's lecture. One of the best Anti-Slavery lectures I ever heard. While listening to him I could not help thinking of Luther of old. Indeed as it has been said of Luther, I believe, "his words were half battles." Glorious indeed they were—those battles for suffering humanity. They excited me to such a degree of enthusiasm, that I could have risen and thanked and blessed him for them, then and there. As Sidney says of the Ballad of Chevy Chase, "they stir the soul like the sound of the trumpet," but to a higher, nobler impulse than that of *physical* resistance; to a stern *moral* resolve of sternest *moral* warfare against the terrible curse of our country and of the age.—Such a lecture renews one's strength; make one feel equal to any labor, for the ennobling of mankind.

Monday, December 22.   Went to hear Dr. [William] Elder at the Lyceum.—Subject "Natural History of Civili-zation." Lecture was not particularly interesting; though he is a very peculiar and comical person. Expected Sarah, but she did not come.—Answered Mr. N. [ell]'s letter.

Tuesday, December 23.   Ellen S. [hearman] gives me such a glowing account of the Fair, that I long more earnestly than ever to see it. If possible I *will* go on Christmas.

Commenced the second volume of the "Conquest" which greatly increases in interest.

Christmas Day, December, 1856.   Spent the day very de-lightfully at the Fair.—Saw many beautiful things and many interesting people. Had the good fortune to be made known to three of the noblest and best of women;—Mesdames [Maria W.] Chapman, [Elizabeth] Follen, and [Lydia M.] Child; who were very kind and pleasant to me. Saw the most distinguished champions of our cause. Mr. [Wendell] Phillips' kind pressure of the hand and beaming smile, I shall not soon forget, nor the cordial greetings of our dauntless pioneer, and his lovely wife. Mrs. [Francis] Drake of Leominster I found a very social and pleasant person. She was anxious to have me go with her to Fitchburg, and attend the Fair. Mrs. Follen has a real *motherly* kindness of manner. She is a lovely looking silver haired old lady; Mrs. Chapman's irresistible sweetness and grace of manner, I have no words to describe. Mrs. [Lydia M.] Child smilingly told me that she visited our house once,—when *I* must have been a "wee toddling." She is not quite so spiritual looking as one would expect to see the author of "Philothea," but is a very charming person nevertheless. I attended our Salem table part of the time, and then assisted Mrs. Follen. One of the most interesting people that I met was Charles R. Whipple, who came up, and commenced talking to me. We had a long a very delightful conversation. He is a fine conversationist (as well as an excellent writer) and a very social and attractive person. Mr. [Charles] Hovey was as genial as usual. Altogether this has been a most delightful day to me; and I am *very* sorry that I cannot accept the numerous invitations that I have received to remain here during the Fair.—Had the very great *honor* and pleasure of walking through the Fair, arm-in-arm—with Mrs. [Maria W.] Chapman.

Saturday, December 27. Commenced translating Cesar's [*sic*] "Commentaries."

Sunday, December 28. Read the last number of "Little

Dorrit," which is exceedingly interesting; an exquisite poem "To E. B. Browning"; and a very favorable criticism of her "Aurora Leigh," which I long to read.

Tuesday, December 30. I went over to Carltonville and had a fine time coasting with Mr. [Joseph] P.[utnam] and Ellen S.[hearman]. It is a most delightful and exhilarating exercise.

Wednesday, December 31. The last day of the Old Year! Many and sad have been the changes since first we greeted thee, old friend! Wednesday, 12 o'clock. The clock strikes twelve! The year has gone! And with it I bid farewell, a last farewell to thee, my Journal! The year has gone! Gone, with its sorrows and its joys.—Gone to join its brethren in the shadowy regions of the Past! Dear, dear friend, who has gone before us to the Spirit Land! In that bright land thou sayest not farewell to the *Old* nor welcomest in the *New. There* all is joy and peace forever more. But for us! Oh! how sadly we say 'farewell' to the closing year,—the year in which thy dear and precious existence closed on earth forever. May I ever remember thy beautiful example. Have I improved the past year as I might have done? Alas! I have not.—Too many hours have been spent in fruit*less* dreamings—golden anticipations of the Future. They are over now; and I commence the New Year a little wiser, I hope, from the experience of the Old.—Dear friends at home;—I think of you to-night. You cannot hear me; but in my heart I wish you a happy *very* happy New Year;—with the earnest, longing hope that ere *it* passes away, I may be with you once again!

JOURNAL TWO

Salem, January 1, 1857–
January 27, 1858

Salem. January 1, 1857. Welcome in, New Year! with thy many changes; thy fullness of joy or sorrow, unknown, undreamed of now,—Have formed many good resolutions for the opening year, but think it wisest to commit none of them to paper. Night—spent most of the day at my beloved Normal School. Enjoyed particularly the recitations in French and Latin. This evening had a fine time coasting down the hill with Mr. [Joseph] P.[utnam]. 'Tis a delightful and exhilarating exercise.—Read several chapters of the "Conquest."—Am shocked at the cruelty and rapacity of the Spaniards. Think Prescott is too lenient in his judgment of Cortes. Certainly he was a great conqueror, but it seems to me that *personal ambition*, rather than love of his religion, was his ruling passion.

Friday, January 2. Felt much disappointment and grieved at not being able to attend the Festival at Faneuil Hall, celebrating the twenty-fifth anniversary of the formation of the Mass. A.[nti]S.[lavery] Society.[1]—Dared to compose a letter to Mr. [Wendell] Phillips—The Spirit moved me!— really could not help it.—Felt as if I *must* say something, something to express my heartfelt gratitude and admiration for the noble friends of the oppressed, who meet in the "Old Cradle of Liberty" to-night. Don't believe I shall have the courage to send it.—Read the "Two Guardians" an interesting book by the author of the "Heir of Redclyffe." Ellen S.[hearman] has gone away so, save our domestic, I am quite alone.

Saturday, January 3. Sarah P.[utnam] and Lizzie C.[hurch] spent the afternoon with me. Thought that S.[arah] P.[utnam] seemed rather low spirited. Lizzie [Church] and I had a pleasant chat over old times,—our early school days.— Then discussed our favorite books and pictures.—Read the "Conquest."

Sunday, January 4. A magnificent snow storm! Ventured to send my letter.—Fear the great man will think me very presumptuous.—but who can resist the Spirit's movings? Paid Mrs. [Jane] P.[utnam] a visit—Read Tennyson and wrote letters all the evening.

Monday, January 5. Still alone, and should be lonesome were not my time so constantly occupied,—teaching all day and reading and studying all the evening. Translated several passages from the "Commentaries," and finished the "Conquest of Mexico," which has interested me greatly. The language of Prescott is elegant, and his style very brilliant and attractive. This account of the Aztec civilization, particularly interested and surprised me. I had no idea that they had reached so high a state of civilization.

Tuesday, January 6. Mr. [Joseph] P.[utnam] spent the evening with me. We read and criticized Tennyson, and then I made him admire some of my favorite passages in Milton's exquisite "Lycidas." But he is not so ardent an admirer of the poem as I am; nor, indeed, of Milton generally.

Wednesday, January 7. Spent the afternoon in studying Latin;—the evening with Mrs. [Jane] P.[utnam] and Mrs. [Helen Putnam] G.[illiard]. I like them exceedingly. The daughter is thoroughly kind, sensible and unassuming. The mother equally kind, and with such depth of feeling, and excellent judgment. Little E.[lizabeth] read "Hiawatha" to us. She reads beautifully, with an evident appreciation really wonderful in so young a child. Mr. P. [utnam] and I coasted a while.

Thursday, January 8.   Bitter, bitter cold! Cannot wonder that S. [arah] does not come. Strange that E. [llen?] does not. Came home from school almost frozen. Studied "Caesar." Find it rather difficult, but am determined to persevere. Excelsior! shall be my motto, now and forever.

Friday, January 9.   Went to Thalberg's concert, for which Mr. [James] Shearman very kindly sent me a ticket. Such glorious strains I never heard before from the piano. They were most inspiring. The singing was very fine;—all in Italian, but, although I understood not a word, I could not wish it changed, so exquisitely rich and musical are the tones of that beautiful language. The singers were a true son and daughter of fair Italy, with the rich glowing complexion and the splendid dark hair and eyes peculiar to that sunny clime.— It was a rare and most delightful treat for me. Read with great pleasure a very interesting account of the Festival (in "Lib. [erator]") and some of the very beautiful and appropriate letters read there.—Those of Rev. Mr. [Octavius B.] Frothingham and Mrs. [Abigail] Foster, liked particularly.

Saturday, January 10.   Greatly disappointed that Sarah [Cassey Smith] does not come.—Commenced Rogers' "Table Talk," and have become much interested in it.—Studied Latin.

Sunday, January 11.   Wrote to—Miss [Harriet] Martineau![2] Am astonished and shocked at my own presumption.— But felt *impelled* to write by one of those Spirit movings' which *will* not be resisted. Have always greatly admired and loved Miss Martineau, and have thought of her much since seeing her exquisite work at the Fair. Felt that I must say *something* to show the admiration and gratitude with which I regard her. It may give her some pleasure to hear in this way from a young colored girl in a distant land. Finished Rogers' "Table Talk"—a delightful book, full of interesting anecdotes of the most distinguished people of his day.

Monday, January 12.   Still quite alone. Read Miss Strickland's "Elizabeth." Like it much better than any other history of the great queen that I have seen. It occupied my time very pleasantly during the evening.

Tuesday, January 13.   This evening [Rev.] Mr. [Octavius B.] Frothingham lectured on "The Relation of the Bible to Slavery." One of the most beautiful, earnest and convincing lectures I have ever heard. It made me feel *very happy.*—Do not know Mr. F.[rothingham] personally, but after the lecture, longed to shake hands with him. Should not have had the courage to do so, had not my friend, Mrs. P.[utnam] presented me to him. His kind pressure of my hand and beaming gracious smile I shall always remember. Of course *he* does not believe that the Bible sanctions slavery, and most clearly and convincingly did he *prove* that it does not. A man with such a heart and mind as his is truly a host in himself,— one of the noblest of all mankind.[3]

Wednesday, January 14.   Attended Mr. Frothingham's lecture on "Epicurus." It was very interesting and instructive but did not compare with the admirable lecture of last evening. Greek scholars would enjoy it.

Thursday, January 15.   As usual read and studied all the evening. Feel a little lonesome at times.—Still no news from Canada. It grieves me deeply that father should act so strangely. It seems as if my only parent has quite forsaken me. I lay awake all last night, thinking about, and could not help crying. I wish he *would* write to me.

Friday, January 16.   Stopped to see Miss S.[hepard] who

told me about Hugh Miller's death. How very sad it is! So noble and gifted a man. I cannot believe that he voluntarily committed suicide. Miss S. [hepard] lent me two of Hillard's new "Readers." They contain excellent selections from the best writers; but with sorrow—with contempt for the author's cowardice, I noticed that he most carefully avoided the *mention* of slavery. Even in quoting from *Whittier*, the true poet of humanity, and in giving a beautiful sketch of him, not one word is said of his noble devotion to the cause of the slave,— not one line of the many glorious ones he has written for freedom, does Mr. H. [illard] *dare* to quote! Such moral pusillanimity is degrading, most pitiable.

Saturday, January 17. Dined with Mr. and Mrs. P. [utnam]. We talked of the wrongs and sufferings of our race. Mr. [Joseph] P. [utnam] thought me too sensitive.— But oh, how inexpressibly bitter and agonizing it is to feel oneself an outcast from the rest of mankind, as we are in this country! To me it is *dreadful, dreadful*. Were I to indulge in the thought I fear I should become insane. But I do not despair. I *will* not despair; though *very* often I can hardly help doing so. God help us! We are indeed a wretched people. Oh, that I could do much toward bettering our condition. I will do *all*, all the *very little* that lies in my power, while life and strength last!

Monday, January 19. Woke this morning to find my floor carpeted with snow; windows and doors completely blockaded. Streets are deserted.—Stores and schools all closed. Such a storm even the oldest inhabitant can hardly remember. I cannot get outside the door. Night—Our domestic, one of Erin's daughters, 'wrapped in the arms of Morphous.' Hear no sound save the meaning of the wind, and the musical ticking of the clock, as I sit before the bright fire and muse.

Have studied a little, and read Mr. [Wendell] Phillips' excellent speech at the Woman's Rights Convention in New York.

Tuesday, January 20. A glorious day. Never saw so much snow in my life before. Streets piled with miniature "Mont-Blancs," presenting in the bright rays of the sun a most beautiful and wonderful sight.—Waded through the snow to the school house.—No school.—Paid a visit to Carltonville, enjoying the fun of climbing the hill in the *deep, deep* snow. Assisted Mrs. P. [utnam] in her store all the afternoon. Mr. P. [utnam] and I had quite a discussion on Woman's Rights, to which he says he is much opposed. But I am seriously inclined to doubt it—(his opposition).

Wednesday, January 21. Our society met at Mrs. William Chase's. She is a very pleasant, lovable woman,—perfectly free from prejudice. Read and studied all the eve.

Thursday, January 22. Came from school cold and weary, found to my joyful surprise a letter from Mr. [Wendell] Phillips.—How *very* kind he was to *write*. I feel *very* grateful to him. He is indeed a noble-hearted man. I can never, never express all the reverence and admiration which I feel for him. How delightful it would be to be admitted to his society. Alas, I can never hope to be fitted for that great privilege. But I *can* love and admire him, and shall ever do so, with all my heart.—Looked over many old letters, which gave me rather a sad and lonesome feeling.

Friday, January 23. Coldest day of all! Bitter, bitter! Suffered much on my way to school.—No school this afternoon.—Studied Latin and French. Don't expect S. [arah] *now. Very* lonesome at meals and bed-time. Ellen [Gilliard] still in Boston.

Saturday, January 24. Was greatly shocked and surprised

to hear that Mr. Jos.[eph] died on last Saturday. Too unwell to attend school. Miss Chase sent me "Gan Eden, or Pictures of Cuba," with a very kind note. Lizzie C.[hurch] and Sarah P.[itnam?] brought me Longfellow's "Kavanagh." It is interesting,—many parts beautiful, but does not compare with "Hyperion."

Sunday, January 25. Read "Pictures of Cuba." Don't like it much. The style is rather extravagant. Was pleased with the author's remarks on slavery, and the mulatto poet— Placide.

Monday, January 26. Attended school.—This evening heard Rev. T.[heodore] Parker's lecture on Franklin. It was admirable. He spoke beautifully of Franklin's anti-slavery views. "He, the most famous man of America, almost of the age, was not ashamed to be known as the President of an Abolition Society." Noticed in Mr. P.[arker,] as I do in all our great liberal men, how much more eloquent they become in speaking of slavery. This ever exciting subject kindles in them a noble enthusiasm, which always finds expression in the most beautiful and elevated language.

Tuesday, January 27. Had our private examination. Vacation commenced. Studied L.[atin] and F.[rench]. Spent the evening at Mrs. P.[utnam's] playing whist. Read "The Rape of the Lock."

Wednesday, January 28. Went to the services at the Tabernacle on the reunion of past pupils of the High School. Gen. Oliver's speech was spirited and excellent; Mr. E. P. Whipple's oration elegant. But I do not like him. He is too conservative. This evening read Tennyson. Like "Maud" much better than I expected. Many parts are very beautiful and impassioned. "The Miller's Daughter" is one of my favorites;—a love poem, but with no sickly sentiment. It is

full of graceful sweetness. Tennyson requires study, but richly
does he repay it.—Greatly admire the lofty pride in that
spirited poem, "Lady Clara Vere de Vere."

Thursday, January 29. Too stormy to go to Boston. Assisted Mrs. P. [utnam] in her store. In the evening Mr.
P. [utnam] went to Boston.—I spent the night with Mrs.
P. [utnam]. Read my beloved Whittier, and in an old number
of "Blackwood," a very interesting sketch of the gifted and
brilliant Prof. Wilson—Christopher North.

Friday, January 30. Went to the meetings with Mrs.
[Jane] P. [utnam] and her daughter. First person whom I
met on entering the Melodian was Mr. [Wendell] Phillips.
He spoke to me *very* kindly. Asked me if I received his note,
and thanked me warmly for writing him so kind a letter.
My heart was too full to say much. Mrs. [Abigail] Foster,
that most excellent of women, gave me so warm and kind a
greeting that I was quite touched. She pressed my hand with
great fervor, and said most earnestly, "God bless you, my
dear, I am most happy to meet you." The speeches were
nearly all excellent. Those of Messrs. [William] Garrison,
[Wendell] Phillips, [Theodore] Parker and [Parker] Pillsbury especially so. Mr. Phillips made the closing speech—a
noble one;—one of the most eloquent I have ever heard even
from his eloquent lips. The meetings were held in the
Tremont Temple, which is very beautiful. The gas lights are
arranged in the ceiling like groups of stars. The effect of the
light falling in this way on the rich carving and gilding of
the room, is enchantingly beautiful.—Like a scene of fairy-
land.

Saturday, January 31. A terribly stormy day. Felt much
disappointment, as there were many places of interest which

I had intended to visit. Went in the midst of the storm to several book-stores, trying to replace Miss Upton's book, but was unsuccessful. Shall leave Mr. [William] N.[ell] to prosecute the search. The store of Phillips, Sampson and Co. is very splendid. Went with Mr. Nell to Rev. T.[heodore] Parker's library. The great man gave me a cordial greeting, which rather surprised me for I had heard that he was cold to strangers. But he happened to be in a genial mood today. Went first to his principal library, which is also his study. It contains *ten thousand* volumes, in almost every language. Mr. Parker showed me the works of the Christian Fathers—one hundred vol[umes]. It was delightful to see so many books. I wanted to spend weeks there. Thought of that exquisite little poem by Anne C. Lynch, "Thoughts in a Library" commencing—

> "Speak low, tread softly through these halls,
>   Here genius reigns sublime,
> Here dwell in silent majesty
>   The monarchs of the mind."

The great man showed us a little chest of drawers in which his mother kept his clothes when he was a child. He opened one drawer and said there was where she used to keep his buttons, and he keeps them there now. Another drawer is filled with toys which he keeps for the amusement of children who come to visit him. These things revealed to me a beautiful trait of character. In a window of this favorite apartment stands an orange tree filled with fine fruit. The table was covered with his writing materials. Some sheets of written paper I thought were probably part of his sermon for tomorrow. Before the table stood his plain, cane-bottomed armchair. He accompanied me around the room talking very delightfully. On leaving he presented me with two of his finest sermons, and cordially invited me to come again.

After leaving this library, which occupies the third story of his house, we descended to the parlor. Part of *its* walls are also covered with books. It contains some of the finest engravings I have ever seen. One of them, "The Angel bearing St. Catharine to Heaven," is exquisitely beautiful. An exquisite wreath of the leaves and berries of the laurel and myrtle appropriately encircles a fine picture of the noble [Charles] Sumner. From the parlor we descended to another room also filled with books. The entire library contains *fifteen thousand* vol[umes]. I shall always remember my visit to it, and my very pleasant interview with its great and learned, yet most genial-hearted owner. Was very desirous of hearing him preach tomorrow, but did not dare to remain lest the road should become blockaded with snow. Came home this afternoon with Mrs. P.[utnam]. Found a kind letter from Annie [Woods Webb]. Felt greatly disappointed at not meeting Sarah [Cassey Smith] here. Read last no. of "Little Dorrit." Studied Latin, and commenced "Eleven Weeks in Europe," by Rev. James F.[reeman] Clarke.

Sunday, February 1. Spent the day at home reading "Eleven Weeks in Europe." It is very interesting; like it exceedingly— as well as if not better than any book of European travel I have read. Nearly all that one most wants to see abroad was seen in eleven weeks and most thoroughly appreciated by one who is a fine scholar, an ardent lover of the beautiful, and a truly noble-hearted man. His descriptions of pictures and of mountain scenery are particularly fine. Again read and committed to memory Coleridge's noble and sublime "Hymn to Mont-Blanc," to which Mr. Clarke beautifully alludes in speaking of the "Monarch of Mountains." Mrs. P.[utnam] came in and we had a pleasant chat. Wrote to Aunt Sarah [Purvis] [4] and Aunt M.[argaretta Forten].

Monday, February 2. No school. Spent part of the day in copying this month's journalisms into my new book. This afternoon went to Mrs. [Caroline] P.[utnam]'s and had a long and interesting talk with her about books of travels, histories, etc. She is a delightful person to converse with. Studied Latin, read the Anti-Slavery papers, and Mr. Clark's interesting book.

Tuesday, February 3. Attended school. Have a new class.— Some very small creatures but bright and interesting. Went to our Society meeting at Miss [William] Chase's. Quite a large and pleasant meeting. Sarah [Cassey Smith] came at last! Rejoiced to see her. We lay awake nearly all night talking about home and distant friends.

Wednesday, February 4. 'Tis delightful to have S.[arah] home again. We have had long talks and consultations of future plans. Much perplexed. Do not know what we shall do. Don't wish to stay with Mr. R.[emond] any longer. Finished "Eleven Weeks in Europe" and commenced "The Autobiography of a Female Slave." The authoress is a gifted young southern lady;—a cousin of Sir. E. L. Bulwer. Received many presents, useful ones from home, sweet home.— Wrote to Hattie P.[urvis] [5]—Saw Miss W.[eston] who told me of poor Marie [Barnes?]'s death. [6] It is hard to realize it.

Thursday, February 5. S.[arah] has gone to bring Frank [Cassey]. Became much interested in the "Autobiography." It is very thrilling. Studied Latin this evening and again looked over "Madeline" by Julia Kavanagh, a tale founded on fact. The character of the heroine, a poor peasant girl of Auvergus, is *very* noble. Her pure, heroic, self-sacrificing spirit affected me much. Strengthened my own aspirations for something high and holy.—My earnest longings to do *something* for the good of others. I know that I am very selfish. Always the thought of *self-culture* presents itself *first*. With that, I think I can accomplish something more noble, more enduring, I will try not to forget that, while striving to improve myself, I may at least *commence* to work for others.

Friday, February 6. After school studied French with Sarah [Cassey Smith]. Played chess with Frank [Cassey]. Studied Latin; read "The Autobiography" and "Little Dorrit."

Saturday, February 7. S. [arah] and I went to see Mrs. Ruth R. [emond]. She is an excellent woman, who has had much sorrow. Received a very kind letter from Ellen A. [lexander?] whom I have always liked exceedingly. It will give me much pleasure to correspond with her. "The Autobiography" is very thrilling. Some parts of it almost too horrible to be believed, did we not know that they cannot exceed the terrible reality. It is *dreadful, dreadful* that *such* scenes can be daily and hourly enacted in this enlightened age, and *most* enlightened republic. How long, Oh Lord, how long, wilt thou delay thy vengeance? Am much grieved to hear that Ada [Putnam] is so ill that her mother is going to N. [ew] Y. [ork].[7] Hope most earnestly that she is not dangerous [*sic*].

Sunday, February 8. Finished "The Autobiography of a Female Slave." To me it is deeply interesting. The writer's style has not, perhaps, that perfect elegance and simplicity which distinguishes the *best* writers, but she evidently *feels* deeply on the subject, and her book is calculated to awaken our deepest sympathies. I thank her for writing it. Hers must be a brave, true soul thus to surmount all obstacles, to soar above all the prejudices, which, from childhood must have been instilled into her mind, and take upon herself the defense of a down-trodden and degraded race! Recommenced Rollin's "Ancient History" which I intend to read regularly, and read several papers of the "Spectator." Committed some poetry to memory. A plan which I shall pursue, as my memory greatly needs strengthening. Mr. and Mrs. P. [utnam] spent the evening. Talked of forming a French class. Probably it will amount to nothing. I shall go on alone with both Latin and French—and *persevere*.

Monday, February 9.   Was glad to meet Miss R. [emond] and some of my other Normal friends, whom I have not seen for some time. This is the first day of their examination. Read with much interest the Hymns. Some of them, especially Miss Norton's and Lucy R.'s[,] are very good. Wrote to Aunt M. [argaretta]. Studied Latin, and read Whittier's new poem "The Last Walk in Autumn." It is exquisitely beautiful, and very characteristic.

Tuesday, February 10.   This afternoon went to Normal School Examination. The exercises were all interesting. Miss Norton's valedictory was *perfectly beautiful*. She is decidedly a *genius*. Met many old friends and school mates. Spent a delightful evening with them at the Hall.

Wednesday, February 11.   Studied Latin before school. This afternoon went shopping with Sarah, and paid a few visits. Night—Have just returned from hearing R. [alph] W. [aldo] Emerson.—Subject "Works and Days" from Hesiod's poem—One of the most beautiful and eloquent lectures I ever heard. The lecturer spoke particularly of the preciousness of time, the too often unappreciated worth of a *day*. We *must live* in the *Present* rather than in the Past and Future, for the *present hour* alone is ours. *Now* we must *act—now* we must *enjoy*. Eternity is boundless,—yet the *present hour* is worth the whole of it. He spoke of the great superiority of *character* over *talent*, and illustrated by an old Grecian fable so beautiful that I must remember it. "Apollo challenged Jove to shoot at a great distance. Mars shook the lots together in his helmet, and it fell to Phoebus to have the first shot. He drew his bow, and his arrow flew into the far West. Jove, at a single stride, cleared the whole distance, and asked, "Where shall I shoot, I see no space over which the arrow may fly." The victory was given to Jove who had not shot a single arrow. Most beautifully did the poet philosopher speak of the earth and sky in many figures, the most beautiful of which was, I think, this—"The earth is a cup of which the sky is the cover, in which is contained the glorious bounty of Nature." Very many other eloquent and beautiful expressions I heard from those eloquent lips, but I vainly try to recall them. But the impression made on my mind will be a lasting one. I have felt strengthened in all earnest and noble purposes since hearing that lecture. Never, never before have I so forcibly felt the *preciousness* of time. And oh, how deeply do the words and the presence of such a man as Emerson, make us feel the utter insignificance, the great inferiority of *our-selves*. 'Tis a sad lesson, but a most *salutary* one, for who, while earnestly feeling that *he is* nothing, *knows* nothing, comparatively, will not strive with all his might to *know* and to be something? Poets and philosophers! the great, the gifted of the earth. I thank you for teaching me this lesson—so sad, so humbling, yet so truly useful and ennobling!

Thursday, February 12. Rose very early and studied French. After school assisted Sarah [Cassey Smith] with her sewing; then read aloud in the "Living Age." "The Young Girl's Story," a simple, yet exquisitely beautiful tale from "Eliza

Cook's Journal." Studied French again. Mr. and Mrs. P.[utnam] called.

Friday, February 13.   Studied Latin and French—This evening went to a spiritual meeting.[8] A rapping medium was present. Many very satisfactory answers were given,—satisfactory because they showed almost conclusively that there was no imposture. But I cannot think there is a spiritual agency. Still I am open to conviction.

Saturday, February 14.   A lovely day, almost a May day. Had a delightful walk and visit to my dear Miss S.[hepard] who lent me "Margaret Maitland." Commenced it this evening after sewing for S.[arah] and studying French. Think I shall like it exceedingly.

Sunday, February 15.   Finished "Margaret Maitland," a charming story by the author of "Meekland." Wrote to Annie [Woods Webb], Helen A.[lexander?] and Miss R.[emond]. Spent the evening at Mrs. P.[utnam]'s. Mr. P.[utnam] entertained us by telling us about his travels in England and France. We felt all quite excited, and eager to go. I *fear I* never shall! But Oh, how earnestly do I long to do so. I *must*, I *will* go, some day!

Monday, February 16.   After school studied French and recited a lesson to Mrs. [Caroline] P.[utnam] while Mr. [Joseph] P.[utnam] and S.[arah] played chess. Afterwards committed to memory a portion of Whittier's exquisite poem.

Tuesday, February 17.   Our society met at Mrs. [Amy] Ives. Had a very pleasant meeting. Miss Chase and I talked about Mr. [James Freeman] Clarke's book. She and Mrs. V. are the most interesting people, to me, in our very small society. Read Rollin's "Ancient History."—S.[arah] had a strange letter from Mr. [Charles Lenox] R.[emond].

Wednesday, February 18.   Went with Miss S.[hepard] to

Mrs. Putnam's store. Looked over a very fine Physical Geography, which I should like to study. Miss S. [hepard] read Whittier's poem, while I wove. Spent the evening at Mrs. P. [utnam]'s studying French and reading "Household Words" while Sarah [Cassey] S. [mith] and Mr. P. [utnam] played chess.

Thursday, February 19. Was much shocked, while on my way to school, by hearing that one of our scholars,—one of the best and brightest,—a beautiful boy,—had been accidentally drowned. It has thrown a gloom over the whole school. Went this afternoon, to his funeral, with the other teachers and scholars.—Mr. [L. F.] W. [arren] [9] wrote a beautiful hymn, which they sung around his grave.

Paid Miss Chase a short visit, and enjoyed it exceedingly. She is *very* pleasant and kind. Had a delightful conversation with her. She lent me Miss Mitford's "Recollections of a Literary Life," which I've long wanted to read.—On returning home, found a ticket for Mr. Alger's lecture. It was "A Parallel between the *Ancient* and *Modern* Chivalry," one of the finest lectures I have ever heard. The lecturer spoke in high terms of the many noble qualities which adorned the knighthood of the ancient time;—was most eloquent and enthusiastic in his praise of those brave old chevaliers, more than one of which was *"sans peur et sans reproche."* Then he spoke earnestly and beautifully of the chivalry of the modern time, of which such philanthropists as Elizabeth Fry, and Howard and Miss Nightingale, are the worthy representatives; and paid an exquisitely beautiful tribute to Mrs. Stowe. He concluded most eloquently by urging all to cultivate those high and noble qualities,—to strengthen those lofty aims which should make them as pure, as high-souled and blameless in the *moral* chivalry of our nineteenth century as were the ancient knights in their martial chivalry of five hundred years ago. This lecture, next to Emerson's, I place in my list of rich and rare "mental feasts."

Friday, February 20. Attended school as usual.—Spent most of the evening alone, reading Miss Mitford's charming book. I like it exceedingly. And I like particularly the depth and enthusiastic attachment to my beloved "priestess of poetry,"—Mrs. Browning.

Saturday, February 21. Assisted Mrs. P.[utnam] in the afternoon. Played chess with her in the evening, and wrote to Aunt M.[argaretta]. Found a note from Miss Chamberlain, inviting me to a meeting of Normalities relative to our holding a convention. Felt quite sorry that I could not attend.

Sunday, February 22. Dined with Mr. and Mrs. P.[utnam]. Addie [Putnam] and her mother have arrived. A.[ddie] looks better than I expected to see her. Studied French. Attended the last lecture of our course, by Mr. Higginson; on "Kansas and the Union." The latter part of it was excellent, though very much the same as I had heard him give at the January meetings. Read Miss Mitford's delightful "Recollections," this evening.

Monday, February 23. Studied French in the morning. Attended school as usual. In the evening went to a Promenade Concert by the Germania Band. The hall was beautifully decorated with flags and flowers, and the music was not inspiring. Had never attended such a concert before and thought it a beautiful sight. Found on my return home, that Mr. [Charles Lenox] R.[emond] has arrived. We were not surprised.

Tuesday, February 24. Saw Miss [Sarah Parker] R.[emond] who looks very well, and is delighted with her tour.[10] Went to our Society meeting at Mrs. Rowditch's.

Read Miss Mitford. Played chess with S. [arah Cassey Smith] and actually checkmated her!

Wednesday, February 25. Paid Addie [Putnam] a visit. She is not so well. Went to see Mrs. Russell. Had a very pleasant visit looking at her beautiful plants and books. She very kindly offered to assist me in French. An offer that I gladly accepted. Feel sorry that *Brownie*[11] has gone. Heard Lowell's lecture on "Dante." It is *very* beautiful. Enjoyed it perfectly. Must read the "Inferno" now. He says that when he opens it, the gates of earth close behind him, and he communes with saints and angels. I liked particularly his saying that "all great poets are necessarily somewhat *provincial*; nothing, that has not had a *living experience*, can have a living expression." For Dante he has an enthusiastic admiration; and most beautifully, as only a true *poet can* speak, did he speak of the nobility of his life—a life which great suffering continued to purify and ennoble,—sustained by a constant faith in God;—sublime trust in His power and goodness. Then he spoke of the high and noble influence which the *human* love of Beatrice, exorted upon him; leading him ever higher and higher to a full appreciation of *Divine* love. Dante, he says, was a *true* poet,—and a highly imaginative one. Not only, may it be said of him that he represents Italy, but almost that he *is* Italy.—This beautiful lecture I cannot place below Emerson's. It is almost too much happiness to have heard both.

Thursday, February 26. Studied French. Spent the evening at Miss R. [emond]'s listening with much pleasure to her animated and interesting account of her lecturing tour; her visit to Niagara, now in all its glorious winter beauty; to Montreal and other interesting places. Read Miss Mitford. Had a nice letter from Hattie [Purvis].

Friday, February 27.   Went with Lizzie C.[hurch] to return Miss Manning's books. This is a very pleasant home; with beautiful books, plants, and fine engravings, one— "Milton at the Age of Twelve," is exquisitely beautiful. I never saw so perfectly angelic a face. I can never forget it— *never;* and *wish* I had it,—I *can't help* wishing so. Lizzie and I had a pleasant talk about our favorite books. Preeminent, of course, is our beloved Mrs. Browning. L.[izzie] thoroughly appreciates the beautiful. She is a lovely girl.—Read a most ridiculous slave holder's letter, which Mr. R.[emond] has. I wonder if this blundering epistle is a fair sample of the productions of the Southern *chivalry*. Am inclined to think it is. 'Tis horrible, horrible to think that such as *these* have uncontrolled dominion over hundreds of their fellow men! When, oh when, will these things cease! Will they *ever* cease? I sometimes ask myself. They *will;*—I do not, *cannot* doubt that God is just, therefore know they will.

Saturday, February 28.   Read in "Harper's" a very interesting account of the "Massacre of St. Bartholomew," by Abbott—the most interesting I've ever read. Most startlingly does it reveal the horrible wickedness and treachery of the notorious Catherine de Medicis. We shrink with horror from one so infamous. It seems as if she were hardly a human being.

S.[arah] and I took our work and spent the afternoon very pleasantly with Mrs. P.[utnam] and her daughters.—In the evening read Tennyson, and played whist, while S.[arah] and Mr. P.[utnam] (with whom she is a great favorite), played chess.—Sat. Night.—and now we must bid thee farewell, old Winter, with thy "aged locks"; and to-morrow we will welcome in not the "delicate-footed May" but stern and blustering March, the war-god's chosen attendant. Ne'er the less, as he ushers in the Spring, we'll greet him gladly, even though his aspect be most lion-like.—I've felt terribly home-sick lately—I know not why, but this longing to see the few dear faces, to hear the kind voices of home is at times almost uncontrollable. Hattie [Purvis] thinks grandmother [Forten] [12] doesn't look so well, and it is plain to see that she is growing old. This makes me feel very anxious. I *wish* I could see her, and Oh! I wish most earnestly that I could have averted the sorrow and fatigue she has lately endured. But it could not be. I can only give her my love and grateful sympathy. How delightful it would be to be able to do all we wish for those we love! This must be *one* source of *true* happiness.

Sunday, March. Read the delightful "Recollections," and learned several poems, among them the exquisite serenade in "Maud," of which Lowell says, "when Tennyson sings his 'Come into the garden, Maud,' every lover feels that he has helped him to write it, and every maiden thinks he has betrayed the reason her shoes were wet with dew the night before." Certainly it is one of the rarest and most beautiful of poetical gems.—was surprised by a visit from Mr. L. [enox?] who came last night. Sallie [Cassey Smith] and I went to see Mrs. [Nancy] S. [hearman] [13] awhile.

Afterwards we read and recited poetry during the whole evening. Have been cheerful within,—without 'tis rather gloomy for the first day of spring.

Monday, March 2. A terribly stormy day.—Had double school. Mr. L. [enox?] called. Accomplished considerable sewing, thanks to his visit, which interrupted my French lesson. Played whist all the evening. Had a little note from Miss S. [hepard]. We greatly regret that we cannot hear Dr. Cheever.

Tuesday, March 3.—Our society met at Mrs. H.[ey-wood?]'s whose house, as is often the case[,] is much more elegant than its mistress. It contains some fine pictures. Received a letter from Aunt M.[argaretta] who also happens to be reading the "Recollections." She admires, particularly, as I do, the chapter on "Authors Associated with Places." Mrs. C.[aroline] P.[utnam] and S.[arah] I think speak rather slightingly of Mrs. R.[ussell]'s ability to assist me in French. But as they do not know her, I don't feel troubled about it. Only I wish people wouldn't say little unpleasant things when they might just as well be left unsaid. Mrs. P.[utnam] has a real gift for such sayings.—Had a long talk with my dear friend Mrs. [Jane] P.[utnam], Sr., about her taking us to board. I think she will consent to do so if she possibly can. Hear that Dr. [George] C.[heever's] lecture was excellent; very radical. 'Twas continued to-night. *Very* sorry that I did not know until too late.

Wednesday, March 4.   After school went to Mr. Russell's. Had a delightful visit. Mr. Russell showed me a very valuable book of splendid engravings from the architecture of the Vatican and other palaces and cathedrals of Rome. How magnificent and how wonderful are those carvings in stone,—the masterpieces of art.—some of them the work of centuries;—all of that great antiquity which has so potent a charm for us;—leading us back from the real and practical Present, through the glorious haunted visits of the ideal Past.

Spent the evening at Mrs. [Jane] P.[utnam]'s, listening again with pleasure to Addie [Putnam]'s delightful music.

Thursday, March 5.   Miss Upton spoke very kindly about the lost volume. Feel exceedingly obliged to her. But should not have been able to meet her could I not have replaced it.

Though very wealthy and high in station, she is perfectly gentle and unassuming, and assured me that she is deeply interested in anti-slavery. Read Miss Mitford, and commenced "Aurora Leigh." Miss [Sarah Parker] R.[emond] spends the night here.

Friday, March 6. Last night Miss R.[emond] entertained me with an account of her tour, and of the delightful day she spent with Mr. [Wendell] Phillips. S.[arah Cassey Smith] and Ellen S.[hearman] soon fell asleep, but I listened with most unwearied attention until the "small hours of the morn" stole upon us.

Well can I appreciate the glorious privilege (though I've never enjoyed it) of being on terms of intimacy with such a man. Am afraid much of envy stole into the pleasure with which I listened to Miss R.[emond]'s animated account, for the friendship of a great, a truly noble *genius* has, since childhood, been one of the most fondly cherished of my many dreams. It can never be realized. 'Tis folly to cherish it;— for *he* could give everything, while *I* can give nothing. "Princes must mate with princes."

Saturday, March 7. Spent the evening at Miss R.[emond]'s—S.[arah] and I went through Mrs. [Nancy?] R.[emond]'s nice little house, and had a long talk about taking it. I hope she will. 'Twould be delightful. Spent part of the afternoon with Sarah P.[itman?] who is quite sick. Am completely fascinated with "Aurora." Think it is perfectly beautiful, earnest, passionate, powerful, noble. More than ever do I love and reverence the richly gifted "priestess of poetry." I may never see her face;—but the thought of her makes my heart beat quicker, and I feel that she is indeed my *friend*. Every sublime and earnest thought (who can boast so many?) every gentle and loving word, which the world listens to and admires, seems written for *me* alone; and herein I suppose lies the poet's greatest power. Beloved friend! I have no words to express my love and admiration for thee, none! May thy sublime and noble nature strengthen me for life's labor! I cannot but believe it will.

Sunday, March 8.   Finished "Aurora." I think it one of the most beautiful books I've ever read. So full of earnest, powerful, beautiful thought. 'Tis a book that I shall want to read often, as one does all Mrs. Browning's poems. Beautiful as they all are, this, which she calls "her most mature work, and the one into which her highest convictions of Life and Art have entered," far exceeds them all.

Went, with Miss Anthony and some friends, to Gallows Hill. Spent the evening at Miss R.[emond]'s. Like Miss A.[nthony] very much indeed. She is a large-hearted, independent woman. Was very kind to me. My dear friend Miss S.[hepard] called for me to go to the Grove. Our walk was a very pleasant, though somewhat sad one. She read some of Whittier's "Questions of Life," full of the perfect beauty, humility and faith which characterize the noble poet.

Monday, March 9.   After school stopped at Mrs. P.[utnam]'s, Sr., a little while. This evening studied French and wrote to Aunt M.[argaretta] while S.[arah] and I were preparing to retire, we heard three loud, distinct raps. There was no accounting for them. I am inclined to think they were spiritual rappings.

Tuesday, March 10.   Our society met at Miss R.[emond]'s. Had a very pleasant meeting. Miss C.[hase] and I looked over Miss R.[emond]'s beautiful album, which contains contributions from the truly great and gifted. Read, wrote, and played chess.

Wednesday, March 11.   Stopped at the Normal and had a

long chat with Olive. Went with S.[arah] to call on Mrs.
R.[uth Remond]'s sister, a gentle, pleasant young lady from
Newport.[14] Went to Mrs. Mannings for some of Whittier's
books for my dear Miss S.[hepard] who is quite unwell. In
the evening read Miss Mitford, and studied French.

Thursday, March 12. Miss Mitford and French, as usual.
All the evening, while sewing, S.[arah] and I studied poetry—"The Prisoner of Chillon," full of grace and fire,—
which none but *he* could have written. What a gallant,
chivalrous knight *he* would have made! I long to read his life
of Lockhart.

Friday, March 13. After school, went to Mrs. P.[utnam]'s
and spent the evening. Read part of "Aurora Leigh" to them.
Every time I read it it seems more beautiful than before.
Coasted with A.[ddie] and Mr. P.[utnam] a while, but did
not feel well enough to enjoy it.

Have an unusually melancholy feeling to-night. Lonely
and home-sick,—longing for I know not what;—a very
foolish state of mind, I know, but still it has the mastery for
the present.—Mr. P.[utnam] rallied me on my "low spirits."
Tried to be cheerful, but came very near crying, which would
have been the silliest thing possible.

Saturday, March 14. Not feeling very well; spent the
afternoon at home studying French—The evening in finishing
Miss Mitford and reading Byron. Have enjoyed the "Recollections" very much. The style so graceful and pleasant.
The selections—all rich and beautiful. There is a large and
most delightful collection from the best poets.

Miss M.[itford], herself, one of the gifted ones, enjoyed
the friendship of many of the best writers, and choicest spirits
of the age.

Sunday, March 15. Spent the day at Mrs. [Cecelia]

B. [abcock]'s[,] the evening at Mrs. P. [utnam]'s, interesting Australian [*sic*] letters. Read "Fresh Gleamings."

Monday, March 16. Stopped at Sarah P. [itman?]'s as she and Lizzie were sitting down to tea in their cozy little Kitchen. They would have me take tea with them. We had a pleasant chat, as usual about favorite books and poets. In the evening played chess and studied French. Received a letter from Aunt S. [arah Purvis]. Poor W. [illiam Purvis] [15] is still very ill, 'tis feared hopelessly so. I am *very* sorry. Mr. [Charles Lenox] R. [emond] goes to Penn. [sylvania] this week. When any one goes home from here I have a woeful attack of home sickness. Feel quite rejoiced that S. [arah Cassey Smith] has at last made the long-desired arrangement with Mr. [Charles Lenox] R. [emond] so I board with *her* now, not with him.

Tuesday, March 17. On my return from school, was delighted and surprised to find a *very* kind and characteristic letter from Miss [Harriet] Martineau. I thank her *very* much for it. 'Twas forwarded by Mrs. [Maria W.] Chapman. [16] Of course I shall always prize it very highly.

Wednesday, March 18. Studied French, and wrote several letters. Spent the afternoon and evening at Mrs. [Cecelia] B. [abock]'s "sewing bee." Quite a large number was present. We had quite a pleasant time.

Thursday, March 19. Had double school, and so the pleasure of spending the afternoon home with S. [arah]. Had a nice time, talking, studying French, and committing to memory the "Prisoner of Chillon." This evening were surprised by a "surprise Party"—quite a large one. Wrote to Mrs. Chapman, and answered a most *icy* letter from Lizzie M. [agee] [17] who seems deeply offended with me for not writing oftener.—Sorry for it.

Friday, March 20. Wrote several French exercises before school. Took tea at Mrs. P.[utnam]'s. Afterwards Addie came over and played chess with me. S.[arah] tells me there has been a terrible "flaring up" between Miss S.[arah] P.[arker Remond] and her sister. She vows she will never enter the store. Such things are *very* unpleasant. Our society it so exceeding[ly] small, it does seem as if they might dwell in peace together. These constant dissensions between people with whom I necessarily come in close contact, are so *very* disagreeable, that I sometimes wish myself far away from Salem. Our once pleasant little circle is entirely broken up now.

Saturday, March 21. Not feeling well[,] stayed at home this afternoon. Did a little washing. Mr. [Joseph] P.[utnam] came in and played chess with me.—Studied French, read "Fresh Gleanings," and the last number, one of the most-deeply interesting of "Little Dorrit."—How beautiful, how wonderful are the writings of Dickens! Exciting us at one time, by their matchless wit,—their thorough exposition of the ludicrous, to most uncontrollable merriment;—again sub-duing us to tears by their touching tenderness and pathos. In this last chapter his description of Mr. Dorrit's last illness and Amy's untiring devotion is *very* beautiful and touching.

Sunday, March 22. As usual read, wrote and studied. S.[arah Cassey Smith] and I went to the Groves. Hard, hard indeed it is to realize that our beloved friend, who one short year ago was with us, is now slumbering there. Spent the evening at Miss Maritchie [Remond]'s.[18] Had some excellent singing from Miss [Susan] Rice and Ellen S.[hearman]. Very sweetly they sang my two favorites "What is home without a mother?" and "Good News from home."

Monday, March 23. Read some passages in "Aurora"

which I wish very much to have explained to me. I wish it were mine so that I could mark them. The book has perfectly bewitched me. Studied French, read Ik Marvel's "Fresh Gleanings," and did wonders in the sewing line while Mr. P.[utnam] and S.[arah] played chess, which I also am beginning to be much interested in.

Tuesday, March 24. Went to the society at Mrs. [Amy] Ives'. Afterwards discussed poetry and poets,—Tennyson and Burns with Mr. P.[utnam]. He does not like T.[ennyson] but is a great admirer of B.[urns] and has promised to lend me his life and works. Received a letter from E. M.

Wednesday, March 25. Spent the afternoon and most of the evening at home busily sewing. In the evening wrote and studied a little. Mrs. J.[ane?] P.[utnam?] was here, and in rather a disagreeable mood, I think. She is not one of my favorites, nor indeed am I one of hers. (I could never be intimate with her).

Thursday, March 26. Lizzie C.[hurch] and S.[arah] D.[alton?] called to see me. Spent the evening at Mrs. Shearman's. Played whist with S.[arah], Mrs. G.[illiard] and Mr. N.[ell] who had just arrived. These little "sociables" are in honor of Miss Rice, I suppose. I'll be glad when they are over, for I need the time for reading and study.

Friday, March 27. Spent the evening at Mrs. P.[utnam]'s. Danced—the first time for a great while. This will be the last of our unusual "dissipations." I'm not sorry, for I *need* all the time I can get. Received through Mr. Edwards a little book on "Scenery" from Prof. Crosby, to whose kindness I am much obliged. It contains some very beautiful and useful thoughts.

Saturday, March 28. Our friend, Mr. N.[ell] to our surprise, left this morning.—Lizzie C.[hurch] and S.[arah]

P. [itman?] came in this morning. L. [izzie] says our ever kind friend Miss L. proposes to give us French lessons. I shall be delighted.—Felt unwell and spent the afternoon and evening at home, reading and studying. Mr. P. [utnam] has very kindly invited me to go to Boston tomorrow, and hear Mr. [Wendell] Phillips at Music Hall. I *hate* to be under obligations to any one, but *this* temptation could not be resisted.

Sunday, March 29. Went very early this morning to Boston with Mr. and Mrs. P. [utnam] and S. [arah] and Miss R. [emond]. Before we left Salem, our conveyance broke down; but we soon obtained a better one, and had quite a pleasant ride. Mr. [Wendell] Phillips, who preached for Mr. [Theodore] Parker (who is ill) was, I thought, almost *sublime* in his eloquence. Truly may he be called, like Herodes of old, *the tongue of our* Athens. Every time I hear him, I like him better, admire him more. This *sermon* was truly *very* beautiful. The music and singing I thought very fine; Went to Mrs. Lockley's. Mary and I took a walk on the Common, and saw some beautiful flowers in the greenhouses. How delightful it is to see flowers now, when there are around us only the "bare woods with outstretched hands," and the bleak, brown hills. In the evening our party, except myself, went to the concert—"Thalang's." Read one of Mrs. Stephens' charming stories, most of which are so superior to magazine tales generally;—and commenced a very interesting book—"Ruins of Ancient Cities."

Monday, March 30. Started from Boston at six.—Lost our road, and, after leaving Lynn, and riding for miles along a beautiful road, completely skirted with fine evergreens, with occasional glimpses of the sea between,—found ourselves near Lynnfield on the road to Lowell. 'Twas provoking, for I wanted to reach home in time for school. But, finding it impossible, made myself as comfortable as possible. Breakfasted at Lynnfield, and after spending some time there to rest our *cheval*, rode leisurely home to Salem. The ride would have been delightful,—I should have enjoyed it perfectly; had not the thought of school disturbed me.

Night. Feel *terribly* depressed. Think of our wrongs, and Oh! the *indifference* of many of us to them. It is *dreadful*. I dare not trust my mind to dwell upon it.

Tuesday, March 31. At last received a letter from Aunt M. [argaretta]. W. [illiam Purvis] is better. Went to see my dear Miss S. [hepard] whom I'd not seen for some time. How very interesting and lovable she is! It is *always* a real *refreshment* and pleasure to meet her.

Our society met at Miss Chase's. Stopped at Mrs. P. [utnam]'s Sr., a little while. Studied French.

Wednesday, April 1. This afternoon went to the Normal School. Saw Lucy R. for the first time since school commenced. Am grieved to hear that my kind and loved friend Miss R. is not well. Fear that earnest, ardent spirit is wearing out the body.—Played chess with Mr. P. [utnam]. Thought Miss R. seemed unusually depressed; she seems to feel herself neglected by L.—very unjustly, I think. Commenced Prescott's "Philip the Second," very kindly lent me by Mrs. Chase. Mr. and Mrs. P. [utnam] supped here.

Thursday, April 2. After school purchased "Fasquelle" and began studying it.—Wrote to father; played chess with Mrs. P. [utnam] and read "Philip the Second" which commences to interest me greatly.

Friday, April 3. Saw my dear Miss R.[emond] a few minutes. Spent the evening alone, studying French and reading "Philip." Also finished committing to mem.[ory] "Prisoner of Chillon."

Saturday, April 4. Took a delightful walk out Lafayette St. with Mrs. G.[illiard] and S.[arah]. Went into an exquisite little house in the style of an Italian villa;—from every window there is a beautiful view, far over the hills even out to the bay—with its blue waters and picturesque white sails. Was perfectly delighted. As usual Mr. and Mrs. P.[utnam] spent most of the evening with us. Mr. P.[utnam] and S.[arah] played and sang, while Mrs. P.[utnam] and I, busily knitting and sewing, listened and enjoyed. The old Scotch airs are my special favorites. I never tire of them; they recall to me my childhood's days, when I so often used to hear father, and Uncles W.[illiam] and T.[homas] [19] sing them.

Sunday, April 5. Another lonely day, and a long and pleasant walk in the pastures with S.[arah] and Mr. P.[utnam]—Looked in vain for the delicate yet brave Hepatica, but enjoyed perfectly the beauty of the hill, the mossgrown rocks,—the sky—the waters,—and the delicious songs of numberless little brooks, whose sparkling waters and picturesque windings gladden the eye, even as their music does the ear. Our walk was, indeed, a *delightful* one. Returned home, from the holy peace and beauty of Nature, to encounter quite a storm of passion from Mrs. [Caroline Remond] P.[utnam] and her sister, Miss [Sarah P.] R.[emond] who are always getting offended at trifles. I wish they *would* be more agreeable. But I'll say no more about it; not even to thee, my journal. We've formed a reading club;—and had our first meeting—this evening.—Commenced "The Queens of England." Though I've read them once, know I shall enjoy, and be benefitted by reading them again.—Read "Philip."

Monday, April 6.   Rain! rain! rain! *such* a storm! Rode home from school feeling quite unwell. Tried to read and study in vain. Spent most of the evening lying on the sofa listening to Sarah's music.

Tuesday, April 7.   Took a little French lesson, from my dear Miss S. [hepard]. Society met at our house,—quite a large and pleasant meeting. Mrs. Ives very kindly offered me a ticket for Mr. [Thomas] Stone's lectures. Am exceedingly obliged to her,—for I know I shall enjoy them. After the meeting, S. [arah] went to spend the night with Mrs. P. [utnam]. Sat up alone, studying French and writing, until quite late.

Wednesday, April 8.   A delightful day. After school, walked down town to escort S. [arah] home. Spent the afternoon at home—washing, sewing, and studying. Mrs. Russell was so good as to bring me a ticket for the Concert. Knowing that Sarah had never heard Mrs. Wentworth, persuaded her to take my ticket. This evening had a very interesting French lesson from my friend Miss S. [hepard]. Her society is always delightful to me. Read "Philip the Second."—Wrote to Aunt M. [argaretta].

Thursday, April 9.   Attended Mr. Stone's lecture on the "Drama." It was very interesting. The lecturer considered the drama principally in its connection with religion. He read some passages from Shakespeare. After the lecture, studied a French lesson, and gave Sarah one. Mr. P. [utnam] paid us a visit at noon. Greatly enjoyed his and S. [arah]'s music and singing. Miss R. [emond] spent the night here. As usual we lay awake till morning, talking about her lecturing experiences.—No letters!

Friday, April 10. Read "Phillip." Gave Mrs. P. [utnam] and S. [arah] [*sic*] who have almost exchanged their beloved chess for this more social amusement.

Saturday, April 11. One of the loveliest of days;—a *rare* day. This afternoon paid Lucy R. a visit. A very interesting girl,—'Tis always pleasant to see her. She told me of Lizzie Swan's death. Was much too shocked to hear of it. *Two* deaths in our class. She and poor Maria were friends. Soon they have followed each other to the better land. Both were fine scholars and excellent girls. M. [ary] S. [hepard] tells me that *Whittier* is coming. Paid Mrs. R. [uth] R. [emond] a visit. Little Celia B. [abcock] [20] and I had a delightful walk by the water, through Nauvro.—Spent the evening busily sewing.

Sunday, April 12. Another *rare* day. How delightful it is to hear the song of the Robins when one wakes in the morning. I *love* these spring mornings. The air is so pure, sky and earth are so beautiful. I could *live* out of doors. This is Easter, and my thoughts go back to my childish days, when Annie [Woods Webb] and I joyfully welcomed in the "feast of eggs." When we used to go to the Catholic Church and admire and enjoy, as children *do*, the beauty of its decorations,—the singing,—the incense, and the grand tones of the organ. And with these memories comes that of the dear, motherly face, whose kind, loving smile beamed on us day by day, making our lives better and happier. Beloved mother! *more* than mother to me;—I long to see thee again; thee and my *own* mother—the darling brother, *all* the loved ones who have gone before. Sometimes I feel that it will not be long,— not *very* long, ere we all meet again. How often it comes over me!—this longing for a mother's love,—a mother's care.

I *know* there is none other like it. 'Tis a selfish feeling, but I cannot *control* it.

Walked to Romewood with S. [arah] and Mr. P. [utnam]. 'Tis a beautiful place in the English style. Through some of the windows we could see magnificent rooms, with carved oak ceilings, and massive and elegant furniture. In the eve. [ning] our reading circle met at Mrs. Putnam's. There was more music than reading. Received Colman's very entertaining letters.

Monday, April 13. Rain poureth! Went to school and got thoroughly drenched. Sewed, read "Philip" and studied French.

Tuesday, April 14. Our friend Mr. N. [ell] sent us "John Halifax," which Aunt M. [argaretta] strongly urged me to read. Commenced it, and like it *exceedingly*. Mr. P. [utnam] and S. [arah] sang a beautiful song, "When the swallows homeward fly." Sewed and gave Mrs. P. [utnam] a French lesson.

Wednesday, April 15. "John Halifax" is, without exception, one of the best novels I have ever read. The hero is a nboel character,—no "perfect man sublime," but, a true high-souled friend, husband, father. "Nature's nobleman" in every sense of the word. The book is beautifully written,—by an English lady, I believe. Addie came and played chess with me. I was victor. Afterwards she played and sang charmingly for me. Spent the evening with Miss Remond.—To our great surprise who should walk in but Master Henry [Cassey]. We all sat up, talking till nearly midnight.

Thursday, April 16. Have holiday the rest of the week. Read "Philip," which greatly interests me, and wrote considerably before breakfast.—Fast Day.—Wrote to Brownie. Mr. Nell came in. Spent the evening very pleasantly at Mrs.

Putnam's. Took a walk with Mrs. P. [utnam] and Mrs. G. [illiard] to the Grove.—Friday, Miss Chase *very* kindly sent her carriage for me to go to Mr. Stone's lecture. *Very* sorry I could not.

Friday, April 17.   Mr. N. [ell] spent the day with us.— Did considerable sewing and more talking. In the afternoon Mr. and Mrs. P. [utnam] came in, and we had music and singing.—This evening played whist, and amused ourselves writing impromptus;—very comical most of them were. Had altogether, a very pleasant evening.

Saturday, April 18.   Studied French and sewed busily in the morn. Assisted Mrs. P. [utnam] this afternoon. Mr. P. [utnam] read to us the last number of "Little Dorrit." Called to thank Miss Chase for her kindness. Returned home, and found very joyfully—two letters,—one from Lizzie M. [agee] who is still in a most desponding mood, and a long letter from Cousin Robert [Purvis, Jr.]; the first I have ever received from him. It is very characteristic.—Felt grieved to hear that William [Purvis] is worse. Grandmother gives him up entirely, but his parents[21] still think that he may recover. God grant that it may be so! R. [obert] will visit Salem again this summer,—to "regain his health." We shall be very glad to see him.

Sunday, April 19.   The robin's song awoke me this morning. Lay awake a great while, musing as usual.—Spent the day at home. Read "Philip the Second." Commenced writing a story—subject "prejudice against color." Henry and Sis. [Sarah Cassey Smith] kindly interest themselves in it, and encourage me to go on. 'Twas commenced on the impulse of the moment. 'Tis not possible that it will ever be finished—or if finished, worth publishing. I'm *quite sure* it will not. Still am determined to write on; and trust to fate for its success.

Monday, April 20.   Attended Mrs. [Frances] Kemble's reading;—"Merchant of Venice." Was perfectly enchanted. Her power of voice is very wonderful—her power of expression scarcely less so. Rarely have I felt so excited. Wish I could attend her other readings, but 'tis impossible. *This* I shall never forget.

Tuesday, April 21.   Dreadful storm. Had double school. Sewed, read "Philip," studied French and Latin with H. [enry]. Received a letter from Aunt M. [argaretta].

Wednesday, April 22.   Read and studied in the morning. Mrs. G. [illiard] and Addie [Putnam] spent the afternoon and evening with us. 'Tis a real treat to hear A. [ddie]'s delightful music. She and I played several fine duets. How strange, how sweet, yet sad, is the power of music! It effects me greatly at times. Received a letter, and a package of "Home Journals" from Mr. Nell.

Thursday, April 23.   Had unusually bad lessons, and felt rather dispirited till this evening, when I went to Mr. Stone's lecture on the "Song." It was *very* beautiful—the noblest sentiments, finely expressed. It is delightful to hear such, when, as in this case, we know they come from the *heart* of the speaker,—that his *practice* ever accords with his teachings. He spoke of all the great poets from Chaucer to Tennyson, his idea was that the true "song" is an inspiration; this is particularly true of the sonnet;—and after alluding to the sonnets of Shakespeare, of Wordsworth, and other great poets, he concluded by paying a beautiful tribute to the sonnets of Jones Very, and quoted that really exquisite one—"Wilt thou not visit me?" The poet was present, and must have felt gratified at *such* a tribute from *such* a man. I hope these lectures will be published. I want to study them. Studied a long French lesson.

Friday, April 24. An uneventful day. Felt truly *grieved* that I could not hear Mrs. [Frances] Kemble. "Twas *pecuniarily* impossible. Wrote to Mr. N. [ell]. Studied French all the evening.

Saturday, April 25. After school assisted Mrs. P. [utnam] in the store. Am going to try to earn three dollars in four weeks, that I may go with my dear Miss R. [emond] to Bridgewater. Spent the evening at Miss R. [emond]'s sewing, while S. [arah] read to us some excellent letters from Mr. [Aaron] Powell and Miss [Susan B.] Anthony. I *love* to hear good letters.

Sunday, April 26. A *lovely* day. Had a delightful walk to Castle Hill with S. [arah] and Mr. P. [utnam]. Sky, hills, rocks, and streams—enchantingly beautiful. Spent the afternoon at home reading "Philip." Had a short visit from Addie and E. L. Old Mr. [John] R. [emond] [22] supped here. He's a peculiar person, *very.* Spent the evening with S. [arah] at Mrs. P. [utnam]'s. Mr. P. [utnam] read to us the last number of "Little Dorrit." Deeply interesting, but *very* sad.

Monday, April 27. Took an early walk at five, in the Pastures, with Sarah P. [itman?]. Found a few Hepaticas. Made some pies, studied a little French and Latin; but feel too tired and unwell to accomplish much of anything this evening. Mr. and Mrs. P. [utnam] took tea with us. Never felt less like seeing company. To thee, my journal, however sad and weary I may be, I will always say a word—My faithful friend, my comfortee! Somehow thou seemest always to give me a mute consolation and sympathy. I *wish* I were not so selfish,—This loneliness, this despondency, it is all *selfishness.* Would that I could banish it forever! Received a very kind letter from Annie [Woods Webb].

Tuesday, April 28. Finished the last volume of "Philip"

which I've thoroughly enjoyed. Returned it to Miss Chase, and received the second volume. Assisted Henry [Cassey] with his Latin. Met with the Society at Mrs. Heywood's. Afterwards wrote a very long letter to Aunt M.[argaretta]. Felt quite communicative.

Wednesday, April 29.   Commenced second volume of "Philip," studied French, took a walk with Addie. Played chess with her nearly all the evening, she checkmated me constantly. Received a very kind notice from my dear Miss S.[hepard]. I can *never* repay her for all her goodness to my unworthy self. S.[arah] who had been to Boston, returned and gave me a glowing account of "Neighbor Jackwood," as performed at the Museum. I'm quite impatient to read the book.

Thursday, April 30.   Played ball at recess with the children. 'Tis fine exercise. This evening, Mr. [Thomas] Stone's lecture, "The Essay." 'Twas excellent, but not so interesting to me as the "Song." He spoke particularly of Bacon and Montaigne, with whom I am not familiar. I best appreciated and liked his allusion to Emerson the "poet philosopher," to whom he paid a beautiful and well deserved tribute. Mrs. [Amy] Ives lent me "Neighbor Jackwood." It does not interest me quite as much as I expected.

Friday, May 1.   A beautiful May-day. Went "Maying" in the "Pastures." Met several parties of girls with wreaths on their heads. They looked quite picturesque. Found few flowers but had, as usual, a most delightful walk. Came home, thoroughly tired; and finished "Neighbor Jackwood." It's radical and antislavery. I like very much. But in the book, generally, I am rather disappointed. Played a game of chess with Mr. P.[utnam] and checkmated him for the first time. Read "Philip" and some of Flood's most amusing

"Pugsley Papers." Went into the Normal School, saw Lucy R. and Mr. [Richard] E. [dwards] who spoke to me most kindly. Played grace hoops some time with Olive B.

Saturday, May 2. Heard through Miss R. [emond] that poor W. [illiam Purvis] is growing worse. Fear there is no hope of his recovery. 'Tis very sad. Spent most of the afternoon at home, alone, sewing—and day-dreaming. Paid a short visit to Miss S. [hepard] who told me that I came very near getting a situation in her school, but it was found that I was "very popular in my district" and thought best not to remove me. I am glad if I do give general satisfaction, but I cannot help feeling grieved that I cannot be with Miss S. [hepard]. 'Twould make me very happy. This evening received some "Edinburgh Reviews" from Mr. N. [ell]. I shall enjoy reading them. A book of "Parlor Dramas" contains some good plays,—one of which "The Oddity" would be quite suitable for us as it has only one gentleman and several ladies.

Sunday, May 3. The loveliest day of the season. Had a delightful walk over to Mrs. B. [abcock]'s and spent most of the day there. My dear Miss R. [emond] paid me a visit. 'Twas delightful to see her. How very kind and lovable she is! Miss R. [emond] and Mr. and Mrs. [Caroline] P. [utnam] spent the evening here. Among other things we read a "Journey Due North[,]" an interesting paper from "Household Words," and discussed some of the "Parlor Dramas." Read my beloved Whittier's "Chapel of the Hermits."

Monday, May 4. A miserable day; came from school *very* weary, and found to my joyful surprise, a letter from father,—at last. He says he had written several times, and has not heard from me. 'Tis very strange. He thinks of going to

England or Scotland! If so, I shall go. But I must not anticipate it would be too delightful.

Tuesday, May 5. Studied French and sewed. Felt too unwell, this evening to go to the Society meeting. Spent the evening alone, dreaming.

Wednesday, May 6. After school went on the hills with some of my scholars, and found some violets;—the first I've seen this season. Beautiful violets! Very joyfully do I welcome them, and the delicate and fairly-like anemone. Gathered quite a bouquet of both, and took them to Miss S. [hepard]. I like to give flowers to one who so truly loves and appreciates them. Had a long talk with her about Antislavery. Beckie H. came in as I was leaving. She *does* interest me, though I know full well, on subjects of vital importance to me, there is little sympathy between us.

Thursday, May 7. Wrote to Cousin R. [obert Purvis]. Never, since I've been teaching, have my scholars done so miserably as they have this week. I feel almost utterly discouraged and miserable. I will not indulge the feeling, I *must* not. Sometimes I'm fairly desperate. Went to Mr. [Thomas] Stone's last lecture on the "Sermon." It was very fine! and made me feel better and happier. After he had concluded, a gentleman moved that the thanks of the audience be offered to Mr. Stone, for a series of lectures,—so beautiful and so instructive. It was unanimously adopted, and Mr. Stone's reply was most beautiful and touching.

Friday, May 8. School prospects do not brighten. I cannot fully enjoy even this delightful May weather. I am disappointed about Bridgewater, as Mr. Edwards gives vacation a week sooner. Tis too bad. In addition to other cares, a perfect *weight* of sewing presses upon me. Felt somewhat cheered by a pleasant walk, this evening, with Lucy R. and Sarah P. [itman?]. We walked by the water, in the light of a magnificent moon, now in the very fullness of its glory. Played chess with H. [enry Cassey].

Saturday, May 9. After school gathered some beautiful flowers on Gallows Hill,—violets and anemones—a quantity of them. Spent most of the afternoon at home, sewing. Took my flowers to Mrs. G. [illiard] who is quite unwell, and spent the evening with her. The view from their windows, of the water, rippling in the brilliant moonlight, was *beautiful, most beautiful.*

Sunday, May 10. Spent most of the day in constant and varied employment. The evening at Miss [Sarah Parker] R. [emond]'s reading a most delightful book—Mrs. Jamieson's "Characteristic of Woman."

Monday, May 11. Lizzie C. [hurch] sent me those beautiful lines which Miss Morton had, "A lovely day in the lap of May." Gave S. [arah] P. [itman?] a French lesson. Sewed busily.

Tuesday, May 12. Gathered some lovely flowers for Mrs. P. [utnam] at whose house the society met. S. [arah] came from Boston, bringing me a letter from dear Aunt M. [argaretta] forwarded by Mrs. Chew.[23] She sends me an excellent letter from Mrs. Martineau to grandfather [James Forten, Sr.],[24] on giving him her "Hour and the Man."

Wednesday, May 13. Gathered more flowers for Mrs. S. [hearman]. Spent the afternoon at home with S. [arah] busily engaged in sewing. Walked down town with her this evening. A lovely night. H. [enry] brought some exquisite anemones and columbines. Studied French and Latin with H. [enry]. Played chess with S. [arah] and,—checkmated her!

Thursday, May 14. Our friend Mrs. Chew came. Was

delighted to see her. She looks remarkably well. How strangely pleasant it is to see any one from home! She and S. [arah] and I have nice long talks together.

Friday, May 15. Weather still continues so stormy, so un-like May, that our friend can see none of the beauties of Salem. I regret it. Mr. and Mrs. P. [utnam] spent the evening with us. We had music and singing which Mrs. C. [hew] enjoys. She is a very kind person.

Saturday, May 16. Spent part of the afternoon in talking and sewing. The evening at Miss Remond's. Mr. P. [utnam] and I taught Mrs. C. [hew] to play whist. Felt quite unwell, and very stupid.

Sunday, May 17. Read "Philip"; took a walk with Mrs. C. [hew]. Spent the evening at Mrs. Putnam's, but felt too sick to enjoy myself; though the very excellent and spirited singing (all the old Methodists' Hymns being brought to life) did revive me a little.

Monday, May 18. Our friend left us today, and very lonesome we feel. Went through my school duties mechanically, and felt glad enough to come home and go to bed. Hope I shall not be imprudent enough to get such a cold again very soon.

Tuesday, May 19. Too unwell to attend school. Translated some Latin, did a little sewing, read Chambers' "Life and Works of Burns"; and played chess with Sarah.

Wednesday, May 20. Translated a little of "Marie, on L'Esclavage Aux Etats Unis" which Aunt M. [argaretta] sent me. Sarah P. [utnam] brought me Curtis's "Prue and I."

Thursday, May 21. Weather most dismal. Feel much troubled as I can get no one to teach for me. Read "Prue and I." Am rather disappointed in it. 'Tis dreamy and beautifully written, but does not seem to amount to much. Miss S. [hepard]

came to see me this evening, and read some passages from the "Life of Charlotte Bronte."

Friday, May 22. Felt better this morning. Translated some Latin and French. Lizzie C.[hurch] came in at noon, looking as sweet as an English rose;—bringing me a very kind note from Miss S.[hepard]. She also read some of "Charlotte Bronte" to me, and left me the book. It is very beautifully written, and, of course, deeply interesting. There is in it a portrait of Charlotte, a noble face—which the light of the soul beautifies. Just such a face as one might imagine Jane Eyre's. Played a game of chess with Addie, and *check-mated* her. Feel rather tired, and not so well to-night.

Saturday, May 23. My friends are very kind,—Miss S.[hepard] read "Charlotte Bronte" for me nearly all the afternoon. Mrs. G.[illiard] sent me cake and cologne by Ada, who played and sang for me. Wrote to Aunt M.[argaretta]. This has been a long, long dreary week to me. Rain and sickness.

Sunday, May 24. A lovely day—just as a May day ought to be. Am not strong enough to walk out. Had several visitors, among them Miss W.[eston] whom I was particularly glad to see, and Lucy R. whose loving presence cheered me greatly. Read "Philip," and finished "Charlotte Bronte" (1st vol.). What a noble life was hers. Poverty, illness; many other difficulties which would have seemed insurmountable to a less courageous spirit were nobly overcome by one, who was yet as gentle and loving as she was firm. Such a life inspires one with faith and hope and courage "to *do* and to *endure*." Read some excellent criticisms on different books, in some of the old "Edinburgh Reviews."

Monday, May 25. Rode down town and went with S.[arah] and Mr. [Joseph] P.[utnam] to see a launch, as I had never seen one. It is quite a pretty sight. We had a pleasant seat on some rocks projecting far into the water. Very beautiful the white sails looked in the distance, skimming over the blue waters of the bay; and occasionally a graceful little vessel came near us, cleaving the waves as she glided swiftly along. The delightful, ever welcome sea breeze greatly strengthened and refreshed me. Spent most of the day down town, reading and sewing. Feel much better.—Miss R.[emond] gave me some "Narcissi." How very pure and beautiful they are! Sewed and read Flood's, "Literary Reminiscences." They are very interesting. Received a kind note from Miss L.[enox?].[25] Wrote to her and H.[enry Cassey] took her some very beautiful wild flowers.

Wednesday, May 27. Went to Boston with S.[arah] and Mr. P.[utnam]. Attended the Anti-Slavery meetings all the day and evening. Many of the speeches were excellent. Our noble Garrison and Phillips spoke, as usual most eloquently. Mr. P.[utnam]'s evening speech was particularly fine, I thought. The Common is perfectly beautiful now. The young grass is a fresh bright green; the birds are singing among the delicate leaves, and the delicious music, the coolness, and the beauty of the fountain are the crowning glory of all. I enjoy them all perfectly, perfectly.

Thursday, May 28. Again attended the meetings most of the day and evening. In the afternoon visited some stores, and, saw several fine pictures. Two of them are particularly beautiful. "Shakespeare and his Contemporaries," and "Walter Scott and his Friends at Abbotsford." All the names are written out, and it is delightful to see grouped around the two great master minds, so many others among the noblest and most gifted at that age. Among the many fine faces around "The Wizard of the North" that of "Christopher

North" was particularly striking and noble, and Lockhart's by far the most classically beautiful. It reminded me of Byron's. Mr. [Wendell] Phillips, Mr. [William Lloyd] Garrison, and Mr. [Parker] Pillsbury were of course, the most deeply interesting speakers. Was very glad to meet Miss [Susan B.] Anthony. Like Mr. [Aaron] Powell very much indeed. Lizzie M. [agee] came to-day. She looks better. Also her friends Carrie W. [eston] and Miss M. They seem to be very pleasant and interesting people. Now that the pleasant excitement of the meeting is over, feel *very, very* tired.

Friday, May 29. Despite the rain, went with a large party to Mount Auburn. The ride through Cambridge was most delightful. How often I have longed to see the venerable old town. We saw Longfellow's house, once the headquarters of Washington. It has not the antiquated appearance which I had hoped and expected to see. How *could* the poet have had it renewed. How *could* he allow the traces of the honored hand of Time to be effaced. We could not see Lowell's house, only the noble old trees among which it is completely concealed. It must be truly a fitting home for a poet.

I have no words to describe the beauty of Mt. Auburn; and the glorious view from the observatory. I shall ever remember. It was a splendid picture, a blending of Nature and Art, in which, as ever, the hand of the Great Artist is by far the most visible and skillful. Deeply it is impressed upon my mind, and often it will come to me from the treasure house of Memory, to soothe and gladden me in the sorrowful hours of which I have too many, far too many for my own good, I fear. Carrie W. and all the party were much delighted. In the pleasant and luxurious horse-cars (a great improvement on omnibuses) we rode from Mt. Auburn to Watertown to visit the L. [enox]'s. Dined there, and went afterwards to Cushing's Garden, but just as we were entering it, a thunderstorm commenced, and we were obliged to return without seeing the beautiful flowers. Spent the evening at Watertown looking over some finely illustrated volumes of Shakespeare and playing whist. Sybil H.[inton?] is an intelligent girl. She reads much.

Saturday, May 30.   Returned home very weary. Received an invitation from Miss Upton to ride with her, Miss L. and L.[izzie] C.[hurch] to Wenham Lake. Felt very sorry that I could not go. Lizzie M.[agee], Carrie W.[eston] and Miss M. came; so we have quite a pleasant party now. The excitement makes me feel stronger and better. Mr. [William C.] N.[ell] has not come.

Sunday, May 31.   My friend Miss S.[hepard] brought me the second volume of "Charlotte Bronte." Commenced it, and read some of Mrs. Stowe's "Mayflower." Our usually quiet home is quite lively now. This afternoon went to Mrs. P.[utnam]'s. It was delightful. The water, the grass, the trees, looked beautiful. Took tea with Mrs. P.[utnam] Sr., while all the party went to walk except A.[ddie] and Helen.— Passed the evening very pleasantly at home, listening to Carrie W.[eston]'s lovely conversation; and Lizzie's really fine singing.

Monday, June 1.   Started for school this morning, but feeling very weak and tired, and finding that it did not commence until 9 o'clock, found some one to teach for me and returned home, where I shall stay a few days till I'm perfectly well. Have done little but rest to-day. Went to the doctor's this afternoon. He lent me "Two Years Ago," which I've long wanted to read. Spent the evening at home, reading it, while the rest of our household went to Miss R.[emond]'s.

Tuesday, June 2.   One of the rare days. Finished "Two

Years Ago." I like it much. There are some excellent things about slavery in it. Addie came over and we played chess. This afternoon was persuaded to go with our large party to Marblehead Beach. The ride there was delightful. Thought I had never seen the country look so beautiful. Our sparkling, winding Forest River called forth the admiration of the party. Arrived at the beach, we found the tide high. As usual, I enjoyed perfectly the grandeur of the Old Ocean, and sat long on the bold rocks watching the waves as they dashed furiously against them. All our party were much delighted. The ever welcome sea breeze strenghtened me for the time, but afterwards felt very, very tired. Came home, and found Mr. [William C.] N.[ell] and Mr. [William Wells] B.[rown] at the stage office. They and the P.[utnam]'s spent the evening with us.

Wednesday, June 3. Slept nearly all day. Read some in "Charlotte Bronte." Spent the evening at Mrs. P.[utnam]'s. Had quite a pleasant time though feeling rather tired. 'Twas pleasant to see the others enjoying themselves so much.

Thursday, June 4. As usual, after the least exertion, feel perfectly exhausted. Our agreeable guests left to-day. We miss them much, especially Carrie W.[eston] whom I like very much indeed. She is so very animated one could not help missing her. I shall be glad to correspond with her. Did little else but sleep all day. This evening my too kind friend Miss S.[hepard] came in, bringing some exquisite flowers and spent some time with me. It was so delightful to have her here. We talked about our noble, our beloved Whittier. She, with her usual self-sacrificing kindness and generosity wishes me to spend a few weeks in the country at her expense. But I feel as if I *ought* not to do it. I know how *she* feels about it. But it would not be just to her. I *know* that it would not be. We are going to talk it over again. I—so unworthy— am blest indeed, in having so very kind a friend. Her visit did me much good, and her beautiful flowers, with some exquisite lilies of the valley, the kind gift of Miss Manning, were most delightful companions for me all the evening. Flowers! blessed flowers! How dearly I love them! Truly "your voiceless lips, oh flowers! are living preachers." Many a noble and beautiful sermon ye preach for us. I can but thank you for the deep true pleasure you give me always, always.

Friday, June 5. Finished "Charlotte Bronte," a deeply interesting book, the record of a life so good, so noble, so pure, it cannot fail to do us some good. Had a nice letter from Hattie P.[urvis].—Read the "Head of the Family" by the author of "John Halifax." Like it even better, I think. Ada and Mrs. S.[hearman] spent most of the afternoon with me.

Saturday, June 6. Lizzie and S.[arah Cassey Smith] went with Mr. R.[emond] to Prov.[idence]. Wrote to Mrs. Cha[c]e. Felt very sorry that I could not go to see her. Was rather lonesome after they had all gone. Had two kind notes from Miss S.[hepard]. Read my beloved Whittier's "Songs of Labor." Mrs. G.[illiard] and her mother came to see me, also Miss W.[eston] who was very kind, and urged me to go home now, and not return to school till the fall. I wish I could do so. But it is pecuniarily impossible. Ada spends the night with me. Played chess with her all the evening.

Sunday, June 7. Dr. G. came, and examined my lungs. Advises me not to enter school again this summer. Shall be glad to rest if it can only be arranged so that I may have school again in the Fall. If it cannot be so, I know not what I *shall* do. Miss W. [eston], Miss S. [hepard] and Lucy R. have called and been very kind to me, but I shall feel *very* restless and excited until I know what arrangement can be made with regard to my school affairs. Feel that I would rather risk anything than give up my school entirely. Ada spends the day and night with me. Have tried vainly to read or compose my mind. It is utterly impossible. Went through a few pages of "Philip," then closed the book in despair. Received the "Mayflower."

Monday, June 8. Troubled and worried about school affairs. Have seen Mr. [L. F.] W. [arren] but know not exactly what arrangements will be made. Did a little packing.—Am *very,* very tired, and much excited. If I could only *rest* a little. But I cannot—Miss F. taught for me.

Tuesday, June 9. Mr. E. [dwards] came to see me this morning, and greatly relieved my mind. Think the arrangement I desire can be made. How much I owe to Mr. E. [dwards]'s kindness! My dear Miss S. [hepard] came in, and Lizzie C. [hurch]. Also Miss C. [hase] who wishes me to write a hymn for the Normal Convention. I cannot think of it now. Miss R. [emond] came up, and says S. [arah] will not be home till Thursday night. What shall I do without her. Getting ready tires me *dreadfully.* Miss R. [emond] gave me a ring. My friends are all kind, but I long for the quiet of home. My friend Mrs. [Helen] G. [illiard] is extremely kind. Went to Carltonville, probably for the last time before I go home.

Wednesday, June 10. A *rare* day. Walked down town, and rode home. Felt *very* tired. Saw Miss Chase, and bade her good-bye. Several of my scholars came and Sarah P. [itman?]. Commenced Mrs. Jamieson's "Diary of Ennuyee."—Several of my friends and scholars came to see me. Mrs. C.[aroline] P.[utnam] has determined to go with me. Am *very* glad. Rather dreaded to go alone.

Thursday, June 11.   To my great joy Lizzie and S.[arah Cassey Smith] came this morning. Am very, *very* tired packing, and bidding people good-bye. If it be clear tomorrow, this is the last day that I shall spend, (for some time) in New England, dear beautiful New England. Even to go home I shall leave it, not without regret. I shall miss the pure air of the hills, the long, pleasant country walks; but I shall see the dear faces, hear the kind voices of home! sweet home!

Friday, June 12.   Left Salem this morning. It is beautiful now; I cannot leave it without regret. Went to Boston with a large party. S.[arah], A.[ddie Putnam], Mr. and Mrs. [Joseph] P.[utnam]. Spent the morning at a daguerreotypist's. Before I left, Miss S.[hepard] gave me a beautiful locket with her hair and Lizzie C.[hurch]'s. I prize it very highly. Miss U.[pton] sent me a copy of Bryant's Poems in "blue and gold." Rested at Mrs. L.[ockley]'s till it was time to take the cars for Fall River. Our party with the addition of Mr. N.[ell] and Mr. L.[ockley] went with us to the cars. Felt particularly sorry to leave S.[arah]. Got into the invalid car, and had a pleasant ride to Fall River; sometimes reading, sometimes looking out of the window, as I lay on the soft cushions. But there is little worth seeing. We took the boat before dark, and had a delightful sail down the bay until we reached Newport; after that it became very rough, and we hastened to get in our berths. I was not sick, but did not dare to move a finger or even open my eyes lest I should be so. It was a peculiar feeling. Poor Mrs. P.[utnam] was very sick and did not close her eyes all night. Met Miss [Maria W.]

Chapman on the boat; who made herself very agreeable, to
my surprise.

  Saturday, June 13.   Rose before five and went on deck.
The sail past Long Island was beautiful. There was a glorious
sunshine. Was much interested in looking at the prisons and
the shipping. Wonder if Roslyn is near the shore of the
Sound. There were many find residences there, but none, I
thought, quite this as beautiful as Bryant's home. On arriving
at N.[ew] York, found no Mr. [George?] D.[owning?].²⁶
Fortunately we saw his son who took us to his father's who
soon came in. He, the most gallant of escorts[,] had actually
overslept himself. We plagued him considerably about it.
Georgie [Putnam]²⁷ came in. She is looking remarkably
well. Went with her to Mrs. L. Mrs. W.[illiams]²⁸ came
to see me. Thinks she will return with Mrs. P.[utnam]. Am
very glad on S.[arah]'s account. Took the cars in the afternoon. The ride from New York to Phila.[delphia] was very
tedious; the only thing that made it tolerable to me was that
we rode for miles past a canal. As I had never seen one
before, I was rather interested in watching the lazy boats.
They seemed to me a hundred years behind the age. Reached
home this evening. They were perfectly astonished to see us.
It is pleasant to be home again. *Bon nuit*—my journal!

  Phila[delphia]. Sunday, June 14.   Yes, it *is* pleasant to be
home, but how very, very different it is from my dear
N.[ew] England. The air is almost suffocating here. I miss
the pure air of our dear old hills. Spent the day at home,
resting. Wrote to L.[izzie Church] and Miss S.[hepard] and
read the charming "Diary of an Ennuyee." Mrs. P.[utnam]
and Aunt M.[argaretta] went to old Mr. Chew's funeral.
Was much shocked and surprised to hear of his death. Think

grandmother looks rather thin, but everyone and everybody seems very natural.

Monday, June 15.   Went out shopping this morning. This part of the city has not changed much, and is rather pleasant. Went to see Madame G. who was greatly surprised to see me. This afternoon went to the boat with Mrs. P.[utnam] and Aunt M.[argaretta] who are going to Aunt H.[arriet]'s. Saw Robert [Purvis, Jr.] who looks very well. Spent the evening at home, talking with grandmother.

Tuesday, June 16.   Spent most of the day at Mrs. Chew's. On my way there stopped at the Misses H.[opper?]'s. There was a general exclamation. Feel perfectly at home at Mrs. C.[hew]'s. The children have grown finely. Mr. C.[hew] and I were glad to meet each other. Read there a very interesting "Memoir of Shelley," and commenced Schiller's "Thirty Years War" which Mrs. C.[hew] lent me. Aunt H.[arriet] came down. Talked most of the evening; but finished it by communing with thee, my friend, *my* "Diary."

Wednesday, June 17.   Went to Byberry. On the boat met Miss Peabody,[29] and Mattie Griffiths,[30] the author of "Autobiography of a Female Slave." Miss P.[eabody] read to us an account of her last visit to Washington Allston. It was beautifully written and deeply interesting. Miss P.[eabody] is certainly a highly cultivated and intellectual woman. She converses finely.—We spent the day very pleasantly at Byberry. W.[illiam Purvis] looks very poorly. Hattie [Purvis] has greatly improved in *agreeableness* at least. With Mrs. P.[utnam] was a friend of hers, a Mrs. D. C., a N.[ew] E.[ngland] lady, very interesting and intelligent. To see and hear her, one would think that *she* and not Miss G.[riffiths] was the genius. The latter is a plain and unpretending young lady; but she is pleasant and I like her much. Miss P.[eabody]

was the principal talker. She gave us her spiritual experiences, which were really quite wonderful. Tacie T. [ownsend] [31] was there. She is a gentle lovely girl. We had a long conversation together about our favorite books. I hope I shall meet her again. We came down in the afternoon with Miss G. [riffiths] and Mrs. D. C. Our conversation was almost entirely about prejudice. The ladies expressed themselves very warmly against it. On reaching the city, Mrs. P. [utnam] and I were *refused* at two ice cream saloons, successively. Oh, how terribly I felt! Could say but few words. Mrs. P. [utnam] told one of the people some wholesome truths, which cannot be soon forgotten. It is dreadful! dreadful! I cannot stay in such a place. I long for N. [ew] E. [ngland].

Thursday, June 18. Mrs. P. [utnam] had a letter from Salem. They are all well. Mr. G. [illiard] [32] has arrived. Want very much to see him. Took a long walk this morning and saw many fine buildings. The Masonic Hall is particularly beautiful. Wrote to Mrs. P. [utnam] and Miss R. [emond]. Went out with Aunt M. [argaretta] and visited Miss J. [ames] and Mrs. C. [hew,] also went to Independence Hall. The old bell with its famous inscription, the mottoes, the relics, the pictures of the heroes of the Revolution—the *Saviours* of their country—what a mockery they all seemed, *here* where there breathes not a free man, black or white. This evening Ada [Putnam], Mrs. J. [ames] and Miss M. called. The latter, is as usual, a *wonderfully* quiet person. Saw cousin J. [oseph] [33] who is quite a young man. Read "Diary of an Ennuyee." The description of Rome with its palaces, its churches, its endless wonders and glories, is, I think, the finest I've ever read. It is full of beauty and poetry.

Thursday, June 18. Rain, rain constantly. I am sick of it. This morning rose early and found it pouring. Studied French and sewed busily. Visited Mrs. [Sarah] D. [ouglass]'s [34] school. It seems to be well conducted. Read the "Diary." The description of Naples is, if possible, more beautiful than that of Rome. Wrote a long letter to Helen A. [lexander?].

Friday, June 19.   Exceedingly stupid all day. Walked out, talked, read and wrote a little; that is all.

Saturday, June 20.   Went to Byberry with Mrs. P. [utnam] and Aunt H. [arriet]. Had a delightful sail up the river. The country looks beautifully now. It is so *very* pleasant to be on a farm.

Sunday, June 21.   This morning drove out in the pony wagon with Hattie and Mrs. P. [utnam]. The roads are so dreadfully bad, that before we had gone far we stuck fast in the mud and were obliged to turn back. Walked around admiring the beautiful flowers; read the "Correspondence between Goethe and Schiller"; then slept till it was time to go to Tacie. T. [ownsend]'s. Had very pleasant ride and visit. Mrs. T. [ownsend] is a handsome Quaker lady, and has a younger daughter who looks very much like Annie [Woods Webb]. Tacie was, as usual, *very* lovely. She has an excellent library,—a choice selection of the best poets. We looked over some fine pictures together, and found that our tastes agreed perfectly.

While we were there a terrible storm came up. The size and sound of the hail stones were really terrific. The streams we had to cross were much swollen, and seemed dangerous, but we got safely through, and reached home about nine o'clock.

Monday, June 22.   A delightful day. Jumped into the hay wagon drawn by two really handsome grey mules, and took a pleasant ride with Charley [Purvis]. [35] The air, so pure and refreshing, did me much good. Dearly, dearly do I love the country. I have named this Sycamore Lodge from the grand old tree. It is truly a charming place, within and without. Mr. [Robert] Purvis is most entertaining. We had a long talk with him today about the colored people and their wicked folly. It is really deplorable. They do nothing themselves, yet continually abuse their only friends. I am perfectly sick of them. Another terrible thunderstorm. Aunt H. [arriet] and Mrs. P. [utnam] went to bed while Hattie and I read.

Tuesday, June 23. Came to town this morning. Refused again in a salon. This place is totally hateful to me. Spent most of the day lying down, reading "Barnaby Rudge."

Wednesday, June 24. Visited Girard College. It is a very fine building, after the model of the Madeleine in Paris, it is said. The columns by which it is supported are very grand, and were imported from Italy at an immense cost. The lofty marble stair cases in the interior, impressed me particularly. The view from the top of the College is very fine and extensive. But, on contrasting it with the view from the Observatory at Mt. Auburn, I greatly missed the noble hills and picturesque winding river which give to the latter so much beauty and character.

Thursday, June 25. This morning, Mrs. P. [utnam] left. Her *attempt* at departure was a fitting *finale* to our pleasant adventures in this delectable city. She was refused admission to the car in which she wished to go, on the C. and O. Railroad, and was *ordered* to go in the "colored car," which she of course indignantly refused to do, and was obliged to return home and wait for the ten o'clock "Way Line," in which she met with no difficulty. I longed to return with her. I shall be better able to appreciate than ever the blessings we enjoy in N. [ew] England. Finished "Barnaby" and think it is the finest work of Dickens' that I have ever read. Have received several letters this week, from S. [arah Cassey Smith], Miss S. [hepard], and Helen A. [lexander?]. Commenced "Rienzi—the last of the Tribunes."

Friday, June 26.   Read "Rienzi," which is very exciting and gives one much information about the ancient history of Rome. But Oh! the degradation, the ingratitude of the Romans of the seventeenth century! It is truly dreadful, mournful to think how they had forgotten the glorious deeds, the heroic sacrifices of their illustrious ancestors. And to *him* in whom their spirit had survived how shamefully and dastardly ungrateful they were. This afternoon went to Aunt Sarah's. Their place is very pleasant, and with the elegant cultivation which distinguishes Aunt H. [arriet]'s would be far more beautiful. Fairview, it is called. The view is very pretty indeed.

Saturday, June 27.   Have had two delightful rides, and, being allowed to drive, enjoyed them perfectly. The country around is really beautiful. The children, [E]M. [ily] and S. [arah] [36] who came with us, are wild with delight—too wild to suit Aunt M. [argaretta]. I do enjoy rambling over the fields, picking fruit and flowers,—driving in the cows, making butter, and all the et-ceteras of summer country life. Have also been reading Mrs. Jamieson's "Beauties of the Court of Charles 2nd."

Sunday, June 28.   Last night was lovely. We sat on the piazza very late enjoying the delicious moonlight. Aunt S. [arah] and the girls singing very prettily. I do not enjoy "Beauties" as I did "The Diary." It is not the writer's fault, but the character of most of the famous "beauties." Nell Gwynn, Lady Castlemaine, and others, must ever be utterly distasteful to every pure-minded person. In the afternoon drove to Mrs. Lloyd's, who was glad to see me. The pleasant place looks much the same as of old, and recalled to me forcibly the many happy days I've spent there with Annie [Woods Webb] and Sarah [Cassey Smith].

Looking over Aunt Sarah's books I found Irving's "Tales of the Alhambra," and read for the first time the story of "the magic mat Whereon the Eastern lover sat." Now I am filled with a desire to visit Spain and the Alhambra. Shall I ever do so? I will *wait*.

Monday, June 29. Returned to the city. Found a letter from S. [arah Cassey Smith], Mrs. P. [utnam] had arrived safely, but without Mrs. W. [illiams]. Read "Bryant and the 'Thirty Years' War." Commenced Miss Mitford's "Rienzi," and wrote to Miss S. [hepard]. Also studied some French while sewing.

Tuesday, June 30. A dismal, rainy day. Studied French, read, wrote to Lizzie C. [hurch] and Addie [Putnam]. Heard from Annie [Woods Webb], who has been quite sick; and had a long and very entertaining letter from Mr. [Joseph] P. [utnam]. Commenced teaching Uncle W. [illiam] to play chess—with *pasteboard* chess-men, manufactured *impromptu*.

Wednesday, July 1. Went to Mrs. C. [hew]'s. On my way stopped at Mrs. B.'s and had quite a long chat with the girls. Mr. B. did not recognize me. Wrote several letters. Stayed all night at Mrs. C. [hew]'s. Uncle W. [illiam] came down and we made some more *impromptu* chess-men. Several visitors came in.

Thursday, July 2. A letter from my dear Miss [Sarah Parker] R. [emond]. She is better. Helped Mrs. C. [hew] sew; read; in the afternoon Mattie F. [arbeaux][37] came in. She is a lovely girl, and we spent a delightful evening. I gave the others a lesson in whist. They are apt scholars.

Friday, July 3. Still at Mrs. C. [hew]'s for it rains and

has done so every day this week. Had a letter from Sarah P. [itman?]. She very kindly promises to make all my pecuniary arrangements. Sewed very busily. Commenced Cunningham's "Lives of the Painter"; it is quite interesting. Uncle W. [illiam] came and brought a letter from Mrs. P. [utnam] Sr., also a "register" containing a full account of the funeral of Hon. S. C. Phillips, who was lost in the Montreal. A noble man is gone; one Salem could not afford to lose. Am much grieved to hear of this death. Mr. C. [hew], Lu, Uncle W. [illiam] and I played whist till the morning of the glorious "Fourth."

Saturday, July 4. The celebration of this day! What a mockery it is! My soul sickens of it. Am glad to see that the people are much less demonstrative in their mock patriotism than of old. Went marketing with Mrs. C. [hew]. Then returned home, and studied French, read, sewed; in the evening paid (with Sallie) Mrs. D. [ouglass] a visit, and had a very pleasant conversation with her and Grace [Douglass].

Sunday, July 5. At last, at last after hiding for a whole week the sun deigns to show us his face again. Right glad are we to see him. This is truly a perfect day. Mr. C. [hew] came and insisted on taking me to Broadbent's where I had an excellent likeness taken. Miss J. [ames] was there and showed me a daguerreotype of a young slave girl who escaped in a box. My heart was full as I gazed at it; full of admiration for the heroic girl, who risked *all* for freedom; full of indignation that in this boasted land of liberty such a thing *could* occur. Were she of any other nation her heroism would receive all due honor from these Americans, but *as it is*, there is not even a single spot in this broad land, where her rights can be protected,—not one. Only in the dominions of a *queen* is she free. How long, Oh! how long will this continue! Took a long, pleasant walk with Lu. Saw many beautiful houses and splendid churches;—if the number and magnificence of these last were any test of the *religion* of the *people*,—well, this would truly be "The City of Brotherly Love."

We paid a visit to Mrs. F.[,] a real southerner, very hospitable and pleasant,—to Mrs. D.[ouglass]. Stopped in several pretty "squares" to rest, and lastly visited Ada H.[inton]. Read "Lady Lu's Widowhood."

Monday, July 6. Finished "Lady Lu" which I like very much, sewed, and studied French. Spent the eve. with Aunt M.[argaretta] at Mrs. D.[ouglass]'s. She and Miss M. were very agreeable, and we had a really delightful evening. Talked of many things, but principally of our favorite books. Very pleasant it is to me to meet intelligent, well-educated people, with good literary tastes. Alas! among *us* they are too rare.

Tuesday, July 7. Read, studied, wrote to Mr. P.[utnam] and to Sarah P.[itman?]. Received letters from Hon. G.[errit] S.[mith],[38] Lizzie M.[agee], Sis,[39] and a very kind one from Mrs. E.[lizabeth] C.[hace][40] inviting me to spend a week with her. I will if it be possible. Spent the evening at Mrs. C.[hew] playing whist. Phoebus deigns to smile again.

Wednesday, July 8. Another lovely day. Aunt M.[argaretta] and I took a long walk. Stopped at the A.[nti] S.[lavery] Office. Mr. McK.[im] was very gracious and pleasant. Mr. [William] S.[till][41] with his most fascinating smile amazed me by asking, "Have you written any poetry lately?" I paused a moment, at a loss what to say;—then replied, "No, sir, I *never* wrote any," and turned away rather abruptly, to speak to some one else. I fear I must have appeared rude, but I couldn't help it. 'Twas such a queer question from him, a perfect stranger, to ask me. Received a letter from Ada

P.[utnam]. This evening had a pleasant visit from Mrs. J.[ames] and gentle Ada H.[inton].

Thursday, July 9. Read and sewed busily. This afternoon went to the Library and took out Lillian's "Travels in Europe." I went determined *not* to take a book of travels, for already the foreign fever burns high enough. But on opening the book, the magical names of places and people fascinated me, and I could not resist the temptation. It seems to be very interesting. I know I shall enjoy it.

Friday, July 10. Rose at four and took a long walk with Ada to Market Street Bridge from which we could see Fairmont, in all its quiet beauty, in the distance. A.[da] is a lovely girl. Wish I were half as good. We talked of many things, particularly of our much loved S. Mrs. C.[hew] and L.[u] came with an invitation from Mrs. [Sarah] D.[ouglass] which I *cannot* accept. It would be a positive infliction. Must excuse myself somehow. Aunt M.[argaretta] and I sewed busily while E.[liza] read to us. Friend B. called. I had quite a pleasant talk with him.

Saturday, July 11. Felt quite unwell. Read a letter, and sewed till I was sick of it. In the afternoon went to Aunt H.[arriet]'s.

Sunday, July 12. A lovely day,—pleasantly spent,—reading the "Liberator"—the excellent speeches, and Mr. [Wendell] Phillips' chef d'oeuvres. In the evening Miss B. sang beautifully for us. Poor W.[illiam Purvis] is not quite so well.

Monday, July 13. Aunt H.[arriet] went to town and left W.[illiam] under my care. Read "The Ogilivies," an interesting book by the author of "John Halifax." This evening drove to the boat for Aunt H.[arriet]. Came to the city this morning, and immediately left with Mrs. J.[ames] for Annie

[Woods Webb]'s. Anticipated a dismal ride through the sands of Jersey, but the weather was delightful, the roads excellent, and the stage not crowded; so we were pleasantly disappointed. Reached A.[nnie]'s near dark.

Wednesday, July 15. A.[nnie] has changed, has become much more matured and practical. She has two nice little girls.—The place is most dismal, surrounded by woods of dwarf oaks, and not a house within sight. 'Tis far too dreary for her. Had a long and pleasant talk with her. She is as loving and unselfish as ever.

Thursday, July 16. Almost melted by heat and devoured by mosquitoes. Did a little reading and sewing—much talking and idling. In the eve. walked with A.[nnie] and Mrs. J.[ames] to the nearest village,—about a mile distant. Very, very quiet it was; yet rather pleasant. I liked the perfect contrast with the tumult and confusion of the crowded city. Looked over some very old letters written by my dear, lost mother—years ago. As I read the words penned by that dear hand, a strange feeling of tenderness, of sadness, of *loneliness* came over me, and I could not refrain from tears. Dear, dear mother whom I have scarcely known, yet so warmly love;— who art now an angel in heaven,—my heart yearns for thee!

Friday, July 17. A record of one day is a record of all in this intensely quiet place. Last night I lay awake, thinking of my mother's letters. What a pure and noble character they reveal. She must indeed have been just such a being as I have always fondly imagined. Had a long farewell talk with dear Annie. I cannot but love the sister of that mother—so gentle and kind she has always been to me. I grieve to leave her in this dreary place. Mr. W.[ebb][42] is very pleasant to me.

Saturday, July 18. Had an early and rather dismal ride to town. Found a long and *very* entertaining letter from Mr.

[Joseph] P. [utnam]—'Tis a real pleasure to hear from him. In the afternoon took another journey to Trenton. On the way read "Visits in Europe." Had a warm welcome from the girls, and spent with them a quiet and pleasant evening.

Sunday, July 19.   Intensely hot day. Wrote a little and read Dickens' "Cricket on the Hearth," a charming story. In the evening S. [arah Purvis?][43] and I took a pleasant walk past the cottages, which with their grottoes and fountains are quite beautiful.

Monday, July 20.   Still terribly hot. Spent the morning in sewing and reading; the afternoon mostly in *sleeping.* Mr. P. [utnam] came and brought me a letter from dear S. [arah Cassey Smith]. This evening Mr. C. [hew], L. [u] and I took a delightful walk over the bridge to Morrisville, a beautiful little village. We stood long on the bridge looking down into the dark depths of the river, and listening to its music. In the distance the lights of the town gleamed through the darkness,—it was truly a picturesque scene.

Tuesday, July 21.   Met Mrs. C. [hew] and Aunt M. [argaretta] at the cars. They brought kind letters from Mrs. G. [illiard] and Miss S. [hepard]. This afternoon bade farewell to the kind and hospitable H. [opper?]'s.—Had a pleasant ride in the cars to Aunt S. [arah]'s. The country is delightful now; in the very fulness of summer beauty.

Wednesday, July 22.   Lovely morning rose very early; sewed and read; spent the afternoon very pleasantly at Mrs. S. [mith]'s. Drove Aunt S. [arah] and the children home in the evening.

Thursday, July 23.   Returned to town. Went with Aunt M. [argaretta] to bid Mad. [ame] G. farewell. She seemed much affected at leaving all her friends. But 'tis ever so— "Love's watchword is farewell."—Wrote to N. [ellie]

A. [lexander]. Had a long talk with grandmother about father. His behavior is very unaccountable;—very saddening to me.

Friday, July 24. After shopping with Aunt M. [argaretta], sewed busily till afternoon. Then went to Mrs. C. [hew]'s. Met sweet Mattie F. [arbeaux] whom I wish I could have seen more of. She has promised to correspond with me.— This eve. went to Parkinson's Garden. It was like fairy-land. Brilliant lights were gleaming among the trees, fountains were playing—the coolness was delicious. Under a graceful canopy was seated a full orchestra who played finely.—The audience had seats canopied only by the dark blue sky. A Scotch "lassie" sang "Macgregor's gathering" with great spirit. After the concert came splendid fire works. At one of these representing the "cross of the legion of honor" the band played the national air of France. It was most beautiful and inspiring. Altogether the scene was a most delightful and novel one to me.

Saturday, July 25. Had a letter from Miss S. [hepard]. Sewed busily.—Paid Mrs. C. [hew] a visit.—Am very, very tired.

Sunday, July 26. Busy packing. Uncle W. [illiam] read to me some of F. [rederick] Douglass'[44] best speeches;—very fine they were. I wish the man had a *heart* worthy of so great, so gifted a mind.

Monday, July 27. Shopped all the morning. Left for Byberry this afternoon. Arrived there thoroughly worn out. Spent ne'ertheless, a very pleasant evening.

Tuesday, July 28. Left Byberry this morning. Almost immediately on my return, bade everybody a last farewell. Poor W. [illiam], I think I shall never see him again. A long and tedious ride to New York. Went to Mrs. [James Mc-

Cune] S. [mith]'s[45] who gave me a warm welcome. I like her much. N. [ew] Y. [ork] is cleaner than when I was here before; but little pleasanter to me. Played chess with Jimmy S. [mith] all the evening, and was unusually successful.

Wednesday, July 29.   Conversed pleasantly with Mrs. [James McCune] S. [mith] all the morning. This afternoon called at Mrs. L.'s and went to Greenwood with H. [enry Cassey] and G. [eorgianna Putnam]. It is very, very beautiful. I cannot describe it now. Spent some time at Mr. [George] D. [owning]'s "saloon."

Thursday, July 30.   Pouring rain. Went with H. [enry] to N. [ellie] A. [lexander]'s school and got soaked. Saw dear N. [ellie] who does not look well. Mr. R. was very pleasant, as usual.—A prisoner in the house for the rest of the day. This evening Mr. W. called. Intelligent on some subjects,— ignorant of true Anti-slavery. I soon wearied of him.

Friday, July 31.   Returned to Mrs. S. [mith]'s. Left this afternoon in the boat with a very large party,—G. [eorgianna], H. [enry], R. [obert Purvis, Jr.] and N. [ellie] A. [lexander?], Mrs. J. [ames], and Mr. G[illiard?]. The day is lovely; the scenery on Long Island perfectly beautiful, and, with so very pleasant a party, I spent a delightful evening. The sunset was grand; and long after it we sat on deck in the gathering darkness, through which gleamed the lights of the shore and gazed at the water. I *felt a strange happiness.*

Newport. Saturday, August 1.   After a good rocking "in the cradle of the deep," reached Newport after three this morning. It was very dark as we drove through the town; and strange indeed it seemed to us, but we were soon established in a nice boarding house, and slept soundly till daylight. This part of Newport is certainly not very prepossessing; but I like its old-fashioned appearance. H. H. and I walked out on an exploring expedition, and discovered a very beautiful Catholic Church,—received permission to go in, and stood overwhelmed by the beauty, the splendor which burst upon us. The painted glass windows were the most splendid I ever saw; the stone arches, the organ so grand and imposing. It is very splendid. We stood a great while admiring it. There is something so impressive in such a building.

The girls and I walked to the Beach; it was not so fine, nor were there so many people there as I expected; but we were much amused seeing the bathers as they plunged with such hearty rest among the waves; of course I envied them, and longed for one, if only one nice bath in those clear bright waves. Then we walked to the rocks which are far less imposing in this part, at least, than those at Marblehead,— seated ourselves and looked out over the deep blue waters; the little bathing houses with their white roofs looked very prettily in the distance. The Beach presented a very gay appearance enlivened by splendid carriages and horses, equestrians, and bathers in every variety of costume.

Came home very tired and spent the afternoon in bed. This evening visited the D.[ownings]'s in their beautiful "Sea Girt House."[46] Wrote an apology for a Hymn.

Sunday, August 2. Perfectly delightful morning. Took a nice walk. The streets and houses in this part are not at all remarkable for their beauty. Returned home, read and wrote busily. This afternoon went to the "Sea Girt House" and saw the magnificent view from its summit—the view of the ocean. It was grand,—finer even than my favorite view from Mt. Auburn Obs.[ervatory]. We went to vespers in the Catholic Church. The organ is a splendid one, but the singing was poor. The effect of the rich solemn music stealing through that beautiful building, was singularly impressive; in perfect keeping with the grand stone arches, beautiful altars and statues, and exquisite stained windows. After tea, took a long walk on "The Island" past some beautiful houses, and finely kept grounds. Mrs. R. [uth] R. [emond] whom I was delighted to meet again, her father [Isaac Rice] and sister, accompanied us.[47] Our walk was perfectly delightful. We passed the famous "Ocean House," brilliantly lighted up, and looking very bright and cheerful. This sea air is delightful, it greatly strengthens me.

Monday, August 3. Another walk this morn, to the "Forty Steps[,]" a beautiful place. We sat upon the rocks which are very fine, but do not compare with those at Marblehead. Had a delightful time climbing the rocks, and wading in the water. Old Mr. R. [ice] was our escort, and a very pleasant one, too. This afternoon a delightful sail to the Fort. We walked around it on the top, enjoyng the fine view. It is a noble building. When we first entered we contrasted the perfect quiet which reigned around with the din and confusion which must have existed there in time of war, and almost fancied we could hear the thunder of the cannon and the sharp crack of the rifle resounding through the "Fort Adams" of the Revolution. Soon the stillness was broken by carriages' wheels, and in a little time the area enclosed within the walls was filled with splendid carriages of every description each bearing[,] of course, its burden of elegant ladies. I never saw such fine horses.—On the green in the center the Germania Band took their station, and played beautifully. The grand appearance of the Fort, the splendor and brilliancy of the vehicles and their occupants, the beauty of the music, altogether formed one of the most beautiful and picturesque scenes I ever enjoyed. I shall never forget it—nor the charming sail back to Newport. Just as the sun was setting, the water was so beautifully transparent. Spent the evening—our last in this lovely place—at Mrs. R.[uth] R.[emond]'s, listening to some fine singing.

Salem. Tuesday, August 4. Left N.[ewport] with regret;—had a very pleasant sail up the Bay to Prov.[idence]. Felt sorry we could see no more of the city, took the cars to Boston. Very, very pleasant it is to be in the dear Old Bay State again. Told the girls I felt brighter and better the moment I crossed the boundary line, they laughed at me, and wished to know *when* the moment was, which I couldn't exactly tell.—I am glad to be in Salem again. We slept nearly all the afternoon. This evening visited some of my friends and was warmly welcomed.

Wednesday, August 5. Terrible day for our Convention— rain pouring. Sorry my friends cannot attend. Rode to the school-house,—after the exercises there walked to Dr. E.'s Church and listened to the oration by Prof. Felton. Most of it was excellent; but there was one part—a tirade against *Spiritualism,* which I disliked exceedingly; it seemed to me very inappropriate and uncharitable. The dinner at the Bowditch School Room was excellent. Very good and amusing speeches were made, and everybody evidently enjoyed themselves greatly. Mr. E.[dwards] read M. O.'s very excellent and entertaining poem. The room was beautifully decorated with blue and white hangings, with evergreens woven into the names of Mann, Bowditch, Sears and other distinguished friends of education, with portraits of S. C. Phillips, J.[ohn] Q.[uincy] Adams, Sumner and others, and with exquisite bouquets of flowers. The effect was very beautiful indeed. In the evening the girls accompanied me to the Normal Lecture Room, to which the floral decorations had been removed. A large party was assembled; we had toasts and many amusing *impromptu* speeches, and enjoyed the evening very much.— There were fewer familiar faces than I had hoped; but it is very pleasant to see *them* again.

Thursday, August 6. Too tired to keep my engagement to dear Miss S.[hepard] with whom I long to have a talk. Afternoon and evening spent at a little musical party at Mrs. [Jane] P.[utnam]'s which I was too stupid to enjoy. Commenced "The Old Curiosity Shop."

Friday, August 7. A charming day—a day to be marked with a white stone. Spent it at Nahant. Took the cars to Lynn, and carriages from there to N.[ahant]. There were S.[arah], E.[llen?] H.[annah] R.[ice?]. G.[eorgianna], Mr. P.[utnam], Mr. N.[ell], and myself. The ride was perfectly beautiful—a splendid sea view on either side, part of the road shaded by fine trees. Nahant is delightful. The rocks are the most grand that I ever saw. H.[annah?] and I sat long on one completely overhanging the sea to whose wild music we listened reverently. I think that she, more than all the rest of our party[,] understood and sympathized with me. My cup of enjoyment was full. The girls sang beautiful and appropriate songs, songs of praise to glorious Old Ocean. Some of the bravest of us explored dangerous places, looked down with awe into fearful chasms, and felt a wild intoxicating delight in doing so,—at least *I* did. After some hours of perfect enjoyment—to me—left the grand old rocks—the mighty waves, and went towards the Hotel; played at Tenpins and even fired pistols. Our ride back to Lynn! *Can* I describe it? The sun was just setting or rather, near it. The sky was a mass of crimsom and gold, the sea a vast stream of silver, and this glorious picture we enjoyed during the whole ride. It was *too* beautiful. Came home in such high spirits as I seldom enjoy. Everything seemed glorified, transfigured for me—was a reproduction of the beauty and brightness we had seen. Spent some time with Miss S.[hepard] and had a long confidential talk with her about our beloved W.[hittier]. At home danced, and listened to singing this eve.

Saturday, August 8. Am deeply interested in Little Nell. The girls being all musical, and busily preparing for a Parlor Concert,—whereof I,—being unmusical, am to be assistant manager;—so we have music all day long. Quite a pleasant party this evening. Mr. N.[ell] came.

Sunday, August 9. Longed to spend the day in quiet, but as usual visitors came. Did some reading and writing—more *sleeping*, not feeling well, and in the eve. walked to D.[anvers] to hear my dear Mr. [William Lloyd] Garrison. 'Twas delightful to see his beloved face, to hear his familiar voice again, to feel the warm pressure of his hand, and the sudden strength and hopefulness which *his* presence always inspires, even in our weakest and most desponding moods. He spoke as usual, nobly and well, and tonight my heart is filled with thankfulness that God has given us so glorious a Pioneer.

Monday, August 10. I scarcely know myself tonight;—a great and sudden joy has completely dazzled—overpowered me. This evening Miss R.[emond] sent for me in haste saying a gentleman wished to see me. I went wondering who it *could* be, and found——[John Greenleaf] Whittier![48] one of the few men whom I truly reverence for their great minds and greater hearts. I cannot *say* all that I *felt*—even to *thee*, my Journal! I stood like one bewildered before the noble poet, whose kindly, earnest greeting *could* not increase my love and admiration for him;—my heart was full, but I *could* not speak, though constantly tormented by the thought that *he* would think me very stupid, very foolish;—but after a few simple words from him, I felt more at ease, and though

I still could say but very little, and left the talking in part to Miss R. [emond] who can *always talk*, it was such a pleasure to listen to *him*, to have *him* before me, to watch that noble, spiritual face, those glorious eyes—there are no eyes like them—that I felt *very very* happy.—The memory of this interview will be a life-long happiness to me. Shall I try to tell thee, my Journal, *something* of what he said? First we spoke of my old home and my present home. He asked me if I liked N. [ew] E. [ngland]—it was such a pleasure to tell him that I loved it. Well to see the approving smile, the sudden lighting of those earnest eyes! In comparing P. [ennsylvania] and N. [ew] E. [ngland] he spoke of the superior richness of the soil of the former, but said that here, though there were fewer and smaller farms, larger crops were raised on the same extent of ground, because vastly more labor and pains were bestowed upon its cultivation. Then I remembered that the poet was also a *farmer*. By some strange transition we got from *agriculture* to *spiritualism*. Whittier said that he too (having read them), thought that Professor F. [elton]'s views were most uncharitable. Though *he* cannot believe in it; he thinks it wrong and unjust to condemn all interested in it.—The transition of this subject to that of the "future life" was easy. I shall never forget how earnestly, how beautifully the poet expressed his *perfect faith*, that faith so evident in his writing, in his holy and consistent life.

At his request, I took him to see Miss S. [hepard]. The joy and surprise were almost more than she could bear. I stayed but a little while then left them together. The poet gave me a cordial invitation to visit him and his sister at their home. God bless him! This is a day to be marked with a white stone.

Tuesday, August 11.   Busy all day preparing for our Con-

cert, which came off this evening with considerable *éclat*.
The singers looked beautifully and sang beautifully, and were
much applauded. Dr. C. [heever] and Miss W. [eston] spent
a very pleasant evening. H. and C. A. are beautiful singers;
the former a very interesting and lovable girl. We shall be
sorry to part with them.

Wednesday, August 12.. Went with a large fishing party
to Lowell Island. The day was perfect, and though I caught
few fish, I greatly enjoyed myself. N. [ellie?] and I, weary
of fishing, wandered off and found a delightful *nook* among
the rocks, close to the water, and completely shaded by an
immense overhanging rock. There we ensconced ourselves,
listening to what the wild waves were saying, and conversing
so delightfully that I hated to leave the spot. I believe that
N. [ellie?] has the most perfect sympathy in most of my tastes
and feelings, and it is very pleasant for me to be with her. I
have so few to understand me—to give me their loving
sympathy. Miss W. [,] who is quite gifted, does not seem to
me particularly interesting. Perhaps I might not think so if
I knew her better. I thought I had never seen the water so
beautiful—such a deep, deep blue, studded by innumerable
little snowy sails. Dear Old Ocean! I love thee well. Thou
giv'st to me a strange feeling of happiness, of rest. Our sail
home was delightful. Mr. P. [utnam] and I read aloud, in
turn, some passages from the "Old Curiosity Shop," whose
mingled humor and pathos are truly wonderful—or would
be so if written by any other than the inimitable Dickens.
Spent the evening at Miss B. [abcock]'s. Came home thoroughly exhausted.

Thursday, August 13. Bored with company all day. Read
a little. Felt *dreadfully* stupid. C. and I ran over to Carltonville and had a pleasant chat. The sun was just setting, and

sky and water were beautiful in the fading glory. The gentlest of showers *dimpled* the face of the stream, then a glorious rainbow arched itself over the sky. It was beautiful, most beautiful. In the evening had some pleasant games. Greatly to our surprise, who should come in with the P.[utnam]'s but Mr. G.[illiard?] looking remarkably well. It was a great pleasure to me to see him again.

Friday, August 14. Hottest day of the season. Glad enough to stay quietly at home, though strongly persuaded to take a jaunt. Did a little writing and sewing, but devoted most of the day to reading the "Old Curiosity Shop," and finished it. 'Tis very, very beautiful. There could not be a lovelier, a nobler conception than Little Nell; and most of the other characters are, in their way, inimitable. Quilp is most unnatural; but there is a strange and frightful interest attached to the monster, throughout the book; and his horrible wickedness only shows forth in brilliant and beautiful contrast, the true nobility of such characters as Rit, the Garlands, etc., and the angelic goodness of darling Little Nell. I believe I think of Dickens' writings as of Mr. Phillips' speeches;—the last which I read, always seems to me the best;—at any rate, I give now to the "Old Curiosity Shop" the highest place in my admiration of the great author's works, of which, however, I still have many more to read.—Received a letter from the noble Whittier; who requests me to obtain a letter he wrote to grandfather. What treasures his letters are! In the evening heard the *Miserere* and other good music, by the band.

Saturday, August 15. Wrote a long letter to Aunt M.[argaretta]. Had a delightful ride to Marblehead with Mr. G.[illiard] and the P.[utnam]'s. Went in the regular beach wagons, which are very pleasant.—Most of the party went to bathe, and a gay time they had. I sat on the rocks watching them, and recommenced "Jane Eyre." From the Beach we drove to the Fort, from which there is a fine view over the bay; we could see Lowell Island and Nahant. Had a delightful drive home.

Sunday, August 16. Deeply engrossed in "Jane Eyre." Took a long pleasant walk this afternoon. Spent the evening at Mrs. P.[utnam]'s listening to sacred music.

Monday, August 17. My twentieth birthday. Very, very fast the years are passing away, and I,—Ah! how little am I improving them. I thought so to-day after I had finished "Jane Eyre," which has so powerfully interested and excited me. The excitement was not a healthy one, I know—and reason told me I *ought* to have been better employed.—But we have had so much company now that it is impossible to accomplish anything. This afternoon was regularly bored, victimized by two dull people—I do wish they would leave us to do the enjoyment of our own family circle, which is such a pleasant one now.—Twenty years! I have lived. I shall *not* live twenty years more,—I feel it. I believe I have but few years to live. Then I *must*, I *will* improve,—I will pray for strength to keep this resolution; I have broken so many. This *I must* keep.

Tuesday, August 18. A gloomy, rainy day. N.[ell] and I spent the morning among books, glancing at one and another, and talking about all—trying to find a selection for an album—always a tiresome and *bothersome* task. Went with N.[ell] to see my dear Miss S.[hepard] who was, as usual, very charming.—N.[ell] was delighted with her. She told us much that she has heard about the gifted and delightful Browning. It was so pleasant to hear about their devotion to each other. Miss S.[hepard] read the "Namesake's Response" (to Whittier). It is beautiful. Was written by an excellent friend of N. [ell]'s, the "Namesake's" father. In the evening attended a "Bell Concert." Some of the music was singularly sweet;—I liked the Staff Bells, and the harps particularly. The latter are most graceful and beautiful instruments, I think.

Wednesday, August 19. Read and wrote, this morn. Took a pleasant walk with the girls to the Factory Beach. Sat a long while on the rocks, talking over our future plans and prospects. S. [arah] and I have much to think about. This last afternoon that we are to spend together, it was pleasant to talk confidentially with each other. Spent the evening at Mrs. P. [utnam]'s where there were Mr. and Mrs. P. and Sybil.

Thursday, August 20. Our pleasant visitors left this morn. Very lonely the house seems without them. The girls were so lively and attractive. Miss J. so kind and good. I felt very sorry to part with them—with Nellie particularly, for *she* is very dear to me. We are to keep up a constant correspondence. Went to see Miss S. [hepard] and had a long talk with her about our noble Whittier. He has been pleased to speak most approvingly of my poor attempts at letter writing. I thank him, with all my heart. Miss S. [hepard] with her usual great kindness, has made several plans for our mutual enjoyment, during vacation. This afternoon, kept store for Mrs. P. [utnam] and became deeply interested in "Dombey and Son."

Friday, August 21. Spent the day at Mrs. P. [utnam]'s store, alternately reading and weaving. Had a letter from Aunt M. [argaretta]. Poor W. [illiam] is sinking very fast. Enclosed was a letter from father to grandmother—at last. A cold letter, it seems to me. He "is sorry that my health is impaired, hopes that it will be better"—just as any stranger might. I can sympathize with poor "Florence," for I too, have known but little of a father's love. It is hard for me to bear. To thee, alone, my journal, can I say with tears how *very* hard it is. I *have* a loving heart, though some may doubt it, and I long for a parent's love—for the love of my only parent; but it seems denied me;—I know not why.

Saturday, August 22. Again reading "Dombey," and weaving. Mr. P. [utnam] read to me an account of the great mechanic, Stevenson, who, little by little, "inch by inch," won his way upward. I never hear of such noble, energetic characters, without longing to imitate them—without forming new and good resolves, by which I too, may go "inch by inch," upward. *Now* I *will* keep them!

Sunday, August 23. Finished "Dombey and Son." Like it even better than "The Old Curiosity Shop." The death of little Paul is as touching and beautiful as that of Little Nell. Went to see Ada P. [utnam] who is very ill. Walked with Mr. P. [utnam] to Harmony Grove. Wrote to Hattie [Purvis], Mrs. C. [hew] and the noble W. [hittier]. Scribbled all the evening.

Monday, August 24. Worked at Mrs. P. [utnam]'s all the morn. Went to Gallows Hill with G. [eorgianna Putnam] and H. [elen Gilliard]. The view was very fine; the air pure, perfectly delightful. Practised, studied French. This eve., to our great surprise, who should come in but Mr. [Charles Lenox] R. [emond] and Mr. [Charles] Hovey. The former as morose and disagreeable[,] the latter as pleasant, as usual. The sooner I leave this house and Mr. R. [emond]'s presence, the better, I think. I *cannot* stay much longer.

Tuesday, August 25. At Mrs. P. [utnam]'s still. My friend Mrs. S. [hearman] came in. Read a little and studied French. In the eve. went to hear the band.

Wednesday, August 26. Paid a long visit to Miss.

S. [hepard]. Went to see A. [da] who is still very ill. Read "Mosses from an Old Manse." The first chapter—"The Old Manse" is very beautiful—truly poetic prose. Some of the stories are strange and terrible—the offspring of a diseased imagination, it seems to me.

Thursday, August 27. A perfect day. Had a delightful sail to Lowell Island with my dear Miss S. [hepard]. Spent the day on the rocks, reading, talking, and looking out over the "blue expanse of waters," or watching the graceful waves as they came dancing in to the shore. We had "Thallata," Whittier, Hawthorne, and the book which C. [harlotte] Bronte mentions,—"Friends in Council" which I like much. But we did little reading. How *could* we read when glorious Old Ocean lay before us with his infinite variety, his endless charm? We took a rustic dinner and had a pleasant sail home in the evening. This is a day to be marked with a white stone. Received a note and paper from our friend Mr. N. [ell] who has quite lost the little heart he had left, to our charming S. [arah], I think. Poor Man! Took tea with Miss S. [hepard] and listened to ghost stories.

Friday, August 28. A rainy day;—spent most of it at home, studying, sewing and reading "Mosses from the Old Manse."—In the evening played chess very successfully with Frank.

Saturday, August 29. Weaving in the morn.—Sewing in the aft. Spent eve. and night with A. [da Putnam] who is much better. Read there a very interesting account of Lady Hamilton and Lord Nelson, from the "London Times."

Sunday, August 30. One of the *perfect* days. A magnificent sunrise, illuminating sky and water most beautifully. The view from A. [da]'s little study is pretty. Stayed with her a while then came home and made pies. Read some of Thackeray's sketches. Took a pleasant walk to the Factory Beach. The water was studded by many pretty, picturesque sails— large and small. Read the "Mosses," and wrote to Aunt M. [argaretta].

Monday, August 31. Busy working all day. Mr. [Joseph] P. [utnam] read to me some very amusing passages from "Martin Chuzzlewit." This evening took a delightful walk on the Common. 'Twas perfectly lovely. The moon was glancing brilliantly through the graceful branches of the grand old elm trees. Peaceful, happy thoughts came lovingly to me as I paced slowly along under the arching branches. To me there is always a strange, sweet influence pervading these noble elms. I love them.

Tuesday, September 1. Sad news to-day. Cousin W. [illiam] is dead,—died last Friday. Though we have expected so long, it still seems sudden to us. The coming of the Angel of Death is ever unexpected to us. It is *some* consolation to know that one we love has left a world of sorrow and sin and strife to enter into *perfect peace*. Dear cousin! I could almost, almost envy thee that dreamless sleep, that knows no waking! Sometimes my heart is so very sad and heavy, that I long for it.

Wednesday, September 2. Wrote a few words of sympathy to Aunt H. [arriet]. *Words* can give but little consolation at such a time.

Worked, translated some French, paid Miss S. [hepard] a visit and read some chapters in the second part of "Mosses from the Old Manse."

Thursday, September 3. Another *perfect* day. Took a delightful walk at sunrise with Miss S. [hepard]. Spent the morn. weaving at Mrs. P. [utnam]'s; the evening at Miss S. [hepard]'s. Took tea in her charming parlor. The tea set was sixty years old. Had glasses taken from on board a privateer during the Revolution. Miss F. gave us a very interesting account of her visit to Niagara,—Miss S. [hepard] some amusing reminiscences of her childhood. We spent a pleasant evening.

Friday, September 4.   Very hot morning. Took "Corinne" and my French Dictionary and, with S. [arah] and L. [ucy], went to Harmony Grove, where we spent most of the morning. Georgie and Helen S. [hearman] took tea with us. After they had gone, felt one of those strange fits of sadness creeping over me. S. [arah] played and sang some of the old Scotch airs that I love so well, but they rather increased the sadness;—and now, I must say a few more words to thee, my own dear friend,—my journal! I have been examining myself to-night,—trying to fathom my own thoughts and feelings; and I find, alas! too much, too much of *selfishness!* And yet, I know that, in this world of care and sorrow, however weary and sad the heart may be, true *un*selfishness must ever be a source of the purest and highest happiness. Every kindly word, every gentle and generous deed we bestow upon others,—every ray of sunshine which penetrates the darkness of another's life, through the openings which our hands have made, *must* give to us a truer, nobler pleasure than any self-indulgence can impart. Knowing this, feeling it with my whole heart,—I ask thee, Oh! Heavenly Father! to make me truly *unselfish,* to give to me a heart-felt interest in the welfare of others;—a spirit willing to sacrifice *my own;*—to live "for the *good* that I can do!"

Saturday, September 5.   Bade the girls "good-bye." It made me feel quite sad to part from two such pleasant members of our little circle—lessening every day. Commenced learning Mrs. Sigourney's fine poem on Niagara, while sewing. This afternoon played chess with Addie, and took a pleasant walk by the water. L.[izzie] C.[hurch] and S.[arah] P.[itman?] called and asked me to join a French class, which I shall be delighted to do.

Tonight had a splendid walk in Nauvoo, by the brilliant moonlight, along the water's edge. 'Twas perfectly delightful. The surface of the water glittered with diamonds, sparkled with the most magnificent stars.

Sunday, September 6. Delightful day. Wrote to Mrs. Chase, Ada H.[inton] and Mattie F.[arbeaux]. Took a pleasant walk by the water; read all the evening.

Monday, September 7. First day of school. 'Tis pleasant to see the bright young faces again;—but it isn't pleasant to go to work. I hope it *will* be soon. Studied French. Went with Sarah P.[itman?] to see Mr. E.[dwards]. How we shall miss him,—we "Normalities"! What shall we do without him. Miss W.[eston?] came in, whom we were delighted to meet, and had a pleasant walk home with us in the moonlight.

Tuesday, September 8. Rather tired and sad to-day. A most delightful evening;—our first French lesson. M.[onsieur] J.[erome] is a pleasant teacher. We had a nice time. I love *la belle Francais*.

Wednesday, September 9. Taught; wove; studied French. S.[arah], L.[izzie], and I commenced history lessons.

Thursday, September 10. Unexpected holiday from *Training*, wherein Young America delighteth. Wrote to Mr. N.[ell]. Spent the afternoon at Mrs. P.[utnam]'s playing chess with A.[da]. Studied French pronunciations with S.[arah] P.[itman?]. We had a merry time. Played chess with H.[elen].

Friday, September 11. Studied history, and took a French lesson, after school.

Saturday, September 12. One of my scholars brought me a quantity of beautiful flowers. They are smiling on me now, as I write. Doubly precious they are now that we know that we shall miss their bright faces so soon,—truly;

> "Your voiceless lips, oh! flowers are living
>   preachers,
> Each cup a pulpit and each leaf a psalm."

Many a good and beautiful sermon have ye preached to me. Took my dear Miss S. [hepard] some of my flowers. Afterwards took tea with her.

Sunday, September 13. Wrote, studied French, took a long and delightful walk, read my beloved Mrs. Browning. How very, very beautiful, how noble is "Lady Geraldine's Courtship."

Monday, September 14. After school, translated French, studied history, and read the "Mosses," and Mrs. Browning.

Tuesday, September 15. Still no letters from home. I am weary of expecting. Took a French lesson. Played chess with Mrs. Putnam. Studied history.

Wednesday, September 16. Worked, read, studied;—spent a dull evening at Miss S. [arah] R. [emond]'s.

Thursday, September 17. A record of one day is a record of all. Some sad news about Mr. [Jacob] G. [illiard]'s steamer has quite dispirited me.[49]

Friday, September 18. A hard day at school. This constant warfare is crushing, killing me. I am desperate tonight. Even the pleasing variety of my French lesson has not relieved me. I am *desperate*, and shall write no more to-night.

Saturday, September 19. At last a letter from home;—full of scoldings; wove, committed "Maud Muller" to memory. Thank heaven! tomorrow will be a day of rest.

Sunday, September 20. Read our noble Whittier's "Panorama," wrote to Aunt M. [argaretta]. Studied a very long French lesson.

Monday, September 21. Went to the society at Mrs. [William] C. [hase]'s. She is a lovely woman, and has a delightful home. Most beautifully she read a letter of Mrs. [Harriet Beecher] Stowe's commencing "Who shall roll away the stone from the door of the sepulchre?" Very beautiful, very noble are the ideas of spirit life it contains.

Tuesday, September 22. Took my French lesson, read, wrote, and studied history and poetry.

Wednesday, September 23. Went with S. [arah] P. [itman?] to our Normal School to see our friend Mr. E. [dwards] there for the last time. It will never seem like *home* when he is gone.

Composed French sentences all the evening.

Thursday, September 24. Spent the eve. with a very large party of Normalities, at Mr. E. [dward]'s, and bade him a last farewell. Very, very sorry I am that he is going.—He has been a true friend to me.

Friday, September 25. Terribly stupid, tired and unwell. Was glad to retire as soon as possible after my French lesson.

Saturday, September 26. After school slept till four. Then L. [izzie Magee] very kindly gave me a ride with S. [arah] and Mrs. M. [agee]. We went through Swampscot;—the day was perfect,—sky, earth, water most beautiful. 'Twas just before sunset;—a purple haze rested on the surface of the sea, golden and purple clouds glorified the sky. In the eve. studied French. Had a visit from Mr. N. [ell].

Sunday, September 27. A perfectly lovely day. Did not feel well enough to go out. Mr. N. [ell] came in, with his usual budget of scraps for me to read;—some really beautiful poems. Studied French nearly all day. My kind Miss

S. [hepard] came bringing me cake and fruit, and a paper sent her by our noble Whittier.—E. [lizabeth Magee] let me read some old letters.

Monday, September 28.   Society met here. Was very glad to see Mrs. R. [emond] again. Had a nice long talk with her about our dear Brownie; she is a noble girl.

Tuesday, September 29.   Saw my dear Miss R. [emond] this evening. I mention it because it is always so great a pleasure to see her sweet, earnest face. She is truly a *whole-souled* woman. Took my French lesson. M. [onsieur] J. [erome] sang for us the grand old "Marseillaise" most splendidly. It excited me to quite a military enthusiasm. Ah! Rouget de L'Islo! thou hast indeed immortalized thyself.

Wednesday, September 30.   A beautiful letter from Lucy R. so earnest, so thoughtful, so kind! She is richly gifted in heart and mind. Have few friends who interest me so deeply.— Read Dickens "Christmas Carol" a charming story.—One could not read it without feeling more unselfish, more truly *Christian* for a long time.

Thursday, October 1.   After school read "Villette" and studied French.

Friday, October 2.   A long kind letter from Aunt M. [argaretta] and another from Nellie A.—They quite cheered me. Felt too unwell to take my French lesson; sewed and read all the evening.

Saturday, October 3.   A wintry day. Walked down town with S. [arah Cassey Smith] to market, then we paid a visit to poor Helen G. [illiard]. Very ill and sad she looks. I pity her with all my heart. Time is the only healer of such griefs as hers. Miss S. [hepard] read me a little from Una Hawthorne, the author's daughter. She is a girl of thirteen and writes most charmingly. In this letter she describes the Art

Exposition at Manchester. What particularly interested me was her description of Tennyson whom she met there. There is a perfect elegance and yet a child-like simplicity about her writing, which is perfectly charming.

Sunday, October 4. Rarely have I had so pleasant a walk as I had this beautiful October morning with Lizzie M. [agee]. We walked over railroad bridges, selecting the most dangerous, for we were seized with the very spirit of adventure. The tide was high, the water clear and sparkling as crystal, and those exquisite little fleecy clouds, which I think so beautiful, rested most lovingly on the soft blue of the sky. We walked to the old town of Beverly and back again; sauntering most leisurely along, now stopping to listen to the music of the waves, and to look at the myriad of glittering stars, which every moment appeared and disappeared on their surface, and to gaze "o'er the far blue main, where glancing sails to gentle breezes swell"; now looking with loving eyes at the quiet green hills and the moss covered rocks, which I love only less than the dancing waves which sparkle at their feet. This was truly a delightful morning walk—one to be long remembered. L. [izzie] seemed to possess this morn, a truer and fuller appreciation of the beautiful, a warmer love of dear Mother Nature, than I gave her credit for. "Truly our earth is beautiful, most beautiful!" No tears.

Dim the sweet look which Nature wears.—Read Bayne's "Christian Life" and studied French.

Monday, October 5. Read a little; went to the society, and played chess with Addie [Putnam].

Tuesday, October 6. A nice letter from Ada H. [inton?]. Took my French lesson, and commenced Dickens' "Pictures from Italy," which are perfectly charming, I think.

Wednesday, October 7. A perfect day. Went to see Dr.

G. who thinks it will do me no harm to spend the winter here; so I can set Aunt M. [argaretta]'s kind heart at ease.

A delightful walk in the country with Mr. P. [utnam] and S. [arah Cassey Smith]. The air was very pure; hills and rocks, sky and water most beautiful. Was delighted to find awaiting me Howitt's "Homes and Haunts of the British Poets," kindly sent me by Mr. N. [ell]. I anticipate a "rich mental feast" from its perusal.

Saturday [sic], *October 8.*   After school studied French, and read in "Homes and Haunts" some very amusing anecdotes of Wordsworth.

Friday, October 9.   Took my French lesson, and read a beautiful and most interesting account of lovely Mrs. Hemans in "Homes."—Beautiful in person as in heart and mind, she must have been most lovable.

Saturday, October 10.   While sewing, L. [izzie] read to me what Howitt says of gifted, unfortunate "L.E.L."—Read sadly and thoughtfully of Chatterton "the marvelous boy who perished in his pride."

Sunday, October 11.   Spent the morn. in reading and in translating. Had a brief visit from my dear friends Miss R. [emond] and Miss S. [hepard]. With the latter I spent a delightful afternoon. She read to me a beautiful and interesting memoir of Howard. This eve. attended the first lecture of our series by Mr. [Thomas] Stone. 'Twas very good. Tonight I have been reading old letters;—they have made me feel rather sad and home-sick. I have constantly a longing for something higher and nobler, than I have known. Constantly I ask myself Cowley's question "what shall I do to be forever known?" This is ambition, I know. It is selfish, it is wrong. But, oh! how very hard it is to do and feel what is right.

Monday, October 12. Studied and read. Wrote to Mr. N.[ell].

Tuesday, October 13. Double school. Slept nearly all the afternoon. Wrote to Lucy W. Took a French lesson.

Wednesday, October 14. A warm lonely day. Spent part of the afternoon out of doors, enjoying the air and sunshine. Played chess with Ada, and helped Mrs. P.[utnam] to preserve.

Thursday, October 15. Read and studied French all evening.

Friday, October 16. An April day,—alternate smiles and tears. Attended the teachers' meeting at Lynn. As usual 'twas rather uninteresting to me. Walked a little way towards the Beach. Noticed again the singularly soft and beautiful haze hovering "like the white wing of prayer" over the water. This eve. took my French lesson, and read.

Saturday, October 17. Spent the day in Boston. Ascended Bunker Hill Monument from which the view is fine. Salem and the White Mts. can be seen. The view of the bay is extensive. The wind rushed through the Monument sounding like the wail of departed spirits.—The statue of Warren seems to me wonderfully beautiful. In the afternoon had an interesting visit to the Navy Yard. At the Museum saw a beautiful and thrilling "The Sea of Ice" written to illustrate Dr. Rane's perils and adventures. Paid a visit to Mrs. L.[ockley?] to the A.[nti] S.[lavery] Office. Mr. P.[utnam] and Mr. N.[ell] went round with us. Returned home this eve. after a very pleasantly spent day.

Sunday, October 18. Another lovely day. Spent the morning at home writing. This afternoon read with Miss S.[hepard]. Walked to the Grove. Very beautifully the mellow autumnal light fell on the changing foliage. To-night heard one of the most beautiful and excellent Anti-Slavery lectures, by Rev. Mr. [William] F. [urness]. It did my very soul good. Most earnestly and truly did he speak of the terrible prejudice against color. He particularly dwelt on the dreadful effects produced by slavery on the morals of the people; how some of the greatest minds had utterly debased themselves at the bidding of the Slave Power. I have rarely heard anything more eloquent than were many passages of his lecture. My heart was so full of gratitude, of deep and earnest appreciation, I could not help writing a few lines to express to him *something* of what I felt. Thank God for such brave earnest hearts as these!

Monday, October 19.   Not feeling well, spent the evening at home, studying French.

Tuesday, October 20.   Read, wrote to Aunt M.[argaretta] and father, and took my French lesson. Commenced Hugh Miller. A message from Whittier.

Wednesday, October 21.   A wintry day. I fear the beautiful autumnal days are gone forever. This eve. went to a teacher's party at Caddie T.'s. Very old-fashioned people her parents are, and very agreeable. Saw a pair of little shoes—eighty-six years old. We were in such a nice old-fashioned room, with books and shells, and Chinese ornaments and a blazing wood fire. It was quite delightful.

Thursday, October 22.   Read an interesting account of the "homes and haunts" of Pope. Studied French and wrote.

Friday, October 23.   A letter from Mrs. C.[hase] who writes very kindly. Took my lesson; and read in the [Boston] "Transcript" a beautiful and most appreciative tribute to Mrs. Browning; also a very interesting sketch of the gifted sculptress, Miss Hosmer.

Saturday, October 24.   Wrote to Miss R.[emond]. Spent

the evening at Mrs. S. [hearman]'s. Read a very interesting sketch of Swift, the most unclerical of clergymen in "Homes and Haunts."

Sunday, October 25. A rainy day. All the day have the clouds wept. Made pies, studied French. Read about Coleridge in the delightful "Homes."

Monday, October 26. Studied French; went to the society at Mrs. B. [abcock]'s.

Tuesday, October 27. Studied, read Hugh Miller, and "The Homes'" and tried to write; but the ideas come too slowly.

Wednesday, October 28. Spent the afternoon at home, busily sewing. Miss S. [hepard] brought me some beautiful flowers. Took a French lesson, and read "The Atlantic Monthly" just published. It ought to be excellent for the most gifted minds on both sides of the Atlantic are among its contributors. Read aloud a sad but finely written story, "The Mourning Veil"; and a beautiful poetic tribute to Florence Nightingale—"Santa Filomena," by Longfellow.

Thursday, October 29. Saw my dear Miss R. [emond] and Mrs. W. for a few moments. Borrowed from Mrs. V. an interesting Guessing Game of cards, and took them to Mrs. P. [utnam]'s where L. [izzie], S. [arah] and I spent a very pleasant evening. Had some delightful music and singing.

Friday, October 30. Read, wrote and studied as usual.

Saturday, October 31. So bright, so beautiful has thou been, October, I grieve to say to thee "farewell." Took a French lesson and read Hugh Miller.

Sunday, November 1. Mr. N. [ell] gave me heads of Miss Mott, Mrs. Chapman, and Whittier which are especially acceptable. Miss [Mary] W. [ebb] dined with us. This afternoon took a long delightful walk nearly to Swampscot.

'Tis rather too late to see the full glory of the autumn tints, but still they are beautiful. Attended Miss W. [ebb]'s lecture[,] some of which was quite thrilling and much finer than I had expected.

Monday, November 2.   A pleasant society meeting at Mrs. A.'s. She has a beautiful home. Miss W. [ebb] was there, and talked very well. Kept me awake nearly all night,—quoting and reciting poetry which is her "hobby." She is quite a romantic, interesting person.

Tuesday, November 3.   Recited French, read, and sewed very industriously.

Wednesday, November 4.   Went into the Normal and saw my dear Miss R. [emond]. Heard from Aunt M. [argaretta]. Sewed and studied.

Thursday, November 5.   Spent the evening at Miss S. [arah] R. [emond]'s, very unprofitably, playing whist. Afterwards studied French.

Friday, November 6.   Recited French, read, wrote, and did more sewing. I consider myself quite a *martyr.*

Saturday, November 7.   A long and delightful walk by the water—alone. It was very, very, lovely. The water as blue as the sky and both so peaceful. I sat on a rock, and mused a long while.

Sunday, November 8.   Spent a rainy day in reading and writing. In the eve. heard an excellent lecture by Rev. J. [ames] F. [reeman] Clarke.

Monday, November 9.   At school, sick in bed, sewing and writing, all in one day and eve.

Tuesday, November 10.   Sewing again. French, reading and writing.

Wednesday, November 11.   Heard an excellent lecture on education by Rev. Dr. [Henry] Bellows. The real theme of the lecture was the importance of the highest possible education. He quite scourged the Americans for their supreme self-conceit,—for the little gratitude and reverence which they felt toward the Mother Land for the treasures of Art, Science, and Literature in which she so immeasurably surpasses them. I liked his remarks as a whole, exceedingly; though he *did* call the Brownings and Tennyson "beautiful corrupters of the English language" for their many unheard-of and obscure words and expressions. As Miss S. [hepard] says, it made us wince because we could not, enthusiastic admirers of these poets as we are, help acknowledging to ourselves that it was all too true.

Thursday, November 12.   Read, wrote, sewed and studied French.

Friday, November 13.   Spent a little time delightfully at Miss S. [hepard]'s. She told me some interesting things about Prescott and read an exquisite poem of Browning's "By the Fireside" addressed to his lovely and gifted wife. It is *very* sweet and beautiful.

Saturday, November 14.   Spent the afternoon and evening at Mrs. P. [utnam]'s, reading, sewing and playing chess with A. [da]. A bitter cold day.

Sunday, November 15.   Another wintry day. Our constant visitor, Mr. P. [utnam] came in this morning, and we had a pleasant chat about books and people. Read in the "Atlantic Monthly" a very interesting description of the Manchester Exhibition, evidently written by one well versed in Art. Also a poem "Brahma" by R. W. Emerson, remarkable only for its utter obscurity. Can't understand a word of it. Evidently poetry is not the philosopher's forte. Read Spencer in "Homes and Haunts," and wrote to Carrie W. [eston] and translated a French lesson.—Am most impatient to read "Canterbury Tales," and Spencer's "Faerie Queene."

Monday, November 16. Worked, and studied French. Had a letter form Miss R.[emond], who does not understand me, I am quite sure.

Tuesday, November 17. Studied, took my French lesson, and played chess with S.[arah].

Wednesday, November 18. Took a pleasant walk on the Pastures with S.[arah]. The air was delightful, the sky most beautiful. This eve. read an exquisite little story, "The Angel over the Right Shoulder," by the author of "Sunny Side"; and some beautiful thoughts on death by Jean Paul Richter. Also commenced translating "Corinne, on Italie."

Thursday, November 19. Heard from Aunt M. Sewed, studied French, and read "Hugh Miller." Aunt says that poor E. C. is dying.

Friday, November 20. An interesting letter from Nellie A.[lexander?]. Took my lesson. Had quite a discussion on Slavery with Mr. Jerome. Read aloud "The Old Man's Home," a beautiful allegory.—The clouds to-day were *perfect*.

Saturday, November 21. Close of the term. All the scholars met together, and sang most sweetly; it was very pleasant to hear them and to see so many beaming, happy little faces. Played chess with H.[elen]. Took a walk with dear C.[arrie?]. Sewed and read some interesting articles in "Harper's Monthly." Read a very interesting article on "Brahma," and a paraphrase of it, which renders it much clearer, and most comprehensible. Mr. N.[ell] sent me reports of Mackay's "Lectures on Poetry."

Sunday, November 22. Just such a day as the Sunday

before Thanksgiving *ought* to be. I give thanks with all my
heart, and feel in a particularly good humor with myself and
everybody else. Mr. and Mrs. P. [utnam] spent most of the
morn with us. We had a long, pleasant chat. This afternoon
took a long splendid walk of several miles with S. [arah
Cassey Smith] and Mr. P. [utnam], the North wind blowing
in our faces. The keen air was most inspiring; and one never
tires of the moss-grown rocks, the long ranges of brown hills,
with their crowns of evergreen, and the ever-varying, wonderful beauty of the clouds.—Too sleepy, from walking in
the wind, to appreciate Mr. H. [odges]'s lecture. Commenced
Mackay's Lecture. Read Whittier's "Supernaturalism" and
wrote to Mr. Nell.

Monday, November 23.   How nice it is to have vacation
and stay at home for a day or two! Spent most of the morning
in writing. This aft. [ernoon] Mr. P. [utnam] read to us
extracts from some of Mr. N. [ell]'s letters while we were
sewing. Had a *very* pleasant society meeting at Mrs. C. [hase]'s,
always a charming place to visit. She and Miss S. [hepard]
and I had a delightful talk about Whittier. Had a pleasant
letter from Mattie F. [arbeaux?].

Tuesday, November 24.   Studied French all the morning;
paid my dear Miss S. [hepard] a visit. Finished Whittier's
"Supernaturalism," which is very interesting, took my lesson
and read part of Lela's "Two Idle Apprentices." His style is
wonderfully like that of Dickens.

Wednesday, November 25.   Mrs. W. [ebb] and I alone.
Wrote, ironed, and read a little. Spent the afternoon at Mrs.
P. [utnam]'s,—sewing. The eve. playing chess with Mr.
P. [utnam].

Thursday, November 26.   Thanksgiving Day Mr. N. [ell]
and Mr. [Joseph] P. [utnam] spent most of the day with us.

The former told me much that was very interesting about Sumner, whom he has lately seen. Spent the evening at Mrs. P. [utnam]'s playing whist.

Friday, November 27. Spent most of the day busily sewing. This eve. took my last French lesson. I am *very*, very sorry to discontinue them. But I can't afford to keep on. But L. [izzie] P. and I are going to study together all winter. Read the "Homes," and played chess with H. [elen].

Saturday, November 28. A *wonderfully* lovely day. Spent the afternoon at Mrs. P. [utnam]'s store. Mr. P. [utnam] read the first no. of Charles Reade's new story, "Jack of all Trades." It is written in that easy natural style about which there is a peculiar charm,—which characterizes the articles in "Household Words." Mr. N. [ell] very kindly allowed me to read letters from Mrs. [Maria W.] Chapman and Mr. [William Lloyd] Garrison. Played whist this eve.

Sunday, November 29. Visitors as usual in the morn. interrupting my writing and reading. This afternoon walked to S. [outh] Danvers, to hear Parker Pillsbury. As usual "my Luther" was full of fiery, earnest eloquence; and I enjoyed it greatly. This eve. heard our beloved Garrison, and had the very, very great pleasure of shaking hands with him.

Monday, November 30. School again. Children wild and unmanageable, as usual after vacation. Read "Retribution[,]" an impassioned story by Mrs. Southworth. It excited me entirely too much. Studied a French lesson.

Tuesday, December 1. Had a kind little note from dear Carrie W. [eston]. Spent the evening translating "Corinne" with Sarah P. [itman?]. Wrote to Aunt M. [argaretta].

Wednesday, December 2. The afternoon in writing and reading. Had a visit from pleasant Mary O. [sborn?]. In the evening worked for the Fair, and read Tennyson.

Thursday, December 3. A pleasant evening.—translating French, working, and chatting with the P.[utnam]'s.

Friday, December 4. Translated "Corinne" with S.[arah] P.[itman?,] wrote to the noble Whittier and read my beloved "Liberator." L.[izzie] is quite provoked with me for my "hero worship"; thinks it most absurd.

Saturday, December 5. My dear Miss S.[hepard] spent most of the afternoon with me. She helped me pack my books, and a delightful time we had. Mrs. W.[ebb] was charmed with her. Truly she is a charming person, and the best of friends to me. This eve. studied French; then sewed while S.[arah] read to us.

Sunday, December 6. Spent the day in reading, writing and studying. Translated several chapters of the French Testament.

Monday, December 7. Heard Mr. Giles' lecture on the Bronte family. It was very fine. He is an eloquent, energetic speaker.

Tuesday, December 8. Heard Mr. J.[ames] F.[reeman] Clarke's lecture on the "Yankee." An excellent lecture, very amusing and interesting. The true-hearted man was not afraid to speak of slavery, and the most truthfully and beautifully. Afterwards wrote considerably.

Wednesday, December 9. A rainy day; we are positively going to move this week. So nothing have I done but pack, pack all the afternoon. A little reading to-night.

Thursday, December 10. Spent the eve. at Mrs. P.[utnam]'s. Received "The Atlantic Monthly."

Friday, December 11. Lizzie and Mrs. W.[ebb] left early this morning; how much we shall miss them. Studied French—"Corinne"—with S.[arah] P.[itman?].

Saturday, December 12. Packing, packing most busily all

day. This eve. thoroughly tired bade the house good-bye. H.[elen] has gone to D.[anvers]. Sarah and I are established at Mrs. P.[utnam]'s. Could not leave the house which has been my home ever since I have been in Salem, without regret—a little. Have thought much of *her* who was its guardian genius, without whom it seems so changed—so changed! Dear lost friend, *I* shall never forget thee,—never! Received an entertaining letter from old Mr. D. He gives me some encouragement about the draft.—He is a kind old gentleman. Read a little "Peter Still." Am so tired that I shall be glad to retire early. It seems strange, yet pleasant to be here.

Sunday, December 13. Spent nearly all day in writing busily. Determined to finish my story. Took a pleasant little walk with S.[arah] P.[itman?], afterwards finished my "Lost Bride." S.[arah] likes it much, but it seems to *me* silly and flat. I can't see any sense in it. Yet *necessity* compels me to try to publish it.

Wednesday, December 16. Find it delightful to rise so early. Can accomplish so much more. Sent my story to the "Home Journal."[50] Shall have little peace of mind till I know its fate. Had very kind letters from Annie and Aunt S.[arah] P.[urvis]. Spent the afternoon with my dear Miss S.[hepard]. We had a long and confidential talk. This eve. heard a splendid lecture on Toussaint by our noble Mr. [Wendell] Phillips. It was a glorious and well-deserved tribute to the "First of the Blacks." My enthusiastic enjoyment knew no bounds. What heightened it was that a large part of the audience was composed of people who would not go to an avowedly Anti-Slavery lecture. But they had a grand dose of Anti-Slavery and anti-prejudice to-night. It was enough for them to hear him say, as *he* alone *could* say it—"I hate prejudice against colore; I despise it!" In concluding he said, as nearly as I can remember, "I would compare Toussaint to Cromwell, but Cromwell shed much blood in clutching at a throne. Toussaint walked by natural gravitation into the leadership of his people, without a crime. I would compare him to Napoleon, but Napoleon's whole career was *covered* with cheatery.—This black chief *'never broke his word.'* I would compare him to Washington—but Washington held slaves.—This man's hands were clean. There are none worthy to compare with him, in purity of character, save Tell and Jay.—"

Thursday, December 17. S.[arah Cassey Smith] and others of the family gone to the Boston Fair,[51] to which I *long* to go, but cannot, so there's no use of repining. My sad heart was gladdened even more than a visit to the Fair would have gladdened it, by a letter from father,—at last. It is as I thought. He is *utterly unable* to assist me. Ah! if he had only confided this to me long ago, I would *never, never* have asked his assistance. The letter was full of affection. Dear father! he is sorely tired. I wish *I* could be of some assistance to him. I will write and tell him how much I feel with him. Read, wrote, and played chess with E.[llen Shearman?].

Friday, December 18. Read, wrote and translated "Corinne" with Sarah P.[itman?]. Still no news of my poor story. Though of course 'tis too soon. I shall be most impatient till I hear.

Saturday, December 19. As usual, read a little, wrote, studied and sewed. *Tired* to-day.—Longing for letters from home.

Sunday, December 20. Read the "Homes"; called on Miss S.[hepard]. Read "Corinne" and listened to Mr. P.[utnam] reading Burns.

Monday, December 21. Went to an Amateur Concert for the benefit of the poor. Some beautiful singing. The "Mass" I liked, especially. Mrs. Norton's exquisite song—"The Outward Bound" was given by a quartette,—a sister and three brothers,—with fine effect. Rather too much operatic music for me.

Tuesday, December 22. Double school. So had plenty of time for reading and sewing. Can hardly believe that Christmas is so near.

Wednesday, December 23. Went into the dear old Normal and had such a warm welcome as made my weary heart rejoice. Miss L.[ucy] R. arrived, bringing letters and useful presents to me from home.

Thursday, December 24. Christmas eve. Busy preparing to go to Boston, when my kind friend Miss S.[hepard] came in, bringing me a Christmas present from her father;—a complete and most ingenious set of Jack Straws. She spent some time with us.

Friday, Christmas Day. Went to Boston at seven, 'twas bitter cold. Visited several bookstores, and saw many magnificent books among which was Mrs. Clarke's "World Noted Women," splendidly illustrated with engravings of the most distinguished women from Sappho to Florence Nightingale. Then went to the Fair, and saw many beautiful articles; the most beautiful was a set of photographs of the different ruins of Rome executed by Mrs. Jam[i]eson's son-in-law and sent by her from Rome to the Bazaar. The explanations were written by her and accompanied by her autograph. Photographing seems to me the best way of representing columns. One could hardly realize that these were on paper, they seemed to stand out from it in such fine relief. On Mrs. Stowe's table was a statuette of Uncle Tiff executed by a

colored French artist; exquisite statuettes of the Venus de
Medici and Canova's Venus of the Bath;—a model of the
famous Warwick base, *very* beautifully carved. Saw Sumner,
Emerson, Wendell Phillips, all in the Fair at once. It was
glorious to see such a trio. I feasted my eyes. Sumner looks
pale and weak but still bears the unmistakable stamp of
"nature's nobleman." To-night went to the Boston Theatre.
The play—"Satan in Paris," was nothing but I enjoyed seeing
the Theatre. It is so beautiful. The chandelier especially
attracted my attention. Its lights were arranged like groups
of stars, and produced a fine effect on the beautifully painted
ceiling. I had never seen a bona-fide Theatre before.

Saturday, December 26. Spent the day at the Fair. Looked
over those exquisite photographs again, with Mr. and Mrs.
[Samuel] May[,] and was much pleased and benefitted by
their interesting comments. Mrs. M. [ay] is one of the most
refined and truly eloquent women I've ever seen. Saw some
very old French books—more than two hundred years old;
and exquisite illustrations of "Tam O'Shanter." Heard my
queenly Mrs. C. [hapman] speak French "like a stream of
silver" with some interesting French emigrants. Saw Sumner
again, and Giles. Last night of the Fair. Was introduced to
the gifted Mrs. [Caroline] Dall, who said that she had heard
Miss S. [hepard] speak of me. Left with regret and reached
home at midnight. It is a *glorious* night,—a pure white robe
of spotless snow beautifies the earth. Found a letter and a
kind present from Lizzie [Church] awaiting me.

Sunday, December 27. Completely exhausted after such
unwanted excitement. Did little else but sleep. Wrote a little
and read some tales and legends of the "Lake-Side." All the
eve. listened to sacred music and singing.

Monday, December 28. School again. Read, studied French,

and wrote a *very* long letter to dear, kind Aunt M. [argaretta].

Tuesday, December 29. After school translated "Corinne" with S. [arah] P. [itman] and read the "Homes," and played chess with Addie [Putnam].

Wednesday, December 30. Spent most of the afternoon with Miss S. [hepard] who showed me some beautiful New Year's gifts. One book, "Bayne's Biographical Essays," I liked especially. He speaks of Tennyson, Mrs. Browning and other distinguished poets, and pays a beautiful tribute to "Currer Bell." Went to see Miss F. who showed me an exquisite medallion of the "Descent from the Cross"; doubtless taken from Ruben's famous picture. It is certainly the most beautiful I have ever seen. The expression of the faces is perfect. I particularly noticed the wonderful delicacy and beauty of the hands. Miss F. lent me De Quincey's "Literary Reminiscences," which I commenced this eve. and like much.— Sewed busily.

Thursday, December 31. The last night, the last night of the old Year. Sad memories and bitter thoughts have been busy at my heart and brain to-night, but I'm going to drive them away. Read "Corinne," and wrote to Georgie, sending her a "Liberty Bell." Mrs. P. [utnam], H. [elen], A. [da] and I are sitting up to welcome in the New Year. I have just finished Tennyson's "Death of the Old Year"; and now he lies *dead*, and the New Year comes in. Farewell! old year, with thy joys and thy sorrows, thy pleasant happy memories and thy sad experiences.—Farewell! For me;—Ah! I cannot bear to think how I have misspent and lost the precious, precious hours that can return no more. 'Tis sad, very sad to think of.

Friday, New Year's morn. 1858.—Welcome in; New Year! A *perfect day* ushers thee in. I greet thee with mingled tears of joy and sorrow. I will record no *vows*, no good resolutions *this* year,—to shed, at the beginning of the next, bitter, repentant tears over their graves. In the secret depths of my own heart I make some vows. Oh! may God give me strength to keep them!

New Year's Night. Made some calls with A. [da]. At Miss S. [arah] R. [emond]'s, saw an exquisite old picture of Sappho, a most inspired face. Saw Miss S. [hepard]'s beautiful gifts. Heard that the mother of our noble Whittier is dead. Ah! this will be a sad New Year to him. With all my heart I feel for him and his sister in this sad loss. Wrote to father and Nellie A. [lexander?]. Read in De Quincey a very interesting and appreciative sketch of Charles Lamb. The warm praises bestowed on the "Gentle Elia's" Essays have made me very desirous of reading them. And so has passed the first day of the year.

Saturday, January 2. After school sewed busily all the afternoon and eve. S. [arah] and A. [da] entertained us with their brilliant opera airs.—I wonder why it is that I have this strangee feeling of not *living out myself:* My existence seems not *full* not expansive enough. I must need some great emotion to arouse the dormant energies of my nature. What means this constant restlessness, this longing for something, I know not what? Alas! I shall never, never be able to say— "My minde to me a kingdome, is Such perfecte *peace* therein dothe dwelle."

Sunday, January 3. Wrote; took a walk in the Grove with Mrs. P. [utnam] and H. [elen Putnam Gilliard]. We had a long earnest talk about death and immortality. Poor H. [elen], her great grief makes her quite skeptical.[52] I wish I could inspire her with perfect faith. It would be so great a help and consolation to her. Read De Quincey and "Corinne."

Took another long, pleasant walk. Wrote to sweet Mattie F. [arbeaux]. Mr. P. [utnam] read to us some very interesting sketches of travel in India; before the terrible insurrection broke out.

Monday, January 4.   After school, sewed busily; and read De Quincey. What a worshipper of Coleridge he is!

Tuesday, January 5.   Translated Corinne and studied Algebra with S. [arah] whose persevering energy I greatly admire.

Wednesday, January 6.   A stormy day, without and within. Spent it in sewing, reading and *thinking* very sadly.

Thursday, January 7.   Read a little and sewed a great deal. Had a letter from Lizzie.

Friday, January 8.   After school spent much of the eve. in coasting, a most exhilarating and delightful amusement. S. [arah] P. [itman?] came in and we had a splendid time, reluctantly sobered down to sewing for the rest of the eve. Sat up late,—alone,—deliriously *dreaming*.

Saturday, January 9.   For the afternoon and evening sewed busily. At twilight S. [arah] played some old familiar airs which gave me a strange feeling of heart-sickness and homesickness. I could not restrain some bitter tears. Played chess with Mrs. P. [utnam].

Sunday, January 10.   A splendid day. The snow-clad earth glittering in the sun. Wrote letters and in Miss R. [emond]'s exquisite album. Writing in albums is my special aversion. Read "Corinne" and "De Quincey," and took a delightful walk. This evening H. [elen] read aloud Lowell's amusing and excellent "Bigelow Papers" which were new to us.

Monday, January 11.   Walking abominable. Could hardly get to school. Mr. R. [emond] very kindly drove me home. Read "De Quincey" and played chess.

Tuesday, January 12. A letter from dear Aunt M. [argaretta] gladdened my heart. Went to the society at Miss R. [emond]'s and met Parker Pillsbury there. Saw him only a few minutes. Fought quite a hard *chess* battle with Mrs. P. [utnam].

Wednesday, January 13. After school translated "Corinne" with S. [arah] P. [itman?] who spent the evening with us. Read "De Quincey," and played chess with A. [da]. My dear Miss [Sarah Parker] R. [emond] came in. I was rejoiced to see her. Went to Miss S. [hepard]'s and met Lizzie D. [ike].

Thursday, January 14. Sewed, read "De Quincey," and commenced committing "Gray's Elegy."

Friday, January 15. Ditto with Thursday.

Saturday, January 16. Received a prospectus of a magazine to which Mr. P. [atrick?] R. [eason?] wishes me to contribute. I may, occasionally. This afternoon a little girl professing to be a medium, came in. Some raps were produced, but nothing more satisfactory. I grow more and more skeptical about spiritualism. This eve. sewed busily, while Mr. P. [utnam] read aloud Reade's "Jack of all Trades."

Sunday, January 17. Went to a spiritual meeting with H. [elen] and A. [da] which was a sad failure. This beautiful afternoon made calls on Miss R. [emond] and Mrs. R. [emond], had a long and interesting conversation with the latter. Saw as usual, beautiful plants and pictures. An exquisite picture of Raphael, wrote for her album.

Monday, January 18. Sewed busily;—Am tired and depressed. Can think of nothing but that horrid examination. Had two pleasant, characteristic notes from Miss N. I think I could like her very much.

Tuesday, January 19. Sewed and played chess.

Wednesday, January 20. A lecture from [Ralph Waldo]

Emerson—really on the true beauty of Nature, and the pleasure and benefit to be derived from walking amid this beauty. I have rarely enjoyed so rich a mental feast. I am really *grieved* that my mind is in such a stupid state, so "care-laden," that I cannot treasure up, as I once could, the golden words which fell from the poet-philosopher's lips. A walk with Emerson would be intensely yet *silently* delightful. I cannot but believe that he is one of the truest of Nature's interpreters.

Thursday, January 21.   Private examination to-day. Children did admirable. Am *tired* to death.

Friday, January 22.   Sewed busily and read "De Quincey."

Saturday, January 23.   All the afternoon sewing while Helen read to us, "Fashion and Famine."

Sunday, January 24.   Read and wrote. Towards evening took a long delightful walk alone.

Monday, January 25.   Public examination.—Horrid nuisance! Went off very well. *Dreadfully* tired. Heard an interesting lecture by Dr. Gusdorff (which I was almost too stupid to appreciate) on the "Transformation of Matter."

Tuesday, January 26.   Feeling tired and ill, retired so early that I was sick of bed. Rose and sat by the window in the delicious moonlight, recalling Tennyson's fine "Lady Clara Vere de Vere," and many other old favorite poems.

Wednesday, January 27.   Went to the closing exercises of H. [enry]'s examination. He did admirably. Was quite proud of him. Heard the lion-like Dr. [George] Cheever to-night. He was grand and fearless. Miss S. [hepard] and I enjoyed him together. And now farewell to thee! my dear old friend, my *only confidant*—my journal!

JOURNAL THREE

Salem, January 28, 1858–
St. Helena Island, February 14, 1863

Salem. January 28, 1858. A word of greeting to thee, my new friend my new journal! Soon will thy face become a familiar one to me. Wrote to Aunt M.[argaretta] and L.[izzie Magee]. Finished my old journal. Read the "Atlantic Monthly," and the beautiful tragedy of Norma. I long to see the Opera. Played chess with Addie [Putnam] and Mrs. P.[utnam].

Friday, January 29. Took a walk with A.[da]. Spent most of the day busily sewing. Went into the dear old Normal, and paid a few other visits. Played chess all the evening.

Saturday, January 30. Spent the morn. in working, talking, and *trying* to play duets with H.[enry Cassey]. This afternoon visited Miss L. and L. P. who is sick. To my great joy she lent me Reade's "White Lies," of which I *devoured* the two first vols. this eve. It is really a refreshing book, written in such a sparkling, delightful style;—very different from most other novels. I enjoy it exceedingly. Miss S.[hepard] gave me some sweet flowers for A.[da]. Flowers in winter! What treasures they are! A.[da] says the fragrance of the mignonette reminds her of the ball-room. It reminds *me* of that delicious "rarity—a day in June; when the soft blue sky, the genial sunlight, the dewy air, the fresh young murmuring leaves, the sweet song of birds, the rich perfume of the flowers, make it a *blessed privilege* to live." What a silly rhapsody [*sic*] some people would think this! But I don't care. I can say what I please to thee, my indulgent friend, without fear of criticism or rebuke.

Sunday, January 31. Spent most of the day in finishing

"White Lies"—one of the most charming, fascinating books I've ever read. It excited me to such a degree that I was obliged to take a walk to "cool my fever." This eve. read "De Quincey," and had quite an animated talk with Mr. R. [emond] who *can* be agreeable when he so wills it.

Monday, February 1. Read and wrote. Spent the afternoon with Miss [Sarah Parker] R. [emond] and had a long talk about lecturing. Received a letter and papers from Mr. N. [ell] who is *very* kind. Read a very fine essay on Milton by Macaulay. It is written with even more brilliancy than his History. Went to the society at Mrs. [Amy] I. [ves].

Tuesday, February 2. School again. Rain pouring. My heart was gladdened by a letter from Aunt M. [argaretta]. Read "De Quincey," and played chess. This evening H. [enry Cassey] and some of his friends amused us with their magic lantern.

Wednesday, February 3. A *very* beautiful day. Spent the afternoon in the Normal, and heard pleasant Prof. C. [rosby]'s class on Virgil. Paid a few visits. Sat up very late reading "The Days of My Life," a beautiful story by the author of "Margaret Maitland."

Thursday, February 4. A nice little note from kind Miss N. A visit from Miss R. [emond]—after school wrote, studied French, and commenced "Emerson's Essays"—having finished "De Quincey." E. [merson]'s first essay on "The Poet" is very beautiful, and very true, I think.

Friday, February 5. After school studied French, read Emerson and commenced De Quincey's "Confessions of an Opium Eater," which I *know* I shall like.

Saturday, February 6. Read, wrote, studied a *very* long French lesson, and played chess.

Sunday, February 7. Mr. [Joseph] P. [utnam] and I spent

the morning in writing a Parody for Mr. N. [ell] on the "Red, White and Blue." *His* share of it is very good,—mine miserable. Went this afternoon to the New Catholic Church. The stained windows and the exquisitely painted ceiling are very beautiful, but I was disappointed in the rest of the buildings. There are no pictures in it. The music was fine, but the singing rather poor. This eve. read some poetry aloud, and the "Confessions." They are *very* interesting. Mr. P. [utnam] read to us some splendid passages from Macaulay's "Biographical Essays." His description of the Italian of Machiavelli's time, and another—of Johnson's Boswell impressed me as being the finest pen-and-ink portraits that I have ever known of.

Monday, February 8. Read "DeQuincey" and Emerson; went to the society at Mrs. I. [ves].

Tuesday, February 9. Sick and weary, and feeling more discouraged, than I dare acknowledge, even to thee, dear journal!

Wednesday, February 10. Ill nearly all day, but in the evening well enough to read, and play whist with Mr. R. [emond].

Thursday, February 11. Au desespoir to-day. Wrote a *desperate* little note to Miss S. [hepard]. I think I must go home. I am weary! I am weary! And oh, so unsettled and troubled! I know not what to do. I *ought* not to go. I *cannot* stay. I am *heart sick,* and my physical strength is giving way fast; I feel it. If I could go right on and *die soon,* how gladly would I do so. But oh, to drag on so from day to day. I have no longer the heart to do it. And if it be possible for me to feel secure of another situation on my return, I will go home *now.* And write if I can.

Friday, February 12. Feeling a little better—*physically.*

Still thinking of *home*. Finished De Quincey's "Confessions." They are singularly written, original, delightful reading,— though the *subject* is not. My mind is too much occupied and disturbed to think or say much about them now.

Saturday, February 13. My kind and good friend Miss S. [hepard] spent most of the afternoon with me, and greatly cheered me. But I cannot yet say what I shall do. H. [enry Cassey] came and proposed my studying German with him. If I only *could*. Oh, I do hope I *shall* be able to.

Sunday, February 14. Wrote some lines for A. [da Putnam] to set to music. My dear Miss Sh. [epard] kindly sent me the "Eclectic" containing a portrait of our beloved Mrs. Browning. It is beautiful, but it is not my *idea* of her. However I have studied it over and over, and like it much. It has gladdened my heart, as the brilliant constellation (Scott and his Friends at Abbottsford), on the opposite page, has gladdened my eyes. I believe I've quite lost my *heart* to *Lockhart*. He is eminently handsome; a *Byronic* style of beauty.

Monday, February 15. After school read Emerson and played chess. In the "Eclectic" read a very searching criticism on "Aurora"; another finely written one on A. [lexander] Smith's "City Poems"; a beautiful and most appreciative sketch of Mrs. Browning; and the most deeply interesting accounts I have yet seen from India; all from foreign periodicals.

Tuesday, February 16. Read Emerson and Mrs. Browning (my favorite "Lady Geraldine"). Studied a little German with H. [enry]. The pronunciation seems hard, and most unmusical to me, after the sweeter, softer *francaise*. But I wish very much to acquire it. Afterwards, French.

Wednesday, February 17. Wrote and studied German. Played chess and read "Corinne."

Thursday, February 18. Ditto except German.

Friday, February 19. Wrote to dear noble Mr. G.[arrison] requesting his autograph. Had a letter and some papers from Mr. N.[ell]. That poor Ms., its fate is not decided yet. Finished the first volume of Emerson's "Essays." I cannot *quite* understand *everything* that he says; but I understand enough to admire and enjoy, and be benefitted by. He has taught me many a good and noble lesson, for which I thank him with all my heart. Studied French. Read "Corinne."

Saturday, February 20. Again studied German with H.[enry] and, in exchange, taught him a little French. Sewed some. Commenced Emerson's second volume and played chess with A.[da]. *Beat her once.*

Sunday, February 21. Mr. P.[utnam] read me some very fine passages about the French Revolution, from Alison's brilliant "History of Europe." Took a delightful walk in the pure, bright snow. Persuaded Helen to go to my favorite little rustic bridge, where we stood, admiring the beauty of the clouds and the dazzling purity of the snow. Read "Emerson" and wrote to him, requesting his autograph.

Monday, February 22. Wrote to Aunt M.[argaretta] and with considerable trepidation, to the noble [Charles] Sumner, for his autograph. Had a pleasant letter from Mattie F.[arbeaux].

Tuesday, February 23. Half holiday. Spent most of it with my dear Miss S.[hepard] who showed me a beautiful letter from the noble and gifted W.[hittier]. We had a long, confidential talk together. How much greater are her trials than mine! I feel ashamed of my own discontent. Took tea with the P.[utnam]'s. Read Emerson, and played chess. Saw a beautiful flower at L. P.'s.

Wednesday, February 24. Sewed busily all the afternoon and evening, while Helen [Gilliard] read aloud De Quincey's "Klosterheim," a finely written and most exciting, delightful book. I enjoyed it greatly.

Thursday, February 25. Re-read "Shirley," and enjoyed it quite as much as I did the first time; years ago. Shirley is a noble character; Caroline a sweet gentle, womanly creature. Robert Moore is provokingly interesting. Altogether the book is charming, and has all Miss Bronte's originality. Studied French.

Friday, February 26. Read Emerson, "Corinne." Wrote a little note to Mr. [Richard] E.[dwards] asking his opinion about resigning. I feel strongly inclined to do so. This is the most glorious, moonlight night I have ever seen. Mrs. P.[utnam] and I sat up till half past eleven playing chess. I am looking from the little study window, through which a silvery stream pours in, flooding the room. How calm, how peaceful, how gloriously beautiful is the scene. While I gaze on it, a strange longing steals over me. "Oh that I had the wings like a dove!" I would fly away, away to those bright worlds above, and find there the rest which seems denied me in this vain, fruitless longings these!

Saturday, February 27. A day to be marked with a *white stone*. Returning from school, weary and sad, as usual, found *two* parcels from [Charles] *Sumner*. One containing an extract from one of his speeches, and bearing his signature;—the other filled with other valuable autographs, of the Duchess of Sutherland, the Duchess of Argyle, the Earl of Shaftsbury, Longfellow, W.[illiam] H. Furness, Sen. Blair, Jared Sparks, and Lady Napier, the Lady of the British Minister at Washington. The first three particularly surprised and delighted me. How very, very kind it was in Mr. Sumner. To an entire stranger, too. I suppose I have to thank my color for it. I can hardly conceive of any worse handwriting than the Duchess of Sutherland's. Her daughter and the Earl of S.[haftsbury] write much better. Lady Napier, very prettily. Longfellow writes a little like Mr. Nell. I am full of the most joyful surprise.

Sunday, February 28.   Wrote a long letter to Lizzie. Read Emerson's "Essays, and Household Words." In it is an exquisite fairy tale very charmingly told in verse. H.[enry] came in, and we had a very interesting talk about "Klosterheim." Took a little walk. Wrote to Mr. Nell.

Monday, March 1.   Had a very kind note from Miss S.[hepard], and one from Mr. [Richard] E.[dwards], in which he very kindly assures me that he will do all in his power to get me another situation when I shall want one. Now I shall certainly resign. Miss S.[hepard] urges me to do so, and I feel that my health demands it. S.[arah] tells me that Mr. F.[rancis] Webb has received an appointment as postmaster in Jamaica. Probably Annie [Woods Webb] will accompany them. If she *wants* me, I shall be delighted to go. Next week, for home, sweet home! A pleasant day for the first of spring.

Tuesday, March 2.   Waded through a deep snow to school. Miss R.[emond] paid us a visit. Sewed most of the afternoon. This evening wrote to Annie [Woods Webb], and the noble S.[umner]. Wrote my resignation.

Wednesday, March 3.   Announced my determination of leaving; to everybody's astonishment. I am sorely disturbed in mind. Constantly I ask myself "Am I doing right?" Yet I *believe* that I am. If I entirely lose my health *now* of what use will my life be to me? None. I shall only be dependent, miserably dependent on others. I would ten thousand times rather die than that. Lizzie A. [lexander?] arrived.

Thursday, March 4.   A letter and package from home. How astonished they will be to see me. It is a pleasure to go where one is *sure* of a welcome! Tried to read a little.

Friday, March 5.   Went to Boston, to Mr. N. [ell]'s "Attucks Celebration."[1] For me the greatest attraction was hearing Phillips and Garrison once more, perhaps for the last time. Old Faneuil Hall presented quite a gay scene after the meeting. There was a large crowd of finely dressed dancers, of whose movements, I was, for some time an amused spectator. But after I grew terribly tired and was glad to leave.

Saturday, March 6.   Came home in the earliest train. Very beautifully look the "snow clad" hills in the pleasant sunshine, and beautifully they contrast with the dark, shining branches of the ever-greens. After school Mr. Russell and my dear Kitty D. called. Spent the eve. as usual in the rocking chair—feeling dismal enough because my aching head and side prevented my doing anything.

Sunday, March 7.   Had visitors in the morn. Lizzie, and Miss R. [emond]. Spent the afternoon and evening *delightfully* with my dear Miss S. [hepard]. How very kind she is! She showed me all the noble W. [hittier]'s letters, and *very, very* beautiful they are. I shall keep the picture of this afternoon in my mind. Seated by a table in her pleasant, old fashioned room, near the cheerful stove; on the table stands an exquisite vase, of which the leaves and flowers of the lily of the valley form the design,—filled with beautiful flowers—heliotrope pines, mignonette and a bright blue little California flower. The little book-shelf is filled with books, and an air of perfect

and most delicious *repose* fills the whole room. It is as subtle
and delightful as the fragrance of the flowers,—stealing into
the senses, and driving care and unrest away. Miss U. [pton]
came in, and very kindly gave me Mrs. Browning in blue
and gold. Miss S. [hepard] gave me Whittier, in the same;
"Picciola" in French, and the Eclectic containing Mrs.
Browning's picture. How very very much I thank her! Said
farewell to our "English rose"—Lizzie C. [hurch]. Dear
Mary S. [hepard]! I feel sad at parting with thee, for thou
has ever been the best, the kindest, the dearest of friends to
me. Other friends have sometimes seemed cold or unkind,—
thou never! I thank and bless thee! Truly thou art one of the
good and unselfish on earth.

Monday, March 8.　　My last day in school. Feel both
relieved and sad. Had many kind farewells from the scholars.
I *hope* I may never repent the step which I have taken. Read
"Aurora," and played chess with Mrs. Putnam.

Friday, [sic] *March 9.*　　Was surprised and delighted by
a visit from Misses W. [eston] and K. [itty] and a beautiful
letter from dear Lucy. Everybody is very kind to me—much
kinder than I deserve. Busy packing all the afternoon.

Wednesday, March 10.　　The last day in beautiful N. [ew]
England. Had several visitors this afternoon, and all the
"Good Byes" were said. My dear Miss S. [hepard] came to
see me. I *know she* will miss me far more than any one else
in Salem. Addie and Mr. L. [enox] came bringing me a
letter from Mr. N. [ell]; I should have liked to see him.
Helen gave me Longfellow in blue and gold, and Sarah
P. [itman] gave me Bayard Taylor's "Poems of the Orient."

Thursday, March 11.　　Philadelphia. Left Salem at six.
Spent the whole day in the cars. The ride from Boston to
N. [ew] Y. [ork] is rather tedious,—especially when one is

not well. The succession of snow-crowned hills, contrasting with dark glossy ever-greens, and interspersed with villages and towns between is at first pleasing to the eye, but after awhile one wearies of it. Longfellow's sweet and musical rhymes beguiled much of the time. We approached the "Armory," and then I read the poet's beautiful "Arsenal at Springfield"! Arrived here after eleven, thoroughly worn out.

Friday, March 12. Spend the day at home—*resting.*

Saturday, March 13. Too tired to go out. Had several visitors. It is pleasant to be at home. Read Shakespeare a little, and *talked* more than I ought.

Sunday, March 14. Wrote to Mrs. P.[utnam] and Miss S.[hepard]. Such a queer looking visitor as S.[arah] had! Company all the afternoon. This evening read "The Atlantic Monthly," and tried to teach L. and E.[mily Purvis?] "The Day is Done." With proper cultivation L. would make a superior woman, I think. She is an interesting girl. Oh dear! I'm weary of *lounging about.*

Monday, March 15. Home as usual. Aunt H.[arriet] came down. Sweet Mattie F.[arbeaux] and her sister called. Most sweetly she sang for me. Mr. P.[utnam] sent me the "Observer."

Tuesday, March 16. Took a little walk, for the first time, in search of pure air, but found it not. The air is so close, damp and heavy that I can hardly breathe. Oh! for a breath of pure fresh N.[ew] England air! Commenced a shawl for my dear Miss S.[hepard]. Copied some poems for Hattie [Purvis]. Cordelia S. came in. She is an intelligent, interesting girl,—very imaginative, with a great deal of freshness and originality. She is from the South, and needs to be converted to Anti-Slavery. I gave her Whittier's A.[nti]

S. [lavery] poems for a beginning. Wrote a long letter to Mrs. C. [aroline] Putnam.

Wednesday, March 17. Aunt S. [arah Purvis] came in; was delighted to see her. Walked out a little way. Read Longfellow. The S. [mith]'s spent the evening here, and we had music and singing,—quite a pleasant time.

Thursday, March 18. A paper from Salem—from S. [arah] P. [itman?]. Still no letters. Made some calls with S. [arah] and Ada. Saw the "Black Siddons"—Mrs. [Mary F.] Webb, who told me that Annie [Woods Webb] was coming in a few days. Mrs. W. [ebb] is very refined and lady-like, and has a beautiful voice. Went to Mrs. C. [hew]'s.

Friday, March 19. Went to Earle's Gallery, and saw some beautiful paintings. The statue of Beatrice was gone, but there is an exquisite picture of her here. What a sweet, lovely face is hers. How terrible must have been the wrongs which could have driven that gentle, lovely girl to so dark a crime! There is a beautiful little picture of Red Riding Hood; the sweetest little face I ever saw. The soft, violet eyes, the tinted cheeks, the rosebud lips, and the bright scarlet hood so cunningly over her sunny head, all are charming.—Saw also a striking picture which must, I think, represent the murder of Virginia by her father. To my unpracticed eyes this picture is very fine. It is the moment after the fatal blow is received, and the lovely Virginia falls back into the arms of one who is standing near. Her form and features are *perfect*. An expression of horror, not unmingled with awe and admiration rests on the faces of the spectators. The countenance of Virginius, as he raises on high the bloody dagger, is lit up with the loftiest enthusiasm. Saw also a picture of West's, a scene from Hamlet,—where Ophelia comes in mud, and singing as she offers her flowers. Every lover of Hamlet knows how touching this scene is. The artist has represented it finely. Saw "Christus Consolator," with the manacled slave, which the pious people of our land are so careful as to leave out of their prayer books. Saw a picture of "St. Catherine Borne by the Angels," exactly like the one I saw at Mr. [Theodore] Parker's. The legend of St. Catherine is beautiful.

Saturday, March 20. Read, and worked all the morning. In the afternoon, went with S.[arah] and L.[izzie] to visit the Misses S. The prettiest one, Miss Sallie, played and sung very prettily for us, accompanying herself on the guitar. I noticed there a beautiful engraving of Mary, Queen of Scotts, and a fine view of St. Paul's Cathedral. The L.'s are much more interesting than Southerners usually are. I am going to *try hard* to convert them to anti-slavery. This evening read in an old English periodical, a very interesting criticism on, with numerous extracts from "The Reminiscences of Michael Kelly," an actor and stage manager in the days of Mrs. Siddions, Sheridan, Kemble, and other brilliant actors and authors, of whom the writer tells many amusing and interesting anecdotes. Heard from my dear friend, Mary S.[hepard].

Sunday, March 21. Wrote busily all the morn. Letters to S.[arah] P.[itman?], Miss R.[emond] and one to Dr. B. one of the "Era." This afternoon talked with Mr. C.[hew] about Jamaica. How much I should like to go there! Read some poetry. Visited Mrs. [Sarah] D.[ouglass]. Miss M. a quiet but interesting intelligent girl was quite cordial, and played on the melodeon while L. sang for us.

Monday, March 22. Spent most of the day at Mrs. C.[hew]'s. Afterwards went to meet A.[da] at Mr. L.'s, but she did not come. Miss W.[ebb?] entertained us with her "hobby" pretty. She is a peculiar genius. In the evening Mrs. [Mary] Webb[2] read "Uncle Tom's Cabin" dramatized, and portions of "Hiawatha." I thought she read remarkably well. The most humorous portions were perhaps the best—they were read capitally. The pathetic portions were touchingly and beautifully read. Mattie G.[riffith], Prof. C. and several other Abolitionists were present. Mr. [Francis] W.[ebb] showed us a fine portrait of the Duchess of Sutherland[,] the first I have ever seen. She is as beautiful, noble, and queenly looking as I had expected. Saw also a picture of Lady Byron, who looks very old; also a magnificent picture of "Rachel" as Phaedra and another of Ira Aldridge the black tragedian. Rachel is a splendid looking woman. Saw an engraving of the Queen's musician, a very handsome German, who wins ladies' hearts as well as laurels. Mrs. W.[ebb] is a *very* interesting woman.

Tuesday, March 23. Went early to Mrs. W.[ebb]'s, and had a long and pleasant conversation with her. She told me about several distinguished people, among whom were Mrs. Jam[i]eson, and Mrs. S. C. Hall,—the latter, whom I thought *must* be beautiful, is *very homely;* and Mrs. Jam[i]eson, my *ideal* writer, who, I imagined, must be a spiritual beauty,— is a "great, fat woman, who comes into a room puffing and blowing!" Horrible! Horrible! My favorites,—the Howitts, were, I'm glad to say, described as "lovely looking," and Dean Milman as a noble old man, with beautiful, long white hair.—Dear Annie [Woods Webb] arrived with her two little darlings, who have grown finely. A.[nnie] looks thin.— Had a letter from Mrs. [Jane] Putnam, Sr.

Wednesday, March 24. Paid several visits. Went to Earle's Gallery again, with Miss W.[ebb], who went into raptures

over some of the pictures, as well she might. This afternoon
went to Mrs. Farbeaux's. Had a delightful visit. Received
several papers from Mr. N. [ell] and wrote him a *very* long
letter. Wrote also to Georgie Putnam.

Thursday, March 25. Spent most of the day with dear
Annie. She has two sweet, pretty little girls. Had a long
pleasant talk with her. Mrs. W. [ebb] gave me an interesting
account of her visit to Holyrood, and other remarkable places.
I can't help liking her. Spent the evening delightfully at
Mrs. Farbeaux's. Wrote to Miss Shepard, and to Mrs.
C. [aroline] Putnam.

Friday, March 26. Spent all the morning at the da-
guerre's with A. [nnie]'s sweet little girls. Bade Mr. and
Mrs. W. [ebb] farewell. They sail on Sunday. Spent the
afternoon and evening at Mrs. C. [hew]. Came home feeling
quite ill.

Saturday, March 27. Most of the day in bed. Too sick
to accompany S. [arah] to Aunt H. [arriet]'s. In the evening
felt able to read some peotry, and practise.

Sunday, March 28. Commenced Livingstone's "Travels
in Africa." Think I shall like it much. Some strangers came
in. Miss Jennette Miller and Mr. Vogelsang, whom I have
not seen for years. How vividly the sight of them brought
dear Aunt J. [?] to my mind! This afternoon more visitors.
Mr. V. [ogelsang] spent part of the eve. with us. He is very
agreeable and sensible, and we had a pleasant talk.

Monday, March 29. Read Dr. Livingstone. A visit from
dear A. [nnie Woods Webb] and Mrs. C. [hew]. A letter
from Miss R. [emond]. A very pleasant one. Dear Salem! I
wish I could see thee! I feel quite worried at not receiving
some other letters. Some of my friends have forgotten me, I

fear. Lizzie [Magee]³ and I have had a long talk to-day, planning about the future. L.[izzie] is *very* kind hearted; but for me,—I must achieve my destiny—alone. May God give me strength to work *earnestly!*

Tuesday, March 30.   A letter from Sarah P.[itman?]. Wrote to Nellie A.[lexander?]. Spent most of the day with Annie. Sallie L. brought me a beautiful "Heartsease." How it has gladdened my eyes! Felt very unwell, and retired early.

Wedneesday, March 31.   A prisoner at home. Cordelia L. came in, and we read and discussed poetry. She is very familiar with Shakespeare. Received a letter from Mr. [Joseph] Putnam. He is quite unwell. Wrote him a very long letter; wrote also to Ada. Read Dr. Livingstone.

Thursday, April 1.   Sewed; read Bulwer's fine tragedy of "Richelieu." It is beautiful. Went to Independence Square, and sat there a long time, watching the graceful little squirrels as they bounded so lightly over the green grass—as green now—almost as if it were summer, and tried to imagine that I was in dear Old Salem, far away from the crowd and tumult of a great city. But it needed only to turn from the trees, the grass, and the squirrels, and look out upon the busy street, to dispel the illusion. What a crowd went hurrying past; and among them all, how few pleasant and happy faces! how many sad and careworn ones! Wrote to my dear Miss S.[hepard]. To-morrow the girls leave. I dare not trust myself to think how *very* lonely I shall be. Wrote to Cordelia.

Friday, April 2.   L.[izzie Magee] and S.[arah Cassey Smith] left to-day. Oh! how very lonely I am without them! Read "Picciola" with Aunt M.[argaretta]. Practised a long while. Lucy commenced reading to me the tragedy of "Virginius." How desolate the room up stairs looks. Now that all the trunks are removed. Why must these constant partings be. I cannot be intimate with everybody, and Sarah is my only sister. I miss her *dreadfully*.

Saturday, April 3. Practised. Wrote to Mr. N. [ell]. Spent most of the day at Mrs. C. [hew]'s. Worked, and read a charming little English book "Sibert's World," by the author of "A Trap to Catch a Sunbeam." Was much amused by some profound questions about heaven, etc. from little Charlie [Purvis] an interesting little fellow. Returning home found some very acceptable presents from Mr. C. [hew]'s store. He is very kind. The girls reach home to-day. My heart is with them.

Sunday, April 4. This morning looked over some of dear grandfather's[4] old letters. There was a very interesting letter from a gentleman, travelling in France and Italy, and another of equal interest to me because of the writer—N. P. Rogers. And what an insight these letters are into dear grandfather's own character. With how much veneration and respect to himself are they all expressed. And it makes me proud and happy to think how worthy of it he was! Would that some of his family resembled, I grieve to say that they *do not;* far, far from it. Looked over a book of painted flowers. Very, very beautiful they are. The graceful lily, the brilliant carnation, the sweet, modest violet, and my own darling mignonette with many others, were so beautifully and faithfully represented that I felt a thrill of delight when looking at them. "Stars of earth!" how dear to my heart ye are!

Monday, April 5. Practised several hours, and read French with Aunt M. [argaretta]. Went to Mrs. F. [arbeaux]'s where I met Kate A. We had a nice long talk. Mattie F. [arbeaux] sang one of the sweetest songs I ever heard, "Hark, I Hear an Angel Sing." It is *very* beautiful, and most appropriate to this season. Wrote to my dear Sallie.

Tuesday, April 6. Practised as usual. Commenced the opera of "La Favorita," paid a visit to the S. [allie]'s who played and sang to me. Mattie F. [arbeaux] came in. Heard from S. [arah Cassey Smith], Mrs. C. [aroline] P. [utnam], Addie [Putnam] and Helen [Gilliard]. So many letters make me feel better and brighter. Sent letters to S. [arah] and Mrs. P. [utnam]. Saw, in an Italian's store, some beautiful statues and vases.

Wednesday, April 7. Had a manifestation of the wicked, contemptible prejudice, which made my blood boil with indignation. How long, how long will this last! It is *very* hard to bear. Spent most of the day at Mrs. C. [hew]'s. A letter from dear A. [nnie]. Read the "Opera of Ernani," and Dr. Livingstone.

Thursday, April 8. A dismal day. Rain pouring. Aunt H. [arriet] and Emma,[5] whom I was delighted to see, came in. Heard of the death of Mrs. C. [hew]'s brother-in-law, Mr. S. Theirs seems truly to be a fated family. Practised, and read Dr. Livingstone more than I have hitherto. Do not find it quite so interesting as at first. Though I very much like the liberal spirit in which it is written.

Friday, April 9. Read Dr. Livingstone, and practised. Kate A. and Mattie F. [arbeaux] came to see me. The latter sang that sweet song "Hark, I Hear an Angel Sing" most beautifully.

Byberry.[6] *Saturday, April 10.* Had a delightful sail up the river. Found Hattie [Purvis] and Georgia [Purvis][7] waiting for me. Our ride home was very pleasant. Already the country is beginning to look quite summer-like. What a relief it is to escape from the close and crowded city, from the sight of glaring brick walls, with only *patches* of the sky between to the pure, fresh air of the country, to boundless canopy above. Received a warm welcome from my Byberry cousins. In the eve. Hattie sang and played for me. Robert [Purvis] came.

Sunday, April 11. A rainy day. Feel very miserable. Tried to enter into the pleasant conversation which was going on around me. Hattie has a friend here who reminds me very much of Lizzie Church. She is about her size, and has just such long, light hair, and beautiful blue eyes. She is a little poetess,—a sweet, gentle creature. I have fallen quite in love with her. We had quite an animated discussion about Shakespeare's plays, with Aunt H.[arriet] who pretends that she agrees with Miss Bacon. We are quite sure it can only be pretense. I *know* that Shakespeare, and *he* only wrote those immortal plays. To look at that noble unrivalled head alone, would convince me of that. Robert [Purvis, Jr.] left.

Monday, April 12. Rain again. Crocheted very industriously while Aunt H.[arriet] read "The Fire Worshippers" to me. It is certainly very beautiful; far more so than "The Veiled Prophet" which is grand, but too horrible. Feel better and stronger than I did yesterday.

Tuesday, April 13. Still a prisoner. Worked busily on my shawl while Aunt H.[arriet] read Byron to me. Wrote to Miss Sarah. Commenced Mrs. Child's "Letters from New York." This eve. had a long talk with Mr. [Robert] P.[urvis] about family affairs. It made my heart feel very sad and heavy. Oh! if I could have things my way, there should [be] nothing but perfect harmony between the members of one family. These dissensions are really terrible to me.

Wednesday, April 14. Aunt H.[arriet] and Mr. P.[urvis]

went away. Hattie and I had a nice long talk. She read "Jonathan Slick," a very amusing book while I worked. The "Letters" are perfectly charming. Through written in a city, they almost compensate for the loss of sunlight and pleasant walks. The writer's heart is *brimming* full of love to all mankind. Most beautifully she expresses those thoughts which can belong only to a truly loving heart and richly gifted mind. Friend P. [arson?] and his wife returned with Aunt H. [arriet]. What perfect serenity and repose there is in the manner of these old Quaker ladies!

Thursday, April 15.   Aunt Harriet was sick. Spent most of the day in her room. Read in her album two beautiful poems by Mrs. [Lydia Maria] Child and by Whittier, addressed "To the Daughters of James Forten."[8] Finished the delightful "Letters." I love and thank Mrs. Child for writing such a book. This eve. Mr. P. [urvis] talked with me about my dear lost mother; I love to hear of her. What a pleasure it would be to me if I had a portrait of her, my own dear mother!

Friday, April 16.   Yesterday visited poor W. [illiam Purvis]'s[9] grave. It is sad to think that we shall see these we love, no more on earth yet we know they are far happier than they could be with us. Spent to-day in reading, working and talking. Read the A. [nti] S. [lavery] Papers, and Cooper's interesting "Water-witch." Must return to the city to-morrow, though I would fain stay longer. Every one is so kind and pleasant to me. Aunt H. [arriet] wishes me to spend the summer with her, and teach her three youngest children.[10] I should like to, but have not yet decided.

Philadelphia. April 17.   Arrived in town this morning, and found, to my great delight, a *lot* of letters awaiting me. What a blessing letters are! These were from dear Sallie

[Cassey Smith], Mr. [Joseph] P. [utnam], Miss S. [hepard], Annie W. [oods Webb], and Lizzie M. [agee]. Also some papers from Mr. [William C.] Nell. I feel as rich as a queen. But was too tired to go in the country with Aunt M. [argaretta]. Sent a letter to my dear sister Sallie [Cassey Smith]. *Rested* myself.

Sunday, April 18. Have done nothing but write letters the whole day. Wrote *seven* letters; to Mr. and Mrs. P. [utnam], Addie, Helen, Miss S. [hepard], Annie W. [oods Webb], and Augusta L. Completely tired out. Mr. [Joseph] P. [utnam]'s letters are so suggestive, particularly his last, that I always write longer letters to him than I intend. I fear he may not like some things in my last. But it can't be helped. What he said to me about Mr. R. [emond] *had* to be frankly answered. I hope he will not misunderstand me.

Monday, April 19. Read a little. Wrote to Lizzie [Magee]. In the afternoon had "aclarin up" time, as Aunt Dinah says; which has tired me dreadfully.—Taught school all the morning for Aunt M. [argaretta].

Tuesday, April 20. Worked busily all day. In the afternoon Uncle T. [homas Forten] read to us Mr. [Hinton Rowan] Halper's book "The Impending Crisis." It is *excellent*. One of the best arguments against slavery I've ever heard.

Wednesday, April 21. A letter from Annie [Woods Webb]. Paid some visits with Aunt M. [argaretta]. Worked, and practised.

Thursday, April 22. Commenced a *story,* and wrote till breakfast. Studied French an hour. Sewed till 10:30. Latin with Eddie C. [hew], then walked till dinner time. After dinner practised, and sewed. Went with Aunt M. [argaretta] to the Library; an excellent one. Commenced Bayne's "Essays in Biography," which dear Mary S.[hepard] likes so much. Read Tennyson's beautiful "May Queen" to S.[arah]. Received a letter from Miss R.[emond] and one of twelve pages from Lizzie [Magee]. In the eve. crocheted while Suzy read "Harper['s]" to us. I've *enjoyed* the day.

Tuesday, April 23. This morning passed as yesterday's. This afternoon, sewed, practised and read Hayne's "Essays." Had a long letter from Mr. P.[utnam]. I do think he is one of the most provoking as well as delightful people in the world. No letter from Sis. She deserves a good scolding.

Saturday, April 24. Went to the A.[nti] S.[lavery] Office. Was glad to meet Mr. P.[urvis] there. The noble [Charles] Sumner is in town. Oh! if I could only have a *glimpse* of him. It makes my heart ache to think of the wide, wide gulf between us. I shall never meet him, even to hear him converse with others, myself a passive listener; yet how I long to do so. But even a sight of him would do my soul good. I stayed at the Office as long as I could, hoping that he might chance to come in. But I waited in vain. In the evening read Bayne's essays on De Quincey and on Tennyson to Aunt M.[argaretta]. They are most appreciative, and splendidly written. I enjoy them perfectly.

Sunday, April 25. Wrote some letters. While writing the bell rang. I[,] not feeling very well, was still *on dishabille* and made my escape. Afterwards came in and found lovely Mrs. [Lucretia] Mott and some friends, among whom was an English lady; a most delightful and interesting person. She is the wife of an eminent french writer, whose name I can't remember. He has written a book on the Unity of the Races. She is very social and talked with me about N.[ew] E.[ngland] and seemed to appreciate my enthusiasm for it. She resides in Algeria; likes it very much; and thinks the natives—Arabs and Africans are the finest people in the world. Thinks the mixed races superior to any other. *I* think she is truly a "Jewel of a woman." Am perfectly charmed; felt sorry that I could not have seen more of her.

Monday, April 26. After performing the morning's duties, spent the rest of the day at Mrs. C.[hew]'s. This eve. read the "Essays" and Mrs. Browning to Aunt M.[argaretta]. How perfectly, perfectly beautiful are such poems as "The Sleep," "Crowned and Wedded," "Cowper's Grave," and many, many others. Wrote to S.[arah]. Heard from Miss S.[hepard].

Tuesday, April 27. Morn. passed as usual. This afternoon went to the A.[nti] S.[lavery] Office, hoping, I confess, to obtain a glimpse of Sumner, but of course, I had not that great pleasure. Paid several visits, saw in Chestnut St. some beautiful pictures. Two splendid portraits of Victoria and Albert in their robes of state. How magnificently they *look*. Saw at the S.[mith]'s some very fine views of Rome and Venice. Heard from S.[arah].

Wednesday, April 28. Wrote, studied and practised. Aunt H.[arriet] came in, and she and I went to see Rosa Bonheur's famous picture of "The Horse-Fair." What a marvelous picture it is! There are numbers of horses in all positions, splendid looking and wonderfully life-like. Some of the most prominent ones particularly impressed me. There were two powerful white horses near the center of the picture. One cannot realize that they are *painted*, they or the rider who sits on one of them, his head bare, his shirt sleeves rolled up, every sinew of his brawny arms plainly visible as he strains every nerve, uses his utmost strength to hold his horse. These are *real* horses, this is a *real* man. Again, on the left, is a magnificent black horse, his fore feet rearing up in the air, his nostrils distended. How proud, how conscious he is of his own beauty and power! I think he is my favorite. On his left is a beautiful sorrel, very graceful, yet gentle looking. *His* head is not raised so loftily as my favorite's. I think he must be a lady's horse. Still farther to the left is a very fine roan[,] a "strawberry roan"—Aunt H. [arriet], who knows more about horses than I, says. He is a very grand looking horse. All these, and many others are perfect *marvels* to me. Every one *stands out* from the canvas; has a wonderful *individuality*. Aunt H. [arriet] thought the trees almost as marvelous as the horses. They are certainly beautiful. But no description could do justice to this mighty masterpiece of Art. We saw also a smaller picture by the same artist, representing cattle ploughing in Flanders; and hard work it seems, for there are six oxen yoked to one plough, and yet they are toiling on very slowly and heavily.—Returning home we saw in the window of a picture store, two paintings, the same, or copies of the same, that we had previously seen at the Crystal Palace. They both represent market-places at night; probably in Italy or some other country of southern Europe. Groups of people are standing around a fruit stall. The fruit is perfectly natural. The light from a candle on the table falls on the faces of the woman standing near, with very fine effect. But the mournful beauty of one picture I shall never forget. It represents Lady Jane Gray at the moment before her execution. Her eyes are bandaged, and she kneels by the fatal block. Her confessor bends over her, whispering to her the last words of hope and consolation. Her face is white as marble; its expression perfectly resigned, angelic. The beautiful, long hair falls over the uncovered neck and shoulders. One of her ladies-in-waiting has fainted. The other turns shudderingly away. The executioner stands near leaning on the axe. Even on *his* face there is an expression of compassion. This is a most touching picture, and impressed me deeply, I think of it often.

Thursday, April 29. After the morn.'s duties, read the "Improvisatore," a book translated from the Danish of Hans Christian Andersen by Mary Howitt. It abounds in beautiful descriptions of Rome and other Italian cities. The story is impassioned enough for a son of Italy to have written and is intensely interesting throughout. Read also a very interesting sketch of Hans Christian Andersen. Sewed, while Uncle T.[homas Forten] read to me Bayne's "Glimpses of Recent British Art." Very, very beautiful they are, and they have taught me far more about British Painters than I ever knew before. Bayne is a fine writer. Wrote to Mr. Putnam, and sent him some quotations from the essay on "Tennyson," hoping to convert him, for he's an admirer of my favorite laureate.

Friday, April 30. After writing and studying, sat by the window sewing and learning the "May Queen"—while the "Sweet, south wind," the first of the season, kissed my cheek. How warm, how delicious its kisses were. But soon the heat quite over-powered me; the air is now very oppressive, and weighs me down. I feel *miserably* both in mind and body, and *dare not* say another word to thee, my journal.—*Bon nuit.*

Saturday, May 1. Diem perdidi! Yes, I have lost this bright, beautiful May day. Lost it in shopping, for which I am thoroughly ashamed of myself; and am *tired*, dreadfully! This eve. cousin James F.[orten] [11] came in. How greatly he is changed. I should not have known him! Read in the "[National Anti-Slavery] Standard," a very interesting sketch of Dumas, and one of Byron and Shelley from Trelawney's "Recollections." Had a little billet from dear S.[arah] containing a tiny bouquet of May flowers, violets, and a columbine. She gathered them on the dear old hills *expressly* for me. I shall always prize them *very* highly.

Sunday, May 2.   Read aloud the "Maniac," a scene from "Julius Caesar," and some of Whittier's spirited A.[nti] S.[lavery] poems, till I was breathless. Then tried, in some verses to express to S.[arah] my thanks for her dear little flowers. Spent the afternoon and eve. with Aunt M.[argaretta] at Mrs. C.[hew]'s. Sweet Mattie F.[arbeaux] was there. We looked over some very fine engravings of American scenery. I could not help acknowledging that some of it was beautiful and grand, despite my prejudice against everything *Am.*[erican].

Monday, May 3.   Sewed very busily nearly all day. Wrote to Aunt H.[arriet] and to dear Sallie [Cassey Smith]. Latin.

Tuesday, May 4.   Attended the examination of the colored High School,[12] all the day and evening. Many of the exercises were well conducted, and quite interesting. Mrs. [Sarah] D.[ouglass] did beautifully. Mattie F.[arbeaux] read a beautiful composition, "The Pleasures of Memory"; and graduated. Had a letter from Annie.

Wednesday, May 5.   Latin and sewing. Then read a very interesting essay of Bayne's on "The Modern Novel." His criticism of Dickens—*most* of it, seems to me particularly just and appreciative. So also of Bulwer. Wrote to Annie.

Thursday, May 6.   After hearing E.[ddie]'s Latin, and sewing busily nearly all day went to the Library, and read in the "Eclectic" a fine description of Malmaison, and some beautiful stories from "Household Words."—In the evening read to Aunt M.[argaretta] the essay on Currer Bell. How beautifully it is written! What a noble and just tribute it is to that wonderfully gifted woman! This chapter ends the volume.

Seldom have I closed a book with so much regret, and yet with so much admiration. I have truly and thoroughly enjoyed these Essays. The writer is himself a poet, I think.

Friday, May 7.   In looking over what I've said of Bayne, I find I've made no mention of the sketch of Hugh Miller. I'll merely note it here as one of the finest in the book; full of deep, earnest feeling, of poetic beauty, of warm and most cordial appreciation. I can't help thinking that the writer *loved* Hugh Miller more than any one of whom he has written.

Fairview. Saturday, May 8.[13]   Went to Aunt S.[arah]'s. Had a pleasant sail up the river. Met the girls at the landing and rode home. The *sun* was out! Rare sight, indeed, for this *wonderfully* rainy month;—and the country looked beautifully. The trees are loaded with blossoms, pink and white, and the young leaves and grass are of the most delicate, exquisite green.

Sunday, May 9.   The sweet songs of the birds awoke me. Nature is looking her loveliest on this "sweet and dewy morn." Went to the woods with the girls, in search of wild flowers. Found the sweetest violets and anemones, and a delicate little white, bell-shaped flower whose name I do not know. After a while, tired of looking for flowers, seated myself on a picturesque old stump, while my little cousins continued their search. Thoroughly enjoyed the sweet, pure air, the glorious clouds, the blossoming trees, the dewy grass, and the perfect, *stillness* that reigned around me. Returning home we saw the cows and sheep lying in luxurious repose on the soft grass. How beautifully the snow-white little lambs contrasted with the bright, emerald green! "If Rosa Bonheur were here," exclaimed my gipsy-looking little cousin E.[mily Purvis] "what a pretty picture she could paint!" In the afternoon rode a little way on horseback. I did not dare to trot my horse, but walked along very leisurely, and enjoyed my ride greatly. This evening spent at the P. [arson?]'s[,] a pleasant family and friends with whom I talked unceasingly about dear N. [ew] England. Meaning no disrespect to them, for they're good people and I like them, I must confess that I was most interested in a magnificent Newfoundland dog, the handsomest, noblest creature I ever saw. Really could not help coveting him. I do *love* such dogs.

Monday, May 10.   Rain, rain! Imprisoned in the house, sewed, talked, and commenced Pope's "Illiad." Had always fancied that old Homer would be too grand and stately for my comprehension, but am pleasantly disappointed. Find it delightful to leave this matter-of-fact, every-day world and soar into *his* world of grand old heroes and gods and god-desses. Took advantage of a gleam of sunshine to take a long pleasant drive. *I* do most of the driving, to my great delight.

Tuesday, May 11.   Sewed (for it still rains) while S. [arah] read the "Illiad" to me. Took a long drive, despite the rain, and visited Mrs. E. In the evening the children gathered round me and insisted upon my "telling them a story." Delighted them with "Klosterheim."

Wednesday, May 12.   Took my leave of "Fairview," and drove to the station. Found myself an hour too early; and sat in the lonely little car-house knitting, and thinking. Then came the mighty steam-horse, and I was rapidly whirled away to the pretty little town of T. [renton] on the banks of the Delaware, from whence we took the steam-boat, and had a pleasant sail to the city. Found awaiting me, a long, *very* kind letter from dear Sallie. Read also a *very* kind letter *about* me, from Aunt H. [arriet]. She wishes me to spend the summer with them, *without* teaching. But that is not to be thought of. I will gladly pay them a few weeks visit, but if I spend the *summer* there, I *must* do something. I could not do otherwise. Took my sewing, and went to visit my friend Mrs. C. [hew].

Thursday, May 13.   Grandmother is quite unwell, so I was cook and housekeeper. This afternoon heard an excellent lecture by Mr. D. on "Respiration." Spent the eve. at the S.'s and heard some delightful music and singing. All were Southerners save me.

Friday, May 14.   Kept house again this morn. This aft. and eve. spent at Mrs. F. [arbeaux]'s. Rev. Bishop [Daniel Alexander] P. [ayne] [14] was there, and talked with, and prayed for me. He's a singular person, but very kind hearted. He wishes me to contribute to a magazine of which he is editor. [15] I have promised to *try*. Mrs. F. [arbeaux] read to me the interesting account of the A. [nti] S. [lavery] Meetings. Wrote to Miss S. [hepard].

Saturday, May 15.   Worked busily all day, and in the eve. read "Harper's."

Sunday, May 16.   Commenced writing some "Glimpses of New England." Sent my simple verses about the flowers to Bishop P. [ayne]. He is such a critic that I don't believe he'll think them worth publishing. Paid some visits with my sweet friend Mattie, whose mother has given me an elegant gold pencil-case. Wrote busily all the evening.

Monday, May 17.   Worked, and wrote during every spare moment.

Tuesday, May 18.   Had a great surprise in the arrival of Mr. [Joseph] Putnam and Mr. [William C.] Nell. Stood almost transfixed with astonishment. Was delighted to see them, and took them to Mrs. C. [hew]'s.

Wednesday, May 19.   Read my "Glimpses" to Mr.

P. [utnam] and N. [ell] who were pleased to commend them much more highly than they deserve. Then paid a round of visits with them, and spent most of the eve. at Mrs. C. [hew]'s. Returning home found a note from my dear Miss S. [hepard] awaiting me—enclosing a sprig of arbutus gathered by Whittier and his sister. He writes her word that they crossed the Mass. [achusetts] line into N. [ew] H. [ampshire] to gather it. For the poet hands that gathered it, for the loving heart that gave, as well as for its own sweetness and beauty, what a precious treasure it will be to me.

Byberry. Thursday, May 20. Greatly to my surprise received a note full of kind thanks, and a dollar from Bishop P. [ayne] for my simple contribution. The first money I've ever made by *writing*. This afternoon had a delightful sail up the river with our friends. The trees along the shore look beautifully—presenting every variety of green. Arrived at B. [yberry] in the midst of a storm, but it soon passed off and became pleasant. Sweet Tacie T. [ownsend] is here. Passed the eve. with music, singing and pleasant conversation. I think our friends enjoyed it.

Friday, May 21. Had to finish the "Glimpses" this morn, for Mr. [Joseph] P. [utnam] insisted on taking them with him to be published. His kind intentions will be defeated, for he'll find no one willing to publish such stuff. He and Mr. N. [ell] both left this morn. One for N. [ew] Y. [ork] the other for Phila. [delphia]. Drove to the station with Mr. P. [utnam]. The country is beautiful now. Bidding him farewell seemed like taking leave of a part of N. [ew] E. [ngland]. Tacie and I had a nice long talk about our favorite books. She is a gifted girl, and very charming. This afternoon she, Aunt H. [arriet], and Miss [Sarah Parker] R. [emond] who has been spending a few days here, and was very friendly to me, went to the city. Miss R. [emond] leaves for Europe[16] in the autumn. Worked on my shawl, talked with Hattie, and read "Shetland and the Shetlanders."

Saturday, May 22. A charming day. Read "Romans and Reality" by L. E. R. The descriptions of Italy are beautiful. Sketches of fashionable life, and of distinguished literary people abound. And wonderfully graphic and amusing and interesting they are. The ending of the story—one of hopeless love, is so very mournful that I felt really quite sad after reading it. I was soon revived by the entertaining conversation which very pleasantly beguiled our evening. Wrote a long letter to Sallie.

Sunday, May 23. Read, wrote and talked with Tacie [Townsend] and R. [obert Purvis, Jr.]. This morning had a delightful little ride just after breakfast. And this eve. a longer and more delightful one to the boat. I have never seen the country more lovely.

Monday, May 24. Persuaded Mr. Purvis to give me some out-of-door work to do; and raked the freshly cut grass on the lawn, quite busily. The exercise did me good. Then studied French, and chatted with Aunt H. [arriet]. After dinner, went for the mail. Found a letter from Mr. P. [utnam] which I read as I strolled leisurely along. It contains little encouragement about my poor *Ms.; but I will not* despair. Read "Calaynas" a fine tragedy by Boker. This eve. had a delightful ramble over the fields with my bright little cousin Georgie; and gathered some very pretty wild flowers.

Tuesday, May 25. This morn. worked busily out-of-doors. Then read "Picciola," and Boker's fine tragedies. Wrote to Mr. P. [utnam]. I am more and more charmed with Miss Sinclair's book.

Wednesday, May 26. Commenced reading "Paradise Lost,"

to Aunt H. [arriet]. Also commenced botany with H. [attie Purvis] to whom I teach French. Read a beautiful letter from Mr. [William Lloyd] Garrison to Mr. [Robert] P. [urvis] written years ago. Talked a great deal, studied French, read and sewed.—Rain, rain, rain!

Thursday, May 27. Sent letters to Aunt M. [argaretta] and Mr. P. [utnam]. Think it very *mean* that nobody writes to me. Studied French and botany, sewed and read "Paradise Lost," and some fine descriptions of old castles in Scotland.

Friday, May 28. Read, wrote and studied, as usual. This afternoon had a delightful ride to the landing. I do enjoy riding perfectly.

Saturday, May 29. Morn. ditto with yes. Another charming ride to Tonisdale. E. [vening] pleasant [ly] spent at Dr. C.'s. H. [attie] P. [urvis] has greatly improved.

Sunday, May 30. Read "She Stoops to Conquer," and another amusing comedy of Goldsmith's. Felt unwell to-day.

Monday, May 31. The last day of spring. A most *un-May-like* May this has been. Commenced teaching to-day, and found it quite pleasant. The children are well behaved and eager to learn. Studied French and wrote. A long letter from Sallie [Cassey Smith].

Tuesday, June 1. Welcome in, bright summer! Welcome in, thou "rare" month of June! School; then French; a long pleasant walk. Helped Aunt H. [arriet] to plant some beautiful flowers, the sight of which has done me a world of good. Commenced Lady M. Montagu's "Letters," and wrote to my dear Miss S. [hepard].

Wednesday, June 2. Am perfectly charmed with Lady M.'s delightful "Letters." Her descriptions of Turkey are the most interesting I've ever read. What a lovely day this has been. And what a perfect evening! Hattie and I amused ourselves raking hay until the bright stars came out, and "gemmed the brow of Heaven."

Thursday, June 3. French; school, read the charming "Letters," and wrote to Sarah P. [itman?].

Friday, June 4. After the day's duties were over sat on the piazza, and tried to read but if the birds had entered into a conspiracy to prevent me, they could not have been more successful. They were having such a joyous time. There were two sweet little wrens that have the tiniest nest in a little evergreen not more than two or three feet high. I suppose they were adding some finishing touches to their dwelling. How busy and important they were! Their delicate little feet glancing to and fro on the soft velvety grass; flying far away, then returning, so near me that I began to hope they could be tempted to alight on the piazza, but no sooner did their bright eyes encounter the glance of mine than they were off again. Then there were two beautiful robins—lovers I am sure—for after advancing towards each other, they shyly retreating, exchanging inumerable tender glances, they finally met on the maple branches and *kissed* each other. I saw them myself. Beautiful bluebirds and occasionally a splendid, brilliant oriole, alighted for a moment on the lawn, their bright wings flashing like gems in the fading sunlight—then vanished. But what gladdened my eyes most was a pair of tiny humming birds,—the most *jewel* like of all the birds, who were playing at hide-and-seek amid the clustering leaves of the woodbine. How I wished they were tame enough to come and perch on my shoulder, that I might smooth their soft, bright plumage, and have a good look into their sparkling eyes! What nonsense this is! But I do, love birds. They are our *living breathing moving* flowers.

Saturday, June 5. Went to town;—had a delightful sail.

Found the city hot and disagreeable as usual. Grandmother
is better. Called at Mrs. C.[hew]'s and the S.[mith?]'s.
Visited Earle's Gallery and saw some beautiful pictures. Spent
the evening delightfully at sweet Mattie F.[arbeaux]'s.

Sunday, June 6.   Read Miss Austin's "Pride and Prejudice" which I like much. Spent most of the day at Mrs.
C.[hew]'s. Had a pleasant sail up the river in the evening.

Monday, June 7.   After school, read and sewed, walked
and talked, as usual. Heard from Mr. [Joseph] P.[utnam].

Tuesday, Wednesday and Thursday.—Ditto with yesterday.

Friday, June 11.   Spent the evening very pleasantly with
the H. family. With A. I was particularly pleased. She seems
so gentle and sensible. The girls, who are Hattie's teachers,
are all intelligent and agreeable. I like them exceedingly.
What a beautiful shower we had this evening! Leaving the
grass and leaves like dripping emeralds. Returned home, and
read Lady Montagu's charming "Letters."

Saturday, June 12.   Have had a perfect hurricane to-
day.—Just such a wild storm as I like to see. Read in the
"Living Age," a sweet Scotch story, "The Quiet Heart."
Sewed.

Sunday, June 13.   Wrote a long letter to Sallie. Laughed
and talked with R.[obert] till I was completely exhausted.
Read the "Letters."

Monday, June 14.   Wrote to Nellie A.[lexander?], Mrs.
C.[hew], and Annie. After school, read and studied. H.[attie]
and I amused ourselves with making the most ridiculous
rhymes and conundrums, this eve. I've laughed too much
these two days.

Tuesday, June 15.   Have been under-going a thorough
self-examination. The result is a mingled feeling of sorrow,
shame and self-contempt. Have realized more deeply and

bitterly than ever in my life my own ignorance and folly. Not only am I without the gifts of Nature, wit, beauty and talent; without the accomplishments which nearly every one of my age, whom I know, possesses; but I am not even *intelligent*. And for *this* there is not the *shadow* of an excuse. Have had many advantages of late years; and it is entirely owing to my own want of energy, perseverance and application, that I have not improved them. It grieves me deeply to think of this. I have read an immense quantity, and it has all amounted to nothing, because I have been too indolent and foolish to take the trouble of *reflecting*. Have *wasted* more time than I dare think of, in idle day-dreams, one of which was, how much I should know and do before I was twenty-one. And here I am nearly twenty-one, and only a *wasted life* to look back upon.—Add to intellectual defects a disposition whose despondency and fretfulness have constantly led me to look on the dark side of things, and effectually prevented me from contributing to the happiness of others; whose contrariness has often induced me to do those things which I ought not to have done, and to leave undone those which I ought to have done, and wanted to do,—and we have as dismal a picture as one could look upon; and yet hardly dismal enough to be faithful. Of course, I want to try to reform. But how to begin! Hav'nt the least spark of order or method in my composition, and fear I'm wholly incapable of forming any regular plan of improvement. Wish I had some of the superabundant energy and perseverance which some whom I know possess, just to enable me to *keep* the good resolutions which are so easily made and so very easily broken. Wrote to Mr. P. [utnam].

Wednesday, June 16. Finished Lady Montagu's delightful "Letters." Was disappointed to find so little about her quarrel with Pope. His letters to her, previous to it, are full of the most impassioned admiration. Think the outrageous and contemptible slanders, invented by Horace Walpole against her[,] are most unpardonable. I think she was a noble-hearted, high-souled woman, in many respects a century in advance of the age in which she lived;—in her enlightened appreciation of the true dignity of woman, for instance[,] in which she probably found no sympathy from any of her contemporaries. The "Letters" are very entertaining, but it doesn't seem to me as if they evince generally the decided intellectual superiority which their writer certainly possessed. And yet perhaps this is their great charm that they are not full of profound reasonings or sage opinions on intellectual subjects;—but rather consisting of graphic graceful descriptions, and a very fair proportion of gossip. I particularly like the perfect *ease* with which they are written. This eve. was beautiful. Had a glorious sunset. Hattie, C.[harles], G.[eorgie] and I went on a strawberry hunting expedition. Visited Mrs. R. who has the greatest variety of fruit I ever saw. She also has *legions* of roses, and gave us a beautiful bouquet among which were some exquisite moss-rose buds, my favorite—especially. I have always thought "The origin of the Moss-Rose" one of the sweetest little poems in the world. We had abundance of *fun* during our walk. Hattie, who is a capital mimic, amused me exceedingly. Laughed till we nearly exhausted.—Sent Mr. P.[utnam]'s letter this morn.

Thursday, June 17.   After school had a delightful ride to a garden. Saw a large variety of beautiful plants. Quantities of my darling heliotropes. The leaf of the bigonia [*sic*] I thought very singular and beautiful, and also the flower of the elements. The country through which we rode was quite hilly, and much more picturesque than I'd supposed any part of B. [yberry] to be. Returning we saw an old slave who had bought himself. He was hoeing corn very industriously, near a "little hut among the bushes"—and quite a respectable one too,—which he has built for himself. A little farther on was a woman seated by the road-side, her bonnet thrown off, and evidently bent on enjoying the cool of the day. Aunt H. [arriet] was actually wicked enough to call her "Jane Eyre." A bundle through which cakes and oranges were conspicuous, lay on the ground beside her. Altogether she formed quite a picture of ease and comfort. Still farther on was another picture which would have gladdened *Mrs. [Lydia Maria] Child's* heart;—a little sun-burned, barefooted boy, evidently not more than two or three years old; with the brightest pair of eyes, the most *speaking* face that I ever saw, we could not admire him sufficiently. He had such an arch, bright, spirited expression. A little rustic gate of white palings against which he was leaning formed a frame work for this charming picture, which will long "hang on memory's wall." Sweet T. [acie] T. [ownsend] has spent the day with us. She has very kindly lent me Browning's poems.

Friday, June 18. To my great astonishment see that my poor "Glimpses" are published in the "[National Anti-Slavery] Standard."[17] They are not worth it. Have been reading Browning's "Paracelsus." How softly, and yet how gloriously the silvery streams of moonlight are pouring through the leaves of the majestic poplars and the graceful maples, and resting on the lawn. And how sweetly this light summer breeze sings among the leaves; its tones are like the gentle dropping of the summer rain; just as musical to the ear; as sweet and soothing to the heart. Such nights as these it seems to me that the spirits of the dear, departed ones are nearer to us. Spirit vows seem breathing in my ear;—spirit influences, calm and deep and holy, seem twining themselves around my weary heart.—My mother! my loved lost mother! Thou are hovering near me now! Oh! bless and lead aright thy erring child, and let it not be very long ere thou claimest her again for thine own! For I am very weary[;] I *long* for thee, my mother. Oh, take me, take me to thy arms, there to rest forever!

Saturday, June 19. After school, sewed, and learned an exquisite little poem of Alice Carey's "Pictures of Memory." Then read Browning, the "Liberator," and some old papers. Most of the household have gone away. Another delightful eve. Georgie [Purvis] and I walked about, enjoying the moonlight.

Sunday, June 20. The very loveliest of June *country* sabbaths. This *quiet* is delicious. Not a sound is to be heard save the sweet "matin hymns" of the birds who are worshipping in the groves—"God's first temples," and truly most fitting and beautiful ones. Am sitting by the window writing, but pausing often to listen to them, and to watch the sunbeams as they steal so softly through the foliage and rest on the bright green grass of the lawn. Some exquisite roses and geranium are smiling on me as only *flowers can* smile, and I'll venture to say, preaching a sermon far more eloquent and beautiful than many are listening to this morning. Wrote to Mr. N.[ell] and Mattie M.[agee]. Read Browning, Whittier, and Alice Carey's Poems. Another beautiful moonlight night. Had several pleasant visitors.

Monday, June 21. Had a long, delightful letter from my dear Miss S.[hepard] who sent me some of that pretty edging made by her old, old aunt in the most old fashioned of ways, on a cushion. Dear friends! how earnestly I long to see thee, and my dear old S. [arah] once more. I *long* for it these bright June days.

Tuesday, June 22. Took a very pleasant drive this beautiful morn. Stopped at Tacie's whose home is very prettily and romantically situated.—Awful headache most of the day. Delicious moonlight, and a visit from T. [acie Townsend] this eve. Yesterday received a paper (Mr. N. [ell]) and a catalogue of very fine engravings, copies from the old masters,—in B. [oston]. How very much I'd like to see them.

Wednesday, June 23. Had a *Transcript*, full of interesting matter, from Mr. P. [urvis]. After school went to ride with Hen. [ry Purvis] in *the* donkey wagon. Had a very pleasant ride till we got within a little distance of home. Then *M.* [onsieur] *le donkey* took it into his head to be frightened at some cows, and jumped into a ditch nearly upsetting the wagon. Whereupon I took my leave, and preferred to walk home.

Thursday, June 24. Are having *perfect* June days now. Gathered some flowers for Aunt M. [argaretta]. After school Hattie and I took a walk to Dr. C.'s. Met Tacie there. Had a pleasant conversation, and a delightful walk home in the *rising* moonlight. Finished "Wearyfoot Common," a very interesting and well-written story in the "Living Age."

Friday, June 25. Very hot day. Perfectly beautiful moonlight eve. Mr. P. [urvis] drove H. [attie] and me to Tacie's where we spent an hour or two delightfully. Her home is beautifully situated on a gently sloping hill at the foot of which flows a pretty little stream. Her sisters are exquisitely, picturesquely beautiful.

Saturday, June 26. Too hot to do anything. This eve. Tacie came over, and we sat a long while together on the

Piazza*, talking and enjoying the delicious moonlight. Heard from Helen G. [illiard] and Aunt M. [argaretta].

Sunday, June 27. Read "Picciola" with Tacie. Mr. P. [urvis] read the "Prisoner of Chillon" to us. Wrote to Helen G. [illiard]. Hers is a very, very kind letter, and has really gladdened my heart. Read Browning.

Monday, June 28. Sick in bed all day. Have had no rest for several nights; the heat is so intense. Had a long, kind and very interesting [letter] from Mr. P. [utnam] and a kind note from sweet Lizzie C. [hurch]. Wrote to Aunt M. [argaretta]. Had a note and some lines from T. [acie].

Tuesday, June 29. Better and cooler to-day. After hearing Georgie's lessons (my other pupils are in the harvest field) read Browning and the "Living Age." This eve. had a delightful ride. The delicious air—fresh from the N. [ew] England hills (I believe) kissed my cheek. Lost my heart to some fine old walnut trees, whose delicate foliage looked beautifully in the fading sunlight. I hope my beloved elms will pardon the momentary faithlessness; for my heart has already returned to its first love. How much better and happier I feel for this pleasant drive.

Wednesday, June 30. Sadly, sorrowfully I bid thee farewell, thou rare and beautiful month of June! Queen rose of the "rosebud garden" of *summer months!* Fleeting, fleeting as are all the blessings of this earth! But the sweet memory of thee will linger with us still; for thou art "a thing of beauty," and must therefore be "a joy forever." Last night we had quite an amusing *comedy* enacted. Mr. [Robert] P. [urvis] had one of his *sleep talking* attacks, and said the most ridiculous things. I laughed till I was exhausted. Then *Hattie* had the night-mare, and nearly threw herself out of bed, imagining that she saw "something clothed in white" passing through the room, and other horrors. The tone of injured innocence in which she afterwards declared that she *"had'nt* had the night-mare, she *had'nt* been asleep at all was deliciously ridiculous. What with these doings, and the barking of dogs and humming of bugs, I believe I slept about half an hour during the night. This morn. heard Georgie, sewed, and wrote to Tacie.

Thursday, July 1. After school, Tacie [Townsend] came over and read "Picciola," and Cowper's "Illiad," which I like better than Pope's—with me. Gave her sister Lizzie a French lesson.

Philadelphia.—Friday, July 2. Felt unwell the whole day. In the eve. had a pleasant sail down the river, during which I read Browning's "Return of the Druses" which I like very much. City hot and uncomfortable as possible. Grandma better.

Saturday, and Sunday, spent mostly at Mrs. C. [hew]'s. Saw some exquisite flowers which were refreshing and *delight-giving* beyond expression in this hot and brickwalled city.

Monday, July 5. Saw Mrs. C. [hew] start for N. [ew] E. [ngland]. Ah! how I longed to go with her! My own, my beloved N. [ew] E. [ngland], When shall I see thee again!

Spent the afternoon and eve. in trying to rest; but in vain. Patriotic young America kept up a din in celebrating their glorious *Fourth*, that rest was impossible. My very soul is sick of such a mockery. All the day my thoughts reverted to that delightful Grove at Framingham where the noblest and best and most eloquent of our land uttered their testimony against its hypocrisy. And I *yearned* to be there.

Tuesday, July 6. Went to Aunt S. [arah]'s this morn. As usual a scene of confusion and disorder greeted me. What a contrast to the elegance and order of Byberry. Every thing, every body is so very, very different. It grieves me to think of it. Spent the day in sewing. In the eve. had a pleasant walk to the P.'s beautiful place, and to Mrs. Parson's, an interesting and lovable Quaker lady.—Read Browning's "Luria." Like it much.

Byberry. Wednesday, July 7. Had a perfectly delightful ride to Newport, a pleasant little village on the banks of the Neshamming, which are well-wooded, and really quite picturesque. Passed the beautiful "Grove" where Aunt H.[arriet] and the Cassey's used to live; and saw several other very elegant houses,—all beautifully situated,—close to the pretty sparkling little river. Afterwards the girls drove me over to Byberry and very delightful its elegant repose is, after the *whirl* that I've been in for the last few days. Am grieved and disappointed to find no letters awaiting me. Tis very strange that S.[arah] does not write.

Thursday, July 8. Had a letter from Mr. N.[ell]. Sewed, and read the "Illiad." A pleasant drive this eve.

Friday, July 9. Received a long and interesting letter from my dear Sallie [Cassey Smith] who has arrived in Canada. Read the "Illiad." Sat up late on the piazza, watching the stars as they peeped so softly and brightly, like the sweet, loving face of a friend, through the leafy branches of the grand old sycamore. Truly there is something inexpressibly soothing in *night*; as Longfellow so sweetly tells us.—

> "Oh! holy Night from thee I learn to bear
> What man has borne before,
> Thou lay'st thy finger on the lips of care
> And they complain no more."

Saturday, July 10. *Worked* this morn. Afterwards wrote to Lizzie C.[hurch] and Sarah P.[itman?]. A beautiful evening. Tacie came, and we drove to her pleasant home together. Read the "Atlantic [Monthly]."

Sunday, July 11. A day to be marked with a *white stone*. I've enjoyed it greatly, despite the intense heat. Tacie [Townsend] and I spent most of the morning in the woods, close to a pretty little stream, which falls over some rocks, forming a really beautiful cascade, and gladdening our ears with its sweet, dreamy music. We took our books with us, but they were never opened. We did nothing but talk. Tacie told me all about her college life, and many other pleasant things. I know and love her all the better for this day's pleasant intercourse. Spent the afternoon in her pretty little room, where flowers, and books, and pictures all bespeak the character of the occupant. She showed me one of Raphael's cartoons, of which I've often heard, but never had a clear idea. It looks much like an engraving to me. It is the "Seventh Hour of the Night."—Night is personified, and bears a sleeping swan in her arms as she rises in the air. Under her are the cock, and other symbols. T. [acie] has a very nice collection of books. Besides many other interesting things, read in the "Atlantic" a beautiful southern story "Loo-Loo," by Mrs. [Lydia Maria] Child. Aunt H. [arriet] and others came, and we rode home in the beautiful—even unusually bright and beautiful starlight. I shall long think of this very happy day.

Monday, and Tuesday, July 12 and 13. A *little* work and reading, and a great deal of *sleeping*. Feel quite unwell. Wrote a long letter to Mr. P. [utnam] and heard from Aunt M. [argaretta] that grandma is ill.—Wrote to Annie.

Wednesday, July 14. Have just heard some very sad news,—that Mr. Putnam has had a hemorrage [*sic*] of the lungs. Am deeply grieved to hear it. He writes very lightly about it, but I know too well how very dangerous such attacks are. Tis very sad. He tells me that Lizzie [Magee] was married on the Fifth, at Newton by Theodore Parker.[18] Married at last! Poor deluded girl! She has sealed her fate now. A whole lifetime of repentance lies before her. Had very kind letters from Helen [Gilliard] and Ada [Putnam].

Philadelphia. Thursday, July 15. Came to the city with Aunt H.[arriet] this morn. Commenced the "Faerie Queene." Felt unwell and spent most of the day in bed. Passed the eve. very pleasantly with the S. family. Talked about poetry, music and foreign lands. Their father is an educated man who has travelled a great deal, but he's much too conceited, besides being a pro-slavery southerner. Sent a letter to L.[izzie], and Mrs. P.[utnam], *Sr.*

Friday, July 16. Spent part of the day with Lucy H.[opper].[19] Saw some very fine pictures, but not knowing them, except Dante, Tasse, and a few familiar faces, I could not enjoy them as much as I otherwise would. Passed the eve. very pleasantly with my favorites, the F.[arbeaux]'s.

Jersey. Saturday, July 17. Arrived at A.[nnie]'s little "lodge in the vast wilderness" this eve. After a long and tedious ride through the sun and sand of Jersey.

Sunday, July 18. Pass the time as well as I can in this desolate place. Talked, read Talfourd's "Miscellanie" and the "Faerie Queene" a *gorgeous* book.

Saturday, July 24. A record of one day is a record of all here. For the past week have spent the morn. in assisting A.[nnie] in household affairs; the afternoon in *sleeping* and reading—generally the "F.[aerie] Q.[ueene]" and a little French. Then regularly to the Post Office—nearly a mile distant with my little three year old cousin Eddie [Webb], a beautiful and interesting child. The walk is dreary enough,

or would be but for the never failing beauty of the clouds
and the purity of the country air. Only sand and stunted trees
to be met with. But the hope of finding a letter buoys me up
till I get there, but am regularly disappointed, for no letter
comes, and my homeward walk is dejected enough. To-day
determined *not* to go, and to my great joy, the first letter
came,—a long, kind and very interesting one from Sarah
P. [itman?]. I thank her for it with all my heart. On Tuesday
wrote to Mrs. C. [aroline] P. [utnam].

Sunday, July 25. Wrote to Lizzie [Magee] R. [emond]
and Mr. N. [ell]. This afternoon took a ride—with such a
horse! I wish *Dickens* could have been there to see and hear.
He *wouldn't* trot, neither entreaties nor threats, nor the whip
would induce him to do so, except when our little driver
sprang from the wagon and cracked him with the whip. Then
he would gallop at a fine rate. But no sooner did the whipping
cease, and Tom pause to take breath, than the trot degenerated
into the very laziest and most tiresome of *creeps,*—it couldn't
be called a walk. I never saw such a horse. He seems to have
neither feeling nor hearing, as immovable as a block. The
country through which we drove was dismally uninteresting,
except here and there a really fine wood—but these were "few
and far between." However, I tried to make the best of it;
and even found a little enjoyment, thanks to the clouds and
air and a *love* of *driving* which even the laziest of horses and
the dullest of roads cannot *quite* extinguish. Our driver too
amused me—such an odd, wide awake, droll little black boy.

Monday, July 26. Wrote a little poem—"The Angel's
Visit,"[20] for Bishop P. [ayne]'s Magazine, but tis a poor little
concern, fear tis not worth publishing.

Tuesday, July 27. After our household duties were over,
read some French, and the first of "Lectures on Modern

History," by Dr. Arnold, the distinguished and excellent Master of Rugby. This lecture charms me so much, that I'm tempted to quote a portion of it. In commencing, he says— "It has often been remarked that when a stranger enters St. Peter's, for the first time, the immediate impression is one of disappointment; the building looks smaller than he had expected to find it. So it is with the first sight of mountains; their summits never seem so near the clouds as we had hoped to see them. But a closer acquaintance with these, and with other grand or beautiful objects, convinces us that our first impressions arose not from the want of greatness in what we saw but from a want of comprehensiveness in ourselves to grasp it. What we saw was not all that existed; but all that our untaught glance could master. As we know it better, it remains the same, but we rise more nearly to its level; our greater admiration is but the proof that we are becom[ing] able to appreciate it more truly.

Something of this sort takes place, I think in our uninstructed impressions of history. We are not inclined to rate very highly the qualifications required either in the student or in the writer of it. It seems to demand little more than memory in this one, and honesty and diligence in the other. It is, we say, only a record of facts, and such a work seems to offer no field for the imagination, or for the judgment, or for our powers of reasoning. History is but time's followers; she does not pretend to discover, but merely to register what time has already brought to light. Eminent men have been known to hold this language; Johnson, whose fondness for biography might have taught him to judge more truly, entertained little respect for history. We cannot comprehend what we have never studied, and history must be content to share in the common portion of everything great and good;

it must be undervalued by a hasty observer" Note.—(Which I particularly like and perfectly agree with).

"The works of great poets require to be approached at the outset with a full faith in their excellence: the reader must be convinced that if he does not fully admire them, it is his fault, not theirs. This is no more than a just tribute to their reputation; in other words it is the proper modesty of an individual thinking his own unpractised judgment more likely to be mistaken than the concurring voice of the public. And it is the property of the greatest works of genius in other departments also, that a first view of them is generally disappointing, and if a man were foolish enough to go away trusting more to his own hasty impressions than to the deliberate judgment of the world, he would remain continually as blind and ignorant as he was at the beginning. The cartoons of Raphael at Hampton Court Palace, the frescoes of the same great painter in the galleries of the Vatican at Rome, the famous statues of the Laocoon and the Apollo Belvedere, and the Church of St. Peter, at Rome, the most magnificent building perhaps in the world,—all alike are generally found they are excellent, and that he only wants the knowledge and the taste to appreciate them properly, and every succeeding sight of them will open his eyes more and more, till he learns to admire them, not indeed as much as they deserve but so much as greatly to enrich and enlarge his own mind, by becoming acquainted with such perfect beauty. So it is with great poets: they must be read often and studied reverently, before an unpractised mind can gain anything like an adequate notion of their excellence. Meanwhile, the process is in itself most useful: it is a good thing to doubt our own wisdom, it is a good thing to believe, it is a good thing to admire. By continually looking upward our minds will themselves grow upwards; and as a man by indulging in habits of scorn and contempt for others, is sure to descend to the levels of what he despises, so the opposite habits of admiration and enthusiastic reverence for excellence impart to ourselves a portion of the qualities which we admire; and here, as in everything else, humility is the sweet path to exaltation."

Saturday, July 31. This week passed as usual. Nothing occurred worth recording. This morn. received a letter from Mr. P.[utnam] who is better; and a very kind note and pretty little book-mark from Caddie T.

Sunday, August 1. A sad and glad day always for me,— telling me of the freedom of other lands, and bitterly reminding me of the slavery in our own. Wrote to Sarah C.[assey Smith], Caddie T. and Addie [Putnam]. Read the "F.[aerie] Q.[ueene]" and "Ivanhoe," which is always *enjoyable* to me.

Monday, August 2. A rainy and dull day. Hope it does not rain in N.[ew] E.[ngland] and prevent the Celebration in that beautiful Abington Grove. Noble, untiring, eloquent friends of the slave! I am with you in spirit to-day. Studied and read French, sewed, and learned from Mr. W. to play euchre. Like whist better.

Friday, August 6. Had a very kind note from Hattie who says that Mattie G.[riffith] was disappointed at not seeing me at B.[yberry]. I wish I could have met her.

Philadelphia. Monday, August 9. Left J.[ersey] very early this morn. Was really sorry to leave A.[nnie] and her two treasures. The youngest—my darling sweetheart—and our little Gipsy Girl.—Had a long and tedious ride.—A long talk with Mr. Webb, who has much good sense. Arrived here thoroughly worn out. Read "Harper['s]."

Tuesday, August 10. Wrote to Mr. P.[utnam]. Had a

letter from Lizzie [Remond] with more cheerful news. Mrs. [Caroline] P.[utnam] has a little girl—born on the third.[21] L.[izzie] says "it is a most remarkable and beautiful child," and goes into raptures over it. Mrs. P.[utnam] must be highly delighted. She wished so much for a daughter. Had a visit from W.[illiam Wells] Brown. He tells such ridiculous stories, that although I believe as little as I please—I can't help being amused. Spent the eve. very pleasantly at the L.'s listening to very beautiful music and singing. Mr. B.[rown] came home with me, and told me some very discreditable things about Mr. R.[emond]. Poor Lizzie! I truly pity her.

Wednesday, August 11.   Sewed, read in "Harper's" some beautifully written "Criticisms on Italy" and a very interesting paper by a genius Yankee, "Vagabondizing in Belgium." Paid my kind friends—the F.[arbeaux]'s a pleasant visit, wrote to Annie, and Hattie, and went to Lucy H.[opper]— Tis very strange that I don't hear from my dear Mary S.[hepard]. I hope she is not unwell. Feel very anxious about her.

Thursday, August 12.   Sewed, wrote to Aunt H.[arriet] and Miss S.[hepard], read the "Lectures on History," and in the eve. paid some visits with Aunt M.[argaretta].

Friday, August 13.   Spent the day and night with Lucy H.[opper]. Mr. C.[hew] gave me an exquisite bouquet composed entirely of roses and arbor vitae. Dear, beautiful roses! How ye have gladdeneed my heart! For a whole month I had not seen one.

Saturday, August 14.   Read in the "Standard" some excellent and interesting articles. The paper improves weekly. "Bringing Our Sheeves with Us" is a very beautiful and earnest poem from the "Atlantic [Monthly]," which I think

Whittier must have written. Gentle Ada H.[inton] and I visited Mrs. J.[ames] whom I have always liked particularly. Very matter-of-fact, very practical she is, indeed, but so thoroughly sincere and kind, that one can't help liking her. Read in "Harper['s]" an excellent and amusing poem "The Finishing School," which must have been written by the author of "Nothing to Wear."

Sunday, August 15.   Spent the day and night with Lucy H.[opper]. Looked over some beautiful views of Rome and *longed, longed* to go there.

Monday, August 16.   Had a delightful walk with Ellen H.[opper] and saw some splendid buildings. Saw a beautiful painting of the "Women at the Spulchre," and a fine engraving representing Van Dyke taking leave of Rubens on his departure for Italy. Came home and found a very nice letter from Mrs. C.[aroline] Putnam awaiting me, also letters from Mrs. C.[hew], and Mr. N.[ell].

Tuesday, August 17.   My birthday. Twenty-one to-day! It grieves me to think of it;—to think that I have wasted so many years. I dare not, dare not dwell upon the thought! Saw to-day a book of leaves from Rome, and all the "hallowed shrines of Italy." They were beautiful; and ah what a passionate longing—as ever—did such names as the Coliseum, the Forum, the Tomb of Juliet, Venice, St. Peter's, Florence, awake in this too restless,—eager soul of mine. Sacred, sacred spots! Sacred to genius and beauty and deathless fame, ah little did I think, years ago, that twenty-one summers should pass over me without my realizing the cherished all absorbing dream of my heart—the dream of beholding ye! And now when all hope of such happiness should have flown, the dream still lingers on. Foolish, foolish girl! When will you be strong and sensible.

I suppose I ought to rejoice to-day for all the city seems to be rejoicing. The Queen's message arrived safely through the wonderful submarine telegram, the bells are pealing forth merrily. But I cannot rejoice that England, my beloved England should be brought so very near this wicked land. I tremble for the consequences, but I will hope for the best. Thank God for *Home!*

Burlington. Wednesday, August 18. Had a pleasant sail up the river to Burlington. My dear Nellie A. [lexander] is looking much better than I expected. Met the L.'s and the F. [arbeaux]'s and a merry time we had. Think B. [urlington] is a beautiful place. N. [ellie] and I had a delightful walk on the "Banks" and very lovely they are, with their soft carpet of green, and the sparkling river flowing so peacefully at one's feet. The A. [lexander]'s are a very intelligent, interesting people, and I enjoy their society greatly. Of course Nellie is my especial favorite. Saw some beautiful houses, and Bishop Doane's dwelling and church, the latter entirely in the English style, and a most exquisite little building it is—of dark, brown stone, with graceful vines drooping over it, and every window of stained glass. Just my ideal of a church.

Phila[delphia]. Friday, August 20. Passed the day in looking over some beautiful illustrations of Shakespeare, and in pleasant and cheerful conversation. This evening had a delightful sail down to the city in the most beautiful, beautiful moonlight, which N. [ellie] A. [lexander] and I enjoyed perfectly. Drove with them to Mrs. F. [arbeaux]'s and spent the night there.

Byberry. Saturday, August 21. Bade farewell to the city, and came to B. [yberry]. Read Coleridge's "Christabel," what a singular and exquisite poem it is! Found a letter from

Georgie P. [utnam] awaiting me, and a long, interesting one of 12 pages from my dear Miss S. [hepard] who has been enjoying herself at North Conway, among the White Mts.— She described them beautifully.

Sunday, August 22. Read some interesting "H. [ome] Journals," sent me by Mr. N. [ell], the "F. [aerie] Queene" and walked with Georgie [Purvis]. How delightful and refreshing is the quiet of this country Sabbath!

Monday, August 23. Recommenced teaching to-day. Nothing else worth recording occurred.

Tuesday, August 24. French, school. Had some pleasant visitors, among whom was my dear friend Tacie. Afterwards Hat. [tie] and I danced and promenaded in the delicious moonlight.

Wednesday, August 25. Learned a new and quite interesting system of chronology. Had some very amusing tableaux. Dressed G. [rinnel Purvis] and the boys as wandering musicians. Charlie [Purvis] looked like a splendid oriental *magician* in his long scarlet robe and white silk cap with black plumes. Hat. [tie] and I were a bride and groom of the olden time. She made a handsome cavalier in her knee briches and ruffled shirt, and I was very fine in Aunt H. [attie]'s white satin wedding dress and lace, with a gold chain around my hair and a *crocheted shawl* fastened on my head for a wedding veil. Our Irish girls were in ecstasies, and what with their mirth and the children's we had a merry time, of it. We waited for Aunt H. [arriet], Tacie [Townsend] and Mr. P. [urvis] (who were away), as long as we could, but at last had to doff our robes, for they came not. Sat up very late, reading.

Thursday, August 26. Read a sweet little French Poem "Picciola," and a really beautiful poem of Tacie's "A Dream of Eden." I think it is really very fine, and shall urge her to publish it. Read French with her, ("Pic.") and commenced "Telemaque" by myself. Am already charmed with it. Wrote to Mrs. C.[hew].

Friday, August 27. Have been much interested in the very brilliant account of the fortifications at Cherbourg, and the queen's visit to them. I'm sorry she went there. To *me* it seems like demeaning herself, almost. And then to accept such civilities from such a heartless tyrant. Well, the world's turning round the wrong way.—And I can't help it. Read "Telemaque," and a very interesting story—"The Maiden Aunt," in the "Liv.[ing] Age."

Saturday, August 28. Recommenced Latin, read "Telemaque," and wrote to Mrs. C.[aroline] P.[utnam]. In the afternoon drove to Tacie's—H.[attie] and I—and met there two very agreeable friends of hers—the W.'s. Had some very amusing charades acted, and played "Consequences," and capped verses.

Sunday, August 29. Spent the day in reading and talking alternatively. With Bessie W. I'm especially delighted. She is only fifteen, but very intelligent and interesting, and will doubtless make a very superior woman.

She and I had some pleasant talks about favorite books and pictures and on many other interesting subjects, and she exhibited an amount of taste, judgment, and appreciation most remarkable in one so young. Besides she seems to be a truly earnest warm-hearted, and independent girl, but these are qualities too often dimmed and weakened by contact with the hollow and heartless world—yet I cannot but hope and believe that in her case it may not be so. Her sister is quite reserved, but I like her.

Monday, August 30. School, Latin and French. This

evening took a drive in the little pony wagon with G. [rinnel].
Commenced Reade's "It is Never Too Late to Mend." Heard
from Sarah P. [itman?]!

Tuesday, August 31. Bright summer, fare thee well! Summer is going!

> "Now flushes her cheek, and her step goes slow,
>   As she gathers her floating robes to go,
> And with some fair flowers still in her hand,
> Companioned o'erhead by a songster band,
>   She passes on to a Southern land."

This eve. the pleasant W.'s spent with us. Had a delightful
time—music, dancing, and some tableaux. The first—"Rebecca
and Rowena,"—the last scene in "Ivanhoe," Tacie and
Hattie acted well. T. [acie Townsend] made an exquisite
Rowena in her white satin dress and lace mantle, her long
and beautiful light hair flowing below her waist, and bound
with jewels, and a "cloud" made to do service as a veil. She
was perfectly lovely. Hattie in a black silk dress, scarlet robe,
and scarlet and white turban, with her decidedly Jewish
features—made a fine Jewess, and looked very handsome.
Then they changed scene, and improvised "The Jewish Convert"—H. [attie] kneeling with clasped hands and down cast
eyes, and T. [acie]'s hands resting lightly on her head—a
very pretty scene. In the other tableau[,] "The Gipsey,"
Bessie W. made a magnificently horrible looking gipsey
witch. She was entirely enveloped in a long scarlet robe which
was also drawn over her head, her face and arms were
darkened, and the manner in which she contorted her features
as she bent over the hand of the proud girl whose fortune
she was telling, was really wonderful. Lizzie T. [ownsend]
made a very pretty peasant, in a white skirt, red and black

bodice, which contrasted finely with ribbons. Altogether, we enjoyed it greatly, and I am more than ever delighted with the W's.

Wednesday, September 1.   Rose early. A beautiful autumn morning. Studied Latin, read "Telemaque," and after school had a delightful drive to the landing. The country still looks beautifully.

Thursday, September 2.   Studied English History and Latin. To-night sat up very late reading "Never Too Late to Mend," a powerful[ly] written book. The prison scenes are terrible, and have burned into my very soul. *Can* they be true? *Can* such things occur in my own dear England?

Friday, September 3.   History and Latin, school—"Telemaque" which I think *charmant*. Felt rather sad and depressed to-night. A weight seemed to press on my heart. Already it is brightened since I wrote a long, confiding letter to my dear friend Tacie.

Saturday, September 4.   A pleasant sail up the river to Bristol. Han.[nah] and Em.[ily] Pierce met me. This eve. had some very good tableaux. "Rebecca and Rowena" (Hat.[tie Purvis] and H.[annah] Pierce) were the best. I was Pocahantas. C.[harles] P.[urvis], J.[oseph] P.[urvis], Powhatan and Capt.[ain] Smith. A large company was assembled, the room was filled up something like a stage, and we had a very merry, pleasant time. A short visit from Tacie.

Sunday, September 5.   Took a delightful walk this morning with Han.[nah] through Lover's Lane[,] a beautiful walk beside which flows the most winding picturesque stream I ever saw. How delicious was the coolness and quiet of this early morning walk through the green and shady lane! I enjoyed it perfectly. Read some exquisite stray poems, the

"Atlantic," and some of Beecher's "Life Thoughts"[;] passed the evening in the entertaining game of "capping quotations" and in pleasant conversation with the P.[ierce]'s who are intelligent and most hospitable, and with Mr. W., H.[annah]'s betrothed, a very agreeable and sensible young man.

Monday, September 6. Returned home. School, Latin, "Telemaque" and "Never Too Late to Mend." A delightful ride on horseback with Mr. P.[urvis]—the first good ride I've had for years. To my great joy, received a long, kind letter from Sallie, at last. Tis not her fault that she did not write before. Long to see her again. She is in dear Old S.[alem] now.

Tuesday, September 7. A letter from Helen G.[illiard].

Wednesday, September 8. Met a very interesting girl— Agnes W. this evening. Am charmed with her, she is so intelligent and lovely. Tacie spent the night with us. Wrote to G.[eorgie Putnam].

Thursday, September 9. T.[acie] and I rose very early and read several pages of "Picciola." After the day's employments were over, rode to G.'s and spent the night with her. Poor girl! Her father is most unworthy, and makes her home unhappy;—and she has even a deeper source of sorrow,—a disappointed [*sic*] caused by death, as I learned tonight— from some really beautiful lines which she showed me. She is a noble girl, or she could never be so resigned and cheerful as she is. I feel that this revelation of her heart—history has drawn me even closer to her. Had a very long talk with her. Read "Rosamund Gray," a beautiful story by Charles Lamb. [Charles] Burleigh [Purvis] entered school.

Friday, September 10. Commenced teaching Latin to B.[urleigh], H.[enry] and Hat.[tie]. Stupid and unwell today—Read French and an interesting sketch of the gifted Miss Hosmer, which has made me *long, long, long* for the glorious gift of genius!

Saturday, September 11. Heard from Mr. P.[utnam]. Miss S.[arah] P. R.[emond] I hear has burst out most venomously upon my poor "Glimpses"—accusing them of being pro-slavery and heaven knows what all. I *pity* her. Studied Latin and read "Telemaque."

Sunday, September 12. Diem perdidi! Though perhaps it was not my fault, for I really have felt too unwell to do anything. Hat.[tie] and I fasted and spent the day in her darkened little room, for she is quite sick.—Read some of Homer's "Odyssey" (Pope's) and in the eve. drove with Charlie [Purvis] to the landing. Met with quite an adventure; just as we were starting to return, a man sprang forward and seized the horse's head. I was terribly frightened. But the man proved to be intoxicated and only wanted to inquire his way. He was in his shirt-sleeves, his hair uncovered and in wild disorder, and altogether in the deepening gloom he looked quite alarming;—besides he had a companion, and at first we knew not what they might do—for the road was very lonely, not a single habitation near. Quite an adventure.

Monday, September 13. Read the "Odyssey," "Telemaque" and "Picciola" and helped Aunt H.[arriet] about household affairs. Feel much better.

Tuesday, September 14. School and do. with yesterday.

Wednesday, September 15. After school attended the A.[nti] S.[lavery] circle at the H.[opper]'s, and had quite a pleasant time, though there were few present. Saw a brilliant and beautiful comet last eve.

Thursday, September 16. School, reading, and studying as usual. This eve. joined a kind of literary society just formed at the Hall. Joined only because I was urged to. Hope I shall not be called upon to do anything more than write. Indeed it would be utterly impossible for me to read or recite.

Friday, September 17.   A perfect moonlight night. Hat. [tie] and I walked to the H. [opper]'s and admired the comet, which is unusually brilliant tonight. My thoughts revert to dear N. [ew] E. [ngland] on such a night as this. Memories of delightful rambles by the water, in the delicious moonlight,—how vividly they return to me now! Dearly-loved times! When, when, shall I behold you again!

Saturday, September 18.   After school Mr. P. [urvis] drove me to Tacie's. Spent several hours with her—reading our charming "Picciola." T. [acie] came back with us, and we had a delightful eve.—Mr. P. [urvis] reading to us some old letters, written when he was in Europe; and others most interesting from dear Mr. G. [arrison], George Thompson, and other good and distinguished people. T. [acie] showed me today a little story which she has partly written. I like it much. It is very naturally and prettily written.

Sunday, September 19.   Heard the lovely and excellent Mrs. Nots preach at "Friend's meeting." The sermon was, of course, beautiful and radical. She said many good things about Peace, Temperance, and Anti-Slavery. She and Mr. N. [ots] with the P. [arson?]'s and quite a large party dined with us. Howard Gilbert was here. He is quite a literary character,—a hard student and good writer; and though he isn't a general favorite T. [acie] and I quite like him. He explained some passages in "Pic. [ciola]" for us, and talked about the modern languages, in which he is proficient. He is a thorough Garrisonian, but rather bitter in his denunciations; and he and Mr. P. [urvis] had some very spicy discussions.

Though he *is* rather too egotistical, I can't help admiring his earnestness and enthusiasm.

Sunday, October 3. Have been reading a delightful book. "Doctor Antonio" by Ruffini. The hero is a noble Italian— just my *ideal*. The description of Italian scenery, life, and manners are the most beautiful and interesting that I've ever read. Mr. Wise was here today. Talked with [him] much about Carrie. Am truly grieved to hear that her health is in a very bad state. Mr. W. [ise] is a very kind hearted man, and seems to feel for her as warmly as if she were his own child.

Saturday, October 9. A delightful, veritable October day. Tacie and I read French as usual. In the eve. went to the Lyceum, which was quite interesting. Hattie read a very good poem of T. [acie]'s, "The Slave," and read it *excellently*. Hers was incomparably the best reading there. Saw a rare and grand sight to-night as we were returning home. The splendid comet blazing in one part of the heavens and the Northern Lights,—more brilliant than I ever saw them before,—in the other. It was a magnificent spectacle—one to be long remembered.

Sunday, October 10. Read the "Odyssey" and French. In the afternoon had a pleasant ride to Bristol with R. [obert] P. [urvis, Jr.]. Spent the afternoon with the P. [arson]'s. Our homeward ride in the fading sunlight was beautiful—as only an *October* ride *can* be.

Wednesday, October 13. Tacie and Sallie C., a very agreeable girl, spent the day with us. Had a delightful time. In the evening believe we were all a little wild. Recited and read and declaimed in great style until quite a late hour. *Charmed* with S. [allie] C.

Thursday, October 14. Went to the city. Did some shopping with Aunt H. [arriet]. Saw some beautiful pictures, and some silks that were really magnificent—as a work of art. Attended the meeting of the [Philadelphia Female] A. [nti] S. [lavery] Society. Mary Grew and lovely Mrs. Not gave very interesting accounts of the West Chester meetings. Spent the evening at G.'s.

Friday, October 15. Returned home and read a great deal of "Picciola" with dear Tacie. What *should* I do without *her!* She is my constant and sympathizing fellow student.

Saturday, October 16. Attended the sewing circle at Dr. C.'s. Had a long talk with Sallie C. about the prejudice. I am sure that *her* heart is right. She has certainly a true and noble soul.

Sunday, October 17. Did some writing. Read the A. [nti] S. [lavery] papers, and "Homes." This afternoon Hat. [tie] and I walked to Tacie's. T'was a perfect October day, and we enjoyed our walk greatly. T. [acie] walked home with us,—just as the sun was setting—most gloriously. To me it seemed as if "October" were written on every cloud and leaf, and ray of sunlight that fell across our path. This eve. read in the "Atlantic" several beautiful stories, and an interesting account of the famous Faust.

Saturday, October 23. Read "Picciola" and sewed. This eve. Mr. G. [ilbert] came in very unexpectedly, and accompanied us to the Lyceum. Had a sharp discussion on the question "Is a citizen of the United States ever justifiable in breaking the laws of his country if he believes them to be morally wrong?" Some of the debators were usually rude and there was a greater display of ignorance than I have ever before seen, for the especial benefit of the fastidious Mr. G. [ilbert]. He was terribly shocked, I know.

Sunday, October 24. Played several games of chess with

Mr. G. [ilbert]. Beat him once. Then walked over to Tacie's with him, and dined there. Had quite an interesting conversation on poetry, Italy, Germany, &, &. Should like him very much if he were not so egotistical. When he *does* talk about anything but himself, he's very interesting. Read French with Tacie, and a long talk with her about prejudice; she is a dear, good girl full of love and sympathy, and I feel rich in having such a friend.

Saturday, October 30. Overwhelmed with sewing, and should have been in the deepest depths of the cave of Despair had not my good friend T. [acie] come over and helped me a great deal. Rode to the sewing circle at the Jameses. The largest and pleasantest we've ever had. Was delighted to meet Sallie C. Enjoyed myself very much. Driving home met with quite an adventure. There was the thickest fog I have ever seen, and although we had lamps to the carriage it was impossible to see more than a few yards ahead. I was sitting on the front seat with Mr. P. [urvis] and should have enjoyed the novelty of finding our way through the darkness had not Aunt H. [arriet] been so much alarmed. Suddenly the light from the lamps fell on the fact and figure of a man who was walking leisurely along the roadside. He seemed to gaze at us very intently, and had just passed when suddenly the snapping of a pistol near us startled our horse, and frightened us not a little. The man had doubtless done it, but whether to frighten us or really fire at us we know not. At any rate he entirely succeeded in doing the former, and I think we shall not soon venture out again on such a dark night.— Finished some sewing.

Sunday, October 31. Spent most of the morning looking over old letters. How many *pleasing*, but more sad memories such an employment awakens! Read "Quits" an excellent story by the author of the "Initials." Tis a beautiful picture of life in Germany, and the story is deeply interesting. Wrote to Sarah P. [itman?] and Annie W. [ebb?].

Monday, November 1.   October, beautiful, bright October has gone! What a beautiful month it has been! And I have truly enjoyed it. Have had a few pleasant rambles in the woods in search of leaves, but have not found any very beautiful ones for the foliage this year is not so brilliant as usual. Have enjoyed being in the husking field and watching the busy huskers, sometimes helping them gather in the "golden corn," and being rewarded by a ride home on top of the heaped up "cracking wain." Many times I have thought of Whittier's "Huskers" and the beautiful "Corn Song."— Heard from Mr. P. [utnam] and sent letters to Miss S. [hepard] and S. [arah Cassey Smith] and wrote to Mr. N. [ell].

Sunday, November 7.   Passed last week in constant sewing—out of school hours—relieved only by an occasional glance at "Picciola." Never, never, was any one so heartily sick of destestable [*sic*] sewing! Read the "Atlantic." This no. is not so interesting as usual, I think. Contains an excellent article on "Physical Courage" by Mr. Higginson, and a beautiful story "Her Grace the Drummer's Daughter," probably by Miss Cheesboro. Has rained all the week and to-day, for the first time the sun shows his face. It is beautiful. Soft-white, pearly clouds floating over the deep blue sky, and the air pure, bracing and delightful. A little poem "November," that I've just read in the "Atlantic," exactly meets the mood of this lovely Autumn day. T'was written by Mrs. R. H. Stoddard—the poet's wife.

Saturday, November 13.   Rode to Attleboro through a county which must be quite pretty in summer. It is so much more hilly and picturesque than B. [yberry]. Had a large and pleasant sewing circle at the S.'s family of excellent, warm-hearted Quakers. Was glad to meet Tacie and Sallie again. After the circle Hattie [Purvis] and I went home with the latter. Twas a glowing moonlight-night, and, yet, bright as the moon, the stars were also unusually bright—They looked like brilliant jewels.

Sunday, November 14.   Spent the day very pleasantly with Sallie. I like her better and better. I hope she is all that I believe her to be. But I have been so often deceived that I fear I have grown distrustful. Had a merry eve. and a beautiful drive home in the moonlight with H.[attie] and R.[obert].

Monday, November 15.   A gloomy, chilly, and, to me, most depressing day. We have our first snow. It is an earnest of Winter, [*sic*] which I dread more than I have words to express. I am *sick,* today, sick, sick at heart;—and though I had *almost* resolved to forbear committing sad thoughts and gloomy feelings to my pages, dear Journal, and have very rarely done so, yet, tonight I long for a confident [*sic*]—and thou art my only one. In the twilight—I sat by the fire and watched the bright, usually so cheering blaze. But it cheered me not. Thoughts of the past came thronging upon me;— thoughts of the loved faces on which I used to look so fondly;—of the loved voices which were music to my ear, and ever sent a thrill of joy to my heart—voices now silent forever. I am *lonely* tonight. I long for one earnest sympathizing soul to be in close communion with my own. I long for the pressure of a loving hand in mine, the touch of loving lips upon my aching brow. I long to lay my weary head upon an earnest heart, which beats for me,—to which *I* am dearer far than all the world beside. There is none, for me, and never will be. I could only love one whom I could look up to, and reverence and that *one* would never think of such a poor little ignoramus as I. But what a selfish creature I am. This is a forlorn old maid's reverie, and yet I am only twenty-one. But I am weary of life, and would gladly lay me down and rest in the quiet grave. There, alone, is peace, peace! Had a long and interesting letter from dear Brownie.

Friday, November 19.   Went to town with Aunt H.[arriet]. Had a pleasant sail down the river in company with a large party of the P.[ierce]'s and Mr. B.[rown]. Went to see Annie W.[ebb], and was greatly grieved to find my darling little Genie W.[ebb] quite ill. How beautiful she looks! Just like an exquisite, delicate little rosebud. This eve. went to hear Mr. [George] Curtis.[22] I have rarely been delighted with any lecture as I have been to-night with "Fair Play for Women." It is as much Anti-Slavery as Woman's Rights. The magnificent voice of the orator—the finest voice I have ever heard, his youth, beauty and eloquence, and the fear-lessness with which he avowed his noble and radical sentiments before that immense, fashionable, and doubtlessly mostly pro-slavery audience,—all these impressed me greatly, and awak-ened all my enthusiasm. I *will not* despair when such noble souls as his devote the glory of their genius and their youth to the holy cause of Truth and Freedom.

Saturday, November 20.   Spent most of the day at Mrs. C[hew]'s. In the evening played whist.

Sunday, November 21.   Rain poured in torrents. Had a visit from "Dimmock Charlton," an interesting old, African, whose story I read some time ago in the "Standard." Wrote to Mr. Curtis—*dared* to write to him—(anonymously, of course) informing him of the exclusion of colored persons from the Musical Fund, (at which he is to lecture), and trying to express my grateful admiration of his lecture.

Returned to B. [yberry] in the pouring rain, and while on the boat, read "Nile Notes of a Howadj-i"—Curtis. Found Tacie [Townsend] here, and was very, very glad to see her.

Tuesday, November 23. Read "Miles Standish," and like it very much; though it might as well have been written in prose as that "prose poem" "Hyperion," which has even more poetry in it. Think Priscilla is charming, and should have been sorry enough had she have married that grim Puritan, though he was a noble man. And so was John Alden. While sewing this eve. learned "Agassiz's Birthday" and that charming little poem "Children."

Saturday, November 27. Attended the circle at the W.'s and worked busily all the eve. This week while sewing, have learned among others of Longfellow's poems, "The Golden Mile Stone" and "Santa Filomena" both of which, the former especially, are *very* beautiful, I think.

Sunday, November 28. Read poor neglected "Picciola" with Tacie. How pleasant it is to have her here. I do wish we could be always together. How nicely we could get on with our studies. But I wish I was wiser and better, and worthier of being her friend and companion. Wrote to Mrs. Putnam and Sis. [Sarah Cassey Smith].

Monday, November 29. This eve. learned "Sandalphon," which I like best of all the poems in the new volume. Have hardly had time to glance at the "Atlantic." Read "Anis" by Holmes. The story is a touching one[,] that of a poor forsaken colored child in one of the hospitals (I believe) of Mass. [achusetts] who had a disease so disgusting and malignant that no one could be found to nurse her, until a fair and noble young girl of high position, offered her services, and went and kindly and carefully nursed the poor child until she recovered. All honor to the brave, warm heart of that young girl! The poem is really beautiful, and I was particularly pleased with it as it is probably the first really liberal thing that Holmes has ever written. Indeed I am altogether pleasantly disappointed in him since reading some of the really exquisite poems appended to the "Autocrat." I had always supposed that his forte lay entirely in the humorous, and that he would not *dare* to attempt the sentimental. "The Minister's Wooing" is a veritable N.[ew] England story, attributed to Mrs. Stowe. There is but little poetry, and that, it seems to me, not nearly so good as usual.

Tuesday, November 30. November fare thee well! Autumn thou art leaving us,—leaving us to the merciless attacks of stern old Winter. I used to love winter so well. But now I dread it beyond measure. My last two or three experiences have quite disenchanted me. Ah! if I had but the power, how gladly would I fly to sunny France, or beautiful Italy, and evade the Winter in that warm and bright south-land. But it cannot be. I must submit to inevitable Fate. This eve. finished a shirt for the Fair, and committed to memory Longfellow's exquisite "Two Angels." How beautiful is this stanza . . .

> "Then on the house there fell a sudden gloom,
> A shadow on those features fair and thin;—
> And, softly, from the hushed and darkened room,
> Two Angels issued where but *one* went in.—"

Wednesday, December 1. A cold, dismal, cheerless day is this first day in Winter, and I feel greatly depressed and troubled, for I have heard sad news. Isiah tells me that our friend Mr. [Joseph] Putnam has been given up by the physicians. There is no hope of his recovery! I am deeply grieved to hear it. We cannot afford to lose such as he. And then he is so young, and has so much to live for. It seems very hard. And yet—

> "All is of God; if he but wave his hand
> The mists collect, the rain falls loud and thick.
> Till, with a smile of light on sea and land,
> Lo! He looks back from the departing cloud.

> Angels of Life and Death alike are his;
> Without his leave they pass no threshold o'er.
> Who thou would wish or dare, believing this—
> Against his messengers to shut the door!"

And now the "beautiful strange superstition of 'Sandalphon' " is haunting me, and I will copy it from memory.

> "Have you read, in the Talmud of old,
> In the legends the Rabbins have told,
>   Of the limitless realms of the air?
> Have you read it—the marvelous story
> Of Sandalphon, the Angel of Prayer?

> How, erect at the outermost gates
> of the City Celestial he waits;
>   With his feet on the ladder of light,
> That crowded with angels unnumbered
> By Jacob was seen as he slumbered
>   Alone in the desert at night.

> The Angels of Wind and of Fire
> Chant only one hymn, and expire
>   With the song's irresistible stress;
> Expire in their rapture and wonder,
> As harp strings are broken asunder
>   By music they throb to express.

But serene in the rapturous throng,
Unmoved by the rush of the song
With eyes unimpassioned and slow,
   Among the dead Angels, the deathless
Sandalphon stands listening breathless
   To the sounds that ascend from below.

From the spirits on earth that adore
From the souls that entreat and implore
   In the fervor and passion of prayer
From the hearts that are broken with losses
And weary with dragging the crosses.—
   Too heavy for mortals to bear.

And he gathers the prayers as he stands,
And they change into flowers in his hands,
   Into garlands of purple and red
And beneath the Great-Arch of the portal,
Through the streets of the City Immortal
   Is wafted the fragrance they shed.

It is but a legend, I know
A fable, a phantom, a show,
   Of the ancient Rabbinical lore
Yet the old, medieval tradition,
The beautiful, strange superstition
   But holds me and haunts me the more.

As I look from my window at night,
And the welkin above is all white,
   And throbbing and panting with stars
Among them, majestic, is standing
Sandalphon, the angel, expanding
   His pinions in nebulous bars.

And the legend, I feel, is a part
Of the hunger and thirst of the heart,

Of the frenzy and fire of the brain,
That grasps at the fruitage forbidden,
The golden pomegranites of Eden
To quiet its fever and pain.

Thursday, December 2.   Received a letter from Rev. Mr. [Daniel] P. [ayne] and a package of "Home Journals" from Mr. N. [ell].

Friday, December 3.   Have had very sad news to-day. My friend Mr. P. [utnam] has been declared by his physicians hopelessly ill, so S. [arah] writes me. It makes my heart ache to think that I may never again see one who is as dear as a brother to me. I cannot bear to give up all hope.

Saturday, December 11.   Hear from S. Putnam that Mr. P. [utnam] appears a little better. So we try to hope. This eve. the last circle, a mammoth one met at our house. One of Hat. [tie]'s friends, Ellie W. [right,] came. Like her very much,—an independent, intelligent girl.

Tuesday, December 14.   To [*sic*] unwell to go to the Fair, and very low spirited. Dear T. [acie] came over, and did me a great deal of good. Wrote some stanzas which express what I've *felt*. They are the "Two Voices."[23]

Friday, December 17.   Came to the Fair on Wednesday but haven't enjoyed it at all till to-day. Dined with the W. [alton]'s and had a really pleasant time. They are highly cultivated and interesting people. C. [harles?] W. [alton] is quite handsome, and very intelligent. With his brother, J. [ames] had a long conversation this eve. about books, authors, slavery, prejudice, etc. He seems to be very earnest and warm-hearted, and I like him, though I hardly dare to trust myself to do so.

Christmas Day, 1858.   A pleasant day. Dear G. [eorgie] spent it with us. What did I do? Occupied myself part of the day in making evergreen wreaths to adorn the picture frames, so as to give the rooms as Christmas like an appearance as possible. Then looked over my old journals till my heart ached. In the eve. acted charades and read "Lady Geraldine" with Tacie. I like the way it is written in the old edition better than in this—some things in it. But both are very beautiful. Received "Andromeda" (Kingsley's) from Tacie. The "Autocrat" from Mr. [William Wells] Brown, and an exquisite pearl-handled penknife from R. [obert] P. [urvis]. This week sent my "Two Voices" to the "[National Anti-Slavery] Standard." But have no idea that they will publish it. 'Tis not worth publishing. Had a long pleasant walk over the fields with T. [acie] this morning. The air was delightfully exhilarating.

Sunday, December 26.　　Read the two last "Atlantics" (some articles)[,] a pretty little poem of T. [acie's], and several other things, and talked more.

Friday, December 31.　　All the eve. read the "Odyssey" (Pope) and finished it. Sat up to see the old year out with Aunt H. [arriet] and Mr. P. [urvis] and read Tennyson's "Death of the Old Year." I am charmed with the "Odyssey."—How terrible and exciting are the dangers through which Ulysses passed, how spirited the scene of the bending of the bow, and how beautiful many other passages—particularly the meeting of the hero with his sire[,] the old Laertes. But the slaughter of the suitors is too horrible and revolting. It made me shudder.

'Tis twelve! Farewell, old year! And welcome, welcome in the new! One year ago tonight I was in dear old Salem, and little did I imagine that the next New Year would find me here. But so it is! How little do we know. How little *can* we dream of what the future has in store for us. But I must retire,—and spend the first few hours of the New Year in the land of dreams.

New Year's Day, 1859. How strange the date looks to me! Ah! how the years are slipping and sliding away from us. Again T. [acie] is here, and *her* presence opens the year pleasantly for me.—New Year! may'st thou be a year of *triumphs* for me. Of triumphs over all sorrows and trials. A year of brave endurance, and of earnest labor. If I live until this day one year, may I feel that I have *done* something for *others* as well as for myself.—Recommenced Latin. I *will* persevere! Read quite an interesting little story written by T. [acie] when she was quite young.

Sunday, January 30. A whole month, dear Journal, and I have not written a line on thy pages. Well I couldn't help it. Where have I been, what have I done since I wrote last? Very little indeed. On Sat. [urday] Jan. [uary] 9 went to Bristol with Hat. [tie] and Ellie W. [right]. Had tableaux at the P. [ierce]'s. Received a copy of "Racine," complete, from Bess and Annie W. [ebb.] A real treasure it is to me. On Sunday rode in an immense wagon with a large party to the L.'s and had quite a pleasant, merry time. On Thursday, 20th, finished the famous tragedy of Phedre, which I read first because of Rachel; am charmed with it. With all save the last part, the death of poor Hippolyte. It was too horrible. Phedre has a grandeur even in her sorrow and her sin, that one cannot help admiring. On Friday, 21, went to dear Tacie's and spent the night with her. Had a delightful eve. She read me many of her old poems some of which were really beautiful, because they were evidently *heart expressions.*—The stream was swollen high from the plentiful rains, and as I sat in Tacie's cozy, charming room, reading alone (for she had retired) I could hear the little waterfall, distinctly

as it fell over the rocks. The wild sound of the rushing stream
I liked. It brought back to me a thought of [the] sea. But it
brought also the restless longing that the sea always brings to
me, and it was not until I had gazed long at Tacie's sweet,
placid, sleeping face that peace and *restfulness* returned. Saturday morn. had a regular *ploughing* homeward through the
mud with T.[acie]. Our horse was so venerable and feeble
that she *would* only *creep*; so we preferred walking. Read
Goethe's beautiful drama of "Iphigenia in Tauris." Monday,
Jan.[uary] 24, heard very sad news. Poor Mr. [Joseph]
P.[utnam] is no more. He died last Thursday.[24] Have heard
none of the particulars. It has made my heart ache. For I
know few so worthy to live; and to me he has always been
dear as a brother. I cannot realize, *cannot* think that I shall
never see him again on earth. In another and better world, I
have faith to believe that we shall meet. Wrote to his wife
and mother, and to Sarah. Thursday, January 27. Read the
"Iliad" and commenced Racine's "Iphigenie" whose plot I
like better than Goethe's. Find it very easy to read. Heard a
good lecture on Yankee Traits. Friday, January 28. Read the
account of the very interesting [Anthony] Burns celebration
in Boston and N.[ew] Y.[ork]. Emerson's speech and Whittier's and Holmes's poems are beautiful. Saturday, Jan.[uary]
29. Had to open the debate at the Lyceum. Read an intensely
matter-of-fact "Gradgrindish" production. Afterward, the
debate was unusually interesting. Mr. P.[urvis] was very
eloquent; and excelled himself. I think the amount of good
that he does in awakening and rousing these people is incal-
culable. The judges decided in our favor,—that the Constitution *does* sanction slavery. Hat.[tie] recited *well*; with great
spirit and fire. Sunday, Jan.[uary] 30.—A *charming* day.
Went in the fields with G.[eorgie] and felt like staying there,

the sunlight was so pure and sweet, but the mud! the mud! T'was unbearable! and we had to turn back. Read the papers. The "Standard" has a fine poem by Adelaide Proctor; through every line of which an earnest soul infuses itself. Read the "Iliad" and "Iphigenie" and Whittier, and wrote to Tacie who is in town. Walked with H. [attie] to Dr. C.'s.

Sunday, February 6. Read Racine, and Giles, and wrote to Mr. and Mrs. Russell. A lovely winter's day. How silently and softly the large white flakes are falling! The branches of the trees are laden with snow, and the brown fields are covered now with a carpet of pure white. I love these peaceful country Sabbaths.

Thursday, February 10. Went to town. Attended the Annual Meeting. Miss Grew's report was excellent.[25] Read an excellent and most interesting article in the "Westiminster Review" on "The Capabilities of Woman." It was a criticism on several books written written [*sic*] by ladies who were assistant nurses at the Crimea, and [the] thoroughly liberal and appreciative spirit in which it is written pleased me greatly. Visited dear Annie, and Mrs. C. [hew].

Friday, February 11. Went to see T. [acie] at Dr. N. [ot]'s. What a beautiful house he has! Such exquisite pictures, books, ferns, statuettes, and all kinds of elegant little curiosities. Such a home is so fitting for dear T. [acie,] would that she could always have such a one! Went with her to the W. [right]'s and then to Earle's. Saw some fine landscapes by Weber. There was one very striking picture of John the Baptist before Herod. It was fine. I returned home this afternoon.

Saturday, February 12. Read the excellent speeches made at the Boston meetings.[26] Mr. Phillips was especially fine. The A. [nti] S. [lavery] Festival was a complete success;—far more profitable than the Bazaar. I am so glad of it. Tis all owing to Mrs. [Maria W.] Chapman. She is indeed a host in herself. This eve. our Lyceum met. Had a very spirited debate on the question "Do the signs of the times indicate the downfal [*sic*] of this Republic?" Of course, we took the affirmative, and after a long and animated discussion, thanks to Mr. P. [urvis] it was decided in our favor.

Sunday, February 13.   Read Gile's delightful "Essays." That on Don Quixote is excellent. Wrote to Mattie F. [arbeaux] and Sarah P. [itman?] and some doggerel.

Tuesday, February 15.   Wrote to Sallie [Cassey Smith] and to Brownie. Yesterday had a kind letter from S. [arah] P. [itman?].

Monday, February 21.   Dear T. [acie] came home to-day. Was delighted to see her. Brought me "Bitter-Sweet" a singular poem by Holland. Some passages of it are beautiful. The aim of the book is to show the *benefit* accruing from the existence of evil in the world. To make us holier and better through suffering is indeed its mission, but often, too often, the sick and weary heart will not acknowledge because it *cannot* feel this. And in bitter anguish of of [*sic*] soul it cries out, "Why, oh, why is it, Lord, that thou sufferest these things? Why is it that thou allowest the wicked to "flourish like a green bay tree" and the innocent to suffer untold injury and wrong." In those dark hours no response comes to the heart's passionate prayer, and faith becomes weak and blind. God, merciful Father help us to believe wholly, implicitly in thee!

Saturday, February 26.   Hat. [tie] and I are still reading Don Quixote and Shakespeare. She read "Hamlet" to me to-day. Every time I hear it I find new beauty, new grandeur in it. And how many, many passages have become to us "familiar as household words."—Have finished the "Iliad."

Achilles is no hero for me. His treatment of poor Hector's body was outrageous—most unworthy of himself. Am disappointed to find that the "Iliad" closes before the termination of the Trojan war. But 'tis very fine, and I've enjoyed it.

Saturday, March 5. Spring has come, and wonderfully bright and beautiful it is for March. Have been reading "Benvenuto Cellini." It is very interesting, but not quite so much as I expected for there is not so very much about other eminent sculptors and artists as I had hoped. Spent the night with Tacie. I do love to listen to the music of the little waterfall. Looked over our favorite "quilts," and had a nice long talk with dear Z.

Sunday, March 6. What a lovely, lovely morning this is! From T.[acie]'s window I can see the little waterfall and brook sparkling in the sunlight, and how beautifully that sunlight falls across the brown meadow, bathing it in a golden flood! I thank thee, Father, for the beautiful world thou has given us!—The country is delightful now; all alive with the pleasant chirpings of birds—dear, cheerful little spirits! They gladden my heart, and banish from it many a weary, weary ache.

Thursday, March 10. Have commenced the "Rise of the Dutch Republic." Am already charmed with it. Hat.[tie] gave me the beautiful "Christmas Carol." Wrote to Miss S.[hepard]. Heard from Mattie F.[arbeaux].

Monday, April 4. Heard to-day that there has been another fugitive arrested.[27] There is to be a trial. God grant that poor man may be released from the clutches of the slave-hunters. Mr. P.[urvis] has gone down. We wait anxiously to hear the result of the trial. How long, oh, how long shall such a state of things as this last?

Wednesday, April 6.   Good news! After waiting with intense and painful anxiety for the result of the three days' trial we are at last gladdened by the news that the alleged fugitive, Daniel Dangerfield, has been released.—The Commissioner *said* that he released him because he was not satisfied of his identity. Others are inclined to believe that the pressure of public sentiment—which was, strange to say, almost universally on the right side—was too overwhelming for the Com.[mittee] to resist, particularly as his own family—even his wife, it is said, declared that they could discard him if he sent the man into slavery. It is encouraging to know that there was so much right and just feeling about the matter. It gives one some hope even for Philadelphia. Last night the court sat for *fourteen* hours, the longest session that has ever been held in this city. Many ladies stayed during the entire night, among the noble and venerable Lucretia Mott, untiring and devoted to the last. She is truly lovely—saintly in look as in spirit, for a beautiful soul shines through her beautiful face. She is indeed one of the "blest of earth," one of those whose "very presence is a benediction!"

Friday, April 8.   Long, long to be remembered. This eve. attended a large Anti-Slavery meeting at Samson Hall celebrating Daniel [Dangerfield]'s release. A crowd of Southerners was present, and ere the meeting had progressed far they created a great disturbance, stamping, hallooing, groaning etc. so that it was impossible to hear a word that the speakers were saying. In vain did the President strive to preserve order,—the tumult increased every moment, and at one time there was a precipitate rush forward. We thought we should be crushed, but I did not feel at all frightened, I was too excited to think of fear. The veterans in the cause said that it reminded them of the time when the new and beautiful Pennsylvania Hall, which was afterward burned to the ground—was mobbed. But at last the police arrived.

Many of the disturbers were arrested, and order restored. Mr. [Robert] P.[urvis]'s speech was fine; decidely the most effective. A young Englishman spoke fearlessly and well. The meeting was one of deep interest. I shall long remember it.

Saturday, April 9. The hero of the last few days came here to-night. He is a sturdy, sensible seeming man. It makes my heart beat quickly to see one who has just had so narrow an escape from a doom far darker and more terrible than death. Nor is he quite safe yet, for we hear that there are warrants out for his re-arrest. Poor man! there can be no rest for his weary feet nearer than the free soil of Canada. We shall be obliged to keep him very close.

Saturday, April 23. D.[aniel Dangerfield] has left us and we hear with joy that he is safe in Canada. Oh, stars and stripes, that wave so proudly over our *mockery* of freedom, what is your protection. Hear that the noble Whittier is in town, wish, hope that I may have the pleasure of seeing his face again. It would be *too* delightful if he would come up here and see us. But I dare not hope that. Had a delightful sail to town just at sunset, but found, to my great disappointment that Aunt M.[argaretta] had already left her N.[ew] E.[ngland].

Phila[delphia]. Sunday, April 24. Paid several visits, and in the eve. went with Annie [Woods Webb] and Mattie F.[arbeaux] to hear Dr. [William] Furness.[28] Most beautifully he spoke. And his sermon was full of love of *man* and therefore of the love of God. Heard the most exquisite singing there, by a lady, of the Lord's prayer. Dr. F.[urness] is a perfect Christian. How much good it does one to listen to words of truth from the lips of those true ministers—too few, alas! who *practise* what they preach,—whose lives are a beautiful exemplification of their teachings. I *cannot* listen to those who do not live up to their preaching.

Saturday, April 30. Went to town with Mr. P.[urvis], T.[acie] and H.[attie], to see Whittier. Had a delightful visit. He was in one of his most genial moods, and laughed and talked most charmingly. He looks much better than I feared to see him, and says that he feels better. I am glad. It was a real happiness to see him again, and in such excellent spirits. Grand, noble man that he is! Another great happiness is in store for me. Thanks to the kindness of my good friends Prof. Crosby and Mary S.[hepard] I am offered a situation in the school[29] of the latter. *That* is indeed a pleasure, and I shall have time to study some at dear old Normal. I have had a truly kind and happy home here, and have become much attached to it. But the great advantage of attending school, the pleasure of being with Mary S.[hepard] and, above all, my conviction that it is my *duty* to go (some of my friends think it is *not.*) prevent me from hesitating a moment about going. Prof. C.[rosby] and indeed all my N.[ew] E.[ngland] friends are very, very kind and good. At the office I was introduced to Dr. [William] Furness, and had a very pleasant conversation with him. He is as genial and affable as he is noble and fearless. I have a high reverence for him.

Sunday, May 1. A beautiful May-day.—One of the loveliest I've ever seen. Had a delightful drive through the country to Attleborough. The trees are perfectly beautiful— in full bloom. The grass is as green, the birds as mirthful, the sky as cloudless, and the air as warm as in summer. Had a pleasant day at the C.'s delightful place. Am almost as deeply in love with Sallie C. as G. is. She is a dear, warm-hearted girl. Saw some perfect violets.

Friday, May 6. Had a splendid ride of three miles, on horseback, to L.'s greenhouse. Before I reached it the air was laden with the fragrance of mignonette and heliotrope. Within was a scene—beautiful as fairy land,—roses, verbenas, clematic [*sic*], all kinds of flowers, in full bloom. One division of the greenhouse was filled with geraniums in bloom,—the finest collection I've ever seen. My sturdy old horse—"Joe" came back quite rapidly, and I enjoyed the sunset ride perfectly. No exercise is so thoroughly exhilarating and delightful to me as horseback riding. It makes me feel younger and happier.

Saturday, May 7. Went to town, and saw Aunt M.[argaretta] who has just returned from N.[ew] E.[ngland]. Had a talk about the friends in old S.[alem]. Am grieved to hear that Mrs. [Caroline] P.[utnam]'s little girl [Louisa Victoria] is dangerously ill.[30] Poor Mrs. P.[utnam]! I pity her sincerely. But oh, how greatly it grieves and saddens me to think of the death of Mr. [Charles] Hovey.[31] He was so truly good and noble. The cause of light and Truth cannot afford to lose such a friend. Why must such noble, true-hearted men leave us?

Phila[delphia]. Sunday, May 8. Spent the day with my dear A.[nnie Woods Webb] who is going to her country home. We may never meet again. Soon I shall be in N.[ew] E.[ngland] and hundreds of miles be interposed between us. Dear A.[nnie]! the only sister of my lost mother. My heart clings to her and her darling little girls. God grant that we *may* indeed meet once more. This eve went again to Dr. Furness's church. To my surprise and delight who should ascend the pulpit but Mr. [O. B.] Frothingham (of Salem—

once;)—kindred in spirit to Dr. F. [urness] and highly talented. His discourse was on God and was excellent—marked of course by the liberality which characterizes Mr. F. [rothingham]. As a *preacher* I don't like him quite as well as Dr. F. [urness,] as a *lecturer*—better. They are both "Nature's noblemen."—It does one's soul good to listen to such ministers. Wrote to L. F.

Salem. January 1, 1860. Can it be possible that so many months have elapsed since my pen last touched the pages, old friend! Carelessly enough we say "time flies." Do we, after all, realize *how* it flies! How the months, days and hours *rush* along, bearing us on—on—upon their swift, unwearying wings? To me there is something deeply impressive in this strange flight of Time. Standing now upon the threshold of another year, how solemn, how strangely solemn seem the Past and the Future; the *dead* and *newly born* year;—memories, gladdening and sorrowing of the one, eager hopes, desires, resolves for the other;—how they crowd upon us now! Do they avail aught? I ask myself. Alas! to [*sic*] often they do not. Too often past experiences, and high resolves for the future, are forgotten, swallowed up in the excitement of the present moment. I have been reading to-day Arnold's "History of Rome." How it thrills one to know of those heroic deeds done "in the brave days of old." And how blessed it is that all the wealth of the ages can be ours, if we choose to grasp it! That we can live, not in this century, this corner of the world, alone, but in every century, and every age, and every clime! That we can listen to the words of orators, poets and sages; that we can enter into every conflict, share every joy, thrill with every noble deed, known since the world began. And hence are books to us a treasure and a blessing unspeakable. And they are doubly this when one is shut out from society as I am, and has not opportunities of studying those living, breathing, *human* books, which are, I doubt not, after all, the most profoundly interesting and useful study. From that kind of pleasure, that kind of improvement I am barred; but, thank God! none can deprive me of the other kind. And I will strive to be resigned during the little while we have to stay here.—and in that higher sphere do I now *know* the cruelty[,] the injustice of man ceases? *There* do Right, and Justice and Love abide.

Salem. June 22, 1862. More penitent than ever I come to thee again, old Journal, long neglected friend. More than two years have elapsed since I last talked to thee.—Two years full of changes. A little while ago a friend read to me Miss Mullock's "Life for a Life." The Journal letters, which I liked so much, were at first addressed to an unknown friend. So shall mine be. What name shall I give to thee, oh *ami inconnu?* It will be safer to give merely an initial—A. And so, dear A. I will tell you a little of my life, for the past two years. When I wrote to you last,—on a bright, lovely New Year's Day, I was here in old Salem, and in this very house. What a busy winter that was for me, I was assisting my dear Miss S. [hepard] with one of her classes, and at the same time studying, and reciting at the Normal, Latin, French and a little Algebra. Besides I was taking German lessons. How was I not busy, dear A.? Yet it seems to me I was never so happy. I enjoyed life perfectly and all the winter was strong and well. But when Spring came my health gave way. First my eyesight failed me, and the German which I liked better than anything else, which it was a real luxury to study[,] had to be given up, and then all my other studies. My health continuing to fail, I was obliged to stop teaching, and go away. Went to Bridgewater, and in the Kingman[']s[32]

delightful home grew gradually stronger. Then went to the
water cure at Worcester, where the excellent Dr. [Seth]
R.[ogers] [33] did me a world of good—spiritually as well as
physically. To me he seems one of the best and noblest types
of manhood I ever saw. In my heart I shall thank him always.
Early in September, came back from W.[orcester] and recommenced teaching, feeling quite well. But late in October
had a violent attack of lung fever, which brought me very,
very near the grave, and entirely unfitted me for further
work. My physician's commands were positive that I sh'ld
not attempt spending the winter in S.[alem], and I was
obliged to return to P.[hiladelphia]. A weary winter I had
there, unable to work, and having but little congenial society,
and suffering the many deprivations which all of our unhappy
race must suffer in the so-called "City of Brotherly Love."
What a mockery that name is! But over these weary months
it is better to draw the veil and forget. In May I went to
Byberry to see poor R.[obert Purvis, Jr.] who was ill with
lung disease. And all the beautiful summer I stayed there
trying to nurse and amuse him as well as I c'ld. It was so sad
to see one so young, so full of energy and ambition, doomed
to lead a life of inaction, and the weariness which ill health
brings. R.[obert] seemed to improve as the summer advanced, and in the Fall I left him, to take charge of Aunt
M.[argaretta]'s school [34] in the city. A small school—but the
children were mostly bright and interesting; and I was thankful to have anything to do. About this time H.[enry]
C.[assey] [35] arrived, having recently returned from Paris.
He was improved very much, and was a very pleasant
companion for me all through winter. For business detained
him in P.[hiladelphia], which he detests as heartily as I do.
He read much to me, both French and English—consisting

chiefly of Carlyle, that most singular and original of mortals, whom I like, despite his oddities. My dear Aunt A. [nnie Woods Webb] sent me "Hero Worship," and some of "Sarter Resartus," which to me as dear noble, Mr. Furness said it was to him truly a "revelation." I thank Carlyle for writing it. That "Everlasting Yea" in especial is to me most wonderful, beautiful and helpful. Then H. [enry Cassey] read to Aunt M. [argaretta] and me the "French Rev. [iew]" another wonderful book. He knows much more about French history than I do and told me many things necessary to know. He and I have many things in common, and saw much of each other. Of course people talked, and many very sagely said that we were engaged. We heard of it with amusement, for nothing c'ld be more absurd. I sh'ld no more think of marrying him than of marrying my own brother. It is perfectly a sisterly feeling that I have for him. And I know that he does not care nearly as much for me as he does for his sister, which is very natural. So let the world gossip— "never a bit care we," I think Mr. [William F. [urness]'s sermons which I sometimes heard, were almost the only thing that made life tolerable to me in P. [hiladelphia] last winter. Such sermons! So full of vitality, earnest, and practical Christianity—how could they fail to do good? No one would call Mr. F. [urness]'s face handsome, yet it was often beautiful to me. When he was preaching it lighted up so beautifully. The "soul shows through"; the inspiration became evident to all.

In March, poor R. [obert Purvis, Jr.] died.[36] When I saw him lying so cold and still, and witnessed the agony of the loving hearts around him, I wished, dear A.! that I c'ld have been taken instead of him. He had everything to live for, and I so very little. It seems hard; yet we *know* it must be

right. Some weeks ago H. [enry] went to N. [ew] Y. [ork]
on his way to T. [oronto] to see his sister.[37] I missed him
sadly, and was not afraid to say so, let people say what they
might. H. [enry] has a noble nature, and high aspirations,
both moral and mental, which makes him a different being
from the generality of colored young men that one sees;—
though I know that the unhappy circumstances in which these
are placed, are often more to blame than they themselves.
Week before I had a letter from Mary S. [hepard] asking me
to come on and take charge of S. C's classes during the
summer, as she was obliged to go away. How gladly I
accepted, you, dear A., may imagine. I had been longing so
for a breath of N. [ew] E. [ngland] air; for a glimpse of the
sea, for a walk over our good old hills. C. [harlotte] E., a
bright Southern girl of sixteen, who wants to qualify herself
for a teacher, came with me to school. We left P. [hiladelphia]
on Tuesday, the 10th; stopped a little while in N.Y., and
walked on Broadway with H. [enry], who was still there.
Then took the evening boat, and reached here Wed. [nesday]
morn. Mrs. [Amy] I. [ves] gave us a most cordial welcome;
and we immediately felt quite at home. How delightful it
was to see Mary S. [hepard]. Mrs. R. [emond], Mrs. C. [hase?]
and one or two other dear friends! And to see my lovely
elms, now in all their June glory, and to go upon the hills
again! Yesterday A. [my] I. [ves], C. [harlotte] E. and I went
to Marblehead Beach. The tide was coming in, and never
have I seen Old Ocean more gloriously beautiful. We had
an afternoon of rare enjoyment; and it seemed to me as if I
really *could* not tear myself away. I think I should have stayed
all night if any one would have stayed with me. It was too
much happiness to sit upon the rocks, and see those breaking
waves, again. As they receded, my whole soul seemed drawn

away with them, then when they rushed back again upon the
steadfast rocks my being thrilled, glowed, with joyous, ex-
ultant life. Strange, strange, old sea, how something in the
deepest depths of my nature responds to you, how the very
fibres of my being seem to cling to you. But how can I
describe the emotions which you awake in me? Words cannot
do it. They fail, and are worthless, absurd. Well, dear A. [,]
are you weary of my rhapsodizing? But, kind unknown, you
will not tell me if you are. You will not blame nor laugh at
me, but simply listen, and be silent.

It is a lovely June Sunday,—the air sweet and cool, the
birds singing, the sun shining, and soon the church bells will
ring. But I shall not go to church. I shall stay at home and
write. I must write to others besides you, so fare well, for
the present, my indulgent *ami inconnu*. (I give you the
masculine form in French, only because it is more general. I
have no special reason for it, I assure you, none whatever.)

Sunday eve.   Went with C. [harlotte] to Harmony Grove.
It looks lovelier than ever. Went to the graves of those I
loved so well—Mrs. [Amy Matilda] R. [emond] and Mr.
[Joseph] P. [utnam]—the one almost a mother, the other
almost a brother to me. How calmly they rest now.

Sunday, June 29.   Little worth recording has occurred
during the past week. Have taught school, as usual, wrote
letters, played chess, and listened to "Chronicles of Carling-
ford," which Miss S. [hepard] has been reading. It is a
wonderfully, tragically interesting story, by the author of
"Adam Bede." Have had a grand walk on the turnpike this
morning. How fresh and invigorating the breezes were. How
peaceful the green hills, and gray old rocks looked,—sleeping
in the June sunlight. Gathered a quantity of wild roses for
dear Mary S. [hepard]. Mr. Manning of the "Old South,"

preached here this morning; and greatly as I admire this
fearless young apostle of freedom, I could not prevail upon
myself to go to church. I felt such a strong drawing toward
my dear old hills. T'was irresistible.

Sunday, July 6. Let me see? How did I spend last week!
In teaching as usual, until Friday, on which, being the
"glorious Fourth," we had no school, and I went to Framingham to the Grove Meeting.[38] The day was lovely, and
I had a delightful time. Greatly to my disappointment Mr.
[Wendell] Phillips was not there. But it was better that he
sh'ld not attempt speaking in the open air.—His throat was
troubling him much. Mr. [William Lloyd] G.[arrison] and
all his children were there looking as well and happy as
possible. He and Mr. [Ezra] Heywood and Miss [Susan
B.] Anthony made the best speeches. One cannot listen to
Mr. H.[eywood] without feeling that he is a "born orator."
C.[harlotte] and I spent most of the afternoon in taking a
row on the delightful Pond. We had a lesson in rowing from
two good-natured country lads, who were our oarsmen. They
were infinitely amused at our proceedings. But we persevered
despite the heat, determined that we w'ld not be put down;
and some sort of fashion—"by hook or by crook," finally
brought the boat to shore. It was good fun, and good, hard
work, too. I wish I c'ld learn to row. Every day of my life
I feel more and more the great importance of physical
exercise. I know it is most necessary to health, and health is
now the first consideration with me. Without it I feel that I
can never accomplish anything. Met some old friends at
Framingham. Dr. and Mrs. [Seth] Rogers were there from
W.[orcester]. How glad I was to see the Dr. again. But it
grieved me to see him looking so far from well. He has been
quite ill since Feb.[ruary], with pleurisy. He is certainly

one of the most thoroughly good men in the world. Saw Helen M. who goes to Paris the last of the month to complete her medical studies. Enviable mortal! Mrs. P.[utnam] and H.[elen Gilliard] were there and urged me to come to W.[orcester] [39] which I shall try to do in Aug.[ust]. After the meeting, spent a day or two in Boston. Had a lovely walk on the Common, Saturday morning. How fresh and beautiful the grass and trees looked. Spent most of the forenoon with Sarah P.[itman?]. Poor girl! She is looking very weary. On my way home, stopped at Williams and Everett's and saw a magnificent bust of Milton in marble. Saw a picture of "Rahl of the Rhine," which was really startling in its *lifelikeness*. The legend runs this wise.—Rahl and two wild companions were in the habit of meeting to drink together. And one night they took a vow that they w'ld continue to meet on that same night of every year, even though two of them sh'ld be dead. And the vow was kept. The painting, which is large and [a] very fine one, represents Rahl as raising a glass of wine, and at the same moment the four ghostly hands of his two dead companions are stretched out and clutch the other two glasses, while Rahl stands transfixed with horror. There is something very life-like and striking about this picture. One cannot look at it without a shudder.—In the afternoon S.[arah] P.[itman?] and I spent a little time at the [Boston] Atheneum. My attention was particularly attracted by a magnificent bust of John Brown (in marble), and by a landscape—I think it must have been a part of two German Alps—by a German artist. I thought it one of the most beautiful pictures I ever saw, but you know, dear A., that there never was a greater ignoramus than I about matters of Art. Still I believe no one could have helped liking this picture. It was so lovely— Grand mountains, *real* mountains, rising above the clouds in the background, a lovely valley with a clear stream flowing through it at the foot of the mts. Near the stream was a party of gipsies in bright picturesque costumes preparing their meal. Over all bent a sky, blue and beautiful as an Italian sky. It was a most enjoyable picture, and one to be easily recalled. Had but little time to devote to others. Spent the evening quite pleasantly at Mrs. L.[ockley?]'s. To-day— Sunday—had the great happiness of hearing Mr. [Wendell] Phillips. S.[arah] and I went together. Music Hall was crowded.[40] The heat was so intense that I c'ld scarcely breathe. I thought, before the lecture commenced, that I sh'ld certainly have to go out. But after Mr. P.[hillips] commenced speaking I forgot everything else. It was a grand, glorious speech, much as he alone can make. I wish the poor miserable President whom he so justly criticised c'ld have heard it. It grieved me to see him looking so pale and weary. And his throat troubles him much. I cannot bear to think of his health failing. Yet sometimes I fear it is. Oh dear A. let us pray to the good All-Father to spare this noble soul to see the result of his life-long labors—the freedom of the slaves. After *church* S.[arah] and I went on the lovely Common—looking its loveliest on this sweet summer day. We had a long pleasant chat together. Poor dear S.[arah]! I hope the blessed gift of health may yet be hers. Ah, friend of mine, I must not forget to tell you about a little adventure I met with to-day. I was boarding with Mrs. R.[,] a very good anti-slavery woman, and kind and pleasant as can be. Well, when I appeared at the dinner-table to-day, it seems that a *gentleman* took umbrage at sitting at the same table with one whose skin chanced to be "not colored like his own," and rose and left the table. Poor man! he feared contamination. But the charming part of the affair is that I with eyes intent upon my dinner, and mind entirely engrossed by Mr. Phillips' glorious words, which were still sounding in my soul, did not notice this person's presence nor disappearance. So his proceedings were quite lost upon me, and I sh'd have been in a state of blissful ignorance as to his very existence had not the hostess afterward spoken to me about it, expressing the wish, good woman— that my "feelings were not hurt." I told her the truth, and begged her to set her mind at ease, for even had I have noticed the simpleton's behavior it w'ld not have troubled me. I felt too thorough a contempt for such people to allow myself to be wounded by them. This wise gentleman was an *officer in the navy*, I understand. An honor to his country's service isn't he? but he is not alone, I know full well. The name of his kindred is Legion,—but I defy and despise them all. I hope as I grow older I get a little more philosophy. Such things do not wound me as deeply as of yore. But they create a bitterness of feeling, which is far from desirable. "When, when will these outrages cease?" often my soul cries out—"How long, oh Lord, how long?" You w'ld have pitied me during the last part of my ride back to S. [alem] this afternoon. The first part of the ride from B. [oston] to L. [ynn] in the horse cars, w'ld have been quite pleasant but for the heat. One has a good opportunity of seeing the surrounding country traveling in this way. At L. [ynn] we met the stage, or rather omnibus. We packed in;—thirty outside; the inside crowded to suffocation with odorous Irish and their screaming babies;—the heat intense. Altogether it was quite unbearable. The driver refused to move with such a load. Nobody was willing to get off. And I think we must have been detained at L. [ynn] an hour, till at last an open wagon drove up, and taking off part of the load, we started for S. [alem]. We were altogether about three hours going from B.[oston] to S.[alem]. Got home just in time to see my good friend Miss W.[eston?] a few minutes. It was a real happiness, for she is one of those *sincere* and most kindly people that one believes in.

Saturday, August 2. Have spent the last few weeks as usual in teaching, alternating with walking, reading or listening to Mary read. "Salem Chapel" increases in interest. Some letters of Mendelssohn I like exceedingly. I long to know more of the great composer. Those letters show a singularly beautiful and lovable character. Just from reading these, one can feel how truly the character of Seraphael in "Charles Au.[gusta]" is drawn. I never can understand how that wonderful book c'ld have been written at sixteen. Truly it was an inspiration. And one cannot cease to wonder how so great and singular a genius c'ld have been so unappreciated in her own land. School closed to-day. To-day Sallie [Cassey] S.[mith Watson] arrived. It is very pleasant and home-like to see her. What a graceful creature she is. And so very French. It seems as if she *must* have grown up in the atmosphere of Paris. Spent a very pleasant eve. with her at Lizzie [Magee] R.[emond].

Monday, August 4. L.[izzie], S.[allie] and I went to Marblehead Beach. Had a delightful time on the rocks. S.[allie] and I waded and frolicked like a couple of children. Walked back as far as Forest River and thence had a lovely ride home in the cars, just at sunset.

Wednesday, August 6. Spent the day at Nahant. Had a glorious time. There was one place among the rocks that I enjoyed perfectly. It was on a point that extended quite far out into the sea. In a deep chasm between the rocks the waves rushed up, surging and boiling, then rising broke upon the rocks in great sheets of spray, pure and white as new-fallen snow. It was a glorious sight. I sat there a long time enjoying it perfectly. Never, never before, I thought—dearly as I have always loved the ocean,—have I had so delightful an experience of it as I have had today. Dear A. it will be a precious memory to me always. Returning, how much we enjoyed the beautiful drive from N. [ahant] to L. [ynn]—a narrow strip of land with the sea on either hand, and that sea glowing in the sunset. It was very beautiful. Soon after I reached home dear M. [ary Shepard] came, bringing me the kindest note from [John Greenleaf] Whittier in answer to one I had written asking what day we sh'ld come. (His sister[41] had urgently invited us to come before I left N. [ew] E. [ngland].) We are to go on Saturday. My mind is filled with pleasant anticipations. Good night.

Saturday, August 9. Another "day to be marked with a white stone." Mary and I started early at the station whom sh'ld we meet but the C. [hase?]'s and Lizzie R. [emond]. I was delighted; not expecting to see them. We went with them as far as Salisbury. They propose spending to-morrow on the Isle of Shoals. We changed cars at L. [ynn] then proceeded to Amesbury. Did not see Whittier at the station. Drove to the house; met with a warm welcome from his sister. She looks very frail. Just as we entered the door of the house a lady came in behind us, whom we found afterward to be Lucy Larcom[42]—a pleasant mothering, unassuming kind of person, really quite lovable. W. [hittier] was in one of his most delightful genial moods. His sister as lovely, childlike— I had almost said as angelic as ever. The day was showery, and we c'ld not take any walks, but I enjoyed myself perfectly in the house. W. [hittier] told us some amusing anecdotes of how he was pestered by people coming to see him—people who were utter strangers. Sometimes, he said they brought their carpet-bags. "Oh, Mr. W. [hittier], not their carpet-bags!" we exclaimed. "Yes, actually," he replied, smiling quite grimly, "and they all have the same speeches to make 'Mr. W. [hittier] we have read y[ou]r writings and admired them very much, and had such a great desire to see you.' " He said he was thankful to live in such a quiet little place as Amesbury, where nobody said anything to him about his writings, and where he was not thought of as a writer. He said sometimes he had tracked these lion hunters, and found that the same people went to [Ralph Waldo] Emerson and [Henry W.] Longfellow and others. Emerson did not care so much for them. He rather enjoyed studying character in all its different phases. He and his sister told us a comical story about a "Mrs. Hansford's husband," this Mrs. H. [ansford] it seems, being one of the most persistent lion-hunters. The conversation turned on many topics, and was most enjoyable throughout. Miss W. [hittier] showed us photographs of her friends. Among them was one of a Mrs. Howell of Phila. [delphia] (whom gossip once said W. [hittier] w'ld marry)[,] a face faultless in outline and coloring— exquisitely beautiful, yet lacking a little in depth of expression. Miss W. [hittier] says that it does not do her justice. That she is more beautiful than her picture. Then she must look like an angel. The picture of Helen W. [hithe,] the lovely, gifted girl who died in Italy, charmed me. A face at once most gentle and yet most spirited, beautiful, noble, and lighted up by the soul within. A cherished and only child, she died at seventeen. Miss W. [hittier] showed us the picture of an Italian girl, in which she found a striking likeness to me. Everybody else agreed that there was a resemblance. But I utterly failed to see it: *I* thought the Italian girl very pretty, and I know myself to be the very opposite. We left the poet's home with regret. Such a quiet lovely home. It made my heart ache to see his sister looking so frail, knowing what these two are to each other. I was glad to find that she was going away for a while with Lucy Larcom, she is such a motherly person—one by whom it must be a real happiness to be taken care of. W. [hittier] advised me to apply to the Port-Royal Com. [mission] [43] in Boston. He is very desirous that I sh'ld go. I shall certainly take his advice.

Sunday, August 10. My last Sabbath in dear old Salem. Passed the morn. in packing, the afternoon with my dear M. [ary Shepard]. She read me some of the "Home Ballads," and then we had one of our long confidential talks. I am very, very sorry to part with her. And to leave her looking so weary grieves me much. She must stop teaching. It is too hard for her. She can and *must* write. Ah, if I c'ld only bring it about! But I am powerless, powerless, now. Spent the evening with S. [arah] and others at Mrs. [Caroline] P. [utnam]'s. Mr. [John] R. [emond] came in to say goodbye. He has been a true friend to me. And he is an original, genial, and—to me—most interesting person. His wife,[44] dear A., ah I cannot tell you how noble she is. What *restfulness* there is in that deep, calm, earnest nature. I remember when I was very, very ill how it used to rest me and soothe me just to have her sit by my side, and to look into that kind grave face, and meet the glance of those loving earnest eyes. She is a *rare* woman.

Boston. Monday, August 11. Left S. [alem] with Sallie [Cassey Smith Watson] this morn. Farewell, farewell again old town! I know not when I shall see thee again. S. [allie] and I with Mr. L. [enox?] walked from B. [oston] to Bunker Hill. Charmed our eyes with Warren's statue[,] exhausted ourselves with ascending the mon. [ument,] were refreshed again by the magnificent view from the top, descended, went to the Public Library and the Atheneum. Saw nothing new at the latter, but some old pictures of which one never wearies, then dined with Mrs. J. In the afternoon S. [allie] left with Mrs. P. [utnam] and E. [ddie Putnam] who go to W. [orcester] whither I shall follow in a few days. Mrs. J. [,] kind, motherly friend that she is[,] insists on my spending those days with her, which I will very gladly do.

Wednesday, August 13. Had gone to see some members of the P. [ort] R. [oyal] Com. [mission] and finding them all out of town, felt somewhat discouraged, when I rec'd the kindest letter from Whittier, advising me again to apply to the Com. [mission] and giving me the names of several friends of his [to] whom to apply, also his permission to use his name as a reference. How very kind he is. I shall go see those whom he mentions at once.

Watertown. Saturday, August 16. Have not yet succeeded in seeing any of the Com. [mission]. Though I have traversed this hilly city enough; but I don't despair for I have seen Dr. [Samuel] Howe.[45] Was disappointed in his appearance. He is not the benevolent looking, genial person I expected to see. At first he seemed cold and hard, but no wonder, he was being so persecuted with some tiresome people. When I stated my business to him, and showed him W. [hittier]'s letter he was as kind and cordial as c'ld be, and entered with much interest into my wishes. He is not a member of the Com. [mission] but recommended me to go to a Dr. [Solomon] Peck[46] who has been Superintendent of the schools at P. [ort] R. [oyal] and who has great influence with the Com. [mission]. Mrs. J. and I have been to Roxbury to see Dr. P. [eck] but he was not at home[,] will probably be on Tuesday. So I determined instead of going to W. [orcester] to come to Watertown and stay with S. [allie Cassey Smith Watson] till Monday. Had a delightful ride out in the horse cars, through old Cambridge, past Longfellow's home, and Lowell's, the Colleges and Mt. Auburn. This eve. L. [ucy Kingman] brought me "John Brent," which I am eagerly devouring.

Sunday, August 17. My twenty-fifth birthday. Tisn't a very pleasant thought that I have lived a quarter of a century, and am so very, very ignorant. Ten years ago, I hoped for a different fate at twenty-five. But why complain? The accomplishments, the society, the delights of travel which I have dreamed of and longed for all my life, I am now convinced can never be mine. If I can go to Port Royal, I will try to forget all these desires. I will pray that God in his goodness will make me noble enough to find my highest happiness in doing my duty. Since Mrs. J. has given me such sad accounts of the sufferings of the poor freed people my desire of helping them has increased. It is but little I c'ld do, I know, but that little I w'ld do with all my heart. Went to church this morning to hear Mr. Weiss—author of "The Horrors of San Domingo," in the "Atlantic." It was a beautiful earnest sermon, and I enjoyed it, but was rather disappointed that it was not on the times, as I had hoped it w'ld be. *That* is the subject which he usually chooses, I am told. It was a pleasant little church and the altar adorned with the loveliest flowers. I like to see that. The afternoon S. [allie] and I spent in a pleasant little grove. There, lying on the grass in perfect ease, I finished "John Brent." I like it exceedingly. It is a soul-stirring book. That "Gallop of Three" is particularly grand, and reminds one of that splendid poem of Browning's "How They Brought the Good News" etc., which is also a "Gallop of Three." Afterward, S. [allie] and I looked over "Edwin

Brothertoft." I do not like it very much. The scene is laid at the time of the Revolution. It does not interest me. S.[allie] and I had a lovely walk by the riverside. W.[atertown] is a very pleasant little place. I forgot to say, dear A.[,] that Mr. Weiss lives in the house that the lovely Maria Lowell lived in before she married the poet. It is a large comfortable-looking old-fashioned country house with beautiful trees, just one's idea of a pleasant home. The White family, to which the poetess belonged are scattered far and wide now, and strangers dwell in the home which *her* presence must have made almost a Paradise.

Monday, August 18.   Walked from W.[atertown] to Mt. Auburn. It was a delightful walk through the quiet, beautiful country. Spent nearly all day at Mt. A.[uburn]. It was very lovely there. The beautiful chapel with its noble statues, the grand view from the Observatory, the stately monuments, the exquisite flowers—I enjoyed all perfectly. Such flowers! Geranium, heliotrope, mignonette, and everything else that is fragrant and beautiful in profusion. I sat down and *luxuriated*. The whole cemetery is like a flower garden. One or two of the monuments I liked particularly. On one—over a child's grave—was carved a cross and anchor, and twining around them, a morning glory vine also exquisitely carved. The inscription was—"Here in Faith and Hope we placed our Morning Glory." On another simple white headstone, with no name upon it, were the words—"All I loved lies here." It was over the grave of a grown person. There was something very touching in those few, simple words.

Worcester. Tuesday, August 19.   Saw Dr. P.[eck] this morning. He was very kind, and assures me that he thinks there will be no difficulty about my going. He will speak to the Com.[mission] about it and let me know in a few days.

It was very interesting to hear his account of his experiences at Port Royal. He seems deeply interested in the people there. I hope I can go. Bade farewell to my kind friend Mrs. J. and came to W. [orcester] this eve. Here I shall remain until I get news from B. [oston]. I sh'ld have stayed there, but c'ld find no employment, though I tried hard to do so. It is pleasant to be here with my old friends, the P. [utnam]'s, whom I have always liked exceedingly. They are very kind and hospitable. I must say that Mrs. C. [aroline] P. [utnam] manages to make herself intensely disagreeable. She seems to delight in it. A most unfortunate disposition.

Saturday, August 23. Have seen my dear friend Dr. [Seth] R. [ogers] twice. Had a delightful drive and talk with him to-day. He is as good as he can be, *I* think. Went home with him and spent the rest of the day. Was delighted to see Lucy R. and Sarah P. [itman] again. Had a nice long talk. L. [ucy] is a particularly interesting girl.

Thursday, August 28. Yesterday Sallie S. [mith Watson] came down from Mendon, and to-day we went with Mrs. P. [utnam] and T. to Princeton. I drove. It was so foggy we c'ld scarcely see twenty yards in front of us, at times. Not a very promising day to see a mountain; but in the afternoon the mists rolled beautifully away, and we proceeded to the mountain. E. [ddie] and I were soon at the top. Mrs. P. [utnam] and S. [allie] followed more slowly. The view as we drove to the base was very fine. Machusett looked like a great sea monster thrown upon the land. It did not give me the idea of grandeur—this, the first mountain I had ever had a view of. Rather of strength and size and weight. It is not aspiring. Not high enough for that, I suppose. The view from the top was grand, not so extensive as it w'ld have been, however, had not some remnants of the morning's mist still lingered about the horizon. I experienced to the full the sense of freedom that I had longed for. I sh'ld like to camp out there for weeks. In the distance we saw a mountain, grand aspiring, just my idea of one. I thought it at first Mt. Washington, but was told it must have been Monadnock. Probably it was. It pierced the clouds, I thought, and was much more mountain-like than Machusett. Still I enjoyed the latter much, although it is only about 2,000 ft. high; and w'ld fain see it again. The drive home was wild and grand, to me, but most alarming to Mrs. P. [utnam], for it was in a thunder storm—rain pouring in torrents—lightning flashing sharply. Did not reach home till long after dark; and had various difficulties in finding the way. I was the driver, and was wet through. Nevertheless, I enjoyed it greatly, as I always do an adventure. A day not soon to be forgotten. I had nearly forgotten to tell you dear A. what a wonderful hail storm we had yesterday, Wednesday. It came on very suddenly. The hail came down thickly, and some of the stones were nearly as large as a hen's egg. It was the most astonishing sight, I ever saw, and beautiful too. I wish you c'ld have seen those stones leaping about the grass. It was very strange.

Saturday, August 30. All the guests left to-day but me. T'was rather lonly [*sic*] here. After seeing the friends off I went to the Water-Cure and finished the day. S. [arah] P. [itman?] read us extracts from Goethe's "Biography." Then L. [ucy] and I had the loveliest walk to a place called the Hermitage, a little nook in the woods just as delightful as it can be. We roamed about in desultory fashion, and enjoyed ourselves. Discovered a bit of Italy, too—an actual vineyard with some beautiful grapes in it.

Sunday, August 31. "Bright Summer, Fare-the-well!" Went to hear Dr. Cheever preach. He said some grand and stirring things as he always does.

Wednesday, September 3. Have been anxious and disappointed at not hearing from Dr. P. [eck]. But a letter from Mrs. J. to-day tells me that she has seen him, and that he is very sanguine about my going. Dr. [Seth] R. [ogers] and others to whom he spoke about it, wish it. The Com. [mission] meets to-day, and then he will write immediately and let me know the final decision. Last week I heard from home that there was now no doubt of my being able to go from the Phila. [delphia] Com. [mittee].[47] Mr. [J. Miller] McK. [im] [48] had spoken to them about it. So if I cannot go from Boston I am sure of going from P. [hiladelphia] but I w'ld rather go under Boston auspices. Since I have been here have read "Cecil Breems." I liked it better than I feared, but not nearly so well as "John Brent." Still it interested me much. It has the heroic element and much *real* tragedy in it. A picture of Winthrop that I saw at the W. [hittier]'s interested me much. Beautiful, with all a woman's gentleness, and a woman's and man's high heroism and grandeur of soul, and a poet's dreamy grace besides.

Monday, September 8. No further news from B. [oston]. I am determined to go to-morrow and see for myself what the trouble is. Have paid a last visit to the W. [ater] C. [ure]. Am so grieved that I shall not see Dr. [Seth] R. [ogers]. He has gone to N. [ahant]. S. [allie] walked here to see me. We sat on the doorstep in the lovely moonlight, and talked for hours. We talked of self sacrifice. What a girl S. [allie] is! Full of originality and genius—strange and wayward to the last degree. What will become of her? What will her life be? I ask myself often. She interests me deeply.

Phila[delphia]. Sunday, September 14.   Back again in old abominable P.[hiladelphia]. H.[enry] and I went from W.[orcester] to B.[oston] on Tuesday afternoon. I got little satisfaction from the B.[oston] Com.[mission]. "They were not sending women at present" etc. Dr. R.[ogers] promised to do all he c'ld for me, but I am resolved to apply to the Com.[mittee] here. Mrs. J. wrote to me twice to W.[orcester] and I did not get her letters. Strange. Remained in Boston till Friday afternoon. Had the happiness of getting a glimpse of Wendell Phillip's before I left. W'ld not stop him to shake hands with him, and have been sorry every since that I did not. It w'ld have been *such* a satisfaction to me, and I may never see him again. Too late now. Came to N.Y. on the Sound, and had a very rough night of it. On Sat. Henry C.[assey] went with me to Central Park. A delightful place it is. T'will be a perfect fairy-land when the trees are grown. H.[enry] came to P.[hiladelphia] with me. We got there between ten and eleven. Everybody was in bed but Aunt M.[argaretta] who was astonished to see me. All well. House seems strange without the little girls, H.[arriet Purvis] and E.[mily] [49] who have gone to their relatives in Canada. Saw my dear A.[nnie Woods Webb] who is looking poorly, and has a bad cough. I feel troubled about her. Spent the eve. at my old friends the C.[hew]'s!

Monday, September 15.   Through Mr. [J. Miller] McK.[im]'s kindness have seen the Com.[mittee]. They are perfectly willing for me to go. The only difficulty is that it may not be quite safe. They will write to Port Royal at once, and inquire about my going. I shall wait anxiously for a reply.

Saturday, October 11.   For a month past have been busily occupied in sewing. H.[enry Cassey] has read to me a little

French and Eng. [lish] but he cannot read much aloud, poor child. His lungs are so weak. I feel really troubled about him. To-day had the happiness of receiving a note from my dear and noble friend Whittier, God bless him!

Wednesday, October 21.   To-day rec'd a note from Mr. McK. [im] asking me if I c'ld possibly be ready to sail for Port Royal perhaps tomorrow. I was astonished, stupefied, and, at first thought it impossible, but on seeing Mr. McK. [im] I found there was an excellent opportunity for me to go. An old Quaker gentleman is going there to keep store, accompanied by his daughter, and he is willing to take charge of me.[50] It will probably be the only opportunity that I shall have of going this winter, so at any cost I *will* go. And so new to work. In greatest haste.

Met John P. [ierce] on the cars. He was very kind.

At Sea. October 27, Monday.—Let me see. Where am I? What do I want to write? I am in a state of utter bewilderment. It was on Wed. I rec'd the note. On Thursday I said "good bye" to the friends that are so dear, and the city that is so hateful, and went to N.Y. Spent the night with Mrs. [Peter] W. [illiams]. The next morn did not hurry myself, having heard that the Steamer "United States" w'ld not sail till twelve. Mrs. W. [illiams] and I went to "Lovejoy's" to meet the Hunns' and found there a card from Mr. H. [unn] bidding me hasten to the steamer, as it was advertised to sail at nine. It was then between ten and eleven. After hurrying down and wearying ourselves, found when I got on board that it was not to sail till twelve. But I did not go ashore again. It was too bad, for I had not time to get several things that I wanted much, among them "Les Miserables," which my dear brother H. [enry] had kindly given me the money for. He had not had time to get it in Phila. [delphia].

Enjoyed the sail down the harbor perfectly. The shipping is a noble sight. Had no symptoms of sea-sickness until eve. when, being seated at the table an inexpressibly singular sensation caused me to make a hasty retreat to the aft-deck, where by keeping perfectly still sitting on a coil of ropes spent a very comfortable eve. and had a pleasant conversation with one of the passengers. Did not get out of sight of land until after dark. I regretted that.

Went below for the night into the close ladies' cabin with many misgivings which proved not unfounded. Was terribly sea-sick that night and all the next morning. Did not reappear on deck till noon of the next day—Saturday. What an experience. Of all doleful, dismal, desperate experiences sea-sickness is certainly the dolefulest, dismalist, desperate-est!

It was rather a miserable afternoon. Was half sick all the time and scarcely dared to move. There was highly pleasant talk going on around me, to which I could listen in silence—that was all. My companion Lizzie Hunn was sick all the time. Poor girl, she c'ld take no pleasure in anything.

When night came, we both determined that we w'ldn't go below and have a repetition of the agonies of the night before. We heroically resolved to pass the night on deck. A nice little nook was found for us "amidships," and there enveloped in shawls and seated in arm chairs we were made as comfortable as possible, and passed the night without being sick. Two of the passengers—young men from Hilton Head, who were very gentlemanly and attentive, entertained us for some time with some fine singing; then they retired, and we passed the rest of the night in the society of the Ocean alone. How wild and strange it seemed there on deck in the dark night, only the dim outlines of sea and sky to be seen, only the roaring of the waves to be heard. I enjoyed it much. The thought that we were far, far, away from land was a pleasant one to me.

The next day—Sunday—was emphatically a *dismal* day. It rained nearly all the time so that we c'ld not be on deck much of the time. As soon as we established ourselves nicely outside[,] down came the rain and we were driven into the close cabin, which was almost unendurable to me. Tried to read a little in the French Bible which H. [enry Cassey] gave me, but in vain. The day was mostly spent in the interesting occupation of preventing sea-sickness by keeping perfectly quiet and watching the rain drops.

Before night a storm came on. And a terrible storm it was. The steward arranged mattresses and blankets for us in the covered passage way "amidships" and we lay down, but not to rest. It was a veritable grand storm at sea. The vessel rocked and plunged, the planks creaked and groaned; the sea broke upon the boat with thunderous roars, and within[,] one w'ld have though that all the crockery in the establishment was going to pieces. Such a noise I never heard in my life. Such roaring and plunging, and creaking. Afterward we were told that one of the chains of the vessel broke, and indeed for a time she seemed to be at the mercy of the waves. Some one near us—one of the waiters, I think, was dreadfully frightened, and commenced praying and moaning most piteously, crying "Oh Jesus, dear Jesus," in most lamentable tones, till I began to think we must really be in danger. Then the water came into the ladies' cabin, below. One lady who had a baby with her woke up in the night and c'ld not find the child. It had been rolled away from her by the tossing of the ship, the lamps were out, and after some time, and much terror on the part of the poor woman the baby was found by one of the waiters under the berths. She was very quiet, and did not seem at all alarmed at her involuntary journey. Despite all the alarm and distress and anxiety we c'ld not help being amused at this little episode. During all the storm, however, I felt no fear; and now that the danger has passed, I feel really glad that I have at last experienced a "veritable storm at sea." The most astonishing thing was that I had two or three most refreshing sleeps in the very height of the storm.

This morning the sea was still very rough, but I struggled up, and dressed with great difficulty, and with the aid of one of the waiters made my way on deck. The sky was still very much overcast, the great, white capped waves were rising to a great height and breaking against the sides of the vessel. It was a grand sight, and I enjoyed it greatly. It has quite cleared off now, and the day is most lovely. I am feeling well and *luxuriating* in the glorious beauty of sea and sky. But my poor companion is still quite sick, and while I write, sits before me on a coil of ropes, enveloped in shawls, and looking the picture of dolefulness and despair.

How grand, how glorious the sea is, to-day! It far more than realizes my highest expectations of it. The sky too is beautiful[,] a deep, delicious blue, with soft, white, fleecy clouds floating over it. We have seen several sails today, in the distance, but still no land, whereat I am rejoiced.

There is not much to be said about the passengers on board. There are about a dozen beside ourselves, none of whom seem to me especially interesting, except perhaps our friend from Hilton Head, Mr. B. He is very intelligent, and I sh'ld think even a talented young man. He has read and admires all my favorite authors, and I enjoy talking with him about them. I have rarely found a man with so keen and delicate an appreciation of the beautiful, both in Nature and Art. There are no soldiers on board but one officer who stalks about the boat looking well pleased with himself and evidently trying to look quite grand, but *sans* success, for he was rather insignificant despite his good figure, fierce moustaches, and epaulettes.

Of the three ladies on board two go South to join their husbands, and the third accompanies hers. The first two are quite talkative, the latter very quiet. I believe that is all that can be said of them. There is a sea captain here whom I like very much. He is a Cape Cod man; has been to sea ever since he was nine years old. Has visited many lands, and I enjoy hearing him talk about them. The other gentlemen do not interest me, so I shall let them pass. Have only been able to go to the table twice. Then there was no difficulty—as I feared there might be. People were as kind and polite as possible. Indeed I have had not the least trouble since I have been on board. The waiters are as obliging and attentive as they can be, and bring us our meals out on deck every day.

Afternoon. I have just beheld the most glorious sight I ever saw in my life. With the aid of Mr. B. I staggered to the bow of the ship (which still rolls and pitches terribly) and there saw the sea in all its glory and grandeur. Oh, how beautiful those great waves were as they broke upon the side of the vessel, into foam and spray pure and white as new fallen snow. People talk of the monotony of the sea. I have not found it monotonous for a moment, since I have been well. To me there is "infinite variety," constant enjoyment in it.

I have tried to read, but in vain; there is so much to take off one's attention, besides reading makes my head dizzy. One of the most beautiful sights I have yet seen is the phosphorescence in the water at night—the long line of light in the wake of the steamer, and the stars, and sometimes balls of fire that rise so magically out of the water. It is most strange and beautiful. Had it not been for the storm we should have reached Port Royal to-day. But we shall not get there till to-morrow.

Tuesday, A.M. October 28.   How very, very lovely it was last night. Saw at last what I have so longed to see—the ocean in the moonlight. There was a beautiful young moon. Our ship rode gently along over a smooth sea leaving a path of silver echoing it. There was something inexpressibly sweet and soothing and solemn in that soft moonlight. We sat on deck a long time, and the friends from H.[ilton] H.[ead], both of whom have very fine voices, sang beautifully. They were kind enough to change state rooms with us, and we slept up stairs very quietly.

Early this morn. Mr. [John] H.[unn] came to our door to tell us that we were in sight of the blockading fleet in Charleston harbor. Of course, we sprang to the window eagerly, and saw the masts of the ships looking like a grove of trees in the distance. We were not near enough to see the city. It was hard to realize that we were even so near the barbarous place.

Later. We are again in sight of land. Have passed Edisto and several other islands, and can now see Hilton Head. Shall reach it about one. Tis nearly eleven now. The S.[outh] C.[arolina] shore is flat and low;—a long line of trees. It does not look very inviting. We are told that oranges will be ripe when we get to Beaufort, and that in every way this is just the loveliest season to be there, which is very encouraging.

We approach Hilton Head. Our ship has been boarded by Health Officer and Provost Marshal. We shall soon reach the landing. All is hurry and confusion on board. I must lay thee aside, friend journal, and use my eyes for seeing all there is to be seen. When we reach our place of destination I will give to thee, oh faithful friend, the result of my observations. So *au revoir.*

Tuesday Night. T'was a strange sight as our boat approached the landing at Hilton Head. On the wharf was a motley assemblage,—soldiers, officers, and "contrabands"[51] of every hue and size. They were mostly black, however, and certainly the most dismal specimens I ever saw. H.[ilton] H.[ead] looks like a very desolate place; just a long low, sandy point running out into the sea with no visible dwellings upon it but the soldiers' white roofed tents.

Thence, after an hour's delay, during which we signed a paper, which was virtually taking the oath of allegiance, we left the "United States," most rocking of rockety propellers,—and took a steamboat for Beaufort. On board the boat was General [Rufus] Saxton[52] to whom we were introduced. I like his face exceedingly. And his manners were very courteous and affable. He looks like a thoroughly *good* man.— From H.[ilton] H.[ead] to B.[eaufort] the same low line of sandy shore bordered by trees[,] almost the only object of interest to me were the remains of an old Huguenot Fort, built many, many years ago.

Arrived at B.[eaufort;] we found that we had yet not reached our home. Went to Mr. [Mansfield] French's,[53] and saw there Reuben T.[omlinson][54] whom I was very glad to meet, and Mrs. [Francis] Gage,[55] who seemed to be in rather a dismal state of mind. B.[eaufort] looks like a pleasant place. The houses are large and quite handsome, built in the usual Southern style with verandahs around them, and beautiful trees. One magnolia tree in Mr. F.[rench]'s yard is splendid,—quite as large as some of our large shade trees, and with the most beautiful foliage, a dark rich glossy green.

Went into the Commissary's Office to wait for the boat which was to take us to St. Helena's Island which is about six miles from B.[eaufort]. Tis here that Miss [Laura] Towne[56] has her school, in which I am to teach and that Mr. Hunn will have his store. While waiting in the office we saw several military gentleman [*sic*], *not* very creditable specimens, I sh'ld say. The little Commissary himself, Capt. T. is a perfect little popinjay, and he and a Colonel somebody who didn't look any too sensible, talked in a very smart manner, evidently for our especial benefit. The word "nigger" was plentifully used, whereupon I set them down at once as *not* gentleman [*sic*]. Then they talked a great deal about rebel attacks and yellow fever, and other alarming things, with significant nods and looks at each other. We saw through them at once, and were not at all alarmed by any of their representations. But if they are a fair example of army officers, I sh'ld pray to see as little of them as possible.

To my great joy found that we were to be rowed by a crew of negro boatmen. Young Mr. F.[rench—]whom I like— accompanied us, while Mr. H.[unn] went with a flat to get our baggage. The row was delightful. It was just at sunset— a grand Southern sunset; and the gorgeous clouds of crimson and gold were reflected in the waters below, which were smooth and calm as a mirror. Then, as we glided along, the rich sonorous tones of the boatmen broke upon the evening stillness. Their singing impressed me much. It was so sweet and strange and solemn. "Roll, Jordan, Roll" was grand, and another

> "Jesus make de blind to see
> Jesus make de deaf to hear
> Jesus make de cripple walk
> Walk in, dear Jesus,"

and the refrain

> "No man can hender me."

It was very, very impressive. I want to hear these men sing [John Greenleaf] Whittier's "Song of the Negro Boatmen." I am going to see if it can't be brought about in some way.

It was nearly dark when we reached St. Helena's, where we found Miss T.[owne]'s carriage awaiting us, and then we three and our driver, had a long drive along the lonely roads in the dark night. How easy it sh'ld have been for a band of guerillas—had any chanced that way—to seize and hang us. But we found nothing of the kind. We were in a jubilant state of mind and sang "John Brown" with a will as we drove through the pines and palmettos. Arrived at the Superintendent's house[;] we were kindly greeted by him and the ladies and shown into a lofty *ceilinged* parlor where a cheerful wood fire glowed in the grate, and we soon began to feel quite at home in the very heart of Rebeldom; only that I do not at all realize yet that we are in S.[outh] C.[arolina]. It is all a strange wild dream, from which I am constantly expecting to awake. But I can write no more now. I am tired, and still feel the motion of the ship in my poor head. Good night, dear A!

Wednesday, October 29. A lovely day, but rather cool, I sh'ld think, for the "sunny South." The ship still reals [*sic*] in my head, and everything is most unreal, yet I went to drive . . . We drove to Oaklands, our future home. It is very pleasantly situated, but the house is in rather a dilapidated condition, as are most of the houses here, and the and the [*sic*] yard and garden have a neglected look, when it is cleaned up, and the house made habitable I think it will be quite a pleasant place. There are some lovely roses growing there and quantities of ivy creeping along the ground, even under the house, in wild luxuriance—The negroes on the place are very kind and polite. I think I shall get on amicably with them[.]

After walking about and talking with them, and plucking some roses and ivy to send home, we left Oaklands and drove to the school. It is kept by Miss [Ellen] Murray[57] and Miss Towne in the little Baptist Church, which is beautifully situated in a grove of live oaks. Never saw anything more beautiful than these trees. It is strange that we do not hear of them at the North. They are the first objects that attract one's attention here. They are large, noble trees with small glossy green leaves. Their beauty consists in the long bearded moss with which every branch is heavily draped. This moss is singularly beautiful, and gives a solemn almost funeral aspect to the trees.

We went into the school, and heard the children read and spell. The teachers tell us that they have made great improvement in a very short time, and I noticed with pleasure how bright, how eager to learn many of them seem. The singing delighted me most. They sang beautifully in their rich, sweet clear tones, and with that peculiar swaying motion which I had noticed before in the older people, and which seems to make their singing all the more effective. Besides several other tunes they sang "Marching Along" with much spirit, and then one of their own hymns "Down in the Lonesome Valley," which is sweetly solemn and most beautiful. Dear children! born in slavery, but free at last? May God preserve to you all the blessings of freedom, and may you be in every possible way fitted to enjoy them. My heart goes out to you. I shall be glad to do all that I can to help you.—

As we drove homeward I noticed that the trees are just

beginning to turn; some beautiful scarlet berries were growing along the roadside, and everywhere the beautiful live oak with its moss drapery. The palmettos disappoint me much. Most of them have a very jagged appearance, and are yet stiff and ungraceful. The country is very level—as flat as that in eastern Penn. [sylvania]. There are plenty of woods, but I think they have not the grandeur of our Northern woods. The cotton fields disappoint me too. They have a very straggling look, and the pods are small, not at all the great snowballs that I had imagined. Altogether the country w'ld be rather desolate looking were it not for my beautiful and evergreen live oaks.

Friday, October 31. Miss T. [owne] went to B. [eaufort] to-day, and I taught for her. I enjoyed it much. The children are well-behaved and eager to learn. It will be a happiness to teach here. I like Miss [Ellen] Murray so much. She is of English parentage, born in the Provinces. She is one of the most whole-souled warm-hearted women I ever met. I felt drawn to her from the first (before I knew she was English) and of course I like her none the less for that. Miss Towne also is a delightful person. "A charming lady" Gen. Saxton calls her and my heart echoes the words. She is housekeeper, physician, everything, here. The most indispensable person on the place, and the people are devoted to her. And indeed she is quite a remarkable young lady. She is one of the earliest comers, and has done much good in teaching and superintending the negroes. She is quite young; not more than twenty-two or three I sh'ld think, and is superintendent of two plantations. I like her energy and decision of character. Her appearance too is very interesting. Mr. [Richard] S. [oule] [58] the superintendent, is a very kind, agreeable person. I like him.

Sunday, November 2. Drove to church to-day—to the same little Baptist Church that the school is held in. The people came in slowly. They have no way of telling the time. About eleven they had all assembled; the church was full. Old and young were there assembled in their Sunday dresses. Clean gowns on, clean head handkerchiefs, bright colored, of course, I noticed that some had even reached the dignity of straw hats, with bright feathers. The services were very interesting. The minister, Mr. P. [hillips?] [59] is an earnest N. [ew] E. [ngland] man. The singing was very beautiful, sat there in a kind of trance and listened to it, and while I listened looked through the open windows into the beautiful grove of oaks with their moss drapery. "Ah w'ld that my tongue c'ld utter the thoughts that arise in me." But it cannot. The sermon was quite good. But I enjoyed nothing so much as the singing—the wonderful, beautiful singing. There can be no doubt that these people have a great deal of musical talent. It was a beautiful sight,—their enthusiasm. After the service two couples were married. Then the meeting was out. The various groups under the trees forming a very pretty picture. We drove to the Episcopal Church afterward where the aristocracy of Rebeldom was to worship. The building is much smaller than the others, but there is a fine organ there on which Miss W. [ay?] [60] played while some of the young superintendents sang very finely, and then we came home. It is all like a dream still, and will be for a long time, I suppose; a strange wild dream. When we get settled in our own house and I have fairly entered into teaching, perhaps I shall begin to realize it all. What we are to do for furniture I know not. Our sole possessions now consist of two bureaus and a bed-stead. Mr. H. [unn] had not time to get the mattresses in N. [ew] York. So I suppose we must use blanket substitutes till we can do better. I am determined not to be discouraged at anything. I have never felt more hopeful, more cheerful than I do now.

Oaklands. Tuesday, November 4.   Came to our new home to-day. Felt sorry to leave the friends who have been so kind to us, but as they are only three miles distant[,] hope to see them occasionally. But nobody here has much time for visiting. Our home looks rather desolate; the only furniture consisting of two bureaus, three small pine tables and two chairs, one of which has a broken back. L. [izzie] and I have manufactured a tolerable drugget out of some woollen stuff, red and black plaid which will give our "parlor" a somewhat more comfortable look. I have already hung up my lovely Evangeline, and two or three other prints and gathered some beautiful roses. This has been a busy day. A few more such and we hope that our home will begin to look homelike. I am tired, dear A. Good night, and God be with you.

Wednesday, November 5.   Had my first regular teaching experience, and to you and you only friend beloved, will acknowledge that it was *not* a very pleasant one. Part of my scholars are very tiny,—babies, I call them—and it is hard to keep them quiet and interested while I am hearing the larger ones. They are too young even for the alphabet, it seems to me. I think I must write home and ask somebody to send me picture-books and toys to amuse them with. I fancied Miss T. [owne] looked annoyed when, at one time the little ones were usually restless. Perhaps it was only my fancy. Dear Miss M. [urray] was kind and considerate as usual. She is very lovable. Well I *must* not be discouraged. Perhaps things will go on better to-morrow. I am sure I enjoyed the walk to school. Through those lovely woods, just brightening to scarlet now. Met the ladies about halfway, and they gave me a drive to the church. Lizzie H. [unn] tells me that the store has been crowded all day. Her father hasn't had time to arrange his goods. I foresee that his store, to which people from all the neighboring plantations come,—will be a source of considerable interest and amusement. We've established our household on—as we hope—a firm basis. We have *Rose* for our little maid-of-all-work, *Amoretta* for cook, washer, and ironer, and *Cupid*, yes, Cupid himself, for clerk, oysterman and future coachman. I must also inform you dear A., that we have made ourselves a bed, whereon we hope to rest to-night, for rest *I* certainly did not last night, despite innumerable blankets designed to conceal and render inactive the bones of the bed. But said bones did so protrude that sleep was almost an impossibility to our poor little body. Everything is still very, very strange. I am not at all home-sick, but it does seem *so* long since I saw some who are very dear, and I believe *I* am quite sick for want of a letter. But patience! patience! *That* is a luxury which cannot possibly be enjoyed before the last of next week.

Thursday, November 6. Rained all day so that I c'ldn't go to school. Attended store part of the day. T'was crowded nearly all the time. It was quite amusing to see how eager the people are to buy. The bright handkerchiefs—imitation Madras—are an especial attraction. I think they were very quiet and orderly considering how crowded the place was. This afternoon made another bed; and this eve. finished a very long letter to father, the first part of which was begun last month. I wish I c'ld see them all. It w'ld be such a happiness. My dear, dear Quincy [Forten] [61]—I wonder if he w'ld know me now, God bless him! God be with him! Cut out a dress to-day for an old woman—Venus,—who thanked and blessed me enough poor old soul. It was a

pleasure to hear her say what a happy year this has been for
her[:] "Nobody to whip me nor dribe me, and plenty to eat.
Nebber had such a happy year in my life before." Promised
to make a little dress for her great-grandchild—only a few
weeks old. It shall be a bright pink calico, such as will delight
the little free baby's eyes, when it shall be old enough to
appreciate it.

Friday, November 7.   Had a lovely walk to school. The
trees,—a few of them are thinning beautifully now, but they
have not the general brilliant hues of the northern woods.
The mocking birds were singing sweetly this morn. I think
my "babies" were rather more manageable to-day, but they
were certainly troublesome enough. This afternoon L. [izzie]
and I went round to the "quarters." Some of the people are
really quite interesting, and all were pleasant and seemed glad
to see us. One poor woman has a very sick child. The poor
little thing is only a few months old, and is suffering dreadfully with whooping cough. It is pitiful to hear it moan. If
our good doctor Miss T. [owne] were only here. But she does
not come to-day.

Saturday.   This eve. after sewing, read part of "Alexandre" aloud. I must practice my French every day, or I
shall entirely forget it. I wish I had my chessmen.

Saturday, November 8.   Spent part of the morn. in the
store which was more crowded than ever. So much gold and
silver I've not seen for many months. These people must
have been hoarding it up for a long time. They are rather
unreasonable, and expect one to wait on a dozen at once. But
it is not strange. Miss T. [owne] came this afternoon, and
gave medicine to Tilla's baby, which seems, I think, a little
better; and all the other children. Everyone of them has the
whooping cough. I've put my books and a vase of lovely

roses and oleanders on our little table. The fire burns brightly, and the little room looks quite cheerful and homelike. Have done some sewing and reading.

Monday, November 10. We taught—or rather commenced teaching the children "John Brown" which they entered into eagerly. I felt to the full the significance of *that* song being sung here in S.[outh] C.[arolina] by little negro children, by those whom he—the glorious old man—died to save. Miss [Laura] T.[owne] told them about him. A poor mulatto man is in one of our people's houses, a man from the North, who assisted Mr. [Samuel D.] Phillips[62] (a nephew of Wendell P.[hillips]) when he was here, in teaching school; he seems to be quite an intelligent man. He is suffering from fever. I shall be glad to take as good care of him as I can. It is so sad to be ill, helpless and poor, and so far away from home. This eve. though I felt wretchedly, had a long exercise in irregular French verbs. The work of reviewing did me good. Forgot bodily ills—even so great an ill as a bad cold in the head for a while.

Thursday, November 13. Was there ever a lovelier road than that through part of my way to school lies? Oh, I wish you were here to go with me, *cher ami*. It is lined with woods on both sides. On the one tall stately pines, on the other the noble live oaks with their graceful moss drapery. And the road is captured with those brown odorous pine leaves that I love so well. It is perfectly lovely. I forgot that I was almost ill to-day, while sauntering along, listening to the birds and breathing the soft delicious air. Of the last part of the walk, through sun and sand, the less said the better. Talked to the children a little while to-day about the noble Toussaint.[63] They listened very attentively. It is well that they sh'ld know what one of their own color c'ld do for his race. I long to

inspire them with courage and ambition (of a noble sort),
and high purposes. It is noticeable how very few mulattoes
there are here. Indeed in our school, with one or two
exceptions, the children are all black. A little mulatto child
strayed into the school house yesterday—a pretty little thing
with large beautiful black eyes and lovely long lashes. But so
dirty! I longed to seize and thoroughly cleanse her. The
mother is a good-looking woman, but quite black. "Thereby,"
I doubt not, "hangs a tale." This eve. Harry, one of the men
on the place, came in for a lesson. He is most eager to learn,
and is really a scholar to be proud of. He learns rapidly. I
gave him his first lesson in writing to-night, and his progress
was wonderful. He held his pen almost perfectly right the
first time. He will very soon learn to write, I think. I must
inquire who w'ld like to take lessons at night. Whenever I
am well enough it will be a real pleasure to teach them.
Finished translating into French Adelaide Proctor's poem "A
Woman's Question," which I like so much. It was an experiment, and I assure you, *mon ami,* tis a queer translation. But
it was good practice in French. Shall finish this eve. by
copying some of my Journal for my dear Mary [Shepard].

Sunday, November 16. Felt too tired to go to church to-
day. Some of the grown people came in this morn. I read
them the Sermon on the Mount. And then they sang some of
their own beautiful hymns; among them "Down in the Lonesome Valley" which I like best of all. I want to hear it every
day. This afternoon some of the children came in and sang a
long time. Then I commenced teaching them the 23d Psalm,
which Miss M. [urray] is teaching the children in school.
Ours here are too ill with whooping cough to attend school.
I have enjoyed this day very much. For my own especial
benefit, have read and re-read my dear Mrs. Browning. Can

anything be more exquisite than those "Sonnets from the Portuguese." Is *any* man, even Browning himself, worthy of such homage from such a soul? yes, yes, *he* is, I do believe. But few others are. This eve. finished my Journal for Mary S.[hepard]. Tis so voluminous, so badly written, and so stupid that I am ashamed to send it. But I suppose almost anything from this region w'ld be interesting to people at the N.[orth] so it might as well go.

Monday, November 17. Had a dreadfully wearying day in school, of which the less said the better. Afterward drove the ladies to "The Corner," a collection of negro houses, whither Miss T.[owne] went on a doctoring expedition. The people there are very pleasant. Saw a little baby, just borne [*sic*] today—and another—old Venus' great grandchild for whom I made the little pink frock. These people are very grateful. The least kindness that you do them they insist on repaying in some way. We have had a quantity of eggs and potatoes brought us despite our remonstrances. Today one of the women gave me some Tanias. Tania is a queer looking root. After it is boiled it looks a little like potato, but is much larger. I don't like the taste.

Tuesday, November 18. After school went to the Corner again. Stopped at old Susy's house to see some sick children. Old Susy is a character. Miss T.[owne] asked her if she wanted her old master to come back again. Most emphatically she answered. "No *indeed*, missus, no indeed dey treat we too bad. Dey tuk ebery one of my chilen away from me. When we sick and c'ldnt work dey tuk away all our food from us; gib us nutten to eat. Dey's orful hard Missis." When Miss T.[owne] told her that some of the people wanted their old masters to come back, a look of supreme contempt came to old Susy's withered face. "That's cause dey's got no sense den, missus," she said indignantly. Susy has any quantity of children and grandchildren, and she thanks God that she can now have some of them with her in her old age. To-night gave Cupid a lesson in the alphabet. He is not a brilliant scholar, but he tries hard to learn, and so I am sure will succeed in time. A man from another plantation came in for a lesson. L. [izzie Hunn] attended to him while I had Cupid. He knows his letters, and seems very bright.

Wednesday, November 19. A steamer is in! Miss T. [owne] had letters from Phila. [delphia] to-day. The mail is not yet all distributed. If I don't get any I shall be *perfectly* desperate. But I surely will get some to-morrow. To-night had another pupil—Robert—brighter than Cupid—not so bright as Harry. He will do well I think.

Thursday, November 20. Had letters from Aunt M. [argaretta], Annie [Woods Webb], and Sarah P. [itman?]. Was delighted to hear from them, but so disappointed at not hearing from my dear brother Henry [Cassey]. Aunt M. [argaretta] writes me that he did not receive any letter from me. Strange! When I wrote to him the same time that I wrote to her. Am very sorry. Wrote to-night to Aunt M. [argaretta], Lizzie C. [hurch?], Charlotte, E. [llen Shearman?], Sarah P. [itman?] and to Whittier asking him to write a little Christmas hymn for our children to sing. I hope he will do it. Asked Aunt M. [argaretta] to see Mrs. Rachel Moore about sending some thick clothing for the people, and some blocks, etc. for our "babies." I hope they can get here by Christmas. It w'ld be so nice to distribute them for Christmas presents.

Saturday, November 22. Had the loveliest walk this afternoon to Mr. [T. Edwin] R. [uggle]'s [64] our nearest neighbor's. The path lay partly through woods[,] principally pines and live oaks. The air was delicious, the sunlight bright, the brown pine leaves odorous as usual, and I noticed some green leaves that had turned a rich dark, almost copper color. Plucked some for my dear Miss M. [urray] whom I heard express a wish for some a day or two ago. Found that Miss [Amanda] R. [uggles]⁶⁵ was not at home. They have a pleasant little place, rather more civilized looking than ours. Returning, just at sunset saw a beautiful, beautiful sight. In some parts of the wood the branches of the live oak formed a perfect ceiling overhead and from them depended long sprays of that exquisitie moss lighted up by the sun's last rays. I c'ld think only of some fairy palace, at first, then the sight suggested the Mammoth cave as I had seen it once in an excellent Panorama. Those sprays of moss, glowing in the sunlight, were perfect stalactites, as I saw them illuminated. If they lacked the sparkling crystals they quite made up for the loss in airy grace and lightness. I wanted you my dearest A.,—and several dear friends of mine who like you have a most keen and delicate perception of the beautiful—to look upon that scene with me. And since that c'ld not be, I longed to be an artist that I might make a sketch and send it to you.

Sunday, November 23.   Attended church to-day. T'was even a pleasanter experience than before. Saw several new arrivals there—old ones returned, rather—among them Mr. S. [amuel] Phillips, a nephew of *the* Phillips. He has not the glorious beauty of his illustrious relative, but still has somewhat the Phillips style of face. He is not at all handsome; has bright red hair, but a pleasant face, and an air *distingue*. After the sermon an old negro made a touching and most effective prayer. Then the minister read Gen. Saxton's Proclamation for Thanksgiving⁶⁶—which is grand—the very best and noblest that c'ld have been penned. I like and admire the

Gen. [eral] more than ever now. Six couples were married to-day. Some of the dresses were unique. Am sure one must have worn a cast-off dress of her mistress's. It looked like white silk covered with lace. The lace sleeves, and other trimmings were in rather a decayed state and the white cotton gloves were well ventilated. But the bride looked none the less happy for that. Only one had the slightest claim to good looks, and she was a demure little thing with a neat, plain silk dress on. T'was amusing to see some of the headresses. One, of tattered flowers and ribbons, was very ridiculous. But no matter for that. I am *truly* glad that the poor creatures are trying to live right and virtuous lives. As usual we had some fine singing. It was very pleasant to be at church again. For two Sundays past I had not been, not feeling well.

This eve. our boys and girls with others from across the creek came in and sang a long time for us. Of course we had the old favorites "Down in the Lonesome Valley," and "Roll, Jordan, Roll," and "No man can hender me," and beside those several shouting tunes that we had not heard before; they are very wild and strange. It was impossible for me to understand many of the words although I asked them to repeat them for me. I only know that one had something about "De Nell Am Ringing." I think that was the refrain; and of another, some of the words were "Christ build the church widout no hammer nor nail." "Jehovah Halleluhiah," which is a grand thing, and "Hold the light," an especial favorite of mine—they sang also with great spirit. The leader of the singing was Prince, a large black boy, from Mr. R. [uggle]'s place. He was full of the shouting spirit, and c'ld not possibly keep still. It was amusing to see his gymnastic performances. They were quite in the Ethiopian Methodists' style. He has really a very fine bass voice. I enjoyed their singing so much, and sh'ld have enjoyed it so much more if some dear ones who are far away c'ld have listened it to [*sic*] with me. How delighted they would have been. The effect of the singing has been to make me feel a little sad and lonely to-night. A yearning for congenial companionship *will* sometimes come over me in the few leisure moments I have in the house. 'Tis well they are so few. Kindness, most invariable,—for which I am most grateful—I meet with constantly, but congeniality I find not at all in this house. But silence, foolish murmurer. He who knows all things knows that it was for no selfish motive that I came here, far from the few who are so dear to me. Therefore let me not be selfish now. Let the work to which I have solemnly pledged myself fill up my whole existence to the exclusion of all vain longings.

Tuesday, November 25. Am deeply disappointed, at not receiving any letters by the mail which came to-day. I shall stop expecting. Shall *try* very hard to stop. They *might* write to me. A letter is such a luxury here. Miss [Ellen] M.[urray] is teaching the children in school "Sound the Loud Timbrel." They like the words so much that I think they will soon learn them. Saw the "Standard" tonight. Twas welcome as the face of an old friend. Read also a few numbers of "Salem Chapel," which is as intensely interesting and exciting as ever. This eve. gave Harry and Rob.[ert] their lesson. Yesterday had some visitors in school—Miss T.[ambling?] and her brother,[67] and a Miss [Chloe] Merrick[68] from Syracuse. I liked the latter's face. She looks like an earnest worker. Miss T.[ambling?] is pretty, but does not look like a person of much character. I have heard that she is a genius. She does not so impress me.

Wednesday, November 26. Miss T.[owne] was not at school, and Miss [Ellen] M.[urray] and I had sole charge.

After school told the children a little about sun, stars etc., and then Miss M.[urray] taught them some verses of "Sound the Loud Timbrel" which she wants them to learn for the New Year. Had a lovely walk in the woods gathering leaves and berries wherewith to decorate the church to-morrow.

Thursday, November 27. Thanksgiving Day. This, according to Gen. [Rufus] Saxton's noble Proclamation, was observed as a day of "Thanksgiving and praise." It has been a lovely day—cool, delicious air, golden, gladdening sunlight, deep blue sky, with soft white clouds floating over it. Had we no other causes the glory and beauty of the day alone make it a day for which to give thanks. But we have other causes, great and glorious, which unite to make this peculiarly a day of thanksgiving and praise. It has been a general holiday. According to Gen. Saxton's orders an animal was killed on each plantation that the people might to-day eat fresh meat, which is a great luxury to them, and indeed to all of us here. This morning a large number—Superintendents, teachers, and freed people, assembled in the little Baptist church. It was a sight that I shall not soon forget— that crowd of eager, happy black faces from which the shadow of slavery had forever passed. "Forever free!" "Forever free!" Those magical words were all the time singing themselves in my soul, and never before have I felt so truly grateful to God. The singing was, as usual, very beautiful. I thought I had never heard my favorite "Down in the Lonesome Valley" so well sung. After an appropriate prayer and sermon by Rev. Mr. Phillips, Gen. Saxton made a short but spirited speech to the people—urging the young men to enlist in the regiment now forming under Col. T.[homas] W.[entworth] Higginson.[69] That was the first intimation I had had of Mr. H.[igginson]'s being down here. I am greatly rejoiced threat. He seems to me of all fighting men the one best fitted to command a regiment of colored soldiers. The mention of his [name] recalled the happy days passed last summer in Mass.[achusetts], when day after day, in the streets of W.[orcester] we used to see the indefatigable *Capt.* H.[igginson] drilling his white company. I never saw him so full of life and energy—entering with his whole soul into his work—without thinking what a splendid general he w'ld make. And that too may come about. Gen. Saxton said today that he hoped to see him commander of an army of black men. The Gen. told the people how nobly Mr. H.[igginson] had stood by Anthony Burns,[70] in the old dark days, even suffering imprisonment for his sake; and assured [them] that they might feel sure of meeting with no injustice under the leadership of such a man; that he w'ld see to it that they were not wronged in any way. Then he told them the story of Robert Small[s],[71] and added "Today Robt. came to see me. I asked him how he was getting on in the store which he is keeping for the freed people. He said he was doing very well—making fifty dollars a week, sometimes. 'But,' said he[,] 'Gen. I'm going to stop keeping store. I'm going to enlist!' When you can make fifty doll[ar]s. a week keeping store? 'Yes Sir,' he replied, 'I'm going to enlist as a private in the black regiment. How can I expect to keep my freedom if I'm not willing to fight for it? Suppose the Secesh sh'ld get back here again? what good w'ld my fifty doll[ar]s. do me then? Yes, Sir, I sh'ld enlist if I were making a thousand dollars a week.' " Mrs. [Francis] Gage then made a few beautiful and earnest remarks. She told the people about the slaves in Santa Cruz, how they rose and conquered their masters, and declared themselves free, and no one dared to oppose them. And how, soon after, the governor rode into the market-place and proclaimed emancipation to all the people of the Danish W. [est] I. [ndies]. She then made a beautiful appeal to the mothers, urging them not to keep back their sons from the war fearing they might be killed but to send them forth willingly and gladly as she had done hers, to fight for liberty. It must have been something very novel and strange to them to hear a woman speak in public, but they listened with great attention and seemed much moved by what she said. Then Gen. Saxton made a few more remarks. I think what he said will have much effect on the young men here. There has been a good deal of distrust about joining the regiment[,] the soldiers were formerly so unjustly treated by the Government. But they trust Gen. Saxton. He told them what a victory the black troops had lately won on the Georgian coast, and what a great good they had done for their race in winning: they had proved to their enemies that the black man can and will fight for his freedom. After the Gen. had done speaking the people [sang] "Marching Along," with great spirit. After church there was a wedding. This is a very common occurrence here. Of course the bridal costumes are generally very unique and comical, but the principal actors are fortunately quite unconscious of it, and look so proud and happy while enjoying this—one of the many privileges that freedom has bestowed upon them—that it is quite pleasant to see them. Beside the Gen. and Miss. G. [age] there were several other strangers present;—ladies from the North who come down here to teach. In Miss T. [owne]'s box came my parcel—so long looked for—containing letters from my dear Mary S. [hepard], Aunt M. [argaretta], Nellie A. [lexander?] and Mrs. J. and a "Liberator," the first that I have seen since leaving home. How great a pleasure it is to

see it. It is familiar and delightful to look upon as the face
of an old friend. It is of an old date—October 31st—but it
is not the less welcome for that. And what a significant fact
it is that one may now sit here in safety—here in the rebellious
little Palmetto State and read the "Liberator," and display it
to one's friends, rejoicing over it in the fulness of one's heart
as a very great treasure. It is fitting that we sh'ld give to
this—the pioneer paper in the cause of human rights—a
hearty welcome to the land where, until so recently, those
rights have been most barbarously trampled upon. We do
not forget that it is in fact directly traceable to the exertions
of the editor of this paper and those who have labored so
faithfully with him, that the Northern people now occupy in
safety the S. [outh] C. [arolina] shore; that freedom now
blesses it, that it is, for the first time, a place worth living
in. This eve. commenced a long letter to Mr. [William
Lloyd] Garrison. Composed partly of to-day's journalism,
and partly of other things that I thought w'ld interest him.
He can publish it in the "Liberator," if he thinks it worth
printing, which I do not.[72] Truly this has been a delightful
day to me. I recal [*sic*] with pleasure the pleasant Thanksgiving days passed in N. [ew] E. [ngland] in Mass. [achusetts],
which I believe I am in the habit of considering as *all* N. [ew]
E. [ngland]. But this has been the happiest, the most jubilant
Thanksgiving day of my life. We hear of cold weather and
heavy snow-storms up in the North land. But here roses and
oleanders are blooming in the open air. Figs and oranges are
ripening, the sunlight is warm and bright, and over all shines
gloriously the blessed light of Freedom—Freedom forever-
more!

Friday, November 28.   Kept store nearly all day, and

found constant sources of interest and amusement in it. I had nearly forgotten to tell you, dear A., to tell you about a very old man—Dr. Crofts, they call him—(his name is Scipio rightly) who came into the store yesterday. He was rejoicing over the new state of things here, and said to Mr. [John] Hunn, "Don't hab me feelins hurt now. Used to hab me feelins hurt all all de time. But don't hab em hurt now, no more." Poor old soul! We rejoice with him that he and many like him no longer have their "feelins hurt," as in the old time.

This evening finished my letter to Mr. G.[arrison] and wrote to dear Tacie [Townsend], Mr. H.[unn] brought me a paper from the office—a "Boston Transcript," sent by Sarah P.[itman?]. It is pleasant to see a Boston paper.

Saturday, November 29. Have decorated our little sitting room with ivy and autumn leaves and berries till it looks quite bright. Have hung a wreath of ivy around my lovely Eva. which makes her, if possible, lovelier than ever. We have a clock, which is quite a treasure here. It is like the face of an old friend. Accomplished a little sewing. Had a lovely sunset walk to and from the church. This eve. devoured "Aurora Leigh" for the *very manyth* time. Every time I read it I discover new beauty in it.

Sunday, November 30. Farewell Autumn! It seems so very long since we came here, and yet, as they pass, the days seem short enough. But to look back upon the times seems very long. Attended church. Mr. [David] Thorpe,[73] one of the young Superintendents, a N.[ew] E.[ngland] man, was so kind as to send his wagon for us. L.[izzie Hunn] did not feel well enough to go, but I went and had a very pleasant drive with old Jack—Mr. T.[horpe]'s foreman, as he told

me. He is a *very* polite old man, and seemed quite pleased
and proud at driving a lady. It was very kind in Mr.
T.[horpe]. I like him much, and Mr. S.[amuel] Phillips
also. The latter invited me to come and get some slips from
his garden. And oh, dear A.[,] he has japonicas in bloom. I
shall not go, of course, but live in hourly hope that he will
be moved by the spirit to bring me some japonicas. Mr.
P.[hillips] the minister, is an excellent man, but certainly
not an interesting preacher. To-day he was unusually dull,
and I got very tired. I thought I sh'ld go to sleep. Fortunately
I did not. We had a bit of a Sunday School, taught the
children a hymn—"Heaven is my Home." After Church
three couples were married. This eve. heard Harry read,
then the children came in and sang for us, and had a regular
"shout" in the piazza, of which, of course Prince was the
leader. He is the most comical creature I ever saw. Besides
the old songs they sang two new ones, so singular that I must
try to note down the words—some of them. But of the tune
and manner of singing it is impossible to give any idea. The
first is—

> "Old elder, old elder, where hab you been
> When the gospel been flourishin
> All over dis world
> I have somethin fur to tell you
> From the secret of my heart
>   Mary King Jesus
> And no more to part."

Then

> "Young sister, young sister where hab you been, etc.
> Young bruder, young bruder where hab you been,
> Young member, young member where hab you been,"

Another commences

> "My mudder's gone to glory and I went to git dere too
>   Till dis warfare's over hallelujah
>   Chorus—Hallelujah, hallelujah
>   Till dis warfare's over, hallelujah, etc.
>   All de member's gone to glory, etc.
>   Then chorus.
>   Cinda gnaw my sin, hallelujah."
>   Chorus

The singular hymn that I heard them sing in school one day, about the graveyard begins thus.—

> "I wonder where my mudder gone,
>   Sing oh graveyard!
> Graveyard ought to know me
>   Sing Jerusalem!
> Oh carry my mudder in de graveyard
>   Sing etc.
> Oh grass grow in de graveyard
>   Sing etc.
> Lay my body in de graveyard
>   Sing, etc."

It is a very strange wild thing. I am quite in love with one of the children here—little Amaretta who is niece to our good old Amaretta. She is a cunning little kittenish thing with such a gentle demure look. She is not quite black, and has pretty close hair, but delicate features. She is bright too. I love the child. Wish I cld take her for my own. Am in a writing mood to-night, and think I will give to you, my dearest A.[,] a more minute description of the people around than I've yet given to anyone. I shall write down their names too, that I may remember them always. Don't know them thoroughly enough yet to say much about their characters. To begin with the older ones. First there is old Harriet. She is a very kind, pleasant old soul. Comes from Darien G.[eorgia]. Her parents were Africans. She speaks a *very* foreign tongue. Three of her children have been sold from her. Her master's son killed somebody in a duel, and was obliged to "pay money" H.[arriet] says. I suppose she means to give bail. And she and her children were sold to this place, to raise the money. Then there is her daughter Tillah. Poor creature, she has a dear little baby, Annie, who for weeks has been dangerously ill with whooping cough and fever. Our good Miss T.[owne] attends it, and does all that can be done, but the baby is still very ill. For Tillah's sake I hope it will get well. She is devoted to it night and day. T.[illah]'s husband is a gallant looking young soldier—a member of the black regiment. H.[arriet]'s mother, Bella, is rather a querulous body. But who can blame her? She has had enough to try her sorely. One by one her children at a tender age have been dragged from her to work in the cotton fields. She herself has been made to work when most unfit for it. She has had to see her own children cruelly beaten. Is it strange that these things sh'ld have embittered her? But she has much of the milk of human kindness left her yet. She nurses her poor baby faithfully, and often, old as she is, sits up the entire night with it. Harry is another of her sons. I have told you, dear A., how bright, how eager to learn, he is. His wife, Tamar, is a good-natured easy soul. She has several nice little children, and the baby—Mary Lincoln—as Mr. [T. Edwin] R.[uggles] the Superintendent has named her—is a very cunning little creature, an especial pet of ours. Celia is one of the best women on the place. She is a cripple. Her feet and limbs were so badly frozen by exposure that her legs were obliged to be amputated just above the knees. But she manages to get about almost as actively as any of the others. Her husband, Thomas, has been a soldier, and is now quite ill with pneumonia. She has several children—Rose, who is our little maid, Olivia the eldest, Dolly, a bright little thing who goes to school with me every morn. and who likes to go. Lastly Aikin, whose proper name is Thomas. He is an odd little fellow, very much spoiled. Amaretta, Celia's sister is our laundress and cook. I like her very much. Then there is Wilhelmina, a mulatto (the others are all black). She comes from Virginia, and speaks therefore quite intelligibly. She is a good sensible woman, and both she and her husband Robt.,—who is one of my night pupils—are most anxious for their three little ones to learn. Cupid our major-domo. is as obliging as possible. A shrewd fellow, who knows well what he is about. His wife Patience, is Tamar's sister, and lives across the creek at Pollywana. Their children—two of them—come to our school. They are good scholars. I do enjoy hearing Cupid and Harry tell about the time that the Secesh had to flee. The time of the "gun shoot," as they call the taking of Bay Point, which is opposite Hilton Head.[74] It delights them greatly to recall that time. Their master had the audacity to venture back even while the Union troops were occupying Beaufort. H.[arry] says he tried to persuade him to go back with him, assuring him that the Yankees w'ld shoot them all when they came. "Bery well sur," he replied[,] "if I go wid you I be good as dead, so if I got the dead, I might's well dead here as anywhere. So I'll stay and wait for the Yankees." He told me that he knew all the time that his master was not telling the truth. Cupid says the master told the people to get all the furniture together and take it over to

Pollywana, and to stay on that side themselves, "so" says Cupid, "dey c'ld jus' swap us all and put us in de boat. And he telled me to row Patience and de chilens down to a certain pint, and den I c'ld come back if I choose." "Jus' as if I was gwine to be sich a goat" adds Cupid, with a look and gesture of ineffable contempt. The *finale* of the story is that the people left the premises and hid themselves so that when the master returned not one of all his "faithful servants" was to be found to go into slavery with him, and he was obliged to return, a disappointed, but it is to be hoped, a wiser man.

Monday, December 1. The first day of winter. It is hard to realize it here. Tis almost as warm as June to-day, and almost as lovely.

Tuesday, December 2. After school went with the children to the Episcopal Church, where Miss [Ellen] M. [urray] played on the organ "Sound the Loud Timbrel," while the children sang. They enjoyed it very much. Fear some of it is too difficult for them, but Miss M. [urray] is determined they shall learn it, and I hope they will. It w'ld be so very appropriate. The road to the church is very beautiful. It is lined with the noble live oaks, and carpeted with brown pine leaves. The woods looked particularly inviting to-day. One tree—a green tree was all a-flame in the sunlight. Every leaf looked as if it were steeped in rosy wine. Have rarely seen so beautiful a sight. Miss M. [urray] and I secured as many of the leaves as we c'ld carry. I wanted to bring away the whole tree. Found a letter awaiting me at home—a kind letter from my dear Mrs. P. [utman]. It was very pleasant to hear from her. But why does not my brother Henry [Cassey] write? I feel very anxious at not hearing from him. Fear he must be ill. Every day I expect a letter from him, and every day, am disappointed. Has he forgotten his stupid little sister, I wonder? Or is he ill. I do wish I c'ld know. This eve. gave Harry his lesson.

Wednesday, December 3. Wrote to Jane [Putnam] this morn—Miss T. [owne] was so kind as to let me have her "Standard" of Nov. [ember] 22. It is full of interesting matter. I devoured Mr. [Wendell] Phillips' fine Music Hall speech. Mr. French's account of the victory won by the black troops on the Georgian coast is very interesting. They did splendidly. I feel quite proud of them. See that Lucy McKim[75] has set to music some of the songs of the "contrabands" here. She has sent "Poor Rosy, poor gal" as the first of a series, to "Dwight's Journal." It is much liked.

Thursday, December 4. After school went again to the Episcopal Church with the children. Miss M. [urray] and I preferred walking. Gathered some more of those exquisite leaves. After the children had done singing and all had gone, stayed some time and practiced on the organ;—some of my old pieces, and one or two from the book of Church music, among them "Sound the Loud Timbrel" which I am anxious to learn so as to relieve Miss M. [urray]. Tis hard for me to learn the simplest thing. Have forgotten so many of my notes. Had a good long walk home in the light rain, which I enjoyed much. Heard to my surprise, that Wilhelmina has a little girl. Shall suggest as a name, Jessie Fremont,[76] dear to all lovers of freedom.

Friday, December 5. Rained all day so that I cldn't go to school. Has been a sad day. Heard this afternoon of the death of the young Mr. [Samuel] Phillips of whom I've already spoken to you. It was very sudden; after only a few days' illness. Do not know when anything has made me feel so sad. He was a good young man, much loved by all the people.

Saw him last Sunday at church in perfect health. And now he is dead. My heart aches for his poor mother. He was an only son. It will be a terrible shock to her. It has cast a gloom over every thing here. The people grieve for him much. Another death—tonight. One of the old men has just come in to tell us of the death of his little grandson—Hercules— or "Harkles," as they call it. The little fellow has been ill a long time with whooping cough and fever; and now he has gone to rest.

Sunday, December 7.   Poor Mr. P.[hillips] was buried to-day, or rather the funeral services were said at the church. The body is to be sent home. Was not well enough to go but Mr. H.[unn] says there were many people there, and that they were much affected. Everybody who knew him loved him. His poor, poor mother I can only think of her with her aching heart. Little "Harkles" was buried, across the creek, this morn. This afternoon the people had a meeting in front of his grandparents' cabin. There was singing—a kind of funeral chant—very sad and dismal, and then an old preacher made a prayer, and afterward a few remarks. I did not stay to hear him but went in to see poor Tillah's baby, who is worse to-day. The poor little creature looks very ill. I fear poor Tillah must lose it. This eve. wrote a long letter to Henry. We did not have our usual singing. The children said it was too cold. And truly it has been wintry to-day. I can't get warm.

Monday, December 8.   Almost froze in school to-day. It was intensely cold. Grew milder at night, and the children came in. They have been singing gloriously all the eve. Several new hymns were sung. I will try to note them down for you dear A. I can't describe to you the effect that the singing has on me to-night. I believe I was quite *lifted out* of myself. Oh it was glorious! They all sing beautifully; but one of our girls, Grace, has the strongest voice for a child that I ever heard. And Aaron—the leader has really a magnificent voice. I want you dearest, I want everybody to hear his wonderful singing.

Tuesday, December 9. Wrote a long letter to Henry [Cassey] which will be mailed tomorrow. Am feeling very anxious about him. Am sure he must be ill, poor child. I wish I c'ld hear from or of him.

Thursday, December 11. After lessons we went again to the Epis. [copal] Church and practiced the hymn with the children. The woods around seemed more beautiful than ever. I longed to explore some of those lovely paths. Came home, and soon afterward, to my great grief, heard that poor Tillah's dear little baby was dead. It was really a shock to me; for only this morn. we thought the little creature seemed better. I hastened at once to the cabin. The baby had just died, and lay on old Nella's lap, looking as if it were sleeping sweetly. The poor mother sat by looking so very sad. My heart aches for her. During eight weeks she has been constantly devoted to this child—her only little girl—and we hoped she w'ld be rewarded by having it spared to her. But it has gone to heaven. It was one of the loveliest, most interesting babies I ever saw. We are going to bury it tomorrow, over at Polawany; I am so sorry that William, its father, will not get to see it. It looks very lovely. It's death is a great grief to its mother and grandparents, and a sorrow to us all.

Friday, December 12. This morn. Mr. R. [uggles] beaming with delight, informed me that there was a large mail in by the "Star of the South." I am afraid I answered somewhat impatiently that I was disgusted with mails, and that I wasn't going to expect any more, I had been so often disappointed. Nevertheless I *did* expect, despite myself. I did hope for those letters this time. And when we heard that there were letters for us at the Oars, we at once despatched our trusty Cupid there. With what a beating heart did I await his coming. Calm outwardly, but what a flutter of expectation within. I never sh'ld have thought that I sh'ld become so *insane* about letters. At last Cupid came, and only *one* letter for me, and that not from home. It was entirely unexpected—from Mr. McK.[im]. Certainly it was very kind in him to write to me. He reminds me that he expects to have a line from me. And indeed I ought to have written to him before. But I am *so* disappointed. Why do I not hear from Mary S.[hepard]. I thought she w'ld certainly have written to me during her vacation. I am very much troubled at not hearing from her, and from H.[enry]. Aunt M.[argaretta] has probably written and put her letter in the box, which I suppose will not get here for a month. I am quite sick at heart to-night, and must go to bed.

Saturday, December 13. Had some new no.'s of "Salem Chapel" which I devoured eagerly. It keeps up the interest. Sewed on some bags—sewing bags that we are going to give our children Christmas.

Sunday, December 14. What a night last night was! A night worth telling you about, dear A. We retired early. I was very sleepy, but what with the headache, the fleas, and Miss [Elizabeth] H.[unn]'s *tremendous* snoring I got very nervous, and it was a long time before I c'ld get to sleep. At last sleep came. It seemed to me that I hadn't slept more than ten minutes when I was awakened by what seemed to me terrible screams coming from the direction of the Quarters. Three or four times they were repeated, and then, with infinite difficulty I succeeded in awaking Miss Hunn. We both heard the shrieks repeated. I thought somebody was insane or dying, or that something terrible had happened. Sometimes I thought it might be that the rebels had forced a landing, and were trying to carry off the people. We were in a state of great alarm; and sleep was impossible. At last the sounds ceased. And then near day, I had a short and troubled sleep which did me no good. Consequently I felt rather wretched this morn but the day was so beautiful I determined to go to church. L. [izzie] and I started, but met Mr. T. [horpe]'s wagon in the lane, coming for us. How very kind he is. But I am hardly willing to be under such an obligation to a stranger. And yet we can't very well refuse. How very sad Mr. T. [horpe] looked to-day. I know he must greatly miss Mr. Phillips, with whom he was so intimate. I pity him.

There were several new arrivals at church to-day. Among them Miss T. [owne]'s sister—Miss Rosa T. [owne]. She does not look at all like Miss Laura. Is very fair, and has light hair; an English looking person, as I told her sister. A Miss [Harriet] Ware [77] was also there, sister to Mrs. Windsor. A lovely but good face. Not the least resemblance to Mrs. W. [indsor] whom I think very fine looking. Nearly everybody was looking gay and happy; and yet I came home with the blues. Threw myself on the bed, and for the first time since I have been here, felt very lonely and pitied myself. But I have reasoned myself into a more sensible mood and am better now. Let me not forget again that I came not here for friendly sympathy or for anything else but to work, and to work hard. Let me do that faithfully and well. To-night answered Mr. McK. [im]'s letter, and commenced one to my dear A. [nnie Woods Webb] whom I feel very anxious.

There, dear A., I have forgotten to tell you the cause of our fright last night. Two of the colored soldiers had come to visit their friends who live across the creek. And they blew a kind of whistle that they have so that somebody on the opposite side might send a boat over for them. That was the shrieking we heard. And it seems we were the only people who heard it on the place. And yet it was heard across the creek. They must be sound sleepers here. The rebels w'ld have a good chance to land without being discovered.

Monday, December 15.   Had a perfectly *immense* school to-day. 147, of whom I had 58, at least two-thirds of whom were tiny A.B.C. people. Hardly knew what to do with them at first. But I like a large school. It is inspiring. Miss Rosa T.[owne] was there. Had a good long talk with her while her sister and Miss M.[urray] went doctoring. Like her exceedingly. She is very social and enthusiastic. She is delighted with things down here. Never heard the children sing as well as they did to-day. There were so many of them. It was quite grand. To-night wrote to A.[nnie], Aunt M.[argaretta] and Aunt H.[arriet]. The days of my writing are nearly ended. Eyes are beginning to fail. And besides nobody writes to me.

Wednesday, December 17.   This eve. Mr. R.[uggles] with another Sup.—Mr. N. spent a little time with us. I like Mr. R.[uggles]. He seems to me a whole-souled kind-hearted man. The negroes like him much. I asked him a little about the people on his plantations. Some are industrious, but many are not inclined to work, he says. But he thinks it is because they are so irregularly and poorly paid. He thinks if they were promptly and fully paid they w'ld work willingly. I think he is a true friend of the people; but some of the Sup.'s seem to me strongly prejudiced against them and they have a contemptuous way of speaking of them that I do not like. It shows a lack of sympathy with them. Such people sh'ld not come here. Miss H.[unn] told me an interesting story of a man who was in the store this afternoon. He had been carried off by the rebels about a year ago and left a wife and children on this island. It was not until a short time since that he had a chance to get a way from Jacksonboro[,] the place to which he had been taken. He and two relatives, a man and woman, got away in the night while the family were in bed. They traveled a long distance on foot, and at last reached a stream, which they had no convenience for crossing. He made a kind of raft out of a board and some part of a ruined house, and they crossed in safety. They concealed themselves in the woods during the day, and traveled at night. They came to another stream and again he built a raft, this time from the roof of the piazza of an old house near. On this they crossed a little Edisto, where they procured a boat from a boat-house and in this went to the blockading fleets. The captain of one of the gunboats took them and provided them with a boat on which they came to this island. He said it was "almost like death" to his family to see him. They had feared they sh'ld never see him again. He expressed himself very grateful to the Lord for his escape. He said the Lord had been merciful to him. He was a God of mercy and Justice. He said "Put your faith in the Lord and he will give you talents to do anything." They were several days making their escape, during which they lived on hominy of which they carried a peck in tin buckets.

Thursday, December 18. A truly *wintry* day. I had not half as many scholars as usual. It was too cold for my "babies" to venture out. But altogether we had nearly a hundred. They were unusually bright to-day and sang with the greatest spirit.

"Sound the Loud Timbrel," was a grand success. After school the children went into a little cabin near, where they had kindled a fire, and had a grand "shout." While they were performing, two officers rode up, and asked Miss M. [urray] if they might look on. She assented, and they dismounted, and came to the cabin door. The children stopped at first, evidently a little alarmed at the presence of soldiers, the latter spoke so kindly to them that at last they were reassured, and went on with their "shout" with great spirit. The visitors seemed much interested and amused. Had two Salem papers from Charlotte. It was good to see them. But I am truly sorry to see the notice of the death of my kind and genial old French teacher, Mr. Jerome. He died on Thanksgiving Day, aged 56. I sh'ld have thought him much older. What good times we used to have studying French with him. It is very hard to realize that he is dead.

Friday, December 19. Miss M. [urray] and I had school to ourselves. Miss T. [owne] was not able to come on account of the illness of her sister, Miss Rosa. Had 127. T'was terribly cold. Mr. [James H.] Palmer,[79] one of the other teachers on the island, came in towards the close of school. He very kindly assisted us to put away our books. I was pleasantly disappointed in him. He seems much more agreeable than he looks. Spent most of the afternoon in the store. Had a crowd. Enjoyed it very much. Felt so tired that I went to bed at seven, and consequently missed seeing Mr. and Miss Ruggles who spent the eve. here. Am sorry, for I like them.

Saturday, December 20. Went round to see the people, of whom I haven't seen so much this week, being even unusually busy. Had as usual a very pleasant time talking with them all, big and little. Came home, and worked busily. Made before school this morn. a red flannel jacket for poor old Harriet who is far from well. The good old woman and her husband seemed very grateful. I wish I c'ld do ten times as much for these people. This afternoon a solider, a private from the 8th Maine, came in, and we gave him some dinner. The poor fellow seemed glad to get into a comfortable house, and talked about his home and his family quite confidentially, and told us how his little brothers ran out when he went to visit his home. He seemed a simple, kindly, good hearted fellow, and I was glad that we gave him a good dinner. These poor privates have rather a hard time of it, I fear. They look weary and forlorn, while the officers have a most prosperous, well-to-do-look. Had a call from Rev. Mr. P. [illsbury] and his wife and children. They seem good, kindly people, though not very cultivated.

Sunday, December 21. Went to church, and victimized myself sitting in a cold church, and listening to the dullest of sermons, but was amply rewarded after church when Mr. [J. S.] Severance came from B. [eaufort] and I had four letters—from dear Mary S. [hepard], and Hattie [Purvis] and Charlotte E., and, last and best of all, the kindest letter from the noble Whittier, and with it a beautiful little hymn for our children to sing at the Celebration.[79] Also his photograph—a perfect likeness. How very, very kind it was in him to write it; when he was ill too. It grieves me to hear that his dear sister is ill also. She sends me the kindest messages. I am very, very much obliged to Mr. W. [hittier] for everything but his sending my letter to the "Transcript." as Mary S. [hepard] tells me he did. He ought not to have done that. It was not worth it. How dear Miss M. [urray] and I rejoiced over the hymn. With what pleasure we will teach our little ones to sing it.

Monday, December 22.   Commenced teaching the children Whittier's hymn. We told them who had written it; what a great friend he is to them, and that he had written it *expressly* for them, whereat they seemed greatly pleased. After school, with some of the larger children we three went into the woods in search of evergreens to decorate the church. Had a delightful ramble and got a quantity of greens. Wrote to Miss Grew, Nellie A. and Mattie F. [arbeaux].

Tuesday, December 23.   We commenced decorating the church, and worked hard till dark. They w'ld insist upon my dressing the pulpit, which I was unwilling to do, for that is the most conspicuous place. Finished it to-day. Made a drapery all around it with the lovely hanging moss, and a heading of casino berries and holly. It looks quite pretty. Came home tired but sat up till after 11 sewing on the little aprons for Christmas presents. I *cannot* realize that Christmas is so near.

Wednesday, December 24.   Called the children together, and let them sing for some time and then dismissed them and devoted ourselves to finishing the decorations. Miss M. [urray] and Miss T. [owne] made the festoons, while I made wreaths for the walls. In the afternoon Miss M. [urray] came, bringing evergreen letters of the words "His people are Free." She and Mr. [M. J. D.] M. [cKay] [80] put them up. Mr. [Josiah] F. [airfield] [81] came in also, and helped us. It was quite dark when we got through. Miss W. [insor] [82] was so kind as to drive me home. Sat up till after midnight, finishing my little Christmas gifts. Saw Christmas morn. But it does not seem like Christmas to me.

Christmas Day, 1862.   A bright and lovely Christmas day. We were waked early by the people knocking at our window and shouting "Merry Christmas." After breakfast we went out and distributed the presents;—to each of the babies a bright red dress, and to little Jessie a white apron trimmed with crochet braid, and to each of the other children an apron and an orange. To each of the workers a pie—an apple pie, which pleased them much. Then we went to school. How pretty the evergreens looked in the bright light, after we had thrown open the windows. T'was a long time before the other teachers got there, and I had to keep all the children from getting restless. I kept them out of doors, and had them sing old songs and new. They sang with great spirit. After the others came, we opened school, and at once commenced distributing the presents. First Miss M. [urray]'s class, then mine, then Miss T. [owne]'s. Most of the children were much delighted with their gifts, and well they might be, for they were useful ones,—principally dresses for the girls, and material for shirts and pantaloons for the boys. For the larger ones, also there were little bags, nicely fitted out with sewing utensils which Miss M. [urray] and Miss T. [owne] arranged. The larger children behaved well, and by great exertions I managed to keep the "babies" quiet.

After the gifts were distributed, they were addressed by Lieut. Col. [Liberty] Billings[83] of the 1st reg. [iment] S. [outh] C. [arolina] Vol. [unteers]. He is a N. [ew] E. [ngland] man of very gentlemanly and pleasing manners. A good man, and much interested in the people, I sh'ld think. I liked him. Then Mr. Fairfield spoke to them about the birth of Christ. Afterward they sang; among other things, "John Brown," Whittier's "Hymn," "Sing oh Graveyard," and "Roll, Jordan Roll." There was no one present beside the teachers, our household, Col. B. [illings], Mr. T. [horpe], Mr. F. [airfield] and Miss Rosa and Miss W. [insor]. I enjoyed the day very much. Was too excited and interested to feel weariness then, but am quite exhausted to-night. The children have been in, singing for us. My pet *petite* Amaretta has a sweet voice and quite strong for such a little one. She was full of music to-night. "All I want to do is sing and shout" she said to me with her pretty, dimply smile. There is something very bewitching about that child. All the children had the shouting spirit to-night. They had several grand shouts in the entry. "Look upon the Lord," which they sang to-night, seems to me the most beautiful of all their shouting tunes. There is something in it that goes to the depths of one's soul.—I am weary and must stop.

Dear friends, up North! my heart is with you to-night. What w'ld I not give for one look at your dear faces, one grasp of your kindly hands! Dear ones! I pray with my whole heart that this may have been to you a very, very happy Christmas.

Friday, December 26. Kept store nearly all day. I like it occasionally. It amuses and interests me. There was one very sensible man in to-day, whose story interested me much. He had been a carpenter, and had been taken up by his master on the mainland, on "the main," as they call it, to help build houses to which the families of the rebels might retreat when the Yankees sh'ld come. His master sent him back again to this island to bring back a boat and some of the people. He was provided with a pass. On reaching the island, he found that the Union troops had come, so he determined (indeed he had determined before) to remain here with his family, as he knew his master w'ld not dare to come back after them. Some of his fellow servants whom he had left on the "main," hearing that the Union troops had come[,] resolved to try to make their escape. They found a boat of the master's, out of which a piece about six feet square had been cut. In the night, secretly, they went to the boat which had been sunk near the edge of the creek, measured the hole, and went to the woods and, after several nights' work, made a piece large enough to fit in. With this they mended the boat, by another night's work, and then sunk it in the same position in which they had found it. The next night five of them embarked, and after passing through many perils in the shape of the enemy's boats, near which they were obliged to pass, and so making very slow progress, for they c'ld travel only at night, and in the day time, ran their boat close up to the shore, out of sight—they at last passed the enemy's lines and reached one of our gunboats in safty [*sic*]. They were taken on board, and their wants attended to, for their provisions had given out and they were much exhausted. After being there some time they were sent to this island, where their families, who had feared they w'ld never see them again welcomed them rejoicingly. I was much interested in the story of their escape, and give it for y[our] especial benefit, dear A.

Spent the eve. in making wreaths for our windows and [for] my lovely Eva. Had a letter from Sarah W.[atson] [84] enclosing a tiny bouquet—pansies, mignonette, geranium, and something else that I do not know, very prettily arranged and pressed by the Dr. It was good to hear from dear S.[arah]. Still no letter from H.[enry]. I know not what to think. I am weary of conjecturing and expecting. It is very strange. A letter from Sarah P[itman?] delights me much for it tells me that my dear friend Dr. [Seth] Rogers,[85] sailed last week for P.[ort] R.[oyal] so of course he has come in this steamer. I c'ld clap my hands and shout for joy. I am so very, very glad. This is the very place for him, and he is of all men, the man for the place. He is to be surgeon in Col.

H[igginson]'s reg. S.C., Vol. It is splendid. I am most impatient to see him.

Sat. December 27. A rather dreary day. So the less said about [it] the better. Worked quite hard. Then Miss T.[owne] and Miss M.[urray] paid us a brief visit. Capt. [Edward W.] H.[ooper] [86] whom everybody likes, has come, and brought me a letter, which I rec'd wonderingly from Miss M.[urray]'s hands. The handwriting was strange to me. It was postmarked "Boston." On opening it I found it to be from a stranger—a lady in W. Gloucester, who says she has read with interest my letter in the paper, and expresses her great interest in the work here. A very kind and pretty letter. Enclosed in it was a "Proclamation Song," written by a friend of hers, to be sung to the air "Glory Hallelujah," on 1st Jan.[uary]. Not exquisite poetry, but a very good and appropriate song. It touched me receiving such a letter from a stranger. I think I must write and thank her for it. Had a lovely walk in the woods this morn. Twas almost like June.

Sunday, December 28. At church had the pleasure of seeing Gen. S.[axton] and his father, who has come down to visit him. The Gen. presented him to me. He is a pleasant old gentleman, and spoke warmly in praise of Dr. R.[ogers] who came on the same steamer with him. His nephew James R.[ogers] [87] accompanies him. Saw also the much loved Capt. Hooper, whose looks and manners I like much. He made a very good speech to the people, as also did Gen. S.[axton] urging them to enlist, and inviting them all to come to the camp near B.[eaufort] on N.[ew] Year's Day, and join in the grand Celebration, which is to take place there. I long to go, and hope I shall. Capt. H.[ooper] handed me a letter from my dear Mary S.[hepard]. It was unexpected, and so all the more delightful. I sh'ld have been very, very glad to have had letters from home and from H.[enry] for Christmas gifts. But as it was not, I must try to be content.

Tuesday, December 30. This eve. Mr. and Miss R.[uggles] spent with us quite pleasantly. It is very rarely we have company, and so I note it down.

Wednesday, December 31. Mr. [David] T.[horpe] and Mr. [Edward] H.[ooper] dined with us to-day. I think they are—Mr. T.[horpe] especially, the most anti-slavery of the superintendents. And they are very gentlemenly [*sic*] and I like them. This afternoon Mr. and Mrs. [George M.] W.[ells] [88] called. He is very agreeable, she *not* so agreeable, to me. I count the hours till to-morrow, the glorious, glorious day of freedom.

Thursday, New Year's Day, 1863. [89] The most glorious day this nation has yet seen, *I* think. I rose early—an event here—and early we started, with an old borrowed carriage and a remarkably slow horse. Whither were we going? thou wilt ask, dearest A. To the ferry; thence to Camp Saxton, to the celebration. From the ferry to the camp the "Flora" took us. How pleasant it was on board! A crowd of people, whites and blacks, and a band of music—to the great delight of the negroes. Met on board Dr. [Solomon] and Mrs. Peck and their daughters, who greeted me most kindly. Also Gen. S.[axton]'s father whom I like much, and several other acquaintances whom I was glad to see. We stopped at Beaufort, and then proceeded to Camp Saxton, the camp of the 1st Reg.[iment] S.[outh] C.[arolina] Vol[unteer]s. The "Flora" c'ld not get up to the landing, so we were rowed ashore in a row boat. Just as my foot touched the plank, on landing, a hand grasped mine and a well known voice spoke my name. It was my dear and noble friend, Dr. [Seth]

Rogers. I cannot tell you, dear A., how delighted I was to see him; how *good* it was to see the face of a friend from the North, and *such* a friend. I think myself particularly blessed to have him for a friend. Walking on a little distance I found myself being presented to Col. Higginson, whereat I was so much overwhelmed, that I had no reply to make to the very kind and courteous little speech with which he met me. I believe I mumbled something, and grinned like a simpleton, that was all. Provoking, isn't it? that when one is most in need of sensible words, one finds them not. I *cannot* give a regular chronicle of the day. It is impossible. I was in such a state of excitement. It all seemed, and seems still, like a brilliant dream. Dr. R.[ogers] and I talked all the time, I know, while he showed me the camp and all the arrangements. They have a beautiful situation, on the grounds once occupied by a very old fort, "De La Ribanchine," built in 1629 or 30. Some of the walls are still standing. Dr. R.[ogers] has made quite a good hospital out of an old gin house. I went over it. There are only a few invalids in it, at present. I saw everything; the kitchens, cooking arrangements, and all. Then we took seats on the platform. The meeting was held in a beautiful grove, a live-oak grove, adjoining the camp. It is the largest one I have yet seen; but I don't think the moss pendants are quite as beautiful as they are on St. Helena. As I sat on the stand and looked around on the various groups, I thought I had never seen a sight so beautiful. There were the black soldiers, in their blue coats and scarlet pants, the officers of this and other regiments in their handsome uniforms, and crowds of lookers-on, men, women and children, grouped in various attitudes, under the trees. The faces of all wore a happy, eager, expectant look. The exercises commenced by a prayer from Rev. Mr. [James H.] Fowler,[90]

Chaplain of the Reg. An ode written for the occasion by
Prof. [John] Zachos, originally a Greek, now Sup. [erintendent]
of Paris Island, was read by himself, and then sung by the
whites. Col. H. [igginson] introduced Dr. [William]
Brisbane[91] in a few elegant and graceful words. He (Dr.
B. [risbane]) read the President's Proclamation,[92] which was
warmly cheered. Then the beautiful flags presented by Dr.
[George] Cheever's Church[93] were presented to Col.
H. [igginson] for the Reg. in an excellent and enthusiastic
speech, by Rev. Mr. [Mansfield] French. Immediately at
the conclusion, some of the colored people—of their own
accord sang "My Country Tis of Thee." It was a touching
and beautiful incident, and Col. Higginson, in accepting the
flags made it the occasion of some happy remarks. He said
that *that* tribute was far more effecting than any speech he
c'ld make. He spoke for some time, and all that he said was
grand, glorious. He seemed inspired. Nothing c'ld have been
better, more perfect. And Dr. R. [ogers] told me afterward
that the Col. was much affected. That tears were in his eyes.
He is as Whittier says, truly a "sure man." The men all
admire and love him. There is a great deal of personal
magnetism about him, and his kindness is proverbial. After
he had done speaking he delivered the flags to the color-
bearers with a few very impressive remarks to them. They
each then, Prince Rivers,[94] and Robert Sutton,[95] made very
good speeches indeed, and were loudly cheered. Gen. Saxton
and Mrs. Gage spoke very well. The good Gen. was received
with great enthusiasm, and throughout the morning—every
little while it seemed to me three cheers were given for him.
A Hymn written I believe, by Mr. Judd, was sung, and
then all the people united with the Reg. in singing "John
Brown." It was grand. During the exercises, it was announced

that [John C.] Fremont was appointed Commander-in-Chief of the Army, and this was received with enthusiastic and prolonged cheering. But as it was picket news, I greatly fear that it is not true.[96]

We dined with good Dr. R.[ogers] at the Col.'s table, though, greatly to my regret he, (the Col.) was not there. He partook of some of the oxen, (of which ten had been roasted) with his men. I like his doing that. We had quite a sumptuous dinner. Our party consisted of Dr. [Seth] R.[ogers], Adjutant [G. W.] D.[ewhurst],[97] Capt. [James] R.[ogers], Mr. and Miss Ware (Mrs. Win[d]sor's brother and sister[,] Mr. [William?] Hall, their cousin, whom I like much, and Mr. [John] and Miss [Elizabeth] H.[unn] and me. We had a merry, delightful dinner. The only part that I did not enjoy was being obliged to read Whittier's "Hymn" aloud at the table. I wanted Dr. R.[ogers] to do it. But he w'ld insist on my doing it. So of course, it was murdered. I believe the older I grow the more averse I get to doing anything in public. I have no courage to do such things. Col. H.[igginson] invited us into his tent—a very nice, almost *homelike* one. I noticed a nice secretary, with writing utensils and "Les Miserables" on it. A *wreath* of beautiful oranges hung against the wall, fronting the door. I wanted to have a good look at this tent; but we were hardly seated when the Dr. and the Col. were called away for a moment, and Lieut. Col. [Liberty] Billings coming in w'ld insist upon our going into his tent. I did not want to go at all, but he was so persistent we had to. I fear he is a somewhat vain person. His tent was very comfortable too, and I noticed quite a large piece of "Secesh" furniture, something between a secretary and a bureau, and quite a collection of photographs and daguerres. But I did not examine them, for my attention

was occupied by Col. H.[igginson] to whom I showed
Whittier's poem, letter and photo. "He looks old," he said
to me sadly, as he handed back the picture. Dr. R.[ogers]
introduced me to Dr. [J. Milton] H.[awkes] [98] and his wife
[Esther Hawkes]—pleasant people, and *good* anti-slavery.
They mentioned having "Liberators" with my letters in
them. [99] I am sorry they have come down here. Col.
H.[igginson] asked me to go out and hear the band play,
which I very gladly did. But it stopped just as we stepped
outside the tent. Just then one of the soldiers came up to the
Col. and said "Do Cunnel, do ask 'em to play Dixie, just for
me, for my lone self." The Col. made the request, but the
leader of the band said he feared they w'ld not be able to play
the whole thing as they had not the necessary pieces. "Nebber
mind," said the man[,] "jus' half a tune will do." It was
found impossible to play even that but the leader promised
that the next time they came they would be fully prepared to
play Dixie for him. The Dress Parade—the first I have ever
seen—delighted me. It was a brilliant sight—the lone line of
men in their brilliant uniforms, with bayonets gleaming in
the sunlight. The Col. looked splendid. The Dr. said the
men went through the drill remarkably well. It seemed to me
nothing c'ld be more perfect. To me it was a grand triumph—
that black regiment doing itself honor in the sight of the
white officers, many of whom, doubtless "came to scoff." It
was typical of what the race, so long down-trodden and
degraded will yet achieve on this continent. After the parade,
we went to the landing, intending to take a boat for Beaufort.
But the boat was too crowded, and we decided to wait for
another. It was the softest, loveliest moonlight. We sat down
among the ruins of the old fort. Just as soon as the boat had
reached a favorable distance from the shore the band in it

commenced playing "Home, Sweet Home." It was exquisitely beautiful. The lovely moonlight on the water, the perfect stillness around seemed to give new beauty to that ever beautiful old song. And then as my dear friend Dr. R. [ogers] said, "It came *very near* to us all." Finding the night air damp we went to the tent of Mr. [James] Fowler, the chaplain, whom I like much better in private conversation than as an orator. He is a thoroughly good, earnest man. Whither came Col. H. [igginson] and Dr. R. [ogers]. We sat around the nice fire—the *chimney* and fire place, made by Mr. F. [owler]'s own skillful hands. Col. H. [igginson] is a perfectly delightful person in private.—So genial, so witty, so kind. But I noticed when he was silent[,] a care-worn almost sad expression on his earnest, noble face. My heart was full when I looked at him. I longed to say, "I thank you, I thank you, for that noble glorious speech." And yet I *c'ld* not. It is always so. I do not know how to talk. Words always fail me when I want them most. The more I feel the more impossible it is for me to speak. It is very provoking. Among other things, Col. H. [igginson] said how amusing it was to him—their plan of housekeeping down here. "This morning I was asked 'Well, Colonel, how many oxen shall we roast to-day.' And I said, just as calmly as I w'ld have ordered a pound or two of beef, at home—well I think *ten* will do. And then to be consulted as to how many gallons of molasses, and of vinegar, and how many pounds of ginger w'ld be wanted, seemed very odd." I wish I c'ld reproduce for you the dry humorous tones in which this was said. We had a pleasant chat, sitting there in the firelight, and I was most unwilling to go, for besides the happiness of being in the society of the Col. and the Dr. we wanted dreadfully to see the "shout" and grand jubilee which the soldiers were going to have that night. But it was already late, and hearing that the "Flora" was coming we had to hasten to the landing. I was sorry to say good-bye to Dr. R.[ogers]. What an *unspeakable* happiness it was to see him. But I fear for his health. I fear the exposure of a camp life. Am glad to see that he has warm robes and blankets, to keep him comfortable. I wish I c'ld do something for him. He has done so much for me. Ah, what a grand, glorious day this has been. The dawn of freedom which it heralds may not break upon us at once; but it will surely come, and sooner, I believe[,] than we have ever dared hope before. My soul is glad with an exceeding gladness. But before I close, dear A. I must bring our little party safe home to Oaklands. We had a good time on the Flora. L.[izzie] and I promenaded the deck, and sang "John Brown," and "Whittier's Hymn" and "My Country Tis of Thee," and the moon shone bright above us, and the waves beneath, smooth and clear, glistened in the soft moonlight. At Beaufort we took the row boat, and the boatmen sang as they rowed us across. Mr. [William W.] Hall[100] was with us, and seemed really to appreciate and enjoy everything. I like him. Arrived at St. Helena's; we separated, he to go to "Coffin's Point" (a dreadful name as Dr. R.[ogers] says) and we to come hither. Can't say that I enjoyed the homeward drive very much. T'was so intensely cold, yes *intensely*, for these regions. I fear some of the hot enthusiasm with which my soul was filled got chilled a little but it was only for a short time. Old friend, my good and dear A. a very, very happy New Year to you! Dear friends in both my northern homes a happy, happy New Year to you, too! And to us all a year of such freedom as we have never yet known in this boasted but hitherto wicked land. The hymn, or rather one of the hymns that these boat men sang is singing itself to me now. The refrain "Religion so . . . sweet" was so sweet and touching in its solemnity.

Sunday, Jan. 4.   On Friday was delighted to receive a letter from my dear Mrs. Crosby, a long kind interesting letter. She kindly offers to send me some books for our children. Had just mailed a letter to her. To-day we had a little celebration at our church on our own account. Gen. [Rufus] Saxton spoke. [Brig.] Gen. [Truman] Seymour[101] was present. Mr. [Mansfield] French and others made very good addresses. The children of Mr. L.[yon?]'s[102] school sang a beautiful hymn. And our children sang "Sound the Loud Timbrel," and "Whittier's Hymn." I thought they did not sing so well as usual. But the people seemed pleased. Our children wore badges of red, white and blue which delighted them much. Capt. H.[ooper] handed me a letter which on opening I found to be from Mrs. Howery. I was surprised enough at getting a letter from her. Speaks very kindly of my letters from P.[ort] R.[oyal]. So much more so than they deserve. This afternoon Mrs. [Hannah] H.[unn][103] arrived with her children. So of course there was great rejoicing in the household. I like her appearance. She seems a gentle, lady-like person. The little girl has a look of refinement.

Monday, January 5.   Went to school, but as Miss M.[urray] and I were both far from well, and it was very damp and chilly, had no school. To-night wrote to Mrs. C.[hew] and to Mr. [P. B.] Hunt.[104] I dreaded the last performance.

Wednesday, January 7.   Yesterday and to-day quite unwell with a bad cough, and hear that dear Miss M.[urray] is quite ill. My good physician, Miss. T.[owne] came. How kind she is to me. She said she thought it decidedly best that we sh'ld give up school for this week. I demurred at first, but afterward agreed, seeing the prudence of the thing. This afternoon was lying on the lounge feeling rather ill, and decidely low-spirited, when the door opened and who sh'ld enter but my dear friend Dr. R.[ogers]. Wasn't I glad to see him. It did me never so much good. He came on purpose to see me, but c'ld only stay a very little while. How much I enjoyed that brief visit no words can tell. He is looking well, but from what he said I fear he is *not* well. It grieves me to think it. I was so sorry to have him go.—Dear noble, kind friend! There are few as good as he is. He said he w'ld write to me often if I w'ld write to him. I shall do so gladly, for the sake of having letters from him. I don't deserve it I know. Our people here are very kind; several have been in to see me. I will not, must not be ill here.

Thursday, January 8. Feel better to-day. Went round to see the people. Then my good Miss T.[owne] came and took me as far as the church, just for the sake of the drive. But she w'ld not let me go in, while she put away the books. Had a very pleasant talk with her by the way. It always does me good just to see her bright, cheerful face. Did some sewing and considerable writing to-day.

Sunday, January 11. Rec'd to-day my hat, and my box of chessmen from Aunt M.[argaretta] with a note;—nothing else that I wanted. I am so disappointed, for I needed the things sadly. But it c'ld not be helped. Had also a note from Hat.[tie Purvis] and the box of clothing, which I am very glad to get. Drove out to the Oaks for a little while this afternoon.

Monday, January 12. A bright, lovely day. Feel much better. Had school out-of-doors—in the bright sunlight. T'was delightful. Imagine our school-room, dear A.—the soft brown earth for a carpet; blue sky for a ceiling, and for walls, the grand old oaks with their exquisite moss drapery. I enjoyed it very much. Even the children seemed to appreciate it, and were unusually quiet.

Thursday, January 15.   After school drove to the Oaks, and practised for some time. Then went upstairs and had a pleasant little chat with the ladies in their homelike room. Had a letter mailed to my good friend Whittier. Dear Miss M.[urray] is quite unwell which grieves me much. Miss T.[owne] sent me the Dec.[ember] "Atlantic." Enjoyed it this eve. especially Dr. [Oliver Wendell] Holmes's excellent article, wherein he speaks of our friend Charley W. very pleasantly. It is an excellent no. That article is "My Hunt after the Captain."

Saturday, January 17.   Spent the afternooon with Miss R.[uggles]. She is a kind soul, though somewhat garrulous. Met there a new arrival, a Mrs. [E.] Clarke[105] whom I don't admire particularly, and a Mr. [Jules] De la Croix[106] who seems to me decidedly *lap-dogish*. Had a delicious tea; which is worth recording being the first we have taken from home. Miss R.[uggles] lent me "Ravenshoe," by Henry Kingsley. Some parts of it are good; others seem to me not worth reading. Don't like him as well as Charles K.[ingsley] his brother.

Sunday, January 18.   Had a lovely drive partly through the woods. The pines were singing "The slow song of the sea." It recalled the old Bridgewater days, when we used to lie on the brown leaves and listen dreamily to that wondrous song. We lost our way, which made it all the more delightful, of course!

Monday, January 19.   Cold disagreeable day. Was too

unwell to go to school. Miss T. [owne] came to see me and did me good, as usual with her good medicines and her sunshiny face. Sewed in a most exemplary way.

Tuesday, January 20. Terrible storm all last night and to-day. I thought "God pity those who sail the seas to-night."

Wednesday, January 21. Had letters from Mattie F. [arbeaux] and Mrs. J. Was very glad. But still no letter from A. [nnie Woods Webb] nor from Henry [Cassey]. I know not what to think. No box, no package;—nothing but waiting, waiting. I grow very weary and heart-sick sometimes; but I must, must wait patiently.

Friday, January 23. Had a kind little note from my good friend, Dr. R. [ogers]. His reg[imen]t. goes on an expedition to-day. He asks me to pray for their success. And indeed I will, with my whole soul and for his safety, too—dear, kind friend that he is. I wish I cld have seen him again before he went. How he rejoices in [Major] Gen. [David] Hunter's [107] coming. And how I rejoice with him!

Saturday, January 24. Had to-day the pleasantest visit I've had since I've been here. L. [izzie] and I drove to Mr. Thorpe's plantation to call on Mrs. Harrison[,] [108] a new arrival. She is a pleasant lady-like, *exceedingly* quiet person. That is all I can say of her. The gentlemen took us round to see the people of whom there are 150 on the place. 100 have come from Edisto. There were no houses to accommodate so many, and they had to find shelter in barns, outhouses and any other place they cld get. They have constructed rude houses for themselves—many of them which do not, however[,] afford them much protection in bad weather. I am told that they are all excellent, industrious people. One old woman interested me deeply. Her name is Daphne, and she is probably at least a hundred years old. She has had fifty grandchildren, sixty-five great-children, and three great, great grandchildren. She is entirely blind, but seems quite cheerful and happy. She told us that she was brought from Africa to this country, just after the Revolution. I asked her if she were glad that all her numerous family were now and forever free. Her bright old face grew brighter as she answered. "Oh yes, yes missus." She retains her faculties remarkably well for one so old. It interested me greatly to see her. As Mr. H.[unn] said "it was worth coming to S[outh] C.[arolina] to see that old relic of a past time." 15 of the people on this place escaped from the mainland, last spring. Among them was a man named Michael. After they had gone some distance—their masters in pursuit—M.[ichael]'s master overtook him in the swamp. A fierce grapple ensued—the master on horseback, the man on foot;—the former drew a pistol and shot the slave through the arm, shattering it dreadfully. Still the brave man fought desperately and at last succeeded in unhorsing the master, and beat him until he was senseless. He then with the rest of the company escaped. With them was a woman named Rina, now cook at Mr. T.[horpe]'s. She was overtaken by her master's cousin, and nearly run over by his horse. But he, having a liking for her, wheeled his horse around, when he saw who it was, without saying a word, and allowed her to escape—a story which I record because it is a rare thing to hear anything good of a rebel. I had the pleasure of shaking hands with Rina, and congratulating her on her escape. She is very neat, a sensible looking black woman. Mr. T.[horpe]'s place—which used to be the property of one of the numerous family of Fripp's—Thomas by name—is most beautifully situated in the midst of noble pine trees, and on the banks of a large creek which deserves— almost—to be dignified by the name of river. Tis the pleasantest place I've seen yet. And Mr. T. [horpe] says it is quite healthy. Of *course* we lost our way coming back, and I, in trying to turn the horse, ran up against a tree and there our *"shay"* staid. In vain did L. [izzie] and I try to move the horse, and then the wheels. Both were equally immovable, till fortunately we saw a man at a little distance and called him to our aid. With his assistance we soon got righted again. All this I tell you dear A. as a great secret. Wldn't have anybody else know of my *un*skilfulness. Despite this little *contretemps* we had a delightful sunset drive home.

Sunday, January 25. Saw a wonderful sight to-day. 150 people were baptized in the creek near the church. They looked very picturesque—many of them in white aprons, and bright dresses and handkerchiefs. And as they, in procession, marched down to the water, they sang beautifully. The most perfect order and quiet prevailed throughout.

Monday, January 26. Rec'd another kind note from Dr. R. [ogers] written prior to the other. In it he gives me some account of what he is doing; and I am so glad to know. It is so good to hear from him, I fear he has not got my note. Not that 'twas of much importance, but I w'ld like him to know how constantly I think of him.

Tuesday, January 27. J. [ack] brought me from B. [eaufort] to-day a package from home containing a letter from Aunt M. [argaretta], some delicious candy from our good Emma, and a pair of quite nice pants, from Mrs. Chew, sent especially to Cupid. How delighted he was to get them. He cldn't say much, but I wish Mrs. C. [hew] c'ld have seen the marvelous bows and *scrapings* which he made.

Wednesday, January 28. A memorable day because we had a snow storm—a miniature. When I got up this morning some of the roofs had a white layer on them, but it did not stay on the ground. The "storm" lasted but a little while. Towards eve. there was another slight attempt at snow, which was unsuccessful. A cold, dreary day. Miss R. [uggles] sent me "Say and Seal" and a bunch of lovely white flowers, which it does my soul good to see. She is very kind.

Thursday, January 29. Was very fortunate to-day. Miss T. [owne] brought me letters from Mrs. C. [hew], Mrs. Crosby, Libby, Aunt M. [argaretta], Aunt H. [arriet], Jane, [109] and several Boston papers. Am delighted. But still no letter from H. [enry Cassey]. And dear A. it troubles me. I think he c'ldn't have written. Yet he assured me he w'ld write often. And the thought of that makes me fear that he may be ill. I can only wait, wait. Mrs. C. [hew] tells me she is getting up a box for me, which I am very glad to know.

Friday, January 30. Finished "Say and Seal," some of which I like very much. But it is rather religious to suit me. I don't know but it seems to me the author's works have a little *cant* about them. Now Mrs. [Harriet Beecher] Stowe always has something about religion in her books, but it is so differently *administered*, that it is only pleasant and beautiful. Wrote to Aunt M. [argaretta] and to dear Annie [Woods Webb].

Saturday, January 31. L. [izzie] and I went to Beaufort— after bread. We had a lovely row across,—at noon—in the brightest sunlight. But neither going nor coming did the boatman sing, which disappointed me much. The Sergeant said these were not singers—*that* is most surprising. I thought *everybody* sang down here. Certainly every boat crew *ought*. As we drove to the ferry, we noticed how fresh and green everything looked;—so unlike winter. The trees are nearly all evergreen. Bare branches are rarely to be seen. What a lovely morning it was!—like a May morn. up North. Birds singing on every side. Deep green in the pines and "deep delicious blue" in the sky. Why is it that green and blue together are so lovely in Nature, and so unlovely elsewhere? In B. [eaufort] we spent nearly all our time at Harriet Tubman's[110] otherwise [*sic*] "Moses." She is a wonderful woman—a real heroine. Has helped off a large number of slaves, after taking her own freedom. She told us that she used to hide them in the woods during the day and go around to get provisions for them. Once she had with her a man named Joe, for whom a reward of $1500 was offered. Frequently, in different places she found handbills exactly describing him, but at last they reached in safety the Suspension Bridge over the Falls and found themselves in Canada. Until then, she said, Joe had been very silent. In vain had she called his attention to the glory of the Falls. He sat perfectly still—moody, it seemed, and w'ld not even glance at them. But when she said, "Now we are in Can. [ada]" he sprang to his feet—with a great shout and sang and clapped his hands in a perfect delirium of joy. So when they got out, and he first touched *free* soil, he shouted and hurrahed "as if he were crazy"—she said. How exciting it was to hear her tell the story. And to hear her sing the very scraps of jubilant hymns that he sang. She said the ladies crowded around them, and some laughed and some cried. My own eyes were full as I listened to her—the heroic woman! A reward of $10,000 was offered for her by the Southerners, and her friends deemed it best that she sh'ld, for a time find refuge in Can. [ada]. And she did so, but only for a short time. She came back and was soon at the good brave work again. She is living in B. [eaufort] now; keeping an eating house. But she wants to go North, and will probably do so ere long. I am glad I saw her—*very* glad. At her house we met one of the Superintendents from P.[ort] R.[oyal] I.[sland], a Boston man—Mr. S.—who is intelligent and very agreeable. He kindly went with us to Mrs. Hawkes'[111]—the wife of the Sur.[geon] 1st Reg. S.C.V., but she was at the camp with her husband who did not go with the Expedition. Was sorry not to see her. Went, afterward, to the Judd's for letters, and found there one from A.[nnie]. Am delighted to have it and to know she is not ill. Mr. J[udd]'s house is beautifully situated. In the same street with Gen. Saxton's. On the Bay—as they call it. Saw the building which was once the Public Library. It is now a shelter for "contrabands" from Ferandino. How disgusted the rebels w'ld be. I suppose they w'ld upturn their aristocratic noses and say "To what base uses etc." It does *me* good to see how the tables are turned. The market place also we saw. Mr. S. said doubtless human beings had been sold there. But there is not a certainty of it, as that business was generally transacted in Charleston. The Arsenal is a fine large stone structure—fine—I shld say for this region. The entrance is guarded by two handsome brass canon, and a fierce looking sentinel. Nearly all the houses in B.[eaufort] have a dismantled desolate look. Few persons are to be seen in the streets, some soldiers and "contrabands." I believe we saw only three ladies. But already Northern improvements have reached this southern town. One of them is a fine new wharf which is a convenience that one wonders how the "Secesh" c'ld have done without. They were an uncivilized people. I noticed more mulattoes there than we have on St. Hel.[ena]. Some were very good-looking. Little colored children—of every hue were playing about the streets looking as merry and happy as children ought to look—now that the dark shadow of slavery hangs over them no more. We did our few errands and were quite ready for the four o'clock boat, which was not, however, ready for us until sometime afterward. I missed the singing, in our row back.

Sunday, February 1. Quite a number of strangers at church to-day,—among them our good Gen. [eral] whom it is always a pleasure to see. Reuben T. [omlinson] was there. I was glad to see him. It recalled the old Phila. [delphia] days—the pleasantest of them. This afternoon went into the woods, and gathered some casine berries and beautiful magnolia leaves and exquisite ferns. How beautifully they contrast, on my table, with the daffodils and narcissus which are in full bloom now. Think of these flowers blooming out of doors in Jan. and Feb. Isn't it wonderful? I can't tell you how much pleasure they give me. What sunbeams they are to warm and cheer my heart.

Monday, February 2. Have just heard to-night of the return of the 1st Regt. They came back with laurels—and Secesh prisoners. Have heard no particulars, but am *glad,* emphatically glad to know that they come back completely successful. That is grand, glorious! In the joy of my heart sat down and wrote a congratulatory note, to my dear friend, Dr. R. [ogers]. I know how rejoiced he must be. Thank God that he and the noble Col. [Higginson] have come back safe.

Saturday, February 7. One day this week Tina, an excellent woman from Palawana came in, and told us a very interesting story about two girls, one about ten and the other fifteen, who having been taken by their master up into the country about the time of the "Gun Shoot," determined to try to get back to their parents who had been left on this island. They stole away at night, and travelled through woods and swamps, for two days without eating. Sometimes their strength w'ld fail and they w'ld sink down in the swamps, and think they c'ld go no further, but they had brave little hearts, and struggled on, till at last they reached Port Royal Ferry. There they were seen by a boat-load of people who had also made their escape. The boat was too full to take them but the people, as soon as they reached these islands, told the father of the children, who immediately hastened to the Ferry for them. The poor little creatures were almost wild with joy, despite their exhausted state, when they saw their father coming to them. When they were brought to their mother she fell down "jus' as if she was dead" as Tina expressed it. She was so overpowered with joy. Both children are living on Balta now. They are said to be very clever. I want to see the heroic little creatures.

Another day, one of the black soldiers came in and gave us *his* account of the Expedition. No words of mine, dear A.[,] can give you any account of the state of exaltation and enthusiasm that he was in. He was eager for another chance at "de Secesh." I asked him what he w'ld do if his master and others sh'ld come back and try to reenslave him. "I'd fight un Miss, I'd fight un till I turned to dust!" He was especially delighted at the ire which the sight of the black troops excited in the minds of certain Secesh women whom they saw. These vented their spleen by calling the men "baboons dressed in soldiers' clothes, and telling them that they ought to be at work in their masters' rice swamps, and that they ought to be lashed to death." "And what did you say to them?" I asked. "Oh miss, we only tell us 'Hole your tongue, and dry up,! You see we wusn't feared of *dem, dey cldn't hurt us now.* Whew! didn't we laugh to see dem so mad!" The spirit of resistance to the Secesh is strong in these men.

Sunday, February 8. Mr. T.[horpe] and Mr. John Alden

dined with us to-day. The latter, I believe, a veritable
descendant of *the* John;—a modest youth but with a twinkle
of fun about the eyes, which bespeaks him not so demure as
he seems. Towards night, after the other had gone, Dr.
R[ogers] came. Wasn't I glad to see him. He looks none the
worse for his late experience. He brought his notes of the
Ex.[pedition] taken on the spot, and very kindly read them
to us, to-night. They are very, very interesting, more so to
me even than Col. H.[igginson]'s excellent Report, (which
the Dr. also brought) because entering more into particulars.
He will not have them printed for which I am sorry. They
ought to be printed. They, and the report also, show plainly
how nobly and bravely the black soldiers can fight. I am
delighted. I think the contemptuous white soldiers will cease
to sneer soon. Dr. R.[ogers] described beautifully the scenes
through which they passed, particularly the night journey up
St. Mary's River with the good old funeral oaks on either
side. How strange and solemn it must have been. At one
place, Alberti's Mill, they went up to the plantation, and
found the mistress, living in solitary splendor. She and her
husband (now dead) come from the North, but have lived a
long time down South and had a large plantation and great
wealth. Dr. R.[ogers] describes Mad.[ame] A.[lberti] as a
very superior woman. She spent a long time in trying to
convince Dr. R.[ogers] that she and her husband had devoted
themselves to the good of their slaves, and lamented their
ingratitude in all deserting her—as they have all done except
one or two petted house servants. Robt. Sutton, now Corporal
in the Regt. was formerly her slave, and said the people were
cruelly treated, and the jail on the place, where chains and
handcuffs were found, bears witness to that. The soldiers
brought off cattle, horses and lumber, all of great value to

the Gov. They behaved gallantly under fire from the rebels and entered into their work with zeal. Three of them saved the life of their brave Col. He, as usual, was at one time in advance, when a rebel pistol was fired at him by an officer, who immediately drew another and was about to take more fatal aim (the Col. not perceiving it) when three of the soldiers seeing his danger, fired at once, killing the rebel officer. Dr. R. [ogers] says that several who were badly wounded did not report to him, fearing that they w'ld be obliged to leave their posts. The noble Robt. Sutton whom Col. H. [igginson] calls "the Leader of the Expedition" was wounded in three places, and still kept at his post. Dr. R. [ogers] speaks of him as does Col. H. [igginson] in the highest terms. He says he thinks he must be the descendant of some Nubian king. He is a grand man. My heart is filled with an exceeding great joy to-night. I can never thank Dr. R. [ogers] sufficiently for bringing me those notes. It was very kind. And it makes me so happy to see him safe back again. The kind, loving words he spoke to me to-night sank deep into my heart. "As a brother," he told me to consider him. And I will gladly do so. He read me Emerson's noble "Hymn," [112] written for the grand Jubilee Concert, on Emancipation Day in Boston. Dr. R. [ogers] read it to the Regt. he told me, during the service, this morning. I am glad. He was in full uniform to-day. Makes a splendid looking officer. I looked at him and his horse with childish admiration.

Monday, February 9. Dr. R. [ogers] walked part of the way to school with me, and we had a nice, long talk. He said he wished he lived nearer that he might come in and read to me sometimes. Ah! wldn't *I* enjoy that, unspeakably. It is too bad that I can see so seldom the only old friend I have here,— and such a friend! Dear Miss T. [owne] was not well enough to be at school to-day. I am very sorry. Miss M. [urray] and I did the best we c'ld without her. With what eager interest and delight Miss M. [urray] speaks of the success of the Regt. I believe she is as rejoiced as I am and that's saying a great deal. It does me good to see it.

Frogmore. Wednesday, February 11.   Quite unwell yesterday and to-day. This morn. the Townes—my good physician and her sister—came in declaring that I need a change of air, forcibly bore me off to Frogmore. Well, I was glad to go, and here I am. The place is delightfully situated, on an arm of the sea, which, at high tide, comes up to within a few feet of the house. There are lovely trees around, and an almost sea air, which is most invigorating after the somewhat oppressive atmosphere farther inland. This is a very large plantation. There are nearly 200 people living on it. Ah! how pleasant this salt smell is. It recalls the dear old Marblehead days.

Thursday, February 12.   Have done little else but sleep. It is very quiet here. Have had most delicious rest, both for soul and body. Miss Rose T. [owne] is as kind as possible. Here is a beautiful kindness, that does one good thoroughly. I love her. This afternoon wrote to my dear Mrs. Russell.

Found the first snowdrop today;—a lovely, pure, little darling, growing at the foot of the piazza steps. Miss Laura T. [owne] came to-day. To-night some of the little boys came in and danced for us. It was *deliciously* comical. Miss L. [aura] rewarded them by giving them belts with bright buckles, which pleased them mightily. To-night there was a bit of a shout in the "Praise House," but there were not enough to make it enjoyable. They sang beautifully however one song I have not heard before. Must try to get the words. "Jacob" and "wld not let me go," are in it.

Saturday, February 14.   Valentine's Day *at home*. Who will send me one? A dark, gloomy, stormy day without, but cheery within. Miss W.[are] and Miss M.[urray] came to-day, and we have quite a large party—five ladies and two gentlemen. Stormed so much this afternoon they c'ld not go, and will be obliged to spend the night with us. That is *jolly*. I know Mr. F.[rench?] thinks so. *Wasn't* he rejoiced to see Miss M.[urray]. Ah! love. 'Tis a queer thing, but very amusing—to lookers-on. Helped Miss Rosa fill bags with sewing utensils for the people—a pleasant task. We both enjoyed it. To-night—a wild stormy night—went out on the piazza and listened to the roaring of the sea. How wild it sounded. Occasionally we c'ld hear a great wave break upon the shore. That sound of the sea is music to my ears. I c'ld not bear to come away from it. It brought N.[ew] E.[ngland] near to me. But the air was dangerously damp, and I had to tear myself away. Miss L.[aura] T.[owne] told us some delightfully horrible stories and then Mr. F.[rench] told us some stories from Virgil, in which he seems well read. We had a very pleasant, social evening. Goodbye, old journal friend.

JOURNAL FOUR
St. Helena Island, February 15, 1863–
May 15, 1864

Oaklands. Sunday, February 15. Home again! Left Frogmore[1] this afternoon. T'was so lovely there I did not want to leave it at all, and dear Miss Rosa urged me to stay. But I c'ld not. The water was clear and beautiful, and even today we c'ld hear the sea, but rather a distant murmur, not the grand roaring of last night. The day has been bright, lovely, and most spring-like. Two soldiers dined at F.[rogmore] with us. They are part of the patrol, which it has been found necessary to place here, on account of the depredations made by some of the soldiers, who have recently landed. They have stolen poultry, and everything else they c'ld get on the plantations, cheated the Negroes, and in some instances even burned their houses. These outrages are said to have been committed by deserters. It is too bad. We are all most indignant about it, but hope now, since more vigilant measures have been taken that things will be in a better state. Found awaiting me here letters from Mrs. Crosby, Mrs. Chew, Mr. Hunt, and Mary S.[hepard], also a "Boston Journal" and two "Liberators," was delighted, of course, to get them all. Oaklands seems rather cramped and close after the larger grounds, and pleasant water view and sea breezes of Frogmore; but we have the snuggest little sitting room I've seen yet and it's pleasant to get into it again. I am much better, thanks to change of air, rest, and Miss Rosa's loving care. I feel quite ready for to-morrow's work.

Tuesday, February 17. To-night rec'd a box from Phila.[delphia] containing nice little alphabet-blocks and pic-

ture cards for my little ones. They'll delight the little creature's hearts, I know. Had also letters from Mrs. C. [hew]
and Aunt M. [argaretta] and from Sallie P. written in her
usual original and entertaining style. She has a faculty for
writing.

Wednesday, February 18. Too rainy this morning for
school. This afternoon cleared up beautifully and we had a
lovely drive to the Oaks. Was grieved to find Miss G. [age?] [2]
still quite unwell. Coming back saw the loveliest cloud
scene—a picture not to be forgotten. Read some good things
in Beecher's "Eyes and Bars."

Thursday, February 19. Who sh'ld walk into school to-
day but my good and dear Dr. R. [ogers]. *Wasn't* I glad to
see him! Miss M. [urray] w'ld have my children read for
him, and they read remarkably well. He praised them. They
sang beautifully too, which delighted him. He came home to
dine with us, and then we—just he and I—had the loveliest
horseback ride to Mr. Thorpe's place. It was lovely through
those pines and we found the most exquisite jessamine. The
ground had been burnt, and so attracted the sun's rays, and
the greater heat made the flowers much larger than ours.
Nothing c'ld be more perfect than the color, more delicious
than the fragrance. Dr. R. [ogers] broke off long sprays and
twined them around me. I felt grand as a queen. How good
Mr. H. [unn] opened his eyes when he saw me so gloriously
adorned. Mr. T. [horpe] (whom Dr. R. [ogers] wants to
know) was not at home, so we made no stay. Dear A. I can
give you no idea of the ride homeward. I know only that it
was the most delightful ride I ever had in my life. The young
moon—just a silver bow—had a singular, almost violet tinge,
and all around it in the heavens was a rosy glow, deepening
every moment, which was wonderfully beautiful. I shall never

forget how that rosy light, and the moon and stars looked to us as we caught them in glimpses, riding through the dark pines. How wild and unreal it all seemed and what happiness it was, as we rode slowly along to listen to the conversation of the dear friend who is always so kind, so full of noble sympathy, and of eager enthusiasm in the great work in which he is engaged. No wonder the soldiers love him so much, no wonder that, as Col. H.[igginson] says, he has such a hold upon them. So that one of them said to him "Why Dr., don't you know there ain't a man in de regiment—but what *dotes his eyes on you.*" There is a magnetism about him impossible to resist. I can never be thankful enough that he came here. But oh, I do not want him to be ill, or to die. Most gladly w'ld I give my life that one so noble so valuable might be preserved. He brought me a note from Col. H.[igginson]. So very kind! I shall not say anything about its contents or about what Dr. R.[ogers] said to me relating to it, even to you, yet my dear A. for it is a profound secret, which I must not trust to paper. But rest assured you will know all about it ere long. After tea the Dr. read to us a grand article, in the Feb.[ruary] "Atlantic" by his friend Mr. Wasson called "The Law of Costs." It is in relation to the war, and is certainly the best thing I have yet seen on the subject. Full of noble truths told in the most beautiful language. He also read us Lowell's last "Biglow Paper" on the same subject—a capital thing; far superior to anything he has written of late.

Friday, February 20. Dr. R.[ogers] went this morn. I rose earlier than usual, and plucked some lovely jessamine for him and the Col. I shall see him again to-morrow, for we are to go to Camp Saxton. After school read Jan.[uary] "Atlantic" which Dr. R.[ogers] very kindly brought me. Then S.[usannah?][3] and I made some cakes, one large one

apiece for the Col. and the Dr. Mr. T.[horpe] spent the
night with us. He is intelligent and agreeable, and really
interested in the people here. I like him.

Saturday, February 21. Ah, what a day I've had! Another
day "to be marked with a white stone." We—that is Mr.
T.[horpe], Mrs. and Miss H.[unn] and I drove to the
landing and at noon took a nice boat, with four oarsmen. The
tide was very high, the air exhilarating, the sunshine joyous.
It was a perfect row—an ideal row, through those dancing
laughing waves we flew along and reached camp Saxton in
half an hour. Beaufort looks really quite beautiful from the
water. The sky wore its best blue. Everything smiled upon
us, and the boatmen sang several singular and beautiful hymns
which I have never heard before. Noted them down as well
as I c'ld. C'ldn't understand the words very readily. Had a
warm welcome from the Col and Dr. The adjutant[4] was
married last Sunday, in a hollow square. His bride is pleasant,
intelligent looking, and ladylike. We dined at the Col.'s
table, and had the happiness of listening to his always entertaining talk. After dinner paid several visits. Am so glad the
Dr. has a nice large tent, with a stove in it, and as many
things to make him comfortable as one can have in a tent.
The adjutant's tent has a carpet in it—a wonderful luxury in
camp—and indeed down here, everywhere. Saw the battalion
drill and the dress parade, both of which were fine sights to
me. The Dr. took us to a cypress swamp about half a mile
from the camp. It is a wonderful place. Never saw one
before. The trunks of the trees, near the base are fluted, just
as perfectly as if done by art. The branches are hung with
moss, through which the sunlight was streaming. The surface
of the water is covered with a plant having fine leaves of a
vivid green. But the most wonderful thing about it is the

variety of forms which the roots take. In many places they come up a foot or more in height and bear a striking resemblance to monks with long cloaks and shaven crowns. Others take the form of birds. But the monks are the most distinct and are most remarkable. The Dr. got one for me and whittled off the end so as to make it more shapely. Some very fine beautiful moss on it. I've put it in water, hoping the moss will grow. The whole swamp looks wonderfully like some old cathedral, with monks cloaked and hooded, kneeling around it. Col. H. [igginson] showed us at the camp one of the finest live oaks I have ever seen. A grand old tree heavily draped with moss and with delicate little ferns growing on some of the limbs. While in the Dr.'s tent Rob't Sutton came in. It was very interesting to hear him talk about the expedition. His manner is very simple and earnest and his words, full of eloquence and enthusiasm, flow forth with wonderful ease. It was amusing to hear him say with perfect simplicity— "now if de Connel had done so and so, as I told him, we c'ld a taken all dem rebels right off." And the Col. bowed his noble head, and acknowledged Robt's superior wisdom. The Colonel seems to have entered into firing houses at St. Mary's with great zest. We were laughing and talking about it when he turned to me with great gravity (I c'ldn't imagine what was coming) and said "Now Miss Forten, what in your opinion is the best place to begin with in setting a house on fire?" I laughingly replied that I feared I hadn't considered the subject sufficiently to venture an opinion. "Well," he said, "some authorities say to the leeward, others to the windward. I've tried both and I don't see that it makes any difference—It seems to me the very best place is just under a shelf in a closet or cupboard." He talked to me, alone, for sometime, about the plan proposed in his note. How can I

ever thank him for his kindness? I can only say in my heart—
how noble, how splendid he is! While the brightest day must
come to a close and so mine came. I didn't want to come
away at all, but come must. It was nearly dark when we again
stopped into "our dug out." Capt. R.[ogers] came with us.
How he is improved since the old Worcester days, he seems
a fine fellow now. The wind was high, the water quite rough
to-night and our boatmen worked too hard to sing. So we
had to console ourselves, by singing, as well as we c'ld
ourselves. Mr. T.[horpe] has quite a good voice. The moon
and stars smiled down upon us. It was a wild row; and all
the more delightful for that. I wished for the Dr. to enjoy it
with me. Then the dark drive home—Mrs. H.[unn] driving, Mr. T.[horpe] and Capt. R.[ogers] on horseback as
escort. T'was all enjoyable.

Sunday, February 22. Mr. T.[horpe] and Capt. R.[ogers]
spent most of the day with us. Had a very pleasant time. Did
a great deal of chatting. Copied several of the people's hymns
for the Col. and Dr. and gathered jessamine and ivy for
them. The children came in and sang and then had some
grand shouts on the piazza, which delighted the gentlemen
exceedingly. Capt. R.[ogers] and I had two games of chess,
wld'nt that shock some people! in both of which I was most
ignominiously defeated. Nevertheless I enjoyed them. After
dinner the Capt. left, and then Mr. T.[horpe] and I had a
good little ride on horseback, in which old Edisto, usually so
slow, quite distinguished himself. He came home at a full
gallop. This eve. Mr. and Miss R.[uggles] came in, bringing me letters from Mr. Hunt, dear Nellie, A.[nnie] and
the most flowery letter from a gentleman in Wash.[ington]
who must have read Mr. [William Wells] Brown's silly
book,[5] I must send it home to make them laugh.

Wednesday, February 25.   Had no school, as the teachers went to Camp Saxton. Had a splendid ride to the Oaks, and back. Old Edisto behaved admirably. The day was delightful. Was riding nearly all the morn. This eve. wrote to Mr. Hunt.

Thursday, February 26.   To-day several gentlemen from the 21st Mass. [achusetts] came in school. They listened with evident interest to the recitations and singing, and at the close expressed themselves much pleased. Wrote four pages more to Mr. Hunt. Suspect he'll open his eyes in amazement to see a letter of eight pages from me.

Friday, February 27.   Wrote to Mary S. [hepard], Aunt M. [argaretta] and to Miss Fitler[6] thanking her for the blocks and cards.

Saturday, February 28.   Had a nice long talk with some of the people this afternoon. The more one knows of them the more interested one becomes in them. I asked if there used to be people sold at auction in the market-place at Beaufort. They said, "yes, often." Last night finished "Salem Chapel," which ends just as I thought it would.

Sunday, March 1.   Went to church and was victimized with one of Mr. Phillips' dull sermons. Rec'd my pass. Tis necessary we sh'ld all have passes to show to the patrol on the island. Read some good things in the "Atlantic." March, usually so blustering with us, comes in here soft and mild as June. These are indeed June days. Quantities of flowers are in bloom, snow drops, daffodils, narcissus, japonicas, a beautiful fine white flower whose name I do not know, and as for the yellow jessamine, large—flowered and fragrant, the woods are perfectly golden with it. On Friday, coming from school, I saw the loveliest mistletoe that ever eyes beheld. Large branches heavily laden with white berries, pure and beautiful as pearls. My children and I went busily to work. With long sticks bore down the branches so we c'ld reach them, and enriched ourselves with the treasures thereon. And each one of [*sic*] marched home triumphantly, bearing long sprays of pearls. They are hanging over our broken mirror, and drooping over my little table of books now. Mr. H. [unn] has brought in a large branch of jessamine, laden with exquisite blossoms, which adorns another table. So altogether our little room is made quite splendid. Plum and peach blossoms are all out now, perfuming the air, and looking most beautiful and May-like.

Wednesday, March 2.   Rushing along the road from school to-day, in a shivering condition—for our stove w'ld do nothing but smoke—what sh'ld I encounter but Gen. Saxton's carriage, and, in it, himself and Mrs. Gage. The Gen. said "Col. Higginson wants you to go to Florida with his regt." in his usually rather abrupt way.[7] Now although I knew this before, for dear A. *this* is the weighty secret Dr. R. [ogers] imparted to me when he was last here, the suddenness of the Gen.'s speech took me by surprise, and if I looked as surprised as I felt, the Gen. who had of course been told that I knew all about it,—must have thought me a little hypocrite. I hardly knew what to say. Believe I stammered something about leaving my school. Mrs. Gage said I must get some one else to take it. She wants me to go to Fla. If I go, it will be to teach the soldiers. I shall like that. So much depends on these men. If I can help them in any way I shall be glad to do so. I shall be sorry to leave my dear children and Miss T. [owne] and Miss M. [urray] to whom I am most warmly attached; but if I can really do more good by going, I shall be content. And then I shall have the society of my dear and noble friend Dr. R. [ogers] and perhaps of the good and noble Col. too, and these are very, very strong inducements. The climate also is healthier, and oh how I *crave* good health. How can one work well without it? They think it will be safer there for me, too, but of that I do not think. I have never felt the least fear since I have been here. Though not particularly brave at home, it seems if I *cannot* know fear *here.* To-night had letters from Dr. R. [ogers] so kind, so noble. He has sent me a little friend, whose name I am not to mention. But it is a beautiful and true friend. Also a little note of Bell's full of touching and beautiful affection. Indeed it is very kind in him to let me see this little note. It somehow brings me nearer to him. The Regt. will leave to-morrow, he says.[8] I shall not see him before he goes, perhaps never again, for it is an enterprise full of danger on which they go. The thought makes my heart ache. I am willing to give up my life—which is nothing—but I do not want one so good and noble as he to die yet. The world cannot afford to lose such. And yet as he says[,] "let us think how much better it is to die in this sublime struggle for universal freedom, than live to see another generation of slavery." Rec'd also to-night a pass from Gen. Saxton, who highly approves my going. This permit, Dr. R. [ogers] says, is equivalent to a Commission. So I shall go. I am determined now. Dr. R. [ogers] tells me to be ready to join them at an early day.

Thursday, March 5.   Talked over my Fla. plan with Miss T. [owne] and Miss M. [urray]. Although they do not want me to go, they cannot help acknowledging that it would be a wider sphere of usefulness than this.

Saturday, March 7.   Had a long pleasant drive to Mr. B. [ryant]'s[9] place, near "Land's End." It is a fine, stately house, beautifully situated, with much water near it. Two very fine long piazzas, one above the other were favorable for promenading. The water view from these w'ld be fine were it not for the marshes. But the air is fresher and more healthy than with us. After dinner, played euchre, for the first time since I have been here. Driving along the road noticed an oak tree, which looked very singular. One of the limbs, after growing out, bent itself back and grew into the tree again. A very strange thing. Dr. W. [akefield] [10] who pointed it out to us, said that he had seen only one like it on Cape Cod.

Tuesday, March 10. Was very unwell Sunday and yesterday. Felt better today and went with Mrs. Hunn to Beaufort, intending to do some shopping and to go to Camp Saxton and see Mrs. Dewhurst [11] to make inquiries about our going— I am to go with her and Mrs. Hawkes. [12] The Quartermaster [13] very kindly lent us his carriage and we drove off in fine spirits. Our driver[,] Jonas, assured us that he knew where the camp was. But he mistook the place that we wanted to go to, and drove us many miles out of the way. It was the longest drive I have had yet down here. Probably between thirty and forty miles. Camp S. [axton] is only four miles from Beaufort.

The weather was almost oppressively warm, the air laden with the fragrance of jasmine and fruit blossoms. At last our driver was made to understand where we wanted to go, and we reached Camp Saxton. Saw Mrs. D. [ewhurst] and Mrs. H. [awkes]. We may not have to go for 3 weeks. But there is no certainty about it. Returned to B. [eaufort] just in time for the last boat. So no shopping was done. By the Arago had letters from Mary S. [hepard] and Miss T. Wrote to Aunt M. [argaretta] and sent her a spray of moss, by Miss Rosa [Towne], who will probably leave to-morrow.

Friday, March 13. Have been busily sewing this week, though still far from well. Miss H. [awkes] has taught for

me. Went to Beaufort again to-day, and did some shopping.
Saw Gen. [Rufus] S.[axton] who was married to Miss
[Matilda] T.[hompson] [14] last Wed. He looked quite ra-
diant. A strange marriage, it seems to me. Coming over in
the boat, the men sang one of the most beautiful hymns I
have ever heard.

> "Praise believer, praise God, I praise my God until I die
> Jordan stream is a good old stream and I aint but one
>   more river cross
> I want some valiant soldier to help me bear the cross."

It is a beautiful thing. Yesterday I had a book—A.[lexander]
Crummell's "Future of Africa," from Whittier. Also a letter
from him, and a precious little note from his sister[,] both
very kind and beautiful. Also by Miss T.[owne], my Tennyson, some newspapers, letters from Aunt M.[argaretta
Forten], F. E., Lizzie C.[hurch], Hattie [Purvis] and
Henry [Cassey]. The latter has rec'd and answered all my
letters. Also sent me some "Atlantics" and the letter paper,
and yet, I have rec'd nothing from him. It is very strange. I
quite despair of ever getting them now. It is too bad!

Saturday, March 14.   Drove to Coffin P.[oint] to visit
Miss Ware—a sister of Dr. Winsor's wife. A long dreary
drive it was thro' deep Carolina sand. And we did not find
Miss W.[are]. But the house[,] a large, old-fashioned one,
is beautifully situated on the sea shore. There is a lovely path
leading directly thro' the garden down to the beach. Oh it
was *good* to stand upon that beach, feel the cool sea breezes,
and listen to the gentle murmur of the waves. I was most
unwilling to leave it. The sitting room was the pleasantest I
have seen down here, with its books and pictures. And an
excellent piano was there—Gilbert's of Boston—which was

most refreshing to listen to after the tuneless instruments one hears generally down here. Altogether this is a place I sh'ld like to go to for a week, to rest in, thoroughly, before I go down to Florida.

The Oaks. Saturday, March 21. Miss Nellie[15] came and took me to the Oaks. Think the change will do me good. Have been unwell of late. Victimized myself in the dress-maker's hands. To-night Miss M.[urray] and I had some good games of chess. Mr. [Frederick] E.[ustis][16] is staying here. A man of a good deal of wit. Don't think I shall like him from what I've heard of his behavior towards the people. His manners are not at all attractive to me.

Sunday, March 22. Chilly, disagreeable day. Unusually small attendance at church. Some of the people sang "Glory Be to my King Emmanuel." It is one of their grandest hymns. Must have the words. Mr. T.[horpe] and Miss Nellie, sang beautifully for us to-night. Both have fine, rich voices.

Tuesday, March 24. Miss T.[owne] came from B.[eaufort] to-day bringing me news that the ladies had sailed for Fla. this morn. Their letters just came to me to-day. But I am to go with Gen. Saxton day after to-morrow; which is just as well. Had a little note from Dr. R.[ogers]. They are expecting me. He says "we have to keep a sharp lookout for the rebels, but I think we shall hold the town." I shall enjoy the 'spice' of danger. With Miss T.[owne] came the interest[ing] arrival—Mr. [Edward] Pierce[17]—the former *pioneer* down here. His manners are exceedingly pleasant—I can't help acknowledging that, though I had a preconceived dislike for him, because I had heard that he said he "wanted no colored missionaries nor teachers down here." His conversation at table to-night was most entertaining and genial.

But I shall take an early opportunity of asking an explanation of that speech. If he said that, of course, there's no possibility of my liking him. Still, I must confess, it is pleasant to see somebody fresh from Boston, and full of Boston energy and spirit. It is pleasant to hear the dear, noble[,] familiar names again; to meet one who has so lately breathed the same air and trod the same streets with such as Wendell Phillips and dear Mr. Garrison. Then Mr. Pierce himself did a great work down here, and proved himself a true friend of the people who all regard him with love and gratitude. That is a great deal in his favor. Miss T.[owne] lent me some hymns to copy, which I have not.

Wednesday, March 25.   Went to school to-day for the last time. Said good-bye to my little ones with a full heart. Gave them each a book for a parting gift. How that delighted them. Mr. P.[ierce] came in and listened to a little reciting. Some of my tiny ones "did up" the alphabet quite beautifully. Kind Miss T.[owne] came to Oaklands and packed my trunks, for which I am inexpressibly thankful, for I seem to have no strength at all. Said good-bye to old Oaklands. Shall I ever see it and its inmates again, I wonder? Cupid drove me to the Oaks in the beautiful still moonlight. To-morrow we go to Beau.[fort].

Thursday, March 26.   Just too late for the earliest boat, which was provoking. But I supposed we should have time enough, as we were not to go to Fla. till this afternoon. Had the satisfaction of seeing the boat about half-way across. Established ourselves as well as we c'ld on the landing—Miss T.[owne] on a stump and I on a basket; while Mr. P.[ierce] devoted himself to our entertainment—Read a little from "Bull Run Russell's" book, and talked a great deal. While we were sitting there saw the "Flora" pass down the stream, and by the flag, knew that the Gen. was on board. I began to feel uneasy,—thinking that the hour of starting had been changed, and that the boat was off to Fla. without us. But Mr. P.[ierce]—who is also going to Jacksonville—was so secure that it was not so, and so composed about it that I was reassured. At last the ferry boat returned. On reaching B.[eaufort] went at once to Capt. H.[ooper]'s[18] office, and were there told that Gen. S.[axton] had just gone down to Hilton Head to see Gen. Hunter[19] from whom he had just rec'd a dispatch saying that he had ordered the evacuation of Jacksonville. The Gen. returns at once. I waited to see him. Dined at the Judd's.[20] Like them and Miss R.[uggles] also very much. At last Gen. S.[axton] came. Mr. P.[ierce] saw him at once. It is true. Jacksonville is to be evacuated. Gen. Hunter needs the white troops and the gunboats to join the Ex.[pedition] to Charleston, and as the rebels are gathering in great forces near the town, the black regiment alone w'ld be entirely overwhelmed. The Gen. promises to send them back when Charleston is taken. But when will that be? Things move "warily and slow" down here. I think our noble Col. will be bitterly disappointed; it is too bad, too bad. Surely with all the troops that have been raised at the North enough might be sent here to take Charleston and hold Florida too, but it is always so. Always something lacking somewhere. One can't help feeling a little discouraged sometimes. Am back at St. H.[elena] to-night. Saw exquisite orange blossoms opening—on the Gen's grounds, perfuming the whole atmosphere.

Friday, March 27. After school returned to Oaklands. I see it sooner than I thought to. I shall hardly hope to see Florida now.

Monday, March 30. Dreadfully raw, disagreeable day,

very unwell with the worst cold I've had. It *stupifies* me. Who sh'ld come in, all in a shiner, but Mr. Pierce. Had a good long talk with him, over the fire, during which took occasion to ask him about that speech. He emphatically denies ever having made it. Talked a long time on the subject and the result is that we are good friends. I'll allow myself to like him now; which is very much easier than *disliking* him, *Je vous assure, my chere* A.

Thursday, April 2. Drearily, drearily the days drag on. Can do nothing but knit, and that grows wearisome. Have discovered a music box that was taken from a "Secesh" house in Beaufort—a remarkably fine one. Only wants a little cleaning to be perfect. The tone is exquisite. The airs are all gems and all familiar, and oh, how they recall home. This music box is the only comfort I have just now. Had a call to-day from Mr. French, Mr. and Mrs. L.[ennon?] from N.Y. and Miss R.[uggles]. Mr. L.[ennon?] I like—an exceedingly kindly and pleasant manner. His wife has much *hauteur*. To-day, news is *good*. They say the black soldiers fought the rebels bravely; drove them off from J.[acksonville,] fired the town, and returned in triumph.[21] They marched thro' B.[eaufort] this morn. How I long to see Dr. R.[ogers] and hear all from his eloquent lips. I can think of nothing but this regt. How proud of it I am! Mr. Hunt writes to L.[aura Towne] that he has not heard from me. Strange, when I have written to him so often. Wrote to him again to-night, again enclosing my account. On Tuesday Mr. P.[ierce] paid us another visit and took dinner and tea. Had a delightful talk with him about people, literature, politics,—everything. He gave us a very interesting account of his experiences with the "contrabands" in Va. Mailed a long letter to dear Tacie, to-day.

Friday, April 3. This morn., had a nice little note from Dear Dr. R. [ogers] and a very light, pretty rocking chair, from Fla., of course. He says he will see me soon and tell me *all*. I hope it will be very soon, indeed. I do so long to see him. Had a long talk with one of the soldiers—a connection of the Hunns. I find that the prevailing feeling among the troops is impatience at the long delay, and also a kind of discouragement caused by the want of enthusiasm on the part of the officers. It is a sad thing to hear this. He said "it's not the soldiers' fault that something isn't done,"—and I believe it. Oh, if we c'ld only have the noble Fremont for a leader! Mr. Pierce came in again this afternoon, and stayed to tea. We had another nice long talk; about everything, *prejudice,* among the rest. Suspect I got rather excited and talked too much, as I always do on this subject. But how can I help· it? Mr. P. [ierce] gave us some very pleasant reminiscences of his first acquaintance with the noble, noble, glorious Sumner.

Saturday, April 4. Drove with Mrs. H. [unn] to our new home "Seaside." Lost the way of course, taking the wrong road thro' the woods, which detained us. Reached Seaside about noon. It is delightfully situated—when the tide is in, which it was *not* while we were there. Saw not a drop of water, nothing but marsh. The house I like. It has such an old look. The parlor is painted a kind of grey, with oak panelings and white and darker wood work interspersed, and over the chimney is quite a pretty fresco painting—a landscape. The whole room has an air of taste and elegance about it that I've not seen before, down here. There is a tolerable piano and a delightful piazza which can be enclosed with blinds at will. That looks inviting. Altogether the house is on a much finer scale than this; and—what is far more important—the situation is a very much healthier one. So we and the store will probably move this week. Had the loveliest drive home, just at sunset.

Sunday, April 5. Lovely day. So warm, thought I might venture to go to church. But t'was so dreadfully chilly and damp inside that I was afraid to stay. Had letters from Mr. and Mrs. R.[emond] and the brightest, sunshiniest little letter from dear Mary S.[hepard]. Mr. Pierce came for me to go and dine with them at the Oaks. Had another long pleasant chat with him as we drove thither. He saw dear Dr. R.[ogers] yesterday. I shall certainly see him this week. Saw Dr. Brisbane, and listened with much interest to his account of his first convictions with regards to slavery. Shall note down some of the things he said. In 1833, he thought, he, being then editor of a paper in Charleston, wrote an article defending slavery from the scriptures, in reply to an anti-slavery pamphlet which had been sent him. He thought seriously on the subject of slavery though not all considering it as morally wrong. Some time after this, in another article, he said that *Onesimus* was not a slave. For making this simple statement he was loudly abused and threatened with lynch law. Then he made up his mind that though Ones.[imus] was not a slave *he* was. And he determined to live no longer in a place where he was not allowed to express his opinions. But so far was he, at that time, from being convinced of the wrongfulness of slavery that he *sold* his slaves, and removed to Cincinnatii [*sic*]. He was there a year and a half before he became converted to anti-slavery. When that happened his conscience reproached him with having sold his slaves. He returned South, bought back his slaves, brought them North and freed them. Only one man was not bought. Do not exactly understand why except that he was old and very sickly. Suppose they tho't he w'ld not live very long. The Dr. said he always felt troubled afterward, about that man. When he came down here, a few months ago, this, his former slave, was one of the first men he met,—now free and still living. Dr. B.[risbane]'s friends tho't when he proposed rebuying his slaves in order to free them, that he w'ld be wronging his son by so doing. He asked his son what *he* tho't about it, and the latter nobly replied that we w'ld rather have that deed to be proud of than all the money his father c'ld leave him. Was much interested in listening to an old man whom Mr. P.[ierce], the unwearied, was questioning. This man, Don Carlos, by name, was a slave, originally from Vir.[ginia] and living here in the family of the Allston's. He knew the Gov. Allston whom Aaron Burr's daughter married, and was well acquainted with her mournful story. He also knew Mr. Pierpont when he was teaching in the Gov's family—teaching the sons of his second wife. Carlos has been taught to read by him and seems to be a man of considerable intelligence. He, and afterwards, Dr. B.[ribane], gave us some interesting reminiscences of the Denmark Vesey Insurrection.[22] Spent the night at The Oaks.

Tuesday, April 7. Drove with Mrs. H.[unn] to call on Miss R.[uggles] who gave me some of the loveliest roses I ever saw, and an exquisite flower—the pettisporum which is a hothouse plant at home, but is blooming out of doors here. It is deliciously fragrant—almost as delicious as orange blossoms. Had a perfectly lovely drive. The air is delicious today. Surely there is healing in it. This eve. had notes from Dr. R.[ogers] and Mr. Pierce. The latter's, indeed[,] was quite a letter and gives me a very interesting account of his visit to the 1st S.[outh] C.[arolina Volunteers]. My good friend Dr. R.[ogers] wants me to pay them a visit and Mr. P.[ierce] very kindly offers to escort me; and as I am banished from school for a time, I think I shall go. Perhaps the change will do me good.

Oaks. Wednesday, April 8. Mr. P. [ierce] came to-day, and as he will probably be obliged to go Sat. [urday] on the "Arago," urged me to go to The Oaks with him this eve. From there we shall go to "Head Quarters" to-morrow. He gave me a beautiful, pearl handled knife which once belonged to Charles Sumner. How I shall treasure it. He is very good to give me anything so precious. I am *unspeakably* obliged to him.

Milne's Plantation. Thurs.[day], April 9. Came to B. [eaufort] this morn. with Mr. P. [ierce]. We were met by the news that the "Washington," one of our boats lying near the Ferry[,] had been shelled by the rebels. It has got aground. Of course the news created quite a sensation. And Mr. Pierce feared at first that it might not be safe for me to go to where the regiment is stationed, which is not more than a few miles from where the boat lies. But after making some inquiries he, to my great joy, concluded that I might go for the day, but not to stay all night. I demurred not, but took my carpet bag nevertheless, believing I sh'ld stay. We had a lovely drive along the shell road that leads to the Ferry, and Mr. P. [ierce] talked very entertainingly all the way. I think I never before met a stranger with whom I c'ld talk so easily. Can't generally talk to strangers at all. But there's something in his manner—such a graceful geniality—that makes it very easy to talk with him; to say whatever comes into one's head. How delightful and June-like everything looks; how fresh and beautiful! The roadsides white with Cherokee roses which contrast beautifully with the bright green leaves around them. I have rarely enjoyed a drive so much. Arrived at the Plantation, we found the Dr. busy attending to the wounded from the Washington. Mrs. Dr. [Hawkes] [23] was also engaged with them, so Mr. P.[ierce] and I walked to a duck pond at a little distance, and amused ourselves watching some tiny ducklings. Then he entertained me with talk about our noble Sumner whom he knows well, and quoted parts of some of his finest speeches. Did it well, too. Then we returned to the house and had a warm welcome. Am delighted to see the Dr. looking so well. The Col. appeared at dinner. It is *good* to see him and dear Dr. R.[ogers] again. After dinner Mr. P.[ierce] went. I was really sorry to part with him. The "Arago" *may not* go till Monday. If so he will come out here on Sunday, speak to the soldiers, and take me home. Walked with the Col. and Mr. and Mrs. D.[ewhurst] in the garden, which is a delightful one. Here found some exquisite roses— a species of Tea rose, I think—the most beautiful I ever saw, and the lovely, fragrant pettisporums. Arranged a basket for the Col. Then we went to the Dr.'s sunny little room; the Dr., the Col., Mrs. D.[ewhurst], the Chaplain and I—and sat around the beautiful blazing fire talking very pleasantly. How I have enjoyed this first night here.

Friday, April 10. How perfectly lovely it is to-day. This morn. walked round the grounds. There are lovely trees all around. The situation is delightful but do not like it quite so well as Camp Saxton. Miss the water. Around the house are lovely locust trees now in full bloom. The air is laden with their fragrance. Went to ride with Dr. R.[ogers] on the nicest of roads. He canters splendidly. Rode to Seabrook, where Mr. [Charles] Follen is superintendent. Was very glad to see him. He is very gentlemanly and agreeable, though somewhat peculiar in manner. His place is pleasantly situated. From the piazza one sees a beautiful arch formed by two trees at the end of a short avenue which leads to the water's edge. Some of the 1st Regt. are on picket duty here. We rode along the water's edge to a point whence they said the rebels are frequently to be seen on the other side. But to my great regret saw not one. Visited two other plantations, and had a delightful ride home. This afternoon went out to see the Dress Parade. There were about six companies. The others are stationed at different points on picket duty. This eve played euchre with Mrs. D. [ewhurst], Dr. R. [ogers] and Dr. [Thomas] M. [inor].[24] Oh, I must not forget to tell you, dear A. that yesterday on our way hither, we met Col. [James] Montgomery[25] with some of his men. I've long wanted to see the Kansas hero. He is tall, muscular, with a shrewd face, browned and wrinkled. I like his look of quiet determination. Dr. R. [ogers] tells me that although so full of fearless enthusiasm, he is very economical of human life,— never allowing his men rashly to throw away their lives. In talking with the officers I find the feeling of deep disappointment general because of their being obliged to leave Florida just as they had obtained a foothold there. They are sure they c'ld have held Jacksonville with perfect security. They had driven the enemy back, and burnt the railroad for several miles. There are two gunboats constantly stationed at the mouth of the St. John's which c'ld just as well have been brought up for their protection, and that w'ld have been sufficient for their protection. I think this last order of Gen. Hunter has created universal dissatisfaction. It is too bad. As Dr. R. [ogers] says[,] "it is a sad putting off of the day of deliverance for the oppressed."

Saturday, April 11. Had a perfect ride to-day with Col. H. [igginson] and Dr. R. [ogers]. Went to Rose's plantation, and Capers. There the Col. left us to go on board one of the gun boats. Dr. and I rode on to Barnwell's which is the most

beautiful place I have yet seen. It is filled with magnificent
live oaks, magnolias, and other trees. Saw there a grand old
oak said to be the largest on the islands, some of its branches
have been cut off, but the circumference of those remaining
is more than a hundred feet. It is a wonderful tree. The
grounds slope down to the water—Broad River, and here
again we went to a point whence the rebels are sometimes to
be seen[,] and though we and one of the black soldiers
strained our eyes[,] we c'ld discover none. How shall I tell
you, dear A. about our ride home first through an avenue of
beautiful trees—mostly live oaks draped with moss—and then
for miles and miles through the Pine Barrens. The air was
soft, Italian, only a low faint murmur c'ld be heard among
the pines,—hardly "the slow song of the sea." The ground
was thickly carpeted with ferns of a most delicious green, and
to crown all we found Azaleas of a deep pink color and
perfect fragrance. Found also sand violets, very large purple
ones, and some kind of grass which bears an exquisite fine
white flower, some of the petals just tinged with a delicate
lilac. The flower is a little like spices. We rode though the
Barrens. I think I never enjoyed anything so perfectly. I
luxuriated in it. It was almost "too much, too much." Dr.
R.[ogers] and I had a long and interesting talk. How kind,
how good he is! It is very pleasant to know he cared so much
for me, even although I *know* he thinks far better of me than
I deserve. The brightest and most delightful experiences must
come to an end, and at last but too soon we emerged from
the Pine Barrens and came out into the shell road. It was like
leaving Paradise. Yet this is a very pleasant road, too. Noticed
the finest live oak, almost the finest, I ever saw. Not quite so
large as the Barnwell, but far more beautiful. Found also the
most exquisite white violets I ever saw—such delicate, won-

derful penciling. They are fragrant too. Had a good canter on the nice hard road. On reaching home we were met by the news that the rebels were supposed to be bringing up pontoon bridges, were expected to make an attempt to cross near the Ferry, at a place about two miles distant from here. The news created quite a little excitement. The Col. had not yet returned. A messenger was dispatched for him, and another to Gen. Saxton at B.[eaufort] that gunboats and artillery may be sent up. Capt. Rogers seems to enjoy the prospect of a fight, promises me I shall see a shell this afternoon.—The Col. has now returned. Couriers are coming in every few minutes. One of the Supts. whose place is near the Ferry has been watching thro' his glass the movements opposite, and reports that the rebels are gathering in large force. Meanwhile I sit composedly down taking notes; and shall now occupy myself with darning a pair of stockings for the doctor until something further occurs which is *writable*. Have no fear.

Night.—Finished the stockings, then took a pleasant walk with Dr. [Thomas] Minor in the garden; where we discovered a lovely magnolia just opened, some perfect rosebuds, and a *strawberry* nearly ripe. At supper everybody in good spirits, gay and cheerful. We heard that the gunboats had arrived, and all this eve at intervals, we hear the guns. Did not know at first which side they were on, but am incapable of fear. Can hear plainly the explosion of shells. Are sure now that the firing is from our gunboats. Being so very near us, of course it sounds heavy. The Col. has just been reading me (a magnificent reader he is) some of the ballads of the old Cavaliers. How grand, how stirring they are. And how Robt. *Browning* is too. Afterward the Dr. read me a little of the "Faerie Queene" and then some letters which have just come.

The battery has arrived from Beaufort. And I am told young Mr. [Eli] Merriam[26] of Boston is here. He is always ready to fight. Mrs. D. [ewhurst] and I will now composedly retire. We don't fear an attack; but if it comes—why let it. Our men will fight bravely we know. As for myself, I do not fear. W'ld far rather be killed than that our noble Col. or the equally noble and good Dr. R. [ogers] sh'ld be. This has been an exciting day, I have enjoyed it, yes truly enjoyed it. The "Arago" sailed this morn. So I shall not see my good friend Mr. P. [ierce] again, for which I am sorry. Regret very much that he will not be here to-morrow to speak to the soldiers. I like so much his kind genial way of speaking to these people, and Dr. R. [ogers] says he does too. It gives them entire confidence in him. He has promised to call and see grandmother. I am very glad.

Sunday, April 12. Slept more soundly last night than I have before. Was only wakened once or twice by couriers coming "in hot haste." That was all. Woke quite late, to find a lovely morning. Dr. Minor and I had a grand ride. Same programme as yesterday—Rose's Capers' and then Barnwell's; thence another perfect ride thro' the Pine Barrens. Found exquisite white azaleas this time, and the largest violets I've yet seen. T'was a lovely, dreamy kind of morning—half sunlight, half shade. How exquisite the shades of green are now. The bright, fresh green of the young oaks and plums, and gum trees contrasting most beautifully with the dark, sombre pines. I think the air to-day must be like that of Italy. Had a pleasant talk with Dr. Minor. He is very young, full of enthusiasm and courage. I like him much. Dr. R. [ogers] has a very high opinion of him. There's something so earnest, singlehearted about him. He has talent, too. Lives in Conn. [ecticut] now. Was born in Ceylon he tells me. I enjoyed hearing him talk about that far away island. Rode his horse, a noble spirited fellow, but gentle as can be. He canters splendidly; but a little more roughly than the road I've ridden hitherto. The Col. has a splendid horse, Rinoldo. So has the Dr. They came from Florida. Had nearly four hours ride. Got home just so as to miss seeing Gens. Hunter and Saxton, who have been paying us a visit. Wanted to see Gen. H.[unter]. Found that Mr. Judd had come according to Mrs. P.[eck?]'s arrangement to take me to B.[eaufort]. And so unwillingly had to take my leave. How very, very much I have enjoyed this visit. Have promised the Col. that when another person can be found to take my place in school here, I will come and teach the soldiers. I shall be glad to do it. Found it hard to leave my kind friend Dr. R.[ogers]. He has been very good to me. Had a pleasant drive to B.[eaufort] with Mr. J.[udd] and Miss R.[uggles]. Passed the fortifications which are quite complete now. The cannons look like stern and efficient protectors. There was a Negro funeral at the burying ground. We c'ld see the crowd of people and hear them singing hymns;—not their own beautiful hymns, I am sorry to say. I do so fear these will be superseded by ours, which are poor in comparison, and which they do not sing well at all. From B.[eaufort] Capt. Hooper kindly escorted us across the ferry. In B.[eaufort] saw Gen. Hunter in the street, but had not a good look at him.

The Oaks. Monday, morn. April 13.   Came hither last eve., and spent the night. In the night was sure I heard some one try my door. Asked "Who's there?" No answer. The noise was repeated—the question asked again. Still no answer. Woke Miss W.[are] who had the adjoining room. She lit the candle and we took our revolvers,—all ready for rebels. Waited awhile. Then as all continued quiet, put our pistols under our heads and composed ourselves to sleep. The wind or rats, I supposed afterward. At first I was sure it was some person but thought it more likely to be a robber than a rebel.

Oaklands—Night. Have had a wearisome day at school, so many little ones. And nearly all in a state of rebellion, owing to their teacher's long absence. Had some newspapers, but no letters, which disappointed me greatly. Spent the eve. in writing.

Tuesday, April 14. Windy, disagreeable day. Very small school. How deliciously fragrant the air is now with orange blossoms. They've been open a week. Roses too in full bloom. We have some superb buds in our garden. The largest I ever saw; and of an exquisite color—something between a pink and a buff.

To-night it is rumored that there are rebels—cavalry—on the island. I do not believe it. It is said they can blow brandy into their horses' noses and that will enable them to swim a long distance. And so it is tho't they may have been able to cross from Edisto over some of the little creeks. There's no probability of it. Mrs. H. [unn] is somewhat alarmed. Reports are most numerous here, always. So it is better not to believe them at all.

Some rebels were nicely caught a few days ago. They were at a picket station on or near Edisto. Capt. Dutch of the "Kingfisher," hearing that they were there from a Negro, one of their servants, went with some of his men to the house and took them all prisoners. There were nine or ten of them.—The aristocracy of the islands. Am delighted to think they were taken.

Seaside. Wednesday, April 15. After school rode to "Seaside" on my faithful horse—Edisto. Shall take up my abode here for the present. Had a delightful ride hither through the woods. Enjoyed it perfectly. House is still barely furnished, and has rather a comfortless look; but I suppose it will soon seem like home. Tis pleasant to have a piano, though it is a poor one.

Saturday, April 18. Had a pleasant little ride to Dr. White's, a plantation a few miles from here. The grounds must once have been beautiful, but have a somewhat decayed look now. The house is rather poor looking though large. Tis painted a dull red, in which it differs from the other houses down here, most of which are white. Edisto went with great spirit to-day—quite distinguished himself—passed the other horses with astonishing ease.

Sunday, April 19. Went to church, and afterward to Oaklands where we dined. Mr. Tomlinson who is now Gen. Supt. instead of Mr. Soule[27] (who has resigned and gone home) dined with us. I enjoyed his society very much. He is so genial and happy. Makes sunshine wherever he goes. And is also deeply interested in the people here. Think he will make a splendid Supt.

Saturday, April 25. All this week have ridden to school on horseback and enjoyed it very much though Ed.[isto] is rather rough.

Yesterday had a very kind letter from P. B. Hunt.

To-day went on horseback with L.[izzie] and Mrs. H.[unn] to the village which is about eight miles from here. Had a lovely ride through June woods;—the air laden with the fragrance of the locust; the birds singing merrily, the golden sunlight pouring its flood of beauty upon the delicious green of the young leaves. The village is delightfully situated on quite a large and pleasant stream of water. The ladies upon whom we went to call were not at home, but Lieut. [J. M.] B. [ingham] [28] was there, and we dined with him, then walked around under the trees and enjoyed the water.

Had a lovely ride home through the pines just at sunset. The beauty of these wonderful days sinks deep, deep, into my soul.

The people on the place have grand "shouts." They are most inspiring. Went to one Thursday night. There is an old blind man, Maurice, who has a truly wonderful voice, so strong and clear.—It rings out like a trumpet. One song— "Gabriel blow the Trumpet"—was the grandest thing I have yet heard. And with what fire and enthusiasm the old blind man led off. He seemed inspired.

Sunday, April 26. After church dined at Oaklands and had another perfect ride home through the woods. Ah how I revel in these days. They are almost "too much, too much."

This eve. attended in the "Praise House," the grandest shout I have yet seen. Several of the soldiers who had come home on a visit joined in the shout with great spirit. The whole thing was quite inspiring. How thoroughly Mr. [Charles P.] W. [are] [29] enjoyed it, too. I like him exceedingly. He is such a thoroughly good abolitionist—a friend of Mr. Garrison's too—so *of course* I like him. He is very intelligent, gentlemanly and pleasant. He is Supt. of our plan. [tation] and now lives with us.

Wednesday, April 29. Last night Capt. [J. C.] D. [utch] [30] and one or two others called. The Capt. came to make arrangements for our accompanying him to Edisto. He is going to take every precaution for our safety. But as Lieut. B. [ingham] says there are 5000 Union troops on the island[;] I sh'ld'nt think there'd be any danger. I am not afraid, at any rate, I think I sh'ld enjoy going very much. We are to go to the village early to-morrow morning, and thence take boats to the "Kingfisher," Capt. D.[utch]'s boat.

Thursday, April 30. Fast Day. Started this morn. with Mrs. H.[unn] and L.[izzie] to go to the village, but my poor horse was too sick to go, I myself felt far from well, so gave up the expedition and went to Oaklands,—thence to church, where young Mr. W.[are] preached. There was but a small attendance. Am housekeeper now that the others have gone—No sinecure—for it is not easy to get anything to eat. Barely escape starvation. 'Tis fortunate that we shall have our rations in a few days.

Friday, May 1. A lovely May Day. Sunny and bright— not unpleasantly warm. Rode with Mr. P.[eck?] this morn. to visit Mr. Sumner's[31] school. Found but a very small attendance. Just missed one class, and was too soon for the first, which comes in the afternoon. Am sorry to have missed it. Mr. S.[umner] is very witty and original. Don't know half the time, however, whether he is in jest or earnest— which is provoking. While we were there Dr. and Mrs. S. came in. She is pretty, graceful, and lady-like—has a pleasant face—which he has not. Decidedly scornful expression. Nephew of Amos S.—Am told that he came here for his health; and, from what I hear, sh'ld judge that he has not much[,] if any, interest in the people.

Rode a nice little horse belonging to one of the men. It canters very fast—has a swift bounding motion which is most exhilarating. Her name is Linda. Shall hire her, and let my poor Jeanie have a good rest before I use her again.

This is a glorious moonlight night. From the window I can see the water in silver waves shining in the clear soft light. Sat a long time on the piazza listening to the low tones of the piano or the equally musical murmur of the wind in the tree tops, and thinking of some loved ones who are far, far away. How old memories crowd around one on such nights as these! And how dreamy, strange and unreal the present seems. Here on the piazza of this old southern house I sit and think of friends a thousand miles away—of scenes that have past, never, never to return again. Shall I ever see the dear ones "up North" I wonder? Something answers "never" but for to-night at least, I will not listen to that voice. Here the fleas interpose. Farewell to all reminiscenses. Now for tortures unendurable! Oh the *fleas!!* The fleas!! The fleas!!

Sunday, May 3. Too weary and ill to go to church, which I regretted for I always like to see the people, looking so bright and cheerful in their Sunday attire, and to hear them sing. This eve. Mr. T.[horpe] and a friend were here. The people, after "Praise" had one of their grandest shouts, and L.[izzie] and I, in a dark corner of the Praise House, amused ourselves with practicing a little. It is wonderful that perfect time the people keep with hands, feet, and indeed with every part of the body. I enjoy these "shouts" very much.

Oaks. Wednesday, May 6. Miss M.[urray] and I spent the day in procuring flowers and decorating the church for Miss Nellie's marriage.[32] She is to be married to-morrow. Arranged three bouquets for the pulpit and twined ivy around the little pillars supporting it; while Miss M.[urray] arranged beautiful hanging baskets for each side of the pulpit and another for the table. The church has been nicely cleaned by some of the people. To-night have been very busy arranging flowers for the house. Such exquisite roses! It is a real happiness to work among them. We had a tub partly filled with most exquisite flowers. I felt rich as a queen.

Thursday, May 7. Miss N.[ellie] and Mr. F.[airfield] were married to-day. The little church was quite pretty in its dress of flowers, and the bride in her pure white muslin was, of course, most lovely. Nearly all the Superintendents and teachers were there, and the bride's scholars, and the older people from the Oaks. Was sorry there were not more of the freed people there. T'was a very quiet wedding. I think it will prove a happy marriage. How beautifully Miss T.[owne] decorated the table at the Oaks, to-day. All the cakes were wreathed with lovely flowers—and *the* bride cake—which came from Boston was completely imbedded in pure white roses.—Well—a day! After all a marriage is a solemn thing. The more I think of it the more I am impressed with its solemnity. Think *I* sh'ld dread a funeral much less.

Friday, May 8. L.[izzie] and I had a lovely ride on horseback to and from Oaklands. Played chess with Mr. P.[eck?] to-night and beat him twice, whereat I was of course quite triumphant. He plays very well.

Sunday, May 10. Went to church. Taught Sunday School. Had letters from Aunt M.[argaretta] and Mary S.[hepard]. And a pamphlet from Mr. Pierce;—his speech before the Legislature. He called at our house in Phila.[delphia]. Aunt M.[argaretta] writes that they were delighted with him. Mr. McK.[im] thinks I did him good, which is certainly absurd, to say the least.

Monday, May 11. Recommenced school to-day. We had vacation last week on account of Miss N.[ellie]'s wedding. The church looks bright, clean and cheerful now.

Sunday, May 17. Did not attend church. This eve. had a lovely ride on horseback with Mr. S.[umner]. How witty and entertaining he is. Rode J.[eanie]'s pony, which flies along with such wonderful ease it gives one the feeling of being borne along by the wind.

Monday, May 18. After school rode to Mr. T.[horpe]'s with L.[izzie] and Mrs. B.[arnard?].[33] Had a delightful ride through the woods. Returning Mr. T.[horpe,] and Mr. A.[lden?][34] came with us. T'was *intensely* dark. I rode Mr. T.[horpe]'s horse[,] a splendid, swift, high spirited creature. C'ld hardly hold him. But enjoyed the ride exceedingly. I like Mr. T.[horpe]. Report says that he more than likes me. But I *know* it is not so. Have never had the least reason to think it. Although he is very good and liberal he is still an American, and w'ld of course never be so insane as to love one of the prescribed race. The rumor,—like many others is entirely absurd and without the shadow of a foundation. How strange it seemed riding to-night through the woods—often in such perfect darkness we c'ld see nothing—how strange and wild! I liked it.

Found, at home, to my great pleasure my friend Dr. R.[ogers] and also Mr. R.[uggles]. Dr. R.[ogers] brought me a letter from our Col. who thinks it best I sh'ld not join the regt. just now. He fears scandal. There have been of late very scandalous reports of some of the ladies down here, so of course as usual, *all* must suffer to some extent. I am very sorry, and so are the Col. and Dr. It is most annoying that one sh'ld be prevented from doing what one feels to be one's duty just because Mrs. Grundy will not mind her own affairs.

Friday, May 22. Weather still continues intensely hot. Find driving or riding to school between ten and eleven A.M. very fatiguing. Fear, sometimes, I shall not be able to stand it. Had delightful letters to-day from Mr. Pierce and Dear Mary S.[hepard]. Read "Cosette."

Saturday, May 23. L.[izzie] and I drove down to call on gentle Mrs. H.[unter].[35] A long drive, but very pleasant returning in the "cool of the evening." Had a pleasant call from Mrs. Philbrick and Mr. Hall.

Wednesday, June 3. Spent last night at The Oaks, and this morn. went, with the household to the Village. There we found Capt. D.[utch] awaiting us with boats. This morn. was clear and delightful[,] had a lovely row to the "Kingfisher." 'Tis a delightful floating palace; everything perfectly ordered and elegant. The officers were all very kind and polite; and I enjoyed listening to their explanations about the guns. Dined there; then, about three started in two row boats for Edisto. Mr. Rhodes,[36] one of the officers, accompanied us, and the boats' crews—sailors from the ship, armed with guns and cutlasses. There was no actual danger, but still, as Mr. R.[hodes] said we were going into the enemy's country, so it was best to take every precaution, against surprise.

Reached Edisto near sunset. Went to a part called Eddingsville, which was a favorite summer resort of the aristocracy of the island. It has a fine beach several miles long. The houses have a dismal deserted look. We walked along the lovely beach, preceded at some distance by armed sailors who explored some distance, and returned to report "all quiet, and nobody to be seen," so we walked on fearlessly. Gathered tiny and beautiful shells which were buried deep in the sands, and saw for the first time a shark's egg, which looks like an oblong piece of India rubber. The absence of stones here, as on all of these islands strikes one as very singular—especially in contrast with our stony, rocky N.[ew] E.[ngland] Coasts.

Night approached and we retraced our steps to make preparations for supper. As we approached the house saw one of the most singular sights I ever saw. From a very dark

cloud in the sky the most vivid flashes of lightning were
continually breaking. There seemed not a second's pause
between the flashes. And they assumed a variety of singular
form[,] each succeeding one being more dazzling than the
other. This wonderful display lasted sometime, and impressed
us all very much. All around this dark cloud, the sky flushed
with the loveliest, rosy sunset hues. It was a sight not soon
to be forgotten. One of the men found a table for us which
was placed in a room of the deserted house in which we
intended to spend the night, and was soon spread with the
eatables which we had brought with us. For seats we used
bureau drawers, turned up edgewise. Had a very merry
supper. Afterward set for awhile on the piazza in the lovely
moonlight, then had another delightful stroll on the beach.
How very, very lovely it was. I did not want to go in at all.
But there was my good friend and physician Miss T. [owne]
to preach prudence to me, so at an unreasonably early hour—
I thought—we went to bed. We four ladies occupied one
room, and the three gentlemen the other. The marines were
stationed in the adjoining house, in which they had lighted a
large fire, and they danced about the room and sang and
shouted to their hearts content.

Thursday, June 4. We, of course[,] had no beds, but
made ourselves as comfortable as we c'ld on the floor with
boat cushions, blankets and shawls. We had no fear of rebels.
There was but one road by which they c'ld get to us and on
that a watch was kept. So, despite the mosquitoes, we had a
good sound night's sleep.

After breakfast we explored the house, but found nothing
in it except the remains of a bureau, and a bedstead. Afterwards, while the others were packing up their things I went
down to the shore, and sitting there alone had a long delightful

communion with Old Ocean. The morning air was fresh and pure, and merrily the waves leaped and sparkled in the bright sunlight, or softly they kissed the shore with that low, sweet murmur which is the most musical of all sounds. It was very pleasant, and I was sorry enough to be summoned away.

We took our boats again, and followed the most winding little creek I ever saw. In and out, in and out, our boats went. Sometimes it seemed as if we were going to the very heart of the woods. How easy it w'ld have been for rebels secreted behind those thick bushes to fire into us! But there chanced to be none in that region. Sometimes—so narrow was the stream—we got aground, and it was hard work to pull out of the thick marsh grass. But at least we reached our journey's end—the Eddings plantation, whither some of the people have preceded us in their search for corn. This must once have been a beautiful place. The grounds were evidently laid out with great taste and are filled with beautiful trees, among which I noticed particularly the magnolia tree with its wonderful white blossoms, large, pure, dazzlingly white as they shone among the rich, dark, shining leaves. The garden was filled with lovely flowers. We explored the house, but found nothing but rubbish, and an old bedstead, and a very good bathing tub which Lieut. R.[hodes] graciously consented to my appropriating. It is quite a treasure in these regions. I must not forget the lovely oleanders, of which we brought away great bouquets. But when we went down to the shore to take our boats, lo! the tide had gone down so that the boats c'ld not be brought up to the landing, and between us and them was the marsh covered with water too deep for us to walk through, too shallow for the boats. What was to be done? Mr. T.[omlinson] rolled his pantaloons up, took off boots and stockings, and waded across. Lieut. R.[hodes]

and Mr. F. [airfield] were each carried across on the back of a sailor. But what were we Ladies to do! Suddenly the bathing tub suggested itself to somebody. A brilliant idea, and one eagerly acted upon. Mrs. [Nellie] F. [airfield] and I, successively, seated ourselves in the tub which was raised to the shoulders of four stout sailors, and so, triumphantly, we were borne across. But through a mistake the tub was not sent back for Misses T. [owne] and M. [urray] and they had to be brought over on the crossed hands of some of the sailors, in the "carry a lady to London" style, whereat we were all greatly amused.

Back again we rowed, through the creek, out of the creek, into the open sea—among the grand, exhilarating breakers. Well tossed we were, and Mr. T. [omlinson] and I both feeling just a little apprehensive of sea-sickness, kept exceedingly quiet. However, being very hungry we ate pound cake and drank lemonade—though in fear and trembling. We were pleasantly disappointed by finding ourselves better afterward, and so agreed that we had found, in pound cake and lemonade, the true prevention of that most dismal of all sicknesses—sea-sickness.

We reached the "Kingfisher" at last. Miss T. [owne] and Miss M. [urray] being sick, preferred returning home at once, and Mr. and Mrs. F. [airfield] accompanied them. But the hospitable Capt. w'ld insist on Mr. T. [omlinson] and I staying to dine with him. While waiting for dinner, he took me over every part of the ship, into all the storerooms, in the medical department, and even into the kitchen. And throughout all the arrangements were perfect, and seemed more like those of an elegantly appointed house than of a ship. We dined with the Capt. and other officers, and were elegantly entertained. In the afternoon we bade farewell to the "Kingfisher" and its gentlemanly and hospitable officers, and were rowed across with the Capt. in his own beautiful "gig" to St. Helena. It was a lovely sunset row, which I enjoyed perfectly. Tired enough when we arrived there.

Mr. T.[omlinson] drove me to the Oaks, on which occasion I proved myself an exceedingly entertaining companion—going to sleep long before we reached there—having seated myself in the bottom of the buggy with my head on the seat—and sleeping most profoundly till I was waked by Mr. T.[omlinson] on our arrival at The Oaks.

A few more words about Edisto. It was, as everybody knows, at one time in the possession of our troops, but was afterward evacuated by them—why, I know not,—most people here think it a blunder. At the time of its evacuation the freed people were removed to the adjoining islands—many of them to St. Helena. They were very reluctant to leave their beautiful home. Only the fear of again falling into the hands of the "Secesh" induced them to do it. And they still have a warm attachment for it, and cherish the hope that they may one day return to it in safety. As we drove through the island, yesterday, on our way to this village, the people came around the carriage, and eagerly inquired "Is you gwine to Edisto"? "Shall we give your love to Edisto?" asked Miss T.[owne]. "Oh yes, yes, please misses!" And when we came back they asked us "How does Edisto stan'?"

Tuesday, June 30. Nearly a month since I have written to you, dear A. The intense heat must plead my excuse. Day after day I have driven home from school, thoroughly exhausted, and gone to bed there to remain till dark. In the evenings we have a good breeze generally. Were it not for that I think we c'ld not live through the heat. We spend our evenings on the piazza, sitting up quite late generally in fear of the fleas, which torture us so that bed, to me at least[,] is almost unendurable—sleep almost impossible.

This eve. Mrs. H.[unn], L.[izzie] and I rode with Col. [Quincy] G.[illmore][37] down to see the 54th Mass.[achusetts][38] which is encamped at Land's End. We were caught in a thunder shower, which prevented the Regt. from having its Dress Parade and spent the time in Major H.[allowell]'s[39] tent. It was very pleasant to see my old friend J.[ames] W.[alton].[40] He is a Lieut. in the 54th. But surely he is not strong enough to be a soldier. Cheerful little Mr. T.[horpe?] was there, and we had a very pleasant time. Col. G.[illmore] insisted on our taking tea with him. Then we must stop to play whist, so it was midnight when we got home. Had a delightful ride in the bright moonlight. Heard the mocking birds singing as we rode along. Sometimes they sing all night.

Thursday, July 2. Col. [Robert] Shaw[41] and Major H.[allowell] came to take tea with us, and afterwards stayed to the shout. Lieut. W.[alton] was ill, and c'ld not come. I am perfectly charmed with Col. S.[haw]. He seems to me in every way one of the most delightful persons I have ever met. There is something girlish about him, and yet I never saw anyone more manly. To me he seems a thoroughly lovable person. And there is something so exquisite about him. The perfect breeding, how evident it is. Surely he must be a worthy son of such noble parents.[42] I have seen him but once, yet I cannot help feeling a really affectionate admiration for him. We had a very pleasant talk on the moonlit piazza, and then went to the Praise House to see the shout. I was delighted to find that it was one of the very best and most spirited that we had had. The Col. looked and listened with the deepest interest. And after it was over, expressed himself much gratified. He said, he w'ld like to have some of the hymns to send home. I shall be only too glad to copy them for him. Old Maurice surpassed himself to-night in singing "The Talles' Tree in Paradise." He got much excited and his gestures were really quite tragic. I c'ld see with what astonishment and interest our guests watched the old blind man.

Saturday, July 4.   Had a very pleasant celebration to-day. The people and children all assembled in the grove around the Baptist Church. The old flag was hung across the road between two magnificent live oaks, and the children being grouped under it sang "The Star-Spangled Banner"—which we had taught them for that occasion. Then addresses were made by Mr. [Edward] Pierce, Mr. [James] Lynch[43] (a colored minister) and other gentlemen, there was more singing by the children and by the people, who made the grove resound with the grand tones of "Roll, Jordan, Roll." Then they were all treated to molasses and water—a great luxury to them—and hard tack. Among others from Beaufort, Mrs. [Jean] Lander,[44] and Mr. Page,[45] the [Chicago] "Tribune" Correspondent were there. I had met them before—they had called to see me—and Mrs. L.[ander] insisted on my returning to B.[eaufort] with them; promising that I sh'ld see Col. H.[igginson] and Dr. R.[ogers]. Of course the temptation was strong, and I went. Mrs. L.[ander] seems to be a person of great deal of character, and beneath the stage manner there is a real warmth and kindness of heart which are very attractive. Before we drove to the Ferry we—that is Mrs. L.[ander], Mr. P.[age], and I ensconced ourselves very comfortably under a great tree and had a charming picnic dinner. Then Mrs. L.[ander] read us Buchanan Read's exquisite poem "Drifting." She reads, of course, very finely. A long drive to the ferry, made tolerable only by being in

Mrs. L.[ander]'s easy carriage, then a pleasant row across in the Gen.'s handsome "gig" and we were at B.[eaufort]. Spent a delightful eve. with Dr. [Rogers] and Col. [Higginson]. We had been much disappointed in not having the Colonel at our celebration. He was engaged to make an oration before a Penn.[sylvania] regiment. In the eve. he came in to Mrs. L.[ander]'s and we asked him what he said. "Well I don't remember everything" he said "but at the close I know I told them that we of the 1st S.[outh] C.[arolina] V.[olunteers] [46] had no ill-feeling towards them, we had no prejudice against color, and liked white people just as well as black—if they behaved as well! Evidently they were well pleased with these remarks as they applauded them more loudly than anything else I said." The patriotic people of Beaufort sent up three or four rockets that night—and that was all the celebration of the Fourth that I saw there. The Col. and I had a pleasant walk along the bank.

Sunday, July 5. Too unwell to-day for anything but lying down, and so missed the horseback ride I was to have with Mrs. L.[ander] who is a splendid horsewoman, and Mr. Page. Mrs. L.[ander] took kind care of me, and in the afternoon I felt a little better. Had a visit from Mr. [Edward] Pierce, whom it is always pleasant to see. Dr. R.[ogers] spent the eve. with me. How very, very good and noble he is!

Monday, July 6. Came up from B.[eaufort] to Land's End to-day in the "Hunter." Mr. [Edward] Pierce kindly accompanied me on shore, and helped me into my most unique and ancient looking vehicle,—which the soldiers greeted with shouts of laughter, and styled the "Calathumpian." Drove hours, changed horses, and drove to school. After school, though very tired, did not neglect my invitation to tea with the officers of the 54th. Drove down to Land's End with J.[ack], Mrs. H.[itchcock] and L.[izzie]. Met Col. [Quincy] G.[illmore] who went with us. Were just in time to see the Dress Parade. Tis a splendid looking regt. An honor to the race. Then we went with Col. Shaw to tea. Afterward sat outside the tent and listened to some very fine singing from some of the privates. Their voices blended beautifully. "Jubilo" is one of the best things I've heard lately. I am more than ever charmed with the noble little Col. [Shaw]. What purity[,] what nobleness of soul, what exquisite gentleness in that beautiful face! As I look at it I think "The bravest are the tenderest." I can imagine what he must be to his mother. May his life be spared to her! Yesterday at the celebration he stood, leaning against our carriage and speaking of mother, so lovingly, so tenderly. He said he wished she c'ld be there. If the regt. were going to be stationed there for some time he sh'ld send for her. "But you know," he said "we might be suddenly ordered away, and then she w'ld have nobody to take care of her." I do think he is a wonderfully lovable person. Tonight, he helped me on my horse, and after carefully arranging the folds of my riding skirt, said, so kindly, "Good-bye. If I don't see you again down here I hope to see you at our house." But I hope I shall have the pleasure of seeing him many times even down here. He and his men are eager to be called into active service. Major H.[allowell] rode with L.[izzie Hunn] and me to Col. [Quincy] G.[illmore]'s tent where Lieut. and Mrs. H.[unn] were. The rest of the party played whist till a very late hour but I was thoroughly exhausted. Lay down part of the time. And part of the time sat close to the water's edge, and watched the boats, and the gleaming lights over the water, and the rising moon. A deep peace was over everything—not a sound to be heard but the low, musical murmur of the waves as they kissed the shore.

Wednesday, July 8. Mr. T. [horpe] came over and drove down to Land's End for Lieut. W. [alton] who is still quite ill. The regt. has gone. Left this morning. My heart-felt prayers go with them—for the men and for their noble, noble young Colonel [Shaw]. God bless him! God keep him in His care, and grant that his men may do nobly and prove themselves worthy of him!

Monday, July 20. For nearly two weeks we have waited, oh how anxiously for news of our regt. which went, we know[,] to Morris Is. [land] to take part in the attack on Charleston. To-night comes news oh, so sad, so heart sickening. It is too terrible, too terrible to write. We can only hope it may not all be true. That our noble, beautiful young Colonel [Shaw] is killed, and the regt. cut to pieces![47] I cannot, cannot believe it. And yet I know it may be so. But oh, I am stunned, sick at heart. I can scarcely write. There was an attack on Fort Wagner. The 54th put in advance; fought bravely, desperately, but was finally overpowered and driven back after getting into the Fort. Thank Heaven! they fought bravely! And oh, I still must hope that our colonel, *ours* especially he seems to me, is not killed. But I can write no more to-night.

Beaufort, July 21. Came to town to-day hearing that nurses were sadly needed. Went to Mrs. L. [ander]'s. Found Col. H. [igginson] and Dr. R. [ogers] there. Mrs. L. [ander] was sure I sh'ld not be able to endure the fatigues of hospital life even for a few days, but I thought differently, and the Col. and Dr. were both on my side. So at last Mrs. L. [ander] consented and made arrangements for my entering one of the hospitals to-morrow.

It is sad to see the Col. at all feeble. He is usually so very strong and vigorous. He is going North next week. The Dr. is looking very ill. He is quite exhausted. I shall not feel at peace until he is safe in his northern home. The attachment between these two is beautiful, both are so thoroughly good and noble. And both have the rarest charm of manner.

Wednesday, July 22. My hospital life began to-day. Went early this morning with Mrs. L.[ander] and Mrs. G.[,] the surgeon's wife, saw that the Dr. had not finished dressing the wounds, and while I waited below Mrs. S.[axton] gave me some sewing to do—mending the pantaloons and jackets of the poor fellows. (They are all of the 54th.) It was with a full heart that I sewed up bullet holes and bayonet cuts. Sometimes I found a jacket that told a sad tale—so torn to pieces that it was far past mending. After awhile I went through the wards. As I passed along I thought "Many and low are the pallets, but each is the face of a friend." And I was surprised to see such cheerful faces looking up from the beds. Talked a little with some of the patients and assisted Mrs. G. in distributing medicines. Mrs. L.[ander] kindly sent her carriage for me and I returned home, weary, but far more pleasantly impressed than I had thought possible, with hospital life.

Thursday, July 23. Said farewell to Col. H.[igginson] who goes North in the "Arago" today. Am very sorry that Dr. R.[ogers] c'ld not go with him, not having been able to get his papers. He is looking so ill. It makes me very anxious. He goes to Seaside for a few days. I hope the change, and Mrs. H.[unn]'s kind care will do him good. Took a more thorough survey of the hospital to-day. It is a large new brick building—quite close to the water,—two-storied, many win-dowed, and very airy—in every way well adapted for a hospital. Yesterday I was employed part of the time in writing letters for the men. It was pleasant to see the brave, cheerful, uncomplaining spirit which they all breathed. Some of the poor fellows had come from the far west—even so far as Michigan. Talked with them much to-day. Told them that we had heard that their noble Colonel was not dead, but had been taken prisoner by the rebels. How joyfully their wan faces lighted up! They almost started from their couches as the hope entered their souls. Their attachment to their gallant young colonel is beautiful to see. How warmly, how enthusiastically they speak of him. "He was one of the best little men in the world," they said. "No one c'ld be kinder to a set of men than he was to us." Brave grateful hearts! I hope they will ever prove worthy of such a leader. And God grant that he may indeed be living. But I fear, I greatly fear it may be but a false report. One poor fellow here interests me greatly. He is very young, only nineteen, comes from Michigan. He is very badly wounded—in both legs, and there is a ball—in the stomach—it is thought that cannot be extracted. This poor fellow suffers terribly. His groans are pitiful to hear. But he utters no complaint, and it is touching to see his gratitude for the least kindness that one does him. Mrs. G. asked him if he w'ld like her to write to his home. But he said no. He was an only son, and had come away against his mother's will. He w'ld not have her written to until he was better. Poor fellow! that will never be in this world.*

Another, a Sergeant, suffers great pain, being badly wounded in the leg. But he too lies perfectly patient and uncomplaining. He has such a good, honest face. It is pleasant to look at it—

---

*He has since recovered. I am surprised to hear.

although it is black. He is said to be one of the best and bravest men in the regiment.

When I went in this morning and found my patients so cheerful some of them even quite merry, I tho't it c'ld not be possible that they were badly wounded. Many, indeed have only flesh wounds. But there are others—and they among the most uncomplaining—who are severely wounded;—some dangerously so. Brave fellows! I feel it a happiness, an honor, to do the slightest service for them. True they were unsuccessful in the attack of Fort Wagner. But that was no fault of theirs. It is the testimony of all that they fought bravely as men can fight, and that it was only when completely overwhelmed by superior numbers that they were driven back.

Friday, July 24. To-day the news of Col. Shaw's death is confirmed. There can no longer be any doubt. It makes me sad, sad at heart. They say he sprang from the parapet of the fort and cried "Onward, my brave boys, onward"; then fell, pierced with wounds. I know it was a glorious death. But oh, it is hard, very hard for the young wife,[48] so late a bride, for the invalid mother,[49] whose only and most dearly loved son he was,—that heroic mother who rejoiced in the position which he occupied as colonel of a colored regiment. My heart bleeds for her. His death is a very sad loss to us. I recall him as a much loved friend. Yet I saw him but a few times. Oh what must it be to the wife and the mother. Oh it is terrible. It seems very, very hard that the best and the noblest must be the earliest called away. Especially has it been so throughout this dreadful war.

Mr. P. [ierce] who has been unremitting in his attention to the wounded—called at our building to-day, and took me to the Officers Hospital, which is but a very short distance from here. It is in one of the finest residences in Beaufort, and is surrounded by beautiful grounds. Saw Major Hallowell, who, though badly wounded—in three places—is hoped to be slowly improving. A little more than a week ago I parted with him, after an exciting horseback ride, how strong, how well, how vigorous he was then! And now thoroughly prostrated! But he with all the other officers of the 54th, like the privates, are brave, patient—cheerful. With deep sadness he spoke of Col. Shaw and then told me something that greatly surprised me;—that the Col. before that fatal attack had told him that in case he fell he wished me to have one of his horses—He had three very fine spirited ones that he had brought from the North. (I afterward found this to be a mistake. He only wished me to take charge of the horses until [they] c'ld be sent North to his wife.—) How very, very kind it was! And to me, almost a perfect stranger. I shall treasure this gift most sacredly, all my life long.

Home. Saturday, July 25. After my hospital duties were over came home to St. Helena, to pass Sunday. Shall return to B. [eaufort] on Monday. Am delighted to find our patients, Dr. R. [ogers] and Lieut. W. [alton,] both looking much better. Was caught in a heavy shower on my way from the Ferry, and got quite wet. Nearly every afternoon we have these sudden showers, generally accompanied by severe thunder and lightning. They last but a little while. Then the sun shines out brightly, the skies are blue, and clear again, and the trees and grass look fresh and more beautiful for the rain. But I miss our rich green grass. There is very little of it here. Nor is there a rock or the slightest approach to a hill on the island.

Sunday, July 26. Had a pleasant morning under the trees,

near the water, while Dr. R.[ogers] read Emerson to us. Then had a long talk with him, after which came to the very sudden determination to go North in the next steamer. It is necessary for my health, therefore, it is wiser to go. My strength has failed rapidly of late. Have become so weak that I fear I sh'ld be an easy prey to the fever which prevails here, a little later in this season. A few weeks since I stopped going to the church finding it impossible to drive there longer through the heat of the day, and opened a small school for some of the children from Frogmore in a carriage house on our place. Most of the children are crude little specimens. I asked them once what their ears were for. One bright-eyed little girl answered promptly "to put rings in." When Mrs. H.[unn] asked some of them the same question, they said "To put cotton in." One day I had been telling them about metals; how they were dug from the ground, and afterward, in review, I asked "Where is iron obtained from?" "From the ground" was the prompt reply. "And Gold?"—"From the sky!" shouted a little boy. I have found it very interesting to give them a kind of object lesson with the picture cards. They listen with eager attention, and seem to understand and remember very well what I tell them. But although this has been easier for me than teaching at the church—where, in addition to driving through the hot sun to get there, I was obliged to exert my lungs far above their strength to make myself heard when more than a hundred children were reciting at the same time in the same room—yet I have found my strength steadily decreasing, and have been every day tortured by a severe headache. I take my good Dr.'s advice, therefore, and shall go North on a furlough—to stay until the unhealthiest season is over.

At Sea—Friday, July 31. Said farewell to Seaside and its

kind household, white and black, and very early this morn.
Lieut W.[alton]'s boy drove me to Land's End, whence we
were to take the steamboat which was to convey us to the
steamer at Hilton Head. Mr. [C. F.] W.[illiams?] [50] and
his son who were to be our companions were behind in
another carriage. I was barely in time for the boat, and it
was with great difficulty that the Capt. was prevailed upon to
wait for Mr. W.[illiams]. Our trunks were at least two
miles behind in one of the tedious mule carts, so of course,
there was no hope of getting them on board. Mr. E.[phraim
P.] W.[hite?] [51] waited for them, intending to take a row
boat and follow us at all speed down to Hilton Head. He
was quite sanguine of getting there before the steamer left.
But he did not. And here we are, homeward bound but minus
our baggage. I am sorry for Mr. E.[phraim] W.[hite?]'s
disappointment. His health is so poor, it is really important
that he sh'ld go North as soon as possible. The "Fulton"
sailed from Hilton Head between eight and nine. We have
quite a pleasant party on board. Several friends of mine—
Mr. P.[ierce], Dr. R.[ogers], Mr. and Mrs. H.[arrison] [52]
and Mr. and Mrs. F.[airfield] and Mr. [William] Hall [53]—
all good people.

We have had a perfect day. Besides our party there are
two or three ladies and many gentlemen, principally officers,
whom I do not know. The waves are a rich deep green[,]
the sky a lovely blue, the sun shines brightly, it is very, very
pleasant at sea. Early this afternoon we came in sight of
Charleston, and stopped outside the harbor for an hour or
two. Saw plainly the steeples of the hateful little rebel city.
Had an excellent view of Fort Sumter, which seems to rise
out of the water—bold, grim, and most formidable looking.
In the distance we c'ld see the smoke from the guns on Morris

Island, and through a glass caught a very indistinct view of Fort Wagner. I shudder at the thought of that place, remembering the beautiful and brave young colonel [Shaw] who found a grave there, and his heroic men, some dead beneath the walls—some prisoners, doomed, doubtless, to a fate far, far worse than death. Our captain is an immense man—a perfect Falstaff indeed, but wonderfully active for such a "mountain of flesh." He informs us that he is a Cape Cod man, and had been going to sea for nearly fifty years. Surely he ought to be most thoroughly *en rapport* with Old Ocean. I cannot help envying him.

Saturday, August 1.   How perfect last night was. Mr. P. [ierce] and I sat on deck late in the lovely, lovely moonlight, talking very pleasantly. This morn. [,] after several hours of a most doleful experience in my stateroom [,] I at last succeeded in getting dressed, and struggled up on deck. There I literally *dropped* down upon the nearest seat feeling unspeakably woebegone. My kind Mr. P. [ierce] secured the best seat he c'ld for me, and afterward read Dickens' "Christmas Stories" to me. After a time felt better. Spent the day on deck—talking, or listening to Emerson and Tennyson, very kindly read to me by Dr. R. [ogers] and Mr. Hall. Another very lovely day. The sea is unusually calm, and of the most beautiful emerald hue. Am rather sorry that nothing has occurred. Think I sh'ld like a storm if I c'ld be outside and see its full grandeur. Our captain says we shall reach N.Y. to-morrow. I have thought of the faithful ones who have gathered at Abington to celebrate this day in that lovely pine grove. It w'ld be very pleasant to be with them. God bless them!

N.Y. Sunday, August 2.   Came in sight of land to-day, and this afternoon had a lovely sail up the beautiful harbor, with its stately shipping and fair, green islands on every hand. We, ladies and all, mounted to the deck from which there was a lovely view. Staten Island seemed to me particularly beautiful. Towards sunset our steamer touched the landing. There was a great crowd collected on shore, (how odd it seemed to see so many white faces!) and we c'ld not land till sometime after dark. Said good-bye to my pleasant traveling companions, and accompanied by Mr. P.[ierce] came to Mrs. [Peter] W.[illiams]'s[54] to spend the night. It seems so strange to be in a great city again. The Southern dream is over for a time. The real life of the Northland begins again—Farewell!

Phila.[delphia]. Monday, August 3.   Had the hottest and most disagreeable rides to P.[hiladelphia]. Took everybody by surprise. Eat [*sic*] some ice cream—how refreshing it is! What an unspeakable luxury it is! Am thoroughly exhausted, and only fit to go to bed at once. Too tired to think.

Thursday, August 6.   Having endured the intense heat of the city, till I c'ld bear it no longer, came with Mr. [Edward] P.[ierce] to Byberry[55] to-day. How delightful it is to breathe the sweet country air, to get into this quiet country home again. Dear H.[attie] Purvis looked better than when I saw her last. Constant outdoor exercise has brought back the roses to her cheeks. G.[eorgianna Purvis] has grown almost out of my remembrance, and so has S.[arah Purvis]. The others have not changed. It is very, very pleasant to see them all again. We sat on the piazza very late talking with Mr. Pierce, who goes to-morrow morning, first to Washington, afterward to Port Royal.

Sunday, August 9.   B.[essie] W. came up yesterday afternoon, bringing sunshine with her. She certainly is a charming most refreshing girl. We spent the morning at the piano playing "Roll, Jordan" and other songs of the freed people. The afternoon in talking—the eve. mostly with dear T.[acie] T.[ownsend][56] whom it is a great happiness to see again. She is as good and true as ever.

Tuesday, August 11. Came to town to-day but found no laggard trunk awaiting me; am quite *au desespoir,* having almost literally "nothing to wear,"—certainly nothing at all presentable. Went to see dear [Aunt] A.[nnie Woods Webb] who has arrived in town. She has a lovely baby, but is looking wretchedly ill herself. My heart aches for her. She has a very, very hard life. I must try to lighten it as much as I can.

Thursday, August 13. In despair brought a dress, had Miss S. make it, and this afternoon went to call on Col. (formerly) Major [Edward] Hallowell. Found him much improved; sitting up, and looking quite cheerful and happy. Truly theirs is worthy of having it said "the house called beautiful." It seems as if one c'ld not but get well in such a lovely place and with such tender care. Had a very pleasant chat with the Col. recalling our southern life, but w'ld not stay long lest I should weary them. His stately mother and sisters were very gracious.

Monday, August 17. This evening left Phila.[delphia] and Mr. P.[ierce] and I were whirled away to N.Y. Night graciously drew vail [*sic*] over the dreary fields of N.J. We had a pleasant talk. Arrived at N.Y. Went to Mrs. W.[illiams]'s for the night. My twenty-sixth birthday.

Tuesday, August 18. Left for Boston this morn. Mr. Pierce and Mr. [Francis] Shaw[57] met me at the Station. The latter has a good, noble face, but very sad. Said goodbye to them, and was whirled away eastward. Buried myself in "At Odds" which I read with interest, and then had time for a good long look at the dear old hills as we glided along. Reached Salem in the eve. and went to Mrs. [William] C. [hase]'s—Mrs. [Amy] I. [ves] not being at home—but Mary S. [hepard] had not come. Spent the night there.

Wednesday, August 19. Spent most of the day with dear Mrs. [Nancy] R. [emond]. Am grieved to see her looking so ill.

Thursday, August 20. Went to Mrs. [Amy] I. [ves]'s to-day. Shall spend a week with her. It is pleasant to see her kindly face again. But oh, I am very, very tired.

Monday, August 24. Dear Mary S. [hepard] came to-night. How well she looks, and what glowing descriptions she gives of life among the N. [ew] H. [ampshire] hills.

Thursday, September 1. Went to Boston to-day and had an interview with Dr. B. he examined my lungs very thoroughly, but did not give an opinion about them. Advised me to spend four or five months among the Mts. of P[ennsylvani]a. before returning to South. It is not possible. Prescribed Fusel Oil and whiskey. He is very, very kind. I like him exceedingly.

Wednesday, September 2. Mary [Shepard] and I had a lovely day at Amesbury. It was delightful to be with the Wittiers again. I showed them a beautiful and touching letter from Mrs. [Sarah] Shaw, with two excellent photographs of her noble son. I can never thank her enough for sending me these pictures. We amused ourselves with Whittier's droll parrot, walked in the garden, stood in the yard to see the returned soldiers pass; and had much pleasant quiet talk with Mr. W. [hittier] and his sister in the little vine-clad porch. She is as lovely as ever, but so very, very frail. Every time I part with her I have the fear that I may not see her again.

Saturday, September 5. Had a delightful drive with Miss

A. and Mary to-day; to Essex; there through the loveliest woods from E. [ssex] to Manchester. Stopped at a little hotel there, where Miss A. ordered a room. We (or rather Miss A.) had brought baskets of good things with us, including even coffee, all ready [*sic*] boiled, and were going to have a nice picnic in doors.—It was too cool for an out-door one. Had our feast in a pleasant room fronting the village store, and adorned with too [*sic*] extraordinary portraits, doubtless representing the master and mistress of the house, the former very meek, the latter very fierce looking. Those two faces told volumes. They were executed in the highest style of— sign-painting art! They afforded us infinite amusement. Drove home just at dusk through the lovely sea-road. It was perfectly delightful.

Sunday, September 6. Spent most of the day with Mary [Shepard] who read me some beautiful hymns, and passages from Mrs. [Frances] Kemble's book, which interested me greatly. It is indeed painfully interesting, and bears the impress of truth on every line. It fills one with admiration for the noble woman whose keen sense of justice, whose true humanity shrank with the utmost loathing from the terrible system whose details she saw day after day. Such a book, such a thorough exposé of slavery must do good, in this land, and in England as well.

Monday, September 14. Saturday afternoon Mary [Shepard] and I went to Amesbury. Miss [Elizabeth] W. [hittier] had urged our coming again, but I feared at first that I c'ld not. But I c'ld not resist so great a temptation. We had a perfectly delightful visit. Spent Saturday evening in pleasant talk. Sunday was rainy and gloomy without but very cheerful within. We c'ld not go to meeting as we had intended, but we had a very happy time indoors. The poet was in one of his most genial moods,—told much about his early life—a very rare thing for him to do—and was altogether as charming as he c'ld be. His drollest of parrots amused us with its astonishing performances. In the afternoon Mr. Palmer, who lives only two miles from here, came in and took tea with us. It was very pleasant to see him again. I do not forget how very kind and obliging he was to us, down South. In the eve. the poet told us more about his boyhood, and showed us a venerable old book, "Davider's" being a history of David, written in rhyme by Thos. Elwood, a friend of Milton. It was the only book of *poetry*[,] he told us, that he had to read when a boy. And a very, very quaint book it is. We left with great reluctance this morning. Our visits there have always been delightful but this was the best of all. It will be very, very pleasant to look back upon when I return South. If I c'ld only persuade the W.[hittier]'s to come down next winter, as they w'ld like to do. It w'ld be *too* splendid.

Tuesday, September 15. My last day in Salem. During all my visits have only been able to go once to my dear old hills, and not at all the sea-shore. It is a great disappointment, but I had not the strength. I must be contented to do less than I am used to. Made several farewell calls. Took tea with the Crosbys, who are so kind and pleasant as ever,—and spent the eve. with dear Mary S.[hepard].

Worcester. Wednesday, September 16. Left Salem this morn. While in Boston, went to The Lorings, and got "Sacred and Legendary Art" which Mr. P.[ierce] kindly lent me. He got it from a rebel's house—in Florida, I think. It is a very fine English copy. I expect to *luxuriate* in it. In the A.[nti]-S.[lavery] Office met Mr. [William Lloyd] Garrison, and had a very interesting conversation with him. It has done me good to see his face again. Read with great interest some of

Miss Alcott's "Hospital Sketches." She writes with great vivacity—somewhat in the Gail Hamilton style. Read it in the cars. Mrs. Browning's "Last Poems" which Mary S. [hepard] has given me. Reached W. [orcester] this afternoon. Found the P. [utnam]'s well as usual, and rec'd a warm welcome.

Saturday, September 19. Went to the old Water Cure which is now only a boarding house. Saw Miss C. [hase?], Jennette, and had a long and pleasant talk with Mrs. Higginson. I think I shall like her. She is an invalid, and has been so for years. She looks older than her husband. Her manners are kind and pleasant. She asked many questions about Port Royal, and says she has some thought of going down next month. She heard from the Col. [Higginson] a few days ago. His health has greatly improved, but the Major[58] and Adjt.[59] are both very ill; the former dangerously so. I am *very* sorry to hear it. This eve. Addie [Putnam] played and sang some beautiful things for me. It is really delightful to hear some good music again.

Tuesday, September 22. Had six letters to-night. One from Mr. [Edward] Pierce. He is in Boston, and I shall not see him again, I am *very* sorry. Also letters from Port Royal, which I was very glad to get.

Wednesday, September 23. Left W. [orcester] to-night in steam-boat train.

Phila. [delphia]. Thursday, September 24. Arrived in Phila. [delphia] this afternoon, very tired. Had a kind letter from Whittier. Found the little household quite well.

H. [attie] and I spent the night with the W. [alton]'s. Had a delightful time. J. [ames] W. [alton] thinks of returning to Port Royal at the same time that I do, which will be very pleasant.

Tuesday, October 6.   Attended sweet Mattie F. [arbeaux?]'s wedding. T'was large but pleasant. The bride looked very lovely.

N.Y. Friday, October 9.   Left Phila. [delphia] to-day. Arrived in New York to-night and went with H. [attie] to see Nellie A.

Saturday, October 10.   Secured my passage on board the "Fulton." She sails to-morrow (Sunday) morn.

St. Helena. Seaside, Friday, October 16.   Left N.Y. on the morn. of the 11th. Did not reach Hilton Head until Thursday morning. In spite of the pleasant company with me (Dr. R. [ogers], Col. H. [allowell] and James Lee) had a rather dreary voyage being half sick nearly all the time. On reaching Hilton Head met with a very inhospitable reception. Were told that an order had just been issued by Gen. Gillmore forbidding any lady to land unless provided with a pass from himself or the Secretary of War. One lady was taken ashore despite the guards by the surgeon of the hospital in which she was to be nurse. But Mrs. H. [unter?] and I remained on board while the gentlemen went to Beaufort to see what c'ld be done for us, and a dreary time we had of it, with the pleasant prospect before us of being obliged to return to New York; and watched closely meanwhile by no less than three lynx-eyed guards. We stayed there until the following afternoon, when Mr. Hunn appeared with an order for our release. Came up to Land's End, where we all three squeezed into my "sulky," and reached home this eve. glad to get on terra firma again, and nearly exhausted.

Sunday, October 18.   Went to church. it was very pleasant to see the people gathered together again, and to receive their warm welcome.

Came home from the village to-day to find my good Col.

Higginson here. How it rejoiced me to see him. But am grieved to find him so far from well. He will spend a few days with us trying to recruit. Is not really ill, but very much reduced in strength.

Our noble Col. [Higginson] has left us, feeling a little better. Commenced school on the Perry Place, which is one of Mr. W.[illiams]'s plantations, between two and three miles from here. Most of the children were former pupils of Mr. [Arthur] Sumner. Some of the older ones are quite advanced. Have forty names. Have a comparatively comfortable room with a fire in it,—much preferable to the church.

Wednesday, November 25. For the past few weeks our minds have been much and sadly occupied with the dangerous illness of dear Miss [Ellen] Murray. For some time we feared that we sh'ld lose her. And it w'ld have been an irremediable loss. But now she is getting rapidly better; is entirely out of danger, and I, for one feel as if a great weight had been taken off my mind.

Lizzie, Dora and I, spent to-day in decorating our parlor with moss and cedar. It looks very pretty.

Lieut. [Francis Lee] Higginson, a distant cousin of the Col.'s, is spending a few days with us being also an invalid. He is peculiar, but very intelligent and gentlemanly.

Thursday, November 26. Thanksgiving Day. We had quite a large dinner party—fifteen or sixteen,—and a very merry eve.—dancing, games. Of course Mr. Sumner was the life of the party. He is so very witty and entertaining.

Oliver Fripp Plantation. Sunday, May 15, 1864. How many months have elapsed since I last communed with thee old friend, old journal. I will sketch rapidly a few of the principal events, personal, that have occurred. Some are so painful, I cannot dwell upon them. Others are very cheerful. Early in December, 1863, I came here. Our household consists of Mr. [Arthur] Sumner and Mr. [C. F.] Williams and Mrs. [Martha] Kellogg.[60] They are all most pleasant and congenial companions, and on the whole our winter has been passed pleasantly together.

The people on this plantation are not I think so interesting and pleasant as on many others. They have a bad reputation. Their near vicinity to Land's End and the soldiers there has not tended to improve them.

The place has an unhealthy situation so that we cannot live here in the summer. The owner used to leave in the spring, and go down to the Village. The house is comparatively new, and the best built and most comfortable one I have seen here.

On Christmas Eve., went to Beaufort, and Miss K.[ellogg] and I started to go to the Heacocks[61] with whom we were to spend Christmas. After several mishaps, such as losing our way several times and having one of our horses give out, we at last in the cold, moonlight night arrived at the H.[eacock]'s house, and were ushered into a cosy little sitting-room, all aglow with the light of a blazing wood-fire. The H.[eacock]'s are the pleasantest, cheeriest people, whom it does one good to meet. And A.[nnie] is the veriest little sunbeam I ever saw.

Early Christmas morning we were awakened by the merry sound of children's voices shouting "Merry Christmas." Later in the day there was a Christmas tree exhibited to the wondering eyes of the children, from whose branches numerous gifts were taken down and distributed. How joyous and happy they were! At dinner beside the family and ourselves there were Miss [Helen] Ireson[62] of Lynn and A. G. Brown of Salem, the new Treasury Agent. Another carriage and pair came for us in the afternoon—the Gen. [Saxton]'s orderly accompanying the driver, so we had a sufficient escort, and reached B. [eaufort] without any mishaps. Had a very pleasant party at the Gen.'s in the eve;—games, charades, very good singing, etc. Miss K. [ellogg] and I spent the night there. Mrs. [Jean] Lander, Gen. and Mrs. S. [axton] took part in the charades. They were very amusing.

JOURNAL FIVE
Jacksonville, November 1885–
Ler, July 1892

There is a wide field for missionary labor among the lower class[,] I should think.[1] I hope we may be able to accomplish something in this line as well as in our direct church work.

We have a comfortable boarding place, but boarding is so much more expensive here than we had supposed that we have decided to keep house. I have taken a four-roomed cottage into which we hope to move but we shall be obliged to live in picnic fashion for a time, & gather together a few pieces as we can. Bishop [Daniel A.] Payne[2] spent the evening with us & we enjoyed his conversation very much. Afterwards we escorted him home in the lovely moonlight.

Friday November 13. To-night a very pleasant reception was given us at the church. There were between one and two hundred present, & everyone was most kind and cordial. There was singing, speeches by Bishop Payne & other ministers and laymen, and an address of welcome by Mr. Gibbs to which Frank [Grimké][3] responded very happily, finally refreshments. Mrs. Onley and Mrs. Menard, two of the most active members of the church,[4] and other ladies had charge of the affair and it was very enjoyable and successful. The church is very small, but comfortable, and the people are so much pleased at having F.[rank] here that they are going to build a larger one very soon. They own a fine lot on Laura St. in one of the best locations in the town.

Sunday, November 15. To-day we went into the Sunday School a little while before church time, and were pleased to find how nicely the children are doing. Some of the very smallest ones seemed bright and attentive. The school is small, but constantly growing, we are told. The church was nearly filled. Frank spoke from the text "The love of Christ constraineth us,"—an excellent sermon, and I think it made a fine impression. We took dinner with the kind and friendly Onley's in their pleasant cottage a little way out of the city. On the way we stopped to see the Sulphure Springs, and drank of the water, the odor of which is horrible to me and the taste rather nauseous. Yet it is said to have wonderful medicinal properties. In the evening we attended the Baptist Church. A Mr. Bailey from Tallahassee preached. By a singular coincidence his text was the same as Frank's. The sermon had some good ideas, and the speaker was very earnest,—a good conscientious man, I should think, but not very grammatical, nor connected in his thoughts, and with one of those trumpet like voices which are dreadful to a weak head. Mine ached sadly. Why must these colored ministers *scream* so, in the pulpit? It is most unfortunate for their hearers, and ruinous to their own lungs, one would think. Liked the appearance of Mrs. Ross, the minister's wife.

Saturday, November 21st. Have been busy during the past week superintending the repairing of our little cottage. Workmen move so slowly in this Southern land, that I fear we shall not be able to get into the house for some days yet. Thursday night we had a call from Rev. Dr. Allen, Secretary to the Freedmen's Committee, & his wife. The latter gave me an interesting account of the meetings of the [Presbyterian] Synod of Atlantic, & messages from Mrs. Williams and Mrs. Carr informing me that I was appointed a member of the Women's Synodical Committee.

Sunday, November 22nd. In the morning F. [rank] preached

from the text "Blessed are they which hunger and thirst after righteousness,"—one of his best sermons I think. Dr. and Mrs. Allen were present, & quite a good-sized audience. In the afternoon Dr. Allen preached a fine sermon from the text "He that hath this hope in him purifieth himself," & afterwards made very earnest and appropriate remarks to the people, urging them to hold up the hands of their new minister, and to do all in their power for their own elevation, & also to help others.

Mr. Spencer Murray from Washington came in to see us, & brought us messages from friends. He told us of the death and burial of Mr. Montague.

Ivy Cottage. Thursday, November 26th. Thanksgiving Day. A bright beautiful day, just cool enough to require a little blazing open fire. Our hostess gave a fine dinner party in our honor, at which Mr. & Mrs. Ross, the Onleys, Mr. and Mrs. Artrel and others were present. We had a very pleasant evening. Last night, Wednesday, the church people gave us a very kind surprise. We were asked to go to the church, and were then escorted to our new home, which we found brightly lighted up, & our sitting room and bedroom very comfortably furnished for us, besides a handsome writing table for F. [rank]'s study, and a kitchen table, plates, & other useful articles. We greatly appreciate this kindness, & it makes us feel that the people are really interested in us. Our little cottage consists of four rooms, with a hall through the centre,—a style I have always liked,—study and bedroom on one side, & sitting-room and kitchen on the other. Our pictures and books make the place look very homelike. We have quite a number of orange trees in our yard, one of which has borne fruit. The others are small. Over one side of the piazza is trained a pretty English ivy, and I have given our cottage its name from that. It is a cosy little home, and I think we shall enjoy it.

Sunday, November 29th. Began teaching the Sunday School today,—have a class of the large girls,—think I shall like it very much.

Frank preached an excellent sermon from the text—"Add to your faith virtue; and to virtue knowledge; and to knowledge a temperance; and to temperance patience; and to patience godliness; and to godliness brotherly kindness; and to brotherly kindness charity." There was a good attendance; and all seemed interested. After church dined with Mrs. Onley. Took tea with Mrs. W. [illiams] and then went to the A.M.E. church [5] to hear Mr. Culp preach. Received a day or two ago a letter from dear Mr. [John Greenleaf] Whittier. He says he is "sensibly nearing the end." [6] "My heavenly Father has been good to me, beyond my desert here, and I trust He will be so in the next life." He speaks touchingly of the old friends, anti-slavery and literary, who have gone before. Lloyd Wright was buried the day before he wrote. Mr. Whittier & Mr. [Robert] Purvis are now the sole survivors of those who signed the Anti-Slavery Declaration in 1833. [7] This letter is a very beautiful and characteristic one,—full of faith and hope. I earnestly hope I may have the happiness of seeing him again in this life.

Sunday, December 6. F. [rank] preached from the text (Acts 19:2). He said unto them "Have you received the Holy Ghost, since ye believe? and they said unto him, We have not as much as heard whether there be any Holy Ghost." It was an earnest, thoughtful sermon clearly explaining the function of the Holy Ghost.—Was too unwell to attend service in the evening.

Thursday, December 10.   F. [rank] made an excellent Missionary address before the Women's Miss. [ionary] Soc. [iety] of the A.M.E. church. It was organized by our friend Bishop [Daniel A.] Payne, & it was at his request that F. [rank] was asked to deliver the address at their first Quarterly meeting. The attendance was small. I told the president[,] Mrs. Day, how sincerely I could sympathize with her in her struggle to make the Society a success. It will be a joyful day when we can see the women of our colored churches really & deeply interested in mission work. I shall organize a Woman's Miss. [ionary] Soc. [iety] in our church just as soon as the holidays are over. We are busily preparing now for a Christmas Entertainment by the children of the Sabbath School.

Sunday, December 13.   F. [rank] preached today on the subject "The Nature and Mission of the Church." It is a fine sermon & gave[,] I think, general satisfaction. In the evening he gave an exposition of the 2nd Psalm, which was very interesting.

Monday, December 14.   Mr. S. [pencer] Murray called to see us to-day, & reported all well in W. [ashington, D.C.] as far as he knew,—weather very cold—city gay & brilliant. Sent by him to Mrs. Lee's care Miss Piper's album & Mr. Hill's book. On *Saturday* sent my MS. entitled "One Phase of the Race Question,"[8] to Col. [Thomas] Higginson, asking if he thought it possible that I could get it into the "N. [orth] A. [tlantic] Review," & if not whether he could try to get it in the "Congregationalist" for me, or some other Boston paper which Gail Hamilton & other orthodox people could see. Read (yesterday) a beautiful sermon on "Heaven," by Rev. Mr. Waite of Brooklyn, & F. [rank] read to me a fine sermon by Dr. Stone on "Faith in God."

Wednesday, December 16. F.[rank] read to me some extracts of speeches by Dr. Hazzard on the Education of the Negro. They are very fine. He seems to be by far the most liberal and the most Christian friend of the colored people. This evening attended prayer-meeting at our church,—a very small gathering. Mr. Onley conducted the meeting. The first chapter of Philippians was read, & and F.[rank] gave an excellent and constructive talk upon it. The meeting was an interesting one. After it the financial arrangements of the church were considered and committees appointed to attend to those and to discussing plans for a new building. A lovely moonlight night, but the air was raw, & we were glad to get back to our cheerful fire. We are having dreadfully cold nights & mornings,—heavy frost and even ice,—in the sunny South!

Saturday, December 19th. We have been married seven years today,[9]—they would have been seven happy years had it not been for that one great sorrow![10] Oh my darling, what unspeakable happiness it would be for us to have her with us to-day. She would be nearly six years old, our precious New Year's gift, & how lovely and companionable I know she would have been. But I must not mourn. Father, it was Thy will. It *must* be for the best. I must wait.

Sunday, December 20. Frank preached a very fine sermon from the text "Behold I bring unto you good tidings &c." It was on the mission of Christ, and the glorious progress that Christianity has made in the world, and the wondrous changes it has brought. In the evening he preached a good temperance sermon, as he always does just before the holidays. I earnestly hope, & believe it will do good, in preventing the social drinking,—that pernicious habit which is so fully indulged in at this season,—especially at the South.

Monday, December 21. F.[rank]'s sermon has already borne good fruit. One of the members,—a young man who says he has always indulged in egg nog at Christmas, & offered it to others, came in to say that he was much impressed by the sermon, & should have no eggnog this year. How encouraging such instances are! How it would gladden a pastor's heart if they were more frequent. I know we must not always expect *immediate* results, but when they do follow it is very gratifying.

Wednesday, December 23. Had a very small but pleasant little prayer meeting. The chapter was the 2nd of Philippians. F.[rank] made an excellent little talk upon it. The elders lead in these meetings, but F.[rank] always gives some explanation of & comment upon the chapter, which is both interesting and profitable.

Thursday, December 24. Christmas Eve. Spent most of the day helping prepare the Christmas tree and entertainment for our Sabbath School this evening. Went down town with Mrs. C.[arr] & enjoyed visiting the shops & seeing the varieties of people. Many of the country people come in today in gala attire, & all look bright and happy. We went to the market, which is really beautiful & picturesque in its decoration of green—magnolia, holly & various other kinds, & some of the stalls were adorned with great bunches of oranges with their background of leaves. The very hogs were decorated with leaves & had strings of cranberries, for beads, around their necks. Even the fish were adorned with green. The fruit stalls were beautiful. Of course there was a noisy, bustling, but good-natured crowd. This evening we had our Entertainment which passed off very pleasantly. The little ones were delighted, & when Elder Mac D. disguised as Santa Claus, appeared & distributed the presents from the

laden tree, their happiness was complete. The recitations &
singing passed off nicely. Some of the children have really
beautiful voices.

Christmas 1885. A year ago today we were in Washington. I remember we dined with Mr. Fred. [rick] Douglass
at his beautiful home upon the hill.[11] How little we thought
then that we should now be in The Land of Flowers. It is a
lovely day,—bright sunshine, air as mild as our earliest
October, at the North, & one can hardly realize that it is
Christmas when one looks at the orange trees heavy with
golden fruit which is most beautiful as it gleams through the
dark shining leaves. Spent most of the morning making
decorations for our room, with S.'s help,—at the same time
cooking a turkey which had been sent us. Our rooms look
very pretty with their decorations of holly and cedar & moss
& wreaths hung in the windows. Received some lovely
Christmas cards from friends at the North. This afternoon
went to see Miss L.,—a sick lady,—& take her some of our
Christmas cheer. On our way encountered some masquerad-
ers—negroes mounted on horses & mules,—some of them
being fantastically dressed,—masked & wearing bright yellow
& blue gowns &c. They looked very ridiculous, and were
beating & furiously urging on their poor steeds in a way that
made us indignant. There seems to be a good deal of drinking
and wild revelling here at Christmas. How sad it is that the
day should be so desecrated. In the evening F. [rank] went
to the Sabbath School Entertainment at the Baptist Church,
but as I was very tired, remained at home and refreshed
myself by reading the Christmas number of the "Independent,"—a charming number.

Sunday, December 27. F. [rank] preached a fine sermon
from the text "We shall all stand before the judgment seat of

Christ." Dined at Mrs. Onley's & looked over plans for the new church which they propose building at once. This evening F.[rank] preached from the text "Master what shall I do to inherit eternal life," a beautiful & interesting sermon, but there were so few out & they seemed so unresponsive that I think F.[rank] felt somewhat discouraged. I tried to cheer him. The people here have been so long without a pastor that they do not quite understand how to show their appreciation. But I believe they *do* appreciate F.[rank] & after awhile they will show more enthusiasm. They surely cannot be unawakened by his earnest preaching. Doubtless small numbers have rather a chilling effect; and when we have a more attractive place of worship we shall have a larger attendance, & more enthusiasm will be manifested.

Monday, December 28. Bishop [Daniel A.] Payne dined with us. It is a great pleasure to have him; he is so thoroughly interested in literature & all that is improving. What a grand example to the rising generation,—if they would only follow it.

Tuesday, December 29. Spent the evening quite pleasantly at Mrs. Menard's. Saw a good many young people. Talked with Bishop P.[ayne] about forming a Literary Society here. I hope we shall be able to do so, & interest the young people in something higher than dancing & other frivolous amusements.

Wednesday, December 30. After the prayer-meeting, had a congregational meeting at which new Trustees were elected, and Building Committee appointed, who will go to work at once. Heard from Dr. Parsons.

Thursday, December 31. The last day of the Old Year. Spent the evening quietly at home. F.[rank] read the "Independent" to me, & I read to him, Tennyson's "Death of the Old Year," & "Ring out Wild Bells," & so we sat until the bells rang, & ushered in the New Year.—

> "There's a new face at the door, my friend,
> A new face at the door!"

New Year's Day 1886. The first day of the New Year is bright and beautiful, & as warm as one of our loveliest May-days. This is the time for good resolutions. I have made some but shall record only one,—lest I fail,—to read some French & German every day: if only a small quantity. Other far more important resolutions I trust that God will enable me to keep.—Dined with a family opposite, & afterward went out for a time to see some colored guards, who looked quite fine; had good music, & listened to sensible and improving addresses from some of the ministers & others.

In the evening Frank read to me some extremely interesting extracts from Mr. Crafts' "Temperance Century," showing what had been accomplished in the good cause during the past century & also containing many valuable suggestions for work in the present.

Sunday, January 3. F.[rank] preached from the text "Lord what will thou have me to do,"—one of his very best sermons,—and he closed with a clear & earnest statement of the work which lies before us[,] a church during the present year.

Mr. Waters dined with us and told us many interesting facts about his work here. At night Frank gave an excellent and interesting exposition of the 3rd Psalm.

Wednesday, January 6. Bishop Payne took us to East Jack.[sonville] to see a wonderfully sweet and energetic woman, who has a fine vegetable garden which she cultivates herself, with the help of her two children, and makes money enough from it to supply her family with groceries. The garden is beautifully kept, and it was very surprising to us to see peas four feet high, & lettuces almost headed, strawberries in blossom, and violets and narcissus in bloom. There were quantities of other vegetables. Mrs. J. was once a slave. I am going out alone some day to have her tell me her story, which, the Bishop says[,] is very interesting. Had a teachers' meeting this evening before the prayer meeting,—a business meeting. We hope to begin our meetings for the study of the lesson next week. Had a very interesting prayer meeting. The chapter considered was the 3rd of Philippians.

Thursday, January 7. Some of the ladies met at our house to make arrangements for a Fair, which we hope to hold next winter, for the purpose of helping to raise money for the new church building which is to be begun very soon. F.[rank] read to me this evening some extremely interesting passages from Mr. Crafts' "Temperance Century."

Friday, January 8. Went with Mrs. Sherman to call on Mrs. Susan and her husband who are here from Michigan for their health. He is a very successful gardener in Bay City. She is a bright pleasant person. Did not see him. To-night a terribly cold wind came up. It promises to be very cold tomorrow. Can scarcely realize that this is Florida.

Sunday, January 10. We are indulging in the coldest weather that they have had here for years, if ever before. The Land of Flowers has become the land of ice. It is almost impossible to keep warm, in these summer houses. We lay awake last night, suffering from the cold; with *five* blankets on the bed & two spreads! Charming for the "sunny South!" The church was cold; but F.[rank] preached a fine and stimulating sermon, from the text—"Simon, son of Jonas, hearest thou Me?" There was a mere handful out to-night, to listen to his admirable Exposition of the 4th Psalm. The people here are very much afraid of the cold, being so unused to it.

Wednesday, January 13.   The intense cold still continues. People are suffering, and to crown our miseries the supply of wood in the city has given out! Oh[,] the shiftlessness of Southern people! We are obliged to economize with our fires as much as possible. Went to Mrs. O.[nley]'s and helped with some things for the Fair. A *very* small attendance at the prayer meeting tonight, & the church was very cold. Nevertheless we had a good meeting. F.[rank] explained in a very interesting manner the 4th chapter of Philippians.

Sunday, January 17.   Was too unwell to attend church to day.

Wednesday, January 20.   Went with a party in the cars to Bruce City (named for the ex-senator)[12] which is ten miles beyond Palatka. Some enterprising young newspaper men got it up free to induce persons to go out & buy lots. The city exists only on paper however. We got out of the cars in the midst of the pine woods,—no sign of human habitation near. However, the lots were indicated, & I believe quite a number were sold. The place is high & being in the midst of the pines ought to be healthy. A flourishing city may exist there some day,—in the distant future. We enjoyed the place for the day was lovely, like June, almost[,] & we sat a long time on some logs under the pines, drinking in the delightful air. The ride was very pleasant too, with frequent glimpses of the beautiful river whose shores were fringed with the live oaks hung with its lacy silver-gray moss. We passed plantations of orange trees but, alas, the severe cold has blighted them all, & they look very pitiful with their dried, shrunken leaves & ruined fruit. Passed through Palatka which has a pleasant look, more tropical than Jacksonville. Did not get home till nearly 8 o'clock.

Sunday, January 24. F.[rank] preached a fine sermon from the text "If any one would be my disciple, let him deny himself & take up his cross and follow me." In the evening the weather was very bad & Bishop Andrews preached at the A.M.E. Church, for which reasons our attendance was very small & we had only a little prayer-meeting.

Have received some copies of the "Boston Commonwealth," containing my article in reply to Gail Hamilton on "Race Prejudice." I hope she will see it, but as I do not know her address, cannot send it to her.

Wednesday, January 27. Frank left this afternoon for Tuskegee, Ala.[bama] where he has been invited to address the students of the Normal School,[13] & also to preach on Sunday. I am glad to have him visit the school, of which we hear the highest praise. It is entirely under *colored* management [Booker T. Washington]. But oh, how lonely I feel. How very, very much I miss him. Our prayer-meeting this evening was very small. I wish all the members would attend, and cannot understand why they do not. The meetings are always interesting and helpful.

Thursday, January 28. Spent the evening entirely alone, reading the "Independent,"—an exceedingly interesting number,—as usual.

Tuesday, February 2. Frank returned to-day, well, and much pleased with his visit to Tuskegee. Found the school very flourishing, and the teachers excellent in every way. It is delightful to have him home again.

Arbor Day. February. Attended the exercises at the Stanton School[14] which consisted of Recitations, singing, addresses, and finally planting trees in the school-yard, which were named for various distinguished persons—Mr. Douglass, Gov. Perry and others. It was quite an interesting occasion. We were much pleased with the appearance and exercises of the children. Prof. Artrell is Principal of this school. All the teachers are colored.

March. Held our Fair. Cleared nearly $200.

April———— Went to Green Cove Springs. Have seen nothing lovelier than St. David's Walk, the path leading from Green Cove to Magnolia. It is through lovely woods in which there are immense water-oaks, whose leaves of vivid hues contrast most beautifully with the gray hanging moss with which they are draped; great magnolia trees, whose dark shining foliage forms a lovely contrast with the great snowy blossoms; then the Judas vine with its brilliant trumpet like flowers canopied some of the trees. Everywhere there were lovely glimpses of the river through the trees and the innumerable vines, which formed a succession of lovely leafy bowers. The Cove has Sulphur Springs and baths, and we saw one charming cottage literally embowered in roses. The hedge was formed of the exquisite Cherokee rose, with its pure white blossome & leaves of the most delicious green. We had a delightful day. Mrs. Dichusen and her husband were with us. Mrs. D. [ichusen] has been especially kind to me. How much we shall miss them both when they go,—which will be soon.

Also in April, lovely drives through the woods,—mostly pines to Mrs. M. G.'s place.—A visit to Arlington, where we got quantities of magnolias, and oleanders from a tree growing wild on the river bank, and heavily laden with flowers of the richest rose color. In some places the ground is carpeted with a species of phlox which grows wild here,

& is of many exquisite hues. There are lovely views of the river at Arlington, too. It is a delightful place.

May— Our Sunday School Picnic was at Brooklyn, a pleasant place on the water but a bad headache prevented me from enjoying it. The children had a fine time.

June———— Went early in the morning to Pablo Beach, a very wide and fine one, & I enjoyed the sight of the sea again, while the others bathed. But there are no rocks, not a single bit of shade, and the sun soon drove me into the Pavilion, where I was obliged to remain until it was time to return home. It was interesting to watch the people when the trains brought down,—nearly all colored people of the better class. They enjoyed themselves quietly and decorously. And oh for a day at Nahant or Newport! Just to sit on those grand rocks, completely shaded, & watch the waves as they rush in, and break at one's feet! What happiness it would be!

I neglected my journal for many weeks because I was so so ill that I could not write. I am better now, and hope to be more faithful.

Monday, July 5th. The "glorious" Fourth was celebrated to-day, not so much in the city as by immense excursions to the beaches & other places. We have passed the day at home quietly. It has been *intensely* hot. Fortunately we have cool breezes nearly every evening. Otherwise we should hardly be able to bear the heat. F. [rank] has read to me this spring "Letters from Hile" a very striking book, translated from the Danish. Of course it is intensely painful. We are now reading a "Life of Locke" which is very interesting & tells us that he was a delightful, genial man as well as a great philosopher. How pleasant is the record of his life at the Mashams. Such a friendship that is as beautiful as it is rare.

Wednesday, July 7. Had an important meeting, preparatory to communion, to-night. There were very few there,—many of our little band are out of town, but we had an earnest interesting meeting. F. [rank] spoke impressively and beautifully of the preparation needed before partaking of the Lord's Supper. We walked home in the soft, lovely moonlight. These Florida summer nights are certaintly very beautiful. The days are too warm, & I dare not venture out in the sun. It has burned up most of the flowers. The exquisite crape myrtle, and a very beautiful pink lily are among the last. I wish I could paint the latter so that my northern friends c'ld have some idea of its loveliness. It is too frail to send away.

Our new church has been begun, and is progressing satisfactorily. Think it will be very pretty and convenient.

St. Augustine. Friday, August 27. Arrived here this evening. For many weeks I have been ill,—a weary & most trying, illness,—& am almost worn out. Hope the pure sea breezes of the old town will give me health and strength. The few glimpses that I caught of it as we drove from the station, showed one it was very quaint and interesting. Was most kindly received by Mr. & Mrs. R. in their pleasant home & think I shall be happy, although I miss F. [rank] sadly. But he will join me in a few days.

Thursday, September 2. F. [rank] came to-day, to my great joy. Have been too unwell to do any walking, but have enjoyed the pure sea air, & hope to be better soon.

Sunday, September 26. Attended Miss Mathew's Sabbath School which is held in a chapel built by her efforts. It is doing good work among the young people of both sexes.— Have written a sketch of this quaint old town, which I hope may one day be printed.

Jacksonville, Christmas 1886.   Dined with Mr. and Mrs. J. E. Onley, and afterwards took a walk with them to Oaklands. The air was as soft as May, but the country was not particularly interesting.

Washington, May 1887.   Came here very unexpectedly on an Excursion. It is most beautiful. The trees and the parks are *ravishingly* green. It seems as if we could never see enough of them. We had a warm reception & are delighted to see so many old friends. I am grieved that Frank must return so soon. My health is so poor that I am to remain North for the summer.

Newport, July 1887.   Beautiful, beautiful Newport! In spite of illness I enjoy being here, & never weary of the sea & the rocks. Mrs. D.[owning][15] is most kind & does everything to make me happy. If my dear, dear F.[rank] were only here to share the happiness with me.

Jacksonville, October 1887.   Back again in my home with my dearest F.[rank]. How glad I am to see him again & to find him well. I hope we shall not be separated again.

I regret having been able to write only at long intervals in my journal. My head and eyes are so bad that I cannot use them much of the time. I see I have made no mention of our new church. We have such a pleasant one. It was finished last winter, almost entirely through F.[rank]'s exertions, and was dedicated in January. Fortunately Dr. John Hall was here and preached a most beautiful & simple & impressive dedication sermon for us. The exercises were all very interesting and we raised more than $40 towards paying for the church.

December 17, 1887.   The 80th birthday of Whittier. The children of the colored public school[16] sent him a box of oranges & a cane of orange-wood. (He acknowledged these with much pleasure & wrote me that he had received more than 1000 callers & messages on his birthday. He was particularly gratified at receiving so many tokens from colored people. I am so glad of that!)

Christmas, 1887.   A lovely Christmas Day. Our dear friends the G.'s, whom we are soon about to lose, had their dear little baby christened at church. Afterwards we dined with them,—a lovely mild day.

December 26.   Had our Christmas tree for the Sabbath School children to-night. What a happy time the little ones had,—and the older ones, too. It adds greatly to our pleasure to have our dear friend, Mrs. D.[owning,] from Newport with us this year.

March 1888.   Held a nice Fair for our church, & cleared about $175. Our debt is nearly paid now. We have had an ideal Florida winter,—air soft & delightful, flowers blooming,—have sat with doors & windows open part of the time. Meanwhile we hear of dreadful storms & blizzards at the North. Our little church prospering.

April 1888.   Unusual heat, and with it much physical suffering for me.—Mosquitoes & fleas already dreadful. If one could only spend six months here, & the remainder of the year at the North! Sometimes I become dismayed at my almost continuous ill health. It unfits me for work,—and there is so much to be done here. But I must not murmur.

> "All as God wills, who wisely heeds
>   to give or to withhold,
> And knoweth more of all my needs
>   Than all my prayers have told!"

Phila.[delphia]. Wednesday, May 14.   Very unexpectedly we find ourselves in the city of Brotherly Love. Through the

urgent invitation of Rev. Mr. A. [llen?], we suddenly decided,—not before last Saturday, to leave J. [acksonville],—
F. [rank] to attend the Centennial of the Pres. [byterian]
General Assembly in this city, and I to seek health in another
summer at the North. I spent last night in W. [orcester] with
the Lees, & saw many old friends & came here this evening.
Am very pleasantly situated with Rev. Mr. A. [llen?] just
opposite Girard College, whose beautiful grounds are green,
& shaded & most refreshing to look upon. Enjoy much the
society of bright, interesting Dr. [Caroline Still Wiley]
A. [nderson?] [17] & her kind husband, also Dr. H. another
bright lady graduate of the Woman's Medical College, who
is going to train nurses in connection with Rust University,
Miss. [issippi].

Later. There are staying here quite a number of young
colored ministers from the South. Some of them are very
bright & intelligent. The great question which comes up
before the Gen. Assembly this year is the union of the
Northern churches. During some of the meetings which I
have been able to attend, the subject has been discussed, & I
must confess I have been quite disgusted with the *cringing*
spirit manifested by the Northern churches. They are so
anxious for union that they are willing to purchase it at any
sacrifice of their colored brethren which will gratify the
prejudices of the South. The latter, however, are in no such
hurry, & both sides have decided to wait until another year.
But our Gen. Assembly has plainly showed its spirit toward
the colored brother, & that spirit is not a Christian one.
Frank wrote a fine letter on the subject for the N.Y. "Evangelist," and many have spoken of it very highly. I think it
has had its influence in the matter.

Thursday, June 21. I took a heavy cold from the change

of climate; the weather here in May being cold & rainy,—
& I have been confined to my room for weeks. Am only now
convalescent, & feel as if I could hardly bear the great sorrow
of parting from my dear F.[rank] who has left today, on his
way to Florida. It is very, very hard. But I am unable to go
with him. I can only pray that God may keep him safe and
well in the midst of all the heat and unhealthiness.

Kenneth Square. Saturday, June 30. Came down to this
quiet country place to-day, hoping to gain strength.

Monday, July 2. Had no letter from my dearest F.[rank]
to-day. I suppose he has reached J.[acksonville] to-day. My
heart is with him. I think I shall like this place very well. It
is cool & green & quiet, & the air delightfully pure; the
landlady exceedingly kind, & everything nice & comfortable.
It is, however, very lonely, as I can't use my eyes much.
Read in Psalms in a little book of selections for every day
from the Bible & from Whittier, & a little of the "Life of
Agassiz." Took a short walk.—the country around is very
pretty & hilly. If only I had F.[rank] to enjoy it with me.

Thursday, July 5. Heard from F.[rank]. He had reached
home safely. I suppose he is well, as he seems to have done
some vigorous housecleaning immediately upon his arrival.
Oh, how very, very much I miss him. Read a little of the
"Life of Bishop Huntington[,]" a most lovable and noble
character.

Friday, July 6. Dr. Lord's "Great Women" opens with
"Cleopatra," a very interesting sketch. He has taken great
pains to inform us that she had no *Negro* blood & that Story
has made a mistake in giving to his statue the African features.
If I may venture to criticise,—there seems to me a little too
much repetition in these lectures of Dr. Lord's.—Doubtless

it was less perceptible in listening to than in reading them. Still they are very interesting & entertaining. He has chosen his subjects most happily.

Sunday, July 8. A lovely day. I was not able to walk to church. Read some Psalms, & thought of my dear F.[rank] and wished I could be listening to his earnest, helpful words. May God bless & strengthen him, and keep him safe & well! Took a short walk in the quiet lanes.

Thursday, July 12. Had a most kind letter & his picture from dear F.[rank]—the one he had taken in Phila.[delphia]. It is fine,—the best he has ever had. But oh the sight of it makes me long more than ever for him.

Friday, July 13. A letter from Annie [Woods Webb], bringing the sad news that Mrs. W.[ebb] has lost her only son. He was drowned while bathing on the Fourth of July. I am deeply grieved for her. It is a terrible shock to her. Only the dear Father, who never chastens in vain, can give her help & strength in such an hour. It is not very long since she lost her husband.

Sunday, July 15. A bright beautiful day, but I am not well. Read with great interest in the "Christian Register" the Memorial Services to Ja[me]s. Freeman Clarke. He will be greatly missed. The poem which he wrote on his 78th birthday, not long before his death, is very beautiful. Wrote to dear F.[rank].

Monday, July 16. Received a delightful letter from dear F.[rank], and several copies of the "Independent." It is so pleasant to see it again.

Wednesday, July 19. Another letter from F.[rank]. Says they had such a lovely Sabbath, and pleasant communion service. I wish I could have been with them. Read in the

"Independent" a sketch of Mrs. Browning by R. R. Stoddard which is very delightful. He ranks her as "the greatest of female poets," and bestows warm praise upon her prose, too. Wish I could see the volumes of her letters, edited by R. H. Horne. They must be very charming.

Phila.[delphia]. Saturday, July 21. Left Kenneth [Square] late this afternoon & had a charming ride through the green & pleasant country. Received a warm welcome from the J.'s. Found two letters from dear F. [rank] awaiting me,—the best welcome of all.

Sunday, July 22. Heard an excellent sermon from Dr. Reeve from the text—"Let no man think more highly of himself than he deserves."

Monday, July 23. Had so severe an attack of coughing this morning that I decided to see Dr. Kyser. He examined my heart & lungs, & said he could find no organic disease,— only weakness. He prescribed for me. He was just as kind & cordial as ever. Of all my numerous physicians I like him best,—except, of course, my dear Dr. Parsons.

Newport, July 24 Beautiful, delightful Newport again! Left Phila.[delphia] this morning for New York, and came on by the Shore Line. Had a lovely ride from N.Y. to Newport.—The alternating hills and woods & frequent glimpses of the Sound were charming, & the woods were rich in ferns & lighted up by flowers—wild roses, azaleas, while water lilies, daisies, pansy, red lilies, golden caneopis &c. made the roadside more a "Land of Flowers" than our part of Florida. Found a letter from F. [rank].

Thursday, July 25. Mrs. D. [owning] & I went down to the rocks. Oh how delightful it was to see Old Ocean again; to feel that deep thrill which the sea only can give. There is an unspeakable fascination about it to me—

"Age cannot wither *it*, nor custom stale.
Its infinite variety."

As usual the Avenue was filled with fine carriages whose languid & bored looking occupants were less interesting to me than the beautiful horses which drew them.

Received a letter from dear F. [rank] he still keeps well & says the weather is unusually pleasant. But some of our friends are ill. May God protect him, & keep him in health & strength! Had a call from dear Mrs. Bell.

Saturday, July 28.   Went to the beach with little M. & sat a long time, alternately reading & watching the bathers. Although the day was cool & cloudy, there was quite a number of them, & the scene was, as usual, a very lively one. Called at the Downings & found Ada Hinton[18] there. Had a letter from Bishop Payne yesterday. He is coming to Newport next month.

August 1888.   Dear F. [rank] is with us. The yellow fever is in J. [acksonville]. And he was urged to leave immediately. Most of our church people are out of town, and the authorities are anxious to have every one come away who is not acclimated.

January 1889. Jacksonville.   Back again in Florida. How sad and dreary it seems after that dreadful fever! Many who left the city have not returned. There have been many deaths. We shall remain but a short time, as Frank has accepted the urgent invitation of the church in Washington[D.C.][19] to return to them again. I shall be sorry to leave Fl[orid]a. for some reasons. It is a good field for missionary work, and we are much attached to the people and to our little church; but it is very unhealthy,—for me, at least,—half the year, and it is not so wide a scope for Frank's talents as he ought to have. So I am willing to return to Washington again.

March 1889. Back in Washington. Mrs. [Fannie S.] Smyth[20] has kindly taken us in until we can find a permanent home, and we are in all the excitement and confusion of the Inauguration. This is the great day, but I, not being well, dare not venture out, as it is very stormy. It is said to be one of the most crowded and enthusiastic Inaugurations that we have ever had. I hope [Benjamin] Harrison[21] will fulfill all the great expectations which the country has of him.

Ler, Mass.[achusetts],[22] *July 1892.* The last three years have been full of work and of changes, but, on the whole, happy ones. The greatest drawback has been constant ill health, which seemed to culminate this summer, and I was obliged to leave W.[ashington] with its intense heat, sewer gas, and malaria, before it was time for Frank to leave. I am so sorry to leave him, but hope he will join me next week.

NOTES

INTRODUCTION

1. Charlotte Forten Grimké (1837–1914) completed five journals that together make up this volume. The dates and locations of each journal are as follows: Journal One, 1854–1856, Salem, Massachusetts; Journal Two, 1857–1858, Salem and Philadelphia, Pennsylvania; Journal Three, 1858–1863, Salem, Philadelphia, Boston, Massachusetts, and St. Helena Island, South Carolina; Journal Four, 1863–1864, St. Helena Island, Philadelphia, and Salem; Journal Five, 1885–1892, Jacksonville, Florida, Washington, D.C., Philadelphia, and Ler, Massachusetts. Journal citations are given in these notes by reference to journal number and journal entry date. The manuscript copies of Grimké's journals are located in the Moorland-Spingarn Research Center, Howard University, Washington, D.C.

2. Gloria C. Oden, *"The Journal of Charlotte L. Forten:* The Salem-Philadelphia Years (1851–1862) Reexamined," *Essex Institute Historical Collections* 119 (1983): 121; Rayford W. Logan and Michael R. Winston, eds., *Dictionary of American Negro Biography* (New York, 1982), 233–234 (cited hereafter as *DANB*).

3. William C. Nell, *The Colored Patriots of the American Revolution* (1855; New York, 1968), 168–173; *DANB*, 234.

4. As late as 1838 and 1849, occupational census records document that the large majority of blacks employed in Philadelphia were unskilled laborers if they were male, and washerwomen if female. Philip S. Foner and Ronald L. Lewis, eds., *The Black Worker: A Documentary History from Colonial Times to the Present. Vol. 1. The Black Worker to 1869* (Philadelphia, 1978), 117–124; Nell, *Colored Patriots*, 173–175; *DANB*, 234.

5. The Fugitive Slave Law of 1793 allowed slave owners to

seize their runaway slaves in any location in the United States, slave or free, and upon documentation of ownership to a federal or state magistrate, could return the fugitive to his former residence and status. Moreover, this law stipulated that it was a criminal act for anyone to knowingly harbor fugitive slaves or to aid their evasion of arrest. John Hope Franklin, *From Slavery to Freedom: A History of Negro Americans*, 3rd ed. (New York, 1967), 151–152; Peter M. Bergman and Mort N. Bergman, *The Chronological History of the Negro in America* (New York, 1969), 73.

6. Bergman and Bergman, *Chronological History of the Negro*, 83.

7. Howard Holman Bell, *A Survey of the Negro Convention Movement, 1830–1861* (New York, 1969), 10–37; Nell, *Colored Patriots*, 177–178; *DANB*, 235; Franklin, *From Slavery to Freedom*, 237–241.

8. Bell, *Negro Convention Movement*, 43–53; Nell, *Colored Patriots*, 178–179; *DANB*, 235.

9. Oden, *"Journal of Charlotte L. Forten . . .* Reexamined," 122.

10. Dorothy Sterling, ed., *We Are Your Sisters: Black Women in the Nineteenth Century* (New York, 1984), 119–120; "To the Daughters of James Forten," Francis Grimké Papers, Moorland-Spingarn Research Center.

11. Mary Virginia Woods, Charlotte's mother, was not married to Robert Bridges Forten in 1833, the year of the formation of the Philadelphia Female Anti-Slavery Society. They were married in 1836. For an informative account of the lives of Charlotte Forten's parents, see Janice Sumler Lewis, "The Fortens of Philadelphia: An Afro-American Family and Nineteenth Century Reform," Ph.D. Dissertation, Georgetown University (1979), 14–128, *passim;* Sterling, *We Are Your Sisters*, 119–120.

12. Lewis, "Fortens of Philadelphia," 43–44, 61; Sterling, *We Are Your Sisters*, 114, 120–121.

13. Sterling, *We Are Your Sisters*, 121.

14. Sterling, *We Are Your Sisters*, 114.

15. William Wells Brown, *The Black Man: His Antecedents, His Genius, and His Achievements* (1863; New York, 1969), 253–259; R. C. Smedley, *History of the Underground Railroad in Chester and the Neighboring Counties of Pennsylvania* (1883; New York, 1968), 353–354; *DANB*, 508–509.

16. Smedley, *Underground Railroad*, 354–356; *DANB*, 509.

17. *DANB*, 509.

18. Lewis, "Fortens of Philadelphia," 14–128, *passim; DANB*, 509; Bergman and Bergman, *Chronological History of the Negro*, 164.

19. Lewis, "Fortens of Philadelphia," 24–128, *passim*.

20. Journal One, June 10, 1854; Oden, *"Journal of Charlotte L. Forten* . . . Reexamined," 121–122.

21. Journal One, June 10, 1854.

22. On Wednesday, May 24, 1854, U.S. Commissioner Edward G. Loring issued a warrant for the arrest of an alleged fugitive slave, Anthony Burns, who was at that time residing in Boston, Massachusetts. Burns had escaped from his owner, Charles F. Suttle, a merchant of Alexandria, Virginia, on March 26, 1854. His trial attracted abolitionists from all over the Northeast. The court proceedings, which consisted of summations on behalf of the defense and the plaintiff by their counsel rather than a trial by jury, continued after two postponements from Monday, May 29, until the evening of May 31, 1854. The decision of the court was in favor of the plaintiff, Charles F. Suttle. In 1855, Burns was purchased and freed for $1300 by the Reverend Leonard A. Grimes of Boston and his parishioners. Burns later lectured on the antislavery circuit and studied theology at Oberlin and Fairmont Theological Seminary in Cincinnati. Burns, an ordained Baptist minister, died in Canada in 1862 at the age of 28. *Liberator*, June 2, 1854; *National Anti-Slavery Standard*, June 3, 1854; *DANB*, 80–81.

23. Journal One, June 10, 1854.

24. Lewis, "Fortens of Philadelphia," 14–128, *passim*.

25. Oden, *"Journal of Charlotte L. Forten* . . . Reexamined," 121.

26. Journal Three, April 15, 1858.

27. Journal Two, July 17, 1857.

28. Journal Two, February 28, 1857.

29. Journal One, July 26, 1854.

30. Journal One, September 3, 1854; Journal Two, February 14, 1857, April 12, 1857.

31. Journal One, October 23, 1854.

32. Oden, *"Journal of Charlotte L. Forten . . . Reexamined,"* 125–126.

33. Brown, *The Black Man*, 246–247; *DANB*, 520–521.

34. Journal Two, March 6, 1857; *DANB*, 522–523.

35. Oden, *"Journal of Charlotte L. Forten . . . Reexamined,"* 124–134.

36. Journal One, August 15, 1856.

37. Journal One, September 1, 1856.

38. Journal Two, January 18, 1857.

39. Journal Two, April 5, 1857.

40. Journal Two, March 20, 1857.

41. Journal Two, June 17, 1857.

42. *National Anti-Slavery Standard*, June 18, 1858.

43. *Liberator*, March 16, 1855.

44. Journal One, March 28, 1855.

45. *Liberator*, August 24, 1856.

46. Journal Two, January 5, 1857.

47. Journal Two, January 6, 1857.

48. Journal Two, January 7, 1857.

49. Journal Two, January 8, 1857.

50. Journal Two, January 9, 1857.

51. *Liberator*, August 24, 1856.

52. Journal One, July 1855; Journal Two, February 5, 1857, April 27, 1857, September 4, 1857; *Liberator*, August 24, 1856.

53. Journal One, July 1855.

54. Journal Two, September 4, 1857.

55. Journal Three, June 15, 1858. See also Journal Two, February 5, 1857, August 17, 1857.

56. Journal One, September 27, 1854, October 23, 1854, March 16, 1855, March 28, 1855, February 21, 1856; Journal Two, January 15, 1857, May 4, 1857, July 23, 1857, August 21, 1857, December 17, 1857.

57. Journal One, September 3, 1854.

58. Journal Two, August 21, 1857.

59. Journal One, February 21, 1856.

60. Journal Two, May 4, 1857.

61. Journal Two, December 17, 1857.

62. Charlotte Forten does not mention in her journals that she saw her father after he left the country in the fall of 1855. Mr. Forten returned to the United States from England in 1862. Charlotte may have seen him during a trip to Philadelphia in 1863, but she doesn't mention doing so in her journal.

63. Journal Two, April 12, 1857, July 16, 1857; Journal Three, June 18, 1858.

64. Brown, *The Black Man*, 196–199.

65. Journal One, May 1, 1855.

66. Journal One, June 4, 1854.

67. Journal One, September 12, 1855.

68. Journal One, May 26, 1854.

69. Journal One, May 27, 1854.

70. Journal Two, June 4, 1857.

71. John B. Pickard, ed., *The Letters of John Greenleaf Whittier, Vol. 3, 1861–1892* (Cambridge, 1975), 97.

72. *Salem Register*, July 24, 1856.

73. Journal Three, June 22, 1862.

74. Journal Three, August 9, 1862.

75. Journal Three, April 11, 1858.

76. Journal Four, July 23, 1863.

77. Journal One, May 25, 1855, August 18, 1856; Journal Two, September 1, 1857; January 3, 1858; Journal Three, June 22, 1862; Oden, *"Journal of Charlotte L. Forten . . .* Reexamined," 121.

78. Journal Two, June 7, 1857.

79. Journal Two, June 9, 1857.

80. Journal Two, June 12, 1857 to July 28, 1857.

81. Reprinted in the *Liberator*, March 26, 1858.

82. Journal Three, March 3, 1858.

83. Journal Three, May 20, 1858.

84. *National Anti-Slavery Standard*, June 18, 1858.

85. *Liberator*, May 27, 1859; *National Anti-Slavery Standard*, January 15, 1859.

86. *National Anti-Slavery Standard*, January 14, 1860.

87. Journal Three, June 18, 1858.

88. Journal Two, April 19, 1857.

89. Journal Three, June 22, 1862.

90. Journal Three, August 9, 1862.

91. Willie Lee Rose, *Rehearsal for Reconstruction: The Port Royal Experiment* (1964; New York, 1967), xiii–xvi, 17–31; Henry Lee Swint, *The Northern Teacher in the South, 1862–1870* (Nashville, 1941), 3–22, 77–93, *passim*; New England Freedmen's Aid Society, *Annual Report, 1862–1863* (Boston, 1864), 4.

92. Journal Three, August 13, 1862 to October 22, 1862.

93. Journal Three, August 17, 1862.

94. Journal Three, November 30, 1862; and "Life on the Sea Islands," draft in the Francis Grimké Papers, Moorland-Spingarn Research Center, Howard University.

95. Journal Three, November 7, 1862, November 18, 1862.

96. William Vaughan, *Schools for All: The Blacks and Public Education in the South, 1865–1877* (Lexington, 1974), 28; James McPherson, *Abolitionist Legacy: From Reconstruction to the NAACP* (Princeton, N.J., 1975), 162–198.

97. Journal Three, October 29, 1862, November 7, 1862, November 23, 1862.

98. Journal Three, November 23, 1862.

99. Rose, *Rehearsal for Reconstruction*, 159–160.

100. Journal Three, November 27, 1862.

101. Thomas Wentworth Higginson, *Army Life in a Black Regiment* (Boston, 1870), 1–3.

102. Journal Four, March 2, 1863.

103. Higginson, *Army Life in a Black Regiment*, 1–5; Journal Four, February 19, 1863, March 2, 1863, March 26, 1863.

104. Journal Three, October 31, 1862; Swint, *Northern Teacher in the South*, 44–45.

105. Journal Three, October 27, 1862.

106. Swint, *Northern Teacher in the South*, 90, 161, 194; Journal Three, October 28, 1862, November 22, 1862; Journal Four, March 24, 1863, March 30, 1863, May 18, 1863.

107. Rose, *Rehearsal for Reconstruction*, 248–250.

108. Journal Four, July 2, 1863, July 6, 1863.

109. Journal Four, July 20, 1863; Rose, *Rehearsal for Reconstruction*, 252–260.

110. Photographs of Charlotte Forten Grimké, Francis Grimké Collection, Moorland-Spingarn Research Center, Howard University; Sterling, *We Are Your Sisters*, 285.

111. Journal Three, November 30, 1862, January 31, 1863; *DANB*, 606–607.

112. Journal Three, November 15, 1858.

113. Journal Three, June 22, 1862, December 2, 1862, December 9, 1862, December 12, 1862, December 26, 1862.

114. Journal Three, December 26, 1862.

115. Journal Three, June 22, 1862.

116. Journal Three, July 6, 1862.

117. Journal Three, August 23, 1862, August 30, 1862.

118. Journal Three, January 1, 1863.

119. Journal Three, January 1, 1863, January 7, 1863, January 26, 1863, February 8, 1863, February 9, 1863, Journal Four, February 19, 1863, February 22, 1863, March 2, 1863, April 11, 1863, July 25, 1863.

120. Journal Three, January 7, 1863, January 26, 1863; Journal Four, February 19, 1863, March 2, 1863, April 3, 1863.

121. Journal Three, February 8, 1863.

122. Journal Three, December 26, 1862, February 8, 1863; Journal Four, February 19, 1863.

123. Journal Three, January 1, 1863, February 8, 1863; Journal Four, February 19, 1863, July 5, 1863.

124. Journal Three, January 1, 1863.

125. Journal Four, February 19, 1863.

126. Journal Four, March 2, 1863.

127. Journal Three, February 8, 1863; Journal Four, March 2, 1863.

128. Journal Four, July 31, 1863, September 23, 1863, October 16, 1863; Higginson, *Army Life in a Black Regiment*, 269.

129. *Liberator*, December 12, 1862; *Liberator*, December 19, 1862; *Atlantic Monthly*, May 1864; *Atlantic Monthly*, June 1864.

130. Lewis, "Fortens of Philadelphia," 126–128.

131. Pickard, *Letters of John Greenleaf Whittier, Vol. 3*, 97, 98, nn. 1, 4. Whittier wrote to Theodore Dwight Weld concerning Charlotte Forten's desire to seek a place at Lewis's establishment, asking Weld if he could arrange a "reduced" price for her. Pickard quotes a letter of Whittier's dated September 13, 1865, in which Whittier mentions Forten's request and notes that she did not go to the sanatorium because all concerned thought it unwise. He did not give a reason for this decision, but only wrote, "To take her at all would I fear be hazardous to his enterprise, and I am sure Charlotte would not wish to run the risk of that"; Sterling, *We Are Your Sisters*, 284.

132. Emile Erckmann and Alexandre Chatrain, *Madame Thérèse; or, The Volunteers of '92*, Charlotte Forten, trans. (Boston, 1869).

133. Sterling, *We Are Your Sisters*, 284–285.

134. Sterling, *We Are Your Sisters*, 238.

135. Sterling, *We Are Your Sisters*, 283.

136. Pickard, *Letters of John Greenleaf Whittier, Vol. 3*, 233.

137. Sterling, *We Are Your Sisters*, 283.

138. *New National Ear*, July 3, 1873.

139. *DANB*, 507.

140. Pickard, *Letters of John Greenleaf Whittier, Vol. 3*, 278.

141. Sterling, *We Are Your Sisters*, 285–286.

142. *DANB*, 273–274.

143. *DANB*, 272.

144. *DANB*, 274.

145. *DANB*, 274–275.

146. Anna Julia Cooper, "Reminiscences," Francis Grimké Papers, Moorland-Spingarn Research Center, Howard University.

147. Copies of Charlotte Forten Grimké's writings from this period are all part of the Francis Grimké Papers, Moorland-Spingarn Research Center, Howard University.

148. *DANB*, 272–273; correspondence of Charlotte Forten Grimké to Angelina Weld Grimké dated September 23, 1899, January 23, 1903, May 7, 1911, June 4, 1911, July 18, 1911, August 4, 1911, August 25, 1911, Francis Grimké Papers, Moorland-Spingarn Research Center, Howard University.

149. "Dr. Grimké's Obituary, July 23, 1914," Francis Grimké Papers, Moorland-Spingarn Research Center, Howard University.

JOURNAL ONE

1. Caroline Remond Putnam was a prominent black woman of Salem, Massachusetts, and a close personal friend of young Miss Forten during the time she lived there. She and her husband, Joseph Putnam, owned and operated a hairworks establishment in Salem. Mrs. Putnam, as well as other members of her family, was an active abolitionist in Salem and throughout the Northeast. For several years she was a member of the Salem Female Anti-Slavery Society, serving as its president in 1859. Caroline Putnam was the sister of Charlotte's Salem host, Charles Remond, and formed an important part of the small coterie of abolitionists who helped to strengthen her commitment to abolition and equal rights. Charlotte resided in the home of Caroline and Joseph Putnam for a brief while after leaving the home of Charles Remond in 1857. Journals One, Two, and Three, *passim; The Salem Directory . . . An Almanac for 1853* (Salem, 1853), 127; *The Salem Directory . . . An Almanac for 1859* (Salem, 1859), 236.

2. Probably Mr. Jonathan Buffum and family. Buffum was an active member of the Massachusetts Anti-Slavery Society and, there-fore, part of the close circle of abolition activists that frequented the home of Charles Remond in Salem. Mr. Buffum was by occupation a publisher and bookseller. For a time he was in partnership with William C. Nell, the well-known black abolitionist, writer, and publisher, who was also a friend of the Remonds and Charlotte. The Buffum-Nell business establishment was located at 23 Chorn-hill, Boston, Massachusetts. *Liberator*, August 3, 1855, November 16, 1855.

3. On Wednesday, May 24, 1854, a warrant was issued by U.S. Commissioner Edward G. Loring in the city of Boston, Massachusetts, for Anthony Burns—an "alleged fugitive" slave "from the 'service and labor' " of Charles F. Suttle, a merchant of Alexandria, Virginia. Burns escaped on March 26, 1854 and had been a resident in Boston for several weeks prior to his arrest. He was "discovered" after writing a letter to his brother, also a slave of Suttle's. Although the letter bore a Canadian postmark, Burns indicated in his correspondence that he had found occasional work in the clothing shop of Deacon Pitts on Brattle Street in Boston. He was apprehended at the corner of Brattle and Court streets and taken to the Boston City Jail. Counsel for Suttle were Seth J. Thomas and Edward G. Parker. Richard Dana, Jr., Charles Ellis, and Robert Morris volunteered their legal services to defend Burns. On the morning following the arrest, Burns was arraigned before Commis-sioner Loring in the Boston Court House. William Brent, a mer-chant from Virginia, identified Burns as Suttle's "chattel." A decision on the case was postponed by the Commissioner until Saturday morning at the request of the defendant's counsel, and the prisoner was reprimanded into the custody of the U.S. marshal. *Liberator*, June 2, 1854; *National Anti-Slavery Standard*, June 3, 1854.

4. Located on Beckford Street in Salem, the Higginson Gram-mar School was under the direction of Mary F. Shepard, its principal for several years, including those during which Charlotte Forten

was enrolled (1853–1855). Robert Forten, Charlotte's father, sent his daughter to Salem to be educated in its public schools because they were not segregated as Philadelphia's were. The Higginson School was one of the better grammar schools in the city. Charlotte's relationship with Mary Shepard became more than just that of teacher and pupil; Charlotte counted her as one of her dearest friends, and a lifelong one. *Annual Report of the School Committee of the City of Salem,* February 1854 (Salem, 1854), 29–32, 35; Journal Three, March 7, 1858.

5. Born in 1813 in Philadelphia, Charlotte's father—Robert Bridges Forten—was the second son of James and Charlotte Forten. In 1836, Robert Forten married Mary Virginia Woods, and they had one child, Charlotte Forten, born August 17, 1837. Mary Woods Forten died in 1840 at the age of twenty-six. Robert Forten later remarried and had two sons, Edmund Quincy and Wendell Forten. Janice Sumler Lewis, "The Fortens of Philadelphia: An Afro-American Family and Nineteenth Century Reform," Ph.D. Dissertation, Georgetown University (1978), 14–128, *passim.*

6. Sarah Cassey Smith was the daughter of Amy Matilda (Williams Cassey) Remond and Joseph Cassey. Gloria C. Oden, *"The Journal of Charlotte L. Forten:* The Salem-Philadelphia Years (1851–1862) Reexamined," *Essex Institute Historical Collections* 119 (1983): 125–126.

7. P. Elizabeth Church, originally from Nova Scotia, was a close friend of Charlotte during her stay in Salem. Like Charlotte, Miss Church came to the city to take advantage of the fine public schools. She too attended the Higginson Grammar School and the Salem Normal School. In 1857, "Lizzie" Church became an assistant in the Higginson School. Lewis, "The Fortens of Philadelphia," 117; *Annual Report of the School Committee of the City of Salem,* February 1857 (Salem, 1857), 10.

8. Anthony Burns, the escaped slave, was in custody until June 2, 1854.

9. Mrs. Cecelia Remond Babcock was the sister of Charlotte's

Salem host, Charles Lenox Remond. She owned a wig establishment with her sister, Maritchie Juan Remond, at 18 Washington Street, Salem. *Salem Directory, 1853,* 37.

10. On May 30, 1854, the New England Anti-Slavery Society began its annual convention at the Melodeon in Boston. *National Anti-Slavery Standard,* June 3, 1854.

11. Wendell Phillips (1811–1884) was a wealthy Boston aristocrat who used his energies and inheritance to pursue the reform issues that interested him—abolition, women's rights, labor reform, and academic conservatism. Educated at the Boston Latin School, Harvard College, and Harvard Law School, he was an intelligent and able debator. Phillips began his career as orator at twenty-six, when he responded publicly to a statement made by the Attorney General of Massachusetts, who had defended Elijah P. Lovejoy. From this point on, Phillips was a vehement antislavery advocate and remained dedicated to this cause, though his family regarded him as a fanatic. He was one of the young Miss Forten's favorite heroes. Ernest G. Bormann, ed., *Forerunners of Black Power* (Englewood Cliffs, N.J., 1971), 62–123; Journal Two, March 6, 1857.

12. William Lloyd Garrison (1805–1879) was the single most important figure in the U.S. antislavery movement. He was born in Newburyport, Massachusetts, the son of a pious Baptist mother and an alcoholic father who deserted the family when Garrison was only three. Brought up as the ward of a local family, Garrison prepared himself early for a career as a newspaper man, first by becoming an apprentice to a newspaper at the age of thirteen and later by editing papers in Newburyport, Boston, and Birmington. In 1828, Garrison met Benjamin Lundy, a New Jersey Quaker and long-time abolitionist. Lundy asked Garrison to move to Baltimore in 1829, to help him edit the *Genius of Universal Emancipation.* Several months later, Garrison was convicted of libel and jailed for censuring a Massachusetts shipowner who had been supplying slaves to the South. The fine of $50 was paid by New York merchant

Arthur Tappan, and Garrison was released. He decided, however, to issue his own newspaper and began publishing the *Liberator* on January 1, 1831. Aided by Issac Knapp and relatively no capital, Garrison received most of his financial aid from black supporters, such as Charlotte's grandfather, James Forten. For thirty-five years, Garrison used the *Liberator* as a forum to denounce slavery, slaveholders, and any U.S. citizen or institution that supported the practice of slavery.

On January 6, 1832, primarily through the efforts of Garrison, the New England Anti-Slavery Society was formed. The constitution of this organization, signed by such persons as Garrison, Knapp, Arnold Buffum, and Joshua Coffin, was the first to insist on immediate emancipation. In that same year, Garrison published a pamphlet entitled "Thoughts on African Colonization" and, in it, accused the American Colonization Society of being an anti-black, pro-slavery organization. In 1833, Garrison helped establish the American Anti-Slavery Society. As editor of the *Liberator* and the holder of numerous important offices in national antislavery societies, Garrison remained at the forefront of the movement for its entirety.

Although he attracted a great amount of support through the years, he also gained a number of enemies, both inside and outside abolitionist circles. Some believed Garrison to be a brilliant, zealous, stubborn crusader who was unyielding in his moral fights, and they appreciated him as such. Others characterized him as fanatic, impractical, disorganized, and overtly obnoxious in his attempts to make the abolitionist movement a successful one. Because many were discontent with Garrison's way of doing things and because he insisted on female representation among the officeholders of the American Anti-Slavery Society, the organization was split in 1840. Lewis Tappan, who opposed Garrison and his followers, went on to form the American and Foreign Anti-Slavery Society. The American Anti-Slavery Society remained the stronger of the two organizations, still an active group after the Civil War, while its rival, the American and Foreign Anti-Slavery Society, ceased to exist in the

1850s. Louis Ruchames, *The Abolitionists: A Collection of Their Writings* (New York, 1964), 15–24; Bormann, *Forerunners of Black Power*, 94–96.

13. Theodore Parker was born in Lexington, Massachusetts, in 1810, the youngest of eleven children in the household of a poor farmer. Although he was for the most part self-taught, he passed the Harvard entrance exams, but was too poor to enroll. Between 1834 and 1836, he studied at the Harvard Divinity School and was ordained a minister on June 21, 1837. Afterward, Reverend Parker was named pastor of the Spring Street Unitarian Church in West Roxbury. He eventually took the required student examination at Harvard and was made an honorary master of arts in 1840.

Although Parker's unorthodox religious beliefs (he questioned the special authority of the Bible, the supernatural origin of Christianity, and the supernatural character and divine mission of Christ) caused many of the Unitarian clergy to ban him as an "infidel," his congregation continued to support him and, in 1842, arranged for the publication of his *Discourse of Matters Pertaining to Religion*. Parker continued to meet opposition from members of the Unitarian clergy, but he refused to resign, and the Unitarian Church did not force him to do so. In 1846, he became pastor for the Twenty-eighth Congregational Society of Boston.

Parker was a well-known abolitionist and the champion of other reform movements as well. He participated in the Massachusetts Vigilance Committee and was instrumental in the escape of several fugitive slaves, most notably Ellen and William Craft. Parker was also a member of the secret committee that supported John Brown's raid. Throughout his life, he used his pulpit as well as his pen to support abolition. He died in Florence, Italy, in 1860. *Who Was Who in America: Historical Volume, 1607–1896*, rev. ed. (St. Louis, Mo., 1967), 466.

14. Born in 1809, in Canterbury, New Hampshire, Stephen Seymonds Foster has been characterized as second only to Garrison in importance during the early years of the antislavery movement. Foster attended and graduated from Dartmouth, and later enrolled

in the Union Theological Seminary, but disagreed with its policies and soon left. It was after this incident that he began his antislavery speeches. For Foster, slavery was not a Southern institution but an American one and, therefore, all of America was guilty of moral wrong. He also believed that institutions—churches, businesses, and political bodies—indirectly sanctioned slavery. A man of strong convictions, he was known to interrupt church services to address the members regarding their personal views on slavery.

Like Garrison, Foster was a radical reformer with many interests. Aside from the issue of abolition, he was a champion of women's rights and suffrage, temperance, and labor reform. Although he moved to a farm in Worcester, Massachusetts, after his marriage to Abigail Kelley, Foster remained active in the reform movements. He died in 1881. Bormann, *Forerunners of Black Power*, 103–104.

15. Born in Pelham, Massachusetts, in 1810, Abigail Kelley Foster was one of the most important advocates of women's rights and suffrage in the nineteenth century and considered the leader in the movement after 1850. She was also a strong advocate of abolition. In 1837, Kelley, along with Angelina Grimké, conducted an anti-slavery campaign in Massachusetts, making her the first Massachusetts woman to address sexually mixed audiences regularly. In 1840, Foster was chosen as a member of the executive committee of the American Anti-Slavery Society, but her election to the position led to a split in the organization, resulting in the creation of the American and Foreign Anti-Slavery Society. It was also in 1840 that Foster served as a delegate to the World Anti-Slavery Convention.

Abigail Kelley and Stephen S. Foster were married on December 31, 1845 and continued to pursue their causes. Mrs. Foster died on January 14, 1887 in Worcester, Massachusetts. Ruchames, *Abolitionists*, 22; Bormann, *Forerunners of Black Power*, 103–104; *Who Was Who in America*, 257.

16. Sarah Parker Remond (1815–1894), daughter of John and Nancy Remond of Salem, was a lecturing agent for the American Anti-Slavery Society and toured the Northeast as well as Europe. In

the fall of 1858, she embarked on a European tour, which included the major cities of England, Ireland, and Scotland, and in 1864, the Ladies London Emancipation Society published one of her pamphlets entitled *The Negroes as Freedmen and Soldiers*. She continued her work as an advocate of black civil rights after the Civil War and eventually settled permanently in Italy, where she received a Doctor of Medicine degree from the Santa Maria Nuova Hospital. Rayford W. Logan and Michael R. Winston, eds., *Dictionary of American Negro Biography* (New York, 1982), 522–523 (hereafter cited as *DANB*).

17. Nancy Lenox Remond was the mother of Charlotte's Salem host, Charles Lenox Remond, and his siblings—Caroline Remond Putnam, Sarah Parker Remond, Susan H. Remond, Nancy Remond Shearman, Maritchie Juan Remond, John Lenox Remond, and Cecelia Remond Babcock. Born in Newton, Massachusetts, Nancy Remond was the daughter of a Revolutionary War soldier, Cornelius Lenox, and Susannah Toney. Remond and her husband, John, were hairdressers and caterers in Salem. Oden, *"Journal of Charlotte L. Forten . . . Reexamined,"* 127–129.

18. Harriet Forten Purvis was the second daughter of James and Charlotte Forten, Sr., and the sister of Robert Bridges Forten, Charlotte's father. Reared and educated by private tutor in a home whose members were deeply involved in reform and particularly abolitionist activities, Harriet Forten also engaged herself in the fight against slavery. She was a founding member of the Philadelphia Female Anti-Slavery Society in 1833 and held various offices and responsibilities in that organization. In 1837 and 1838, for example, she represented the organization at the Anti-Slavery Convention of American Women.

In 1832, Harriet Forten married Robert Purvis, an important member of the abolitionist movement in Pennsylvania and throughout the Northeast. Lewis, "The Fortens of Philadelphia," 44, 60–63.

19. Helen Putnam, daughter of Jane and George Putnam of Salem, married Jacob Gilliard of Baltimore, Maryland, on June 1,

1854. She was married by Octavius Brooks Frothingham, the Harvard-trained pastor of the North Church in Salem. *National Anti-Slavery Standard*, June 3, 1854; Dumas Malone, ed., *Dictionary of American Biography*, vol. 4 (New York, 1960), 44 (cited hereafter as *DAB*).

20. Little is known about Helen Putnam's husband, Mr. Gilliard. The *National Anti-Slavery Standard*, which announced their marriage in its June 3, 1854 edition, indicated that he was a resident of Baltimore, Maryland. *National Anti-Slavery Standard*, June 3, 1854.

21. On June 2, 1854, the U.S. Court at Boston ruled that Anthony Burns was the escaped property of Charles F. Suttle, a merchant of Alexandria, Virginia, and ordered that he be returned immediately to his master. *Liberator*, June 2, 1854.

22. Security forces surrounding Anthony Burns after the court's decision on June 2, 1854 were substantial, as they had been throughout the period of his arrest and trial, because of the intense protest and agitation his apprehension generated. On Friday, May 26, two days after the arrest, a crowd of protestors filled Court Square, where Burns was being held, and their numbers grew when they were joined by a contingent meeting at Faneuil Hall. Some actually attempted to rescue Burns by using axes and battering rams against the door of the jail, but this was met with opposition from armed policemen. A struggle between the police and members of the crowd ensued, and an officer, Mr. James Batchelder, was shot and killed. Nelson Hopewell, a local black, was arrested and charged with the crime. The Boston artillery, the Columbian artillery, and additional forces from Fort Independence were ordered to maintain peace and to prevent further attempts to rescue Burns. The next morning Anthony Burns was brought into the courtroom handcuffed and guarded by five armed men. Moreover, passageways in the courthouse were "all strongly guarded" by the U.S. marines and "files of soldiers occupied all the stairs." This level of security was maintained throughout the trial. *Liberator*, June 2, 1854; *National Anti-Slavery Standard*, June 3, 1854.

23. Charlotte was enrolled in the Higginson Grammar School from the time she first arrived in Salem (1853) until her final examinations in March 1855.

24. Mary Shepard, Charlotte's teacher and the principal of the Higginson Grammar School.

25. Charlotte is referring to her stepmother, Mary Forten.

26. Charlotte's half-brothers, Edmund Quincy and Wendell Forten, were her only siblings.

27. Henry Cassey was the son of Amy Matilda (Williams Cassey) Remond and Joseph Cassey of Philadelphia. Oden, *"Journal of Charlotte L. Forten . . . Reexamined,"* 127.

28. Adelaide Putnam ("Addie") was the daughter of Jane and George Putnam, hairdressers in Salem, Massachusetts. Oden, *"Journal of Charlotte L. Forten . . . Reexamined,"* 133.

29. Amy Matilda (Williams Cassey) Remond was Charlotte's Salem hostess from 1853 until her death in August 1856. Amy Remond was the daughter of the Reverend Peter Williams of New York, a prominent abolitionist who had been an associate and friend of Charlotte's grandfather, James Forten, Sr. Amy Williams's first marriage was to Joseph Cassey, a wealthy Philadelphia black activist. The Casseys and their children—Alfred, Peter, Sarah, Henry, and Frank—had been neighbors to the Fortens in Philadelphia during the time that Charlotte was growing up there. Mr. Cassey died in 1848, and his widow later married Charles Lenox Remond and moved to Salem. *DANB*, 60–61; Oden, *"Journal of Charlotte L. Forten . . . Reexamined,"* 125–126.

30. The person referred to here is Annie Woods, the youngest sister of Charlotte's deceased mother, Mary Woods Forten. A thorough search of the Philadelphia City Directory for the period (1830–1860) as well as the family papers of the Fortens has not resulted in any information regarding this woman, whom Charlotte was obviously close to during her youth. What information is known about her is extremely scarce and is drawn primarily from Charlotte's diaries. Annie Woods was much younger than Charlotte's mother

and married a Mr. Webb in the late 1840s. After her marriage, she moved from Philadelphia to Trenton, New Jersey, and eventually had two daughters. Charlotte visits her whenever she travels to Philadelphia. Journals One, Two, Three, and Four, *passim;* Oden, *"Journal of Charlotte L. Forten . . .* Reexamined," 134–135.

31. Jane Putnam, wife of George Putnam, owned a hairworks shop in Salem. She was the mother of Joseph Putnam, husband to Caroline Remond Putnam, as well as of Helen, Georgianna, Jane, and Adelaide. It was to Jane Putnam's home—where her son Joseph and his wife Caroline lived as well—that Charlotte came to reside in 1857. Oden, *"Journal of Charlotte L. Forten . . .* Reexamined," 133.

32. This is probably Georgianna Putnam. See Journal One, n. 31.

33. Here it is difficult to determine if Charlotte is referring to Mrs. Jane Putnam or her daughter-in-law, Caroline Putnam.

34. The *Liberator*, founded by William Lloyd Garrison, began publication on January 1, 1831. At this time Garrison, who served as editor, issued a statement outlining his aims for the paper, which stated:

> Assenting to the "self-evident truth" maintained in the American Declaration of Independence, "that all men are created equal, and endowed by their Creator with certain unalienable rights—among which are life, liberty, and the pursuit of happiness," I shall strenuously contend for the immediate enfranchisement of our slave population.

The motto of the *Liberator* was "Our country is the World—Our countrymen are all mankind." The official publication of the New England Anti-Slavery Society, it was published weekly out of Boston and cost $2.50 for an annual subscription. Ruchames, *Abolitionists*, 30–32.

35. Frank Cassey was the son of Amy Matilda (Williams Cassey) and Joseph Cassey of Philadelphia. Oden, *"Journal of Charlotte L. Forten . . . Reexamined,"* 125.

36. Prominent singers and abolitionists, Asa and John Hutchinson toured throughout New England. As friends of the Remonds, they often visited their Salem home. *Liberator*, August 17, 1855.

37. Joseph Putnam was the son of Jane and George Putnam. He was both a teacher and businessman and married Caroline Remond Putnam. Oden, *"Journal of Charlotte L. Forten . . . Reexamined,"* 130.

38. John Greenleaf Whittier was born in December 1807 near Haverhill, Massachusetts, the son of a Quaker farmer, John Whittier, and Abigail Hussey Whittier. The poet had little formal education but as a youth read extensively. His first published poem appeared in William Lloyd Garrison's Newburyport *Free Press* when he was nineteen. Garrison readily recognized Whittier's raw talent and tried, unsuccessfully, to aid him in obtaining a more formal education.

Through the aid of a local editor, Whittier was finally able to attend Haverhill Academy during 1827 and, in 1829, with Garrison's help, became editor of the *American Manufacturer* in Boston. The following year, he became editor of the Haverhill *Gazette* and remained in this position until 1837. From 1838 to 1840, he edited the *Pennsylvania Freeman*, and while in Philadelphia he befriended Charlotte's grandfather, James Forten, as well as other members of the family. Later, the poet served on other editorial staffs, including that of the Middlesex *Standard* (Lowell, Massachusetts), the *Essex Transcript* (Amesbury, Massachusetts), and the *National Era* (Washington, D.C.). While editor of these papers, Whittier published numerous volumes of poetry and actively participated in the abolitionist movement.

Whittier publicly announced his views as an abolitionist in 1833 when he published a pamphlet, *Justice and Expediency*. Using both politics and writing to influence popular thought, he served in the Massachusetts State Legislature in 1835 and ran, unsuccessfully, for

Congress on the Liberty ticket in 1842. Whittier is also credited as being one of the founders of the Republican Party. He became known as the poet of the antislavery movement and published several volumes of poetry, as well as short stories, essays, and a novel. He became friends with Charlotte during her stay in Salem. Stanley Kunitz and Howard Haycraft, eds., *American Authors, 1600–1900* (New York, 1983), 811–813; Charlotte Forten Grimké, "Personal Recollections of Whittier," *New England Magazine* 14, New Series 8 (June 1893).

39. Charles Lenox Remond was Charlotte's Salem host from 1854 to 1857. He was born in February 1810 in Salem, Massachusetts, the son of free black parents, John and Nancy Remond, and received an excellent education, as did Charlotte, in the public schools of Salem. Remond was the first black agent of the Massachusetts Anti-Slavery Society and the most important black participant in the abolitionist movement before Frederick Douglass came on the scene.

During the Civil War Remond served as a recruiting officer for the black regiment, the 54th Massachusetts Infantry. He was appointed inspector in 1865 and later became a clerk in the Boston Custom House. Charles Remond died in December 1873. *Liberator,* June 23, 1854; *DAB*, vol. 3, 499–500; *DANB*, 520–522.

40. Lydia Maria Child was born in February 1802 in Medford, Massachusetts, the youngest child of a baker, Convers Francis, and his wife, Susannah (Rand) Francis. Child received some instruction in the local schools but was principally educated by her brother, a professor at the Harvard Divinity School. She attended and taught at a seminary in Medford for one year and conducted a private school in Watertown, Massachusetts, from 1825 to 1828. In 1828, she married David Lee Child, a Massachusetts lawyer and politician. The two became deeply involved in the abolitionist movement and, in 1833, Child wrote the first book published on the topic of antislavery entitled *Appeal in Favor of That Class of Americans Called Africans*. Child's strong association with the abolitionist movement interfered with her literary career. *Juvenile Miscellany*, a bi-monthly

magazine begun by Child, was abandoned in 1834, largely as a result of the publication of her *Appeal*.

In 1852, the Childs moved from New York to a small farm in Weyland, Massachusetts, their home for the remainder of their lives. There they continued to participate in and support various causes, principally abolition and women's rights. Lydia Child died October 1880. *DAB*, vol. 2, 67–69.

41. The Kansas-Nebraska Act of 1854 in effect repealed the Missouri Compromise of 1850. The Compromise prohibited the practice of slavery north of the 36°30′ line in U.S. territories. The Kansas-Nebraska Act, sponsored by Senator Stephen Douglas of Illinois, allowed the voters of Nebraska and Kansas to decide, through majority representation, if the institution of slavery would be allowed in these states. Peter M. Bergman and Mort N. Bergman, *The Chronological History of the Negro in America* (New York, 1969), 205; *Webster's Encyclopedia of Dictionaries: Outline of U.S. History* (New York, 1978), 1116–1117.

42. Cecelia Remond Babcock and her husband, James Babcock, had three daughters—Gertrude, Agnes, and Cecelia. Charlotte could have been referring to any one of them. Oden, *"Journal of Charlotte L. Forten . . . Reexamined,"* 129–130.

43. Miss Margaretta Forten was the sister of Robert Bridges Forten, Charlotte's father, and the oldest daughter of James and Charlotte Forten. She was teacher and administrator of the Lombard Street School, an institution of learning dedicated to the black youth of Philadelphia. Charlotte felt particularly close to her Aunt Margaretta, as the frequent entries concerning her in the journals indicate. Lewis, "The Fortens of Philadelphia," 43–44, 61.

44. Thomas Wentworth Higginson was born in 1823 in Cambridge, Massachusetts, and was a graduate of Harvard College in 1841. Upon graduation, he taught for two years, returning to Harvard to further his studies and enter the Divinity School. After graduation in 1847, Higginson became minister of the First Religious Society of Newburyport, Massachusetts. Actively involved in

various reform efforts, such as temperance, abolition, and women's rights, Higginson tried to spread his influence to the political arena, but was defeated in his bid as a Free Soil candidate to the U.S. Congress. In 1852, Higginson and his first wife, Mary Channing, moved to Worcester, Massachusetts, where he became pastor of the "Free Church." He held this position until 1861, but all the while, became more and more involved in the abolitionist movement. He not only used his pulpit as a forum for abolition, but also wrote on the subject. He gained some notoriety in 1854 when he participated in the attempt to free the fugitive slave Anthony Burns. Two years later, Higginson traveled to Kansas for the abolitionist cause, and there he met and befriended John Brown.

Higginson volunteered for the army after the outbreak of the Civil War and was commissioned as Captain of the 51st Massachusetts Regiment. Later, General Rufus Saxton chose Higginson to be the commander of the all-black First South Carolina Volunteers, and he served in this capacity from 1862 to 1864. After his service, Higginson returned to the Northeast. There he spent the remainder of his life writing several book-length works, primarily biographical accounts of the lives of associates and relatives, as well as two autobiographical pieces. *DAB*, vol. 5, 16–18.

45. William Cooper Nell (1816–1874) was the son of William G. and Louisa Nell of Boston. Educated in Boston grammar schools, Nell was particularly interested in the movement to desegregate public education. He was a writer who used his skills to enhance the reform movements in which he was involved, especially the abolitionist cause. He began to work with William Lloyd Garrison on the *Liberator* in the early 1840s, contributing numerous articles and taking charge of the Negro Employment Office associated with the journal. A close associate of Frederick Douglass, Nell began to edit Douglass's *North Star* in 1847. He ran for office in the Massachusetts State Legislature in 1850 on the Free Soil Party platform, but his bid was unsuccessful. William Nell was not only a journalist, abolitionist, and politician, but a historian as well. In

1855, he published *The Colored Patriots of the American Revolution* and, in 1861, became one of the first blacks to receive a federal post—that of a postal clerk in Boston.

Prominent in New England abolitionist circles, an avid reader, and largely a self-taught scholar, Nell was one of Charlotte's favorites. He was a close friend not only of the Remonds, but of the Fortens of Philadelphia. *DANB*, 472–473; William Wells Brown, *The Black Man: His Antecedents, His Genius, and His Achievements* (1863; Boston, 1969), 238–241.

46. Helen Shearman was the eldest daughter of Nancy Remond Shearman and James L. Shearman. She is referred to in the journals as both Helen and Ellen. Oden, *"Journal of Charlotte L. Forten . . .* Reexamined," 131.

47. William Deas Forten was the youngest son of James Forten, Sr., and Charlotte Forten, Sr., of Philadelphia. Oden, *"Journal of Charlotte L. Forten . . .* Reexamined," 122.

48. Charles Sumner (1811–1874) was one of the most influential national politicians to support the abolitionist cause. Born in Boston, Sumner graduated from Harvard College (1830) and the Harvard Law School (1833). He never particularly liked the routine duties of a lawyer and early on devoted himself to acquiring knowledge on a variety of subjects by traveling to Europe and reading widely. His sharp legal mind and his reputation as a powerful orator and a morally astute man led him to a most prestigious career in the U.S. Senate, to which he was first elected in 1851. In office, he immediately took on the controversial issues related to the institution of slavery, most notably the Fugitive Slave Law of 1850 and the Kansas-Nebraska Act of 1854. Indeed, his virulent denunciation of the Nebraska Bill and its supporters precipitated a bloody beating which left him unconscious. It was three years before Sumner recovered sufficiently to resume his seat in the Senate.

Sumner was instrumental in the formation of the Republican Party and was later rewarded when the party gained control of the Senate and appointed him chairman of the Committee of Foreign Relations in 1861. Sumner was the first influential Senate member to call for emancipation of slaves after the Civil War began. Moreover, he insisted on the right of Congress to oversee the reconstruction process, mandating legislation that would allow Confederate states to reenter the Union only after they established state constitutions guaranteeing the suffrage of black males. *DAB*, vol. 9, 208–214.

49. William Wells Brown was born a slave near Lexington, Kentucky, in 1814. Owned by three successive masters, Brown managed to escape slavery in 1834. He took his names, Wells and Brown, from a Quaker that he met while traveling to Canada. When he returned to the United States, Brown moved first to Cleveland, Ohio, and then to Framingham, near Buffalo, New York, where he was active in the Underground Railroad and the temperance movement. He also became a lecturer for several anti-slavery societies, touring the United States and England. While abroad, British associates and supporters purchased his freedom so that he could return to the United States without fear of arrest as a fugitive slave. Charlotte met Brown in 1854, soon after his return to this country where he continued to lecture for abolition and temperance. During the Civil War, he helped recruit blacks for the 54th Massachusetts Regiment.

An amateur writer and historian, Brown published at least a dozen pamphlets and books. His autobiography, *Narrative of William W. Brown, A Fugitive Slave Written by Himself*, first appeared in print in 1847. He produced other autobiographical works, as well as one of the first novels published by a black in the United States: *Clotel; Or the President's Daughter: A Narrative of Slave Life in the United States* (1853; later editions appeared under the title of *Clotelle*). His other writings included two dramas—one, *The Escape; Or, a Leap for Freedom*, is mentioned in Charlotte's journal. He also wrote early histories of blacks in the New World, including *St. Domingo: Its Revolutions and Its Patriots* (1855); *The Black Man: His Antecedents, His Genius, and His Achievements* (1863)—which contains sketches of the life of Charlotte Forten, her uncle Robert Purvis, her Salem host Charles Lenox Remond, and family friend

William C. Nell—and *The Rising Son; Or, the Antecedents and Advancement of the Colored Race* (1874). Brown died on November 6, 1884. *DANB*, 71–72; Brown, *The Black Man*, 190–198, 238–240, 253–258.

50. The Luca family were a quartet of black singers and instrumentalists who often performed at antislavery conferences and related events. The founder of the group, Alexander Luca, was born in Milford, Connecticut, but as an adult settled in New Haven. He and his wife were both trained musicians. The singing quartet consisted of his sister-in-law, Dinah Lewis, two sons, and himself. When they performed as instrumentalists the composition of the group changed slightly to include Luca's four sons. The group disbanded in 1860 when Cleveland Luca migrated to Liberia. *DANB*, 406–407.

51. Amy Ives was president of the Salem Female Anti-Slavery Society. *The Salem Directory . . . An Almanac for 1855* (Salem, 1855), 189.

52. Lucy Stone was born in Brookfield, Massachusetts, in 1818. Reared in a family that strongly believed in the inequality of the sexes, she rebelled when her father refused to send her to college as he had done her brothers. Stone worked locally as a teacher for several years while studying independently and saving money for her education. She eventually entered Oberlin College, where she worked as a teacher in the summers and as a domestic to support herself. She graduated with honors in 1847. Later that year, Stone gave her first women's rights lecture. An abolitionist as well as a feminist, she lectured widely on both subjects. In 1855, Lucy Stone married abolitionist Henry Blackwell, but retained her own surname. She continued to be a pioneer in the efforts to increase women's rights and, in 1869, helped establish the American Woman Suffrage Association, serving as chairperson of its executive committee for nineteen of the following twenty years. Stone participated in the suffrage campaigns in Kansas (1867), Vermont (1870), Colorado (1877), and Nebraska (1882) and served as editor of *Woman's Journal*. Frances Willard and Mary Livermore, eds., *A*

Woman of the Century: Fourteen Hundred-Seventy Biographical Sketches, Accompanied by Portraits of Leading American Women in All Walks of Life (Buffalo, 1893), 693–695.

53. Eddie Putnam was the son of Joseph and Caroline Remond Putnam of Salem. Journal One, September 17, 1854.

54. Henry Ward Beecher (1818–1887) was born in Litchfield, Connecticut, the son of the noted clergyman, Lyman Beecher. He graduated from Amherst College in 1834 and then entered Lane Theological Seminary in Cincinnati. It was here that Beecher began to involve himself in the abolitionist movement. His first work as a minister was in Indiana but, in 1847, he accepted the pastorate of the Plymouth Church in Brooklyn, New York. During his forty-year tenure at Plymouth Church, Beecher lectured widely within the United States and England. He served as editor of the New York *Independent* and the *Christian Union. The National Cyclopaedia of American Biography*, vol. 3 (New York, 1921), 129–130.

55. Lucretia Coffin Mott (1793–1880), born in Nantucket, Massachusetts, moved with her family to Boston in 1804. There she completed her education and in 1808 began to teach. One year later, she moved to Philadelphia with her parents. Lucretia Coffin married another teacher, James Mott, in 1817. After her marriage, she continued to teach and also became a minister in the Society of Friends. Early on, Mott was interested in abolition and was present at the formation of the American Anti-Slavery Society in 1833. Seven years later, as a delegate to the World Anti-Slavery Convention, Mott was subjected to gender discrimination. She persisted, however, and was allowed to address the audience. In 1848, she was one of the four women who called the first convention of women concerned with the promotion of women's political and legal status in the United States—the well-known Seneca Falls (New York) convention. She dedicated the remainder of her life to the causes of women's rights and abolition. Willard and Livermore, *Woman of the Century*, 526.

56. Richard Edwards was principal of the Salem Normal School. Journal One, June 18, 1856.

57. Ruth Rice Remond of Newport, Rhode Island, was the wife of John Lenox Remond. John Remond was the brother of Charlotte's Salem host, Charles Lenox Remond. Oden, *"Journal of Charlotte L. Forten . . . Reexamined,"* 131.

58. Charlotte's poem, "To W.L.G. on Reading His 'Chosen Queen,' " reads as follows:

> A loyal subject, thou, to that bright Queen,
> To whom the homage of thy soul is paid;
> Long to her cause devoted hast thou been,
> And many a sacrifice for her hast made.
> *Thy* chosen Queen, O champion of Truth,
> Should be th' acknowledged sovereign of all;
> Her first commands should fire the heart of youth
> And graver age list heedful to her call.
> Thou, who so bravely dost her battles fight,
> With truer weapons than the blood-stained sward,
> And teachest us that greater is the might
> Of *mortal* warfare, noble thought and word,
> On thee shall rest the blessing of mankind,
> As one who nobly dost the Right defend;
> Than thee, thy chosen Queen shall never find
> A truer subject nor a firmer friend.

Liberator, March 16, 1855.

59. Colonizationists advocated the removal of free blacks from American society. They argued that free blacks would never be treated as equals in the United States and, therefore, it would be to their benefit to live elsewhere. The American Colonization Society was founded in 1816. Its members and supporters varied greatly in attitude with regard to abolition, the place of resettlement, and the means of support for such efforts. Some proposed gradual emancipation. Others did not want to "interfere" at all with the institution of slavery, but merely argued the removal of those persons of African descent who were already free. Some black colonizationists

believed in an immediate emancipation of all slaves and a voluntary removal. The most popular location for the "colony" of removed free blacks was Liberia, although some also proposed Haiti, various locations in South America, and the American West. Colonizationists solicited funding from both private and public sources. John Hope Franklin, *From Slavery to Freedom: A History of Negro Americans*, 3rd ed. (New York, 1967), 237–241; Bergman and Bergman, *Chronological History of the Negro*, 103.

60. Mr. Smith is the husband of Sarah Cassey Smith, Charlotte's good friend and Amy Matilda Remond's daughter.

61. William Wells Brown had two daughters with his first wife, Elizabeth Schooner. It is difficult to ascertain which daughter Charlotte is speaking of in this entry. *DANB*, 71.

62. The exact date that Robert Forten, his second wife (also Mary), and their two sons, Edmund Quincy and Wendell, moved to Canada is unknown. Sometime in the fall of 1855 is the date Charlotte indicates in this entry.

63. The Salem Female Anti-Slavery Society was organized by a group of black women on February 22, 1832. The organization was never racially segregated and soon attracted Anglo-American abolitionists. The goals of the society as outlined in its constitution included the self-improvement of its members as well as a commitment to universal emancipation. Dorothy Sterling, ed., *We Are Your Sisters: Black Women in the Nineteenth Century* (New York, 1984), 113.

64. On October 21, 1835, William Lloyd Garrison was attacked by a mob of anti-abolitionists in Boston. The mob had formed outside the offices of the Boston Female Anti-Slavery Society, which had advertised a lecture by the British abolitionist George Thompson. Protestors hoped to disrupt Thompson's speech and do him bodily harm, but he never arrived; Garrison had taken his place. After a chase, the mob caught him and placed a coiled rope around his body with the intention of dragging him through the street. Garrison, however, was able to rid himself of the rope and was escorted through the crowd by two men who shielded him. They

took Garrison to the mayor's office for protection; later, city officials decided he should be placed in jail to avoid further attack. George M. Fredrickson, ed., *William Lloyd Garrison* (Englewood Cliffs, N.J., 1968), 38–46.

65. Mary Webb was a free black dramatist from Philadelphia who performed throughout the Northeast. She was related to Charlotte through marriage—Charlotte's maternal aunt, Annie Woods Webb, was the wife of Mary Webb's brother-in-law. Oden, *"Journal of Charlotte L. Forten . . .* Reexamined," 134.

66. Charlotte's "A Parting Hymn" was chosen from among the poems written by the students in her graduating class to be read at their commencement from the Higginson Grammar School. (Charlotte refers to the actual graduation ceremonies in her entry of February 12, 1856.) The poem reads as follows:

> When Winter's royal robes of white
> From hill and vale are gone
> And the glad voices of the spring
> Upon the air are borne,
> Friends who have met with us before,
> Within these walls shall meet no more.
>
> Forth to a noble work they go:
> O, may their hearts keep pure,
> And hopeful zeal and strength be theirs
> To labor and endure,
> That they an earnest faith may prove
> By words of truth and deeds of love.
>
> May those, whose holy task it is,
> To guide impulsive youth,
> Fail not to cherish in their souls
> A reverence for truth;
> For teachings which the lips impart
> Must have their source within the heart.
> May all who suffer share their love—
> The poor and the oppressed;

So shall the blessing of our God
Upon the labors rest.
And may we meet again where all
Are blest and freed from every thrall.

Brown, *The Black Man*, 191.

67. Nathaniel Banks (1816–1894) was born in Waltham, Massachusetts, and served as both a congressman and the governor of Massachusetts. On February 2, 1856, Banks was elected as speaker of the House of Representatives on the 133rd ballot. His election was acclaimed by abolitionists largely because Banks criticized the repeal of the Missouri Compromise through the passing of the Kansas-Nebraska Act in 1854. See Journal One, n. 41. *DAB*, vol. 1, 577–580.

68. Charlotte was elected to write this poem, entitled simply "Poem for Normal School Graduation," for her graduation exercises.

In the earnest path of duty,
    With the high hopes and hearts sincere,
We, to useful lives aspiring,
    Daily meet to labor here.

No vain dreams of earthly glory
    Urge us onward to explore
Far-extending realms of knowledge,
    With their rich and varied store;

But, with hope of aiding others,
    Gladly we perform our part;
Nor forget, the mind, while storing,
    We must educate the heart,—

Teach it hatred of oppression,
    Truest love of God and man;
Thus our high and holy calling,
    May accomplish His great plan.

Not the great and gifted only
    He appoints to do his will,
But each one, however lowly,
    Has a mission to fulfill.

Knowing this, toil we unwearied,
    With true hearts and purpose high;—
We would win a wreath immortal
    Whose bright flowers ne'er fade and die.

Liberator, August 24, 1856.

69. Charlotte's uncle through marriage, Robert Purvis, Sr. (1810–1898), was born in Charleston, South Carolina, the son of a wealthy cotton broker, William Purvis, and a free woman of color, Harriet Purdah. As a youth, Purvis moved with his family to Philadelphia and there completed his formal education. In 1831, he married Charlotte's paternal aunt, Harriet Forten. It was about this time that he also became actively involved in the antislavery movement and the various other campaigns which addressed the needs of free blacks. Purvis served for several years as the vice-president of the American Anti-Slavery Society and as president of the Pennsylvania Anti-Slavery Society. Perhaps his most important contribution was his work in establishing the Underground Railroad in Pennsylvania, the first of such organizations in the state. For a more detailed account of his activities, see the "Introduction." Brown, *The Black Man*, 253–259; R. C. Smedley, *History of the Underground Railroad in Chester and the Neighboring Counties of Pennsylvania* (1883; New York, 1968), 353–354.

70. Maria Weston Chapman (1806–1885) was born in Weymouth, Massachusetts. After completing her education in England, she retained a position as principal of a high school for young ladies in Boston. In 1830, Maria Weston married Henry Chapman and, four years later, became actively involved in the abolitionist movement. For several years, Chapman was the treasurer of the Massachusetts Anti-Slavery Society. She also co-edited the *National Anti-*

Slavery Standard from 1844 to 1848. After her husband's death, she went to France from 1848 to 1856 but continued to espouse abolition through her writing. She kept up her activism after her return to the U.S. in 1856. Chapman was particularly known for her administration of the annual bazaars sponsored by the New England Anti-Slavery Society. *National Cyclopaedia of American Biography*, vol. 2, 315.

71. Robert Purvis, Jr., was the son of Harriet Forten Purvis and Robert Purvis, Sr.

72. Mrs. Peter Williams was the mother of Amy Matilda (Williams Cassey) Remond.

73. Charles Lenox was the cousin of Charles Lenox Remond. Oden, *"Journal of Charlotte L. Forten . . . Reexamined,"* 135.

74. No known record exists that identifies Sarah Putnam and her apparent relationship to the Putnam family. Perhaps Charlotte is actually referring to Sarah Pitman, her classmate at the Salem Normal School.

75. Peter Cassey was the son of Amy Matilda (Williams Cassey) Remond and her first husband, Joseph Cassey. Oden, *"Journal of Charlotte L. Forten . . . Reexamined,"* 125.

JOURNAL TWO

1. Charlotte is referring to the twenty-fifth anniversary of the New England Anti-Slavery Society organized by William Lloyd Garrison and eleven other white men in the schoolroom of the African Baptist Church in Boston on January 6, 1832. The stated purpose of the organization was the immediate abolition of slavery and the improvement of the political and economic status of free blacks. Leon Litwack, *North of Slavery: The Negro in the Free States*, 1790–1860 (Chicago, 1961), 214.

2. Harriet Martineau (1802–1876), English writer and reformer, gained considerable prestige among U.S. abolitionists through her support of their activities. Martineau suffered from deafness

most of her life, but did not allow this to hinder her research and writing. She was particularly interested in issues of political economy and philosophy. After visiting the United States on an extended tour from 1834 to 1836, she wrote an important work, *Society in America* (1837), in which she was critical of the institution of slavery as well as other political and economic shortcomings of Americans. Valene Pichanick, *Harriet Martineau: The Woman and Her Work, 1802–76* (Ann Arbor, Mich., 1980), 1–104, *passim;* Gillian Thomas, *Harriet Martineau* (Boston, 1985), 1–58, *passim.*

3. Octavius Brooks Frothingham (1822–1895) was born in Boston, Massachusetts, and attended Harvard College, from which he graduated in 1843, and then Harvard Divinity School. On March 10, 1847, he was ordained and made pastor of the North Church of Salem. He later left his Salem congregation over the question of slavery and moved to Jersey City in 1855 to become pastor of a new Unitarian society.

Reverend Frothingham's reputation as a man of great spiritual power spread quickly and, in 1859, a group of New York admirers organized the Third Congregational Unitarian Society (later known as the Independent Liberal Church) with Frothingham as their pastor. Influenced greatly by Theodore Parker, Frothingham was regarded as his "intellectual heir," though his beliefs seemed further removed from traditional Christianity than Parker's. He became one of the founders of the Free Religious Association in Boston in 1867 and served as its first president. In 1879, Frothingham began to suffer from severe health problems and was forced to retire. After a year abroad, he returned to the United States to reside in Boston until his death in 1895. Dumas Malone, ed., *Dictionary of American Biography*, vol. 4 (New York, 1960), 44 (cited hereafter as *DAB*).

4. Sarah Louise Forten Purvis, abolitionist and women's rights advocate, often used her skills as a writer to advance the political and social causes she supported. Sarah Forten was married to abolitionist Joseph Purvis and resided at "Fairview" in Bucks County, Pennsylvania. For a more detailed account of her life and activities, see the "Introduction." Dorothy Sterling, ed., *We Are*

Your Sisters: Black Women in the Nineteenth Century (New York, 1984), 121–126.

5. Harriet ("Hattie") Purvis was the daughter of Harriet Forten and Robert Purvis, Sr.

6. Charlotte is probably referring to her former classmate and friend, Maria Barnes.

7. Adelaide ("Addie" or "Ada") Putnam was the daughter of Jane and George Putnam and a good friend of Charlotte's. A musician, she had moved from Salem to New York City to work as a music teacher. She returned when she became seriously ill.

8. Meetings were a popular pastime for followers of "spiritualism"—a philosophy which centered on the belief that one could make contact and communicate with deceased persons through the efforts of "mediums." Mediums communicated with spiritual beings in numerous ways. During the late antebellum period, it was popular to do so through "rappings"—that is, the medium and spiritual being "rapped" out messages in code to each other. Sydney Ahlstrom, *A Religious History of the American People* (New Haven, 1972), 488–490.

9. Mr. L. F. Warren was the principal of the Epes Grammar School in Salem, Massachusetts. Charlotte had her first teaching job at Epes.

10. Miss Sarah Parker Remond and her brother, Charles Lenox Remond, were returning from a lecturing tour that took them to New York and Canada. The trip had been sponsored by the Massachusetts Anti-Slavery Society. Sterling, *We Are Your Sisters,* 176; Journal Two, February 26, 1857; Rayford W. Logan and Michael R. Winston, eds., *Dictionary of American Negro Biography* (New York, 1982), 522 (cited hereafter as *DANB*).

11. Brownie is Charlotte's friend and former classmate, Sarah Brown.

12. Charlotte is referring to her paternal grandmother, Charlotte Forten (1784–1884), for whom she was named. Like her husband and children, Charlotte Forten, Sr., was active in abolitionist circles and, in 1833, helped found the Philadelphia Female Anti-Slavery

Society. Charlotte was very close to her aging grandmother, who had helped raise Charlotte after her mother died in 1840. For more information on Charlotte Forten, Sr., and her relationship with her granddaughter, see the "Introduction." Sterling, *We Are Your Sisters*, 119.

13. Nancy Remond Shearman, the oldest child of Nancy and John Remond. Her husband, James Shearman, was a Salem oyster dealer. Their daughter, Ellen (Helen), was a close friend of Charlotte. Gloria C. Oden, *"The Journal of Charlotte L. Forten:* The Salem-Philadelphia Years (1851–1862) Reexamined," *Essex Institute Historical Collections* 119 (1983), 131.

14. Susan Rice of Newport, Rhode Island. She was the sister of Ruth Rice Remond, wife of John Lenox Remond. Oden, *"Journal of Charlotte L. Forten . . . Reexamined,"* 131.

15. William Purvis, son of Harriet Forten and Robert Purvis.

16. Maria Weston Chapman was a Boston abolitionist who annually organized the antislavery bazaar. For more information, see Journal One, n. 70.

17. Elizabeth Magee was a friend of Charlotte and the future wife of Charles Lenox Remond. Oden, *"Journal of Charlotte L. Forten . . . Reexamined,"* 125, n. 18.

18. Maritchie Juan Remond, daughter of Nancy and John Remond, owned a hair salon with her sister Cecelia Remond Babcock.

19. Thomas Deas Forten was the son of Charlotte and James Forten of Philadelphia and, therefore, Charlotte's paternal uncle.

20. Little Celia is the daughter of Cecelia Remond and James Babcock. Oden, *"Journal of Charlotte L. Forten . . . Reexamined,"* 129.

21. William's parents are Harriet Forten and Robert Purvis.

22. John Remond, born in Curaçao in 1788, was a Salem hairdresser and caterer. He was married to Nancy Lenox. Oden, *"Journal of Charlotte L. Forten . . . Reexamined,"* 128–129.

23. Charlotte felt close to Mrs. Chew of Philadelphia, who was an old family friend, and would often visit her when in Philadelphia.

24. Charlotte's paternal grandfather, James Forten, Sr. (1766–

1842), was a prominent Philadelphia sailmaker, abolitionist, and temperance advocate. He was a founding member of the American Anti-Slavery Society, member of the American Moral Reform Society, and an important force behind the Negro Convention Movement during the 1830s. His friendship and support of Garrison helped to secure the founding of the *Liberator* magazine. For a more detailed description of James Forten's life and activities, see the "Introduction." *DANB*, 234–235; William C. Nell, *The Colored Patriots of the American Revolution* (1855; New York, 1968), 171–181.

25. Charlotte is probably referring to a cousin of Charles Lenox Remond.

26. George Downing (1819–1903) was born of free parents in New York City and educated at the Mulberry Street School in New York City and Hamilton College in Clinton, New York. Downing was an active abolitionist, served as an agent for the Underground Railroad, and aided in efforts to desegregate public schools in Rhode Island. After the Civil War, he continued in the struggle to secure greater civil rights for blacks. During the 1840s and 1850s, Downing established a lucrative catering service in both New York City and Providence, Rhode Island. He also opened the popular Sea Girt Hotel, a plush resort facility in Newport. *DANB*, 187–188.

27. Georgianna Putnam was the daughter of Jane and George Putnam. To broaden her horizons as a teacher, she left Salem and sought work in Brooklyn. There she became principal of a grammar school. In the journals, Charlotte often refers to Georgianna as "Georgie." Oden, *"Journal of Charlotte L. Forten . . .* Reexamined," 134.

28. Mrs. Peter Williams is the mother of Amy Matilda (Williams Cassey) Remond.

29. Elizabeth Palmer Peabody was born in Billerica, Massachusetts, in 1804. A precocious child, she read widely and studied many disciplines. Through her self-study, Peabody not only gained a thorough knowledge of the classics, history, literature, and mathematics, but mastered ten languages as well. At one time she taught history at the experimental school of Bronson Alcott. As a social

reformer, she worked for abolition, female suffrage, education for women, and special facilities for the handicapped. Peabody was also an active participant of the Transcendental Club. Frances Willard and Mary Livermore, eds., *A Woman of the Century: Fourteen Hundred-Seventy Biographical Sketches, Accompanied by Portraits of Leading Women from All Walks of Life* (Buffalo, 1893), 562.

30. Mattie Griffiths was an important abolitionist, lecturer, and author of *Autobiography of a Female Slave*. Mattie Griffiths, *Autobiography of a Female Salve* (New York, 1857).

31. Tacie Townsend was a young Quaker and abolitionist. She was a friend of the Purvises, through whom Charlotte first met her, and the second wife of Robert Purvis, Sr. *DANB*, 510.

32. Jacob Gilliard was the husband of Helen Putnam.

33. Joseph Purvis was the son of Sarah Forten and Joseph Purvis, Sr.

34. Sarah Mapps Douglass (1806–1882) was born of free parents in Philadelphia where she was reared as a Quaker. Her formal education was provided by private tutors and through them she gained a deep appreciation of intellectual pursuits. Thus during the 1820s she opened a school for black children in Philadelphia and, in 1853, began to teach at the Institute for Colored Youth, where she remained until her retirement in 1877. Douglass was an active member of the Philadelphia Female Anti-Slavery Society. In 1855, Sarah Douglass married the Reverend William Douglass who was then rector of the historic St. Thomas Episcopal Church of Philadelphia. *DANB*, 186–187; Sterling, *We Are Your Sisters*, 127–133.

35. Charles Burleigh Purvis was the son of Harriet Forten and Robert Purvis.

36. These children were the daughters of Sarah Forten and Joseph Purvis. Oden, *"Journal of Charlotte Forten . . . Reexamined,"* 123.

37. Mattie Farbeaux was a close friend of Charlotte's from Philadelphia.

38. Gerrit Smith (1797–1874) was born in Utica, New York, and educated at Clinton Academy and Hamilton College, from

which he graduated in 1818. A successful businessman, Smith first became interested in aiding blacks in the 1830s and opened a manual labor school for black youth at Peterboro, New York, in 1834. Initially a member of the American Colonization Society, Smith donated a considerable sum of money to support schools in Liberia, one of the relocation sites popular among colonizationists. In 1835, Smith parted from the colonizationists and instead joined the New York State Anti-Slavery Society. He served as president of this organization from 1836 to 1839. At this time, he began to espouse abolition and civil rights for free blacks and published letters, pamphlets, and speeches on the subject. In 1859, Smith offered John Brown moral and financial support for his planned revolt, but later suffered a nervous breakdown, partially the result of guilt at having aided what he viewed was a disaster at Harper's Ferry. Smith was institutionalized only briefly and resumed his support of black civil rights through the Civil War and Reconstruction eras. Gerald Sorin, *The New York Abolitionists: A Case Study of Political Suasion* (Westport, Conn., 1971), 26–38.

39. Charlotte refers to Sarah Cassey Smith as "Sis."

40. Born in Providence, Rhode Island, in 1806, Elizabeth Buffum Chace was an active abolitionist who worked closely with Samuel May to organize antislavery meetings throughout Rhode Island. After the Civil War, she dedicated her energies to prison reform efforts and the women's movement, serving as president of the Rhode Island Woman Suffrage Association for more than twenty years. Willard and Livermore, *Woman of the Century*, 163–164.

41. William Still (1821–1902) was born free in Burlington County, New Jersey, the son of an ex-slave, Levin Steel (Still), and a fugitive slave, Charity Steel. As a youth, Still received little formal education and, in 1844, moved to Philadelphia, where he worked odd jobs. Three years later, he obtained janitorial and clerical work in the office of the Pennsylvania Society for the Abolition of Slavery, and it was here that he began to aid fugitive slaves. He continued to work for this office until 1861, during which time he championed many civil rights causes. An active man, he served on the Freedmen's

Aid Commission and was a member of the Philadelphia Board of Trade. During his lifetime, Still was successful in ending racial discrimination on the street cars of Philadelphia and in establishing a YMCA for blacks in the same city. In 1872, his important history, *The Underground Railroad*, was published. *DANB*, 533.

42. This was the husband of Charlotte's maternal aunt, Annie Woods Webb.

43. Charlotte is probably referring to her cousin Sarah Purvis.

44. Frederick Douglass (1817–1895) was the most important black civil rights advocate of the nineteenth century. Born a slave in Tuckahoe, Maryland, he escaped to freedom in 1838. He initially fled to New York City, where he was helped by David Ruggles of the New York Vigilance Committee. In New York, Douglass married Ann Murray, a free black woman that he had met while working as a slave in Baltimore. They moved to New Bedford, Massachusetts, soon after their marriage. It was in 1841 that Douglass first began to lecture for the Massachusetts Anti-Slavery Society, and in May 1845, he published the first of three autobiographies, *Narrative of the Life of Frederick Douglass*.

With the publication of his life story came the threat of recapture, so Douglass left the United States in the summer of 1845 for a twenty-one-month lecturing tour of England, Scotland, and Ireland. He was extremely popular abroad and gained many affluent and influential friends who were able to raise enough money for Douglass to purchase his freedom and to start an abolitionist newspaper back in the United States. Against Garrison's advice, Douglass began to publish the *North Star* out of Rochester, New York, in November 1847. The paper later became the *Frederick Douglass Paper* and then, in 1860, the *Douglass Monthly*. In 1870, he accepted the editorship of the *New National Era*, which he later bought.

Douglass advocated racial solidarity in the face of prejudice and discrimination, and throughout his long career, he lectured widely for abolition, civil rights for blacks, and women's rights. He was also a committed supporter of vocational training for blacks. Initially, he espoused political action as the most appropriate means of accomplishing his goals, and yet he wholeheartedly supported John Brown's raid on Harper's Ferry, West Virginia, in 1859. Uncertain about whether he would be arrested as an accomplice, Douglass moved to Canada and stayed there briefly. With the outbreak of the Civil War, he urged Lincoln to arm free slaves and blacks, and when blacks were finally allowed to enlist in the Union army in late 1862, Douglass served as a recruitment officer.

During and after the war, Douglass fought to secure the vote for black males. A keen supporter of the Republican Party, he received numerous federal appointments, culminating in his appointment, by Benjamin Harrison in 1890, as minister-resident and consul general to Haiti and chargé d'affairs for the Dominican Republic.

Charlotte is criticizing Douglass here probably because he broke with Garrison, whom she idolized. *DANB*, 181–186.

45. Mrs. James McCune Smith was the wife of the prominent New York physician, abolitionist, scholar, and writer. The Smith family had been parishioners in the church of the Reverend Peter Williams, whose widow lived with them. Thus Charlotte contacted the Smiths whenever she visited New York. *DANB*, 660; Oden, *"Journal of Charlotte L. Forten* . . . Reexamined," 125, n. 22.

46. The Sea Girt was a resort hotel in Newport, Rhode Island, and was owned by the Downings.

47. Charlotte is referring to the family of Ruth Rice Remond, wife of John Lenox Remond. A native of Newport, Rhode Island, Mrs. Remond still had family who lived there. Her family members included her father, Isaac Rice, and three sisters, Susan, Hannah, and Sarah. Oden, *"Journal of Charlotte L. Forten* . . . Reexamined," 131.

48. For information on John Greenleaf Whittier, see Journal One, n. 38.

49. Jacob Gilliard, Helen Putnam's husband, was ship's barber aboard the *Central American* when it sank on September 8, 1857. Oden, *"Journal of Charlotte L. Forten* . . . Reexamined," 134.

50. There is no information regarding the fate of Charlotte's story "Lost Bride."

51. Charlotte is referring to the annual antislavery bazaar held during the Christmas season in Boston.

52. Charlotte is referring to the recent death of Helen Putnam Gilliard's husband, Jacob Gilliard.

JOURNAL THREE

1. William C. Nell organized the first Crispus Attucks celebration on March 5, 1858 as an act of protest against the Dred Scott decision. The case of *Dred Scott* v. *Sanford* in which a slave, Dred Scott, sued for his freedom on the basis that he had resided on free soil (Illinois and Wisconsin Territory) had been settled in favor of Sanford by the U.S. Supreme Court on March 6, 1857. Nell believed his celebration of the first patriot to fall in the conflict over American independence—Crispus Attucks, who was killed on March 5, 1770—was an appropriate symbol of the injustice of society that would condemn a black man to slavery and sanction the institution in newly settled territories where, according to the Northwest Ordinance and the Missouri Compromise, slavery was illegal. Rayford W. Logan and Michael R. Winston, eds., *Dictionary of American Negro Biography* (New York, 1982), 472, 548–549 (cited hereafter as *DANB*); Peter M. Bergman and Mort N. Bergman, *The Chronological History of the Negro in America* (New York, 1969), 212.

2. Mary Webb was a popular black dramatist. She was also the sister-in-law of Charlotte's maternal aunt, Annie Woods Webb.

3. Elizabeth ("Lizzie") Magee was a friend of Charlotte's and the future wife of Charles Lenox Remond.

4. James Forten, Sr. For further information see the "Introduction" and Journal Two, n. 24.

5. Emma was an acquaintance of the Fortens and Purvises who occasionally did domestic work for the families.

6. Byberry in Bucks County, Pennsylvania, was the home of Robert Purvis, Sr., his wife, Harriet Forten, and their children, Robert, William, Harriet, Charles Burleigh, Henry, Grinnel, and

Georgianna. Gloria C. Oden, *"The Journal of Charlotte L. Forten: The Salem-Philadelphia Years (1851–1862) Reexamined," Essex Institute Historical Collections* 119 (1983), 122.

7. Georgianna Purvis was the daughter of Harriet Forten and Robert Purvis, Sr.

8. The poem by John Greenleaf Whittier was written in 1833 as a tribute to the daughters of James Forten, Sr., and his wife Charlotte. Whittier became a close friend of the Forten family while he resided in Pennsylvania. The poem is quoted in full in the "Introduction."

9. Charlotte is referring to her deceased cousin, William Purvis, the son of Harriet Forten and Robert Purvis, Sr.

10. Aunt Harriet's youngest were Henry, Grinnel, and Georgianna Purvis.

11. James Forten, III was the son of Charlotte's paternal uncle.

12. Charlotte is referring to the Institute for Colored Youth, the funding of which initially came from a West Indian slaveholder, Richard Humphreys, who had come to live in Philadelphia. When Humphreys died in 1832, he bequeathed the sum of $10,000 to the Society of Friends to establish within Philadelphia an institution "having for its object the benevolent design of instructing the descendants of the African race in school learning, in the various branches of the mechanic arts and trades, and in agriculture, in order to prepare, fit and qualify them to act as teachers." The Institute was established in 1837 and received its charter in 1842. It was considered one of the foremost institutions of its kind. The Institute for Colored Youth later became Cheyney State College. W. E. B. Du Bois, *The Philadelphia Negro* (1899; Millwood, N.Y., 1973), 87; *DANB*, 187.

13. "Fairview" was the home of Sarah Forten Purvis, her husband, Joseph, and their children, Joseph, Jr., James, William, Sarah, Emily, Alfred, Harriet, and Alexander. It was located in Bucks County, Pennsylvania. Oden, *"Journal of Charlotte L. Forten . . . Reexamined,"* 122–123.

14. Daniel Alexander Payne (1811–1893) was born of free

parents in Charleston, South Carolina. Educated at the school of the Minor Moralist Society as well as by private tutor and through apprenticeship, Payne was a young man of noted intelligence and skill. In 1826, he joined the Methodist Episcopal Church and, two years later, started a small school for free blacks and slaves. He left South Carolina in 1835 because newly legislated restrictions outlawed his teaching activities. He settled in New York and through further study was able to gain a license to preach in 1837. A year later, he was ordained by the Franckean Synod of the Lutheran Church. In 1840, Payne opened another school for blacks, this time in Philadelphia, and there became a member of the African Methodist Episcopal Church. In 1842, he became part of the African Methodists' traveling ministry, working first in Washington, D.C., at the Israel Bethel Church and then at the Ebenezer AME Church, which he soon left because church members criticized him as too "uppity." When Payne left this institution, he began to write a history of the African Methodist Episcopal Church (*History of the African Methodist Episcopal Church* [1891]). While writing, Payne continued to travel with his ministry, helping to edit the *Christian Recorder* and to establish schools for blacks. In 1863, Payne purchased Wilberforce University in Xenia, Ohio, and became its president. *DANB*, 484–485; Bergman and Bergman, *Chronological History of the Negro*, 95–96.

15. Payne was editor of the *Christian Recorder*.

16. Miss Sarah Parker Remond went to England in January 1859 to lecture on antislavery. For three years she spoke in some twenty cities in England, Scotland, and Ireland. While abroad she also attended the Bedford College for Ladies (1859–1861). *DANB*, 522.

17. Charlotte Forten's essay, "Glimpses of New England," appeared in the *National Anti-Slavery Standard* on June 18, 1858. *National Anti-Slavery Standard*, June 18, 1858.

18. Elizabeth Magee married Charles Lenox Remond at Newton, Massachusetts, on July 5, 1858. Oden, *"Journal of Charlotte L. Forten . . . Reexamined,"* 125, n. 18.

19. Lucretia (Lucy) Hopper was a friend and former classmate of Charlotte's cousin, Hattie Purvis. Hopper was the granddaughter of the feminist and abolitionist Lucretia Mott. Dorothy Sterling, ed., *We Are Your Sisters: Black Women in the Nineteenth Century* (New York, 1984), 187.

20. Charlotte Forten's poem, "The Angel's Visit," eventually appeared in William Wells Brown's *The Black Man: His Antecedents, His Genius, and His Achievements* (Boston, 1863). Brown, *The Black Man*, 196–199.

21. Louisa Victoria Putnam, daughter of Caroline Remond Putnam and Joseph Putnam of Salem, Massachusetts, was born on August 3, 1858. She died as an infant in May 1859. Oden, *"Journal of Charlotte L. Forten . . .* Reexamined," 130–131.

22. Charlotte is referring to a lecture given by author, lawyer, and orator, George William Curtis (1824–1892). Dumas Malone, ed., *Dictionary of American Biography*, vol. 2 (New York, 1960), 614–616 (cited hereafter as *DAB*).

23. The text of Charlotte's poem, "The Two Voices" (c. 1858), reads as follows:

> In the dim December twilight,
> By the fire I mused alone;
> And a voice within me murmured
> In a deep, impassioned tone—
>
> Murmured first, and then grew stronger,
> Wilder in its thrilling strain—
> "Break, sad heart, for, oh, no longer
> Canst thou bear this ceaseless pain.
>
> "Canst thou bear the bitter anguish,
> All the wrong, and woe, and shame
> That the world hath heaped upon thee,
> Though it hath no cause for blame?
>
> "True it is that thou dost give it
> Hate for hate, and scorn for scorn;

True it is that thou would'st gladly
  Make it bear what thou hast borne.

"But does such a vengeful spirit
  Soothe thee, make thee calm and strong?
No, thy lamest life it poisons,
  Makes the strife more fierce and long.

"Would'st thou live, oh, foolish dreamer?
  What to thee are life and joy?
Know'st thou not the cruel future
  All thy visions shall destroy?

"Wouldn'st thou live, oh, homeless outcast,
  Tossed upon life's restless wave?
Thou canst find a haven only
  In the quiet of the grave.

"There a sweet and soothing stillness
  From thee never shall depart;
There the angel Peace shall fold thee
  Closely to her loving heart."

To the earnest voice I hearkened,
  And within my troubled breast
Deeper, stronger grew the longing
  For the blessed boon of rest.

"Grant," I prayed, "O gracious Father!
  Grant the simple boon I crave,
Let me leave this weary conflict,
  Let me rest within the grave!"

Deep the silence that succeeded;
  Gleamed the firelight warm and bright,
But, for me, its warmth and brightness
  Gladdened not the cold, dark night.

But, without, the dreary night-wind,
   With its wild and mournful moan,
From the sad soul of the pine trees,
   Found an echo in my own.

Then another voice spoke to me,
   Spake in accents strong and clear;
Like the proud notes of a trumpet
   Fell its tones upon my ear.

"Shame," it cried, "oh, weak repiner!
   Hast thou yielded to despair?
Canst thou win the crown immortal
   If the cross thou wilt not bear?

"Hast thou nothing left to live for?
   Would'st thou leave the glorious strife?
Know, the life that's passed in struggling
   Is the true, the only life.

"Canst thou see the souls around thee
   Bravely battling with the wrong,
And not feel thy soul within thee
   In the cause of Truth grow strong?

"Art thou, then, the only wronged one?
   With thy sorrows will all cease?
Thou forgettest other sufferers,
   In thy selfish prayer for peace.

"Live for others; work for others;
   Sharing, strive to soothe their woe,
Till thy heart, no longer fainting,
   With an ardent zeal shall glow.

"Of thyself thou art unworthy,
   To all thy early vows,

If thy once unbending spirit
  Now beneath its burden bows.

"Prayest thou for death? pray, rather,
  For the strength to live, and bear
All thy wrongs with brave endurance.
  Scorn to yield thee to despair;

"Knowing that to strive and suffer,
  With a purpose pure and high,
In a holy cause, is nobler
  Than ingloriously to die.

"Sweet the grave's unbroken quiet
  To thy aching heart would be;
But, believe, to live for others
  Is a higher destiny."

Ceased the voice; again, in silence,
  By the fire I mused alone;
Darkly closed the night around me;
  But my soul had stronger grown.

And I said—"I thank Thee, Father,
  For the answer Thou hast given.
Bravely will I bear earth's burdens,
  Ere I pray to rest in heaven."

24. Charlotte notes that her friend Joseph Putnam, husband of Caroline Remond, died on January 27, 1859.

25. Miss Grew was reporting on the annual meeting of the Philadelphia Female Anti-Slavery Society. Mary Grew was an abolitionist, women's rights advocate, and preacher from Hartford, Connecticut. Grew first moved to Boston, where she was a member of the Boston Female Anti-Slavery Society, and later went to Philadelphia and joined the Female Anti-Slavery Society of that city, serving for many years, as she did in 1859, as its corresponding secretary. She lectured publicly in support of abolition as well as

contributed to bazaars and fairs which lent financial security to the movement. After the passing of the Fifteenth Amendment in 1870, Grew focused most of her energies on the women's suffrage movement, helping to establish, for example, the Pennsylvania Women's Suffrage Association. *National Anti-Slavery Standard,* February 5, 1859; Frances Willard and Mary Livermore, eds., *A Woman of the Century: Fourteen Hundred-Seventy Biographical Sketches, Accompanied by Portraits of Leading Women from All Walks of Life* (Buffalo, 1893), 341.

26. Charlotte means the annual meeting of the Massachusetts Anti-Slavery Society held in Boston on January 27, 1859. *Liberator,* February 4, 1859.

27. Charlotte is referring to the capture and temporary incarceration of the alleged fugitive slave Daniel Webster ("Dangerfield"). Webster was arrested on April 2, 1859 as a runaway slave from Athensville, Virginia. His trial, attended by many abolitionists, was held in Philadelphia on April 5 and the following day. Webster was acquitted and released, and the decision sparked a celebration in abolitionist circles. *Liberator,* April 8, 15, 1859.

28. Dr. William Furness of Boston, Massachusetts, was a Harvard-trained clergyman and religious scholar. For more than fifty years, Furness served as pastor to the Unitarian Church in Philadelphia, where he was assigned in 1825. Furness became active in the abolitionist movement as early as 1824 and considered it, along with his religious scholarship, the greatest interest of his life. *DAB,* vol. 4, 80.

29. Charlotte was offered a position at Higginson Grammar School, where Mary Shepard was principal.

30. Louisa Victoria Putnam, daughter of Caroline Remond Putnam and her husband Joseph, died in May 1859.

31. Charles Hovey, successful merchant, abolitionist, and temperance supporter, died on April 28, 1859. *National Anti-Slavery Standard,* May 7, 1859.

32. Charlotte visited the home of her friend and former classmate Lucy Kingman.

33. Charlotte sought the medical attention of Dr. Seth Rogers who ran a hydropathic clinic in Worcester, Massachusetts. Dr. Rogers, an abolitionist as well as a physician, became, in December 1862, one of the surgeons of the all-black regiment commanded by Colonel Thomas W. Higginson, the First South Carolina Volunteers. Thomas W. Higginson, *Army Life in a Black Regiment* (Boston, 1879), 269.

34. For most of her adult life, Margaretta Forten was a teacher and administrator in a small school for black youth in Philadelphia. Sterling, *We Are Your Sisters*, 120.

35. Henry Cassey was the son of Amy Matilda (Williams Cassey) Remond and Joseph Cassey.

36. Robert Purvis, Jr., the son of Harriet Forten and Robert Purvis, Sr., died on March 19, 1862. *Liberator*, April 4, 1862.

37. Sarah Cassey Smith Watson was Charlotte's long-time friend and "sister." She married Dr. Samuel C. Watson of Chatham, Canada, on February 28, 1861. Oden, *"Journal of Charlotte L. Forten . . . Reexamined,"* 126–127, n. 30.

38. Charlotte is referring to the annual meeting of the Massachusetts Anti-Slavery Society held on July 4, 1862 at Framingham Grove, Massachusetts. *Liberator*, July 11, 1862.

39. The Putnams, Jane and George, along with their daughters, Adelaide and the widowed Helen Gilliard, moved to Worcester, Massachusetts, in 1860. Oden, *"Journal of Charlotte L. Forten . . . Reexamined,"* 134.

40. Charlotte is referring to the meeting of the Congregational Society held on July 6, 1862. *Liberator*, July 11, 1862.

41. Elizabeth Whittier was the sister of the poet John Greenleaf Whittier.

42. Lucy Larcom was born in Beverly, Massachusetts, but her widowed mother moved the family to Lowell when Lucy was quite young. There she attended grammar school and, as a teenager, went to work as an operative in one of the early cotton mills of Lowell. Her experiences were publicized in her *Idyl of Work* (Boston, 1875) and *A New England Girlhood* (Boston and New York, 1890). Larcom

pursued her studies after leaving her job and eventually gained a teaching post at the Wheaton Seminary. She was also a poet of some note. Willard and Livermore, *Woman of the Century*, 448–449; Catherine Clinton, *The Other Civil War: American Women in the Nineteenth Century* (New York, 1984), 25.

43. Charlotte hoped to obtain a position with the Boston Educational Commission as teacher of the newly freed slaves residing on the islands off the coast of South Carolina. This society was organized in February 1862 in response to a request by Edward L. Pierce, special agent of the Treasury Department. Secretary of the Treasury Chase chose Pierce to supervise the labor and activities on the Sea Island plantations, then under Union control. After touring the area, Pierce wrote to the Reverend J. M. Manning and Samuel Cabot, Jr., of Boston asking for material and educational aid for the freed people. Henry Lee Swint, *The Northern Teacher in the South, 1862–1870* (Nashville, 1941), 15–16.

44. John Remond's wife is Nancy Lenox Remond.

45. Dr. Samuel Gridley Howe helped organize the Vigilance Committee of Boston which aided fugitive slaves. Howe was both a politician and abolitionist of some prominence, and it was through these activities that he became a close associate of John Andrew, President of the Boston Educational Commission. Charlotte wanted to secure the position of teacher by interviewing with Dr. Howe, hoping that he would then recommend her to Andrew, who was at the time unavailable to meet her. Swint, *Northern Teacher in the South*, 144.

46. Dr. Solomon Peck of Roxbury, Massachusetts, was one of the first missionaries to arrive at Beaufort, South Carolina, to aid the contraband in January 1862. Peck served as both minister and protector to the contraband slaves and opened a school at which he could teach about sixty students. Edward L. Pierce, *The Freedmen of Port Royal, South Carolina: Official Reports of Edward L. Pierce* (New York, 1863), 314.

47. In March 1862, in response to call for aid from General T. W. Sherman and Admiral Dupont, the Port Royal Relief

Association of Philadelphia was organized to benefit the contraband slaves residing in the Sea Islands off Port Royal Sound. This organization was later renamed the Pennsylvania Freedmen's Relief Association. It was responsible for supporting some sixty teachers from 1864 to 1868 and aiding with the relief efforts at a total cost of $3,500 to $4,000 per month. Swint, *Northern Teacher in the South*, 17–18.

48. J. Miller McKim was the person most responsible for the establishment of the Port Royal Relief Association. A prominent Philadelphia abolitionist, he served for many years as the corresponding secretary to the successor organization, the Pennsylvania Freedmen's Relief Association. Swint, *Northern Teacher in the South*, 158.

49. Emily is the daughter of Sarah Forten and Joseph Purvis.

50. Mr. John Hunn and his daughter Elizabeth were going to Port Royal to open a store for the freedmen on St. Helena Island, South Carolina.

51. In November 1861, U.S. Commodore S. F. Dupont and his naval fleet waged a successful attack on Confederate batteries located in the Port Royal Sound. As a result of the defeat of the Confederate forces, the wealthy planters who occupied the Sea Islands off the coast of South Carolina evacuated their plantations and left behind about ten thousand slaves. The U.S. government confiscated the remaining slaves as "contraband of war," used them in the Union army, and eventually freed them. For more information, see the "Introduction." Willie Lee Rose, *Rehearsal for Reconstruction: The Port Royal Experiment* (New York, 1967), xiii-xiv, 13–62, *passim*.

52. In May 1862, Brigadier General Rufus Saxton traveled to Port Royal, South Carolina, under orders from Secretary Edwin Stanton to take control of the abandoned plantations and the remaining residents who were primarily contraband slaves. Saxton's orders were to ensure the proper cultivation of the lands as well as to protect, govern, and employ the residents. Rose, *Rehearsal for Reconstruction*, 152.

53. Reverend Manfield French helped to solicit the participation

of missionaries in the "Port Royal experiment" and acquired material and financial support in the New York area for the contraband of the Sea Islands. French first went to Port Royal at the request of the American Missionary Association to survey the situation and to inform the organization how they might be useful to the Sea Island blacks. Rose, *Rehearsal for Reconstruction*, 26–27, 30.

54. Reuben Tomlinson was a plantation superintendent from Philadelphia. Rose, *Rehearsal for Reconstruction*, 78.

55. Frances Dana Gage was an abolitionist, writer, and women's rights advocate, originally from Washington County, Ohio. Growing up on the Ohio frontier, Gage became familiar with the plight of fugitive slaves and the issues related to slavery. In 1862, Gage, accompanied by her daughter, went to serve as nurse and missionary to the contraband at Port Royal, South Carolina. She remained in the area for thirteen months. After the war, Gage continued to support the temperance movement, civil rights for the freedmen, and women's rights. Though crippled by a stroke in 1867, she continued to write and gained some acclaim as the author of juvenile stories. Willard and Livermore, *Woman of the Century*, 308–309.

56. Miss Laura Towne was a teacher and physician from Philadelphia. Towne was one of the first of the Northerners to arrive determined to aid the newly freed slaves of the South Carolina Sea Islands. In the summer of 1862, she along with Ellen Murray, opened a school in a local Baptist Church on St. Helena Island. This school became the Penn School. Towne, unlike other teachers and missionaries, dedicated the remainder of her life to her work and stayed on St. Helena administering her school and providing medical service to the residents. Rupert Holland, ed., *Letters and Diary of Laura M. Towne, Written from the Sea Islands of South Carolina, 1862–1884* (Cambridge, 1912).

57. Ellen Murray of Milton, Massachusetts, was a teacher on St. Helena Island. Swint, *Northern Teacher in the South*, 191.

58. Richard Soule was a superintendent at the Frogmore plantation on St. Helena Island. Rose, *Rehearsal for Reconstruction*, 69.

59. Charlotte is probably referring to the minister Mr. Phillips.

Elizabeth Ware Pearson, ed., *Letters from Port Royal Written at the Time of the Civil War* (1906; New York, 1969), 103, 115, 244, 269.

60. Charlotte probably means Miss E. E. Way of Chatham, Pennsylvania, a teacher on St. Helena Island. Swint, *Northern Teacher in the South*, 199.

61. Charlotte is referring to her brother, Edmund Quincy Forten, the son of Charlotte's father and his second wife.

62. Mr. Samuel D. Phillips from Boston was a teacher at Port Royal. Swint, *Northern Teacher in the South*, 193.

63. François-Dominique Toussaint L'Ouverture (1750?–1803), the black slave who became the most important military and political figure to emerge out of the violent struggle for abolition and black civil rights, played a prominent role in the slave insurrection on Haiti. A mass revolt, which began in August 1791, was led by Toussaint, Jean Jacques Dessalines, and Henri Christophe and established the first black independent nation in the New World. Toussaint was most powerful during 1794 and 1802, but he was taken prisoner by Napoléon's forces in 1802, escorted to a French prison, and left there to die. Napoléon, however, did not regain control of Haiti. Bergman and Bergman, eds., *Chronological History of the Negro*, 75, 85, 86.

64. T. Edwin Ruggles was a plantation superintendent from Philadelphia. Swint, *Northern Teacher in the South*, 194.

65. Miss Amanda Ruggles from Milton, Massachusetts, was a teacher on St. Helena Island. She was the sister of T. Edwin Ruggles. Swint, *Northern Teacher in the South*, 194.

66. General Rufus Saxton proclaimed that November 27, 1862 should be a day of "Thanksgiving and praise"—a general holiday to celebrate the Union military victories and the freedom of the slaves in the Port Royal region, which had officially occurred on July 17, 1862. Journal Three, November 27, 1862; Higginson, *Army Life in a Black Regiment*, 8.

67. Charlotte may be referring to Nellie Tambling and her brother, C. L. Tambling, who later went to teach the contraband

of Natchez, Mississippi. Swint, *Northern Teacher in the South*, 167.

68. Chloe Merrick was a teacher from Syracuse, New York, who worked with the freed slaves at Fernandina, Florida, and New Bern, North Carolina. Swint, *Northern Teacher in the South*, 191.

69. Colonel Thomas Wentworth Higginson was commander of the all-black regiment, the First South Carolina Volunteers. For further information, see Journal One, n. 44.

70. See Journal One, nn. 3 and 8.

71. Robert Smalls (1839–1915) was born a slave in Beaufort, South Carolina, and as a young man, acquired skills as both a seaman and coastal pilot. Employed later on the Confederate dispatch boat *Planter*, he and eight other blacks were able to steal the vessel and sail to the Union blockade off the South Carolina coast. Smalls surrendered the boat, but was employed by Union forces to pilot the *Planter* until 1866. After the Civil War, he rose to military and political prominence in South Carolina, eventually obtaining the rank of brigadier general in the state militia and serving in the lower and upper houses of the state legislature. He was elected to the U.S. Congress in 1874. Following the return of a Democratic majority in South Carolina in 1876, however, he became the target of numerous investigations regarding his activities while in public office. He was accused and convicted of accepting a bribe while in the state senate. Later he gained a full pardon and was reelected to the House of Representatives in 1880 and 1884. Smalls ended his career in government service as a customs collector in Beaufort, since ill health forced him to decline positions as the minister to Liberia and as a commissioned officer in a black regiment engaged in the Spanish American War. *DANB*, 560–561.

72. "Interesting Letter from Miss Charlotte L. Forten" appeared in the December 19, 1862 edition of the *Liberator*. *Liberator*, December 19, 1862.

73. Mr. David Thorpe was a plantation superintendent from Providence, Rhode Island. Swint, *Northern Teacher in the South*, 197.

74. The newly freed people of the South Carolina Sea Islands

referred to the Union defeat of Confederate forces in Port Royal Sound in November 1861 as the "gun shoot." For further information, see Journal Three, n. 51.

75. Charlotte is referring to the daughter of J. Miller McKim of the Port Royal Relief Association of Philadelphia.

76. Charlotte suggested that the child be named for the abolitionist, politician, and military officer General John C. Frémont (1813–1890). Frémont had been the 1856 Republican Party nominee for the presidency. He had angered Lincoln but pleased abolitionists when in 1861, while serving in Missouri, he declared martial law and proclaimed that all slaves of owners who did not recognize U.S. authority were free. Lincoln demanded that Frémont rescind the order. *DAB*, vol. 4, 72; Rose, *Rehearsal for Reconstruction*, 13.

77. Harriet Ware was a missionary from Boston who first arrived on St. Helena Island in April 1862. Her brother, Charles Ware, a plantation superintendent, soon followed. Rose, *Rehearsal for Reconstruction*, 77.

78. Mr. James H. Palmer was a teacher from South Hampton, New Hampshire. Swint, *Northern Teacher in the South*, 192.

79. Charlotte is referring to the hymn she asked John Greenleaf Whittier to write for the contraband children to be sung at the celebration of the Emancipation Proclamation on January 1, 1863. It was sung to the tune of "I Will Believe." Holland, *Letters and Diary of Laura M. Towne*, 96–97.

80. Charlotte is perhaps referring to M. J. D. McKay from Allegheny City, Pennsylvania, who was a teacher at Hilton Head, South Carolina. Swint, *Northern Teacher in the South*, 190.

81. Mr. Josiah Fairfield was a plantation superintendent on St. Helena Island. Rose, *Rehearsal for Reconstruction*, 211.

82. Nelly Winsor was a teacher on St. Helena Island. She married the plantation superintendent Josiah Fairfield on May 7, 1863. Rose, *Rehearsal for Reconstruction*, 211.

83. Lieutenant Liberty Billings served with the First South

Carolina Volunteers from January 1, 1862 to July 28, 1863. Higginson, *Army Life in a Black Regiment*, 269.

84. Charlotte is referring to her good friend Sarah (Cassey Smith) Watson.

85. Captain Seth Rogers, Charlotte's friend and physician from Worcester, Massachusetts, was surgeon of the First South Carolina Volunteers from December 2, 1862 (when he was first commissioned) until December 21, 1863. For more information regarding their relationship, see the "Introduction." Higginson, *Army Life in a Black Regiment*, 269.

86. Edward Hooper was a young lawyer who served as personal aid and secretary to Edward Pierce. Rose, *Rehearsal for Reconstruction*, 50–51; Swint, *Northern Teacher in the South*, 187.

87. Captain James S. Rogers, previously of the 51st Massachusetts Regiment, served with the First South Carolina Volunteers from December 6, 1862 to October 20, 1863. Higginson, *Army Life in a Black Regiment*, 270.

88. George M. Wells from Providence, Rhode Island, was a teacher at Port Royal, South Carolina. Swint, *Northern Teacher in the South*, 199.

89. January 1, 1863 was the date set by Lincoln in his celebrated Emancipation Proclamation and it was used as a legal guideline to determine the status of U.S. slaves. The proclamation freed all enslaved persons residing in areas of the country that had seceded from the Union. However, those slaves who lived in states and territories that had remained loyal—Delaware, Kentucky, Maryland, Missouri, parts of Louisiana, Virginia, and West Virginia, some 800,000 out of about 4.4 million slaves—were not freed as a result of conditions in the proclamation. Bergman and Bergman, *Chronological History of the Negro*, 231; Gerald Sorin, *Abolitionism: A New Perspective* (New York, 1972), 152–153.

90. Reverend James H. Fowler was chaplain for the First South Carolina Volunteers. Higginson, *Army Life in a Black Regiment*, 270.

91. Dr. William H. Brisbane was a planter in the South Carolina Sea Islands. He had sold his slaves and left South Carolina in 1830 because he felt restricted by the lack of freedom of speech. While residing in Ohio, Brisbane became an abolitionist and returned to South Carolina to repurchase his slaves, carry them North, and free them. Rose, *Rehearsal for Reconstruction*, 202.

92. Charlotte is referring to President Abraham Lincoln's Emancipation Proclamation.

93. Dr. George Cheever was representing the Church of Puritans in New York City.

94. Prince River was a sergeant in the First South Carolina Volunteers. Higginson, *Army Life in a Black Regiment*, 41.

95. Robert Sutton was a corporal in the First South Carolina Volunteers. Higginson, *Army Life in a Black Regiment*, 41.

96. The rumor regarding Frémont was false. *DAB*, vol. 4, 72.

97. First Lieutenant G. W. Dewhurst was adjutant of the First South Carolina Volunteers. Higginson, *Army Life in a Black Regiment*, 270.

98. J. M. Hawkes was assistant surgeon in the First South Carolina Volunteers. Higginson, *Army Life in a Black Regiment*, 269.

99. Charlotte's letters to the *Liberator* about life on the Sea Islands appeared on December 12, 1862 and December 19, 1862. *Liberator*, December 12 and 19, 1862.

100. William W. Hall was a plantation superintendent. Pearson, *Letters from Port Royal*, 127, 150, 183, 184, 196, 197.

101. General Truman Seymour was born in Burlington, Vermont, and educated at Norwich University and West Point. He was captain of artillery during the defense of Fort Sumter. After serving in several Civil War battles, Seymour returned to South Carolina and commanded the unsuccessful assault on Fort Wagner in Charleston Harbor in July 1863. He was taken prisoner by Confederate forces in May 1864, but freed through a prisoner exchange in August of that year. *DAB*, vol. 9, 12.

102. Charlotte is perhaps referring to M. E. Lyon from Putnam,

Connecticut, a teacher at Port Royal. Swint, *Northern Teacher in the South*, 190.

103. Charlotte is referring to John Hunn's wife, who was a teacher on St. Helena Island. Swint, *Northern Teacher in the South*, 187.

104. P. B. Hunt was an officer of the Pennsylvania Freedmen's Relief Association, the organization which sponsored Charlotte's position. Swint, *Northern Teacher in the South*, 174.

105. Mrs. E. Clark was a teacher on St. Helena Island. *New England Freedmen's Aid Society Annual Report* (Boston, 1864), 80.

106. Mr. Jules de la Croix was a plantation superintendent. Pearson, *Letters from Port Royal*, 141, 142, 143.

107. Major General David Hunter was made Union commander of the Department of the South in March 1862, succeeding General T. W. Sherman. Hunter was praised by abolitionists because of his early (May 9, 1862) proclamation that all slaves in South Carolina, Georgia, and Florida were free since those states were under martial law. He was also determined to draft able-bodied black males into the Union army. His high-handed manner in doing so, however, gave rise to criticism from plantation supervisors and teachers. Rose, *Rehearsal for Reconstruction*, 144–148.

108. Mrs. Harrison was a teacher in the Sea Islands.

109. Charlotte is referring to Jane Putnam, the daughter of Jane and George Putnam.

110. Harriet Tubman (1821–1913) was born a slave in Dorchester County, Maryland. In 1849, in response to a rumor that all of her deceased owner's slaves would be sold, Tubman ran away to Philadelphia. Praised by abolitionists as the "Moses" of her people, Tubman returned to the South about nineteen times to help as many as three hundred slaves reach freedom safely. In the South, a bounty of $40,000 was placed on her head. During the Civil War, Tubman volunteered to aid the Union army and served as scout, spy, nurse, and cook to the troops at Hilton Head, South Carolina. It was here that Charlotte met her.

After the Civil War, Tubman continued to be an advocate of

black civil rights—helping to found schools in North Carolina and establishing a home for the aged and impoverished. She was also active in women's rights and temperance groups. Henrietta Buckmaster, *Women Who Shaped History* (New York, 1966), 99–121; *DANB*, 606–607.

111. Mrs. Esther Hawkes was the wife of the assistant surgeon of the First South Carolina Volunteers, J. M. Hawkes.

112. Charlotte is referring to Ralph Waldo Emerson's "Boston Hymn," which was performed at the Boston celebration of the Emancipation Proclamation on January 1, 1863. *Liberator*, January 30, 1863.

JOURNAL FOUR

1. Frogmore was a plantation on St. Helena Island. Elizabeth Ware Pearson, ed., *Letters from Port Royal Written at the Time of the Civil War* (1906; New York, 1969), 205, 206, 301.

2. Miss Gage was the daughter of Mrs. Frances Gage, who came with her daughter to Port Royal to volunteer as missionary, teacher, and nurse.

3. Susannah was probably a contraband woman who worked as a domestic servant and seamstress for some of the teachers on St. Helena Island. Rupert Holland, ed., *Letters and Diary of Laura M. Towne, Written from the Sea Islands of South Carolina, 1862–1884* (Cambridge, 1912), 23, 30.

4. First Lieutenant G. W. Dewhurst was adjutant of the First South Carolina Volunteers. Thomas W. Higginson, *Army Life in a Black Regiment*, (Boston, 1879), 270.

5. Charlotte is referring to the book by her friend, the prominent abolitionist Williams Wells Brown, entitled *The Black Man: His Antecedents, His Genius, and His Achievements*, which included an essay on Charlotte's talents and experiences. It was published in 1863. Brown, *The Black Man*, 190–199.

6. Miss Filter donated toys, household items, and clothing to

the Pennsylvania Freedmen's Relief Association to be distributed among the Sea Island blacks.

7. Colonel Thomas W. Higginson, commander of the First South Carolina Volunteers, asked Charlotte to join his regiment on their expedition to Florida and to serve as the soldiers' teacher.

8. In January 1863, Colonel Higginson and the First South Carolina Volunteers traveled to lower Georgia and Florida where they were involved in several raids and skirmishes. Fighting along the St. Mary's River, on the border of Georgia and Florida, they captured much needed supplies, such as bricks, lumber, and iron, from Confederate forces. In March 1863, they helped to raid and occupy Jacksonville, Florida. James McPherson, *The Negro's Civil War: How American Negroes Felt and Acted During the War for the Union* (New York, 1965), 166–168. Higginson, *Army Life in a Black Regiment*, 62–129; Willie Lee Rose, *Rehearsal for Reconstruction: The Port Royal Experiment* (New York, 1967), 245.

9. Mr. Bryant was a plantation superintendent on St. Helena Island. Pearson, *Letters from Port Royal*, 108, 116, 122.

10. Dr. Wakefield was a plantation superintendent on St. Helena Island. Pearson, *Letters from Port Royal*, 41, 45, 51, 196; Holland, *Letters and Diary of Laura M. Towne*, 83.

11. Mrs. Dewhurst was the wife of the adjutant of the First South Carolina Volunteers, First Lieutenant G. W. Dewhurst. Higginson, *Army Life in a Black Regiment*, 270.

12. Mrs. Esther Hawkes was the wife of the assistant surgeon of the First South Carolina Volunteers, J. M. Hawkes. Higginson, *Army Life in a Black Regiment*, 169.

13. First Lieutenant J. M. Bingham was the quartermaster for the First South Carolina Volunteers. Higginson, *Army Life in a Black Regiment*, 401.

14. On May 11, 1863, General Rufus Saxton married Miss Matilda Thompson, considered by many the "beauty" of St. Helena Island. Rose, *Rehearsal for Reconstruction*, 211, n. 25.

15. Nellie Winsor, a plantation superintendent, later married Mr. Josiah Fairfield, who was also a plantation superintendent.

Rose, *Rehearsal for Reconstruction*, 211, n. 25; Holland, *Letters and Diary of Laura M. Towne*, 76.

16. Mr. Frederick A. Eustis was superintendent of a Ladies Island plantation of which he was part owner. Pearson, *Letters from Port Royal*, 8.

17. Edward L. Pierce was a Boston lawyer and abolitionist who joined the army just prior to the outbreak of the Civil War. In 1861, Pierce's first station was Fortress Monroe, Virginia, where the first contraband slaves arrived in Union military camps. There Pierce supervised the work of the contraband and publicized his belief that they were able and willing to act on behalf of the Union in an article published in the *Atlantic Monthly* (November 1861). As a result of Pierce's experiences in Virginia, Secretary of the Treasury Salmon P. Chase chose him to supervise the activities of the contraband on the Sea Islands of South Carolina, and he held this position until April 29, 1862 when General Rufus Saxton assumed responsibility. Rose, *Rehearsal for Reconstruction*, 21–23, 152–153.

18. Charles W. Hooper was captain of the First South Carolina Volunteers. Higginson, *Army Life in a Black Regiment*, 271.

19. General David Hunter, commander of the Department of the South, ordered the withdrawal of Higginson's First South Carolina Volunteers from Jacksonville, Florida, in preparation for an attack on Charleston, South Carolina. Higginson, *Army Life in a Black Regiment*, 130–151, *passim*; Rose, *Rehearsal for Reconstruction*, 245.

20. Charlotte is referring to Mr. and Mrs. H. G. Judd. Mr. Judd was general superintendent on Port Royal Island. Rose, *Rehearsal for Reconstruction*, 177, 291.

21. Colonel Thomas Higginson and the First South Carolina Volunteers helped capture and occupy Jacksonville, Florida, in March 1863. Higginson, *Army Life in a Black Regiment*, 62–151, *passim*.

22. Denmark Vesey (1767–1822) was the slave of Joseph Vesey,

an African slaver, until 1800, when Vesey purchased his freedom and opened a carpentry shop in Charleston. As the years passed, his business flourished, and Vesey became an important figure among free blacks as well as slaves in the Charleston area. Inspired by his knowledge of the Haitian revolution of 1791, Vesey planned an intricate and widespread rebellion of blacks that was to affect Charleston and its surroundings. He and his followers hoped to capture all arsenals and powder magazines, block passage of any informants on bridges and roads, and kill all whites in the vicinity. The revolt was to occur on July 14, 1822. Efforts at recruitment proved fatal, however, when two domestic servants revealed details of the plot to their owners. Vesey tried to save the plan by moving forward the day when they would strike to June 16, 1822, but cautious whites heeded the warnings and were able to quell any attempts of violent activity by the blacks. It is estimated that more than 9,000 blacks were ready to participate. Of those arrested, 35 along with Vesey were hung, 43 were deported, 15 acquitted, and 38 released due to lack of evidence. Vesey was hung on July 2, 1822. Rayford W. Logan and Michael R. Winston, *Dictionary of American Negro Biography* (New York, 1982), 618–619 (cited hereafter as *DANB*); Peter M. Bergman and Mort N. Bergman, eds., *The Chronological History of the Negro in America* (New York, 1969), 44, 118.

23. Mrs. Esther Hawkes was the wife of J. M. Hawkes, assistant surgeon of the First South Carolina Volunteers.

24. Dr. Thomas Minor was assistant surgeon of the First South Carolina Volunteers. Higginson, *Army Life in a Black Regiment*, 269.

25. Colonel James Montgomery was commander of the Second South Carolina Volunteers, an all-black regiment recruited in the Sea Islands. Montgomery's men joined Higginson's in the raids on Georgia and Florida and helped with the capture and occupation of Jacksonville in March 1863. McPherson, *Negro's Civil War*, 167; Rose, *Rehearsal for Reconstruction*, 244.

26. Charlotte is referring to Second Lieutenant Eli C. Merriam of the First South Carolina Volunteers. Higginson, *Army Life in a Black Regiment*, 271.

27. Mr. Richard Soule was a superintendent at the Frogmore plantation on St. Helena Island. Rose, *Rehearsal for Reconstruction*, 69.

28. J. M. Bingham was first lieutenant and adjutant of the First South Carolina Volunteers. He died on July 20, 1863 of "exhaustion on a military expedition." Higginson, *Army Life in a Black Regiment*, 270.

29. Charles P. Ware was a Harvard graduate who followed his sister, Harriet Ware, to St. Helena Island. He was a plantation superintendent. Pearson, *Letters from Port Royal*, viii; Rose, *Rehearsal for Reconstruction*, 77.

30. Captain J. C. Dutch was commander of the Union blockade vessel *Kingfisher*. The captain was a man described by Laura Towne as "bold and enterprising." Holland, *Letters and Diary of Laura M. Towne*, 108–109.

31. Mr. Arthur Sumner left Cambridge, Massachusetts, to teach at Port Royal and St. Helena Island. Harry Lee Swint, *The Northern Teacher in the South, 1862–1870* (Nashville, 1941), 197; Pearson, *Letters from Port Royal*, 68.

32. Nellie Winsor married Josiah Fairfield on May 7, 1863. Rose, *Rehearsal for Reconstruction*, 211, n. 25.

33. Charlotte is perhaps referring to Mrs. Barnard, a relation of Mr. Barnard, who was a plantation superintendent. Holland, *Letters and Diary of Laura M. Towne*, 86.

34. John Alden was a plantation superintendent on St. Helena Island. Holland, *Letters and Diary of Laura M. Towne*, 80.

35. Charlotte is referring to Mrs. Hunter, wife of General David Hunter. Pearson, *Letters from Port Royal*, 262; Holland, *Letters and Diary of Laura M. Towne*, 71.

36. Laura Towne confirms that Captain J. C. Dutch's mate, Mr. S. W. Rhodes, accompanied their touring group to Edisto Island. Charlotte mistakenly refers to the ensign as a lieutenant. Holland,

Letters and Diary of Laura M. Towne, 109.

37. Charlotte is referring to Brigadier General Quincy Gillmore who had temporarily relieved General David Hunter as commander of the Department of the South in June 1863. Peter Burchard, *One Gallant Rush: Robert Gould Shaw and His Brave Black Regiment* (New York, 1965), 113.

38. In January 1863, Governor John Andrew of Massachusetts received authorization from the War Department to raise a regiment of black soldiers in his state. Andrews then asked the prominent abolitionist George Stearns to coordinate efforts to recruit men from throughout the Northeast. Stearns hired several prestigious black abolitionists—Frederick Douglass, Charles Lenox Remond, William Wells Brown, and Martin R. Delaney, among them—to aid in these efforts. The regiment was named the 54th Massachusetts and was the first regiment of black males from the Union to serve in the Civil War. Their first commander was Colonel Robert Gould Shaw. Black regiments were not allowed to have black commissioned officers. McPherson, *Negro's Civil War*, 173–179.

39. Charlotte is referring to Major Edward N. Hallowell of Philadelphia, an officer in the 54th Massachusetts. His brother, Norwood, was an officer of this regiment as well.

40. James Walton, an officer of the 54th Massachusetts, was an old abolitionist friend of Charlotte's from Philadelphia.

41. Colonel Robert Gould Shaw was the first commanding officer of the 54th Massachusetts. He was born on October 10, 1837 in Boston and studied at St. John's College Roman Catholic School at Fordham, an academy in Switzerland, and Harvard. After college, Shaw worked for a time in the mercantile firm of his uncle, Henry P. Sturgis, in New York City, but was anxious to participate in the war, if indeed there was going to be one. In early 1860, he joined the 7th Regiment of the New York State Militia and, later that year, went to Camp Andrew in West Roxbury, Massachusetts, where he enlisted in the Massachusetts 2nd Regiment, under the command of Colonel George H. Gordon. On January 30, 1863, Governor Andrew of Massachusetts offered the command of the

54th Massachusetts to Shaw. Andrew thought Shaw an appropriate choice given his youth, vitality, intelligence, and strong abolitionist sentiments. Burchard, *One Gallant Rush*, 4–71, *passim*.

42. Colonel Shaw was the son of prominent abolitionists who wholeheartedly supported his position as commander of the 54th Massachusetts. His mother was Sarah Blake Sturgis and his father, Francis G. Shaw, and both were active in efforts to aid freedmen. Francis Shaw served as president of the National Freedmen's Relief Association and as vice-president of the American Freedmen's Union Commission, among other related commitments. Swint, *Northern Teacher in the South*, 165; Burchard, *One Gallant Rush*, 4–71, *passim*.

43. Reverend James Lynch, a black minister from Baltimore, Maryland, was chaplain of the 54th Massachusetts. Luis F. Emilio, *History of the Fifty-Fourth Regiment of Massachusetts Volunteer Infantry* (Boston, 1891), 50, 232.

44. Jean Lander was the supervisory nurse for the troops stationed at Beaufort, South Carolina. Journal Four, July 21, 1863.

45. Mr. Page, a writer for the Chicago *Tribune*, was writing a series of articles on the activities of the freedmen in the Port Royal region as well as the missionaries, teachers, and plantation superintendents who were involved with the ex-slaves. Pearson, *Letters from Port Royal*, 235.

46. The First South Carolina Volunteers were the all-black regiment commanded by Colonel Thomas Wentworth Higginson.

47. On July 18, 1863, the 54th Massachusetts, commanded by Colonel Robert Gould Shaw, led an attack on Fort Wagner, a Confederate battery on Morris Island that guarded entry to Charleston Harbor. Colonel Shaw and many of his men were killed as they stormed the battery. Though their attempt failed, the courage and determination they demonstrated brought them widespread fame and greater support of the black military effort. Edward Hallowell became commander of the regiment after Shaw's death. McPherson,

Negro's Civil War, 190–191; Burchard, *One Gallant Rush*, 132–147.

48. Robert Gould Shaw married Annie Haggerty on May 2, 1863 in New York City. Burchard, *One Gallant Rush*, 189.

49. Colonel Shaw's mother was Sarah Blake Sturgis Shaw.

50. Charlotte is probably referring to C. F. Williams, a plantation superintendent on St. Helena Island. Pearson, *Letters from Port Royal*, 134, 141, 193, 310.

51. Charlotte is perhaps referring to Ephraim P. White of the First South Carolina Volunteers. Higginson, *Army Life in a Black Regiment*, 271.

52. Mr. Harrison was a plantation superintendent on St. Helena Island. Pearson, *Letters from Port Royal*, 262.

53. Harvard-trained William Hall was a teacher at two schools on St. Helena Island. Pearson, *Letters from Port Royal*, 127.

54. Charlotte is referring to Mrs. Peter Williams, the grandmother of Charlotte's friend Sarah (Cassey Smith) Watson.

55. Charlotte's Aunt Harriet (Purvis), her husband, Robert, and their children lived in Byberry, Pennsylvania.

56. Charlotte is referring to her old Quaker friend from Byberry, Tacie Townsend.

57. Francis Shaw is the father of Robert Gould Shaw.

58. Charles Trowbridge was major of the First South Carolina Volunteers. Higginson, *Army Life in a Black Regiment*, 269.

59. First Lieutenant G. W. Dewhurst was adjutant of the First South Carolina Volunteers. Higginson, *Army Life in a Black Regiment*, 270.

60. Martha Kellogg was a teacher at Hilton Head, South Carolina. Swint, *Northern Teacher in the South*, 188.

61. Annie, Gayner, and Jessie Heacock were teachers at Port Royal. Swint, *Northern Teacher in the South*, 186.

62. Helen Ireson of Lynn, Massachusetts, was a teacher at New Bern, North Carolina. Swint, *Northern Teacher in the South*, 188.

JOURNAL FIVE

1. The first page of Journal Five is permanently missing. The opening date is November 1885. Charlotte is now married to the Reverend Francis Grimké (1950–1937), and the two have moved from their home in Washington, D.C., to Jacksonville, Florida, where Francis Grimké accepted the pastorate of the Laura Street Presbyterian Church.

2. Bishop Daniel A. Payne (1811–1893) was a church historian, civil rights advocate, and president and chancellor of Wilberforce University in Xenia, Ohio. He was an old friend of Charlotte's and, as an elderly adult, spent most of his winters in Jacksonville, Florida. Rayford W. Logan and Michael R. Winston, eds., *Dictionary of American Negro Biography* (New York, 1982), 484–485 (hereafter cited as *DANB*).

3. Francis Grimké was born a slave on the outskirts of Charleston, the son of Nancy Weston and his owner, Henry Grimké. After the Civil War, Francis and his brother Archibald traveled North where they both graduated from Lincoln University in 1870. Francis Grimké also received a graduate degree from the Princeton Theological Seminary in 1878. He and Charlotte were married on December 19, 1878. For more information on Francis Grimké, see the "Introduction." *DANB*, 273–275.

4. Francis Grimké was minister of the Laura Street Presbyterian Church in Jacksonville, Florida, from 1885 until 1889. *DANB*, 274.

5. Charlotte is probably referring to the Mount Zion African Methodist Episcopal Church of Jacksonville. Barbara Ann Richardson, "A History of Blacks in Jacksonville, Florida, 1860–1895: A Socio-Economic and Political Study," Ph.D. Dissertation, Carnegie-Mellon University (1975), 167.

6. Charlotte's close friend, John Greenleaf Whittier, was born in 1807 in Haverhill, Massachusetts. Whittier was almost 80 years old when he wrote to Charlotte of "sensibly nearing the end."

7. Charlotte is referring to the American Anti-Slavery Society of Philadelphia, which was formed in 1833. Both her uncle, Robert Purvis, and John Whittier were signers of the declaration that established this organization. Gerald Sorin, *The New York Abolitionists: A Case Study of Political Suasion* (Westport, Conn., 1971), 39; *DANB*, 509.

8. In October 1885, Charlotte wrote an essay called "One Phase of the Race Question," in which she responded to Gail Hamilton's article, "Race Prejudice," which was published in the November 1884 edition of *North American Review*. Charlotte's essay was published as a letter to the editor of the *Boston Commonwealth*. Charlotte Forten Grimké, "One Phase of the Race Question," Francis Grimké Papers, Moorland-Spingarn Research Center, Howard University, Washington, D.C.

9. Charlotte Forten and Francis Grimké married on December 19, 1878.

10. Charlotte is referring to the death of her daughter, Theodora Cornelia Grimké, born January 1, 1880. The child died later that year.

11. Charlotte is referring to Frederick Douglass's mansion "Cedar Hill" in the Anacostia section of Washington, D.C. The home, previously owned by a virulent racist, was property that Douglass bought from the Freedmen's Bureau. The Douglasses were close friends of the Grimkés, and in 1884, Francis Grimké performed the wedding ceremony when Douglass married his second wife, Helen Pitts. Charlotte wrote an essay entitled "At the Home of Frederick Douglass" after the great man died in 1895, and in it she recalls the time she spent at Cedar Hill with him. *DANB*, 181, 185, 186; Charlotte Forten Grimké, "At the Home of Frederick Douglass," Francis Grimké Papers, Moorland-Spingarn Research Center, Howard University.

12. Charlotte is referring to Blanche K. Bruce (1841–1898) who was born a slave near Farmville, Virginia. As a young man, Bruce was taken by his master to Missouri, but escaped to freedom in Kansas. There he opened the first elementary school for blacks in

the state and, after emancipation, went back to Missouri where he opened another school. Concerned with his own intellectual development, Bruce attended Oberlin College for a short while. Later, in 1869, he left for Mississippi looking for opportunities for advancement. Bruce held a number of political offices, culminating in his election to the U.S. Senate in 1874. After his tenure in the Senate (1875–1881), he also served as register of the treasury (1881–1885; 1897–1898) and recorder of deeds for the District of Columbia (1889–1893). *DANB*, 74–76.

13. Charlotte is referring to Tuskegee Normal and Industrial Institute in Tuskegee, Alabama. The school was founded by Booker T. Washington (1856–1915) in 1881. The institute provided blacks with a practical education—occupational skills and academic subjects related to daily experience. Unlike most other institutions at the time, the staff at Tuskegee was predominantly black. *DANB*, 633–634.

14. Charlotte is referring to the Stanton Graded School, founded in 1868 in Jacksonville, Florida. The school was named for Edwin M. Stanton who served as the Secretary of War from 1862 to 1867. The school had eight grades that accommodated students in the primary and intermediary levels as well as those advanced enough to train as teachers in the school's normal department. Richardson, "History of Blacks in Jacksonville," 143–144.

15. Serena Leanora De Grasse Downing was the wife of George Thomas Downing, a civil rights advocate and businessman in New York City and Providence. Serena Downing was born in New York, the daughter of George De Grasse, a wealthy landowner from Calcutta, and a German woman, Maria Von Surley. The Downings owned prosperous catering services in New York City and Providence as well as the popular Sea Girt Hotel in Newport, Rhode Island. *DANB*, 187.

16. Charlotte is referring to the Stanton Graded School.

17. Charlotte is probably referring to Dr. Caroline Still Wiley Anderson (1848–1919), the daughter of black activist, writer, and businessman, William Still, and his wife Letitia. Caroline was born

in Philadelphia and educated at the Institute for Colored Youth, Oberlin, and the Woman's Medical College of Pennsylvania. Dorothy Sterling, ed., *We Are Your Sisters: Black Women in the Nineteenth Century* (New York, 1984), 443.

18. Ada Hinton was an old friend of Charlotte's from Philadelphia.

19. In 1889, Reverend Francis Grimké accepted an invitation to return to the pastorate of the Fifteenth Street Presbyterian Church in Washington, D.C. Grimké previously served as pastor of this church from 1878 to 1885. *DANB*, 274.

20. Charlotte is referring to her close friend, Mrs. Fannie S. Smyth, whose husband, John H. Smyth, was the U.S. minister to Liberia. Sterling, *We Are Your Sisters*, 431.

21. Benjamin Harrison (1833–1901), a Republican, served as president of the United States from 1889 to 1893.

22. The location of Ler, Massachusetts, is unknown. It was probably a seacoast resort community, but there is no source to substantiate this information.